FINDING AND USING ECONOMIC INFORMATION
A Guide to Sources and Interpretation

FINDING & USING

ECONOMIC INFORMATION

A Guide to
Sources and Interpretation

David B. Johnson
Lousiana State University, Baton Rouge

Under the General Editorship of
Alan S. Blinder

BRISTLECONE BOOKS

Mayfield Publishing Company
Mountain View, California
London · Toronto

To my wife Janet, for many good reasons.

Library of Congress Cataloging-in-Publication Data
Johnson, David Bruce.
    Finding and using economic information : a guide to sources and interpretation / David B. Johnson : under the general editorship of Alan B. Blinder.
       p.   cm.
    Includes index.
    ISBN 1-55934-100-9
    1. United States--Economic conditions--Statistical services--Handbooks, manuals,
etc.   2.   United States--Economic conditions--Statistical methods--Handbooks, manuals,
etc.   3.   Economics--Statistical methods--Handbooks, manuals, etc.   I.   Title.
HC106.J63   1992
016.33'0973--dc20   91-36786
                                                                                         CIP

Manufactured in the United States of America
10   9   8   7   6   5   4   3   2   1

Bristlecone Books
Mayfield Publishing Company
1240 Villa Street
Mountain View, California

Production editor, Sharon Montooth; copy editor, Carol Dondrea; text and cover designer, Joan Greenfield. The text was set in 10/12 Palatino by TypeLink and printed on 50# Finch Opaque by Maple Vail.

CONTENTS

289053

PREFACE

This book was born out of frustration. Frustration of dealing with data that were hard to locate, difficult to interpret, and troublesome to use. It was hatched out of the weariness and dismay of searching through data and statistics books in which the English language was put to the rack and stretched beyond the endurance of all but professional purists. Data books will never rival *Macbeth, The Rise and Fall of the Roman Empire*, or *Pogo* but they should keep the reader awake beyond the second page and, on occasion, they should impart a bit of knowledge, dampen some phobias, and provide useful guidance to those unfortunate souls who have to get the facts. This book will, I hope, accomplish some of these tasks.

The first draft of this preface included what is now contained in the Foreword. Since prefaces are supposed to be short, pithy accolades to those who share the blame for what follows, much of the original material was moved to Chapter 1. Read the Foreword! It will help you to use the book!

This is my second book published by Bristlecone/Mayfield and guided by its sagacious economics editor, Gary Burke. Though the tyranny of a blank page makes writing a loathsome task at times, Gary's patience, gentleness, and optimism, and his unlimited ability to analyze and to accept new ideas, made the task almost enjoyable. Carol Dondrea and Sharon Montooth received a manuscript that was — well, unique might be an understated description — and quickly whipped it into shape. Because the book is directed at a wide audience, we had reviewers drawn from many professions. Their appreciated laudatory remarks made their critical comments more valuable. A debt is owed to Lawrence C. Marsh, Professor of Econometrics at Notre Dame, Lisa Lapin of the *San Jose Mercury News*, Professor Lawrence L. Lapin of San Jose State University, Professor George D. Brower of Moravian College, and Robert Sanders, a research chemist. Professor Alan Blinder, at Princeton University, made astute suggestions.

The author's "deep-in-the-bowels-of-the-library" research efforts were aided by the cheerful assistance of Smittie Bolner and her entire staff in the BA/DOCS division of the Louisiana State University Library, especially Tom Diamond, Wilson T. Plunkett, and Jim Noel. A hardworking group of librarians staffing the Baton Rouge Parish Library's reference desk patiently answered numerous requests for information necessary to complete this book. During the final days of completing the manuscript Debra (Pope) Pontiff, an LSU MBA student, provided smiles and valuable research assistance and John Kelly, a long-time friend and astute accountant, reviewed the accounting section of the manuscript. My gratitude to all of them and to my wife, who proofread the historic data sections—and who brought me cookies, Cokes, and encouraging words while I worked in my study.

CHAPTER 1

HOW TO USE THIS BOOK

This book is written for the millions of students, teachers, journalists, researchers, editorial writers, and others who are tyrannized, overwhelmed, bored, or bedazzled by a plethora of economic data and a paucity of knowledge about such data. It is written for those who have to use data in a term paper, a sales plan, a financial report, an article on the "state of the economy," and for those who simply want to understand (and often correct) the evening news broadcast. This book is written for a journalist reporting on the effects of the latest increase in the unemployment rate in the local community; an attorney working up a case on compensated damages who needs some background on the consumer price index; an analyst employed by the Chamber of Commerce who needs to gather local personal income estimates; an economics student who wants to understand the concepts presented in class or who has a paper to write. This book is for those who have wondered about the meanings of M1, GDP, PPI, options, futures, stocks, bonds, interest rates, national savings, balance of payments, the Dow Jones average, NASDAQ quotes, oil prices, budgets, deficits, input-output matrixes, and flow-of-funds tables. If you have ever wondered who put together those seemingly precise unemployment rates, doubted the accuracy of price changes, or thought that no one really counted exports and imports at our nation's ports and airports, this book is for you. Have you ever wondered what economic data mean, how they are collected, where you can find them, and how you can use them? This book is for you. Have you ever wanted a book of historical economic data that would enable you to put current economic data in historical perspective? This book is for you!

Psst!! Students in economics! I have a dark and closely kept secret to share with you. We economists receive very little training on the sources and meanings of data series or on data collection procedures. We are indeed grateful to our academic godfathers who instructed us so thoroughly on the virtually unlimited number of ways to torture data with sophistication and élan, but without mercy, until the data confess what we need for the court of our peers. We know how to process and manipulate data but not how it is collected or produced. Economists, like most other scientists, are victims of specialization. We are thoroughly familiar with the data within our narrow fields of specialization, but when we teach more general courses we often do not possess that knowledge of data sources that inquiring undergraduate students or reporters would like to know about.

Students, you now have an easy and ready source of answers to your very reasonable questions. Don't irritate the prof; use this book. Use this book to bone up on those infuriating realities of the real world so you will be prepared to answer the natural inquiries of the novices.

ORGANIZATION

The organization of this book is simple. Chapters 2 and 3 contain some useful information about data series and how they are constructed, dozens of useful data tips, and fairly lengthy discussions on sampling error, index numbers, and accounting. These chapters will be especially useful to two classes of people (to which neither the reader nor the author belong but which, unfortunately, include so many of our friends and colleagues): (1) those who seldom, if ever, use statistics and consider them boring, irrelevant, and the curse of a limited intellect—those who generally believe they can convince the world by offering "proof" through loud and repeated assertions; and (2) those who frequently view processed data as factual manna from an incorruptible divine source— those who like to convince the world by using statements such as "as we have just seen, the data irrefutably prove that" when other data, other assumptions, other massaging techniques would have produced different conclusions.

Subsequent chapters are organized by major topics such as national income; money, credit, and interest rates; financial markets and instruments; capital markets; price indices; labor markets; and regional, international, industrial, and commercial economic data. At the beginning of each of these chapters is a "Read Me First" section that provides an overview and possibly some analysis of the data series in that chapter. This topical organization enables the reader to learn about the major data series and their explanations without searching through the book. The major topics/chapters, and the data series within them, are listed alphabetically. If you want to look up a particular term or data series, glance through the Table of Contents or Index to get to the appropriate data series. When you reach the specific data series or topic, you will notice that there is a standardized format. Most data series or topics will begin with a heading that will look something like the following (explanatory comments in capitals). If the entry is not relevant for the data series, the line will be omitted:

Name: NAME OF DATA SERIES OR TOPIC WILL BE FOUND HERE

Alternative name: INFORMAL TITLES, NICKNAMES

Agency/Institution: AGENCY OR INSTITUTION GATHERING THE DATA, WHICH WILL OFTEN BE DIFFERENT FROM THE MOST CONVENIENT SOURCE OF THIS DATA

Address: ADDRESS OF DATA GATHERER OR INSTITUTION THAT MAINTAINS THE DATABASE

Telephone number for data: NUMBER YOU CAN CALL TO OBTAIN THE DATA; OFTEN A RECORDING

Telephone number for inquiries: NUMBER TO CALL FOR INFORMATION ON DATA SOURCES, INTERPRETATION OF TERMS, METHODOLOGIES, AND SO ON. OFTEN THE TELEPHONE NUMBER FOR DATA AND INQUIRIES WILL BE THE SAME

Sources: MOST CONVENIENT SOURCES OF CURRENT INFORMATION ON THE DATA SERIES

Frequency: DATA PUBLISHED DAILY, WEEKLY, QUARTERLY, ANNUALLY

When available: HOW QUICKLY THE DATA ARE AVAILABLE

Revisions: HOW OFTEN THE DATA ARE REVISED. IS THERE A CONSISTENT POLICY ON MAKING REVISIONS?

Historic data: SOURCE OF HISTORIC DATA, IF ANY.

Cross-references: CROSS-REFERENCES TO OTHER SOURCES OR TOPICS IN THIS BOOK

A Quick Look

The "Quick Look" section summarizes the data series and, if necessary, explains the terms and numbers used in the series. This section is the one you should focus on if you are using a data series and you don't know what a particular term means or if you don't know how to interpret the data. If you have a specific question you want answered quickly, here is where you look. If you are reading a newspaper quote on commodity options, for example, and you don't know the meaning of "strike price," look up "strike price, commodity options," in the Index or find Commodity Options in the Table of Contents. Turn to the listed page and read "A Quick Look"—it will contain easy-to-understand definitions of all the terms used in commodity options quotations.

A Closer Look

The "A Closer Look" section provides a mini-course on the data series and the subject to which it relates. If you really want to learn about the uses, weaknesses, importance, meaning, and application of a data series, this is where you look. If you want to learn about the gross domestic product, for example, look up "gross domestic product" in the Index, turn to the page and look for the "A Closer Look" section. Every major data series has a corresponding "A Closer Look" section. (The less significant data series have only "A Quick Look" section.) Don't worry about the material being "over your head." Nothing worthwhile in economics is over anyone's head if the material is written well and read carefully.

Historic Data

If you have never tried to obtain consistent economic data over a period of years, you might not initially appreciate this section, which is published for all major data series. The first time you must compare current data with historic data, you will be willing to pay twice the price of the book for this feature alone. It is fairly easy to obtain current information on the unemployment rate, gross national product, consumer price index, and Dow Jones Industrial Average, but historic data are often hidden in obscure publications, some of them no longer readily available. You might painfully discover that the historic data series you found after hours of searching has been revised many times since it was published. Even the best of the computer services do not have historical data series for more than a couple of decades. Most major data series in this book have historical data sections that contain data for as far back as the series goes, or back to 1900. These historic data series are compatible with the current data series in 1991. One useful application of this section is to look up historical data in order to put current economic news in perspective. If you hear that the current rate of inflation is, for example, 6.3 percent, you can look up the historical data section for the Consumer Price Index and see how many years we have had inflation above 6.3 percent. If the TV news announces that the average duration of unemployment is 12 weeks, you can look up the historical data section in the employment section to see the trend over the past 30 years.

You will soon find that this book has little, if any, competition. It is a source book, an economic dictionary, an economic encyclopedia, and a mini-textbook. Most importantly, it is readable. Look up a number, ferret out a definition, learn the methodologies of the data-mongers. Most economic books are infallible cures for insomnia and this book is probably no exception. But it costs less than a year's supply of sleeping pills, and your friends should be impressed with your choice of a natural cure.

CHAPTER 2

PROBLEMS IN COLLECTING, USING, AND INTERPRETING DATA

LIVING AND LYING WITH STATISTICS

We Americans might not be efficient or prolific producers of steel or cameras, but we can produce data like no other country on earth. Unfortunately, many Americans think that the data generated by the federal bureaucracy are often false and that they are concocted to favor some social or economic class or a political party. Some cynics are even convinced that the federal government consistently manipulates data to make the current administration look better. But—although an occasional number can get swept under the thick Oriental carpet in the Office of the Secretary, or a critical study can get buried in the burrows of the bureaucracy—the simple but unexciting truth is that virtually all government data are clean. Despite some sharp budget cuts in the late 1970s and early 1980s, the United States has the most honest, most thorough, and most sophisticated data collection and processing system in the world. Simply too many people—many of them members of the party not in power—would have to be involved in the falsification of an important data series in order to keep it a secret. The American media would jump on a story that revealed such falsifications to the public, and the reporter who broke the story would be assured of the congratulations of colleagues, hundreds of invitations to address university graduation ceremonies, and probably a promotion. Perhaps most important, data-gathering personnel in the federal government have a long history of professionalism, and no political appointees (often called "political hacks" by the professionals) are going to tell these professionals (often called "mere technicians" by the political appointees) to "look the other way."

Many countries in the world do not have a free press, a tradition of professional independence, or alternative employers. In such countries, data are often deliberately manipulated to support the views, philosophies, and interests of those in power. But most of the major industrialized countries gather data professionally and without political interference.

This does not mean that every study reported by the media or every bit of datum published is the truth, the whole truth, and nothing but the truth. Data are often incorrect or misinterpreted for a variety of reasons. Budget constraints force statisticians to choose smaller samples, poorly trained interviewers ask fuzzy questions, and so on. Those who use or interpret published data, including independent institutions and companies, as well as government bureaucracies, often make errors in their interpretation or slant the data to suit their objectives. Such sins of commission and omission darken the souls of these data users, but they do not affect the integrity of the perfectly innocent data or those dedicated saints who gather and process the data.

The following sections point out some reasons why we should exercise caution in using and interpreting data and the results of empirical studies. We should not conclude, simply because most empirical studies have many inherent problems, that these studies should be ignored or discarded. Data and statistical studies are absolutely essential — not only for scientific progress, but for rational discourse and for effective private and public decision making. Just as a book on English grammar points out the most frequently committed errors in order to enable people to communicate more efficiently, we point out problems in data usage in order to facilitate statistical communication. Where possible, we suggest some solutions to these problems. Unfortunately, unlike most rules for correct grammar, the rules for "correct" statistical processing are often complex and, thus, beyond the scope of this book. A basic text in statistics or in scientific methodology would be a good starting point for those whose confidence in all statistical studies is shaken by the following pages. The point to remember about statistical pitfalls is: "Beware but don't despair."

PROBLEMS WITH STATISTICS

The Media

The misuse of statistics begins with the media. Unfortunately, members of the media are not like most economists, who have time to contemplate certain conditions and then to consider alternatives. News reporters and writers are vassals of the clock; they must gather data quickly and condense it into a few sentences of print or seconds of airtime. Although some media people have undergraduate and graduate degrees in economics and finance, most reporters and commentators do not have such training. Many reporters report economic data, terms, and news that might not be correct or the most relevant.

Although the official press releases of federal, state, and private data-gathering agencies generally state whether the data are annualized, seasonally adjusted, or price adjusted for inflation, the news media often omit such "refinements," with the result that the public does not really know what is being reported. One frequent convention is to report increases in the gross domestic product (which includes increases in prices) when the data actually refer to the real gross domestic product (which does not include changes in prices). Often the media do not mention whether changes in the consumer price index are seasonally adjusted (most probably they are), or whether the monthly rate being reported is the single monthly rate or the annualized rate. Media personnel often seem far too eager to get a number — any number — from an "expert" without inquiring into the meaning and relevance of that number in the context to which it is being applied. However, we should not be too critical of the media. Locating that rare economist who is capable of using the English language in such a way that the average person can understand what is being communicated is a difficult task.

Human Processing Error

All data are collected, processed, and published by people, and people make mistakes. A few years ago, economists at the Federal Reserve System, as well as monetarist economists, who are camp followers of the Fed, were shocked by a sudden change in the money supply data. Numerous explanations were offered for the change. Eventually it was discovered that a new clerk at one of the large New York banks was filling in the wrong information on the bank's money report to the Fed. When I was researching input-output tables for this book, I could not replicate some data contained in the benchmark I-O table published by the Bureau of Economic Analysis. After two hours of futile attempts, a call to Washington confirmed the suspicion that an entire row of 40 numbers had been inadvertently shifted one column to the right.

In March 1992, a clerk at Salomon Brothers Inc. read a form that instructed the company to sell $11 million of stock. Instead, the clerk instructed the computer to sell 11 million shares of stock. A second clerk who was supposed to check the first clerk's work failed to do so. As a result of the large sale of stock, there was a major fall in stock prices and in the Dow Jones Industrial Average.

Computers seldom make mistakes but people fill out forms incorrectly, punch transposed numbers into computers, and make programming errors. These show up as errors in the published data.

Data Filters

Few students get through classes on probability theory without hearing their professor say that if you put 1000 monkeys at a keyboard, they will eventually type Shakespeare's *Hamlet*. There is a corollary to this well-worn thread: If you put 1000 economists, accountants, scientists, pollsters, statisticians, doctors, and social scientists at a computer keyboard, they will eventually produce a study with the results desired by the originator. If the first study doesn't prove that Grin toothpaste prevents tooth decay, send the study to the shredder and the researchers back to their labs to do a second, a third, and a fourth study. Eventually they will produce a study that shows Grin toothpaste is Number 1 in preventing tooth decay. Another way of achieving desirable results is to concentrate on a small number of test cases. It is easy to get a 25 percent decrease in tooth decay if the sample has only four people; a sample of 2500 people is much less likely to yield such impressive results. Most large samples would show a small change of 1 or 2 percent, either negative or positive, or even show no change at all. But if only one person in a sample of four shows fewer cavities, Grin has "shown" that it can reduce tooth decay by 25 percent.[1] For the toothpaste company there is "safety in small numbers."

Don't believe that grubby, profit-oriented companies advertising their wares are the only parties guilty of passing along favorable information and destroying unfavorable information. Politicians repress studies that show their opponents winning; unions and religious organizations do not reveal data that show they are losing members. Government agencies hide, in the deepest burrows of their bureaucracies, studies that show that demand for their services is decreasing; and universities *never* mention that the state financial support they receive is far above the national average. Pity the poor data, which must depend on humans for their distribution and recognition. Most get trapped by human filters and never meet the eyes of the average citizen.

Statistical Alchemy

The search of medieval man for the secret of turning base metal into gold has been resuscitated by the modern alchemist who, as econometrician or statistician, attempts to turn poor data into good data by running them through several sophisticated econometric and statistical treatments. Although such treatments might improve the analysis of the data and the conclusions drawn from them, we should always remember the univer-

---

[1]Did you catch the deliberate misuse of "25 percent"? It was applied to tooth decay when it should have been applied to the number of people or the number of teeth showing less tooth decay. What does "25 percent less tooth decay" mean to you? How would you measure it?

sal validity of GIGO: "Garbage-In, Garbage-Out." Unfortunately, this modern alchemy is encouraged by the lack of training (and interest) of many statisticians and econometricians in the more humble tools related to their professions, such as accounting standards and tax laws, that generate the fundamental data. These people run complicated tests on GNP, profits, savings, and investment without really knowing the composition of these data or the effects of other variables (such as changes in tax laws or generally accepted accounting procedures) on their integrity or consistency. Don't let strange sounding terms such as *Border Hessians, heteroscedasticity, limited-information-single-equation-maximum-likelihood-method, contemporaneously uncorrelated terms,* and *idealized uniequation* scare you into accepting conclusions you might otherwise not accept.

The Elusive Average

You go down to city hall to complain about the latest tax assessment on your house, angrily pointing out to the harassed clerk that a recent study shows that the average price of homes in your neighborhood is only $60,000, while you were assessed $70,000. You brag to your brother-in-law about the exclusive upper-income neighborhood in which you live, mentioning that "a recent study shows that the average value of homes in the neighborhood is a 'cool' $80,000." You tell your neighbors about a recent study showing that the average price of homes in the neighborhood is $70,000. No, you are not lying to the assessor, to your brother-in-law, or to your neighbors. You are simply quoting the results of a recent study that gave three averages. You did what any other person would do in similar circumstances — you used the average that was most favorable to the point you were trying to make in each situation.

Assume, for the sake of simplicity, that the study had obtained the sale prices of seven homes in the neighborhood that were recently sold. The prices were:

$$\begin{array}{ll}
\$130,000 & \\
110,000 & \text{Mean} = \dfrac{\$560,000}{7} = \$80,000 \\
80,000 & \text{Median} = \$70,000 \\
70,000 & \text{Mode} = \$60,000 \\
60,000 & \\
60,000 & \\
\underline{50,000} & \\
\$560,000 &
\end{array}$$

The average called the **arithmetic mean** is the sum of all the numbers in the set divided by the total number of elements of the set. This is the "average" most people have in mind when they use the term. The arithmetic mean in the example is $80,000. Since it is the highest average, you select it to impress your brother-in-law. The **median** is the number that divides a set of numbers so that half the elements in the set are larger and half are smaller. Here the median is $70,000. That is the figure you give to your neighbor, since it gives the best representation of the value of homes in the neighborhood. The **mode** is the number in a set of numbers that occurs most frequently. This is the average you quote to the avaricious tax assessor because it is the lowest: $60,000. Since you are an honest person, you would not and did not lie. You simply engaged in that perfectly natural human tendency to select the data that prove your point.

Some data sets, such as the heights of persons, will have the mean, median, and mode close to each other; others, such as data sets on incomes and property values, are likely to produce means, medians, and modes that are far apart. As a data user, you must be alert to these differences among the averages.

When the mayor of Bentonville, Arkansas, proudly announces that the average income per household in the city is $200,000, you should immediately wonder what kind of average he is reporting. You might recall that Bentonville was the home of the late Sam Walton, founder and owner of the Wal-Mart chain and one of the richest persons in America. If his income were excluded, the average (= mean) income per household in Bentonville might only have been $20,000. One of the problems with using a mean average is that it can be distorted by a few very high or very low numbers. The median would be the preferred number to report here.

Another problem with the elusive average is that individuals sometimes base their decisions solely on the average without examining variances from it. The story about the 6-foot statistician who drowned in a stream with an average depth of 2 feet is painfully well known. Less well known are the builders in the 1960s who built too many three-bedroom homes after reading that the average family consisted of a couple with two children. They built plenty of homes for the average family but ignored the millions of smaller and larger families. Shoe manufacturers seem to be committing the same error now. Try to find a 14D shoe, for example. When a corporation advertises that it has one million stockholders, who hold an average of 20 shares each, don't happily point out the capitalistic egalitarianism in this until you look behind the statistic. It may be that 100 stockholders hold 95 percent of the shares, with the remaining 5 percent distributed among 999,900 stockholders.

Occasionally we come across the terms **geometric mean** and **harmonic mean**. To help explain these terms, we'll compare them to the arithmetic mean. The arithmetic mean measures the central value of the range of prices:

$$\text{Arithmetic mean} = \frac{\text{price } 1 + \text{price } 2 + \text{price } 3 + \cdots + \text{price } N}{N}$$

where N = number of units or observations. For example, assume we are calculating the average price of three commodities:

$$\text{Arithmetic mean} = \frac{50 + 75 + 100}{3} = 75$$

The geometric mean or average is used when there is a large spread between the lowest and highest values of a set. The geometric mean is selected because it is not as heavily weighted by extremely large values as is the arithmetic mean. It is used fairly frequently, and it is determined by taking the nth root of the product of N observations. The geometric mean is always less than the arithmetic mean and always greater than the harmonic mean.

$$\text{Geometric mean} = (\text{price 1} \times \text{price 2} \times \text{price 3} \times \cdots \times \text{price } N)^{1/n}$$

For example,

$$\text{Geometric mean} = (50 \times 75 \times 100)^{1/3} = 72.1$$

One very popular use of the geometric mean is estimating the average percent increase in sales, production, income, or other variable over a period of time. A slight modification is made to the formula when calculating the average percent increase:

$$\text{Geometric mean} = \left(\frac{\text{value at end of period}}{\text{value at beginning of period}}\right)^{1/(n-1)} - 1$$

For example, if the population of Podunk is 500 in 1980 and 2000 in 1990, what is the average annual percentage increase in population?

$$\left(\frac{2000}{500}\right)^{1/(11-1)} - 1 = 0.1487 = 14.87 \text{ percent}$$

Note that there are 11 years between 1980 and 1990, so $n = 11$. Always count the beginning and ending years when using this formula.[2] Podunk's population grew at an annual rate of 14.87 percent. This formula for calculating the average percent increase over a period of years is a very useful one, so remember where you found it.

The harmonic mean is obtained by taking the reciprocal of the arithmetic means of the reciprocals of the individual prices. That definition is tough to follow. Read it again after looking at the example. The harmonic mean is always less than the geometric average.

---

[2]Even sophisticated data users make mistakes in counting the number of years. There are 11 years of data between 1980 and 1990 including the first and last year. Hence, we must enter $n = 11$ in our formula. If we compute the average annual growth rate between 1982 and 1987, we need to use $n = 6$ because there are 6 years of data. If Podunk's population grew from 500 to 550 from 1980 to 1981, $n = 2$ because there are two years of data. The percentage increase using the geometric mean would be:

$$\left(\frac{550}{500}\right)^{1/(2-1)} - 1 = 0.10 = 10 \text{ percent}$$

$$\text{Harmonic mean} = \frac{N}{\dfrac{1}{\text{price 1}} + \dfrac{1}{\text{price 2}} + \dfrac{1}{\text{price 3}} + \cdots + \dfrac{1}{\text{price } N}}$$

For example,

$$\text{Harmonic mean} = \frac{3}{\left(\dfrac{1}{50}\right) + \left(\dfrac{1}{75}\right) + \left(\dfrac{1}{100}\right)} = 69.2$$

The harmonic mean is used in production management to determine the average time needed to complete one unit of production. The harmonic mean is also useful when the observations are expressed as opposites of what is required in the average. For example, if store A charges $1 for three apples, store B charges $1 for four apples, and store C charges $1 for five apples, what is the average price per apple? The data are expressed in "apples per $1," but we want to know average price per apple. The average price at each store is A = $0.333; B = $0.25; C = $0.20. The harmonic mean is

$$\frac{3}{\dfrac{1}{0.333} + \dfrac{1}{0.25} + \dfrac{1}{0.20}} = \$0.25$$

The Slippery Base

We often see comparisons made among data that are related to an inappropriate base. During the 1970s, safety campaigns urged drivers to buckle up because "80 percent of all accidents occur within 10 miles of home." This gave the snobs at the University of Texas the opportunity to joke that the Texas Aggies, upon learning these statistics, began moving more than 10 miles from their homes. Aggie jokes aside, the safety message strongly implied that it was more dangerous to drive near one's home. Since people tend to do most of their driving within 10 miles of their home, it is not surprising that most accidents occur within that radius. The relevant base is not simply the number of accidents, but the number of accidents (as well as injuries and deaths) that occur per 100,000 miles traveled within 10 miles of the victims' homes. Clearly, the accident rate per 100,000 miles driven may actually be lower near home than on the long drive to grandmother's house.

Another irksome set of grim but meaningless automotive statistics are those provided by the National Safety Council during every holiday period. More deaths do occur on "long" holiday weekends than on normal weekends, but that doesn't mean the highways are less safe on holiday weekends. We expect more deaths from automotive accidents during these times because more automobiles are on the road and there are more occupants per car. More useful for a family about to embark on the trip to grandmother's house for Thanksgiving or Christmas would be the comparative death rates per 100,000 person-miles traveled on long holiday weekends. But such data are seldom, if ever, given to the public.[3]

Data are also misinterpreted when the user fails to consider that the population being examined has a different age distribution from that of the base population. For example, recruiters for the armed forces often claim that death rates in their services are lower than the average death rate in the nation. They seldom quote studies or reports that show such comparisons, but even if they had the numbers to support their statements, such numbers would be meaningless. The general population consists of many aged and chronically ill persons, who have high death rates. The proper comparison is not with the general population but with young men and women who are the same age and condition of health as those who enter the armed forces.[4]

Comparisons of accidents, crimes, and income among ethnic and racial groups often ignore significantly different age distributions among these groups. Young people of all races and ethnic backgrounds tend to have higher accident rates, higher crime rates, and lower incomes than adults. Thus, if you were comparing accident rates, crime rates, and income levels between, say, Jewish citizens and Hispanic citizens, you would find that, as a group, Hispanics have higher accident rates, higher crime rates, and lower income levels than Jews. One reason for this is the relative youth of Hispanics; the median age of Hispanics is more than ten years lower than the median age of Jews. Thus, any such study unadjusted for age distribution is comparing oranges and bagels.

The slippery base is often used intentionally. Consider companies reporting their profit rates. When they want to minimize their profit rates, such as when they report to consumer groups, corporations show annual profits as a percentage of sales. For example, the company's public relations flyer might say that the company's profit rate was only 1.5 percent last year. "Hmm," you might say, "that is even lower than the 5.5 percent I earn on certificates of deposit at the bank." Of course, that's exactly what the company's PR people want you to believe. While reporting profits as a percentage of sales yields valuable information about the proportion of

---

[3]In the unlikely event that you do see such data reported next holiday weekend, you can compare them with the number of traffic-related deaths per 100 million vehicle-miles in 1989, which was 2.4, one-half of the 1970 rate. Automotive travel is much safer now than it was two decades ago.

[4]There is some evidence that service in the armed forces, especially for 17- to 19-year-old males, does reduce the chances of an early death. Young men in the military drive vehicles much less frequently than their civilian buddies, thus sparing them the terribly high automotive death rates incurred by young civilian males. (More than 80 percent of 17- and 18-year-olds killed in automotive accidents are males.) The relative drug-free environment in the military also reduces the death rate.

the consumer's dollar that goes to profit, the really relevant variable when discussing return on investment is the amount of profit[5] divided by the amount of owner investment in the business. Conversely, critics of capitalism often report that corporations earn "hundreds of millions of dollars." A hundred million dollars is a large amount if stockholders have only $200 million invested, but if they have $2 billion invested, the rate of return is only 5 percent, which is about what one could earn on deposits at the corner bank.

Politicians use the slippery base in reporting all sorts of data. My favorite is the veteran mayor who brags about the wise decisions he made early in his career. "If we had to build the stadium (museum, city hall, dog pound) today, it would cost three times as much as it cost us back in 1970." It seems almost unfair to point out to the mayor that prices in general have increased by more than three times since 1970 and that if the costs were adjusted to constant dollars it would actually be *cheaper* to build it today. Furthermore, cost aside, the decision to build the stadium may not have been a good one from the start. Perhaps the benefits of building it were far *less* than the costs, measured in either 1970 or current dollars.

Slippery Percentages

Watch those percentages, for they can be as slippery as eels. (Have you seen any data supporting the assertion that eels are more slippery than other fish?) Though most advertisers are fairly sophisticated today, back in the 1960s it was not uncommon to see a sign saying something like "100% OFF REGULAR PRICES OF NEW SHOES." Taking the sign literally, I once asked the clerk for a free pair of shoes because the sign obviously said that the shoes were now being sold at a zero price. The clerk pointed out that the shoes, which had been selling for $40, were now selling for $20. He insisted the sign was correct because, since the shoes were now selling for $20, they had been reduced by $20, and thus the markdown was 100 percent. I tried to point out that the initial base was $40 and the price was now one-half of the initial price, so the markdown was 50 percent, not 100 percent. I left the store without the shoes and without convincing the hapless clerk, but I consoled myself that I had another story I could pass along to students illustrating that we humans will hold tightly to our chest the accumulated ignorance of the past whenever it conveniently serves our self-interest.

Remember to search for that slippery base when reading percent changes. Have you come across sales that enable customers to take 50 percent off the red tag merchandise that has already been reduced 30

---

[5]"Profits" are what certain accountants, tax lawyers, and the IRS say they are. See Chapter 3, page 48, for a discussion of accounting principles.

percent? A coat that originally sold for $100, for example, will have been reduced 30 percent to $70, and then an additional 50 percent will be taken off so that its red tag sale price is $35. No problem with that. One store, however, once advertised: "Shop our Red Tag Sale! 80 percent off!" But you couldn't buy a $100 coat for $20, as stated clearly by the 80 percent reduction. The manager of the store had simply added up the 30 percent and the 50 percent to get the 80 percent, without realizing that this was a slippery base error. The total percentage reduction, of course, was 65 percent. You probably understand the lesson of the slippery base accurately if you understand the following: (1) When you go to a red tag sale, there is no difference between 50 percent off the price of a product that is already reduced by 30 percent, and 30 percent off the price of a product that has already been reduced by 50 percent. (2) If your salary is cut in half, your income needs to increase 100 percent in order to get back to its original level. (3) One of the most important but least understood principles in macroeconomics is that the difference between a 2 percent annual growth rate and a 3 percent annual growth rate is not 1 percent but 50 percent.

Correlation Does Not Mean Causation

Correlation measures the relationship of one variable to another. For example, weight might be correlated to height and lung cancer to smoking. Correlation studies can be very useful, but a serious problem in data usage occurs when writers and their readers attribute correlation to cause and effect. Students who have suffered through a sophomore statistics course may have heard the story about the high correlation between the incomes of Methodist ministers and the price of whiskey. If you plotted the incomes of the ministers and the price of whiskey, you would notice that they have increased at about the same rate year after year for more than 50 years. Does this mean that when ministers got a raise they went out to the local distillery and drove up the price of whiskey? Nah! Both the ministers' incomes and the price of whiskey were strongly affected by a third variable known as inflation. Few people blame ministers for driving up the price of whiskey, but many people equate correlation with causation.

When high school and college students studied Latin, the "correlation is causation" fallacy was known as the "post hoc ergo propter hoc" fallacy. *Post hoc ergo propter hoc* is translated as: "After this, therefore because of this." This means that if B follows A, A causes B. In a 1948 movie adaptation of Mark Twain's story, *A Connecticut Yankee in King Arthur's Court*, Bing Crosby dupes the medieval knights into committing the "correlation is causation" or the "post hoc" fallacy. Crosby gestures at the sun and the sun darkens (Bing knows there is going to be an eclipse). He gestures again and the sun begins to reappear. Surely, they reason, in a classic "post hoc ergo propter hoc" mode, he can control the sun so he must possess magical powers. Many statisticians illustrate the "correlation is causation" fallacy by noting that, upon the appearance of dark clouds in the sky, Indian medicine men showed their power by beating their tom-toms to make it rain. Baseball enthusiasts claim there is a high correlation between the years in which the American League has won the World Series and years in which there is an expanding economy. If correlation really implied causation we could fight economic recessions by inducing good pitchers to join the American League!

On the serious side, we can point to the frequently cited cause-and-effect relationship between education and income. The data usually show that individuals with more education have higher incomes — at least up through a bachelor's degree. But we should be careful about accepting this correlation as necessarily implying a cause-and-effect relationship. The problem is that rich and bright kids go to college, and they tend to have higher incomes. If rich and bright kids skipped college and went into the work force, they would still tend to have higher incomes. Also, much of the income and education data are unadjusted for age. For example, most people born in the early part of the century had a grade school education, and today they often live on Social Security checks. Those who were born later in the century and are at the peak of their income-earning years are more likely to have gone to college. The data show low educational achievement coupled with low income because a relatively high percentage of those with low educational achievement is now retired, and retired persons tend to have relatively low incomes. Remember that even if statisticians claim the correlation results are "highly significant" or that "there is an excellent fit," correlation does not mean causation.

The Respondent Selection Problem in Polls and Surveys

Data obtained from polls and surveys can generate a number of distortions. Assume, for example, that you wanted to determine student attitudes about the size of the university's athletic budget as compared with the university's library budget. You surveyed students coming out of the library on a crisp, clear Saturday afternoon in October and found that 90 percent of your respondents stated that the library's budget should be increased and the athletic department's budget decreased. You would not conclude from your survey that 90 percent of the students on the campus held such views. You would realize that only a few scholarly types would be in the library on that day, while most students would be at the football game or participating in a 50-mile charity bicycle marathon. The results would be worthless because your respondents would be primarily students who preferred the library to sports. The students you interviewed would not be representative of all students.

Now assume that you are interested in determining student attitudes about, and participation in, model railroading. You put an ad in the student newspaper saying, "Students interested in participating in a scientific poll related to model railroading should meet in Room 105B of the Student Union." Would the students responding to this ad represent the "average" student? No, most respondents would be model railroad buffs who would tell you that they spend many enjoyable hours building truss bridges, wiping rails, and oiling the rods of a brass Union Pacific Big Boy.

Assume that you are still determined to get responses about model railroading from a representative group of students, so you ask the registrar to have the computer randomly select 500 student names.[6] Now, you might wallow in the assurance that a randomly selected sample will give representative results. You call the first student on the list and tell him you want to conduct a ten-minute survey on his model railroad preferences. You will probably hear a loud click. After hearing many such negative responses, you might finally come across a railroad buff who will answer your questions. Although you used a random selection procedure to select your respondents, those who respond positively to your questions will not be a random sample of students. There is some evidence that a smaller percentage of individuals today will respond to surveys, which has increased the significance of self-selection errors.

Surely, you think, no one is going to believe the results of the rail survey because they will know that it was distorted by respondent self-selection. However, in the 1950s, Dr. Albert Kinsey published two best-sellers, *Sexual Behavior in the Human Male* (1948) and *Sexual Behavior in the Human Female* (1953), based on similar methodology. Through various means he publicized that he wanted to interview men and women for a sexuality study he was conducting. Although he tried to avoid the worst problems of self-selection, a large percentage of those who responded had an abnormal interest in sex. As a result, the findings were rather severely skewed. Yet, despite the nonscientific methods used to procure respondents, Kinsey's work was widely quoted in newspapers and on television, where it was invariably referred to as a "scientific study of human sexuality."

Assume you want to conduct a door-to-door survey of people's reading habits. Do you think respondents will tell you that they read *True Confessions, Playgirl, Playboy, Romantic Adventures,* comic books, and the *National Enquirer*? Or will they try to impress you by saying that they read the *New Yorker,* the *New England Journal of Medicine,* and if they are really uptown snobs, the *New York Times Book Review.* The published circulation data show that *True Confessions,* the *National Enquirer,* and comic books far outsell the latter publications. But even the circulation data don't tell us

---

[6]Old methods, such as throwing dice and drawing names out of hats, have been replaced by the use of random numbers generated by a computer.

whether the material was actually read. The magazines might merely have been filed on bookshelves next to dusty collections of *Foreign Affairs* and *National Geographic* which are in the same unblemished state of virginity as the moment they came off the press. We could probably get an accurate view of people's reading habits by rummaging through their trash in the dead of night and tabulating the number of pages with turned corners, and with jam and dirt on them.

People tend to lie not only on apparently trivial matters such as their reading habits, but on more substantial matters as well. When asked in a survey whether they had donated blood during the past five years, more than 20 percent of the respondents said they had — the actual proportion, however, is less than 5 percent. Ninety-five percent of Americans surveyed agreed with the statement that every American citizen has a responsibility to vote, but only one-third actually do vote in congressional elections in years when there is no presidential contest. Most survey results indicate that nearly twice the number of Americans reported they voted in the last election than actually voted. Although political polls have improved considerably since they predicted that Thomas Dewey would defeat Harry Truman by a landslide in 1948, they occasionally underestimate the strength of candidates — when respondents are simply too embarrassed to name the candidate they are actually supporting. The age, sex, and race of interviewers are also likely to affect results. During World War II, when blacks were asked by white and black interviewers whether they thought they would be treated better if the Japanese defeated the United States, black respondents interviewed by black surveyors were more than four times as likely to respond affirmatively as were blacks interviewed by whites.

Polls give misleading results for new commercial products as well. Only the most naive marketing pollster believes the raw poll results. Mature and seasoned pollsters know that Americans tend to respond far too enthusiastically, for example, to products "they will buy" if placed on the market — many respondents simply don't want the pollster to think that they are too cheap to buy the product. When you read the seemingly endless number of surveys that claim to reveal the personal habits and preferences of the "average American," always keep in mind that Diogenes' search for an honest man would not end with those who respond to such surveys.

ANNUALIZATION AND SEASONAL ADJUSTMENTS

Many data series, including all GDP/GNP data and the Consumer and Producer Price Indexes, which report data on a weekly, monthly, or quarterly basis, have annualized numbers. Annualization converts periodic data to an annual basis. If two million cars are sold in one quarter, the annual rate of sales will be eight million. Reporting annualized data makes it much easier to compare months, quarters, and years. However, the data user or reporter must be absolutely certain that he or she does not mistakenly substitute the annualized number for the unannualized number. For example, if two million cars were sold last quarter and the annualized number of eight million is reported in the data series, we cannot say that eight million cars were sold last quarter — this is incorrect. Rather, we should say that "cars sold last quarter at an annualized rate totaled eight million."

Most monthly or quarterly data can be adjusted to an annual basis simply by multiplying by 12 or 4, but rates of change, or percents, cannot be annualized so easily. If the sales of cars increased by 2 percent over the previous quarter, the annualized increase is not 8 percent but 8.24 percent. Assume that 100 cars were sold in the fourth quarter of 1990 (1990:IV) and 102 cars were sold in the first quarter of 1991 (1991:I). If the 2 percent increase during 1991:I is annualized as 8 percent, it would understate the true annualized percentage increase. A 2 percent increase each quarter means that total car sales at the end of the year would be 108.24:

1991:I	100	$\times 1.02 = 102.00$
1991:II	102	$\times 1.02 = 104.04$
1991:III	104.04	$\times 1.02 = 106.12$
1991:IV	106.12	$\times 1.02 = 108.24$

If car sales in each quarter grow by 2 percent, the entire year's sales will have grown by 8.24 percent. Thus, the appropriate annualized equivalent of a 2 percent growth rate per quarter is 8.24 percent. Use the following formula to annualize a percent increase:

$$AR = (1 + r)^n - 1$$

where AR is the annualized rate of increase, r is the periodic (month/quarter) rate of increase, and n is the number of periods per year. In our example,

$$AR = (1.02)^4 - 1 = 0.0824 = 8.24 \text{ percent}$$

The annualized rate of increase can also be calculated directly from the raw data:

$$AR = \left(\frac{Q_t}{Q_{t-1}} \right)^n - 1$$

where Q_t is the relevant quantity in the present quarter, Q_{t-1} is the relevant quantity in the previous quarter, and n is the number of periods per year. In our example, if 102 cars are sold in this quarter compared to 100 cars in the previous quarter the annualized rate of increase is

$$AR = \left(\frac{102}{100}\right)^4 - 1 = 0.0824$$

Virtually all annualized data are also seasonalized or seasonally adjusted. Most data are subject to normal and expected seasonal fluctuations due to climatic conditions, school schedules, number of shopping days, vacations, buying patterns, and so on. Retail sales of toys are high in November and low in January; automobile sales are good in May but lousy in February; airline tickets sell well during long weekends and holidays; heating oil sales peak in January and plummet in July. If data are to be compared from one quarter to the next, or from one month to another, these normal seasonal fluctuations need to be smoothed out. Hence, we must first always determine whether a data series is seasonally adjusted or not. If the series is seasonally adjusted, then any week, month, or quarter can be compared with any other week, month, or quarter, or with annual data. If the series is not seasonally adjusted, then comparisons can be made only with the same week, month, or quarter of another year.

Economic researchers who use seasonally adjusted data frequently take such adjustments for granted and too often assume that the adjustments are always "correct" — that is, that the adjustments will smooth out the fluctuations perfectly. This is seldom the case. Although we now possess fairly sophisticated seasonal adjustment models, they are not perfect. When seasonal patterns change, the adjusted data will be incorrect. For example, the percentage of Christmas retail sales made in the last week before Christmas has increased sharply during the past couple of years. Until the change in seasonal patterns (if indeed they have really changed) is integrated into the model, the seasonally adjusted sales in November will be abnormally low and the seasonally adjusted sales in December will be abnormally high. Comparisons with other months will also be distorted.

DATA REVISIONS

One frustrating problem in dealing with data is that data series are revised so frequently. After searching the library for some bit of data for the year 1960, we finally find a book that has the data we want. We write down the number but later we come across another source with data for the same year, except that the values are different. There is a different number for the same year! Which one is right? Why are they different? Which one should I use? If this has ever happened to you, you have just learned a valuable, if jarring, lesson in data research. Many data series are revised annually or every few years. The specific datum presented for any month, quarter, or year depends on the year in which the source was published. For example, GDP/GNP data for the second quarter of 1992 were revised during the following two quarters, and will be revised again for the annual data reported in July 1993, and then revised again in July 1994 and July 1995. It will then remain stable until the benchmark revisions, which are made every five years.

Benchmark revisions reflect new methodologies, definitions, or data sources. Thus, if you are looking up the 1956 GNP in a source published in 1957, you will find one value for the GNP. If you look for the 1956 GNP in that same source published in 1958, you will find that it is different. A source published in 1960 will have yet another figure for the 1956 GNP. That poor 1956 GNP value will never be put to rest. It will change slightly every five years, as long as benchmark revisions are being made. Data collected and reported by the federal government are frequently revised, while data collected by local, state, and private agencies are revised much less frequently. To help readers be aware of data revisions, every major data series in this book has its revision policies clearly stated.

THE UNDERGROUND ECONOMY

The term *underground economy* refers to the billions of dollars in unreported income that results from (1) cash payments for products and services, (2) barter exchanges (of one good or service for another), or (3) services rendered by business firms and independent contractors that are not recorded in the firms' accounting statements. When waiters and taxi drivers fail to report their tips, when doctors and dentists do not report cash payments, when a student tutor does not report his fees, when an independent contractor does business off the books, and when street vendors fail to file an income tax return, they are part of the underground economy. The underground economy also includes illegal activities, which generate income from drugs, prostitution, stealing, gambling, and so on. Estimates of the size of the underground economy run as high as 15 percent of the nation's GDP and involve as many as one in four persons in the work force. Since 1984 the Bureau of Economic Analysis has estimated the value of the underground economy and included it in the gross national product. The revision for 1984 increased the GNP by $44 billion, or 1 percent.[7] The real significance of the underground economy is that much of the national, regional, and local data are incomplete because reliable

---

[7] See Carol S. Carson, "The Underground Economy: An Introduction," *Survey of Current Business*, May 1984; and Robert P. Parker, "Improved Adjustments for Misreporting of Tax Return Information Used to Estimate the National Income and Product Accounts," *Survey of Current Business*, June 1984.

estimates do not exist for it. Not only are some values underestimated but some are underestimated more than others so that comparative distortions also appear in the data.

THE STANDARD INDUSTRIAL CLASSIFICATION CODE (SIC)

Many companies and agencies use government data from various industries and firms to determine competitive pressures, design new markets, and compare costs, revenues, employment, and prices. Prior to 1945 each government agency defined industries in its own way. Some agencies would place a firm producing brooms and towels in the broom industry; others would place it in the towel industry; and still others would put it in both. Since 1945, the classification of firms into specific industries has been standardized in the *Standard Industrial Classification* (SIC) *Manual* published by the Office of Management and Budget. The Standard Industrial Classification (SIC) is an important tool for economists, government regulators, managers, professional organizations, and marketing departments. It enables researchers to classify and compare prices, costs, sales, inventories, and so on within more than 1000 industries. The SIC places each establishment into an industry grouping based on the primary activity of the establishment. An **establishment** is an economic unit — generally at one physical location — where business is conducted, services performed, or goods manufactured. Examples of establishments are factories, mines, stores, motels, warehouses, and offices. A single company might consist of several establishments. At the broadest classification level there are 11 divisions:

A. Agriculture, forestry, and fishing
B. Mining
C. Construction
D. Manufacturing
E. Transportation, communication, electric, gas, and sanitary services
F. Wholesale trade
G. Retail trade
H. Finance, insurance, and real estate
I. Services
J. Public administration
K. Not elsewhere classified

These divisions are further segmented into major groups that have two-digit SIC codes; then into industry groups that have three-digit codes; and, finally, into industries that have four-digit codes.

In order to observe the level of detail in the SIC codes, let's trace the chewing gum industry in the SIC listings. We begin by looking under Manufacturing, continue to the Food and Kindred Products industry, then to the Sugar and Confectionery Products section, and finally get to Chewing Gum.

SIC Code

Manufacturing	D
Food and Kindred Products	20
Sugar and Confectionery Products	206
Chewing Gum	2067

The Food and Kindred Products industry is called a two-digit industry; Sugar and Confectionery Products is a three-digit industry; and Chewing Gum is a four-digit industry.

The Census of Manufacturing, published every five years by the Census Bureau, has five-, six-, and seven-digit classifications for certain industries. Until recently the SIC system was based on the classification manual published in 1972. However, a revised SIC manual, based on 1987 reports, became available in 1990.

There is also a Standard International Trade Classification System (SITC), which facilitates price and other comparisons among international products and industries. Most Western countries use this classification system for their internationally traded goods.

METROPOLITAN AREAS

When looking for regional, state, or local data you are likely to come across such acronyms as MSA, CSMA, PSMA, and NECMA, which all refer to types of metropolitan areas. When World War II veterans returned home and moved to the newly constructed suburbs, the population statistics of the old central cities lost much of their meaning and significance. The population of Cleveland, for example, did not increase a great deal, but the *total* Cleveland area, including the new suburbs, grew significantly. Because of these changes, the bean counters in the Bureau of the Budget (now OMB) developed the concept of a standard metropolitan area (SMA) to include not only the central city but the communities adjacent to the central city. The name was changed in 1959 to Standard Metropolitan Statistical Area (SMSA) and again in 1983 to the Metropolitan Statistical Area (MSA). A Metropolitan Statistical Area does not have to be very metropolitan. The Atlanta, Georgia, Metropolitan Statistical Area would be considered by most people to be metropolitan but not many people, except those living in Dulac, Louisiana, would consider the Houma-Thibodaux, Louisiana, Metropolitan Statistical Area to be metropolitan. It's not hard to qualify as an MSA; there are 267 of them. At the current time the criteria for MSA classification are the following:

1. One city with 50,000 or more inhabitants or an urbanized area with 50,000 population plus a total MSA area population of at least 100,000.

2. MSAs consist of counties (except in New England) adjacent to the central city that have at least 50 percent of their population in the urbanized area. Other counties are included if they meet certain requirements of commuting patterns to the central counties and metropolitan criteria such as population density and urbanization. In New England the MSAs are defined in terms of cities and towns rather than counties.

Unfortunately, the metropolitan waters were muddied in 1983 by the addition of Primary Metropolitan Statistical Areas (PMSAs) and Consolidated Metropolitan Statistical Areas (CMSAs) and by the elongation of area names. New York, San Francisco, Chicago, and Houston are no longer Metropolitan Statistical Areas. The official name for the New York metropolitan area is: "New York-Northern New Jersey-Long Island, NY-NJ-CT Consolidated Metropolitan Statistical Area." The area around the "toddling town" is now known as "Chicago-Gary-Lake County (IL), IL-IN-WI Consolidated Metropolitan Statistical Area." You might be tempted to simply call it the "Chicago Metro area." However, people might not know whether you were referring to the Consolidated Metropolitan Statistical Area (CMSA) or another new area called the Primary Metropolitan Statistical Area (PMSA). After casting a wide net with the CMSA, the bean counters came back and said, "Well, we would really like to differentiate between the extensive metropolitan areas and the more central, but limited, metropolitan areas. Hence, they created PMSAs, which are smaller metropolitan areas that exist within CMSAs. They meet certain criteria, including having a population of 1 million or more. Any metropolitan area containing one or more PMSAs is called a Consolidated Metropolitan Statistical Area. Thus, the Chicago-Gary-Lake County (IL), IL-IN-WI Consolidated Metropolitan Statistical Area consists of six PMSAs: Aurora-Elgin, IL PMSA; Chicago, IL PMSA; Gary-Hammond, IN PMSA; Joliet, IL PMSA; Kenosha, WI PMSA; and Lake County, IL PMSA.

One further complication: The New England MSAs, unlike MSAs in the rest of the country, are composed of cities and towns instead of counties, so statistical data that are compiled only for counties cannot be compiled for these New England MSAs. Consequently, the Census Bureau has defined another type of metropolitan area called the New England County Metropolitan Area (NECMA), which provides county-based metropolitan areas for New England but does not replace the traditional

MSAs in New England. Why didn't the Census Bureau simply redefine the MSAs in New England so that they would be based on counties instead of cities and towns? Possibly because of local political pressure or because they wanted to maintain continuity with the older series. In 1991 there were 267 MSAs, 21 CMSAs, 73 PMSAs, and 16 NECMAs.

OTHER GEOGRAPHIC AREAS

Other geographic areas frequently mentioned in government publications (especially the census) and many private publications include the following:

Minor civil divisions (MCDs):   Minor subdivisions of counties such as towns and townships or not legally defined.

Special economic urban areas (SEUAs):   Townships in New Jersey and Pennsylvania and towns in the six New England states with a 1980 population of 10,000 or more.

Incorporated place: A political unit that is legally incorporated as a city, village, or town.

Census designated places (CDPs):   Formerly called unincorporated places, CDPs are closely settled areas of population without legally established limits. They generally have a population of at least 1000 people. There are about 3000 CDPs.

Census tracts: Statistical subdivisions of counties in metropolitan areas and large counties that average about 4000 in population. Economic data are widely available for the approximately 45,000 census tracts. A medium-size metropolitan area of around 500,000 will have about 100–150 census tracts. The importance of census tracts, other than the smallness of the area they cover, is that their boundaries basically do not change. When a tract's population increases, the tract is divided into smaller tracts, but the boundary of the original tract remains constant. Assume a certain tract on the fringe of a metropolitan area is numbered 50. As it gains in population, it could be divided into tracts 50.01, 50.02, and 50.03 with the three tracts comprising the same total area of the original tract 50. Census tract boundaries may cross place, MCD, and CBD (see below) boundaries, but they never cross state or county boundaries. Blocks and block groups do not cross census tract boundaries.

Census blocks: The smallest type of census areas. These are subdivisions of census tracts that comprise one or a few city blocks that are small rectangular areas bounded by four streets. They are identified in urban areas and include about 70 people. No sample data are published for blocks, and 100 percent, or complete-count, data might be suppressed if they would reveal information about a particular household.

Enumeration districts (EDs):   Used where census blocks are not used. Average population in EDs is about 600.

Central business districts (CBDs):   Areas of high land value, traffic flow, and concentration of retail businesses, offices, theaters, hotels, and service establishments. They are defined in any SMSA central city and any other city with a population of 50,000 or more and a sufficient concentration of economic activity.

Major retail centers (MRCs):   Concentrations of retail stores located in SMSAs but outside the CBDs. MRCs can be malls or shopping districts. They must have at least 25 retail establishments and one or more large general merchandise or department stores.

GEOGRAPHIC CODES

The federal government is increasingly using geographic codes, or geocodes, in presenting its state and local data. There are different coding structures, but the most widely used one is the Federal Information Processing Standards (FIPS) code. Although the hierarchical structure lacks systematic organization, you will probably come across these codes in government and private publications.

The state FIPS code is a two-digit code assigned in alphabetical sequence: Alabama is 01, Alaska is 02, and so on. However, for reasons unknown, some numbers have been skipped. For example, there is no 07; nor is there a 43. Wyoming, the last state according to the alphabet has a FIPS code of 56.

Metropolitan Statistical Areas (MSAs), Consolidated Metropolitan Statistical Areas (CMSAs), and Primary Metropolitan Statistical Areas (PMSAs) have four-digit codes in alphabetical sequence at the national level: Abilene, Texas, MSA is 0040; Albany, Georgia, MSA is 0120. A code of 9999 designates a place as a nonmetropolitan area. CMSAs have their own two-digit code added to their four-digit code. These two-digit codes are also assigned alphabetically. For example, the Dallas-Fort Worth, Texas, CMSA has a geocode of 1922 31. A size code is also given for each MSA/CMSA/PMSA based on its population:

Under 250,000	1
250,000 to 499,999	2
500,000 to 999,999	3
1,000,000 and over	4

Within each state, counties are assigned a three-digit FIPS code in alphabetical sequence. In most states, the codes begin with 001 and generally continue in increments of two—that is, 001, 003, 005, and so on. Agricultural censuses use a different three-digit coding system for counties, which is based on neighborhood groupings.

The place (city, town, municipality) code is a four-digit code assigned in alphabetical sequence within each state. Unincorporated municipalities with populations of fewer than 2500 and rural areas are designated as "rest of county" and assigned a place code of 9990. In addition, there is a size code for places:

Population	Size Code
Under 2500	0
2,500 to 4,999	2
5,000 to 9,999	3
10,000 to 24,999	4
25,000 to 49,999	5
50,000 to 99,999	6
100,000 to 249,999	7
250,000 to 499,999	8
500,000 and over	9

As an example of how these codes work, assume you were searching through a census publication and came across the following entry:

Geocodes

Place	State	County	Place	PS	MSA/PMSA
Dayton City	48	291	1105	2	3360
Del Rio City	48	465	1130	5	9999

By looking up the data in the front of the publication, you would find that both cities are located in Texas (state code 48), that Dayton is located in Liberty County (county code 291), Dayton's own code is 1105, its size is between 2500 and 4999 (size code 2), and it is also located in the Houston, Texas, PMSA (code 3360). Del Rio is not located in any metropolitan area (9999).

CATEGORIES AND SUBCATEGORIES IN DATA STATEMENTS

Inexperienced researchers might have some trouble understanding the format frequently used for reporting categories and subcategories. The descriptions of the main categories of data begin at the far left-hand margin with subcategories indented to the right. Totals are derived by adding together the figures at the next indented level. The following example of categories/subcategories is simple and easy to understand, but data formats can be lengthier and more complicated, and care must be exercised in reading and interpreting them.

Population of Podunk	100,000
Males	45,000
Caucasians	35,000
Blacks	8,000
Native Americans	2,000

Females	55,000
Caucasians	49,000
50 years or older	8,000
Less than 50 years	41,000
Blacks	5,000
Native Americans	1,000

Notice that total population of 100,000 is equal to the population of the two divisions at the next indented level: Males and Females. The total number of females is equal to the sum of the three divisions at the next level of indentation: Caucasians, Blacks, and Native Americans. The total of female Caucasians is equal to the sum of those 50 years and older and those younger than 50.

MISCELLANEOUS TIPS ON USING DATA[8]

1. **Abbreviations**

   a. Who pays the freight?

   c.i.f.   Stands for "*cost, insurance, and freight.*" If something is sold "c.i.f. — buyer's dock," it means that the shipper or seller is paying the costs of getting the goods to the buyer's unloading dock.

   f.a.s.   Stands for "*free alongside ship.*" If something is sold f.a.s., the seller (exporter) pays the costs of getting the goods to the port. The buyer has to pay the costs to get the goods loaded onto the ship and transported to the importer's location.

   f.o.b.   Stands for "*free on board.*" If something is sold f.o.b., it means the buyer pays the freight and insurance costs to get the products from the seller's dock.

   b. What do the letters in the tables mean?

   ar: Annualized *rate.* If the rate of increase remained the same for all months/quarters of the year as it was this month or year, this would be the rate of increase for the year.

   d: Figure withheld to avoid *disclosure of information pertaining to a specific firm or individual.

   n.a.:   Means that the data relevant for that month/year are *not available.* It might mean that the series was discontinued, or the number of respondents was too small for the data to be relevant. Often it means that the data were not collected and processed in time to meet the publication date. Look at the same table in the following week, month, or year.

---

[8]If you use security or interest rate data and are unfamiliar with securities markets, calculations of interest rates, yields, and so on, see Read Me First in Chapter 9, on bonds.

n.e.c.:   Means that the data is *not* *e*lsewhere classified so it is included here.

ns: Percent change irrelevant or insignificant.

nsa: *N*ot seasonally *a*djusted.

p: *P*reliminary data that will be revised. Often, preliminary figures are issued on the basis of partial information and will change substantially when all the data are collected.

r: *R*evised. The data have been revised because of more recent data or because of changes or refinements in the methodology.

sa: Seasonally *a*djusted so that normal seasonal limitations have been smoothed out.

2. Prior to 1977, the federal fiscal year started on July 1 and ended 12 months later on June 30. Beginning in 1977, the federal fiscal year changed, to begin October 1 and end September 30. For most state governments, the fiscal year begins July 1 and ends June 30; for many local governments, the fiscal year ends December 31. Much of the census data, however, have been adjusted to show local, state, and federal data for fiscal years ending June 30.

3. Per capita data are generally based on population existing in the middle of the fiscal or calendar year. Most of the time the population series used to calculate the per capita data exclude armed forces based overseas. Therefore, these per capita figures are slightly higher during wartime.

4. The quarters of a year are often denoted by roman numerals following the year — thus, 1991:I designates the first quarter, 1992:II, the second quarter, and so on. The months of the year are designated by the month's number following the year and a colon; for example, 1991:2 designates February.

5. Current dollar figures represent prices and costs that actually exist during the period. Constant dollar figures are prices and costs that have had the effects of price changes removed. Generally, this is done by dividing current dollar estimates by a price index such as the Consumer Price Index. Any changes in a constant dollar series represent actual changes in real output, expenditures, or income.

CHAPTER 3

SAMPLING ERRORS, INDEX NUMBERS, AND ACCOUNTING

Chapter 2 presented a number of tips for data users. This chapter concentrates on three more topics that are important for all data mongers: samples and sampling error, index numbers, and accounting principles. Readers without any previous knowledge of these subjects are advised to read this material with some care. Even those who have had some exposure to the topics should glance over the pages. At times, the material will become a mite technical, but it is written so that anyone willing to spend a few minutes reading and thinking will be able to comprehend it without undue mental pain. Each section is completely independent of the other two sections, so the material can be consumed in small bites, allowing the joy of acquiring this new knowledge to be savored over many days.

SAMPLES AND SAMPLING ERROR

Censuses and Samples

When the word *population* is used in ordinary conversation, it refers to people in some area. In statistics, the word *population* has a much broader meaning. It refers to the whole of anything. The population could consist of blue pick-up trucks with bald tires, female scientists under the age of 30, red wagons with three wheels, or the CEOs of Fortune 500 companies. The thing we are counting must be clearly defined and must be included in the count. When we count the population, or the universe, as it is sometimes called, we are taking a census.

Given the widely known problems inherent in conducting a census today, it might surprise the reader to learn that censuses are at least as old as recorded history. There were censuses of population (people) in ancient Babylonia as far back as 3000 B.C. The Romans were the first to systematically take regular censuses, which were administered by Roman magistrates called *censors*. In fact, the word *census* comes from the Roman word *censure*, which means "to tax." The Roman census had three purposes: (1) to determine the number of Roman citizens and other persons; (2) to determine the number of men eligible for military service; and (3) to determine the tax capacity of each citizen. The latter two reasons might explain why people have hated and mistrusted censuses since Roman times.[1]

After the fall of the Roman empire censuses apparently disappeared until more recent times. One of the first complete censuses was taken in Canada in 1663, but the first large modern nation to take a census was the United States. The widely publicized censuses of population taken every ten years since 1790 is required by the U.S. Constitution for the purpose of apportioning congressional representatives among the states. The first census was taken by United States marshalls; civilian enumerators were not used until 1880.[2] The U.S. Bureau of the Census was established in 1902 as a permanent office in the Department of Commerce. The Census Bureau conducts about 30 major censuses, including the Census of Manufacturing, Census of Mineral Industries, Census of Transportation, Census of Retail Trade, Census of Service Industries, and Census of Agriculture, which are conducted every five years. Most data series published by government and private sources, however, are obtained not from a census but from personal judgments, extrapolations of past trends, nonrandom sampling, and scientific or random sampling.

Scientific samples, which are used because they are quicker and cheaper than censuses, were started during the 20th century. In fact, they were first widely used during and immediately after World War II. If you were interested in obtaining information on the television viewing habits of American households, you could conduct a census that would require interviews with about 100 million households. If you had only a few general

---

[1]Indications that people disliked censuses show up in early biblical accounts. When King David proposed taking a census about 1000 B.C., Joab warned him that this was an "affront to the Lord." After the king went ahead with the census, God presumably sent a plague upon the people of Israel. This attitude that censuses are evil and to be avoided continues today. When some former colonies in Africa and Asia attempted to take their first census, many enumerators were killed or driven off. Today, many people in the United States still avoid census enumerators.

[2]A "census" of people is more precisely an enumeration, and an *enumerator* is the person who actually counts the people.

questions on TV viewing habits, you would find it much less expensive to obtain the same information through a random sample of about 2000 households. However, small samples cannot be used to obtain detailed social-economic-racial characteristics of respondents. For example, if you were interested in obtaining data only on TV programs watched by American households, a random sample of 2000 households would provide reasonably accurate information. If you were interested in the relationship among the income, race, and sex of members of the TV audience and the programs watched by these various subsets of the audience, the sample size would have to be much larger, a minimum of about 50,000 respondents. Samples are the preferred vehicle for obtaining repetitive information that is not overly concerned with relationships among respondent and subject characteristics. The size of the labor force, the unemployment rate, and numerous monthly price indexes are based on (large) random samples that do not provide detailed information.

Two fundamental errors can cause an estimate derived from a sample to differ from the actual value of its population or universe. The first type of error is called the sampling error and the other, not surprisingly, is called the nonsampling error. Many factors responsible for nonsampling error, such as nonresponse bias, lying, imperfect recall, and poorly worded questions, were mentioned in Chapter 2. Accordingly, we will concentrate on sampling error in this section.

Sampling error arises from the use of a sample rather than a census (a complete counting) to estimate some data. Assume that you randomly select 100 balls from an urn containing 10,000 red and black balls.[3] Assuming that you conduct a random sample and pull out 45 black balls and 55 red balls, you might reasonably conclude that approximately 45 percent of the balls in the jar are black and 55 percent are red. However, you cannot be certain this is the correct ratio of black and red balls because you are basing your estimate on the results of only one sample. You should be concerned that your estimate might be wrong due to sampling error; that is, the results of the sample that you took are not the same results you would get if you took another sample or if you tallied the colors of all 10,000 balls.

If a sample is a random sample, we are able to estimate the likelihood of the occurrence of an error arising from the use of the sample as opposed to the use of a census. The calculation of this sampling error is based on the distribution of the averages (means) in a large number of samples drawn from the same universe. Any single sample is just one of

---

[3] A sample is random if every item in the defined population has an equal chance of being selected.

a large number of samples that could have been selected using the same selection process. If you return to the jar the balls selected in the first sample and take other samples, you will probably get slightly different estimates of the ratio of red and black balls. A second sample of the balls might produce 51 black and 49 red balls instead of 55 red and 45 black. A third sample might have still other results. In other words, each sample could have different estimates or mean averages. The *standard error*, which is the major ingredient in determining sampling error,[4] measures the variation among the estimates derived from all possible samples.

Let's pause here to examine the Census Bureau's sampling of households to obtain monthly data on employment, unemployment, wages, and other characteristics of the labor market. If the Census Bureau took a census, or complete enumeration, of all households in the United States in order to determine the monthly unemployment rate, it would have to contact 95 million households every month. Obviously, this would be prohibitively expensive, even for the federal government, so the Census Bureau uses a sophisticated system called *multistage probability sampling*, which is an attempt to obtain a sample that is representative of various social and geographical groups in society. In order to be able to report such detail with any acceptable degree of confidence, the Bureau has to use a large random sample (56,000 households). It combines personal interviews and telephone contacts with these households to obtain monthly data on labor market participation. The Bureau could use the same procedures to select another sample of 56,000 households, which would yield different estimates, and then select another sample, which would yield yet other results. Each sample would provide slightly different information about the employment situation in the nation. Rather than take a number of samples to observe this variation, the Bureau takes only one sample but then estimates the sampling error associated with it. This sampling error is an estimate of the variation among the results derived from all possible samples.[5] In simple English, it gives us the odds that the sample value is correct. Without going into unnecessary detail and exceptions, let's simply state that when the sample size is a small

---

[4]Unfortunately, some statisticians use the terms *sampling error* and *standard error* interchangeably. Sampling error refers to errors that arise from the use of a sample instead of a complete enumeration. It is, in effect, the total, or bottom line, error after the level of confidence has been selected. The standard error is the first building block in the construction of the sampling error. This footnote will make more sense after you have finished this section.

[5]For those with a bit of statistical training, the standard error is the standard deviation of the means taken from repeated samples. We will present a simplified discussion of this shortly.

percentage of a large universe (which is true for most data series in this book), the standard error is calculated as follows:

$$\text{Standard error} = \frac{\text{standard deviation}[6]}{\sqrt{\text{size of the sample}}}$$

For example, assume the United Auto Workers Union commissions a statistician to estimate the average income of union automobile workers. The statistician takes a random sample of 1000 union auto workers and finds that the average (mean) income of the workers is \$34,300 and the standard deviation is \$8550. The standard error would be:

$$\text{Standard error} = \frac{\$8550}{\sqrt{1000}} = \$270$$

This standard error doesn't mean much yet, but we will use it to construct intervals — called *confidence intervals* — by adding one or more standard errors *to* the mean and subtracting one or more standard errors *from* the mean. The confidence intervals obtained by adding and subtracting these standard errors are the following (skim over them and jump to the example below):

1. Assume that we take repeated samples of some universe or population and calculate the sample mean and standard error for each. Then we generate from each of these samples a confidence interval equal to the sample mean plus or minus 1 standard error. Based on certain statistical theories, we would know that the true population mean will fall within these confidence intervals (mean ± 1 standard error) approximately 68 percent of the time.

2. Assume that we take repeated samples of some universe or population and calculate the sample mean and standard error for each. Then we generate from each of these samples a confidence interval equal to the sample mean plus or minus 1.65 standard errors. Based on certain statistical theories, we would know that the true population mean will fall within these confidence intervals (mean ± 1.65 standard errors) approximately 90 percent of the time.

---

[6]The *standard deviation* is a measure of the dispersion of the sample results, which gives greater weight to the largest deviations. To obtain the standard deviation, calculate the mean (average) of a sample and subtract each observation (value) from the mean to obtain deviations from the mean. Square each of these deviations and sum the squares of the deviations. Then take the square root of this sum to obtain the standard deviation. If this makes no sense, see David B. Johnson, *Statistics for Numerophobiacs: How to Enjoy Learning, Living, and Lying with Statistics* (Mountain View, CA: Mayfield, forthcoming).

3. Assume that we take repeated samples of some universe or population and calculate the sample mean and standard error for each. Then we generate from each of these samples a confidence interval equal to the sample mean plus or minus 1.96 standard errors. Based on certain statistical theories, we would know that the true population mean will fall within these confidence intervals (mean ± 1.96 standard errors) approximately 95 percent of the time.

The preceding discussion is not easy to read and comprehend the first time through. Try it again after reading the following examples, which will simplify the concepts.

Example A: Assume that we return to the autoworkers' income example, where we found the average income from the sample responses to be $34,300 and the standard deviation to be $270. If we were to take repeated samples of 1000 size of the same union membership, we could expect that:

i. In 68 percent of the samples the true average (mean) income would be found within the interval of $34,030 and $34,570: ($34,300 − $270 = $34,030 and $34,300 + $270 = $34,570).

ii. In 90 percent of the samples the true average (mean) income would be found within the interval of $33,855 and $34,745. (*Note*: 1.65 × $270 = $445.)

iii. In 95 percent of the samples the true average (mean) income would be found between $33,771 and $34,829. (*Note*: 1.96 × $270 = $529.)

If you were going to interpret the results of the survey to some guy who has not read this book, you might select, say, the 95 percent confidence level (iii) and then describe it as follows: "A recent survey reported that the average income of automobile workers was $34,300. Since this average was obtained from a random sample, we would like to think it is a reasonably accurate representation of the true average income of all autoworkers, but we cannot be certain. However, we can be 95 percent certain that the true mean will fall within plus or minus $529 (1.96 × $270) of the reported average. That is, we can be 95 percent certain that the true average income of all autoworkers is somewhere between $33,771 and $34,829."

The larger the standard error, the wider will be the generated intervals into which the true value of the population will fall. Thus, if the standard error were $500 instead of $270, we would say that at the 95 percent level of confidence the true average income would be found between $33,300 and $35,300 (rounding 1.96 to 2 standard errors). The smaller the standard error, the smaller the generated confidence intervals. The smaller the confidence intervals, the more precise the mean obtained from the sample.[7] If, for example, the sample mean is $34,300, with a 95 percent confidence interval of $34,299 to $34,301, we know we have a precise and accurate sample mean!

Example B: The Census Bureau's estimate of total civilian employment in February 1990 is 116 million. The standard sampling error for total employment in the nation is approximately 300,000. Hence, we can expect that in 95 percent of the samples, the true or actual employment will be between 115.4 million and 116.6 million (rounding the 1.96 standard errors to 2.0). Remember that the standard error is applicable to the total employment figure and that estimates of local area employment, or employment for certain age, racial, or ethnic groups will have higher relative standard errors.

Most government publications do not report the absolute standard error but rather a relative standard error known as the **coefficient of variation** (cv). The coefficient of sampling variation is a measure of the relative size of the standard error. It is calculated by dividing the standard error by the mean. In the autoworkers' income example, the standard error was $270 and the mean was $34,300; hence, the coefficient of sampling variation is:

$$cv = \frac{\$270}{\$34,300} = 0.00787$$

Because the standard error is now expressed as a percentage of the mean, it can be compared with the standard errors of samples taken from much different populations. For example, assume that we are interested in knowing the average income of lawyers, and from a sample of 1000 lawyers we obtain an estimated mean of $34,300 and a standard error of $1000. A quick check on the relative precision of the average autoworker's income and the average lawyer's income could be obtained easily. The coefficient of sampling variation for lawyers' average income would be 0.025 ($1000/40,000), which is much higher than the cv of 0.00787 for automobile workers. Hence, we know the autoworkers' average is more precise or reliable than the lawyers' average.

We could state this comparison another way. Let's assume that we want to be 95 percent confident that the true universe mean is within a certain range. The 95 percent confidence interval for the autoworkers' mean income is between $33,771 and $34,829. The 95 percent confidence range for the lawyers' income is between $32,340 and $36,260. Although we are 95 percent certain that the autoworkers' average income falls somewhere between $33,771 and $34,829, the 95 percent confidence range for the lawyers' income is a much wider range — $32,340 to $36,260.

---

[7]When interpreting the standard error as being large or small, we must always compare its size relative to the mean, an important qualification we will discuss below.

Hence, we know the lawyers' average is less precise. In fact, if we generated for the lawyers' average income the same confidence interval of $33,771 to $34,829 used for autoworkers' income, that interval would be equivalent to a 40 percent confidence level for the lawyers' average income.[8]

Interpreting Sample Results: Nonproportional Variables

Now to the real nitty gritty! How are we to interpret the following announcement on the evening news: "A recent survey has shown that the average income of lawyers is $34,300 with a margin of error of 'X' percent." Is that "X" percent equivalent to the 2.5 percent of the standard error divided by the mean of lawyers' income? Most definitely not, although I have often seen it reported this way. The sampling error of all nonproportion (not a percent) data should be stated in dollar or quantity amounts, such as this idealized TV spot: "A recent random sample showed that the average income of lawyers was $34,300. Because of possible sampling error, we can only be 95 percent confident that the true average income of lawyers will be somewhere between plus or minus $1960 of this average." That is the correct way of announcing the results because it states the margin of error in dollar amounts around the mean and it gives the level of confidence associated with that error range.

Assume that your news editor has read this far in the book and reports: "The average lawyers' salary was $34,300, with a margin of error of plus or minus $1960." Anything wrong? Are you pounding your fist on the table or cursing at the cat? You should be! Based on this news report you have no idea what level of confidence the $1960 sampling error is associated with. It could be 10 percent, 50 percent, 68 percent, 95 percent, or 99.99 percent. If it were only 10, 50, or 68 percent, you could throw out the reported average as being meaningless. The usual convention among major polling firms is to report the "margin of error" on the basis of a 95 percent level of confidence, but there are no penalties for using other (and unreported) levels of confidence. Unless the news report explicitly states the level of confidence, be wary about the reported "margin of error."

Interpreting Sample Results: Percentage Variables

Although quantity values are reported for thousands of samples taken during each year, the sample results we hear most often, especially around election time, are stated in terms of percentages or proportions. A typical example is: "A recent scientific poll shows that congressional candidate, George "Bubba Hots" Alsoran has 60 percent of the vote with a 3

---

[8]Unless you have a table showing the area under a normal curve and possess an analytical mind, don't try to calculate this confidence level.

percent margin of error." Once again, we wonder what that "3 percent margin of error" really means. The bottom line answer is that we don't know because not enough information has been given to us. But if we become slightly more educated, we can make some educated guesses. We will begin this education by discussing the standard error of a proportion or percentage.

The standard error of a proportion is calculated in the same way as the standard error of the mean: that is, it is equal to the standard deviation divided by the square root of the sample size. However, there is a more convenient formula for calculating the standard error of a proportion:

$$s_P = \sqrt{\frac{PQ}{N}}$$

where s_P = standard error of a percentage
P = proportion of favorable responses
Q = proportion of unfavorable responses
N = size of sample

If 60 percent of 1000 respondents said they were going to vote for Bubba Hots, then,

$$s_P = \sqrt{\frac{(.60)(.40)}{1000}} = \sqrt{0.00024} = 0.01549$$

At a 95 confidence level the limits of the confidence interval are

Confidence limits: $= .60 \pm 1.96\ (0.01549)$
$= .60 \pm .03$
$= .57$ to $.63$
$= 57\%$ to 63%

As before, the confidence interval, or limits, enables us to make some inferences about the true percentage of people who would vote for Bubba Hots. If all possible samples of size 1000 were selected from the population and the mean of each sample computed, 95 percent of the intervals computed for the sample mean would contain the true proportion. Five percent would not. The reader should now understand the meaning of the "margin of error of 3 percent" given in the news report. We are 95 percent confident that between 57 and 63 percent of the voters in the state will express a preference for Bubba Hots over his opponent. However, the news report in the above paragraph left out one very important variable that we have added. That's right, it is the level of confidence of 95 percent, sometimes stated as a 5 percent level of significance. If this level is not stated, we can only guess that the pollsters are using the standard convention of 95 percent confidence but we cannot be certain. If the pollsters wanted to impress us with a small margin of error, they might say that it was ± 1.5 percent. This would be correct at a 68 percent level of confidence where the intervals are determined by only 1 standard error. Such a low confidence level, however, would make the margin of error meaningless.

Before leaving this interesting but mind-boggling section, we need to once again point out the warning — given so strongly in Chapter 2 — about those slippery percentages. Did you catch that slippery percentage in the above paragraph? Shame on you! The 3 percent "margin of error" is really a 5 percent error. The 3 percent refers to three percentage points on each side of the reported 60 percent average, which means that the true percentage of voters hot for "Hots" might be anywhere between 57 percent and 63 percent. This means that the reported 60 percent might be in error by as much as 5 percent (.03/.60).

The next time you are watching TV news and the announcer reports the poll results for Bubba Hots, without mentioning the sampling error, tell your spouse or friend that "The results don't mean a damn thing without the sampling error." If the announcer mentions the sampling error without including the confidence level, say "The results don't mean a damn thing without the level of confidence." If the announcer mentions both the sampling error and the level of confidence, lean back in your easy chair, put on your "smarter than thou" look and say: "We all know that a 60 percent approval rate with a 3 percent margin of error is really a 5 percent error." Then be prepared to duck!

Summary Tips on Samples

The astute reader might be close to acquiring a nervous disorder because the author has included jokes in the discussion of sampling, but he made no mention about the relationship among sampling size, sampling error, and the size of the universe or population. Surely, the size of the sample and sampling error must be affected by the size of the population, or vice versa! Doesn't common sense tell us that the size of the sample necessary to poll Peoria has to be different from the size of the sample necessary to poll California? After all, you might say, poor Peoria has lost "most" of its population to rust bowl disease (Peoria's 1991 population: 110,000) and California has zillions of people running amok (California's 1991 population: 30 million).[9] The wholly unexpected answer to your commonsense inquiry is illustrated by the following quote from the eminent pollster, Dr. George Gallup:

> There is an interesting thing about the laws of probability. This is, that the size of the "universe," or total population group to be sampled, makes no difference at all in the necessary size of the sample. By this I mean when polling the

---

[9]For incurable datamaniacs: Peoria's 1970 population was 127,000 and California's population was 20 million.

United States of America, we don't need any bigger samples than if we are polling New York City, or Trenton, N.J.[10]

As also mentioned in Chapter 2, though, don't abandon your common sense when confronted with expert opinion; the experts might be wrong, they might be making implicit assumptions they are not sharing with you, or you might be misinterpreting their statements. All three possibilities are present in this statement. *Generally*, standard errors and the confidence levels they produce are not affected by the size of the population, which means that the size of the population is *generally* irrelevant to sample size. However, your common sense notion that a sample of 1000 taken from a population of 2000 will yield more precise results than a sample of 1000 taken from a population of 200,000 is absolutely correct. Dr. Gallup's statement is too sweeping and general. A correction factor occasionally has to be applied to the standard error to compensate for the size of the sample (n) in relation to the size of the population (N). That correction factor is

$$\text{Correction factor} = \frac{N-n}{N-1}$$

Table 3.1 shows some applications of the formula to differing sizes of samples and populations.

TABLE 3.1
Correction Factors for Standard Error

Size of Sample (n)	Size of Finite Population (N)	Size of Sample as Percent of Population	Correction Factor
1,000	1,000	100.00	0.000
1,000	1,500	66.67	0.334
1,000	2,000	50.00	0.500
1,000	5,000	20.00	0.800
1,000	10,000	10.00	0.900
1,000	100,000	1.00	0.990
1,000	200,000	0.50	0.995
1,000	1,000,000	0.10	0.999
1,000	2,000,000	0.05	1.000
1,000	4,000,000	0.03	1.000
10,000	4,000,000	0.25	0.998
100,000	4,000,000	2.50	0.975
1,000,000	4,000,000	25.00	0.750
1,500,000	4,000,000	37.50	0.625
2,000,000	4,000,000	50.00	0.500
4,000,000	4,000,000	100.00	0.000

[10]*U.S. News and World Report*, October 5, 1964. Still haven't had enough, have you? New York PMSA has 8.5 million people while the Trenton PMSA has 330,000.

The correction factor is always 1 or less than 1, which means that it reduces the standard error calculated in the normal way. The lower the correction factor, the lower the standard error. Let's return to our autoworker example. If we assumed that the total number, or population, of autoworkers was above 1 million we could use our previous sample of 1000 and ignore the correction factor. Nothing would need to change. However, if the total number of autoworkers was only 10,000 and our sample size was 1000, we would use the correction factor to reduce the standard error from $270 to $243 ($270 × 0.90) and the 95 percent confidence limits from ($33,771 − $34,829) to ($33,824 − $34,776). Alternatively, we could reduce the size of the sample and get the same confidence limits we had before.

The size of the population, or universe, affects the size of the sampling error only when the sample size is a significant proportion of the universe. The size of most nationwide samples are between 1000 and 60,000, with populations ranging from 1 million to 250 million. In most cases, the correction factors will not be used, and only the size of the sample and not the population will determine the sampling error.

Although the size of the population generally does not alter the desirable size of the sample, the level of confidence and the size of the confidence intervals targeted by the pollsters will definitely affect the desirable size of the sample. The higher the level of confidence (for example, 68 percent, 90 percent, 95 percent) and the smaller the error size (for example, $270), the larger the sample should be. If the sample size in the autoworkers' example were increased from 1000 to 2000 while the standard deviation remained unchanged, the standard error would be reduced from $270 to $190, a decrease of 33 percent. If the sample size were doubled again to 4000, the standard error would be $135, or one-half of the original standard error of $270. A quadrupling of the sample size (1000 to 4000) has cut the standard error in half. Sampling error can be cut to *whatever* level is desirable, even to zero. However, increasing the precision of a sample result becomes more and more costly and most pollsters simply believe that the increased precision is not worth the cost.

Most statistics books emphasize statistical theories and their relationship to sampling error. In the real world, however, the most serious errors emanating from samples are not sampling errors. Nonsampling error is caused by a large number of factors. Many of these factors were discussed in Chapter 2. Some subjects in the sample might not respond to the questions, or they might respond with incomplete or inaccurate information; they might make mistakes, or misinterpret the questions; or there might be errors in processing the data. One of the most serious errors is that the variable being measured is not adequately defined in the study or in the publication of the results. What is the meaning of "income" in the autoworkers' example? Is it net or gross monetary income? Does income include health, insurance, pension, and vacation benefits?

Does income include overtime and holiday work? Does it include income from part-time work for other employers? Does it include the use of company-provided cars, uniforms, and parking facilities?[11] Unless these terms are defined precisely in the study *and* in the media release given to the press, the people receiving the information are going to define the terms differently and, therefore, will draw erroneous conclusions from the results.

Various techniques have been developed to recognize and minimize the impacts of certain nonsampling errors (such as nonresponse estimates) on the accuracy of the data. Nothing, however, can protect the data user from poorly designed tests, incomplete or misleading definitions, biased questions, erroneous tabulations, faulty presentations of results, and dozens of other problems.

INDEX NUMBERS

The world is drowning in index numbers. There are index numbers for GNP, crime, population, births, accidents, health, international trade, and every conceivable variety of price. If you want to survive the information age, you had better become acquainted with index numbers. **Index numbers**, which reflect changes in values relative to some base, are found in every nook and cranny of the statistician's office because they are so useful in showing trends and in making comparisons. The important characteristic of an index is that it converts some raw number into a base number. Future changes in the raw numbers are reflected as changes in the index value. To make matters easy for those of us who had trouble with fifth grade arithmetic, indexes are based on data from some period that equal a reference number that is usually but not always given the value of 100. (One exception is the Standard and Poor's Stock Index, which is based on $1941 - 43 = 10$.) This makes it easy to read an index and to compute changes in the index value. For example, if the base period is 1980 ($1980 = 100$) and the index value for the current month is 165, we immediately know that there has been a 65 percent increase in the underlying data between 1980 and the current month. If the index for the current month is 60, the index has decreased by 40 percent since 1980.

Often we want to know the percentage increase in the index value since last month or last year. We can find this out with the help of a simple calculation, as illustrated with the real-world example of the food and beverage component of the Consumer Price Index (CPI) ($1982 - 84 = 100$):

---

[11]Employer-provided parking facilities in the central business district of major cities can easily be worth $400 per month.

January 1992	137.4	$\dfrac{137.8 - 137.4}{137.4} = 0.0029 = 0.29\%$
February 1992	137.8	

The CPI was 137.4 in January 1992 and 137.8 in February 1992, and we want to know the percentage increase during the month of February. As you can see, the series increased 0.29 percent during May, which can be annualized to a 3.54 percent increase $[(1.0029)^{12} - 1]$. Many data series, such as the CPI, are constructed as index numbers and then converted to annualized percentage changes, which are better understood by the average citizen.

Although you can read index numbers without knowing how to construct them, some knowledge of the fundamental steps in their construction will help you to better understand, interpret, and use them. The first step is to determine the items to be included in the index. Usually some of these items will have more significance than other items; that is, you will want to give greater weight to some items than to others. When economists are faced with this formidable task, they revert to the tried and true method of taking a survey. Since surveys are quite expensive, economists are allowed to take broad-based surveys only once every few years, which can lead to distortions in the final results.

Assume that we want to develop a price index for goods purchased by an individual named George. The first thing we would do is survey George's expenditures. Assume that we did so and found that George's total expenditures during the past year (Year 1) were $2000 and were distributed as shown in Table 3.2.

TABLE 3.2
George's Consumer Expenditures in Year 1

(1)	(2) Price Per Unit	(3) Quantity Purchased	(4) Dollars Spent
Steak	$5/lb	100 lb	$ 500
Potatoes	$2/lb	200 lb	400
Beans	$1.50/can	400 cans	600
Beer	$25/case	20 cases	500
			$2,000

Column (1) shows the type of goods in the market basket; column (2), the prices paid by George for each item in his market basket; column (3), the quantity of each good purchased; and column (4) the amount George spent on each item during the year.

Since we want to develop an index showing price changes between two years, we have to tag along after George for another year. Assume that in Year 2 we discover that prices of the goods that George purchased in Year 1 have increased between 5 and 33 percent, as shown in Table 3.3.

TABLE 3.3
Year 2 Prices of Goods Purchased in Year 1

(1)	(2)	(3)	(4)	(5)
	Year 2 Price Per Unit	Percent Increase in Year 2 Prices	Quantity Purchased in Year 1	Year 2 Cost of Buying Year 1 Basket
Steak	$6.00/lb	20%	100 lb	$ 600
Potatoes	$2.10/lb	5	200 lb	420
Beans	$2.00/can	33	400 cans	800
Beer	$27/case	10	20 cases	540
		68%		$2,360

The average increase in price is 17 percent (68 percent/4), but this simple average is meaningless because each of the items constitutes a different proportion of George's budget. We really want to know the weighted average percentage increase in the price of George's market basket, and we have two ways of obtaining those data.

One method is to weight the price increases by the quantities George purchased in Year 1. This method is shown in Table 3.3. By multiplying the prices in Year 2 [column (2)] by the quantities George purchased in Year 1 [column (4)], we obtain the total value of the market basket ($2360). Constructing a price index from this information is simple. We put the value of the market basket in the base period (Year 1) in the denominator and the value of the market basket in the current year (Year 2) in the numerator, multiply the fraction by 100, and we have an index. Thus, the price index for Year 2, using Year 1 quantities (weights), is

$$(\$2360/\$2000) \times 100 = 118.0$$

Using this first method, we find that the price index is 118.0 and that prices have increased by 18 percent during Year 2. Since future price indexes will be based on this base year index, we say that the base period of the index is Year 1 = 100.

Of course, George is unlikely to purchase the same quantities in Year 2 as he purchased in Year 1. His tastes as well as the relative prices he has to pay will change, so he will purchase different quantities of each good during Year 2. Table 3.4 shows the calculations of the price index using Year 2 quantities as weights. However, the cost of this market basket ($2380) *cannot* be compared with the cost of the Year 1 market basket, which utilizes the quantity weights from Year 1. If we incorrectly tried to compare the prices of two market baskets with two different sets of weights, the resulting price index would show the effects of both increases in prices *and* changes in quantities. Therefore, if Year 2 quantities are to be used in calculating the Year 2 price index, they must also be used in calculating the cost of Year 1's market basket. The calculation of the cost of Year 1's market basket using Year 2 quantity weights is shown in Table 3.5.

TABLE 3.4
Year 2 Market Basket Cost Assuming Same Quantities as Year 1

(1)	(2)	(3)	(4)	(5)
	Year 2 Prices Per Unit	Percent Increase in Year 2 Prices	Quantity Purchased in Year 2	Year 2 Cost of Buying Year 2 Basket
Steak	$6.00/lb	20.0	95 lb	$ 570
Potatoes	$2.10/lb	5.0	220 lb	462
Beans	$2.00/can	33.0	350 cans	700
Beer	$27/case	10.0	24 cases	648
				$2,380

TABLE 3.5
Year 1 Market Basket Cost Using Year 2 Quantities

(1)	(2)	(3)	(4)
	Year 1 Prices Per Unit	Quantity Purchased In Year 2	Year 1 Cost of Buying in Year 2
Steak	$5.00/lb	95 lb	$ 475
Potatoes	$2.00/lb	220 lb	440
Beans	$1.50/can	350 cans	525
Beer	$25/case	24 cases	600
			$2,040

Note that the value of any price index depends on the year used for the quantity weights. If Year 1 weights are used, then the index is

$$\frac{2360}{2000} \times 100 = 118.00$$

and the price increase in Year 2 is 18.0 percent. If Year 2 weights or quantities are used, then the index is

$$\frac{2380}{2040} \times 100 = 116.67$$

and the price increase in Year 2 is 16.7 percent.

An index that uses base period (Year 1) weights is known as a Laspeyres index. An index that uses current year weights (Year 2) is a Paasche index. A third method of calculating an index, proposed by economist Irving Fisher and known as the Fisher or Ideal index, is the geometric mean of the Laspeyres and Paasche indexes. Formulas for these indexes are as follows:

Laspeyres index: $I_L = \dfrac{\Sigma P_c Q_b}{\Sigma P_b Q_b} \times I_b$

Paasche index: $I_P = \dfrac{\Sigma P_c Q_c}{\Sigma P_b Q_c} \times I_b$

Fisher index: $I_F = (I_L \times I_P)^{1/2}$

where P_c = prices in the current period
$\quad\;\; P_b$ = prices in the base period
$\quad\;\; Q_c$ = quantities in the current period
$\quad\;\; Q_b$ = quantities in the base period
$\quad\;\; I_b$ = index level or value in the base period

There is no right or wrong way to construct an index, but most statisticians prefer the Laspeyres method because it is much cheaper. They have to determine consumption patterns only during the base year, which they then change infrequently. For example, they may sample the population in 1984 to determine expenditure patterns (weights). These weights — also called market baskets — will then be used to calculate the price index for the next several years. The Paasche method requires that consumption quantities be determined every year. The Consumer Price Index, as well as most other indexes, uses the Laspeyres method.

Index Chaining

Before we leave the topic of indexes, we need to discuss one other useful tool. If you use indexes very much, you often find that an index series calculated on one base year does not "stretch" far enough to cover the years you are interested in. For example, you might find an index series based on 1967 = 100, which covers the years 1960 to 1980, and an index of the same material based on 1987 = 100, which covers the years 1980 to 1990. Inevitably, you will be interested in the years that fall in between, such as the years from 1975 to 1985. Neither index covers all the years in which you are interested.

Before showing you how to solve this pesky problem, let me give you a warning and then offer some advice. The warning involves changing base periods: When base periods are changed, the methodology of the series has likely been changed, which means there will have been a revision of the entire series back to its first year. Hence, when the base period was switched to 1987, the 1970s data was probably revised as well. That old index based on 1967 is likely to be out of date. Revised historical series are hard to obtain, which leads me to offer this bit of advice. Unless you absolutely need precise index numbers (few people do!), go ahead and use that old series because most likely the revisions will be minor and you will save yourself a lot of time and frustration.

Now, back to the problem of trying to span two index series. We'll assume hypothetical data and lead you through one step at a time so you'll understand what you are doing as well as how to do it. Assume that an identical quantity of widgets is purchased each year so that the task of constructing a price index is a simple one. You go to the library one Sunday afternoon and find Index A, based on 1967 = 100 and Index B, based on 1987 = 100. Index A covers the years 1967 to 1982 and Index B covers the years 1980 to 1987. You are interested in obtaining a price index for the years 1975 to 1985.

	Index A 1967 = 100	Index B 1987 = 100	Index C 1967 = 100	Index D 1987 = 100	Index E 1975 = 100
1967	100.0		100.0	22.7	
1975	180.0		180.0	40.9	100.0
1976	192.0		192.0	43.7	106.7
1977	204.0		204.0	46.4	113.3
1978	224.0		224.0	50.9	124.4
1979	240.0		240.0	54.6	133.3
1980	252.0	57.3	252.0	57.3	140.0
1981	268.0	60.9	268.0	60.9	148.8
1982	280.0	63.6	280.0	63.7	155.5
1983		70.0	308.0	70.0	171.0
1984		75.5	331.8	75.5	184.4
1985		81.8	359.8	81.8	199.9
1986		95.5	419.8	95.5	233.2
1987		100.0	439.8	100.0	244.3

You have to stretch at least one of the indexes, but we will construct three indexes—Indexes C, D, and E. The only ingredient required to "chain" an index is at least one overlapping year. In this case, we have three overlapping years: 1980, 1981, 1982. We find the proportional relationship between Index A and Index B in 1980 (252/57.3) and multiply that fixed relationship by the Index B values for each year to obtain Index C. Thus,

$$1981: \quad \frac{252.0}{57.3} \times 60.9 = 268.0$$

$$1982: \quad \frac{252.0}{57.3} \times 63.6 = 280.0$$

$$1983: \quad \frac{252.0}{57.3} \times 70.0 = 308.0$$

and so on.

If you want to extend Index B backward to 1975, you simply invert the ratio:

$$1979: \quad \frac{57.3}{252.0} \times 240.0 = 54.6$$

$$1978: \quad \frac{57.3}{252.0} \times 224.0 = 50.9$$

$$1977: \quad \frac{57.3}{252} \times 204.0 = 46.4$$

and so on to construct Index D.

You can use Index C or D to show the relative prices between 1975 and 1985. If you think it would be easier for your reader to observe relative price changes by converting 1975 to a base year (1975 = 100), you first calculate Index C and convert 180 to a base of 100. Thus, the value of your new index (Index E) in 1976 would be: (192/180) × 100 = 106.7; the value for 1977 would be (204/180) × 100 = 113.3, and so on. As long as you have at least one overlapping year, you can chain two or more indexes together or you can create an index based on an entirely new base year. The year-to-year percentage changes will be the same whether you use Index A, Index B, Index C, or Index D.

Remember that by using this "chaining" process you will not likely have the latest revisions made when the new base year of 1987 = 100 was introduced. The best clue that revisions have indeed been made is that the chained index does not equal the values of the original when they overlap for more than one year. For example, if you constructed Index C from Index A and Index B and found the values to be 269.0 for 1981 and 281.5 for 1982 (which are different from the actual 1967-based index), you would know that some revisions had been made in the 1987-based index (Index B).

A FEW ACCOUNTING PRINCIPLES

Introduction

Although less exciting than its contemporaries, accounting is one of the world's oldest professions. The accounting profession was founded in 1494 by an Italian monk, Luca Pacioli, who laid out double-entry book-keeping for subsequent generations of bean counters. In accounting, every transaction has both a debit, which goes on the left-hand side of a ledger sheet and a credit, which is placed on the right-hand side. Debits are used to record an increase in assets (resources owned by the business), credits are used to report an increase in liabilities (amounts owed to creditors) and net worth (equity or ownership interest). It is important to remember that:

Debits	Credits
Increase assets	Decrease assets
Decrease liabilities	Increase liabilities
Decrease capital	Increase capital

The first rule of accounting is that every debit must have an equal and corresponding credit, or that total debits must equal total credits. If they don't, then the books (though still called "books," they are electronic records) must be checked and the errors found and corrected. The equality of debits and credits does not ensure that the "books" are error free, however. Offsetting errors might have been made or entries could have been made to the wrong accounts. A second rule of accounting, known as the **balance sheet equation**, is that assets = liabilities + net worth. If assets increase, then liabilities or net worth must increase by an equal amount. Following are a few fundamental definitions used in accounting:

Current assets: Sometimes called *working assets*, these are assets that circulate or revolve during the normal operations of the business. Usually, current assets are those that will be converted into cash during the next operating cycle (generally the next few months). They include cash, accounts receivable, inventories, and marketable securities.

Fixed assets: Assets that will not normally be converted into cash during the normal operating cycle of the business. These include property, plant and equipment, investments that are not readily marketable, real estate, and intangibles such as goodwill, patents, copyrights.

Current liabilities: Liabilities that will have to be paid during the operating cycle, including accounts payable, short-term loans payable, taxes payable, accrued wages, and salaries. Current assets are often compared with current liabilities to determine the short-run financial position of the company.

Long-term liabilities: Liabilities that normally will have to be paid off over a period of many years. Long-term bonds and mortgages are examples of long-term liabilities.

Income statement: Also called the *profit and loss statement* or *operating statement*, it reports the revenue, expenses, and profits of the firm during some specific period of time, such as a month, quarter, or year.

Balance sheet: Reports the assets, liabilities, and capital of the entity at some specific date, such as on December 31, 1991.

Cash basis: A method of keeping the books. Revenues are not recorded until cash has been received and expenses are not recorded until payment has been made. Many small firms and virtually all governmental units maintain their records on a cash basis.

Accrual basis: A method of keeping the books. Revenues are recorded for the period in which goods are sold or services performed and expenses are recorded for the period when the costs are incurred or obligated.

Depreciation: The cost of property and equipment that occurs during each accounting period. Depreciation results from physical wear and tear and technical obsolescence, but depreciation charges generally are not related to the actual wear and tear.

Accumulated depreciation: The depreciation expense charged off each year is accumulated and then reported as an offset (deduction) to the property or equipment account to which it pertains.

Simple Transactions Recorded

Debits and credits can be shown in T-accounts or as journal entries. The following simple example shows individual transactions as journal entries, followed by income statements and balance sheets.

1. Assume that Mr. Smith is going to start the new Smith Machine Corporation (SMC) with an initial capital investment of $500,000. His ledger entries will be:

	Debit	Credit
Cash/Deposits	$500,000	
Capital Equity		$500,000

2. SMC gets a loan for $400,000 from the City National Bank.

Cash/Deposits	400,000	
Loans Payable		400,000

3. SMC buys a building.

Buildings	300,000	
Cash or Deposits		300,000

4. SMC buys furniture.

Furniture	100,000	
Cash or Deposits		100,000

5. SMC buys 200 units of metal stampings at $200 per unit.

Inventories	40,000	
Cash or Deposits		40,000

At this point we assume that the Smith Machine Corporation has been operating for the entire month of December. We draw up a simple end-of-month balance sheet to show the initial acquisition and the subsequent shifting of assets. We are assuming there have been no sales or expenses yet.

SMITH MACHINE CORPORATION
Balance Sheet
December 31, 199x

Debits		Credits	
Cash and Deposits	$460,000	Loans Payable	$400,000
Inventories	40,000		
Furniture	100,000		
Building	300,000	Capital Stock	500,000
Total Debits	$900,000	Total Credits	$900,000

Assets are listed on the left-hand (debit) side of the balance sheet whereas liabilities and capital are listed on the right-hand (credit) side. Notice that total debits equal total credits because a debit and a credit are recorded for each transaction. The "cash and deposits account" balance of $460,000 reflects all cash or deposit transactions ($500,000 + $400,000 − $300,000 − $100,000 − $40,000). The owner's equity (capital stock) has remained at $500,000 to reflect the owner's original contribution of capital.

Assume that the following transactions occur during the first quarter of the year:

6. SMC pays wages and salaries.

Wages and Salaries Expense	$ 30,000	
Cash/Deposits		$ 30,000

7. SMC buys more metal stampings.

Inventories	60,000	
Cash/Deposits		60,000

8. SMC buys office supplies.

Supplies Expense	2,000	
Cash/Deposits		2,000

9. SMC sells 150 processed metal stampings at $1000 each; the buyer agrees to pay in 30 days.

Accounts Receivable	150,000	
Sales		150,000

10. SMC makes interest payments to CNB.

Interest Expense	2,000	
Cash/Deposits		2,000

11. SMC records depreciation expenses.

Depreciation Expense	30,000	
Accumulated Depr. Furniture		20,000
Accumulated Depr. Buildings		10,000

12. SMC develops an income statement and determines its taxes and dividends payable, which are as follows.

Income Taxes	24,000	
Income Taxes Payable		24,000
Retained Earnings	11,200	
Dividends Payable		11,200

The company sold 120 processed metal stampings, but it has not received payment, so SMC debits accounts receivable because it is on the accrual basis. Most companies would have an account titled "Estimated Bad Debts" or "Allowance for Bad Debts," which would offset this account, but we will ignore such complications. The depreciation charges recorded in step (11) merit closer evaluation. Our first question, before calculating depreciation expense, is: "What is the depreciable value of the asset?" This is the amount paid for the asset less the estimated salvage value at the end of the asset's useful life. The second question is: "What depreciation method should be used?" There are a variety of depreciation methods; these are usually divided into straight-line depreciation and accelerated depreciation. We assume the company uses straight-line depreciation for both furniture and buildings.

$$\text{Annual depreciation} = \frac{\text{value of asset} - \text{salvage value}}{\text{useful life}}$$

$$\text{Furniture depreciation} = \$20,000 = \frac{\$100,000 - 0}{5 \text{ years}}$$

$$\text{Building depreciation} = \$10,000 = \frac{300,000 - 0}{30 \text{ years}}$$

For ease of computation, we assume that salvage value is zero. We also estimate that furniture will have a useful life of 5 years and that buildings will last 30 years. Depreciation expense is not a cash expense; it is charged off against profits in the income statement. Depreciation expense is often called a "source of cash," but this is not correct. Depreciation is recorded as a current expense, which reduces profits. If the company has a sufficient cash flow, depreciation, as a noncash expense, will represent a "saving" of cash. The depreciation expense recorded each accounting period is accumulated and reported in "Accumulated Depreciation" as a credit offset to the relevant asset in the balance sheet.

We are now going to consolidate and make some sense out of the above transactions. We can begin by developing an income statement for the first quarter of the new year, which should tell us whether the business is operating at a profit or a loss.

INCOME STATEMENT 1
January 1, 199x–March 31, 199x
FIFO Inventory Valuation and Straight-Line Depreciation

Sales Revenue (150 units @ $1000)		$150,000
Cost of Goods Sold:		
Beg. Inventory (200 units @ $200)	$ 40,000	
Plus: Purchases (200 units @ $300)	60,000	
Equals: Cost of Merchandise for Sale	100,000	
Less: Ending Inventory	− 70,000	
(200 units at $300/unit plus 50 units at $200/unit)		
Cost of Goods Sold		30,000
Gross Margin on Sales		$120,000
Expenses:		
Wages and Salaries	$ 30,000	
Supplies	2,000	
Depreciation	30,000	
Interest Payments	2,000	
Total Expenses		64,000
Operating Income		56,000
Less: Corporate Income Taxes		16,800
Equals: After-Tax Income		$ 39,200
Statement of Retained Earnings:		
After-Tax Income		39,200
Less: Dividends Paid to Stockholders		− 7,840
Equals: Retained Earnings		$ 31,360

One of the first steps in calculating profits is to determine the cost of the goods sold during the period. This involves determining the values of beginning and ending inventories. Inventory valuation, in fact, is one of the most significant sources of problems for many data series, including GDP, corporate profits, balance of payments, balance of international indebtedness, and inventories. In this example, we had a beginning inventory (purchased the previous December) of 200 units priced at $200 each, or $40,000. During the quarter, SMC purchased an additional 200 inventory units at $300 per unit, or $60,000. Adding purchases during the period to the beginning inventory produces the cost of the merchandise available for sale: $100,000.

A thorny problem arises when a value has to be attached to the ending inventory. Two of the most widely used inventory valuation methods are the First In, First Out (FIFO) and Last In, First Out (LIFO).[12] FIFO

[12]There are many other types of inventory valuation methods. One of these methods, the weighted average cost method, might have been appropriate to use in this example.

assumes the units that were purchased first are sold first; thus, the units remaining in inventory at the end of the accounting period are those that were purchased most recently. In the current example, we assume that the 150 units sold were the ones purchased for $200 each; hence, the 250 units remaining in inventory include 50 units left over from the first purchase, which were priced at $200 each, plus the 200 units recently purchased at $300 per unit. This FIFO method of inventory valuation gives us a cost of goods sold of $30,000. Most corporations are concerned only with the book value of inventory; they do not attempt to relate inventory costs to the units actually sold. The actual units sold could have been the units bought first or the ones bought most recently.

The balance sheet associated with straight-line depreciation and the FIFO method of inventory valuation is shown below. Notice how the Accumulated Depreciation accounts reduce the book value of the assets and how retained earnings are added to the capital section. If the company had used other depreciation or inventory valuation methods, or had established an Allowance for Uncollected Receivables, the income statement and the balance sheet would be much different. Changes in market value do not affect the values reported on the balance sheet. If the market value of the building had increased or decreased, the book value reported on the balance sheet would remain unchanged. It is important always to remember that reported profits, losses, and balance sheet values are the result of the accounting conventions of those who developed and audited the reports. The "books" might not reflect the conventions or assumptions of those reading the reports or of those who are collecting data for purposes other than reporting financial results for a particular company in a particular industry.

BALANCE SHEET (1)
FIFO Inventory Valuation and Straight-Line Depreciation
March 31, 199x

Cash and Deposits		$366,000	Loans Payable	$400,000
Accounts Receivable		150,000	Taxes Payable	16,800
Inventories		70,000	Dividends Payable	7,840
Furniture	$100,000			
Less: Accumulated Depr.	(20,000)			
Net Furniture Value		80,000	Stockholders' Equity:	
Building	$300,000		Capital Stock	500,000
Less: Accumulated Depr.	(10,000)		Retained Earnings	31,360
Net Building Value		290,000		
Total Assets		$956,000	Total Liabilities and Capital	$956,000

Using Different Inventory Valuation Methods

Two of the most confusing adjustments made to data series are those made to compensate for the use of differing inventory valuation and depreciation methods. In order to understand the adjustments and their effect on the data, readers of corporate-based data series need to understand the differences between FIFO and LIFO and between straight-line and accelerated depreciation. Income Statement 1 (p. 53) was based on the FIFO method of inventory valuation; Income Statement 2 (below) is based on the LIFO method. LIFO assumes that units taken out of inventory during the period were the last units purchased; hence, most of the units remaining in inventory are the units purchased at the earlier price of $200 per unit. As shown in Income Statement 2, the cost of goods sold has risen to $45,000 from the $30,000 calculated with the FIFO method; accordingly, operating income has been reduced from $56,000 to $41,000.

The real cause of the debate about the relative merits of LIFO and FIFO, however, is to be found in the amount of income taxes paid. Taxes paid using the FIFO method amounted to $16,800, whereas they were reduced to $12,300 when LIFO was utilized. Whenever prices are rising in the economy, the use of the LIFO method tends to overstate the cost of goods sold and to understate operating income and income taxes. Thus, during periods of inflation the use of LIFO enables corporations to pay lower taxes than if they had used FIFO. Corporations can use LIFO on their tax reports and FIFO on their other corporate statements.

INCOME STATEMENT 2
January 1, 199x–March 31, 199x
LIFO Inventory Valuation and Straight-Line Depreciation

Sales Revenue (150 units @ $1000)		$150,000
Cost of Goods Sold:		
Beg. Inventory (200 units @ $200)	$ 40,000	
Plus: Purchases (200 units @ $300)	60,000	
Equals: Cost of Merchandise for Sale	100,000	
Less: Ending Inventory	− 55,000	
(200 units at $200/unit and		
50 units at $300/unit)		
Cost of Goods Sold		45,000
Gross Margin on Sales		105,000
Expenses:		
Wages and Salaries	$ 30,000	
Supplies	2,000	
Depreciation	30,000	
Interest Payments	2,000	
Total Expenses		64,000
Operating Income		41,000
Less: Corporate Income Taxes		− 12,300
Equals: After-Tax Income		$ 28,700
Statement of Retained Earnings:		
After-Tax Income		28,700
Less: Dividends Paid to Stockholders		− 5,740
Equals: Retained Earnings		$ 22,960

BALANCE SHEET (2)
LIFO Inventory Valuation and Straight-Line Depreciation
March 31, 199x

Cash and Deposits		$366,000	Loans Payable	$400,000
Accounts Receivable		150,000	Taxes Payable	12,300
Inventories		55,000	Dividends Payable	5,740
Furniture	$100,000			
Less: Accumulated Depr.	(20,000)			
Net Furniture		80,000	Stockholders' Equity:	
Building	300,000		Capital Stock	500,000
Less: Accumulated Depr.	(10,000)		Retained Earnings	22,960
Net Building Value		290,000		
Total Assets		$941,000	Total Liabilities and Capital	$941,000

Depreciation is another source of distorted data. In the previous income statements we assumed that straight-line depreciation was employed by the company. We now assume that SMC uses an accelerated depreciation method, say, the double-declining balance method, which uses a depreciation rate equal to double the straight-line rate. The straight-line depreciation rate was 3.3333 percent for the building and 20 percent for the furniture, so the double declining rate is 6.6667 percent for the building and 40 percent for the furniture. These rates are applied to the declining balances each year. The first year's depreciation for the building is

Building: $300,000 \times 0.06667 = $20,000$
Furniture: $100,000 \times 0.4   = $40,000$

The second year's depreciation is:

Building: $($300,000 - $20,000) \times 0.06667 = $18,668$
Furniture: $($100,000 - $40,000) \times 0.4   = $24,000$

The third year's depreciation is:

Building: $($300,000 - $38,668) \times 0.06667 = $17,423$
Furniture: $($100,000 - $64,000) \times 0.4   = $14,400$

Firms love accelerated depreciation methods while the Treasury hates them. Although accelerated depreciation does not reduce the total tax liability of the firm, as many people believe, it does *postpone* tax liability. It increases depreciation expense and reduces operating income and taxes in the early years of an asset's useful life but reduces depreciation expense and increases income and taxes in the latter years of the asset's useful life. These deferred taxes are the equivalent of an interest-free loan from the Treasury.

Income Statement 3 is based on LIFO inventory valuation (as was Income Statement 2) and the double-declining method of accelerated depreciation. The depreciation expense has increased from $30,000 to $60,000 and after-tax income has been reduced from $28,700 to $7700. Tax liability has decreased from $12,300 to $3300.

INCOME STATEMENT 3
January 1, 199x–March 31, 199x
LIFO Inventory Valuation and Accelerated Depreciation

Sales Revenue		$150,000
Cost of Goods Sold:		
Beg. Inventory (200 units @ $200)	$ 40,000	
Plus: Purchases (200 units @ $300)	60,000	
Equals: Cost of Merchandise for Sale	100,000	
Less: Ending Inventory @ 300/unit	− 55,000	
200 units at $200/unit		
50 units at $300/unit		
Cost of Goods Sold		45,000
Gross Margin on Sales		105,000
Expenses:		
Wages and Salaries	$ 30,000	
Supplies	2,000	
Depreciation	60,000	
Interest Payments	2,000	
Total Expenses		94,000
Operating Income		11,000
Less: Corporate Income Taxes		− 3,300
Equals: After-Tax Income		$ 7,700
Statement of Retained Earnings:		
After-Tax Income		7,700
Less: Dividends Paid to Stockholders		− 2,940
Equals: Retained Earnings		$ 4,760

BALANCE SHEET (3)
LIFO Inventory Valuation and Accelerated Depreciation
March 31, 199x

Cash and Deposits		$366,000	Loans Payable	$400,000
Accounts Receivable		150,000	Taxes Payable	3,300
Inventories		55,000	Dividends Payable	1,540
Furniture	$100,000			
Less: Accumulated Depr.	(40,000)			
Net Furniture		60,000	Stockholders' Equity:	
Building	300,000		Capital Stock	500,000
Less: Accumulated Depr.	(20,000)		Retained Earnings	6,160
Net Building Value		280,000		
Total Assets		$911,000	Total Liabilities and Capital	$911,000

Significance of Accounting Conventions and Variations

Many other accounting changes could have been introduced, but we've decided to spare you the eye-straining agonies of a bean counter. The important point of this entire discussion is that bottom line variables such as corporate profits, inventories, and total assets depend on the accounting conventions employed in each firm. These conventions vary widely among firms within an industry and among industries in the economy. They change over time as tax laws, accounting standards, and social conventions change. With changes in only two variables (depreciation and inventory valuation) in our example, we obtained significantly different outcomes, as shown in Table 3.6.

TABLE 3.6
Outcomes Due to Differences in Inventory Valuation and Depreciation Methods

	Operating Income	Income Taxes	Total Assets
Straight-Line Depreciation and FIFO	$56,000	$16,800	$956,000
Straight-Line and LIFO	41,000	12,300	941,000
Accelerated and LIFO	11,000	3,300	911,000

We know that the fundamental operating data for the SMC Company are the same, no matter how we handle depreciation and inventory valuation. The differences in operating income are due entirely to the different book treatments of depreciation and inventory valuation. Some "bean-counting" investors and, I am sorry to say, many economists, looking only at the bottom line might draw incorrect conclusions about the management, future prospects, and profit rates of the company. If the firm's accountants select straight-line depreciation and FIFO, the company's profits and assets appear to be quite high. If the accountants select accelerated depreciation and LIFO, the company's profits appear to be relatively low. Interpreting "bottom line" data without having a thorough understanding of how the data were put together can result in dangerous interpretations by corporate officers, employees, investors, economists, and the public.

The foundation of much of the economic data published by federal, state, and private sources are these very same accounting records. If you were in charge of gathering inventory data for the Bureau of Economic Analysis, how would you treat the data filed by hundreds of thousands of corporations using LIFO, FIFO, or one of a dozen other methods of inventory valuation? Furthermore, you know that accounting, tax, and industry conventions change periodically, so many companies that used one method last year will be converting to another method this year — or maybe next year. Would you hold your nose and publish the data, mixing apples and oranges?[13]

Sophisticated data users are also affected by these accounting conventions. Assume you have to analyze inventory, profits or asset trends for your boss, or for a paper in a production management class or for a journal article that is guaranteed to get you tenure. Would you attempt to determine whether the appropriate adjustments (whatever they are) have been made to inventory valuation, depreciation, profits, and all the other accounts affected by variable accounting conventions, or would you use one of the following antediluvian excuses: (1) I don't get concerned about such trivial matters; (2) other people, more knowledgeable about these details than I, have made the correct adjustments; (3) there will always be such deviations from the truth, but they will be random and self-cancelling and we can ignore them? Perhaps you will be like the rest of us, who simply plug the data into the latest and most sophisticated econometric model, come to a conclusion, and finish the paper. Diogenes will have to continue his search.

---

[13]The Bureau of Economic Analysis does make various adjustments for inventory valuation and depreciation for some data series. However, not all published corporate-based data are adjusted for inventory valuation and depreciation differences, and many other variable accounting conventions do not get adjusted at all.

CHAPTER 4

THE LABOR MARKET

READ ME FIRST

A nation's most important economic resources are the skills, abilities, and time of its workers, including all employees from janitor to scientist to the company president. To a large extent, the economic vitality and progress of a nation are determined by the number, efforts, and skills of these workers. The labor market is also an important macroeconomic variable, and most politicians and many economists evaluate the current health of the economy by the unemployment rate. If the unemployment rate is rising, the economy is said to be "getting worse" or "sliding into a recession." If the unemployment rate is falling, the "economy is prospering," according to many. Labor market data also include information about wage rates, earnings, hours worked, number of people looking for work, and employment by industry. Few statistics are watched more closely than those associated with the labor market. Surprisingly, systematic labor market data were first obtained only in 1940. Although we do have labor market data going back to 1870, these were estimated during the 1930s from decennial census data.

Data on employment, wages, and hours worked are currently obtained from two different sources. The more widely publicized source of employment data is the Current Population Survey, conducted by the Census Bureau, which is a monthly survey of about 60,000 households across the country randomly selected to represent the U.S. population 16 years of age and older. Each month, one-fourth of the households in the sample is changed so that no single family is interviewed more than four consecutive months. A group of 1500 Census Bureau workers interview the sample families on their labor force activities and participation for the week that includes the twelfth day of the month. Special surveys are conducted to obtain detailed supplementary data. Data are collected in

March on the work experiences of the population during the preceding year and the marital and family status of workers; data are collected in October on school enrollment and employment status. The national unemployment rate widely reported by the media each month is obtained from the Current Population Survey.

The second source of labor market data is the employment, hours, and earnings data compiled from payroll records reported monthly on a voluntary basis to the Bureau of Labor Statistics and cooperating state agencies by more than 340,000 establishments representing all industries except agriculture. Establishment data provide industry-specific data, by SIC codes, for more than 500 industries, information or nonagricultural wage and salary employment, average workweek, and hourly and weekly earnings for the United States, states, and SMSAs. Generally, the sampling probabilities are based on the size of the establishment, so that most large establishments are included in the sample. An **establishment** is an economic unit that produces goods and services at a single location. It could be a plant, an office, store, or warehouse. Unlike the survey data, establishment data exclude unpaid family workers, domestic servants, certain agricultural workers, and self-employed persons, and it double-counts workers who have more than one job. Certain persons on unpaid leave are not counted as employed, but workers under 16, residents of Canada and Mexico who commute to the United States, and institutionalized persons are included. The household survey of the Current Population Survey almost always reports more employment than the employer surveys. As discussed more completely on pages 75 and 76, most of the local and state data on employment and wage rates are obtained from establishment data.

Name: Area Wage Surveys
Agency/Institution: Bureau of Labor Statistics
Address: 441 G Street, N.W., Washington, DC 20212
Telephone number for data and inquiries: 202-523-1763
Sources: Area Wage Surveys; *Handbook of Labor Statistics*, Bureau of Labor Statistics
Frequency: Annually/biannually
When available: Three months after reference month. July data come out in October, for example.
Revisions: Seldom
Historic data: *Handbook of Labor Statistics*

■ A QUICK LOOK: Area Wage Surveys

Currently 90 metropolitan areas have Area Wage Surveys. Thirty-two of the largest SMSAs are surveyed annually, with the remaining 58 surveyed every two years. Employee benefits in these areas are surveyed only once every four years. The Area Wage Surveys provide average straight-time earnings for standard workweeks by sex, by occupation within various industries for each of these metropolitan areas, as well as by major geographic regions (Northeast, South, Midwest, and West). Interarea pay comparisons are also available.

Example of Data Available: Office Clerical
(January–December 1986)

	All Industries	Manufacturing	Nonmanufacturing
Boston, MA	99	98	99
Buffalo, NY	89	90	86
Chicago, IL	101	101	102

The numbers represent the relative pay levels in that occupation compared with the average weekly salaries in the 262 metropolitan areas. The average pay levels for each industry and occupational group in 262 SMSAs are based on 100. Thus, office clerical workers in Buffalo get paid 86 to 90 percent of the metropolitan average, whereas those in Chicago get paid about 1 to 2 percent more than the metropolitan area average. Buffalo, then, is a relatively low wage rate area (for clerical workers) compared with other metropolitan areas; Chicago's clerical wages are just slightly above the metropolitan area average. These numbers are given for numerous occupations (for example, electronic data processing, skilled maintenance, and unskilled plant).

Name: Employment Cost Index (ECI)
Agency/Institution: Bureau of Labor Statistics
Address: 441 G Street, N.W., Washington, DC 20212
Telephone number for data and inquiries: 202-523-1165
Sources: *Monthly Labor Review, Current Wage Developments, Survey of Current Business*
Frequency: Quarterly
When available: One month after reference quarter
Revisions: None, except for changes in seasonal adjustment techniques
Historic data: March issue of *Current Wage Developments, Handbook of Labor Statistics* and *Employment Cost Indexes and Levels, 1975–88*, Bulletin 2319 (Bureau of Labor Statistics)
Further information: *Handbook of Methods*, Bulletin 2285 (Bureau of Labor Statistics) and "Estimation Procedures for the Employment Cost Index," *Monthly Labor Review* (May 1982)

■ A QUICK LOOK: Employment Cost Index

It is not easy to compare changes in the costs of labor because the ratio of labor to capital is constantly changing, as are the various mixes of labor skills and occupations. The **Employment Cost Index**, which measures quarterly changes in the cost of labor, avoids these problems by using a fixed market basket of labor (similar in concept to the fixed market basket of consumer goods used in the Consumer Price Index) to measure changes in employer costs. The Employment Cost Index measures quarterly changes in wages, salaries, and benefits in the private nonfarm economy while holding fixed the industrial, occupational, and geographical mix of workers. The employment cost index includes production workers, executives, managers, and professionals. The following is an example of ECI data:

Employment Cost Index
Compensation, by Occupation and Industry, December 1991
(1989 = 100)

Civilian workers	112.2
By occupation group	
White collar workers	112.8
Blue collar workers	111.1
Service occupations	113.1
By industry	
Manufacturing	112.2
Nonmanufacturing	112.3
State and local government workers	112.6

Employment cost index: Measures changes in the price of labor. The categories listed here are a small sample of the categories listed in the complete employment cost index. Farms and households are excluded; the public sector covers state and local governments but excludes the federal government.

Compensation: Total compensation of labor, including wages, salaries, paid leave, incentive bonuses, supplemental pay, insurance benefits, retirement plans, and other benefits paid by employers. Excluded from compensation are such items as payments in kind, free room and board, and tips. Also excluded are premium pay for overtime and work on weekends and holidays.

The above set of employment cost indexes, which is a small sample of the data actually provided, measures changes in total compensation paid to workers. There are employment cost indexes for union and nonunion workers in manufacturing, service-producing industries, metropolitan areas, health services, white collar occupations, professional and technical workers, sales occupations, machine operators, contract construction, and many more. Two other major sets of employment cost indexes measure changes in wages and salaries and changes in benefits. In addition, smaller sets of indexes measure changes in compensation and in wages and salaries by region and union versus nonunion. The Employment Cost Index is available in seasonally adjusted and nonadjusted form. See Table 4.1.

The major advantage of the employment cost index is its quarterly measurement of changes in the price of labor, free from the influence of employment shifts among occupations and industries. The index holds occupations constant over a ten-year period—but that is also its main disadvantage. Occupations that have a relative shortage of employees also have high wages, inducing firms to substitute other workers or capital for these high-priced workers, thus lowering the wage costs. However, because the employment cost index does not pick up these substitutions, it tends to be biased upward.

TABLE 4.1
Employment Cost Index
Civilian workers, wages, salaries, and benefits
(June 1989 = 100)

1981	70.2
1982	74.8
1983	79.1
1984	83.2
1985	86.8
1986	89.9
1987	93.1
1988	97.7
1989	102.6
1990	107.6
1991	112.2

Name: Index of Help Wanted Advertising in Newspapers
Agency/Institution: The Conference Board
Address: 845 Third Avenue, New York, NY 10022
Telephone number for data and inquiries: 212-759-0900
Sources: *Survey of Current Business*
Frequency: Monthly
When available: First week of the following month
Revisions: None
Historic data: Available from 1960 on BEA's Electronic Bulletin Board

■ A QUICK LOOK: Help Wanted Ads

The Conference Board collects data on the number of help wanted classified ads in 51 cities. All help wanted ads are counted from a single newspaper serving the city and then adjusted for seasonal variation and the size of the labor market in the region. This index is used as one indicator of the state of the labor market. When the index is increasing, it is taken as a sign that the labor market is becoming tighter; that is, the number of job openings is increasing and/or the number of job-seekers is decreasing. This index peaks a few months before the peak of the economy.

The help wanted index was started in 1967 and is based on 1967 = 100; it had a value of 151 in 1989, 129 in 1990, and 93 in 1991. The lowest index value since January 1983 (80) was reached in January 1992, when the index hit 85.

HISTORIC DATA
Index of Help Wanted Ads
(1967 = 100)

1951	64	1961	52	1971	83	1981	118
1952	69	1962	59	1972	103	1982	86
1953	65	1963	59	1973	126	1983	95
1954	42	1964	67	1974	110	1984	130
1955	59	1965	84	1975	80	1985	138
1956	68	1966	104	1976	95	1986	138
1957	58	1967	100	1977	119	1987	153
1958	42	1968	110	1978	149	1988	157
1959	59	1969	121	1979	157	1989	150
1960	56	1970	93	1980	128	1990	129
						1991	93

Name: Hourly and Weekly Earnings (Average)
Agency/Institution: Bureau of Labor Statistics
Address: 441 G Street, N.W., Washington, DC 20212
Telephone number for data and inquiries: 202-523-1172
Sources: *Employment and Earnings* (Bureau of Labor Statistics; monthly) — most complete tables are published here;
Monthly Labor Review (Bureau of Labor Statistics; monthly)
Handbook of Labor Statistics (Bureau of Labor Statistics)
Frequency: Monthly
When available: About three weeks following the month
Revisions: The establishment data are subject to revision during the following month and then are revised each subsequent year for the annual benchmark revisions.
Historic data: Seasonally adjusted and unadjusted data are provided monthly (for most years) between 1909 and 1984. About every four years a reference volume containing employment, earnings, and hours is updated from 1939. SIC two- and some three-digit data are available for total employees and for average weekly and hourly earnings and weekly hours for production and non-supervisory workers by state and about 270 local labor areas (most are SMSAs).

See U.S. Department of Labor, Bureau of Labor Statistics, *Employment and Earnings, United States, 1909–1984*, vols. 1 and 2 (1985) and *Employment, Hours, and Earnings, States and Areas, 1939–82*, vols. 1 and 2 (1984). See historic data below.

■ A QUICK LOOK: Average Hourly and Weekly Earnings

There are two primary sources of data on hourly and weekly earnings. The first is the ongoing Current Population Survey of about 60,000 households selected to represent the civilian noninstitutional population. Hourly earnings are the straight-time wages of workers over the age of 16 paid by the hour. Weekly earnings data are obtained from responses to the question: "How much does _____ usually earn per week at this job before deductions?" Included are overtime pay, commissions, and tips. Data refer to wage and salary workers who work full-time on their sole or primary job. A considerable level of detail is available for median weekly earnings. For example, you can find the average weekly earnings of bartenders, automotive mechanics, computer programmers, and bus drivers.

A second source of workers' earnings is the survey of business establishments, which obtains responses from more than 300,000 employers. Hours and earnings data are derived from reports of payrolls and hours for full-time and part-time production workers and nonsupervisory employees over the age of 16 in manufacturing, mining, construction, and other nonfarm industries. The series excludes managers, professionals, and technical workers. Average hourly earnings are derived by dividing total payrolls by the number of hours; average weekly earnings are obtained by multiplying average weekly hours by average hourly earnings. These earnings include premium pay for overtime and regular incentive bonuses. These earnings series do not measure the total labor costs of the employer since they exclude irregular bonuses, various welfare benefits, payroll taxes paid by employers, and workers not included in the coverage. Gross average weekly earnings are derived by multiplying average weekly hours by average hourly earnings. These earnings do not show wage rates. Weekly earnings are affected not only by changes in gross average hourly wage rates, but also by changes in the length of the workweek, overtime bonuses, part-time work, work stoppages, and absenteeism. Since the earnings include those of part-time workers, the wage rates of the average full-time worker is generally higher than the amounts reported in these hourly and weekly earnings. The earnings do *not* include employer payments for Social Security, unemployment insurance, or health and life insurance. Like other establishment-based data, the earnings series are subject to annual benchmark adjustments made every March. A sample of the data provided is given in Table 4.2.

TABLE 4.2
Average Hourly Earnings of Production or Nonsupervisory Workers in Selected Private Industries

	1989	1990
Private Nonagricultural	$ 9.66	$10.02
Mining	13.26	13.69
Construction	13.54	13.78
Manufacturing	10.48	10.83
Durable Goods	11.01	11.35
Machinery	11.40	11.78
Electric and Electronic	10.05	10.30
Transportation Equipment	13.67	14.10
Nondurable Goods	9.75	10.12
Chemicals	13.09	13.55
Petroleum and Coal Products	15.41	16.23
Rubber and Plastics	9.46	9.77
Leather and Leather Products	6.60	6.90
Transportation and Public Utilities	12.60	12.96
Wholesale Trade	10.39	10.79
Retail Trade	6.53	6.76
Finance, Insurance, Real Estate	9.53	9.97
Services	9.38	9.83

The earnings data are published for industries grouped by two-, three-, and a few four-digit SIC industries and are primarily gathered from state employment security agencies. Workers in the private and public sectors are included, but self-employed individuals, unpaid family workers, farm workers, and domestic workers are not. The same series shows average weekly earnings in current dollars and in constant dollars. Indexes of average hourly earnings, which were provided for many years, were discontinued in 1988.

Historic Data: Average Hourly and Weekly Earnings

	Average Hourly Earnings Total, Private Industry (establishment data)	Average Hourly Earnings Total, Manufacturing (establishment data)		Average Hourly Earnings Total, Private Industry (establishment data)	Average Hourly Earnings Total, Manufacturing (establishment data)
1932		$ 0.44	1955	$ 1.71	$ 1.85
1935		0.54	1960	2.09	2.26
1940		0.66	1961	2.14	2.32
1945		1.02	1962	2.22	2.39
1950	$ 1.34	1.44			*(continued)*

Historic Data: Average Hourly and Weekly Earnings *(continued)*

	Average Hourly Earnings Total, Private Industry (establishment data)	Average Hourly Earnings Total, Manufacturing (establishment data)		Average Hourly Earnings Total, Private Industry (establishment data)	Average Hourly Earnings Total, Manufacturing (establishment data)
1963	$ 2.28	$ 2.45	1977	$ 5.25	$ 5.68
1964	2.36	2.53	1978	5.69	6.17
1965	2.46	2.61	1979	6.16	6.70
1966	2.56	2.71	1980	6.66	7.27
1967	2.68	2.82	1981	7.25	7.99
1968	2.85	3.01	1982	7.68	8.49
1969	3.04	3.19	1983	8.02	8.83
1970	3.23	3.35	1984	8.32	9.19
1971	3.45	3.57	1985	8.57	9.54
1972	3.70	3.82	1986	8.76	9.73
1973	3.94	4.09	1987	8.98	9.91
1974	4.24	4.42	1988	9.29	10.18
1975	4.53	4.83	1989	9.66	10.48
1976	4.86	5.22	1990	10.02	10.83

Name: New Jobless Claims
Alternative name: Average Weekly Initial Claims for Unemployment
Agency/Institution: Employment and Training Administration, Department of Labor
Address: Washington, DC 20212
Telephone number for data: 202-535-0888
Telephone number for inquiries: 202-525-0630
Sources: *Unemployment Insurance Claims; Weekly Bulletin* (Department of Labor); *Survey of Current Business*
Frequency: Weekly
When available: Second week after target week on Thursday morning
Revisions: None
Historic data: See below.

■ A QUICK LOOK: New Jobless Claims

Unemployed persons have to go to their state offices to file unemployment claims. Thus, each state has a record of the number of jobless claims that have been filed during the past week. They report this number to Employment and Training Administration, which publishes the number each week. Many analysts believe that the number of jobless claims is an important indicator of the state of the economy. When the number of jobless claims increases sharply, it is an indication that contractionary pressures are increasing.

The official title of jobless claims is: "Average weekly initial claims for unemployment insurance." These are not total claims or the total number of unemployed persons receiving unemployment compensation. The weekly series reports only the *new* claims made during each week, but the data are also reported by month, quarter, and year. Many publications report annual and quarterly data in terms of average weekly claims. The historic data table shows that average weekly initial claims were 448,000 during 1991. The annual number of initial claims for unemployment insurance in 1991 was 23.3 million (448,000 × 52 weeks). The data are seasonally adjusted for weekly, monthly, and quarterly reports, so they are comparable.

HISTORIC DATA
Initial Claims for Unemployment Insurance,
Average Weekly Initial Claims
(thousands)

1947	187	1960	331	1970	292	1980	480
1948	209	1961	348	1971	291	1981	446
1949	343	1962	299	1972	257	1982	578
1950	232	1963	290	1973	240	1983	438
1951	210	1964	260	1974	351	1984	378
1952	211	1965	228	1975	468	1985	391
1953	218	1966	201	1976	381	1986	373
1954	305	1967	225	1977	368	1987	323
1955	226	1968	194	1978	338	1988	306
1956	227	1969	193	1979	379	1989	329
1957	267					1990	388
1958	370					1991	448
1959	279						

Name: Labor Force, Employment, Unemployment Rates
Agency/Institution: Bureau of Labor Statistics, U.S. Department of Labor, and the Bureau of the Census
Address: 441 G Street, N.W., Washington, DC 20212
Telephone number for data: 24-hour four-minute recorded message (202-523-9658)
Telephone number for inquiries: 202-523-1944
Sources: *Employment and Earnings* (monthly), *Monthly Labor Review* (monthly), *Economic Indicators* (monthly), *Employment Situation News Release, Survey of Current Business*
Frequency: Monthly
When available: First Friday of the following month
Revisions: Household survey data, which provide the most significant national data on employment, are revised in the month after their initial release. The seasonally adjusted data for the year will be adjusted in January for the next five

years. Benchmark adjustments are made every ten years in conjunction with the census. The establishment data, which provide employment data by industry, are subject to benchmark revisions once each year.

Historic data: General sources are: *Historic Statistics of the United States*, March issue of *Employment and Earnings*, and *Handbook of Labor Statistics* (published periodically). Historic data from the Current Population Survey can be obtained from *Labor Force Statistics Derived from the Current Population Survey, 1947–87*, Bulletin 2307 (Bureau of Labor Statistics). The establishment data can be obtained from *Employment, Hours and Earnings, United States, 1909–84*, Bulletin 1312, and annual supplements.

■ A QUICK LOOK: Labor Market Data

The unemployment rate, which is one of the most widely quoted economic data series, is an indicator of the health of the local, state, and national economies, and changes in it are closely watched by authorities responsible for monetary and fiscal policies. Its component parts are used in many social and demographic studies and policies. The Bureau of Labor Statistics releases monthly labor reports, which present total employment, unemployment, and the unemployment rate. The report is released on the first Friday of the following month and is revised in the next three monthly releases. Benchmark revisions in the data are made almost every year. As is true for most data, we have to be careful about using employment and unemployment data. First, there is a series of employment data referring just to civilians, excluding the members of the armed forces. This is called the **civilian labor force**, and all related labor force data exclude the armed forces. Another series, which is known as the **labor force** includes members of the armed forces based in this country. The unemployment rate you hear and read about through the popular media is the civilian labor force unemployment rate. The BLS publishes monthly data that are both seasonally adjusted and unadjusted but the media generally report the seasonally adjusted data. A small sample of the data provided in the monthly labor reports is shown in Table 4.3.

TABLE 4.3
Sample of Employment Data Seasonally Adjusted
(numbers in thousands)

Civilian noninstitutional population	187,669
Civilian labor force	124,886
Participation rate	66.5
Employed	118,116
Employment–population ratio	62.9
Unemployed	6,770
Unemployment rate	5.4

(continued)

TABLE 4.3 *(continued)*
Sample of Employment Data Seasonally Adjusted
(numbers in thousands)

SELECTED UNEMPLOYMENT RATES

Total, 16 years and over	5.4
Men, 16 years and over	5.5
Men, 20 years and over	4.8
Women, 16 years and over	5.4
Women, 20 years and over	4.8
Both sexes, 16 to 19 years	14.7
Married men, spouse present	3.3
Married women, spouse present	3.5
Women who maintain families	7.5
Full-time workers	5.1
Part-time workers	7.1

DURATION OF UNEMPLOYMENT PERCENT DISTRIBUTION

Total unemployed	100.0
Less than 5 weeks	47.4
5 to 14 weeks	32.2
15 weeks and over	20.5
15 to 26 weeks	10.3
27 weeks and over	10.2

REASONS FOR UNEMPLOYMENT PERCENT DISTRIBUTION

Total unemployed	100.0
Job losers	46.8
On layoff	14.9
Other job losers	31.9
Job leavers	17.5
Reentrants	26.5
New entrants	9.2

Civilian noninstitutional population: Includes all residents of the United States who are 16 years of age and over and who are not inmates of hospitals, homes for the aged, or prisons, or members of the armed forces. There is an unemployment series based on the noninstitutional population that excludes the same categories as this one does, except that it includes members of the armed forces stationed in the United States.

Civilian labor force: Comprises all noninstitutionalized persons 16 years of age or over who are either employed or who meet the conditions for unemployment described below (see Unemployed persons). Students in school, housewives, and retirees, those unable to work because of health problems, and those discouraged from seeking employment are excluded. Members of the armed forces are not included in the civilian labor force. Persons who keep house, are voluntarily idle or unable to work, or seasonal workers in the off-season are also not included in the civilian labor force.

Labor force participation ratio: The ratio of the civilian labor force to the civilian noninstitutional population.

Employed persons: Those (1) who worked at least 1 hour for pay or profit during the survey week as paid employees or who worked in their own business, profession, or farm, or (2) who worked at least 15 hours as unpaid workers in a family-owned enterprise, or (3) who were temporarily absent from their jobs due to illness, strikes, bad weather, vacation, or personal reasons. A person working at more than one job is counted only in the job in which he or she worked the greatest number of hours. Persons who work 35 hours or more are classified as full-time; those who work 1 to 34 hours are classified as part-time workers. Persons are counted as full-time employees if they normally work full-time but worked less than 35 hours during the survey week due to noneconomic reasons (illness, vacation, bad weather, labor dispute).

Employment–population ratio: Number of employed persons divided by the civilian noninstitutional population. Provides about the same information as the labor participation ratio, which is much more popular.

Unemployed persons: Those (1) who actively looked for work during the past four weeks, (2) who are currently available for work, and (3) and who do not have a job. Looking for work may consist of *any* of the following:

    Registering at a public or private employment office
    Meeting with prospective employers
    Checking with friends of relatives
    Placing or answering advertisements
    Writing letters of applications
    Being on a union or professional work register

Persons waiting to start a job within 30 days and workers waiting to be recalled to work from a layoff are considered to be unemployed even if they are not actively searching for a job. Thus, the unemployment statistics can include those who have quit their jobs or been fired, new entrants into the labor market, such as high school and college graduates, and experienced workers returning to the labor market after an absence.

Unemployment rate: Number of unemployed persons divided by the civilian labor force. In this series it is seasonally adjusted.

Job losers: Those whose employment ended involuntarily and who immediately began looking for work and persons on either temporary or indefinite layoff.

Job leavers: Those who quit or otherwise terminated their employment voluntarily and immediately began looking for work.

Reentrants: Those who previously worked full-time but who were out of the labor force prior to beginning their job search.

New entrants: Persons who never worked at a full-time job lasting two weeks or more.

Most Americans have seen the monthly unemployment rate given on the evening news, but very few have seen all of the labor market data released by the Bureau of Labor Statistics every month. The labor force participation rate; duration of unemployment; and the unemployment rate by sex, race, age, occupation, industry, and marital status are some of the other detailed information available. You can, for example, find the unemployment rates for black males between the ages of 16 and 19, married Hispanics, mechanics, and accountants.

■ A CLOSER LOOK: Labor Market Data

One important employment indicator is the labor force participation ratio, which is the ratio of the civilian labor force to the civilian noninstitutional population. The participation ratio for men (20 years or older) has fallen steadily since World War II (from 89 percent in 1947 to 77.9 percent in 1990), whereas the ratio for women has increased significantly (from 31 percent to 58 percent). The overall participation ratio has increased slightly and can be expected to continue to increase as the older generations of women, who have a low participation ratio, are replaced by younger generations of women, who more readily enter and remain in the labor force. The net increase in the overall participation ratio will be small because workers, especially men, are retiring at an increasingly early age.

There are many problems with unemployment data. Survey respondents are asked if they are looking for work, and an affirmative response is accepted even if they tell the interviewer they casually chatted with friends about job availability. Unemployed workers in Great Britain and many other countries must physically report to a labor agency before they are counted as unemployed. (This is one of several reasons why unemployment rates among countries are not comparable.)[1] Unlike the United States, most countries do not go out looking for the unemployed; the unemployed are not counted unless they take the initiative to register. Welfare recipients are required to register for work, which is "proof" to the Bureau of Labor Statistics that the survey respondent is available for work and is looking for work — even though the respondent-welfare recipient might be unemployable or have no intention of working but is

---

[1]The BLS periodically compiles a series of unemployment rates adjusted to U.S. concepts for nine foreign nations: Australia, Canada, France, Germany, Italy, Japan, the Netherlands, Sweden, and the United Kingdom. However, even after adjustments are made for these nine countries, unemployment definitions still differ. This International Labor Market data series is discussed on pages 435–437. For further information, see: *International Comparisons of Unemployment*, BLS Bulletin 1979 (August 1978) and Joyanna Moy, "Recent Trends in Unemployment and the Labor Force, 10 Countries," *Monthly Labor Review* (August 1985), pp. 9–22.

registering solely to get welfare. Including such persons in the ranks of the unemployed tends to bias the unemployment rate upward. The BLS has a rule that "labor force activities take precedence over non–labor force activities." Thus, a teenager attending high school who is looking for a part-time job is classified as being in the labor force and unemployed.

Unemployment is typically higher in January and February when it is cold in many parts of the country and construction and other seasonal work is curtailed. Also, retail activity is normally slow during these months. Both employment and unemployment rise in June, when students enter the labor force in search of summer jobs. Hence, it is difficult to tell whether changes in employment and unemployment between any two months reflect changing economic conditions or seasonal fluctuations. To allow monthly comparisons to be made, the BLS uses a statistical technique called **seasonal adjustment**, and it reports the unemployment rate with and without seasonal adjustments.[2] The unadjusted rate should be used for comparison only with the same month of previous years. The seasonally adjusted rate can be used for comparisons with unemployment rates in all months. Be careful when comparing national unemployment rates with state and local unemployment rates. The media generally report the seasonally adjusted national unemployment rate along with state and local unemployment rates, which are not seasonally adjusted and are obtained from different sources. Hence, the two rates are not comparable.

Although the media concentrate on the unemployment rate, the change in the number of employed persons is often a more useful statistic. If the number of employed persons is increasing rapidly, it is a sign that the economy is expanding even if the unemployment rate is stable or increasing. Another bit of information watched closely by labor economists is the duration of unemployment. Before drawing any conclusions about the severity of a certain unemployment rate, economists want to know the average duration of unemployment. For example, in the recessionary month of January 1992, the general unemployment rate was 7.1 percent but nearly 38 percent of the unemployed were without work for less than five weeks. This relatively short duration suggested that the economy was less contractionary than indicated by the simple unemployment rate. Economists also look at the reasons workers are unemployed. During this same month, fewer than 60 percent of the unemployed had lost their jobs; the remaining 40 percent left their jobs or were new entrants or reentrants into the labor force.

---

[2]The official seasonal adjustment method is X-11 ARIMA method, which was developed by Statistics Canada. ARIMA is an acronym for Auto-Regressive Integrated Moving Average. Bet that little bit of knowledge made your day!

Unemployment Rates for States and Local Areas

The 11 largest states and 2 largest metropolitan areas[3] get their monthly employment and unemployment data directly from the household surveys and the Bureau of Labor Statistics. The remaining states and metropolitan areas get their monthly employment data primarily from unemployment insurance data collected and processed by a state agency. This variation in the collection of labor market data has produced considerable confusion.

The Current Population Survey (CPS) produces reliable *annual* estimates for all states, the District of Columbia, and certain metropolitan areas. However, except for the 11 largest states and 2 metropolitan areas, the sample size of the CPS is not large enough to produce reliable *monthly* estimates for local areas. Monthly unemployment rates for the remaining 39 states and the more than 5000 localities for which unemployment rates are published are developed by state employment agencies using estimating procedures established by the BLS. These state and local employment figures are based on surveys of employers derived from unemployment insurance records and the records of nonprofit organizations and government.[4] Nationally based correction factors are then applied to these figures for each of the 39 states and the local areas.[5]

Most states revise their published unemployment rates in each of the two months following initial release and then once each year in March to conform with the new annual census benchmark data. The new March data are then used to revise the previous 12 months' data, which were based solely on samples of employers and previous correction factors. Despite relatively small changes made by the benchmark revisions (see the March issues of *Employment and Earnings* for these revisions), the state establishment data have been widely criticized, and the BLS is working to improve their quality.

The Bureau of the Census' household survey is a count of persons and the establishment (employer) data series is a count of jobs. A jobholder

---

[3]California, Florida, Illinois, Massachusetts, Michigan, New Jersey, New York, North Carolina, Ohio, Pennsylvania, and Texas. The two metropolitan areas are Los Angeles and New York City.

[4]Employment and wage data are compiled from monthly unemployment tax reports submitted to state employment security agencies by employers. From these, the states obtain detailed data on industry wage levels and employment. More than 99 percent of all U.S. wage and salary workers and 90 percent of all civilian workers are covered by unemployment insurance. Proprietors, those self-employed, and farm workers on small farms are excluded. Workers are reported in the state where their jobs are physically located and not in their state of residence, so states must make adjustments to get residence unemployment rates.

[5]For more information, see Chapter 4 of the Bureau of Labor Statistics' *Handbook of Methods*, Bulletin 2134-1 (1982); and its *Manual for Developing Local Area Unemployment Statistics*.

with more than one job, who is counted only once in the population survey, is counted once for *each job* in the establishment data. Although the 39 state monthly unemployment rates are frequently compared with the national monthly unemployment rate, they should not be because different methodologies are used to generate each and because many states do not seasonally adjust their unemployment rates.

HISTORIC DATA: Labor Force Participation Rates
Unemployment Rates, 1900–1991

	Labor Partic- ipation Rate	Unem- ploy- ment rate	Average (mean) Duration of Unemployment in Weeks		Labor Partic- ipation Rate	Unem- ploy- ment rate	Average (mean) Duration of Unemployment in Weeks
1900	55.5%	5.0%	—	1930	55.0%	8.9%	—
1901	55.8	4.1	—	1931	55.2	16.3	—
1902	56.0	3.7	—	1932	55.4	24.1	—
1903	56.2	3.9	—	1933	55.6	25.2	—
1904	56.3	5.4	—	1934	55.7	22.0	—
1905	56.5	4.3	—	1935	55.6	20.3	—
1906	56.8	1.7	—	1936	55.7	17.0	—
1907	57.2	2.8	—	1937	55.9	14.3	—
1908	57.2	8.0	—	1938	56.0	19.1	—
1909	57.2	5.1	—	1939	56.0	17.2	—
1910	57.4	5.9	—	1940	56.0	14.6	—
1911	57.6	6.7	—	1941	56.7	9.9	—
1912	57.4	4.6	—	1942	58.8	4.7	—
1913	57.3	4.3	—	1943	62.3	1.9	—
1914	57.3	7.9	—	1944	63.1	1.2	—
1915	56.8	8.5	—	1945	61.9	1.9	—
1916	56.6	5.1	—	1946	57.2	3.9	—
1917	56.6	4.6	—	1947	57.4	3.9	—
1918	57.7	1.4	—	1948	58.8	3.8	8.6
1919	56.4	1.4	—	1949	58.9	5.9	10.0
1920	55.6	5.2	—	1950	59.2	5.3	12.1
1921	55.9	11.7	—	1951	59.3	3.3	9.7
1922	55.7	6.7	—	1952	59.0	3.0	8.4
1923	55.8	2.4	—	1953	58.9	2.9	8.0
1924	55.5	5.0	—	1954	58.8	5.6	11.8
1925	55.4	3.2	—	1955	59.3	4.4	13.0
1926	55.3	1.8	—	1956	60.0	4.1	11.3
1927	55.2	3.3	—	1957	59.6	4.3	10.5
1928	55.2	4.2	—	1958	59.5	6.8	13.9
1929	55.1	3.2	—	1959	59.3	5.5	14.4

(continued)

HISTORIC DATA: Labor Force Participation Rates *(continued)*
Unemployment Rates, 1900–1991

	Labor Partic- ipation Rate	Unem- ploy- ment rate	Average (mean) Duration of Unemployment in Weeks		Labor Partic- ipation Rate	Unem- ploy- ment rate	Average (mean) Duration of Unemployment in Weeks
1960	59.4%	5.5%	12.8	1976	61.6%	7.7%	15.8
1961	59.3	6.7	15.6	1977	62.3	7.1	14.3
1962	58.8	5.5	14.7	1978	63.2	6.1	11.9
1963	58.7	5.7	14.0	1979	63.7	5.8	10.8
1964	58.7	5.2	13.3	1980	63.8	7.1	11.9
1965	58.9	4.5	11.8	1981	63.9	7.6	13.7
1966	59.2	3.8	10.4	1982	64.0	9.7	15.6
1967	59.6	3.8	8.7	1983	64.0	9.6	20.0
1968	59.6	3.6	8.4	1984	64.4	7.5	18.2
1969	60.1	3.5	7.8	1985	64.8	7.2	15.6
1970	60.4	4.9	8.6	1986	65.3	7.0	15.0
1971	60.2	5.9	11.3	1987	65.6	6.2	14.5
1972	60.4	5.6	12.0	1988	65.9	5.5	13.5
1973	60.8	4.9	10.0	1989	66.5	5.3	11.9
1974	61.3	5.6	9.8	1990	66.3	5.5	12.1
1975	61.2	8.5	14.2	1991	66.0	6.7	13.8

For international comparisons of unemployment rates, see Chapter 17.

Name: Occupational Injury and Illness Data
Agency/Institution: Bureau of Labor Statistics
Address: 441 G Street, N.W., Washington, DC 20212
Telephone number for data and inquiries: 202-501-6410
Sources: The most complete report is contained in *Occupational Injuries and Ill-nesses in the United States, by Industry* (Bureau of Labor Statistics; annual) less complete data are reported in the *Monthly Labor Review.*
Frequency: Annually
When available: More than 12 months after the end of the year
Revisions: None
Historic data: *Handbook of Labor Statistics*

■ A QUICK LOOK: Occupational Injury and Illness Data

In cooperation with state agencies, the Bureau of Labor Statistics collects data on employment-related injuries and accidents, and it issues an annual report from the data collected. Excluded from the survey are the self-employed, farmers with fewer than 11 employees, and federal, state, and local government agencies. In the BLS annual publication, *Occupational Injuries and Illnesses in The United States, by Industry*, estimates are made for industries, number of employees, and severity: fatalities, lost workdays, and nonfatal cases without lost workdays. The following is a sample of some data contained in the *Monthly Labor Review*:

	Occupational Injury and Illness Incidence Rates in 1988 per 100 Full-Time Workers
Private Sector	
Total Cases	8.6
Lost Workday cases	4.0
Lost Workdays	76.1
Manufacturing	
Total Cases	13.1
Lost Workday cases	5.7
Lost Workdays	107.4
Transportation Equipment	
Total Cases	17.7
Lost Workday cases	6.6
Lost Workdays	134.2

Occupational injuries and illnesses: Include (1) occupational deaths, regardless of the time between injury and death; (2) nonfatal occupational illnesses; and (3) nonfatal occupational injuries that involve one or more of the following: loss of consciousness, restriction of work or motion, transfer to another job, or medical treatment.

Lost workday cases: Involve days away from work, or days of restricted work activity or both.

Lost workdays: Number of workdays on which the employee would have worked but could not because of occupational illness or injury, plus the number of days on which the worker worked only part-time, was assigned to other duties, or could not perform all duties normally associated with the job.

Incidence rate: [(Number of injuries/illnesses)/(total hours worked by all employees during year)] × 2,000. The number 2,000 is the number of hours worked by full-time workers working 40 hours per week for 50 weeks.

Data are gathered from the Annual Survey of Occupational Injuries and Illnesses as required by the Occupational Safety and Health Act of 1970. This is an annual mail survey covering virtually the entire private sector except for self-employed individuals, small farms, mining of metal ores and coal, and railroad operations. Data are available for industries at the two- to four-digit SIC level.

Name: Annual Salaries for Professional, Administrative, and Technical Occupations
Alternative name: White Collar Salaries
Agency/Institution: Department of Labor
Address: Dept. of Labor, Division of White Collar Employment, Washington, DC 20212
Telephone number for data and inquiries: 202-523-1570
Sources: *National Survey of Professional, Administrative, Technical, and Clerical Pay (PATC)* (Bureau of Labor Statistics bulletin); *Handbook of Labor Statistics*
Frequency: Annual
When available: Lag of about one year
Revisions: None
Historic data: *Handbook of Labor Statistics*

■ A QUICK LOOK: Salaries of White Collar Occupations

The Department of Labor obtains data on annual salaries for about 30 white collar occupations in fields such as accounting, legal services, personnel management, engineering, chemistry, computer processing, purchasing, drafting, photography, nursing, other health services, and clerical. One of the purposes of the survey is to provide comparisons of the pay of white collar employees in the private sector with those in the federal civil service. Be careful in making comparisons over time because the survey has undergone many changes since it was started in 1961. In 1986, for example, the inclusion of much smaller firms in the survey made accurate comparisons with previous years impossible.

Example of Data Available

	I	II	III	IV	V	VI
Attorneys 1987–88	$33,962	42,589	55,407	69,854	86,940	110,489
Accountants 1987–88	$21,962	26,666	33,028	41,966	53,297	67,950

There are six levels of pay for attorneys and accountants, but other occupations can have more or fewer levels. The levels designate levels of duties and responsibilities.

Name: Weekly Labor Hours
Agency: Bureau of Labor Statistics
Address: 441 G Street, N.W., Washington, DC 20212
Telephone number for data and inquiries: 202-523-1158
Sources: *Survey of Current Business, Employment and Earnings*
Frequency: Monthly

When available: Two months after reference month
Revisions: Benchmark revisions made every year
Historic data: None available

■ A QUICK LOOK: Weekly Labor Hours

Data on weekly labor hours are obtained from the same sources as the establishment data on employment (see Labor Market Data on pages 69–76) and are averages for full-time and part-time employees, including overtime. Data are only for production and nonsupervisory workers; thus, managers, executives, professionals, and technical workers are excluded. Number of weekly hours worked is an early indicator of changes in the utilization of labor and the business cycle in general. It is one of the leading economic indicators. Average weekly hours are given for total private sector, mining, construction, manufacturing, transportation, wholesale, retail, finance, insurance, real estate, and services. Further disaggregations are available for manufacturing (for example, lumber and wood products, furniture and fixtures).

Historic Data: Weekly Labor Hours

Year	Average Weekly Hours of Production and Supervisory Workers, Private Sector	Average Weekly Hours of Production and Supervisory Workers, Manufacturing	Year	Average Weekly Hours of Production and Supervisory Workers, Private Sector	Average Weekly Hours of Production and Supervisory Workers, Manufacturing
1932		38.3	1973	36.9	40.7
1935		36.6	1974	36.5	40.0
1940		38.1	1975	36.1	39.5
1945		43.5	1976	36.1	40.1
1950	39.8	40.5	1977	36.0	40.3
1955	39.6	40.7	1978	35.8	40.4
1960	38.6	39.7	1979	35.7	40.2
1961	38.6	39.8	1980	35.3	39.7
1962	38.7	40.4	1981	35.2	39.8
1963	38.8	40.5	1982	34.8	38.9
1964	38.7	40.7	1983	35.0	40.1
1965	38.8	41.2	1984	35.2	40.7
1966	38.6	41.4	1985	34.9	40.5
1967	38.0	40.6	1986	34.8	40.7
1968	37.8	40.7	1987	34.8	41.0
1969	37.7	40.6	1988	34.7	41.1
1970	37.1	39.8	1989	34.6	41.0
1971	36.9	39.9	1990	34.5	40.8
1972	37.0	40.5	1991	34.3	40.7

Name: Work Stoppages
Agency/Institution: Bureau of Labor Statistics
Address: 441 G Street, N.W., Washington, DC 20212
Telephone number for data and inquiries: 202-523-1320
Sources: *Monthly Labor Review, Current Wage Developments* (both from the Department of Labor)
Frequency: Monthly
When available: First half of month following the reference month
Revisions: If needed
Historic data: *Handbook of Labor Statistics*

■ A QUICK LOOK: Work Stoppages

Work stoppages include all strikes and lockouts involving 1000 or more workers that continue for one full day or shift, or longer. A **strike** is a temporary stoppage of work by a group of employees to express a grievance or to enforce a demand. A **lockout** is a temporary withholding of work by an employer to enforce terms of employment upon a group of employees. All known stoppages, whether or not authorized by a union, legal or illegal, are counted. However, strikes by American seamen or other workers in foreign ports are not counted. The data do not measure the indirect or secondary effects of stoppages on other establishments, whose employees are idled due to material shortages or lack of service. The number of stoppages, the number of workers involved, the number of days idle, and days lost as a percent of total working time are reported in the work stoppage statistics. Data are available by major industry.

CHAPTER 5

PRICE INDEXES:
Measures of Inflation

READ ME FIRST

The experience of Americans who grew up after World War II is that price changes necessarily mean price increases, or **inflation**. In fact, many believe they are highly unlikely ever to witness general deflation.[1] Actually, long-term inflation, which is defined as a sustained rise in the weighted average of prices, did not become a serious problem in the United States until the late 1960s. Prior to 1970, serious inflation was associated only with war and its immediate aftermath.

The most serious inflation in American history occurred during the Revolutionary War, when large quantities of continentals (paper currency) were issued and prices increased by a factor of more than ten. The sharp decrease in the value of money caused subsequent generations of Americans to say that a depreciated and valueless object was "not worth a continental." Deflation followed in the latter 18th century and then strong inflationary pressures erupted during the War of 1812. A period of sharp deflation occurred between 1837 and 1845, caused by decreases in the money supply. Prices more than doubled during the Civil War and then dropped throughout the remainder of the 19th century, especially

---

[1]Prices of some commodities, however, do go down. The GNP fixed-weight price index for printers and computers, based on 1982 = 100 is:

	Printers	Computers
1982	100.0	100.0
1986	20.4	41.7
1987	16.3	37.6
1988	14.7	34.4
1989	12.3	32.0

Source: Survey of Current Business (November 1989 and August 1990).

between 1873 and 1879. Prices rose again during World War I and continued rising until 1920, when they dropped sharply and remained relatively flat until the end of the twenties. Between 1930 and 1933, prices dropped even more sharply, but then rose steadily until 1937, when they dropped slightly again. Prices rose throughout World War II and the early postwar period. Despite the Korean War in the early 1950s, consumer prices increased only 2.2 percent per year during that decade. During the 1960s, too, prices increased an average of only 2.6 percent per year, although they rose more rapidly during the latter half of the decade. The 1970s, however, was a decade of sharp inflation, with prices increasing an average of 7.5 percent per year — and the 1980s, with an average annual inflation rate of 5.1 percent, did not give Americans much respite.

The American experience with high rates of inflation during the past two decades is not unique in the world. Only West Germany, Switzerland, Belgium, and Japan had lower rates of inflation between 1970 and 1990; other countries had higher rates. The following indexes are widely used measures of inflation in the United States. They are used by economists, government officials, corporation managers, and labor union officials. The reader who is unacquainted with some of the fundamentals of index interpretation and construction might want to review the section on indexes in Chapter 3 before tackling the section on consumer prices.

Name: Consumer Price Index
Alternative name: Cost-of-Living Index (incorrect)
Agency/Institution: Bureau of Labor Statistics
Address: Room 3216, 600 E Street, N.W., Washington, DC 20212
Telephone number for data: 202-523-9658 for four-minute tape on various indexes
Telephone number for inquiries: 202-272-5164
Sources: *Monthly Labor Review, CPI Detailed Report, Survey of Current Business,* most newspapers
Frequency: Monthly
When available: The third week of the following month
Revisions: No formal revisions except that each January revisions are made in the seasonally adjusted data for the past five years.
Further information: *Handbook of Methods,* Bulletin 2285 (Bureau of Labor Statistics, 1988); *The Consumer Price Index: 1987 Revision,* Report 736 (Bureau of Labor Statistics, 1987).
Historic data: See below.
Cross-references: Implicit Price Deflator, Producer Price Index

---

■ **A QUICK LOOK: The Consumer Price Index**

The **Consumer Price Index** (CPI) measures the price changes for a market basket of goods and services purchased by consumers. It is used as an indicator of inflation, as an escalator in labor contracts for nearly 10 million workers, and for 55 million Social Security beneficiaries, federal retirees, and food stamp recipients. Many private firms and individuals use the index to keep rents, royalties, and child support payments in line with changing prices. The Consumer Price Index, which measures price changes at the retail level, is one of the most widely reported economic statistics in the world. Incorrectly called the "cost-of-living" index, the CPI is a measure of the average change in prices paid by urban consumers for a fixed market basket of goods and services. See Table 5.1.

TABLE 5.1
Consumer Prices, Not Seasonally Adjusted
(1982–1984 = 100)

	1990	1991	1992 Jan.	1992 Feb.
All Items, Wage Earners and Clerical Workers (CPI-W)	129.0	134.3	136.0	136.4
All Items, All Urban Consumers (CPI-U)	130.7	136.2	138.1	138.6
Commodities	122.8	126.6	127.2	127.6
Commodities, less food & beverages	117.4	120.4	121.6	122.1
Services	139.2	146.3	149.6	150.1
Food and beverages	132.1	136.8	137.2	137.5
Housing	128.5	133.6	135.7	136.1
Shelter	140.0	146.3	149.2	149.8
Fuel and utilities	111.6	115.3	116.2	115.9
Household furnishings	113.3	116.0	116.7	117.3
Apparel and upkeep	124.1	128.7	127.9	130.2
Transportation	120.5	123.8	124.5	124.1
Private	118.8	121.9	122.5	122.0
New cars	121.0	126.0	128.0	128.1
Used cars	117.6	118.1	117.8	116.1
Public	142.6	148.9	151.5	150.7
Medical care	162.8	177.0	184.6	186.4
Seasonally adjusted				
Commodities			127.3	127.8
Food			137.4	137.8
Apparel and upkeep			130.0	131.9
Transportation			124.4	124.2
Services			149.7	150.0

All Items, Wage Earners and Clerical Workers (CPI-W): This index dates back to 1921. It is still maintained for use in labor contracts and escalator clauses, but, for most purposes, it has been replaced by the CPI-U. The "all items" means that it is the general index; the other parts are components of the "all-items index."

Consumer Price Index — Urban Consumers (CPI-U):   The version given on the TV news is the percentage change in the seasonally adjusted all-items CPI-U. The CPI-U is reported in both seasonally adjusted and unadjusted formats.

Seasonally adjusted series: Takes out the normal seasonal fluctuations so that indexes from various months can be compared with each other. The index value is not given for the seasonally adjusted "all items"; only the rates of change are given. Also, seasonally adjusted data are calculated only for months or quarters; there are no seasonally adjusted data for an entire year.

Calculating Percentage Changes in the Consumer Price Index

Let's use the raw index numbers from Table 5.1 to calculate percentage changes in the CPI. From the table, we see that medical care prices are rising much faster than other prices, increasing by more than 86 percent since 1983 — which simply proves what we already suspected. Fuel and utility prices have risen the least. However, the CPI is most useful when percentage changes in the index numbers are calculated from year to year or month to month. If you want to know the percentage change in the consumer price index between any two years, such as 1990 and 1991, you simply divide the absolute difference of the indexes by the index value in the earlier year, as shown below for CPI-U, all items:

$$\frac{136.2 - 130.7}{130.7} = 0.0421 = 4.21\%$$

Thus, prices increased by 4.2 percent between 1990 and 1991.

If you want to know the percentage change from the previous month, you have to decide first if you want the simple percentage change from the previous month or the annualized rate of change between the two months. The simple rate of change can be compared only with the rate of change between the same months of previous years. The annualized change will enable you to make comparisons with price changes in any month, quarter, or year. If you want the simple rate of change, the calculation for the seasonally adjusted *commodity* series between January and February 1992 is

$$\frac{127.8 - 127.3}{127.3} = 0.0039 = 0.4\%$$

This is the nonannualized rate of increase, showing the percentage change between the two months.

If you want the annualized rate of change between the two months you have to use the formula discussed in Chapter 2. Applied to the seasonally adjusted commodity series, it would be

$$\left(\frac{127.8}{127.3}\right)^{12} - 1 = 0.0482 = 4.8\%$$

Thus, there was a 4.8 percent increase in February at an annualized rate. This means that if prices for commodities increased at a simple rate of 0.4 percent each month for 12 months, the equivalent annual increase would be 4.8 percent.

■ A CLOSER LOOK: The Consumer Price Index

The most frequently reported measure of change in the prices of consumer goods and services is the Consumer Price Index (CPI), which is issued by the Bureau of Labor Statistics about three weeks after each reference month. The CPI reports changes in the prices of goods frequently purchased by the average consumer: food and beverages; automobiles; housing; clothes; tickets to movies and plays; repair costs; fees to doctors and lawyers; including all excise, sales, and real estate taxes associated with the purchase or ownership of the item. The CPI is one of the oldest national economic data series. The series known as the CPI-W, for *Consumer Price Index— Wage Earners and Clerical Workers*, was started in 1921. A more recent addition to the CPI series is the CPI-U, the Consumer Price Index — Urban Consumers, which began in 1978 but has been backdated to 1913. Thus, the current CPI is actually composed of two separate data series, the CPI-W and the CPI-U. The CPI-W is based on the spending patterns of urban households in which at least one member worked as a wage earner at least 37 weeks during the year in a craft, clerical, sales, service, or general labor job. The fact that these workers and their families constituted only 40 percent of the population in the mid-1970s was the main reason for the introduction of the broader based CPI-U, which includes all urban consumers, or about 82 percent of the population. The broader based CPI-U is the one reported on television and in the newspapers, while the CPI-W is often used for cost-of-living adjustments in labor contracts.

Chapter 2 warned that misinterpretations can arise when data users are not careful about annualized and seasonalized data series. The Consumer Price Index is reported with and without seasonal adjustments and annualization. Hence, it's important to know which series is being used. Unadjusted data should be used only for comparisons with the same month of previous years; seasonally adjusted data can be compared with any month since the seasonal fluctuations have been taken out. News reports seldom indicate whether the CPI they are reporting is seasonally adjusted or not. In most cases, they are reporting the seasonally adjusted CPI-U, but sometimes they fail to state whether the rate of change is annualized.

There are local as well as national CPI series. For example, 38 local areas, including the metropolitan areas of Chicago, Los Angeles, New York, San Francisco, Baltimore, Miami, St. Louis, Houston, and Detroit, have their own CPI series. The local CPI series, by-products of the national CPI, are based on much smaller samples and are subject to greater volatility than the national CPI. Accordingly, users are cautioned against using local CPIs for escalator clauses.

Although the CPI is frequently called a "cost-of-living" index in labor contracts, federal retirement systems, and Social Security benefit calculations, it is not designed for this purpose for three reasons. First, the CPI measures changes in the prices of consumer goods but it does not measure the cost of maintaining a minimum standard of living. For example, the CPI-U for Chicago might be increasing faster than the CPI-U for New York, but it could cost much more to live in New York than in Chicago. Second, the index reports changes in prices for a fixed group of items and does not reflect changes in buying patterns that a consumer would make to adjust to higher prices. If, for example, the price of steak increases, consumers may shift to eating less steak and more chicken. The CPI does not reflect such substitutions. Third, the CPI excludes all income taxes and personal property taxes, which should be included in a cost-of-living index.

The Bureau of Labor Statistics (BLS), which is responsible for the CPI series, obtains price information by sending field representatives to approximately 25,000 outlets each month (some are visited every other month) to record prices of specific goods and services. How does BLS know what goods to price and how much weight to give to each good? It takes surveys of consumers about every ten years to determine how they spend their money; that is, the BLS determines consumer market baskets through periodic surveys of expenditure patterns.[2] The first study of consumer expenditures was conducted between 1917 and 1919 and provided the weights for the CPI until 1935. The sixth and most recent major consumer survey was taken by the BLS in 1982–84, and the current market basket of goods consists of approximately 370 items. The base period of the CPI was also changed to 1982 – 84.[3] In the consumer expenditure survey of 1982–84, about 20,000 people provided information on their spending habits in a series of interviews. About 18,000 of them kept diaries listing everything they bought during a two-week period. Table 5.2 shows the relative weights of major goods categories in use in February 1992 based on the results of that survey.

---

[2]The CPI is a Lespeyres index, which uses base-year quantity weights. See "The Index Problem" in Chapter 2.

[3]When the BLS changes the base period, it also revises the historical series to that new base period. However, if you are using historical data that have not been revised, you can easily make the revisions. The base or reference period can be reset by dividing each index series by its value for the new base period and multiplying by 100. For example, the CPI-U for February 1987 (based on 1967 = 100) was 334.4. The average value of the index based on 1967 = 100 for the 1982–84 period was 299.5. Hence, [(334.4/299.5) × 100] = 111.7, which is the CPI-U index for February 1987 based on 1982–84 = 100. See the disussion of indexes in Chapter 3 for more information.

TABLE 5.2
Relative Weights Used for Major Products
(CPI, February 1992)

Food and beverages	17.6%
Housing	41.5
Apparel and upkeep	6.1
Transportation	17.0
Medical care	6.7
Entertainment	4.4
Other goods and services	6.7
	100.0%

Data for calculating the price indexes are obtained from about 25,000 retail and service establishments and 60,000 housing units in 85 urban areas. However, most of the 370 items are priced every month only in the five largest areas (New York, Philadelphia, Chicago, Detroit, and Los Angeles); in the other 80 areas most items are priced every other month. Certain items such as food for home consumption, and fuels and utilities are priced every month in all locations. The selection of the retail outlets from which the prices are obtained is based on surveys of where consumers shop. Some data, such as utility rates and rentals, are obtained from mail surveys.

During the late 1970s and early 1980s, the BLS was severely criticized for its calculations of housing costs, which included house prices, mortgage rates, property taxes, and insurance. Before 1983, the implicit assumption was that the average family was buying a proportional share of a house every month. In the early 1980s, however, sharply rising mortgage rates made the housing component of the CPI rise more quickly than it should have. For this reason, since 1983, the BLS has used the rental equivalency value of owner-occupied housing instead. In determining the rental value of homes, the BLS uses a combination of (1) a sample of homeowners' estimates of what it would cost to rent their homes and (2) the actual rents on similar nearby homes that are rented.[4]

CPI data are subject to sampling error, which changes each month but is generally about plus or minus one-fourth of 1 percent. A serious criticism of the CPI is that it uses fixed weights. For example, goods whose prices have increased significantly since the base period are overrepresented in the market basket because consumers normally react to higher prices by decreasing the relative quantity of such goods they purchase,

---

[4]This is one of several revisions that have been made by the BLS during the past ten years. When the BLS makes such revisions, it reestimates the price indexes for previous years. If you are looking at price increases for 1950 in 1955, they will differ from those you will find if you are looking at 1950 price changes in 1960, 1970, 1982, 1985, or 1990. The past is always changing.

but the basket does not reflect such changes. Thus, the CPI tends to exaggerate price increases. The CPI is also criticized for neglecting changes in quality although the Bureau of Labor Statistics attempts to adjust for quality changes. If the known quality of a good, for example, has increased by 10 percent and its price has increased by 10 percent, the BLS reports no increase in price. The problem is one of obtaining reliable data on quality changes and making the appropriate numerical changes. Another criticism of the CPI is that, among the millions of commodities and services actually available in the marketplace, it prices fewer than 400. Many economists prefer using the much broader GDP/GNP deflator, although serious problems exist with that index as well.

Purchasing Power of the Dollar

It is commonly believed that changes in the CPI lead to proportional changes in the purchasing power of the dollar in the opposite direction; that is, if the price index increases by 5 percent, the value of the dollar decreases by 5 percent. Actually, the computation is a bit more complicated because of the problem of "shifting bases." Assume that widgets are priced in the marketplace at 1 cent each, so the purchasing value of a dollar is said to be 100 widgets. Now assume that prices *increase* by 5 percent so the CPI is now 105. The purchasing value of the dollar has not decreased by 5 percent but by 4.76 percent. At $0.0105 per widget, a dollar would purchase 95.24 ($1.00/$0.0105) widgets, which is 4.76 percent fewer than it purchased at the previous price of 1 cent per widget. The purchasing value of the dollar would have fallen by only 4.76 percent. Now assume that the price of widgets *falls* from $0.01 to $0.0095 so the price index will decrease 5 percent from 100 to 95. The purchasing value of the dollar has not increased by 5 percent but by 5.26 percent. At $0.0095 per widget, a dollar will now purchase 105.26 widgets ($1.00/$.0095). Hence, when the price index falls by 5 percent, the purchasing value of the dollar rises by 5.26 percent. The following formula can be used to convert percentage changes in the index to percentage changes in the purchasing power of the dollar:

$$\frac{1}{1 \pm \text{percentage change in price index}} - 1$$

If the CPI increases by 10 percent, the percentage change in the purchasing power of the dollar is:

$$\frac{1}{1 + 0.1} - 1 = -0.0909 = -9.1\%$$

If the raw index values are known, the percentage changes and the value of the dollar can be calculated simply by taking the reciprocal. In

February 1992, the CPI-U index, based on 1982–84 = 100 was 138.6. Thus, the purchasing power of the dollar in July 1990 was:

$$\frac{\text{Index in original period}}{\text{Index in current period}} = \frac{100}{138.6} = \$0.722$$

The purchasing power of the dollar in February was $0.722, which means it had decreased approximately 28 percent between 1983 and February 1992 and that a dollar in February 1992 was worth only about 72 percent of its value in 1983. Based on 1967 = 100, the February 1992 CPI index was 415.2, so the value of the dollar in February 1992, compared with 1967, was 100/415.2 = $0.24. A dollar in 1992 would buy only about one-fourth of what it could have purchased in 1967. If you want to determine the purchasing power of the dollar relative to some year other than the official base year, simply take the base year and divide by the current index, expressing the results in dollars. For example, if you want to determine the value of the dollar in 1989 compared with 1975: 53.8/124.0 = $0.434.

Historic Data: Consumer Price Index, Urban Consumers (CPI-U),
All Items
(1982–84 = 100)

Year	Index	Year	Index	Year	Index	Year	Index
1913	9.9	1935	13.7	1955	26.8	1975	53.8
1914	10.0	1936	13.9	1956	27.2	1976	56.9
1915	10.1	1937	14.4	1957	28.1	1977	60.6
1916	10.9	1938	14.1	1958	28.9	1978	65.2
1917	12.8	1939	13.9	1959	29.1	1979	72.6
1918	15.1	1940	14.0	1960	29.6	1980	82.4
1919	17.3	1941	14.7	1961	29.9	1981	90.9
1920	20.0	1942	16.3	1962	30.2	1982	96.5
1921	17.9	1943	17.3	1963	30.6	1983	99.6
1922	16.8	1944	17.6	1964	31.0	1984	103.9
1923	17.1	1945	18.0	1965	31.5	1985	107.6
1924	17.1	1946	19.5	1966	32.4	1986	109.6
1925	17.5	1947	22.3	1967	33.4	1987	113.6
1926	17.7	1948	24.1	1968	34.8	1988	118.3
1927	17.4	1949	23.8	1969	36.7	1989	124.0
1928	17.1	1950	24.1	1970	38.8	1990	130.7
1929	17.1	1951	26.0	1971	40.5	1991	136.2
1930	16.7	1952	26.5	1972	41.8		
1931	15.2	1953	26.7	1973	44.4		
1932	13.7	1954	26.9	1974	49.3		
1933	13.0						
1934	13.4						

Name: Cost of Living for Urban Areas
Agency/Institution: American Chamber of Commerce Researchers Association (ACCRA)
Address: American Chamber of Commerce Executives, 4232 King St., Alexandria, VA 22302
Telephone number for methodology: 713-658-2466
Telephone number for data and inquiries: 703-998-4172
Sources: *Cost of Living Index*, a pamphlet available by subscription, from P.O. Box 6749, Louisville, Kentucky 40206 (502-897-2890)
Frequency: Quarterly
When available: two–three months after end of quarter
Revisions: None
Historic data: None, but many libraries keep back issues
Cross references: Consumer Price Index

■ **A QUICK LOOK: Cost of Living for Urban Areas**

The association for the country's chambers of commerce (ACCRA) puts together a quarterly pamphlet that measures the relative cost of living in about 290 of the country's urban areas, which contain about 70 percent of the nation's urban population. Members of the association are asked to obtain the prices of certain goods in their metropolitan areas likely to be purchased by midlevel managers. The association then determines the weighted national average of the market basket, and sets that equal to 100. The relative cost of the market basket in each city is then reflected by its relationship to the national average of 100. The following is a sample of the data provided:

Sample of Cost of Living
(Second quarter, 1990)

	Composite	Groceries	Housing	Utilities	Transpor-tation	Health
	100.0%	17%	22%	11%	13%	7%
Augusta GA-SC MSA	98.1	92.4	87.0	117.7	97.7	99.4
Dallas TX PMSA	104.6	104.9	97.6	112.5	115.1	106.1
San Diego CA MSA	131.7	104.6	215.8	73.4	131.9	125.3

Miscellaneous Goods and Services, not shown, account for 30% of the index.

A quick look at the data sample above shows that the cost of living in August, Georgia, is slightly lower than the national average; in Dallas it is slightly above the national average, while in San Diego the cost of living is considerably higher. The cost of living in San Diego is 26 percent higher [(124.5 − 98.7)/98.7] than in Augusta.

This cost-of-living index does not measure changes in prices over time. For example, we cannot conclude that prices are increasing in San Diego faster than they are in Augusta. The data only tell us that the prices in San Diego were higher in the first quarter of 1989 than they were in Augusta, but the San Diego prices could be increasing at a less rapid rate. Use these data with caution because the statistical methodology, market baskets, and clerical accuracy are not comparable with those used to generate the CPI. However, they can be useful as rough guides. There is no doubt that general housing costs are meaningfully higher in San Diego than in Augusta. The Chambers of Commerce volunteer their time to gather and submit the data and some chambers have elected not to participate. ACCRA's quarterly report also shows the average prices of specific goods and services for each of the urban areas.

Name: GDP/GNP Price Deflators
Alternative name: Implicit price deflators
Agency/Institution: Bureau of Economic Analysis, Department of Commerce
Address: Division of GNP, Washington, DC 20230
Telephone number for data and inquiries: 202-523-0828
Sources: *Survey of Current Business* (monthly) and *President's Economic Report* (annual)
Frequency: Quarterly
When available: First estimates are available about 20 days after the end of the quarter.
Revisions: The revisions for the GDP/GNP price deflators are identical to those for the GDP/GNP. The first estimate (called the "advance estimate") is made in the month following the end of the quarter. A revision (called the "preliminary estimate") is published in the following or second month, and the series is revised again the following month with the final estimate. No further revisions are made until the annual revisions, which are published in July. Annual revisions are made for the next two years, and then no further revisions are made until the comprehensive revisions, which are usually made every five years. For example, the advance estimate for the first quarter data of 1993 (1993:I) is released in April. The 1993:I data will be revised in May (preliminary estimate) and June (final estimate). There will be no further revisions of 1993:I until July 1994, when the annual estimates are revised. The 1993 annual estimates will be revised in the July issues of *Survey of Current Business* for the next two years (1995 and 1996) and then will not change until the five-year comprehensive revision (called a "benchmark revision") is made. The most recent benchmark revision was carried out in 1990, but there is a lag in implementing the benchmark data. The GNP deflator for any year, say 1965, changes over the years as new benchmarks are made.
Historic data: See below.

Note: In the fall of 1991, the Bureau of Economic Analysis began converting their GNP and GNP-related data series to a "gross domestic product" (GDP) basis. The GNP price deflators will henceforth be known as the GDP price deflators. Although the following discussion emphasizes the GDP, it occasionally refers to GNP price deflators as well in order to ease the transition for those who are accustomed to "GNP price deflators." The GNP price deflators continue to be published but only for major categories. Unfortunately, some of the price deflator data were not available at the time this book went to press. The BEA has promised that price deflator data will be available by 1993.

■ A QUICK LOOK: The GDP/GNP Deflators

The national income and product accounts (see pages 120–149) produce two widely available measures of price changes that are published quarterly along with the GDP data. Most well known is the **implicit price deflator**, also called the **GDP**, or the **GNP**, **deflator**, which is obtained as a by-product when calculating real GDP and GNP. A sample of this index is shown in Table 5.3.

TABLE 5.3
**Implicit Price Deflator and Fixed-Weight Price Index
for Gross Domestic Product, 1991**
(1987 = 100)

	Implicit Price Deflator	Fixed-Weight Index*
Gross domestic product	117.0	117.6
Personal consumption expenditures	119.3	119.7
Durable goods	107.9	109.4
Nondurable goods	120.0	120.5
Services	121.5	121.8
Gross private domestic investment	—	—
Fixed investment	108.4	110.5
Nonresidential	107.4	110.2
Residential	111.3	111.4
Change in business inventories		
Net exports of goods and services		
Exports	109.9	111.6
Imports	111.3	113.6
Government purchases	116.1	116.3
Federal	115.7	116.4
National defense	115.0	116.3
Nondefense	117.5	116.8
State and local	116.3	116.2

*BEA will publish this index in late 1992 or early 1993.
(For information on converting index values to percent changes, see Chapter 3.)

Implicit price deflator: Also known as the GDP deflator because it is obtained as a by-product of constructing constant-dollar GDP. The value of GDP before correcting for price changes is called "current dollar GDP," or "nominal GDP." It is measured in current prices. The GDP adjusted to eliminate price changes is called "real GDP," or "constant-dollar GDP." Real GDP is obtained by deflating the various component commodities and services in GDP with individual price indexes. These deflated components are added to obtain real GDP. When the nominal GDP is divided by this total real GDP, the result is a price index called the "implicit price deflator."

Fixed-weight price index: This is a more conventional price index also obtained from the GNP accounts. It is similar to the Consumer Price Index in that it uses fixed-period weights or a market basket from some base period. This index measures changes in the prices of this fixed market basket over the years. One advantage of the fixed-weight price index is that it is published for many more commodities and services than the implicit price deflator.

In general, the values of the implicit price deflator and the fixed-weight index are close to each other, but, as would be expected from two indexes that employ such diverse methodologies, there are considerable differences for some categories. Fixed-weight price indexes exist for a wide variety of personal consumption expenditures, with monthly indexes for personal consumption, durable goods, nondurable goods, and services. In the past it was thought that the implicit price deflator was less volatile than the Consumer Price Index, but recent changes in the CPI have made this somewhat less true.

■ A CLOSER LOOK: The GDP/GNP Price Deflators

Current value GDP is obtained by adding together the current market values of all goods and services produced during the year. This number is useful for some purposes but it does not tell us by how much actual output of goods and services has increased since last year or some earlier year. The measure that makes comparisons of actual output possible is the real GDP. It is calculated by deflating the numerous components of current GDP by a number of price indexes to some base year, which is currently 1982. For example, expenditures on gasoline are deflated by a price index for gasoline; men's and boys' clothing expenditures are deflated by a price index for clothing. After deflating the components of GNP by the various deflators, the Bureau of Economic Analysis (BEA) adds the components together to obtain real GNP. In deflating the separate components, BEA uses parts of the CPI, PPI, and special indexes that they constructed. The accuracy of real GDP is enhanced if price indexes exist for each of the several components of the data series. Considerable improvements have been made in such disaggregations during the past couple of decades. For example, until the mid-1970s expenditures on food consumed at home had been deflated by a single index for food at home. These food expenditures were disaggregated, and there are now 16 separate categories and indexes for food at home. In the entire GNP more than 600 categories of goods and services are now deflated separately.

This deflation process yields current year output evaluated at base year prices — for example, 1990 output evaluated at 1987 prices. Thus, the preparation of current and constant-dollar GNP estimates yields a by-product called the *implicit price deflator*. The GDP implicit price deflator is the price index that results from estimating the real and nominal GDP. Assuming that 1987 is the base year:

$$\frac{\text{Nominal GDP}}{\text{Real GDP}} = \frac{1990 \text{ quantity} \times \text{current price}}{1990 \text{ quantity} \times 1987 \text{ price}} = \frac{1990 \text{ price}}{1987 \text{ price}} = \begin{array}{l}\text{Implicit}\\\text{price}\\\text{deflator}\\\text{for } 1990\end{array}$$

Since quantities of final goods and services change from year to year, the weights used to construct the GDP deflator change as well. Thus, the change in the deflator reflects not only changes in prices but changes in the mix of products and services as well.

In addition to the implicit price deflator, the national income and product accounts (see page 127) produce another index of price changes. The *fixed-weight price index (FWPI)* holds constant the purchasing habits or market baskets of the population between the benchmark years, which occur every five years. In contrast to the implicit price deflator, the index is weighted by the composition of the GDP in a fixed base period, so it measures only price changes. Unfortunately, the processing of data can take a number of years. For example, the data from the 1977 survey were not completed and integrated into the FWPI until 1985. The market basket used in the FWPI between 1972 and 1985 was the one generated in 1972. Thus, it did not reflect the product substitution stimulated by the high energy prices that began in 1973–74. When the 1977 benchmark was obtained in 1985, the BEA adjusted the FWPI downward to reflect the fact that prices had not increased as much as they had appeared to. The substitution effects of the 1985–86 price decline in energy will not appear until detected by the 1987 benchmark, which will appear in 1995. The advantage of the FWPI is that it is broad-based, like the implicit price deflator, but unlike the implicit price deflator, it shows price changes only, without commingling the effects of product substitution.

Note: Historical data for the GDP implicit price deflator will not be available until 1993.

Historic Data: Implicit Price Deflator for GNP: 1982 = 100

1929	14.6	1951	25.1	1961	31.2	1971	44.4	1981	94.0
1933	11.2	1952	25.5	1962	31.9	1972	46.5	1982	100.0
1939	12.7	1953	25.9	1963	32.4	1973	49.5	1983	103.9
1940	13.0	1954	26.3	1964	32.9	1974	54.0	1984	107.7
1941	13.8	1955	27.2	1965	33.8	1975	59.3	1985	110.9
1942	14.7	1956	28.1	1966	35.0	1976	63.1	1986	113.8
1943	15.1	1957	29.1	1967	35.9	1977	67.3	1987	117.4
1944	15.3	1958	29.7	1968	37.7	1978	72.2	1988	121.3
1945	15.7	1959	30.4	1969	39.8	1979	78.6	1989	126.3
1946	19.4	1960	30.9	1970	42.0	1980	85.7	1990	131.5
1947	22.1								
1948	23.6								
1949	23.5								
1950	23.9								

Historic Data: Fixed-Weight Deflator for GNP: 1982 = 100

1959	37.6	1970	47.2	1981	94.1
1960	38.1	1971	48.8	1982	100.0
1961	38.4	1972	50.3	1983	104.1
1962	38.7	1973	53.1	1984	108.3
1963	39.1	1974	57.2	1985	111.9
1964	39.6	1975	61.8	1986	114.9
1965	40.1	1976	65.1	1987	119.1
1966	41.1	1977	68.4	1988	124.1
1967	42.1	1978	72.7	1989	129.7
1968	43.7	1979	78.8	1990	133.3
1969	45.6	1980	86.1		

Name: Producer Price Index

Alternative name: Wholesale Price Index

Agency/Institution: Bureau of Labor Statistics, Department of Labor

Address: 600 E. Street, N.W., Washington, DC 20212

Telephone number for data: 202-523-1765 for PPI recorded information

Telephone number for inquiries: 202-272-5108

Sources: Producer price indexes, *Monthly Labor Review, Survey of Current Business*, daily newspapers

Frequency: Monthly

When available: Around third Friday of month for previous month (e.g., third Friday in November for October index)

Revisions: All PPI are subject to one revision, four months after initial release.

Historic data: See page 100 and the *Handbook of Labor Statistics*.

Further Information: *Handbook of Methods*, Bulletin 2285 (BLS)

Cross-references: Consumer Price Index (pages 83–90), implicit price deflator (pages 94–95)

■ A QUICK LOOK: Producer Price Index

The **Producer Price Index (PPI)**, which is widely used as the base for escalation clauses in capital goods and raw materials industries, is reported monthly and is often referred to as the "wholesale price index," which was its official name until 1978. This index measures changes in prices at the raw material, intermediate, and finished goods stages before they are sold to the consumer. Since the Producer Price Index measures price changes at an earlier stage in the production and distribution chain, it is closely watched by some economists as an indicator of future changes in the CPI. There are three major classifications of PPI indexes: (1) stage of processing indexes, (2) commodity indexes, and (3) industry output. See Table 5.4.

TABLE 5.4
Producer Prices, Not Seasonally Adjusted
Selected Indexes
(1982 = 100)

	1990	1991	1992 January	1992 February
All Commodities	116.3	116.5	115.6	115.1
By stage of processing				
Crude materials	108.9	101.2	97.3	99.0
Intermediate materials	114.5	114.4	113.2	113.6
Finished goods	119.2	121.7	121.7	121.9
Finished consumer goods	118.2	120.5	120.0	120.2
Capital equipment	122.9	126.7	128.3	128.3
By Durability of Commodity				
Total durable goods	121.2	122.9	123.4	123.3
Total nondurable goods	112.2	111.7	110.6	110.8
By Industry Output (1984 = 100)				
Mining	70.6	76.4	75.2	75.0
Manufacturing	104.4	109.6	115.9	116.3
Chemicals and allied products	113.0	119.6	123.9	124.6
Furniture and fixtures	111.4	115.6	122.6	122.5

All commodities: This is the Producer Price Index reported by the media and given in the historic data on page 100. It is a weighted average of the prices of all producer goods.

Stage of processing: Organizes products by class of buyer (wholesaler, processor, retailer) and by the degree of fabrication.

Crude materials: Products entering the market for the first time that have not been manufactured or fabricated and that are not sold directly to the consumer. Examples are raw cotton, crude oil, coal, and hides and skins.

Intermediate materials: Supplies, materials, and components that have been processed but require further processing or commodities that are physically complete but are used as inputs by business firms. Examples include flour, yarn, lumber (requiring further processing), diesel fuel, paper boxes, and fertilizers (used as inputs).

Finished goods: Commodities that will not undergo further processing and are ready for sale to the final user or are capital goods used by business firms. Examples are fresh vegetables, bakery products, automobiles, and furniture. Examples of capital equipment are trucks, tractors, and machine tools.

Durable and nondurable goods: Goods that are expected to last at least one year. They include furniture, cars, and televisions. Nondurable goods include food, clothing, and other goods expected to be totally consumed within one year.

Industry output: Price indexes are published for 500 industries, classified according to the Standard Industrial Classification (SIC) code, which means that the industrial classifications are compatible with those for employment, wages, and productivity. The base year for this section is 1984 = 100.

Producer price indexes are currently based on 1982 = 100 and they are reported in both unadjusted and seasonally adjusted form. The unadjusted indexes, such as the one in Table 5.4, are more detailed and show annual data; the seasonally adjusted indexes show only monthly data (no need to show annual data in a seasonal index). The major categories of the PPI are shown in Table 5.4, but many more categories and subcategories are shown in both the adjusted and unadjusted series than are given here. Like other indexes, these raw numbers don't tell you very much. Depending on the source, percentage changes may or may not be given for the price indexes. In any event, the percentage changes are easy to calculate. Calculating percentage changes in indexes, as well as seasonalization and annualization, are discussed thoroughly in Chapter 2. A brief summary applied to this index is explained in the next section.

Calculating Percentage Changes in the Producer Price Index

To find the percentage change in the Producer Price Index between any two years, such as 1990 and 1991, simply divide the absolute difference by the index value in the earlier year:

$$\frac{116.5 - 116.3}{116.3} = 0.0017 = 0.2\%$$

Thus, prices have increased by 2/10ths of 1 percent between 1990 and 1991.

To find the percentage change from the previous month, decide first if you want the simple percentage change from the previous month or the annualized rate of change between the two months. To find the simple rate of change between January and February 1992, for example, calculate for the seasonally adjusted series as follows:

$$\frac{116.1 - 115.6}{115.6} = 0.0043 = 0.43\%$$

This is the nonannualized rate of increase showing the percent change between the two months.

To find the annualized rate of change between any two months, use the formula discussed in Chapter 2. Applied to the monthly data shown in 1992 the formula would be:

$$\left(\frac{116.1}{115.6}\right)^{12} - 1 = 0.0532 = 5.32\%$$

Thus, there was a 5.32 percent increase in February at an annualized rate. This means that if the prices increased at this rate each month for 12 months, the annual increase would be 5.32 percent.

■ A CLOSER LOOK: Producer Price Index

The Producer Price Index (PPI) provides information about price changes in the nonretail sectors of the American economy. The index was revised and improved during the 1980s so that it now reports monthly price changes for the approximately 500 mining and manufacturing industries contained in the Standard Industrial Classification. Monthly price indexes are published for 3100 products calculated from 75,000 quotations per month. Indexes are available for numerous commodity groupings (services are not included). One widely used grouping is stage of production: finished goods, intermediate or semifinished goods, and crude materials. Finished goods are goods ready for sale to ultimate consumers; examples include shirts, computers, and automobiles. Intermediate goods have been processed but require further processing; examples are flour, wool, and steel ingots. Crude materials are unprocessed goods that have not been manufactured or fabricated, such as grains, livestock, crude petroleum, and iron ore.

The PPI is based on a complicated, fixed input-output price index in which it is assumed there are no technological changes and firms are assumed not to change the proportions of their inputs. Prices are f.o.b. and are inclusive of all discounts and exclusive of all excise taxes and transportation charges. Companies are selected to participate on the basis of a stratified sample to ensure proportional representation. Participation is voluntary and confidentiality is assured. The PPI reflects some double counting in that it records price increases in the raw materials, the processed goods, and then the final product. This pyramiding overemphasizes the prices of crude materials, especially when they are rising rapidly. The PPI does not cover services or imported items.

The PPI is used in numerous price escalation clauses on long-term contracts covering raw materials and other basic goods and minerals. It is used also to revalue corporate assets in the replacement cost accounting rules of the Securities and Exchange Commission. Some analysts regard the PPI as a reasonably accurate harbinger of future changes to the Consumer Price Index.

Originally known as the "wholesale price index," PPI calculations started in 1913, although government statisticians have reconstructed the wholesale index back to colonial times.

Historic Data: Producer Price Index, All Commodities
(1982 = 100)

1900	9.7	1920	26.6	1940	13.5	1960	31.7	1980	89.8
1901	9.5	1921	16.8	1941	15.0	1961	31.6	1981	98.0
1902	10.2	1922	16.7	1942	17.0	1962	31.7	1982	100.0
1903	10.3	1923	17.3	1943	17.8	1963	31.6	1983	101.3
1904	10.3	1924	16.9	1944	17.9	1964	31.6	1984	103.7
1905	10.4	1925	17.8	1945	18.2	1965	32.3	1985	103.2
1906	10.7	1926	17.2	1946	20.8	1966	33.3	1986	100.2
1907	11.2	1927	16.4	1947	25.5	1967	33.4	1987	102.8
1908	10.8	1928	16.7	1948	27.6	1968	34.2	1988	106.9
1909	11.7	1929	16.4	1949	26.2	1969	35.6	1989	112.2
1910	12.2	1930	14.9	1950	27.3	1970	36.9	1990	116.3
1911	11.2	1931	12.5	1951	30.4	1971	38.1	1991	116.5
1912	11.9	1932	11.2	1952	29.5	1972	39.8		
1913	12.0	1933	11.3	1953	29.1	1973	45.0		
1914	11.8	1934	12.9	1954	29.2	1974	53.5		
1915	12.0	1935	13.8	1955	29.3	1975	58.4		
1916	14.7	1936	13.9	1956	30.2	1976	61.1		
1917	20.2	1937	14.8	1957	31.1	1977	64.9		
1918	22.6	1938	13.5	1958	31.5	1978	69.9		
1919	23.9	1939	13.3	1959	31.6	1979	78.7		

CHAPTER 6

MONEY, CREDIT, AND BANK INTEREST RATES

READ ME FIRST

Most economists agree that money and credit are important variables in the economy, but they don't always agree on the degree of importance or on the mechanisms through which money and credit influence the economy. Although the precise mechanisms remain somewhat clouded, economists generally agree that increases in the stock of money that are considerably greater than increases in the output of goods and services lead to expansionary pressures in the economy; if the economy is at or close to full employment these expansionary pressures produce inflation. If there are unemployed resources (labor, land, natural resources, capital capacity), these expansionary pressures might produce additional output and employment. Sharp increases in the money supply are thought to produce falling interest rates (at least in the short run), and decreases or slow increases in the money supply are thought to produce rising interest rates. However, changes in the money supply also affect inflationary expectations, which, in turn, affect market interest rates. Thus, sharp increases in the money supply might drive interest rates lower for a short time, but as the additional money supply causes prices to increase, market interest rates soon increase to reflect the heightened expectations of inflation.

You can read volumes on the definition of money, but the bottom line is that money is anything people want to use as money. During the past few hundred years, shells, whiskey, tobacco, cigarettes, cattle, pelts, rocks, and, of course, gold and silver, have been used as money. Contrary to what many economic novices might believe, today's money no longer has any official connection to gold or silver. Money gets its value solely from the fact that people accept it as money.

What about the gold standard? It is history — it no longer exists. The United States went firmly on a gold standard after the Civil War (officially in 1879) and remained on it until it was largely abandoned by President Roosevelt on June 5, 1933. A few gold trappings remained into the latter half of the 20th century, but they had little effect on the supply of money. Until March 1965, the Federal Reserve System was legally required to hold gold certificates, which represented gold held by the Treasury, equal to 25 percent of the reserve deposits held on behalf of member banks. Until March 1968, the Federal Reserve was also required to hold gold certificates equal to 25 percent of all outstanding Federal Reserve Notes (paper currency). Since 1968, however, the Federal Reserve, which is this country's central bank, has had no official gold requirements, and it can make the money supply whatever it wants it to be. The Federal Reserve System is responsible for supplying an appropriate quantity of money and for conducting monetary policy.

Name: Monetary Base
Alternative name: Open Market Operations
Agency/Institution: Board of Governors, Federal Reserve System
Address: Washington, DC 20551
Telephone number for data and inquiries: 202-452-3017
Sources: *Federal Reserve Bulletin*
Frequency: Monthly, reported weekly in some newspapers such as the *Wall Street Journal*
When available: Following week
Revisions: No set policy
Historic data: None available
Cross-references: Money supply, pages 108–112

■ **A QUICK LOOK: The Monetary Base**

The amount of money and credit existing in the economy depends largely on the size of the monetary base, which is composed of both sources (debits) and uses (credits) (although it is almost always defined in terms of its uses). Currency in circulation and reserves held at the Fed are called the components of the monetary base, and they are the primary determinants of the money supply.

THE MONETARY BASE
(Millions of $)
April 1991

SOURCES (Debits)		USES (Credits)	
Federal Reserve credit	$285,272	Reserves at Fed	$23,720
Holdings of securities	$247,775		
Loans and acceptances	233	Currency	287,527
Float	542		
Other Federal Reserve assets	36,722		

(continued)

THE MONETARY BASE (continued)
(Millions of $)
April 1991

SOURCES (Debits)		USES (Credits)	
Gold certificates	11,059		
Special drawing rights	10,018		
Treasury currency outstanding	20,599		
Treasury cash holdings	−640		
Treasury deposits at Fed. Res.	−4,931		
Foreign and other deposits at Fed. Res.	−3,574		
Other FR liabilities and capital	−6,556		
Sources of the base	$311,247	Uses of the base	$311,247

Note: This form of the monetary base is seldom published by the Federal Reserve. The T-account was constructed by the author to isolate reserves and currency on the right-hand side of the ledger sheet. The same data are presented in the *Federal Reserve Bulletin* as "Factors Supplying Reserve Funds" and "Factors Absorbing Reserve Funds." The "Factors Supplying Reserve Funds" are Federal Reserve credit, gold stock, special drawing rights, and Treasury currency outstanding. All the others on the left and right sides of the ledger are "Factors Absorbing Reserve Funds."

Monetary base: The fundamental determinant of the money supply and credit in the economy. It is composed of total reserves plus currency in circulation on the credit or use side. The sources, on the left-hand side of the monetary base, determine the total amounts available for reserves and currency in circulation on the right-hand side. In other words, the monetary base can be changed only if one or more of the accounts on the left-hand side changes. A negative sign preceding the amount indicates that as the "source" increases, the monetary base decreases.

Reserves at Fed: Reserves of depository institutions (banks, credit unions, savings and loans) at the Federal Reserve. Depository institutions are legally required to hold reserves against their deposits.[1] Since these reserves do not earn interest, depository institutions normally do not hold reserves above the amount required. They will buy securities or make loans until their reserves are at or close to the legal minimum.

Currency: Consists of paper currency and coins. Paper currency consists of Federal Reserve notes, which are IOUs of the Fed. Coins have a monetary value far in excess of their commodity value and are issued by the Treasury.

Federal Reserve credit: Whenever the Fed acquires one of the assets listed below, it is extending credit because it pays for the assets by crediting reserves or Federal Reserve notes outstanding.

---

[1]Reserve rates vary by type and total amount of deposits and range from 0 percent to 10 percent of deposits.

Holdings of securities: U.S. government securities held by the Federal Reserve that were purchased through "open market operations" conducted by the Fed. The Fed buys and sells these securities in order to change the money supply and interest rates. It is the primary tool of monetary policy in the United States.

Loans and acceptances: Loans made by the Fed to member depository institutions (banks, credit unions, savings and loans). The interest rate charged on these loans and widely publicized by the media is known as the Federal Reserve discount rate.

Float: Within the Federal Reserve System, occurs when it takes longer to clear a check through the Federal Reserve system than the time listed on the official schedule. When float occurs, the reserves of the bank that sent the check to the Fed are credited (increased) before the reserves of the bank on which the check is drawn are debited (decreased). Thus, an increase in float represents an increase in reserves. The float associated with a particular check may last only a day or two but other delayed checks will be entering the Federal Reserve "pipeline" each day.

Gold certificates: Represent the monetary gold stock of the United States. The gold was acquired and held while the United States was on a domestic gold standard (until 1933) and on an international gold exchange standard (until 1971). When gold was acquired, the monetary base was increased. The gold is valued not at the current market price, which is around $300 to $400 per ounce, but at $42 per ounce, which was the last official monetary price of gold.

Special drawing rights: Known as paper gold, SDRs are credits issued by the International Monetary Fund. They can be used by central banks to purchase foreign exchange. When they are issued, they increase the reserve component of the monetary base.

Treasury currency outstanding: All paper currency consists of Federal Reserve notes, but all coins are issued by the Treasury and are one part of the "currency outstanding" component of the monetary base.

Treasury cash holdings: Since cash held by the Treasury is not in circulation, this is a "negative source" or a decrease in the monetary base. Any cash in the vaults of the Treasury must be deducted from the currency component of the monetary base.

Treasury deposits at Fed Res: The Federal Reserve is the bank for the Treasury. When the Treasury writes those "Do not fold, bend or mutilate" checks, it writes them on its account at the Federal Reserve, but it does not maintain unnecessary balances at the Fed. When the Treasury receives funds from taxpayers or buyers of its securities, it deposits them into "Tax and Loan" accounts at commercial banks. As the Treasury writes checks on its Federal Reserve account, it transfers funds from its "Tax and Loan" accounts in commercial banks to its deposits at the Fed. The Fed carries out this transfer by debiting (decreasing) the reserves of the banks and crediting (increasing) the Treasury's deposit account. Thus, an increase in the Treasury's account decreases reserves and the monetary base.

Foreign and other deposits at Fed Res: Through an international clearing process, an increase in foreign bank deposits at the Federal Reserve decreases reserves and the monetary base.

■ A CLOSER LOOK: The Monetary Base and Open Market Operations

Understanding the monetary base and its components is important for several reasons. First, changes in the monetary base cause changes in money, credit, and interest rates. Second, the Fed has control only over its holdings of government securities and not over the entire monetary base. Hence, it often has to offset changes in other sources by buying and selling securities, as discussed below. Third, the relative sizes of the sources of the monetary base illustrate their comparative importance in money supply determination. About 87 percent of the base is generated by the Fed's holdings of government securities. Although less than one-tenth of 1 percent of the base is generated by the Fed's loans to depository institutions, changes in the discount rate, which presumably affect banks' willingness to borrow, receive much attention from the media. Changes in the discount rate might have some public relations value in signaling the Fed's policy perspectives, but they exert little direct impact on the monetary base or on the money supply. Depository institutions simply don't borrow much from the Fed, regardless of level of interest rates. Some indication of the insignificance of the discount rate is provided by recent experiences with lower discount rates. During 1989 and 1990, the Fed's discount rate was between 6.5 and 7 percent. Beginning in February, the Fed lowered the discount rate in several stages, culminating in a rate of 3.5 percent by the end of December 1991. During the months of November and December 1990 and January 1991, while the discount rate was relatively high, the average daily outstanding balance of Fed loans to banks and other depository institutions was $371 million. During November and December of 1991 and January 1992, when the Fed's discount rate was relatively low, the outstanding balance was only $175 million. The Fed's discount rate went down—and so did the Fed's loans to banks—which is the opposite of what is supposed to happen. The Fed's loans to banks and other depository institutions is simply not significant; the direct impact of the Fed changing the discount rate is not significant. Fed loans, as a percentage of the total monetary base, hover around one-tenth of 1 percent.

The largest and most interesting source of the monetary base is the Fed's holdings of government securities. Because the Fed purchases these securities from dealers—generally large banks—in the open and competitive market, the process is called *open market operations*. When the Fed buys bonds, it credits the selling bank's reserve account and debits its holdings of government securities. Notice that the Fed pays for the bonds simply by crediting the reserve account of the bank; it does not have to obtain or earn these reserves. The Fed creates them with the "stroke" of a computer chip's impulse on electronic ledgers. Banks are willing to accept these credits because they count as part of the bank's legal reserves, and any excess reserves can be lent to other banks or used to make additional loans.

Federal Reserve Bank		
Government securities	$100 Million	Bank reserves $100 Million

Unlike you or me, unlike the state or federal governments, the central bank has no budget constraint. It can purchase an unlimited quantity of bonds or any other asset. When the Fed purchases these securities, it increases the monetary base in the form of bank reserves, as shown in the T-account above. The bank that sold bonds to the Fed now has excess reserves it can lend out; it can use these funds to purchase securities, or it can lend these reserves to other banks, which can lend them out. These funds that banks lend to firms or to individuals get deposited into various banks, which increases the money supply and lowers interest rates. When the Fed wants the money supply and the economy to expand, it increases its purchases of government securities, which increases bank reserves, which induces banks to make more loans (or buy securities), which increases the money supply and lowers interest rates. When the Fed wants to fight inflationary pressures in the economy, it sells bonds, which decreases bank reserves, which induces banks to call in loans and make fewer loans, which lowers the money supply and raises interest rates.

Let's take a simple example. Assume that the country's economy is sluggish and that the unemployment rate is increasing. The Federal Reserve decides to use expansionary monetary policy to fight the recession and purchases $100 million of government securities. After striking an agreement to purchase the bonds, the Fed tells the selling bank that it will credit the bank's reserves. By crediting the bank's reserves, the Fed is said to have injected $100 million of reserves into the banking system. Also, the Fed's decision to buy bonds has increased the demand for bonds, and bond prices will be higher and interest rates lower.[2]

But the effects do not stop there. Since banks now have excess reserves, they can increase their loans or buy securities of $100 million. Firms and individuals borrowing these funds will spend them by writing checks to firms and individuals who, in turn, will deposit them into bank accounts. Since most bank deposits are considered to be part of the money supply, the result is that the money supply increases by $100 million. The check-receiving banks clear the checks through the Federal Reserve. The Fed increases the reserves of the banks by $100 million, of which $10 million is required to support the $100 million of deposits if the reserve ratio is 10 percent. The banks can lend out the remaining $90 million. Borrowers will spend their newly obtained funds by writing checks, which will be deposited in other banks, and the money supply

---

[2]Interest rates decrease for two reasons. An increase in bank reserves and money supply puts downward pressure on interest rates. Also, bond prices are likely to increase and interest rates fall when the Fed buys substantial quantities of bonds in the open market.

will be further increased by $90 million. This lending, spending, and depositing cycle continues through many stages. The amount that is passed on to the next stage is always the amount received less the reserves required to support the new deposits. If there are no leakages or obstacles to this process, it continues until the money supply expands to $1 billion.

$$\text{Maximum increase in the money supply} = \text{increase in reserves} \times \frac{1}{\text{reserve ratio}}$$

$$\$1 \text{ billion} = \$100 \text{ million} \times \frac{1}{0.10}$$

The fraction (1/reserve ratio) is known as the simple money multiplier; it enables us to calculate the maximum increase in the money supply given some increase in banks' excess reserves. Thus, $1 in reserves can support many dollars in deposits (money supply). In this example, each dollar in reserves supports $10 in money supply. When the Federal Reserve engages in open market operations of buying or selling government securities, it increases or decreases banks' reserves, which has a multiple effect on the country's money supply.

The Federal Reserve does not have total control over the monetary base. On a day-to-day basis, it can control only its holdings of government securities through open market operations. The other sources, shown on the left-hand side of the monetary base T-account on page 103, are beyond the direct control of the Fed. Also, the Fed has no control over the form in which people want to hold their money. People can hold their money in currency or in deposits. If they decide to hold more money in currency, they go to their banks and request currency; banks go to the Fed to replenish their currency supplies. The Fed debits (decrease) the bank's reserves and sends currency to the bank. Thus, an increase in people's preferences for currency results in a decrease in bank reserves.

A simple example should illustrate this concept. If banks are required to hold reserves of 10 percent on their deposits, if there is $1000 in bank reserves and no currency in the country, the maximum money supply will be $10,000 ($1000 × 1/.10) in demand deposits. If individuals suddenly want to hold $100 in currency, banks will ask the Fed to send currency to them and to reduce their reserves by $100 to $900. The total maximum money supply will now be $9000 ($900 × 1/.10) in demand deposits plus $100 of currency, or $9100, which is $900 less than before. The greater the quantity of currency demanded by individuals, the lower the maximum potential money supply.

The Federal Reserve has to be alert to changes in people's demand for currency in different seasons and over time. For example, in October and November, the demand for currency increases because of the Christmas shopping season. This would decrease the overall money supply if the Fed did nothing. However, during these months, the Fed purchases government bonds to expand the monetary base to offset the decrease in reserves. Generally, the Fed is prepared to meet these normal seasonal fluctuations, but more often than the Fed would like to admit, it gets surprised, and the money supply changes sharply without its knowledge or consent.

Name: Money Supply
Alternative name: Monetary Aggregates
Agency/Institution: Division of Monetary Affairs, Board of Governors of the Federal Reserve System
Address: Division of Monetary Affairs, Washington, DC 20551
Telephone number for data and inquiries: 202-452-3017
Sources: *Money Stock Measures and Components of Money Stock Measures and Related Items*, H.6 Statistical Release (Federal Reserve); *Federal Reserve Bulletin* (monthly); *Survey of Current Business* (monthly)
Frequency: Weekly money supply figures are released by the Fed every Thursday afternoon. Data are reported weekly, monthly, annually.
When available: M1 is reported weekly on the Federal Reserve's H.6 Statistical Release and is available on the following Thursday. M2, M3, and L are reported on the last H.6 of the month.
Revisions: Revisions are made monthly for the past several months. A benchmark revision, which can revise data as far back as five years, is made every February.
Historic data: *Economic Report of the President* and table below

---

■ A QUICK LOOK: Money Supply

One of the most closely watched economic statistics in the ivory towers of academic economists, in the burrows of Washington policymakers, and in the fast-paced pits of Wall Street is the **money supply**. The Federal Reserve collects and publishes a vast quantity of data about the money supply, banks, interest rates, reserves, credit markets, industrial production, and many other variables. In this section, we focus on the money supply data the Fed provides on a weekly, monthly, and annual basis. Although economists and business analysts talk glibly about *the* money supply, there is no consensus on what constitutes the money supply. Economists use several definitions for the money supply: **M1**, **M2**, **M3**, and **L** (given below). The most frequently used definitions are M1 and M2; the least used is the broad liquidity measure, L.

The components of the narrowest definition of the money supply (M1) and those of the other money supply definitions are as follows:

M1 Components (billions of $)	1990	1991
Currency	$235.5	$259.3
Traveler's checks	7.8	8.3

Demand deposits	277.5	278.9
Other checkable deposits	291.2	312.5

M2 = M1 + savings deposits and CDs of less than $100,000
M3 = M2 + savings deposits and CDs of more than $100,000
L   = M3 + liquid securities, such as Treasury bills

An example of recent money supply data is given in Table 6.1.

TABLE 6.1
Seasonally Adjusted Money Supply
Averages of Daily Balances
(billions of $)

	1990	1991
M1	$ 812	$ 859
M2	3293	3396
M3	4091	4160
L	4930	4987

■ A CLOSER LOOK: Money Supply

Most people can't define it, but they are willing to work for it, to borrow it, to spend it, to save it, and even to steal it. We might not love money, but most of us very much enjoy what money can do for us. Economists not only worry about earning it and borrowing it (seldom lending it), they must also try to define it by drawing lines between money, near money, and credit. And although they might not agree on its definition, they do know that virtually all definitions will become outmoded within a short time, as innovative bankers and brokers create new financial instruments that ordinary Americans soon begin using as money. The definitions of money given below did not exist 20 years ago because many of the financial instruments comprising them did not exist. We should expect that during the next 20 years the definitions of money will undergo further evolution.

Alternative Definitions of Money

M1 = currency in circulation + demand deposits + other checkable deposits + traveler's checks of nonbank issuers

M1 is the narrowest definition of the money supply; it is the most liquid and the one the Fed can control most easily because it has the highest proportion of assets subject to the Fed's reserve requirements. M1 data are provided weekly and monthly. The weekly data are very preliminary, fluctuate widely, and are often substantially revised in the monthly reports.

    a. Currency in circulation: Currency consists of coins issued by the Treasury (pennies, nickels, dimes, and quarters) and Federal Reserve notes (paper money), which are issued by the 12 district banks of the Federal Reserve

System.[3] Federal Reserve notes and coins must be outside of depository institutions, the Treasury, and the Federal Reserve to be considered in circulation and part of the money supply. Currency constitutes only about 29 percent of the M1 money supply and a much lower percentage of the other money supply definitions.

b. Demand deposits: A deposit at a bank that a depositor may convert into currency on demand and without prior notice. Checks can be written on demand deposits. Demand deposits constitute about 36 percent of the M1 money supply and a much smaller percentage of the other money supply definitions.

c. Other checkable deposits: Any deposit or account with a bank or other financial institution on which a check can be written. These deposits, which account for about 36 percent of M1, include NOW accounts and ATS accounts.

    i. NOW accounts: Negotiable order of withdrawal accounts, which is really another name for a checking account, even though these accounts are not legally defined as checking accounts. When banks were prevented from paying interest rates on checking accounts, some innovative banks developed NOW accounts as a way around the restrictions.

    ii. ATS accounts: Automatic transfer saving accounts, another innovation designed to get around the interest rate restrictions back in the sixties and early seventies. When the balance on an ATS account rises above a certain level, the surplus is transferred to a savings account, which pays interest. When a check is written on an ATS account that brings its balance below the stipulated amount, funds are automatically transferred from the savings account.

d. Traveler's checks: Checks that are convertible into currency on demand. Only those issued by nonbanks, such as American Express, are included.

M2 = M1 + savings deposits + small time deposits + Eurodollar deposits and overnight RPs + money market deposit accounts + noninstitutional money market mutual funds

a. Savings deposits: A deposit that bears interest and that does not legally have to be paid on demand even though, in practice, it usually is.

b. Time deposits: A deposit at a financial institution that bears interest and has a fixed term to maturity. Terms may range from one month to many years, and early withdrawal is often possible with a penalty. Often called *certificates of deposit*. Small time deposits are those less than $100,000.

c. Eurodollar deposits: Dollar deposits in banks located outside the United States; for example, a dollar deposit at a London bank. Only overnight Eurodollars held by U.S. residents are included in M2.

---

[3]Look on the left-hand side of the face of the bill to see the name of one of the 12 Federal Reserve district banks that issued the note. These notes are simply the liabilities, or IOUs, of the Federal Reserve banks. They are backed by nothing other than our knowledge that other people will accept them.

d. RPs: RPs are *re*purchase agreements that involve the sale of a security (generally a U.S. government bill or bond) and then the repurchase of that security by the original seller. For example, party A might "sell" a $50,000 Treasury bond to party B and agree to buy it back in 30 days. Actually, the transaction is a 30-day loan from party B to party A with the Treasury security as collateral. M2 includes RPs that are held only overnight and are less than $100,000.

e. Money market deposit accounts (MMDAs): Deposits at commercial banks and thrift institutions that earn higher interest rates than other deposit accounts. They were introduced in 1982 to compete with money market mutual funds offered by brokerage firms. The accounts are insured up to $100,000, but usually only a limited number of checks may be written against these accounts.

f. Money market mutual funds (MMMFs): These are share accounts in money market mutual funds that invest in short-term government and corporate bonds. Started in 1974, these funds compound interest daily and have no redemption penalty. Checks may be written against these accounts, but some restrictions might apply. M2 includes only those MMMFs held by households, individuals, and broker-dealers.

M3 = M2 + large time deposits + long-term RPs and Eurodollars + institution-only money market mutual funds

a. Large time deposits: Those of $100,000 or more.
b. RPs of $100,000 or more, with maturities longer than one day.
c. Eurodollars held for longer than one day (overnight).
d. Institution-only money market mutual funds: Money market mutual funds held by institutional investors such as insurance companies. Usually require a substantial minimum initial investment.

L = M3 + nonbank holdings of U.S. savings bonds + short-term Treasury securities (less than one year) + commercial paper + banker's acceptances

a. Commercial paper: Short-term unsecured promissory notes of well-known businesses.
b. Banker's acceptances: Bankers' agreements to pay bills of customers.

HISTORIC DATA

The following table shows the M1 money stock and its currency component. The table indicates once again that the soothsayers almost always are wrong. Back in the fifties they said that virtually all Americans would own a personal helicopter by 1970; in the sixties they said that by 1980 all of the interstate highways would have wires down the center that would automatically steer our cars; in the 1970s they said that by 1990 we would be living in a checkless and cashless society. The reality, of course, is that the use of cash has not only increased in absolute terms, but its relative role in the economy is greater now than at any other time in history, including the decade of the 1930s, when people fled from "bank money" (deposits) to currency.

Historic Data: M1 Money Supply
(billions of $)
Money Supply; Currency as Percent of M1 Money Supply,
1915–1990

1915	$12.5; 15.5%	1935	$25.9; 18.5%	1955	$134.4; 20.6%	1975	$287.6; 25.3%
1916	14.7; 14.8	1936	29.6; 17.7	1956	136.0; 20.6	1976	306.5; 25.9
1917	17.1; 12.7	1937	30.9; 18.1	1957	136.8; 20.7	1977	331.5; 26.4
1918	19.0; 14.6	1938	30.5; 18.2	1958	138.4; 20.5	1978	358.8; 26.8
1919	21.8; 18.4	1939	34.2; 17.7	1959	140.0; 20.6	1979	386.1; 27.2
1920	23.7; 18.9	1940	39.7; 17.0	1960	140.7; 20.4	1980	412.2; 27.9
1921	21.5; 18.8	1941	46.5; 18.1	1961	145.2; 20.2	1981	439.1; 27.9
1922	21.7; 17.0	1942	55.4; 20.8	1962	147.9; 20.5	1982	476.4; 27.8
1923	22.9; 17.3	1943	72.2; 22.6	1963	153.4; 21.0	1983	522.1; 28.0
1924	23.7; 16.7	1944	85.3; 24.9	1964	160.4; 21.1	1984	551.9; 28.3
1925	25.7; 15.4	1945	99.2; 25.5	1965	167.9; 21.4	1985	620.5; 27.0
1926	26.2; 15.3	1946	106.5; 24.9	1966	172.1; 22.1	1986	724.7; 24.9
1927	26.1; 15.2	1947	111.8; 23.8	1967	183.3; 21.8	1987	750.4; 26.2
1928	26.4; 14.7	1948	112.3; 23.2	1968	197.5; 21.8	1988	787.5; 26.9
1929	26.6; 14.6	1949	111.2; 22.9	1969	204.0; 22.4	1989	794.8; 27.9
1930	25.8; 14.5	1950	114.1; 21.9	1970	214.5; 22.7	1990	812.2; 29.0
1931	24.1; 17.2	1951	119.2; 21.4	1971	228.4; 22.8	1991	859.0; 30.2
1932	21.1; 23.3	1952	125.2; 21.3	1972	249.4; 22.6		
1933	19.9; 25.6	1953	128.3; 21.6	1973	263.0; 23.1		
1934	21.9; 21.2	1954	130.3; 21.1	1974	274.4; 24.4		

Note: Data from 1915 to 1958 are not compatible with data from 1959 to 1991 due to revisions in the money supply definition. The differences between the two series are about 2 to 3 percent, with the latter years having a lower money stock.

Name: Consumer Installment Credit
Agency/Institution: Division of Consumer Spending, Board of Governors of the Federal Reserve
Address: Washington, DC 20551
Telephone number for data and inquiries: 202-452-3206
Sources: Federal Reserve, G19 Statistical Release and *Federal Reserve Bulletin, Survey of Current Business*
Frequency: Monthly
When available: About 30 days after the target month
Revisions: No set policy; revised if needed
Historic data: *Economic Report of the President*

■ **A QUICK LOOK: Consumer Credit**

Consumer credit is the term used to describe credit extended for the purchase of goods by consumers. Charge accounts at department stores and gas companies, as well as loans from automotive finance subsidiaries, general finance companies, banks, savings and loans, and credit unions are included. Prior to World War I, consumer credit simply did not exist. People paid cash or they went without. If they frequently purchased their groceries at the corner store, the owner might allow them to put the week's groceries on a tab, which had to be paid on Friday afternoon. Installment loans for automobile purchases were started around 1920 and quickly spread to the purchase of household appliances and furniture. Like so many other financial and technical institutions, consumer credit became part of the American life during the twenties, and it is now a widely accepted part of the American economy.

Installment credit as a percentage of personal income is closely watched by bankers and retailers as a predictor of current and future retail sales. When that percentage gets relatively high, many analysts believe that consumers are "getting loaned up" and that fewer loans will be made and undertaken and that, as a result, consumer demand for consumer durables will decrease. The percentage of personal income allocated to installment credit was higher in the 1980s than in any other decade. The monthly *Federal Reserve Bulletin* shows consumer installment credit by type of holder (commercial banks, finance companies, etc.), and major type of credit (automobile, revolving, mobile homes).

Historic Data: Consumer Installment Credit
(millions of $)
Installment Credit; Installment Credit as Percent of Personal Income
1946–1991

1946	$3,362; 1.89%	1961	$44,630; 10.48%	1976	$177,172; 12.21%
1947	5,678; 2.98	1962	47,840; 10.55	1977	205,695; 12.79
1948	8,392; 4.01	1963	53,911; 11.32	1978	242,886; 13.40
1949	10,530; 5.10	1964	61,259; 12.00	1979	281,960; 13.86
1950	13,933; 6.10	1965	69,302; 12.55	1980	298,961; 13.26
1951	15,478; 6.04	1966	75,920; 12.64	1981	305,352; 12.12
1952	17,717; 6.46	1967	79,768; 12.38	1982	317,850; 11.90
1953	22,579; 7.77	1968	85,770; 12.13	1983	343,060; 12.08
1954	23,925; 8.16	1969	95,697; 12.38	1984	409,446; 13.16
1955	27,442; 8.73	1970	101,862; 12.25	1985	483,840; 14.54
1956	31,481; 9.34	1971	110,872; 12.40	1986	550,385; 15.61
1957	33,929; 9.52	1972	123,720; 12.60	1987	588,013; 15.57
1958	34,518; 9.41	1973	144,549; 13.12	1988	637,733; 15.69
1959	37,729; 9.65	1974	159,103; 13.15	1989	699,785; 15.81
1960	42,941; 10.49	1975	162,157; 12.36	1990	728,000; 15.67
				1991	730,980; 15.10

Note: These are monthly averages. The data are also reported for the last month of the year, which would be slightly higher.

Name: Federal Reserve Discount Window and the Discount Rate
Alternative name: Federal Reserve Loans
Agency: Division of Monetary Affairs, Federal Reserve System
Address: Washington, DC 20551
Telephone number for data and inquiries: Call the Federal Reserve, 202-452-3244, and you will be referred to the currently correct number.
Sources: Changes in the discount rate are widely reported in the media; the current and recent discount rates can be found in the *Federal Reserve Bulletin* and *Survey of Current Business.*
Frequency: The discount rate, when announced, and quantities of loans made by the Fed are available weekly and monthly.
When available: The discount rate is changed infrequently by the Federal Reserve.
Historic data: The *Federal Reserve Bulletin* publishes a history of discount rate changes.
Cross-references: Federal Funds Rate

■ A QUICK LOOK: The Federal Reserve Discount Window and Discount Rate

The Federal Reserve discount rate is widely used as an indicator of monetary policy although it generally follows rather than leads other interest rates. An example of discount rates is as follows:

	1987	1988	1989	1990	1991	July 10 1992
Discount window borrowing	5.75	6.25	6.93	6.98	5.0	3.0

When commercial banks and other financial institutions borrow from the Federal Reserve, it is called **discount window borrowing** and the rate of interest charged by the Federal Reserve is called the **discount rate**. The Federal Reserve discount rate is an administered rate set by the Federal Reserve banks and the Federal Reserve board of governors. It is changed infrequently and was changed only once during 1990, when it was lowered in December from 7 to 6.5 percent. Generally, the discount rate is the same for all Federal Reserve banks.

■ A CLOSER LOOK: Federal Reserve Discount Rate

Students in elementary economics learn that one of the tools of monetary policy is the interest rate, called the *discount rate*, charged by the Federal Reserve for loans it makes to banks and other depository institutions. The Federal Reserve discount rate is studied in elementary economics courses because changes in the amount of loans made by the Fed affect total bank reserves, which, in turn, affect interest rates and the money supply.

When financial institutions obtain funds by selling their own IOUs to other financial instruments, bank reserves shift among various institutions but there is no net increase in bank reserves or the monetary base. However, when depository institutions borrow from the Fed, the monetary base in the form of reserves is increased. The Federal Reserve credits (increases) the reserves of the borrowing institution and debits its notes receivable. Though the Federal Reserve has liberalized its lending policies during the past decade, it is still more restrictive than other money market sources. And although nonmember banks and thrift institutions, along with member banks, now have access to the discount window, the average outstanding amount of Federal Reserve loans during 1991 was about $400 million.

The quantity of loans made by the Fed depends on the relationship between the discount rate and the rates on other money market funds, especially the federal funds rate. But interest rates are not the only — or even the main — factor determining Federal Reserve loans. The Federal Reserve places several restrictions on the "discount privilege" in Regulation A. Banks, for example, are required to provide collateral for their loans. Generally such collateral is U.S. government securities, but the Fed now accepts state and local government securities and certain commercial notes and mortgages. Most importantly, Regulation A makes nonprice allocation of loans a central feature of Federal Reserve lending. Banks are supposed to confine their use of the discount window to "adjustment credit" to offset unexpected shortages of funds and for seasonal adjustments. Extended credit can be arranged for depository institutions confronting "exceptional circumstances," but the Federal Reserve is very firm that the discount window should not be used as a continuous source of funds to displace normal sources of funds.[4]

Given these restrictions, it is not surprising that the discount window is not a significant source of funds for banks or reserves; hence, it is not an important tool of monetary policy. Banks do have some discretionary access to the discount window. If they have not borrowed recently or have not relied heavily on the window in the past, their requests for a moderate amount of funds are normally accommodated quickly. However, if the size or frequency of their borrowings increase, they are asked to justify their requests. If their justifications are not accepted, they are asked to discontinue their borrowing from the discount window. Although the discount rate is not a powerful determinant of the monetary base, it does generate an "announcement effect," which serves as a source of information about the trend of interest rates and the policy intentions of the Federal Reserve.

---

[4]Banks that borrow on extended credit for longer than 30 days have to pay a higher rate. In 1992, the discount rate (that is, for adjustment and seasonal credit) was 3.5 percent; the rate for extended credit beyond 30 days was 4.85 percent.

Historic Data: Federal Reserve Discount Rate
Average of Highs and Lows,
1915–1992

1915 4.50	1935 1.50	1955 2.00	1975 6.87
1916 3.50	1936 1.50	1956 2.75	1976 5.62
1917 3.25	1937 1.25	1957 3.25	1977 5.62
1918 3.75	1938 1.00	1958 3.50	1978 7.75
1919 4.38	1939 1.00	1959 3.25	1979 10.75
1920 6.00	1940 1.00	1960 3.50	1980 11.50
1921 5.75	1941 1.00	1961 3.00	1981 13.00
1922 4.25	1942 0.75	1962 3.00	1982 10.25
1923 4.25	1943 0.75	1963 3.25	1983 8.50
1924 3.75	1944 0.75	1964 3.75	1984 8.50
1925 3.25	1945 0.75	1965 4.25	1985 7.75
1926 3.75	1946 0.75	1966 4.50	1986 6.50
1927 3.75	1947 1.00	1967 4.25	1987 5.75
1928 4.25	1948 1.25	1968 5.00	1988 6.25
1929 5.25	1949 1.50	1969 5.50	1989 6.93
1930 3.25	1950 1.63	1970 5.75	1990 6.98
1931 2.50	1951 1.75	1971 5.00	1991 5.00
1932 3.00	1952 1.75	1972 4.50	1992* 3.00
1933 2.75	1953 1.87	1973 6.00	
1934 1.75	1954 1.75	1974 7.75	

*July 10, 1992

Name: Federal Funds and the Federal Funds Rate
Agency/Institution: Division of Interest Rates, Federal Reserve System
Address: Washington, DC 20551
Telephone number for data and inquiries: Call the Federal Reserve, 202-452-3244, and you will be referred to the currently correct number.
Sources: Many daily newspapers and the *Federal Reserve Bulletin* (monthly)
Historic summary: None
Cross-reference: Discount rate

■ A QUICK LOOK: Federal Funds and the Federal Funds Rate

Federal funds are the reserves of depository institutions, which are held in the Federal Reserve and which are transferred through "Fedwire," the communications system of the Federal Reserve, from one bank to another. The **federal funds rate** is the rate that banks charge one another when borrowing these federal funds. Although the loans are only for a few days at most, the quoted rate is always annualized. The federal funds rate is watched closely by most market analysts because it is the most sensitive barometer of the costs of funds and the future direction of interest rates. The federal funds rate is also "targeted" by the Federal Reserve, which means it influences the rate by buying and selling securities. The following are examples of federal fund rates:

	1987	1988	1989	1990	1991	July 1992
Federal Funds Rate	6.66	7.57	9.21	8.10	5.69	3.375

The federal funds rate is a market rate determined by competitive forces, and it is constantly changing. The rates for the years shown are average rates for all trading days during that year. The rate for July 1992 is an example of an average rate during the month.

■ A CLOSER LOOK: Federal Funds and the Federal Funds Rate

Depository institutions such as commercial banks, savings and loans, and credit unions must hold a certain percentage of their deposits as reserves in the form of non–interest-earning vault cash and deposits at Federal Reserve banks.[5] Banks sometimes have more reserves than they need or want, while at other times they may be short of reserves and in need of quickly procuring funds to replenish them. Since the 1920s American banks have recognized the advantage of having an efficient market in which banks with excess reserves can lend them to banks with deficient reserves. These reserves that are lent and borrowed through the Fedwire communications system of the Federal Reserve are called *federal funds*, and the interest rate paid on these funds is called the *federal funds rate*.

Federal funds are the reserves of commercial banks and other depository institutions at the Federal Reserve that are sold (lent) and purchased (borrowed) for short periods of time, generally overnight. Banks find lenders and borrowers through personal contacts and banking relationships and through federal funds brokers located in New York City. The parties or the brokers notify the Federal Reserve of the transaction, and the Fed credits the reserve account of the borrowing bank and debits the reserve account of the lending bank. The following day the account is reversed, with an amount added for interest. Financial institutions that do not have reserve accounts are able to participate in the federal funds market by working through correspondent banks. About 80 percent of federal funds are overnight, unsecured borrowings. The remainder is longer term borrowing known as "term federal funds." The federal funds

---

[5]Reserve rates vary between 0 and 12 percent, depending on the type of deposit.

rate, which changes continually (in sharp contrast to the prime and discount rates, which remain fixed for long periods), is often used as a leading indicator of conditions in the money market and of other interest rates. It normally is the first interest rate to reflect changes in the monetary policies of the Federal Reserve as well as reflecting other supply and demand changes in the money market. The federal funds rate is the only interest rate classified by the Bureau of Economic Analysis as a leading indicator.

Historic Data: Federal Funds Rate,
1955–1992

1955 1.78	1965 4.07	1975 5.82	1985 8.10
1956 2.73	1966 5.11	1976 5.05	1986 6.81
1957 3.11	1967 4.22	1977 5.54	1987 6.66
1958 1.57	1968 5.66	1978 7.93	1988 7.57
1959 3.30	1969 8.21	1979 11.19	1989 9.21
1960 3.22	1970 7.18	1980 13.36	1990 8.10
1961 1.96	1971 4.66	1981 16.38	1991 5.69
1962 2.68	1972 4.43	1982 12.26	*1992 3.37
1963 3.18	1973 8.73	1983 9.09	
1964 3.50	1974 10.50	1984 10.23	

*July 10, 1992

Name: Prime Rate
Agency/Institution: Federal Reserve Board of Governors
Address: Washington, DC 20551
Telephone number for data: The Fed is not permitted to give out interest rate information over the phone, but other data are available at 202-452-6459.
Sources: *Selected Interest Rates*, Federal Reserve Release H.15 (519) (weekly), *Federal Reserve Bulletin* (monthly), and Standard & Poor's *Statistical Service Survey of Current Business*
Frequency: Weekly
When available: Monday of every week for previous week
Revisions: None
Historic data: See below

■ A QUICK LOOK: The Prime Rate

The **prime rate**, which originated during the 1930s, is the interest rate commercial banks presumably charge their most creditworthy customers. Each bank determines its own "prime rate," so there is no single prime rate, which is sometimes implied in the media. Most banks use their prime rate as a base for determining the higher interest rates charged to riskier borrowers, and some banks tie their floating or variable rates to the prime rate.

The media give wide coverage to changes in the prime rate, but often these changes do not represent changes in rates actually paid by borrowers. If banks have excess reserves, they will frequently lend money to their most solid borrowers at less than the prime rate. When money is tight, many banks require borrowers to maintain larger compensating balances, which increases the effective rate of interest. For example, if IBM borrows $100 million from Chase Manhattan at the prime rate of 8 percent but is required to keep $5 million as compensating balance, IBM is paying $8 million for borrowing only $95 million and the rate is really 8.42 percent. Another reason the media attention is sometimes misplaced is that the prime generally changes *after*, not *before*, other interest rates have changed.

The Federal Reserve obtains data on the current prime rate by surveying 29 major banks in 6 of the 12 Federal Districts[6] and it gives the average (mean) of the prime rates reported. Sometimes changes in the prime are reported in newspapers but not picked up in the Fed's official list because the banks reporting changes to the media are not part of the group of 29 major banks reporting to the Fed.

Historic Data: Average Prime Rates, 1929–1992

1929 5.75	1950 2.07	1961 4.50	1971 5.70	1981 18.87
1933 2.75	1951 2.56	1962 4.50	1972 5.25	1982 14.86
1939 1.5	1952 3.00	1963 4.50	1973 8.02	1983 10.79
1940 1.5	1953 3.17	1964 4.50	1974 10.80	1984 12.04
1941 1.5	1954 3.05	1965 4.54	1975 7.86	1985 9.93
1942 1.5	1955 3.16	1966 5.63	1976 6.84	1986 8.33
1943 1.5	1956 3.77	1967 5.63	1977 6.82	1987 8.20
1944 1.5	1957 4.20	1968 6.28	1978 9.06	1988 9.32
1945 1.50	1958 3.83	1969 7.95	1979 12.67	1989 10.87
1946 1.50	1959 4.48	1970 7.91	1980 15.27	1990 10.01
1947 1.52	1960 4.82			1991 8.46
1948 1.85				*1992 6.00
1949 2.00				

*July, 1992

---

[6]The Federal Reserve Districts surveyed are Boston, New York, Philadelphia, Cleveland, Chicago, and San Francisco.

CHAPTER 7

GNP ACCOUNTING:
The National Income
and Product Accounts

READ ME FIRST

The American economy is dissected, examined, and diagnosed by more people using more data than all the other economies of the world. So much data are now available that many go unused, either because people don't know they exist or don't know how to access them. Much of the data on the United States economy is based on three fundamental sets of accounts. First is national income and product accounts (NIPAs), which show the value and composition of national output and the distribution of incomes generated in its production. The NIPAs, which include the gross domestic product estimates, are the most widely used measure of the nation's production. They are described in this section. Second is capital finance accounts, also known as flow-of-funds accounts. These show the role of financial intermediaries and financial securities in transforming saving into investment, as well as the changes in assets and liabilities that result from these transformations. See "Flow-of-Funds" on page 222 for a discussion of these accounts. Third is input-output accounts, which trace the flow of goods and services among industries in the production process and show the value added by each industry and the detailed composition of national output. See "Input-Output Tables" on page 291 for a discussion of these accounts.

This section presents the national income and product accounts, also known as the gross domestic/national product accounts. These are the most fundamental set of economic accounts in the nation.

GNP vs. GDP: In late 1991, the Bureau of Economic Analysis (BEA) began changing the emphasis in its national income accounting reports from gross national product (GNP) to gross domestic product (GDP). The BEA will continue to publish GNP data, but it will not emphasize them as it has in the past. One reason for this change is to make U.S. national product reports compatible with those of most other foreign countries, which also emphasize GDP. A second reason is that future GDP will be increasingly faster than GNP. GNP and other "national" measures (such as, net national product) relate to production by labor and other factors *supplied* by residents of the United States. Thus, the income earned by American residents on their investments in other countries is included in the gross national product. Gross domestic product and other domestic measures relate to production by factors physically *located* in the United States, no matter who owns them. The relationship between GNP and GDP is clearly shown below.

Gross National Product
Less: Factor income received from nonresidents
Plus: Factor income paid to nonresidents
Equals: Gross Domestic Product

We have continued to mention GNP and gross national product in the following discussion because readers will find frequent discussions and references to GNP until the conversion process is finished. Some of the historic data and GDP price indexes will not be available until 1993. Also, during the next couple of years, through about 1995, the numerical differences between GNP and GDP will be relatively small. For virtually all purposes, the GDP is interchangeable with GNP.

Name: Gross Domestic Product/Gross National Product
Alternative Name: National Income and Product Accounts
Agency/Institution: Bureau of Economic Analysis, Department of Commerce
Telephone numbers for data and inquiries:
  For recorded GDP estimates: 202-898-2451
      recorded personal income estimates: 202-898-2452
  For inquiries about:
      GDP   202-523-0824
      Personal income and outlays   202-523-0832

Corporate profits	202-523-0888
Personal consumption expenditures	202-523-0819
Gross private domestic investment	202-523-0791
GDP by Industry	202-523-0795
For a listing of the various national income and product account (NIPA) services:	202-523-0669

Sources: The *Survey of Current Business* contains NIPA data in every monthly issue. The July issue contains major revisions for the preceding year and the two previous years.

Other sources include: *Gross Domestic Product* (Bureau of Economic Analysis), a monthly report that features GDP and corporate profits (available on a subscription basis from BEA, $24 per year); *Economic Report of the President*.

Frequency: Quarterly, although some components of the GDP, such as corporate profits, personal income, and personal consumption expenditures are published monthly.

Revisions: The first GDP estimate (called the "advance estimate") is made in the month following the end of the quarter. A revision of the first release (called the "preliminary estimate") is published in the following (second) month and the series is revised again the following (third) month with the final estimate. No further revisions are made until the annual revisions, which are published in July. Annual revisions are made in each of the next two years, and then no further revisions are made until the comprehensive revisions (called "benchmark revisions"), which are made every five years. *Example:* The advance estimate for the first quarter data of 1992 (1992:I) will be released in April. The 1992:I data will be revised in May (preliminary estimate) and June (final estimate). There will be no further revisions of 1992:I until July 1993, when the annual estimates are revised. The 1992 annual estimates will be revised in the July issues of the *Survey of Current Business* for the next two years (1994 and 1995) and then will not change until the five-year benchmark revision is made. The most recent benchmark revision was carried out in 1990 and the next one is due out in 1995, but there is a lag in implementing the benchmark data, which can take an additional two or three years.

Cross-references: After the "Closer Look" discussion below, the best source on the concepts and the detailed methodology used in deriving the national income and product accounts is the collection of methodology papers on U.S. national income and product accounts published by the U.S. Department of Commerce, Bureau of Economic Analysis:

An Introduction to National Economic Accounting, BEA-MP-1, March 1985.

Corporate Profits: Profits Before Tax, Profits Tax Liability, and Dividends, BEA-MP-2, May 1985.

Foreign Transactions, BEA-MP-3, May 1987.

GNP: An Overview of Source Data and Estimating Methods, BEA-MP-4, September 1987.

Government Transactions, BEA-MP-5, November 1988.

Historic data: See below; also see *National Income and Product Accounts, 1929–82; Statistical Tables* (GPO Stock No. 003-010-00174-7; $23) and the September issue of each year's *Survey of Current Business*.

■ A QUICK LOOK: GDP and GNP

The GDP accounts, officially known as the **domestic income and product accounts (NIPA)**, provide an immense amount of data. See the "A Closer Look" section on page 127 for a sample of the detailed data available from these accounts. Those unfamiliar with the GDP or GNP tables should know that the following are just a few of the questions that can be answered by the NIPAs:

- What is the output and income of the economy?
- What is the composition of that output?
- What kinds of income are generated by the output?
- What part of the output is allocated to saving and investment?
- How fast is the economy growing and in what sectors is it growing most quickly?

Gross domestic product is the market value of the final goods and services produced by resources located in the United States. GDP can be measured from both the input (income) side and the output (product) side because the GDP or NIPA accounting system is designed to replicate double entry bookkeeping. This means that the total income generated in the economy will equal the total output produced.

The most well-known version of GDP is the product side, which measures the market value of goods and services sold to final users. The product side, which shows the gross domestic product, is shown on the right side of Table 7.1. The four major components of the GDP on the product side are (1) personal consumption expenditures, (2) gross private domestic investment, (3) net exports, and (4) government purchases.

On the left is the sum of income payments and other costs generated in producing the gross domestic product. The income, or left side of the table shows the charges against GDP—that is, the costs incurred and the profits earned in the production of GDP. The factor incomes—wages, salaries, rents, dividends, profits—are incomes after the deduction of depreciation and other allowances for the capital consumed in the production of the GDP.

The GDP table reflects the truism that the total value of final goods produced in the economy has to equal the total value of income generated in the economy. GDP accountants are concerned only with the goods and services that go to the end user. For example, the GDP does not count both the value of paper sold *and* the value of books sold. Rather, the value reported in the NIPAs (GDP accounts) includes only the value of the books sold. The GDP does not include the value of steel that goes into automobiles *and* the value of automobiles; it includes only the value of automobiles.

TABLE 7.1 Gross Domestic Product (billions of $)

Income Side	1991
Compensation of employees	$3,388.2
Wages and salaries	2,808.2
Supplements to wages and salaries	580.0
Proprietors income with inventory valuation adj. and capital cons. allow	379.7
Rental income of persons with capital cons. allowances	−12.7
Corporate profits with inventory valuation and capital consumption adjustments	306.8
Profits before tax	312.4
Profits tax liability	124.5
Profits after tax	187.9
Dividends	137.8
Undistributed profits	50.2
Inventory valuation adjustment	3.1
Capital consumption adjustment	−8.7
Net interest	480.2
National income	4,542.2
Business transfer payments	31.2
Indirect business tax and nontax liability	471.0
Less: Subsidies less current surplus of govt. enterprises	(0.6)
Plus: Statistical discrepancy	19.0
Charges against net national product	5,062.8
Capital consumption allowances with capital consumption adjustments	622.9
Gross National Product	5,685.8
Plus: Payments of factor income to the rest of the world	121.8
Less: Receipts of factor income from the rest of the world	(135.0)
Charges against gross domestic product	$5,672.6

Product or Expenditure side	1991
Gross domestic product	$5,672.6
Personal consumption expenditures (C)	3,889.1
Durables	445.2
Nondurables	1,251.9
Services	2,191.9
Gross private domestic investment (I)	726.7
Nonresidential	550.1
Residential	195.1
Change in business inventories	−18.5
Net export of goods and services (X)	−30.7
Exports	591.3
Imports	622.0
Government purchases of goods and services (G)	1,087.5
Federal	445.1
State and local	642.4
Gross domestic product	$5,672.6

Wages and salaries: Remuneration of employees, including compensation of corporate officers, commissions, tips, and bonuses.

Supplements to wages and salaries: Employer contributions for social insurance including Social Security and unemployment insurance, plus employer contributions to pension and welfare funds.

Proprietors income: Includes income of sole proprietorships and partnerships and tax-exempt cooperatives. The imputed net rental income of owner-occupied farm dwellings is included. Dividends, interest, and rentals received by proprietors are excluded here but are included in dividends, net interest, and rental incomes of persons.

Rental income: Income from rental of real property, except that primarily engaged in the real estate business. Rental income includes the imputed net rental income of owner-occupied nonfarm dwellings and the royalties received from patents, copyrights, and natural resources.

Corporate profits with inventory valuation and capital consumption adjustments: Income from current production of corporations, mutual financial institutions, private pension funds, Federal Reserve banks, and federally sponsored credit agencies. Capital gains and dividends received are not included. Profits include income earned abroad by U.S. corporations and excludes income earned in the United States by foreigners. All corporate profits are based on the tax return forms filed by corporations and, thus, reflect various treatments of inventory withdrawal and depreciation. In order to convert these tax return profits to a basis that is consistent with other NIPAs, inventory and capital consumption adjustments have to be made. (See Appendix 7B for a thorough but easy-to-understand discussion of these adjustments.)

Inventory valuation adjustment (IVA):   When goods are sold by corporations, they have to charge off the cost of the goods sold—that is, the cost of goods withdrawn from inventory. Some corporations use the most recent prices (replacement costs) in valuing these withdrawals whereas others use earlier (historical) prices. This IVA adjustment converts the value of inventory withdrawals from the mixture of historical and current replacement costs to the more analytically correct system of current replacement costs. The IVA for 1991 was $3.1 billion because current replacement costs were lower than the reported value of inventory withdrawals, and corporate profits were accordingly higher than those reported. (See Appendix 7B for a thorough but easy-to-understand discussion of these adjustments.)

Capital consumption adjustments (CCAdj):   When corporations depreciate their capital assets, they are charging off the costs of capital to the current reporting period. Many assumptions have to be made in determining the depreciation rate, and different corporations make different assumptions, so the data obtained by the BEA are not uniform or correct for NIPA purposes. Generally, firms use the fastest possible depreciation rates in order to lower their corporate income taxes. This CCAdj adjustment converts depreciation charges to a consistent accounting basis of straight-line depreciation, uniform service lives, and current replacement costs. The CCAdj for 1991 was − $8.7 billion, which means that depreciation using the NIPA accounting basis was greater than the depreciation reported by corporations in determining their profits before tax. Thus, corporate profits were $8.7 billion lower than reported.

Profits before tax: Corporate income as defined above except that these profits reflect the inventory and depreciation practices used for unadjusted federal income tax returns. This is sometimes called "book profits" and is not used for GDP accounting purposes.

Profits tax liability: The sum of federal, state, and local income taxes on all corporate earnings; these earnings include capital gains and other income excluded from profits before tax. Not used for GDP accounting.

Profits after tax: Profits before tax less profits tax liability. Dividends include payments in cash or other assets, excluding the corporation's own stock, made by corporations located in the United States and abroad to stockholders who are U.S. residents. Undistributed profits are corporate profits after tax less dividends paid to stockholders.

Net interest: Interest paid by business less interest received by business, plus interest received from foreigners less interest paid to foreigners. Interest payments on mortgage and home improvement loans are included here as interest paid by business because homeowners are treated as businesses.

National income: Income that originates in the production of goods and services attributable to labor and other factors supplied by residents of the United States.

Business transfer payments: Payments made by businesses to persons who did not perform any current services. Examples are liability payments for personal injuries, corporate contributions to nonprofit institutions, and defaults by consumers on their debts to businesses.

Indirect business taxes and nontax liability: Includes taxes paid by businesses such as sales, excise, and property taxes. Corporate income taxes are not included. Property taxes paid by homeowners are included here because their homes are treated as businesses. Nontax payments include regulatory and inspection fees, fines and penalties, rents and royalties, and certain donations.

Subsidies less current surplus of government enterprises: Monetary grants made to businesses and government enterprises. Current surplus is sales receipts of government enterprises less their current expenses.

Charges against net national product: The charges for the inputs into the production of GDP by labor and other resources supplied by residents of the United States.

Capital consumption allowances: More commonly known as depreciation, is based on straight-line depreciation and replacement costs in the NIPAs. The capital consumption allowance reported by firms has been reduced by the capital consumption adjustment, which is the difference between tax-return-based capital consumption allowances and capital consumption based on the use of uniform service lives, straight-line depreciation, and replacement cost. Similar adjustments are calculated for proprietors income, rental income of persons, and nonprofit institutions serving individuals. See Appendix 7B for a thorough discussion of capital consumption allowances and adjustments.

Gross Domestic Product: Market value of the final goods and services produced by resources owned by residents of the United States.

Payments of factor income to the rest of the world: Consists largely of payments to foreign residents of interest and dividends and reinvested earnings of U.S. affiliates of foreign corporations.

Receipts of factor income from the rest of the world: Consists largely of receipts by U.S. residents of interest and dividends and reinvested earnings of foreign affiliates of U.S. corporations.

Personal consumption expenditures: Goods and services purchased by individuals, operating expenses of nonprofit institutions, and the value of food, fuel, clothing, housing, and financial services received in kind by individuals. Net purchases of used goods are also included.

Gross private domestic investment: New structures and equipment purchased by private business and nonprofit institutions, and the value of the change in inventories. This includes purchases of new residential structures.

Net exports of goods and services: Exports are goods and services (including labor and capital) provided by U.S. residents to foreigners; imports are goods and services provided by foreigners to U.S. residents. Imports are initially included in consumer expenditures and inventory components of GDP, but they are subtracted from GDP because imports are not produced in the United States and, consequently, they have not generated income in the United States.

Government purchases of goods and services: Purchases of goods and services by governments are based not on their market values (because they are not sold through the market system) but on the payments made for the inputs—that is, compensation of government employees and purchases from business firms. Transfer payments, interest paid by governments, and subsidies are entirely excluded because such payments represent transfers among individuals without generating new goods or services. Gross investment by government enterprises (such as TVA) is included, but the current outlays of government enterprises are not. Sales and purchases of land and financial assets by government agencies are excluded.

■ A CLOSER LOOK: National Income and Product Accounts

General Background

The U.S. national income and product accounts (NIPAs) are the most complete and readily available set of economic data to be found anywhere in the world. The accounts are released quarterly, the preliminary release being available about 15 to 20 days after the end of the quarter. Quarterly and monthly data are generally presented on an annualized basis, which means that the monthly and quarterly data are shown at their annual equivalents. Virtually all quarterly data published in the national income and product accounts are seasonally adjusted — that is, seasonal fluctuations are taken out so quarters can be compared with each other. (See Chapter 2 for an explanation of annualization and seasonal adjustments.) Seasonally unadjusted estimates are available only in the July issue of *Survey of Current Business*.

The GDP/GNP accounts, as the NIPA are also called, go back to 1929. They provide a continual overview of the condition and direction of the U.S. economy.[1] GDP data are reported in current (nominal) dollars, which means that they include changes in prices as well as changes in real output. Real or constant-dollar GDP, data which are given in terms of some constant year prices (for example, GDP in 1984 dollars), show changes in the quantity of output with price changes taken out. For most purposes, the real GDP is a more informative figure than nominal or money GNP. However, even real GDP data have little value in themselves; they become useful only when converted into changes from some previous year or quarter.

The national income and product accounts represent the nation's economic activity from two perspectives. The demand side (known as the product side) refers to end-use markets for goods and services and is shown as the gross domestic product, or the value of final goods and services provided to the marketplace during some time period (quarter of year). The supply side (known as the income side) refers to the costs involved in producing these goods and services and is shown in the accounts as the wages of workers, profits of business, depreciation, and sales and property taxes. The total value of the output side will equal the total value of the income side, subject to a few minor adjustments.

The term *gross* in gross domestic product refers not to its bad manners but to the fact that the data reported for final goods and services do not include a deduction for the physical depreciation of capital. GDP accountants use another term for depreciation, which is *capital consumption allowance*. These capital consumption allowances are deducted to obtain net domestic product:

Gross domestic product
Less: Capital consumption allowances
Equals: Net domestic product

---

[1]The official series of the national income accounts was first published during the mid-1930s. Its origins were stimulated by the depression and by the writings of John M. Keynes, but the accounts were brought to reality by Simon Kuznets, who was awarded the Nobel prize in 1971 for his efforts. One of the first estimates of national wealth and income was made for England by Sir William Petty in 1665. The first estimates of national income in the United States were made by Professor George Tucker of the University of Virginia in 1843 and were based on the 1840 census. The National Bureau of Economic Research, chartered in 1920, estimated national income and its distributions during the 1920s. Annual estimates of national income were started by the Department of Commerce during the 1930s, but the concept of gross national product was first used during World War II, and the first reporting of gross national product on one side and national income on the other side began in 1953. The term for this double-entry type of bookkeeping was the *national income and product account*.

For example, a car's market value of $15,000 will be reported in the gross domestic product. If the production of that car used up $1000 of machinery and buildings, then this $1000 of depreciation, or capital consumption allowance, would be deducted from GDP in order to obtain the $14,000 "net domestic product" of the car.

Most components of the gross domestic product are valued at market prices, but some important goods and services are not bought and sold through the marketplace, so the value of these goods must be estimated (GDP bean counters use the term *imputed* instead of "guess-timated"). Examples of imputed items include the rental value of housing; agricultural products that are consumed on family farms; food, clothing, and shelter provided by employers; and, just recently added, goods and services generated in the underground economy. Goods and services produced by governments are not sold, exchanged, or valued in the marketplace either. Nor are they imputed. Instead, they are valued at their cost to government — that is, the wages of government workers and the costs of materials purchased by the various governments.

GDP data include only the output of finished products in order to avoid double-counting. For example, if GDP bean counters added the value of steel industry output to the value of automobile industry output, they would be double-counting because the value of the steel is contained in the value of the automobiles. Similarly, there would be double-counting if the accounts included the value of cotton as well as the value of cotton clothing. In order to avoid serious overestimates, GDP accountants use the "value-added" method of determining value, which is illustrated in Table 7.2. (For further information on value added, see "Input-Output" on page 291.)

TABLE 7.2
Example of Value-Added Concept Employed in NIPA Accounting

Stage	Product	Sales	Value-Added	Income Generated (through wages, profits, rents, etc.)
1	Fertilizer, Seed	$0.10	$0.10	$0.10
2	Wheat	0.25	0.15	0.15
3	Flour	0.30	0.05	0.05
4	Baked bread	0.60	0.30	0.30
5	Retail bread	0.75	0.15	0.15
		$2.00	$0.75	$0.75

Stage 1: Chemical and seed companies sell fertilizer and seed to the farmer for 10 cents, which also generates 10 cents of income in these industries.

Stage 2: The farmer uses the fertilizer and seed to grow wheat, which he sells to the miller for 25 cents. The farmer has added 15 cents of value to the product, which is also his income in wages and profits.

(continued)

(continued)

Stage 3: The miller processes the wheat and turns it into flour, which he sells to the baker for 30 cents. He has a "value added" of 5 cents, which also generates income of wages, profits, rents, fees, etc., of 5 cents.

Stage 4: The baker bakes the bread, which he sells to the retailer for 60 cents. The value added by the baker is 30 cents, which is also the income generated by his activities.

Stage 5: The retailer also provides a service to the economy by storing and selling the bread. He sells the bread to the final consumer for 75 cents, thus adding a value of 15 cents.

In the table, the market value of bread is 75 cents, which is also the retail selling price of bread and the amount included in the gross domestic product through the value-added method. If the total sales of all sectors of the economy had been included in the GDP, they would have totaled $2.00, which is more than twice the retail value of bread. Hence, by using the value-added method, the Bureau of Economic Analysis avoids double-counting of the resources used to make the bread.

Note that the total value of the output (GDP) is 75 cents, which is also the total value of the income generated. The output and income approaches are just two different ways of counting the same thing. What would happen if the bread went through this process with the same costs but the retailer was able to sell the bread for only 65 cents? In this case, the value of bread output would be the market price of 65 cents and the income generated would be 65 cents because the retailer's profits would be reduced by 10 cents. Hence, profits (or losses) are the balancing item on the income side.

GDP data are based on the values of goods and services consumed by final consumers. With two exceptions, sales to business firms are not considered to be "final-sales goods." The first exception is capital or investment goods, which are sold to businesses and included in the investment component of the GDP. The second exception is inventory goods sold to businesses. All other goods sold to business firms are excluded from GDP and are assumed to be included in the prices of the goods sold to consumers. For example, the services of an accountant preparing a household's income tax forms are included in GDP; the services of that same accountant preparing a business firm's tax reports are not included. It is assumed that the cost of the accounting services provided to the firm will be included in the price of that firm's final goods. This distinction produces some apparent anomalies in NIPAs' treatment of goods and services. Police services purchased by a local government are included in the final product and in GDP; police services purchased by the local mall are not included. Presumably, they are included in the retail prices of the goods and services sold in the mall—just another factor in producing retail services. When state highways are repaired, the repairs are included in final product. The repair of railroad tracks is not included. If highways were converted to private toll roads and the railroads were nationalized, the treatment would be reversed. A movie produced for showing in theaters or on cable television would be included in final sales and GDP, whereas a movie produced for WTBS, a commercial station, would not be included directly but would be considered an input into the advertising industry.[2]

Let's look a little more carefully at the two sides of the national income and product accounts. The expenditure side is organized around the familiar textbook exposition of Keynesian economics: $Y = C + I + G + X$, where C is consumption, I is investment, G is government expenditures, and X is net exports of goods and services. The income side shows the familiar sources of income: wages and salaries, dividends, interest, profits. We will first discuss the expenditure side.

The Expenditure or Product Side ($C + I + G + X$)

Personal Consumption Expenditures (C)

Personal consumption expenditures (C)[3] is the largest component of the GDP, accounting for about 69 percent of the total GDP (64 percent in 1960). Consumer spending is one of the less volatile components of GDP, and during recessions it decreases at a slower rate than total GDP. Consumption expenditures are divided into durables, nondurables, and services. Durable goods, which have an expected life of three or more years and account for about 12 percent (13 percent in 1960) of consumption expenditures, include automobiles, home furnishings, appliances, books (but not magazines or newspapers), toys, radios, and television sets.[4] Consumer durables are treated as consumption goods and not investment goods. Automobiles, for example, which qualify as investment goods if bought by a business, are treated as consumer durables if purchased by an individual. Nondurables, which account for about 32 percent (46 percent in 1960) of personal consumption expenditures, include food and drink, apparel, medical supplies, gasoline, and oil. Services, which constitute 56 percent (41 percent in 1960) of consumption, include rentals, medical and recreational expenditures, repairs, personal transportation, and utilities.

---

[2]If the government were to nationalize television, as has been done in many other countries, its expenditures for producing television programs would be counted as part of government purchases of goods and services and would raise the GDP. This is one of many problems resulting from a hazy boundary between intermediate products, which are not included in GDP, and final products, which are included.

[3]Economic textbooks refer to consumption expenditures as C; GDP accountants refer to them as *PCE*, for personal consumption expenditures. Both terms mean the same thing — "personal consumption expenditures" is simply more descriptive.

[4]Durable goods account for a small and shrinking proportion of personal consumption expenditures and are quite volatile. In recent years, their volatility has increased.

The Bureau of Economic Analysis, which gathers the GDP data, treats housing in a special way. If a family is renting a home or an apartment, it is "purchasing" the services of the home or apartment, and BEA uses the rental price as a good estimate of the value of the services provided by the home. There is nothing unusual or exceptional about treating rents as approximating the service value of rental homes and apartments. However, BEA also estimates the rental value of owner-occupied homes and includes these estimated rental values in the services section of GDP. The major reason for treating owner-occupied housing as rental property is to avoid certain fluctuations that would otherwise occur in the GDP. If the rental value of these owned homes were excluded from GDP, the GDP would rise whenever a homeowner sold a home and moved into a rental facility, and would shrink whenever a renter bought a home. In order to avoid these changes, GDP accountants devised a system of imputing an annual rental value to owner-occupied homes and then including that value in the services category of personal consumption expenditures.

Gross Private Domestic Investment (*I*)

Investment has a specific meaning to economists that differs from its meaning in everyday conversation. If you purchase the stocks or bonds of General Motors or Exxon, you would consider the transaction to be an investment. However, an economist would say that such a transaction merely involved the security purchaser transferring money to the security seller. There would be no change in total investment or total capital stock in the country. To an economist, investment occurs when there is an addition to or replacement of real productive assets. When you buy a GM bond, no investment takes place and your purchase of the bond does not enter into the GDP. However, if you buy a newly issued bond from General Motors, and GM uses the proceeds to build a new plant, economists would say that GM, but not the bond purchaser, had made an investment. GDP accountants would record the construction of the plant, but not the bond purchase, as part of the investment component of GDP. Investment expenditures are those made for real productive assets (also called *capital stock*) with long lives, such as machines, offices, factories, trucks, business computers, desks, and changes in business inventories. They do *not* include expenditures for stocks, bonds, or other financial securities that are the sources of funds to finance investment assets. Economists are concerned about the quantity of investment because it is influential in determining the future growth rate of the economy and the standard of living enjoyed by Americans. Economists are also concerned about investment because it is generally the most volatile component of the GDP and a major cause of cyclical fluctuations.

Gross private domestic investment (*I*), which was 12.8% of GDP in 1991 (15.2% in 1960), is called "gross" because it is measured before any deduction for depreciation and "private" because it does not include government investments.[5] It is "domestic" because it includes only expenditures made on real capital assets located in the United States. Gross investment expenditures can be used for two purposes: (1) replacement of capital and (2) net additions to capital. They can be used to replace capital goods — buildings, tools, delivery trucks — that were worn out or destroyed during the year. That is, part of the country's gross investment expenditures will have to be used to replace the physical depreciation of capital assets used to produce GDP. The remainder of the investment will be a net addition to the capital stock of the country. Net investment in the economy, then, is equal to gross investment minus depreciation:

	1991
Gross private domestic investment	$726.7
Less: Depreciation (capital consumption allowance)	622.9
Equals: Net private investment	103.8

If the nation invests only an amount sufficient to cover depreciation, the nation's capital stock will not grow and the economy will soon stagnate.[6] Recall that gross private domestic investment is very narrowly defined by the BEA. If trucks, automobiles, and computers are purchased by individuals or by governments, they are considered consumption and not investment goods. They are considered investment goods only if purchased by a business firm or a nonprofit institution. This is contrary to economic theory, in which it is clearly recognized that the purchase of a computer or a pickup truck by a consumer or a government provides the same additional services to the economy that it would if the expenditure were made by a private firm. Furthermore, NIPA accountants treat *all* research and development expenditures by households, governments, nonprofit institutions, *and* business firms as part of current consumption, so they are not included in investment. Since research and development is one of the most significant categories of investment in the economy, its absence from NIPA's investment account means that capital investment is being underreported.

There are three major categories of investment in the GDP accounts: nonresidential construction, residential construction, and change in

---

[5]Many countries include government investment in this category. This is one of several reasons for the incompatibility of GDP data among countries. Although government investment is excluded in the United States, private investment in the NIPA accounts does include investment by nonprofit organizations. Also, government investment expenditures get picked up in government expenditures.

[6]Adjustments to inventory investment, called *inventory valuation adjustments (IVA)*, are necessary because of inflation and inventory valuation practices. These are fully explained in Appendix 7B.

business inventories. *Nonresidential construction* includes producer durables and all structures other than homes or apartments, such as plants, office buildings, shopping malls, and warehouses. *Producer durables* are machinery and equipment — computers, table saws, bulldozers — that have useful lives longer than one year and are depreciated. *Residential construction* includes all outlays for the construction of multiunit apartment buildings, single family residences, and mobile homes, whether they are finished or sold during the period or not.[7] The purchase of a home is not a consumption expenditure but is treated as an investment that the buyer rents to a tenant or to himself or herself.

The last component of investment is the *change in business inventories*. Total output in the economy during any year is either sold to final users (consumers, investors, government, exporters) or added to inventories. Thus, an increase in business inventories represents an increase in investment, which is included in GDP. Inventory accumulation is watched very closely as the first indicator of a recession, but the data are not very reliable. Since inventories are maintained by large and small companies in every industry in every part of the country, the data are difficult to obtain and inventory estimates are considered weak.

Government Purchases (G)

Government purchases (G) are another important component on the product side of GDP accounting. (For a further discussion of government purchases in the NIPAs, see the section on "Government Budgets," Chapter 16.) When government purchases an M-60 tank, pays a local contractor to build a highway, or hires economists and accountants to keep track of the GDP, it is purchasing economic goods (tanks and highways) or services (of economists and accountants). These goods and services are part of the economy's output and GDP. Since governments do not price and sell most of their goods and services, they are valued at the cost of obtaining them. Thus, the "output" of governments is valued by governments' expenditures to purchase goods and services and to pay the wages, salaries, and benefits of their own employees. Government expenditures were 19.2% of GDP in 1991 and 19.5% in 1960.

A significant part of government expenditures is for transfer payments — Social Security, welfare payments, veteran benefits, interest on

---

[7]The residential construction component of GDP has decreased from about 6 percent of GDP in the 1950s to 4–5 percent in the later 1980s. Because of demographic trends in which the baby boomers have now progressed beyond the house-buying stage of their lives, residential construction can be expected to decrease relative to the GDP throughout most of the 1990s until it reaches a lower plateau around 2010.

the government debt, and unemployment compensation. These payments are merely transfers from some citizens (taxpayers) to other citizens (recipients) and do not represent an increase in total goods and services in the economy. Thus, they are not included in GDP or the government component of GDP. Also not included in GDP are foreign economic aid, federal grants to state and local governments, and state grants to local governments. Hence, it is important to always remember that government expenditures in NIPAs are much lower than government expenditures in the official budget, and NIPA data should not be used to estimate all impacts of government on the economy.[8] During the 1980s, federal government purchases in GDP accounts were only about 40 percent of the expenditures reported in the federal budget. For example, in 1990 the federal government's unified budget expenditures were about $1.3 trillion, but government expenditures reported in GDP accounts were only $425 billion. Unlike many other governments, the United States federal government has no capital account in its formal budgetary accounting system, nor is there any in the formal GDP accounts. Hence, all government expenditures are considered part of current consumption and none are treated as investment goods.

Although the government sector in the official GDP accounts does not include transfer payments, "side" accounts in the NIPAs provide considerable detail about *total* government budgets and expenditures, based on NIPA methodology. In fact, the only consistent series of federal budgetary information on a calendar year basis is found within the NIPAs. These "side" accounts include the receipts of the federal government, which include all personal tax receipts, corporate profits tax accruals, excise taxes, customs duties, and receipts of the social insurance funds. Expenditures include all purchases of goods and services, all transfer payments to individuals and local and state governments, interest payments minus receipts, and net subsidies (profits less losses) of government enterprises.

Net Exports $(X - M)$

Goods exported from the country are part of the output of the American economy and generate income in the United States. Hence, they must be included in GDP. Conversely, imports are not produced in the United

---

[8]Other differences between government expenditures in the NIPA accounts and official budgets include: (1) NIPA accounts are given for a calendar year, whereas the budget is shown for a fiscal year; (2) the official budget shows expenditures when checks are paid and receipts when tax payments are received, while the NIPAs record expenditures when the items are delivered and receipts when tax liabilities are incurred.

States and thus generate no income in this country. Since consumer expenditures on imports are included in personal consumption expenditures on the product side but they generate no income recorded on the income side, imports must be deducted from the product side by deducting them from exports. Net exports are U.S. exports minus imports — hence, when total imports exceed total exports, net exports are negative and the net figure is deducted from the product side of GDP.[9]

Let's follow an imported automobile through a few steps in the NIPAs. Although NIPA accountants never have it this easy, assume they know that the value of an automobile imported into the United States is $10,000 (the cost to the importing dealer). NIPA accountants would record the $10,000 auto import as an increase in inventories; when the car is sold to consumers, the inventory account would be decreased and consumption expenditures (durables) would be increased. However, the imported car was not produced in the United States, which means that no income has been generated from its production. Hence, an adjustment is required to deduct the import value of the car from GDP. This is done by increasing the import account by $10,000 and then deducting imports from exports. Thus, imported goods enter into the GDP accounts through increases in inventories and then consumption expenditures, but they are taken out of GDP as import offsets to exports. One problem resulting from showing only net exports in the balance of payments is that net exports understate the importance of international trade in the country's economy. For example, net exports (exports − imports) were $31 billion in 1991 or less than 1 percent of GDP. However, imports ($622 billion) were 11 percent of GDP and exports ($591 billion) were 10 percent of GDP. When evaluating the importance of international trade to the American economy, we need to look at the total amount of imports (or exports). Imports and exports include travel, tourism, and income on investments as well as trade in goods and services. The net export figure is obtained from NIPAs' balance of payments data, and the amount reported is reasonably close to the current account balance in the U.S. balance of payments.

Table 7.1 presented at the beginning of this section is the major table in the NIPAs, but many additional tables present an extraordinary amount of detail. For a number of years NIPAs have been organized and presented in a standard format of nine categories, which are shown in Table 7.3.

---

[9]*Exports* are goods and services provided by U.S. residents to foreigners; *imports* are goods and services provided by foreigners to U.S. residents. Residents are individuals, governments, businesses, trusts, and associations that are physically located in the United States. The United States includes the 50 states, the District of Columbia and U.S. military installations, embassies, and consulates abroad. Unlike the balance of payments accounts, NIPAs do not include U.S. territories and Puerto Rico in the definition of the United States.

TABLE 7.3
Major Categories in National Income and Product Accounts

1. National product and income
2. Personal income and outlays
3. Government receipts and expenditures
4. Foreign transactions
5. Saving and investment
6. Product, income, and employment by industry
7. Fixed weight price indexes and implicit price deflators
8. Supplementary tables
9. Seasonally unadjusted estimates

A wide variety of information is contained in each of these nine categories. For example, personal consumption expenditures is one of the components of national product (category 1). This subsection, personal consumption expenditures, is composed of several subcategories, including food and tobacco, clothing, household operations, and others (see Table 7.4). Each of these subcategories is broken down still further. The subsubcategories are shown only for foreign travel and household operation. Unfortunately, the BEA had not released the detail data for 1991 when this book went to press. This level of detail should give you some idea of the wealth of information available in the NIPAs.

TABLE 7.4
Example of Detailed Data Shown in NIPAs
1991

	Billions of $
Personal consumption expenditures	$3,889.0
Food and tobacco	667.6
Clothing, accessories, jewelry	263.1
Personal care	61.7
Housing	574.7
Medical care	651.6
Personal business	303.8
Transportation	442.8
Recreation	288.4
Private education and research	92.4
Religious and welfare activities	109.7
Foreign travel and other, net	−12.7
Foreign travel by U.S. residents	—
Expenditures abroad by U.S. residents	—
Less: Expenditures in U.S. by foreigners	—
Less: Personal remittances to foreigners	—

(continued)

TABLE 7.4 *(continued)*
Example of Detailed Data Shown in NIPAs
1991

	Billions of $
Household operation	446.1
Furniture, mattresses, bedsprings	—
Kitchen and household appliances	—
China, glassware, tableware	—
Other durable house furnishings	—
Semidurable house furnishings	—
Cleaning and polishing supplies	—
Stationery and writing supplies	—
Household utilities	—
Electricity	—
Gas	—
Water and sewerage	—
Fuel and coal	—
Telephone and telegraph	—
Domestic service	—
Other	—

Detailed data are presented for automobiles (sales, output, exports, government purchases, inventories); social insurance contributions by employees and employers; government revenue and expenditures (by type of expenditure and source, reconciliation with unified budget); foreign transactions (exports, imports, receipts, payments, reconciliation with balance of payments accounts); product, profits, income, and employment by industry; and data on fixed-weight price indexes and implicit price deflators. Some of this information is reported separately in this book in the relevant sections. For example, see NIPA data in "Personal Consumption Expenditures" (page 335) and international trade data in the "Balance of Payments" section (pages 413–415).

The Supply or Income Side

At the beginning of this section we mentioned that the GDP accounts, or NIPAs, had two sides. We have just finished discussing the product side and its components. Now we discuss the income side and the various income balances that are produced. We start with the most inclusive figure, which is gross domestic product, and work our way down to personal and disposable income and even to net saving.

It is often difficult for the economic noviate to understand the conceptual truism that the value of production or output equals total income. When an automobile is produced entirely from resources located in the United States and owned by an American resident, the sales revenue from that automobile represents income to someone in the United States. If a Ford Mustang is sold for $15,000, the dealers, workers, managers, stockholders, bondholders, and resource owners who provided services or resources for its production, transportation, and sales have their incomes increased by $15,000. Thus, in theory, the value of production or sales always equals income. However, in the real world, certain costs of production that enter into the market price, such as depreciation and taxes, do not generate earned income to anyone during that period. Hence, certain adjustments have to be made to the GDP data in order to reconcile the income data. (See Table 7.5).

GDP excludes income earned on American investments in foreign countries and includes income earned by foreigners on their investments in the United States. Hence, we must first obtain GNP by adding in the former and excluding the latter. We can then make a series of further adjustments to obtain personal income. Depreciation, or capital consumption allowance, is part of the gross national product. Since depreciation does not generate any income, it must be deducted from GNP. Deducting depreciation (called *capital consumption allowances*) from GNP produces a figure called **net national product**, which represents the flow of goods and services available to the economy after the capital goods are replaced. If we are making long-run comparisons of output among nations, net national product is a more appropriate measure than GNP because it more closely approximates the goods and services available after making allowances for the capital used up in the production process. However, many researchers ignore NNP because of a widespread belief that the estimates for capital consumption allowances are arbitrary and not very meaningful.

When accountants calculate the values of the various goods and services that constitute GDP, they use prices inclusive of sales and excise taxes. This means that if sales tax rates are increased, both GDP and NNP will increase although there is no increase in real income or output. Hence, by subtracting sales, excise, and certain property taxes — called *indirect taxes* — and deducting business transfers to individuals not connected with current production, we obtain income at factor cost, which is called **national income**.[10] National income is the income counterpart of gross national product and comes closest to the real output–real income (or *Y*) used in macroeconomic models.

Various adjustments shown in Table 7.5 are made to derive *personal income* from national income. Corporate profits are deducted from national income because these profits are not necessarily distributed to the

---

[10]Don't make the mistake of concluding that, since these taxes are subtracted from output, the NIPAs do not include the government sector. Government expenditures *are* included in G, and the income of government workers is included as part of wages and salaries.

TABLE 7.5
Gross Domestic Product: Alternative Presentation of the Income Side
(billions of $)

		1991
Gross domestic product		5,672.6
Plus:	Receipts of factor income from the rest of the world	135.0
Less:	Payments of factor income to the rest of the world	121.8
Equals:	**Gross national product**	5,685.8
Less: Capital consumption allowances		622.9
Equals: **Net national product**		5,062.8
Less:	Indirect business taxes	471.0
	Business transfer payments	31.2
	Statistical discrepancy	19.0
Plus:	Subsidies less current surplus of government enterprises	0.6
Equals:	**National income**	4,542.2
Less:	Corporate profits with inventory valuation and capital cons. adj.	306.8
	Net interest	480.2
	Social insurance contributions	527.4
Plus:	Government transfer payments to persons	733.2
	Personal interest income	718.6
	Personal dividend income	128.5
	Business transfer payments	26.3
Equals:	**Personal income**	4,834.4
Personal income is composed of:		
(1) Wages and salaries from		2,808.3
	Commodity-producing industries	738.7
	Distributive industries	641.2
	Service industries	887.8
	Governments/government indus.	540.6
(2) Other labor income		290.6
(3) Proprietors income		379.7
(4) Personal rental income		−12.7
(5) Personal dividend income		128.5
(6) Personal interest income		718.6
(7) Transfer payments		759.5
	Social Security (OASDHI)	380.0
	Govt. unemploy. ins. benefits	26.6
	Veterans' benefits	18.4
	Federal retirement benefits	99.7
	Aid to families with dep. children	21.8
	Other transfer payments	213.0
(8) Less: Personal contrib. for soc. ins.		238.0
Less:	Personal tax and nontax payments (Includes income, estate and gift taxes)	616.1
Equals:	**Disposable personal income**	4,218.4
Less:	Personal outlays	3,999.1
	Personal consumption expenditures	3,889.1
	Interest paid by consumers to bus.	106.8
	Transfer payments to foreigners	3.2
Equals:	**Personal saving**	219.3

owners (only dividends are distributed) so they do not constitute personal income.[11] If corporate profits are distributed to shareholders, they are included as dividend income from corporations and, along with government and business transfer payments and interest income, are included in personal income.[12] The net interest (just below corporate profits) deducted from national income is the net interest paid by businesses less the amount received by businesses. Thus, it represents a net return to individuals for the capital they lent to the business sector.

Personal income received by households before the payment of income taxes is obtained from wages and fringe benefits, profits from self-employment, rent, interest, dividends, Social Security benefits, unemployment insurance, food stamps, and other income maintenance programs. It is easy to get lost in this table so numbers were added to show the major components of personal income. Personal income is an important statistic that is widely watched by economists and business analysts. It is the most accurate measure of income flows to individuals even though it does not include capital gains or losses that occur in financial markets. Personal income less income, estate, and gift taxes equals *disposable personal income*, which represents the actual purchasing power available to consumers from current income. This statistic, too, is watched closely by producers, wholesalers, and retailers of consumer goods.

If consumption expenditures, certain interest payments, and other minor adjustments are subtracted from personal income, the result is *personal saving*. This figure is widely regarded as the "savings" of consumers and the household sector and is widely used for international comparisons of personal savings rates. Historically, personal savings has been about 5 to 7 percent of disposable income but, since the latter 1970s, it has been just slightly above 4 percent. There is continuing debate about the accuracy of the personal saving figure because it is obtained by subtracting one large number (personal consumption expenditures) from an-

---

[11]Many analysts pay close attention to corporate profits as a valuable indicator of the economy since the NIPAs provide the most complete data on corporate profits. Like all other income flows in the NIPAs, corporate profits are reported before taxes, but, in the more detailed accounts, the associated taxes are reported so that after-tax earnings can be calculated. The after-tax profits are then subdivided into dividend payments and retained earnings. Since corporate profits include profits from increases in the monetary value of inventory valuation, the inventory valuation adjustment (IVA) for corporations is made here. Corporate profits are also adjusted for capital consumption, as reported on pages 125–126. Remember that corporate profits, like all income measures in the NIPAs, do not include capital gains and losses.

[12]Unincorporated businesses are not directly mentioned in the GDP accounts because they are not segregated out as economic entities; the income of unincorporated proprietors goes directly into their personal income.

other large number (disposable personal income). Relatively small errors in either of the two large numbers will have a disproportionately large impact on personal savings.

Personal saving covers a wide variety of saving. It includes financial savings (except capital gains), increase in the cash value of insurance and pension reserves, and increases in personal equity ownerships in land and physical resources. Because the increase in net worth (increase in capital assets and inventories) of unincorporated businesses gets picked up in personal income and is not spent for consumption, personal saving includes these major amounts as well. However, personal saving does not include accumulated capital gains in owner-occupied housing.

Savings and Investment

The NIPAs have a number of tables on savings and investment. As every student learns in the first economics course, the amount of saving in the economy for any given period must equal the amount of investment:

$$\text{Expenditures} = \text{consumption} + \text{investment}$$

$$\text{Income} = \text{savings} + \text{consumption}$$

$$\text{Income} = \text{expenditures}$$

So $\quad$ Saving $=$ Investment

In fact, these relationships are identities: They are equal by definition. The saving side of the identity includes personal saving, retained earnings and depreciation in the business sector, and the surplus of the government sector (a government deficit is "dissaving"). The investment side includes gross private domestic investment (all business investment expenditures plus changes in inventories) plus net foreign investment. See Table 7.6.

TABLE 7.6
Saving and Investment
billions of $

	1991
Gross saving	$715.2
Gross private saving	886.8
(1) Personal saving	219.3
(2) Undistributed corporate profits with inventory valuation adjustment and capital consumption adjustments	44.6
Undistributed profits	50.2
Inventory valuation adjustment	3.1
Capital consumption allowances	−8.7

(continued)

TABLE 7.6 *(continued)*
Saving and Investment
billions of $

	1991
(3) Corporate capital consumption allowances with capital consumption adjustment	383.6
(4) Noncorporate capital consumption allowances with capital consumption adjustments	239.3
Government surplus or deficit (−), NIPA version	− 171.6
Federal	− 201.6
State and local	30.0
Gross investment	$734.2
Gross private domestic investment	726.7
Net foreign investment	7.5
Less: Statistical discrepancy	− 19.0
Gross investment and statistical discrepancy	$715.2

Some of these accounts may be difficult to understand. Personal savings should present no problem. These are the savings of individuals and families that were channeled through the securities markets and financial intermediaries to investors. Undistributed corporate profits are also straightforward. These are the profits, or retained earnings, of corporations that were not distributed as dividends. The corporations reinvested these profits back into the firm. The inventory valuation adjustments and the capital consumption allowances to corporate profits are adjustments made to correct certain problems in inventory valuation and depreciation rates and to make them more realistic. (See Appendix 7B for a detailed but easy-to-understand discussion of these adjustments. You might also want to review the "Accounting" section in Chapter 2.)

Capital consumption allowances (3) is a bit more complicated. Capital consumption allowances are simply fancy words for depreciation that is really a form of saving and a source of funds for investment. If you have no accounting training, you are saying: "Huh??" Don't despair. I'll make it easy for you.

Assume that a corporation has purchased $10 million of machinery and that the real wear and tear on the machinery is $1 million a year. Assume further that the company charges off the correct amount of depreciation ($1 million) to depreciation expense each year. This increases the firm's expenses and reduces profits, but makes an additional $1 million available for investment. In order to show this clearly, assume that the ABC Gear Company has revenue of $14 million, wages and salaries of $6 million, materials cost of $5 million, and depreciation costs of $1 million (Table 7.7). The company would have a profit of $2 million (forget taxes), out of which it would pay $500,000 in dividends to individuals.

TABLE 7.7
Derivation of Savings — Hypothetical Example
millions of $

Revenue from sales			$14.0
Less:	Wages and salaries	$6	
	Materials	5	
	Depreciation	1	
	Total costs		12.0
Equals:	Corporate profits		$ 2.0
Less:	Dividends paid		−0.5
Equals:	Undistributed profits		1.5
Personal income from this firm's activities:			
	Wages and salaries		$ 6.0
	Dividends		0.5
	Total personal income		6.5
Less:	Personal consumption expenditures		−6.1
Equals:	Personal savings (1)		0.4
Plus:	Undistributed corporate profits (2)		1.5
	Depreciation (3)		1.0
	Total private savings		$ 2.9

The corporation has undistributed profits of $1.5 million. Total personal income resulting from this firm's activities are the sum of wages and dividends, or $6.5 million. Assuming that households' consumption expenditures are $6.1 million, they will have personal savings of $400,000, which would go into account (1) of the saving and investment table (Table 7.6). Undistributed corporate profits would get picked up in account (2) of Table 7.6.

The corporation claimed $1 million of depreciation expense, but it didn't pay out any money for depreciation expense. It didn't go to profits; in fact, depreciation expense reduced profits. Where did the depreciation "funds" go? The answer is that funds are still in the company and available for reinvestment. The $1 million depreciation expense was a paper charge against revenue to reflect the fact that one-tenth of the machinery had worn out. This is a real cost to the company because the machinery will have to be replaced someday, but the cost did not necessitate any cash outlay this year. Some accountants like to say that depreciation is a source of cash. This is not really correct because the real source of cash is sales, but a depreciation expense does represent a cash set-aside if there is any cash available. These depreciation "funds" are added to savings along with personal savings and undistributed corporate profits to obtain total private savings.

What funds will the ABC Gear Company have available from private savings? It will have the $1.5 million that it saved in undistributed corporate profits [(2) in Table 7.7], plus it will have the $400,000 of the personal savings of households that it obtained from bond sales (1)[13] and it will have the $1 million in cash savings that are represented by the depreciation expense (3). ABC Gear now has total private savings of $2.9 million. Stay tuned for the next installment on investment, where you will learn what ABC Gear actually does with this savings.

Now you should understand why capital consumption allowances, which represent depreciation expenses, are included in savings. The *capital consumption adjustments* shown in Table 7.6 are necessary because firms often do not charge their depreciation expense accounts with amounts that realistically represent the actual wear and tear on their capital equipment. Hence, BEA makes various capital consumption adjustments to get more realistic amounts for depreciation estimates and, thus, for saving. These adjustments are thoroughly explained in Appendix 7B.

Before turning to the investment side, we need to complete our discussion of saving by discussing government savings. The BEA prepares a separate set of accounts for government revenues and expenditures (see "Government Budgets," pages 365–382). If government expenditures are greater than revenues, the government sector is said to be a net investor. If total government revenue exceeds government expenditures, the government sector is said to be a net saver. The BEA consistently puts the government sector in the savings section even though government has had deficits in virtually every year since 1929. Let's return to our ABC Gear example.

Funds available to ABC Gear from savings:	$2.9 million
Less: Government bonds purchased by ABC	− 1.0
Funds available for investment (gross saving)	$1.9

If the government runs a deficit, it has to finance that deficit by selling bonds. Thus, if the government deficit is $1.0 million, ABC Gear will use $1 million of its funds to buy government bonds, which leaves only $1.9 available for private investment. BEA treats government deficits as negative savings; government deficits reduce the savings that would otherwise have been available for private investment.

Gross private domestic investment ($726.7), listed at the bottom of Table 7.6, and the amount reported as *I* on the product side of the GDP, includes all investment made in the United States regardless of whether the investment was made by an American resident or by a foreigner. However, some of the construction, inventories, and machines were fi-

---

[13]Since the author is a strong believer in the KISS principle, we assume that the employees use their savings to purchase newly issued ABC Gear bonds. What is KISS? *Keep It Simple, Stupid.*

nanced by foreigners. Hence, to obtain investment financed from savings in the United States, the net foreign investment has to be deducted. In 1991, American residents had invested more in foreign countries than foreigners had invested in this country, so the foreign investment account was a net addition to gross investment. The statistical discrepancy is subtracted here to balance the two sides of investment and saving, just as it balanced the overall GDP accounts.

Problems with GDP Accounting

One problem with GDP accounting lies not with the data but with the various BEA releases and the media attention given to them. The media give more publicity to the early releases of the GDP estimates than to the more accurate final or annual releases. The Bureau of Economic Analysis provides at least four estimates of each quarter's GDP data. The advance estimates, released only 15 days after the end of the quarter, are based on data for only the first of the three months in the quarter. Hence, subsequent revisions can make substantial changes in the data. The range of revisions on the seasonally adjusted annual growth rate in the advance estimates varies from about −2.5 to +3.5 percentage points. The preliminary estimates (first revision), which are released about 45 days after the end of the quarter, have a revision range of approximately −2.0 to 2.8 percentage points; the final estimates (second revision), which are released 75 days after the end of the quarter, have a revision range of about −2.2 to 2.7. These are very significant and worrisome ranges, especially since the media give wide coverage to the early estimates (advanced and preliminary) but often ignore subsequent (final and annual) revisions. For example, if the advance estimate of the GDP growth rate from the previous quarter is reported to be an annualized 3 percent, the actual growth rate could range from one-half of 1 percent to 6.5 percent (0.03 − 0.025 to 0.03 + 0.035). If the growth rate is actually at the lower limit of one-half of 1 percent, the economy could be stagnating and unemployment increasing. If the growth rate is at the upper limit of 6.5 percent, the economy is probably experiencing inflationary pressures. Making policy decisions on these advanced estimates can lead to serious errors. The BEA and the media need to educate the public about these simple facts — or the early estimates should not be released, and the resources saved should be allocated to later revisions.

Conceptually, the product and income sides of the GDP accounts should add up to the same total, but the real-life limitations on data collection mean that the two sides seldom are equal in practice. The difference between the totals on the product and income sides is known as the "statistical discrepancy." The reported discrepancy is a net figure because many statistical discrepancies in the individual components offset each other. For example, if a component on the product side has a statistical discrepancy of $20 billion and a component on the income side has a statistical discrepancy of $15 billion, the net reported discrepancy is only $5 billion. Thus, the total distortion in the accounts produced by incomplete data is far more serious than indicated by the statistical discrepancy.

Economists like to define the GDP as the total value of final goods and services produced in the nation. However, private goods and services that do not go through the market mechanism may not be included. Vegetables and flowers grown in the backyard are not included, for example; neither is furniture built by hobbyists. If a homeowner contracts out the addition of a garage to his house, the entire amount of the contract, including wages, materials, and profits, will be included in GDP. However, if the homeowner builds the garage, only the materials purchased will be included in GDP. The GDP does not pick up unreported activities, such as the handyman or maid who gets paid in cash.

The recent increase in the labor participation ratio of women has produced an artificial increase in the GDP. When women stayed home and cleaned the house, took care of the kids, washed and ironed the clothes, and cooked the meals, their efforts were not included in the GDP. Now, with the wife working, the family hires a maid to clean the house, sends the kids to day-care centers, drops clothing off at the dry cleaners, and picks up fast food on the way home from work — and these activities are fully included in GDP. Nevertheless, total goods and services available to consumers are not increased in any real sense. The same services are being provided, but now they are being priced in the marketplace — they were not when the wife stayed home. Before married women worked outside the home, this anomaly enabled economists to wake up their sophomore classes by quipping that the man who married his housekeeper reduced the GDP.

Until a few years ago the GDP did not measure illegal activities because most people do not report income from such activities. The omission of such activities is no trivial matter — the drug trade alone is a multibillion dollar industry. In 1985, GDP statistics going back to 1929 were revised to account for this and other unreported underground activity. The GDP for 1984, for example, was increased by $120 billion, or 3 percent. Nevertheless, many economists thought that larger adjustments should have been made. They continue to argue that GDP underestimates unreported and illegal activities.

Much modern criticism of GDP accounting has been based on the incorrect view that increases in the gross domestic product are always "good" for society. Some critics point out that an increase in military expenditures will cause a corresponding increase in the GDP, and they question whether there has been a net increase in welfare. Some nations seem destined to allocate resources to police the planet, others to ward off cold weather or to recover from typhoons. The NIPAs include expenditures on all these activities even though welfare may or may not be increased. Other critics point out that when a chemical company produces chemicals, the value of the chemicals enters into the GDP. This might be acceptable to them but if, in addition, the chemical production emits smoke and the company has to use expensive scrubbers to cleanse the air, the value of the scrubbers and their maintenance costs are also included in GDP. Thus, the more air, water, and land pollution that must be cleaned up, the higher the GDP. Some critics have quipped that the gross domestic product should be called the "gross domestic cost." One can answer these critics by pointing out that the GDP is essentially an exercise in double-entry bookkeeping. It shows the benefits—the products—on one side of the ledger and income or costs on the other side. The NIPAs do show the costs of using the nation's resources to provide goods and services.

The real source of the critics' complaint, though, is that many people, including most economists, believe that a large increase in real GDP implies a large increase in social welfare. Environmentalists are quite concerned that the degradation of the environment and its ability to support future generations is not priced anywhere in the system. For example, the pollution of a river or the destruction of a forest that had been emitting healthful oxygen are not picked up as costs anywhere in GDP accounting. Perhaps there should be an accounting system called the "gross domestic waste product" to keep track of such costs.

Historic Data: GNP Data
(billions of $)

	Current GNP	Personal Consump. Total	Gross Private Domestic Investment	Exports Less Imports	Govt. Purch.	Real GNP (1982 $)	Real GNP per Capita (1982 $)
1929	$ 104	$ 77.3	$ 16.7	$ 1.2	$ 8.9	$ 709.6	$ 5,822
1930	91	70.0	10.6	1.0	9.5	642.8	5,218
1931	76	60.6	6.0	0.5	9.5	588.1	4,737
1932	59	48.5	1.2	0.4	8.3	509.2	4,075
1933	56	45.9	1.5	0.3	8.3	498.5	3,966
1934	66	51.3	3.5	0.6	10.1	536.7	4,243
1935	73	55.7	6.7	0.1	10.3	580.2	4,555
1936	83	62.0	8.8	0.1	12.2	662.2	5,166
1937	91	66.6	12.1	0.4	12.1	695.3	5,391
1938	85	64.1	6.7	1.3	13.2	664.2	5,111
1939	91	67.0	9.5	1.2	13.5	716.6	5,469
1940	100	71.0	13.4	1.7	14.2	772.9	5,850
1941	126	80.9	18.3	1.4	25.0	909.4	6,817
1942	159	88.7	10.3	0.2	59.8	1,080.3	8,010
1943	193	99.4	6.2	(1.9)	88.9	1,276.2	9,333
1944	211	108.2	7.8	(1.7)	97.0	1,380.6	9,975
1945	213	119.6	11.3	(0.5)	83.0	1,354.8	9,682
1946	212	143.9	31.5	7.9	29.1	1,096.9	7,758
1947	235	161.9	35.1	12.0	26.4	1,066.7	7,401
1948	262	175.0	47.1	6.9	32.6	1,108.7	7,561
1949	260	178.3	36.4	6.6	39.1	1,109.0	7,434

(continued)

Historic Data: GNP Data *(continued)*
(billions of $)

	Current GNP	Personal Consump. Total	Gross Private Domestic Investment	Exports Less Imports	Govt. Purch.	Real GNP (1982 $)	Real GNP per Capita (1982 $)
1950	$ 288	$ 192.2	$ 55.1	$2.2	$ 38.9	$1,203.7	$ 7,935
1951	333	208.1	60.4	4.5	60.4	1,328.2	8,609
1952	352	219.1	53.6	3.2	75.8	1,380.1	8,792
1953	372	232.6	54.9	1.3	82.7	1,435.3	8,995
1954	373	239.8	54.2	2.5	76.1	1,416.2	8,721
1955	406	257.9	69.7	3.0	75.2	1,494.9	9,045
1956	428	270.6	72.6	5.3	79.7	1,525.6	9,069
1957	451	285.3	71.1	7.3	87.4	1,551.1	9,056
1958	457	294.6	63.6	3.3	95.3	1,539.2	8,839
1959	496	316.3	80.2	1.5	97.9	1,629.1	9,200
1960	515	330.7	78.2	5.9	100.5	1,665.3	9,213
1961	534	341.1	77.1	7.2	108.4	1,708.7	9,299
1962	575	362.7	87.6	6.9	118.1	1,799.4	9,644
1963	607	381.8	93.1	8.2	123.8	1,873.3	9,896
1964	650	409.3	99.6	10.9	129.9	1,973.3	10,281
1965	705	440.8	116.1	9.7	138.6	2,087.6	10,741
1966	772	477.3	128.6	7.5	158.6	2,208.3	11,233
1967	816	503.5	125.8	7.4	179.7	2,271.4	11,428
1968	893	552.4	137.0	5.5	197.7	2,365.6	11,784
1969	964	597.8	153.3	5.7	207.2	2,423.3	11,953
1970	1,016	640.0	148.8	8.4	218.2	2,416.2	11,781
1971	1,103	691.6	172.5	6.3	232.3	2,484.8	11,964
1972	1,213	757.6	202.1	3.2	250.0	2,608.5	12,426
1973	1,359	837.3	238.8	16.8	266.5	2,744.1	12,948
1974	1,473	916.6	240.8	16.3	299.1	2,729.3	12,760
1975	1,598	1,012.8	219.6	31.0	335.1	2,695.0	12,478
1976	1,783	1,129.4	277.7	18.8	356.9	2,826.7	12,961
1977	1,991	1,257.2	344.1	1.9	387.3	2,958.6	13,431
1978	2,250	1,403.5	416.8	4.1	425.2	3,115.2	13,993
1979	2,508	1,566.8	454.9	18.7	467.9	3,192.4	14,182
1980	2,732	1,732.6	437.0	32.1	530.3	3,187.1	13,994
1981	3,053	1,915.2	516.1	33.9	588.1	3,248.8	14,114
1982	3,166	2,050.7	447.3	26.3	641.7	3,166.0	13,614
1983	3,406	2,234.5	502.3	(6.2)	675.0	3,279.1	13,964
1984	3,772	2,430.4	664.8	(58.9)	735.8	3,501.4	14,771
1985	4,015	2,709.0	643.0	(78.0)	820.8	3,618.7	15,121
1986	4,232	2,797.5	659.4	(97.3)	872.2	3,717.9	15,385
1987	4,516	3,010.8	700.0	(112.6)	926.1	3,853.7	15,761
1988	4,874	3,238.2	747.1	(74.1)	962.6	4,016.9	16,305
1989	5,201	3,450.1	771.2	(46.1)	1,025.6	4,117.7	16,550
1990	5,524	3,742.6	802.6	(63.6)	1,042.9	4,199.2	16,797
1991	5,685	3,889.1	726.7	(30.7)	1,087.5	4,169.7	16,502

*These are GNP and not GDP data. When this book went to the printer, GDP data were available only as far back as 1959, so we decided to publish a complete GNP series.

ALTERNATIVE GNP MEASURES

The gross domestic/national product formulation discussed in Chapter 3 is the one most frequently reported and used. However, other GDP summaries are also provided by the BEA and used by analysts. This appendix presents the other measures and discusses how they are used.

GROSS DOMESTIC PURCHASES

The GDP data can be summarized in many different ways. A few years ago the BEA began to emphasize a version called gross domestic purchases, which highlights aggregate demand in the United States:

	1991
Gross domestic product	$5,672.6
Less: Exports	− 591.3
Plus: Imports	622.0
Equals: Gross domestic purchases	$5,703.3

Gross domestic purchases are purchases made in the United States, no matter where the goods are produced. By excluding exports, it eliminates those products produced in the United States for foreign consumption, and by including imports, it includes an important part of American domestic demand that is not being met by American firms.

FINAL-SALES GDP

In the regular GDP format an increase in inventories is added to GDP sales and an inventory decrease is subtracted from GDP. **Final-sales GDP** is the same as the GDP, but it excludes inventory changes. This alternative focuses on the demand in the marketplace as evidenced by sales. For example, if sales levels are falling and firms are increasing their inventories, the regular GDP would show a growing economy. In final-sales GDP, an increase in business inventories is deducted; thus, this account tends to show changes in the underlying aggregate demand.

	1991
Gross domestic product	$5,672.6
Less: Increase in business inventories (a decrease is added)	+18.5
Equals: Final sales GDP	$5,691.1

FINAL SALES TO DOMESTIC PURCHASERS

This alternative measure, final sales to domestic purchasers, is calculated as:

	1991
Gross domestic product	$5,672.6
Less: Exports of goods and services	−591.3
Plus: Imports of goods and services	622.0
Equals: Gross domestic purchasers	5,703.3
Less: Increase in business inventories (a decrease is added)	+18.5
Equals: Final sales to domestic purchasers	$5,721.8

This alternative GDP measures final sales in the United States regardless of where goods are produced. It is a combination of gross domestic purchases and final-sales GDP.

COMMAND GNP

Officially known as *command over goods and services, GNP basis*, this version of the GNP summary is commonly known as the **command GNP**. Despite the change to GDP in most reports, the command GNP is still reported on a GNP-basis. Its title reflects its purpose of showing the command over goods and services exercised by American residents and correcting certain distortions that can appear in the real GNP. The command GNP was formulated after economists became aware of an anomaly in the GNP data caused by the sudden and drastic increase in the price of imported oil during 1973–74. Although calculation of the current value of GNP was not affected, the anomaly did produce some distortions in the calculation of the constant-dollar, or real, GNP, which are illustrated in the following example (see Table 7A.1). Assume that the base year is 1967 and current and constant dollar (1967 = 100) prices are the same in that year. Wheat exports, priced at $3 per bushel numbered 300 bushels, so the total value of wheat in 1967 was $900. Oil imports in 1967, priced at $3 per barrel, numbered 200 barrels, so the total value of imports was $600. Since the international trade sector of the GNP is exports minus imports, the GNP's foreign trade sector in 1967 had a surplus of $300. In 1967,

Americans could purchase (import) a barrel of oil by exporting a bushel of wheat.

TABLE 7A.1
Hypothetical Export and Import Data
(base year = 1967)

	Wheat Exports	Oil Imports	Net Exports (Imports)
Current and Real GNP in 1967			
Price	$3	$3	
Quantity	300	200	
Value	$900	$600	$300
Current GNP in 1974			
Price	$3	$10	
Quantity	300	150	
Value	$900	$1,500	($600)
Real GNP in 1974			
Exports and Imports Valued in 1967 Prices			
Price	$3	$3	
Quantity	300	150	
Value	$900	$450	$450

In 1974, the price of wheat exports was unchanged, but the price of oil imports had increased to $10 per barrel. The current value of GNP in 1974 reflected that the trade surplus had turned into a trade deficit of − $600. "Current" 1974 data also showed that the terms of trade for Americans had deteriorated. Americans could no longer get one barrel of oil by exporting one bushel of wheat. They now had to export 3.3 bushels ($10/$3) of wheat to get one barrel of oil. In other words, Americans had lost command over some goods and services. They had to export much more wheat to get the same quantity of oil.

The current GNP for 1974 gave us correct information about the changing realities of the world. However, the real GNP for 1974, which is stated in 1967 prices, told a different — and incorrect — story. Because the oil price increase of 1973–74 was not reflected in 1967 prices, it appeared that net real exports had actually increased from $300 to $450 and that therefore the real GNP had also increased. The higher value of real GNP suggested that Americans had a "command" over a larger quantity of goods and services than, in reality, they had. Higher import prices in 1974 actually meant that Americans had fewer goods available. The appearance that they had more was due to the technique of separately deflating exports and imports by prices that existed in an earlier year when import prices were lower.

In order to correct the distortions produced in the real GNP, the BEA introduced the command GNP. The command GNP corrects such problems by changing the deflation procedure of net exports. Instead of deflating exports and imports separately and then subtracting the deflated (constant $) imports from the deflated (constant $) exports to obtain net exports, command GNP deflates only net exports in a single step. The deflator is the implicit price deflator (1974 price/1967 price) for imports. Thus, in the preceding example, the $600 current-dollar deficit would be deflated by a price index of 333.33 ($10/$3), which would produce constant-, or real, dollar net exports of − $180.

Command GNP for 1991 is obtained by first subtracting the net exports based on the conventional real GNP and then adding back in the command-basis net exports, which have been deflated by the implicit price deflator for imports. In this year, net exports were decreased, and thus real GNP increased, by $10 billion. The following illustrates command-basis real GNP:

	1991 (billions of 1987 $)
Gross national product	$4,860.2
Less: Exports of goods and services and receipts of factor income from the rest of the world	− 652.3
Plus: Command-basis exports of goods and services and receipts of factor income	646.2
Equals: Command-basis gross national product	4,854.1

ADJUSTMENTS TO GDP ACCOUNTS

CAPITAL CONSUMPTION ADJUSTMENT (CCADJ)

The following discussion on capital consumption adjustments, abbreviated as CCAdj, is intended for those who are seriously interested in NIPA accounting or in economic/accounting theory. First, it's necessary to understand clearly the difference between capital consumption *allowances* and capital consumption *adjustments*. **Capital consumption allowances** are the deductions GDP accountants make for physical depreciation — wear and tear on the country's capital stock. **Capital consumption adjustments** are alterations or modifications made to capital consumption allowances to correct for various problems in collecting depreciation data.

The cause of many problems in national income accounting is that the generally accepted accounting principles (GAAP) used in business and tax accounting are not relevant for GDP accounting, or for social decision making. Tax laws often permit businesses to depreciate their structures and equipment more quickly than they are expected to depreciate in terms of real wear and tear. Thus, the GDP accountant is forced to alter the data obtained from business records and from tax records to reflect physical reality. Assume, for example, that there is no inflation and that the tax and accounting laws and regulations permit a $100 million office building with an expected life of 50 years to be depreciated in 10 years. Each year the company reports depreciation costs of $10 million, which lowers the company's profits each year by $10 million, and thus decreases the corporate income tax it has to pay. Although the accounting records say the annual depreciation cost is $10 million, the building is depreciating at a real rate of only $2 million per year. When a NIPA economist/accountant comes across this depreciation information, he will want the depreciation amount in the GDP account to reflect not the $10 million book depreciation reported by the corporation but the $2 million of actual physical depreciation. Hence, the GDP accountant makes a depreciation adjustment, which the BEA insists on calling a "capital consumption adjustment" (CCAdj), by decreasing reported depreciation, which the BEA insists on calling "capital consumption allowances," in the amount of $8 million. In other words, the GDP accountants make the following adjustments in the GDP accounts:

Capital consumption allowances	$10 million
Less: Capital consumption adjustment	− 8 million
Equals: Capital consumption allowances with CCAdj	$ 2 million

The story does not end with the capital consumption adjustment to capital consumption allowances, however. Because the corporation has also reported smaller profits based on inflated expenses due to accelerated depreciation, a positive CCAdj must also be made to profits:

Corporation profits	$100 million
Plus: Capital consumption adjustment	8 million
Equals: Corporation profits with CCAdj	$108 million

These CCAdj's to capital consumption allowances and to corporate profits do not affect total gross domestic product since they offset each other. However, they do affect net national and domestic product and national income because corporation profits are included in these two measurements. When tax laws are liberalized to permit more rapid depreciation, capital consumption adjustments to capital consumption allowances increase in a negative direction and capital consumption adjustments to profits increase in a positive direction. Yes, it makes sense. Read that long sentence again after looking at the accounting entries.

Another cause of capital consumption adjustments is the effect of inflation on the replacement cost of capital assets. The real cost of depreciation to an economy is the need to replace that machine or structure. If prices are stable, depreciation on the basis of historical cost will accurately reflect the cost of replacing the asset since the new asset will cost the same as the old asset. However, if there is inflation, replacement cost will be greater than original cost. In other words, depreciation based on original cost is insufficient to cover the costs of replacing the depreciating asset. Hence, when prices are increasing, an adjustment must be made to increase the depreciation allowance. If the building in the previous example is being depreciated at $2 million per year based on original cost but it is estimated that within 50 years the building will cost twice as much to replace, then annual depreciation should be $4 million instead of $2 million. The following capital consumption adjustment is made on the GDP books:

Capital consumption allowance	$2 million
Plus: Capital consumption adjustment	2 million
Equals: Capital consumption allowance with CCAdj	$4 million

In addition, because book depreciation of the $2 million reported by the corporation does not fully reflect the true depreciation, corporate profits must be reduced by $2 million since depreciation expenses have increased. Hence, the following adjustment is made to the assumed $100 million corporate profits reported in the GNP accounts:

Corporate profits	$100 million
Less: Capital consumption adjustment	− 2 million
Equals: Corporate profits with CCAdj	$ 98 million

Both the tax-incentive CCAdj and the inflation-adjusting CCAdj are made in the GDP accounts, but only the net capital consumption adjustment (CCAdj) is reported. If prices are stable and tax incentives for accelerated depreciation are provided, the capital consumption adjustment is likely to be a negative adjustment to capital consumption allowances and a positive adjustment to corporate profits. If tax incentives are constant but prices are rising rapidly, the capital consumption adjustment is likely to be positive for capital consumption allowances and negative for corporate profits.

INVENTORY VALUATION ADJUSTMENT (IVA)

The "change in business inventories" reported in the GDP accounts is supposed to reflect the physical increase or decrease in inventories, valued at prevailing prices. However, during inflationary periods, the prices of items in inventory go up, which means that the value of inventories goes up even if there is no change in the physical stock of inventory. The reported inventory values thus overstate the physical flow of output into inventories.

The effect of inflation on the value of inventories depends very much on the accounting system used by business firms. One inventory pricing system, called **LIFO** (Last In, First Out), assumes that the last item placed into inventory is the first item taken out when goods are sold. Thus, when inventory is taken, the prices applied to the remaining units are assumed to be the early prices. If all business firms utilized LIFO, the change in business inventories would not be greatly affected by inflation because inventories would be priced on earlier, uninflated prices. However, many firms use **FIFO** (First In, First Out), which assumes that the goods sold are early units (priced low) and those remaining are the last ones added to inventory. When the inventory is taken, those goods remaining are valued at the most recent purchase price and, thus, will be affected by inflation. When firms report the value of their FIFO inventories on various documents, including tax forms, and these values find their way into national income accounts, the inventory component will be overpriced. The purpose of the **inventory adjustment valuation (IVA)** is to adjust those FIFO-valued inventories. The Bureau of Economic Analysis adjusts for the inflationary effects of FIFO inventory valuation by adjusting all inventories to the LIFO method.

Assume a furniture company has 10,000 board feet (bf) of lumber in its inventory, which cost $1 per bf; total inventory value, therefore, is $10,000. If the price remains constant while the quantity of lumber in inventory rises to 11,000 bf next year, the company will report that its inventory has risen from $10,000 to $11,000. This report correctly represents an additional 1000 bf of lumber held in inventory. The BEA will rightly report the change in business inventories as $1000 because that $1000 represents the value of the goods and services that went into producing the 1000 bf of lumber.

Now assume that the country experiences rapid inflation and the price of lumber increases from $1 to $1.50 per board foot. Assume that the inventory at the end of the second year is 10,000 bf, which is the same as it was the first year. Hence, the physical quantity of the inventory has not changed. However, the FIFO method of inventory valuation will report that its inventory rose from $10,000 to $15,000. The FIFO (First In, First Out) method means that the units which are priced at the earlier, lower prices are the ones assumed to have been sold first. Hence, the units remaining in inventory are the ones that were purchased more recently at the higher prices. The FIFO inventory valuation method overstates the value of inventories and undervalues the cost of goods sold, increasing the book profits of the firm. If the BEA reported an increase in inventories of $5000, it would be misleading the reader because the physical inventories have not changed at all—only their monetary value. Hence, BEA uses the inventory valuation adjustment to deduct $5000 from the reported inventory value in the investment accounts.

In addition to having implications for the output side of the GDP accounts, the IVA also has implications for the income side. The overvaluation of inventory resulting from the FIFO method understates the cost of producing the goods, which, in turn, overstates the profits of the corporation. In the above example, the use of the FIFO method had produced "artificial" profits of $5000. The inventory valuation adjustment will reduce corporate profits by $5000. Thus, on the output side, the BEA would have an IVA of −$5000 to "change in business inventories" and, on the income side, it would also have an IVA of −$5000 to corporate profits. In this way, both corporate profits and business inventories are correctly adjusted for the overvaluation of inventory and understating of cost of goods sold.

Business inventories	$15,000
Less: Inventory valuation adjustment	− 5,000
Equals: Business inventories with IVA	$10,000
Corporate profits	$100,000
Less: Inventory valuation adjustment	− 5,000
Equals: Corporate profits with IVA	$ 95,000

CHAPTER 8

THE MONEY MARKET

The term *money market* trips off the tongue of financial novices in class-rooms, at cocktail parties, on golf courses, and in corporate conference rooms. Apart from those who are directly involved in trading in the money market, however, only a few people have a passable knowledge of what the money market does or the components that comprise it. To further complicate matters, the term meant something much different a few decades ago than it means today. At the beginning of the century "money market" was used in a very narrow sense to mean the market for call loans to securities dealers; commercial paper was added to the money market around the time of World War I. A few decades from now it will have a still different meaning.

Today, **money market** means the market for short-term credit instruments that are very liquid, relatively safe, and that offer relatively low yields. The term **very liquid** means that they can be converted into money quickly, easily, and with little chance of a loss. A common distinction is made between the money market and the capital market. The money market deals in securities of one year or less while the capital market deals in longer term securities. The major money market instruments are Treasury bills, commercial paper, repurchase agreements, certificates of deposit, bankers' acceptances, and federal funds. Generally, these money market instruments are issued by firms and institutions with the highest credit ratings. Maturities of some instruments extend beyond one year, but many span only a day or two and most extend fewer than 90 days.

Unlike the organized markets in stocks, bonds, and commodities, there is no specific location or building for the money market. The major participants, which include the large banks in New York City, consist of about three dozen government securities dealers, a dozen commercial paper dealers, a few banker's acceptance dealers, and money brokers. They are all "tied together" by telephones and computers, through which they buy and sell money market instruments. Money market rates are generally lower than the prime lending rates of the large banks, and they have few restrictions on them. Major demanders (users or borrowers) of money market funds are the U.S. Treasury, commercial banks, finance companies, and corporations. Major suppliers of funds are banks, state and local governments, domestic and foreign corporations, and individuals who purchase money market mutual funds and T-bills.

The largest participant on both sides of the market is the Federal Reserve Bank, which is almost always either buying or selling money market securities, primarily Treasury bills. The open market trading desk at the Federal Reserve Bank of New York, which carries out open market operations for the Fed, often buys or sells billions of dollars of Treasury bills in a single day. Unlike other participants, the Fed is not buying and selling securities to earn profits but to stabilize conditions in the money market or to achieve certain monetary policy objectives. The Fed also influences the money market through the interest rate (called the **discount rate**) it charges for its loans to banks and depository institutions and the restrictions it sets on these loans. The Federal Reserve, the Federal Reserve discount rate, and the federal funds rate are discussed in Chapter 6.

Although each money market instrument has its own niche and characteristics, all money market instruments are closely related. Hence, the interest rates on money market instruments tend to fluctuate closely together. When there is a "shock" to one submarket, the rates may diverge from one another — the spread becomes greater — but forces are quickly generated to bring the rates back together again. If, for example, there is a sudden increase in the supply of commercial paper, interest rates on commercial paper will increase and the spread between yields on commercial paper and yields on other money market instruments will increase. These relatively high yields on commercial paper will induce traders to shift funds from CDs and Treasury bills into commercial paper, thus increasing yields of the former and driving down the rates on commercial paper. This shifting of funds from other instruments into the instruments with higher yields (after adjusting for risk variations) is called **interest arbitrage**. Because the money market is large, and extremely efficient, and because the risks are relatively low, interest arbitrage works very efficiently in tying together the interest rates of the various instruments.

The money market is significant to the economy because it enables investors with excess funds to make them available quickly and efficiently to those who need temporary funds. The market is especially important to commercial banks because it enables them to make effective use of their funds, knowing that they can borrow quickly and relatively cheaply if they need to do so. Also, the money market has a vital role to play in distributing the reserves provided by the Federal Reserve system to banks and financial institutions around the country.

Security Prices and Interest Rates

There are four important characteristics of short-term securities (original maturities of one year or less) that all readers should understand. The first is that short-term securities, generally called **bills** or **paper**, do not pay an explicit interest rate. Their "interest" is the difference between the price that an investor pays for the bill and the price that he sells it for. The stated face, par, or maturity value (all mean the same thing) of a short-term security such as a T-bill is the value for which the security will be redeemed. This stated value will not change during the life of the security. Market value is the current market price of the security, and it will change many times each day. If a security with a par value of $1000 maturing one year from today is selling for $900, the market interest rate is 11.1 percent. The investor will receive $100 for giving up $900 for one year; thus, $100/$900 is 11.1 percent. The bill buyer does not have to hold the bill until maturity because he can sell the bill in the secondary market at any time. If the market interest rate remains unchanged at 11.1 percent and the investor sold this bill after six months, he should receive about $947 for it. The closer to maturity, the higher the market price of the bill.

The second characteristic of short-term securities (as well as long-term securities) is that their interest rates are inversely related to their market prices. When the market prices of bills increase, interest rates decrease; when market interest rates decrease, the market prices of bills increase. If this morning's market rate of interest is 11.1 percent, the market price of a one-year bill, as shown in the above paragraph, will be $900. Assume that interest rates in the afternoon decrease to 5 percent. The market price of the one-year bill will have increased to $952.40 because only at this price is the market rate equal to 5 percent:

$$\frac{\$1,000 - \$952.40 = \$47.60}{\$952.40} = 5.0\%$$

Saying that market rates are now 5 percent is equivalent to saying that the price of a bill with one year to maturity is $952.40.

If market interest rates are 11.1 percent in the morning and increase to 15 percent in the afternoon, the price of the one-year bill will fall to $869.60:

$$\frac{\$1,000 - \$869.60 = \$130.40}{\$869.60} = 15\%$$

The market interest rate can be 15 percent only if the price of a one-year bill with maturity value of $1000 is $869.60. The important principle to be learned from this section is that security market prices are inversely related to market interest rates. If interest rates decrease, market prices of bills and bonds increase; if interest rates increase, bill prices will decrease. This inverse relationship between security prices is not some obscure theory that we will never confront in the real world; it is a mathematical necessity that is revealed every time interest rates wiggle even a little bit.

The third characteristic, closely associated with the previous one, is that the longer the time left to maturity, the greater the percentage change in the market prices of the security. For example, when market interest rates decreased from 10 percent to 5 percent, the market price of the one-year Treasury bill changed from $900 to $952.40, an increase of only 6 percent. Assume that instead of a one-year Treasury bill, we are holding a newly purchased zero-coupon Treasury bond that has 30 years left to its maturity date. A zero-coupon bond is similar to a Treasury bill in that it does not pay an explicit interest rate and its interest is obtained from the difference between the buying price and the selling price (or the maturity value). At an interest rate of 10 percent, a 30-year, $1000 par zero-coupon bond will sell for $57.31; if interest rates should decrease to 5 percent, the market price of this bond will increase to $231.38, which is more than a 400 percent increase. If an investor had bought the long-term bond for $231.38 when interest rates were 5 percent and then had to sell the bill the following day, when rates were 10 percent, the investor would receive only $57.31 for the bill and he would suffer a loss of 75 percent. Perhaps the reader can now understand one of the reasons why savings and loans, holding many long-term mortgages, suffered such large capital losses in the early 1980s when interest rates went up. Higher interest rates meant sharply lower security values and significant losses were incurred when S&Ls were forced to sell their mortgages because they were losing deposits.

The fourth characteristic is that the prices of short-term securities are often quoted by their discount rates as well as by the amount per $100 of face value. For example, assume that the reported price for a 91-day T-bill is $98.325. This is the price of the bill per $100 of face value, so if the face value (also called maturity value) of the T-bill is $10,000, the market price of the bill is $9832.50. Another way of quoting the price of the T-bill is to say that it is selling at a discount of 6.6 percent. This discount, also called the *T-bill discount rate*, is calculated as:

$$\frac{\$100 - \$98.325}{\$100} \times \frac{360}{91} = 0.06626 = 6.6\%$$

The T-bill discount rate of 6.626 percent is equivalent to a price of $98.325 per $100 of face value. Prices are quoted and converted from dollar prices to discounts and from discounts to dollar prices, so the reader needs to be familiar with the methods of calculating both. Given the discount or bill rate, the price of a T-bill in dollars per $100 of face value is:

$$100 - [\text{discount rate} \times \left(\frac{\text{days to maturity}}{360}\right) \times 100]$$

In our example,

$$100 - [0.06626 \times \left(\frac{91}{360}\right) \times 100] = 98.325$$

The discount yield shown above is widely used in the bill market, but it is not the true or effective rate (technically called the yield to maturity). The effective rate, or yield to maturity on the T-bill in the example, is calculated as follows:

$$\frac{100 - 98.325}{98.325} \times \frac{365}{91} = .06833 = 6.83\%$$

The T-bill discount rate always understates the effective yield. The difference between the effective yield and the discount yield is greater the longer the time to maturity and the higher the interest rate.

Name: Banker's Acceptances
Alternative name: Bills of Exchange
Agency/Institution: Released by various parties, but the Federal Reserve release is considered the official one.
Address: Publications Services, Federal Reserve System, Washington, DC 20551
Telephone number for data and inquiries: Call the Federal Reserve, 202-452-3244, and you will be referred to the currently correct number.
Sources: *Selected Interest Rates*, H.15 Statistical Release (Board of Governors of the Federal Reserve System; weekly); *Federal Reserve Bulletin* (monthly); *Survey of Current Business*
When available: On Monday for the previous week
Revisions: None

■ **A QUICK LOOK: Banker's Acceptances**

Banker's acceptances (BAs) are a component of the money market and an important part of international finance. A sharp increase in the quantity of banker's acceptances often indicates an increase in either imports or exports or in both, especially those made by small companies. Examples of rates on banker's acceptances are as follows:

	1987	1988	1989	1990	1991
3-months	6.75	7.56	8.87	7.93	5.71

These rates are averages of the closing asked or offered rates (the rates at which they will sell) for all trading days during the year. The rates shown are only for the top-rated banks and may not be representative of all banker's acceptance rates, especially those offered by small local banks. Newspapers generally quote bid and asked rates.

■ A CLOSER LOOK: Banker's Acceptances

Banker's acceptances are part of a broad class of credit instruments known as bills of exchange. *Bills of exchange* are orders to pay a specified amount at a specified time drawn on individuals, firms, or financial institutions. When the person on whom the draft is drawn (called the *drawee*) writes or stamps "Accepted" on the face of the draft, it becomes an acceptance. When the drawee is a bank and it accepts the draft, it becomes a banker's acceptance. When accepted by a firm or individual, it is a trade acceptance.[1]

A banker's acceptance is similar to a check drawn on the bank that is payable on some date in the future. The fact that it is payable in the future makes it a draft. If a holder of the draft presents it to the bank before the due date, the holder will receive less than the face amount of the draft. This is merely another form of discounting a note before its due date. When the draft is presented to the bank for early payment, the bank has two options. It can keep the draft until maturity, or it can guarantee it (stamp "Accepted" on it) and then sell it in the secondary market for a slightly higher price than it paid for it.

Like Treasury bills, banker's acceptances trade on a bid and asked yield basis, as explained earlier. Banks often accept drafts under letters of credit that enable the bank's customers to obtain credit for goods and

---

[1]Bills of exchange, which date back to colonial times, are among the oldest form of credit instruments. When a buyer did not have immediate funds to pay for goods sold to him, he would ask the seller to write a bill of exchange. The seller would draft a note instructing the buyer to pay the seller a specified sum of money on a particular day. The buyer would acknowledge the validity of the note by putting his name, or mark, on the note. Bills of exchange were widely used in the United States, but national banks could not accept time drafts prior to 1913, when the Federal Reserve Act was passed. Between 1913 and 1930, the Federal Reserve not only permitted banks to accept banker's acceptances but encouraged them to do so by buying (rediscounting) them from the banks. Before 1913, much of international trade was financed by banker's acceptances issued by London banks.

services they are purchasing. Today, most banker's acceptances are used to finance foreign trade. Some of the larger daily newspapers publish quotes on banker's acceptances:

Banker's Acceptances:
60–90 days, 7¼ bid; 7 offered

This quote means that the dealer will buy BAs at a discount of 7.25 percent and will sell them at 7 percent. Note that these rates are annualized simple discount rates and are not yields to maturity. The respective price of these bonds are determined in the same way as Treasury bill prices are determined. The following example converts bid and asked prices to dollar prices assuming an 80-day note:

Bid price: $100 - [0.0725 \times (80/360) \times 100] = \$98.39$

Offered price: $100 - [0.07 \times (80/360) \times 100] = \$98.44$

YTM: $[(100 - 98.44)/98.44] \times (365/80) = 7.23\%$

Unlike quotations given for Treasury bills, the BA quotes do not give the YTMs (yields to maturity) so they must be calculated or looked up in a bond table.

The best way to understand banker's acceptances is to work through an example. Assume that ABC Imports, an American company, wants to purchase machine tools from Deutsche Exports, a German company. Because of the long distance involved, the different legal and monetary systems of their respective countries, and infrequent commercial relationships, both companies are hesitant about the transaction. ABC wants to make certain that it does not pay for tools it does not receive in working order, and Deutsch Exports wants to ensure that it does not ship tools for which it will not be paid. This is when the banker's acceptance is very useful. ABC Imports asks its bank, the Fifth National Bank (FNB), in the United States to draw up a letter of credit authorizing Deutsch Exports to draw a time draft upon FNB (requires FNB to redeem the note at some specific date in the future) for the amount of the goods plus interest. Upon receiving the letter of credit, Deutsch Exports goes to its bank, Frankfurt Bank, which helps it draw up the draft and the goods are shipped. Deutsch Exports takes the shipping bill of lading (similar to a title to the goods) and the draft to the Frankfort Bank, which sends the draft and the bill of lading to the Fifth National Bank. Deutsch Exports or its bank could hold the banker's acceptance, but the usual practice is for the exporter to discount (sell) the draft to its bank, which, in turn, will discount the draft with the importer's bank.

When FNB receives the draft, it can either hold it or officially accept it by stamping "Accepted" on its face. Because FNB had been expecting the draft, it stamps "Accepted," which means that it assumes the liability to pay the draft when it matures. A banker's acceptance has now been created. Most likely FNB will pay the Frankfurt bank and give the bill of lading to ABC Imports, which can now go to the docks and claim the goods. However, FNB will obtain in return a trust receipt that obligates the importer to deposit the proceeds from the sale to the FNB in time to pay off the draft.

The bank earns a commission charge for issuing the letter of credit, and it earns the difference between the purchase price (the amount paid to Frankfurt Bank) and the maturity value of the acceptance. In effect, when FNB accepted the draft and paid Frankfurt Bank, it made a loan to ABC Imports. If it sells the acceptance in the secondary market, it has made its commission on the letter of credit, a small fee for the draft, and a small amount on the difference in the price it paid for the draft and the price it sold it for. If FNB sells the acceptance in the secondary market, it is responsible for paying off the banker's acceptance on the maturity date. Unless other arrangements have been made, it will ask ABC Imports to pay the bank for making the letter of credit and accepting the bank draft. Banker's acceptances are considered to be an extremely safe form of investment because they are an irrevocable primary obligation of the accepting bank.

Why do two firms go through such an indirect method of paying for goods? Why, for example, doesn't Deutsch Exports simply tell ABC Exports it has to send a check for the goods before they will be shipped? First, ABC Exports might not trust Deutsch Exports to actually send the goods. Second, it would take about two weeks for the check to clear from Germany and it would take another few weeks to ship the goods. Furthermore, if Deutsch Exports relied on ABC Imports to pay after receiving the goods, it would run the risk of not getting paid. Hence, Deutsch Exports and its bank want to have some assurance that they will get paid. They know relatively little about ABC Imports and are unwilling to extend credit to it. They are, though, willing to trust a large bank, say Citi-Bank, in New York. Essentially what the letter of credit and the banker's acceptance have done is substitute the well-known credit reputation of the FNB (or CitiBank) for the unknown reputation of ABC Imports. After receiving the letter of credit from FNB, Deutsch Exports and its bank can draw the draft with the confidence that it will be accepted and paid by FNB.

Maturities on banker's acceptances range from 30 to 180 days. The rates on banker's acceptances are usually a bit above the Treasury bill rate and just slightly below the rates on commercial paper. About 15 dealers trade in banker's acceptances and "make" the secondary market. About one-fifth of banker's acceptances are held by the accepting banks and most of the rest are held by other banks, corporations, federal agencies, and mutual funds. The rate published for banker's acceptances is the rate of the most representative dealer's closing offered rates for top-rated banks. The Fed says the most representative rate may be, but need not be, the average of the rates quoted by dealers. The reported yields or rates are quoted on a bank discount basis rather than on a yield-to-maturity basis, which would be higher.

Name: Certificates of Deposit
Alternative name: CDs
Agency/Institution: Federal Reserve System
Address: Publications Services, Federal Reserve System, Washington, DC 20551
Telephone number for data and inquiries: Call the Federal Reserve, 202-452-3244, and you will be referred to the currently correct number.
Sources: H.15 Statistical Release (Federal Reserve; weekly) and *Federal Reserve Bulletin* (monthly)
Revisions: None, except for typographical errors

■ A QUICK LOOK: Certificates of Deposit

Large banks issue negotiable certificates of deposit, which can be sold in the secondary market through dealers who quote bid and asked rates for these certificates. The rates shown in the following table are averages of offered (selling) rates made by at least five dealers:

	1987	1988	1989	1990	Week Ending Nov. 29, 1991
1 month	6.75	7.59	9.11	8.15	4.82
3-month	6.87	7.73	9.09	8.15	4.86
6-month	7.01	7.91	9.08	8.17	4.83

■ A CLOSER LOOK: Certificates of Deposit

Certificates of deposit are issued by banks and thrift institutions (S&Ls, credit unions), and earn a specific rate of interest for a given time period ranging from 14 days to several years. They are insured for up to $100,000 by a federal agency and can be either negotiable or nonnegotiable. Nonnegotiable CDs are those issued by thrift institutions in small amounts and normally involve forfeiture of some interest if withdrawn early. Such certificates are not considered to be money market instruments because they cannot be transferred or traded in the secondary market. Negotiable CDs can be transferred to another person, and those issued by large and well-known banks with maturities ranging from 14 to 180 days (average is about 3 months) are widely traded in the secondary money market. Certificates of deposit pay both interest and principal at maturity, which is generally from 1 to 12 months.

There are several types of certificates of deposit: (1) domestic CDs, which are issued by domestic banks; (2) dollar-denominated CDs called *Eurodollar CDs* or, *Euro CDs*,[2] which are issued by banks located in foreign countries; (3) Yankee CDs, which are dollar-denominated certificates of deposit issued by a branch of a foreign bank located in the United States; and (4) thrift CDs, which are issued by savings and loan associations. Most negotiable CDs are issued in denominations greater than $100,000 and are evidenced by a piece of paper, or certificate, explaining the terms of the time deposit. The certificate specifies the amount of the deposit, the maturity date, the interest rate, and the method of calculating the interest rate. More than one-fifth of negotiable CDs are issued by large money center banks located in New York City; the rest are issued by about 200 regional banks.

A secondary market has been established consisting of about 25 dealers for CDs of $1 million or more. One factor affecting the CD market is the reserve requirement on all depository institutions, which the Federal Reserve has varied from time to time. Since January 17, 1991, the reserve requirement on CDs (called *nonpersonal time deposits*) has been zero.[3]

Interest rates on CDs are generally quoted on an interest-bearing basis, with the interest rate computed on the basis of a 360-day year. A $1 million, 90-day CD with an 8 percent annual interest rate would entitle the owner to the following amount at maturity: $1,000,000 \times [1 + (90/360 \times 0.08)] = \$1,020,000$.

Name: Commercial Paper
Alternative name: Prime Commercial Paper and Prime Paper
Agency/Institution: Division of Monetary Affairs, Federal Reserve
Address: Washington, DC 20551

---

[2]The foreign branches of U.S. banks dominate the Euro CD market, but non-U.S. banks, especially Japanese banks, are active in it. Euro CDs, which are centered in London, have maturities that range from 14 days to 5 years, but the shorter maturities are more popular.

[3]The effect of reserve requirements on CDs, or other deposit liabilities of banks and depository institutions, is to raise the cost of obtaining those funds. For example, if the reserve requirement is 3 percent, then only 97 cents of each dollar deposited is available for loans. If the bank's interest rate on CDs is 8 percent, it actually costs the bank $0.08/.97 = 0.0825$, which is 8.25 percent or an increase of 25 basis points. If a bank can obtain funds through some other money market instrument that does not require reserves, such as selling T-bills, at 8 percent it will have an incentive to switch from CDs.

Telephone number for data and inquiries: Call the Federal Reserve, 202-452-3244, and you will be referred to the currently correct number.

Sources: Many newspapers and other financial reports, *Federal Reserve Bulletin* (monthly), *Annual Statistical Digest* (Federal Reserve; annually), Moody's Bond Survey

Frequency: Monthly

When available: About a three-month lag

■ A QUICK LOOK: Commercial Paper

Commercial paper is unsecured short-term promissory notes issued by corporations and resold in the secondary market. The rates, which are averages of the rates during the week/year, are always annualized. Commercial paper rates are highly sensitive to changes in other money market rates. The following are examples of commercial paper rates:

	1987	1988	1989	1990	Week Ending Nov. 29, 1991
1-month	6.74	7.58	9.11	8.15	4.91
3-month	6.82	7.66	8.99	8.06	4.94
6-month	6.85	7.68	8.80	7.95	4.84

■ A CLOSER LOOK: Commercial Paper

Commercial paper is short-term unsecured promissory notes sold on a discount basis to institutional investors and corporations. Commercial paper is unsecured, which means that it has no associated collateral and the paper is backed only by the reputation of the issuer. Thus, commercial paper is generally sold by large corporations, including foreign and multinational firms, with high credit ratings. Commercial paper is sold to raise large sums of money quickly and for short periods of time. Finance companies, such as Beneficial Finance, sell commercial paper, also known as finance paper, to finance their consumer loans or as interim finance between the issuance of their long-term bonds. Nonfinancial companies use commercial paper to finance inventories, payrolls, and tax payments; bank-holding companies sell commercial paper to finance leasing, mortgage banking, and consumer finance. Investors in commercial paper include money center banks, pension funds, foundations, investment firms, state and local governments, and savings and loan associations.

Most commercial paper is sold in amounts of $100,000 or more, with the average size being greater than $3 million. The Securities and

Exchange Commission exempts from its complicated and expensive registration requirements all commercial paper with original maturities less than 271 days. Almost all commercial paper easily meets this requirement because the average original maturity is only 30 days. Large finance companies generally market their own paper directly to investors, whereas other companies utilize one or more of the half-dozen dealers who charge about a one-eighth percent commission.[4] Unlike T-bills and negotiable CDs, there is no secondary market for commercial paper because of its short-term maturities.

Commercial paper is rated by Moody's Investors Service, Standard & Poor's, and Fitch Investor Service. From the highest to the lowest, Moody's ratings are P-1, P-2, P-3; Standard & Poor's, A-1, A-2, A-3, and Fitch's, F-1, F2, F-3. The costs of issuing commercial paper include the fees paid to rating services,[5] backup lines of credit,[6] and fees to commercial banks to handle the paper work and collect the proceeds from the sale.

Name: Eurodollars, Eurodollar Market
Alternative names: Offshore markets, Eurocurrency market
Telephone number for data and inquiries: Call the Federal Reserve, 202-452-3244, and you will be referred to the currently correct number.
Sources: Eurodollar data are published in *World Financial Markets*, which is the monthly newsletter of the Morgan Guaranty Trust Company of New York; *Federal Reserve Bulletin*, and *Survey of Current Business*; also see *Euromoney*, a monthly publication
Frequency: Daily
When available: The following day

■ A QUICK LOOK: Eurodollar Rates

Eurodollar deposits are dollar-denominated deposits in banks located outside of the United States. Accordingly, it is difficult to determine rates on Eurodollar deposits since they are found in banks throughout the

---

[4]If a firm places $100 million in commercial paper, the dealer's commission will be $125,000.

[5]Annual fees for rating the commercial paper of one issuer range from about $10,000 to $50,000.

[6]Most issuers back up or insure their commercial paper with lines of credit established at banks that they can draw upon if necessary to pay off the paper. Between World War II and 1970, commercial paper was thought to be very safe. Only five defaults occurred during the entire decade of the 1960s. In 1970, however, Penn Central's default made investors very wary of commercial paper and rates increased; just as the commercial paper market was settling down, the defaults of some real estate investment trusts (REITs) and the failure of Franklin National Bank in 1974 once again made investors aware of the risks.

world. However, Eurodollar rates are very competitive, so the rates obtained from a few banks are likely to be indicative of the rates found throughout the world. The Eurodollar rate most frequently quoted in Europe is the London interbank rate (LIBOR), which is the arithmetic average of the offer rates quoted by six major banks in the London wholesale market — that is, the rate at which they lend to each other at a certain time in the morning. The LIBOR plus the appropriate spread (less than 1 percent to 2 percent) is the lending rate to borrowers of Eurodollars. The following are examples of Eurodollar deposits:

	1987	1988	1989	1990	Week Ending Nov. 29, 1991
3-month Eurodollar deposits	7.07	7.85	9.16	8.16	4.90

■ A CLOSER LOOK: Eurodollars

Eurodollars are deposit liabilities, denominated in U.S. dollars, of banks located outside the United States.[7] For example, if IBM had a deposit of $10 million (denominated in dollars and not in British pounds) in a London bank, it would own a Eurodollar deposit, or simply Eurodollars.[8] Surprisingly, the term *Eurodollars* can be credited to an action taken by the Soviets during the height of the cold war in the mid-fifties. Fearing a possible freeze of funds by American authorities and also, like good capitalists, not liking the low interest rates in the United States, the Soviet government moved its funds from New York to banks in Europe, including a dollar-denominated account in a Paris bank whose telex was Eur bank. It did not take long for the European financial community to begin calling these dollar-denominated deposits Eurodollars, and the name has stuck even though many Eurodollars are actually dollar deposits in Hong Kong, Japan, Singapore, or the Bahamas. A few months later, through a

---

[7]It is the location and not the ownership of the bank that determines whether a dollar-denominated deposit is a Eurodollar. A foreign-owned bank or a branch of an American bank can hold Eurodollar deposits if it is located outside the United States. A Eurocurrency is a deposit that is denominated in a particular currency and physically located outside the country that issues that currency. For example, Eurodollars are one type of Eurocurrency, a British pound deposit in a French bank or a deutsche mark deposit in an Italian bank are other examples of Eurocurrency.

[8]The Eurodollar market is a subset of the broader Eurocurrency market, which consists of banks that accept deposits and make loans in foreign currencies — for example, banks in Italy that accept deposits of French francs and banks in London that accept deposits and make loans in deutsche marks. This non-Eurodollar Eurocurrency market is expanding, but its major component is still Eurodollars, and the Eurodollar market is most relevant to American financial institutions.

bank located in London, the Soviets lent $800,000 to a London merchant, and the Eurodollar market, headquartered in London, was born. London banks, and then banks located in other European money centers, paid higher interest rates on Eurodollar deposits and charged lower interest rates on loans than banks located in the United States.

Slightly more than 1000 banks from more than 50 countries are active in the Eurodollar market. London is by far the largest and most active Eurodollar (offshore) banking center, followed by Luxembourg—yes, Luxembourg, which does not have a central bank and virtually no domestic capital market has almost as many Eurodollar deposits as London. Hong Kong, Singapore, Nassau, and other Caribbean islands have developed as offshore centers because of lenient tax laws and virtually no regulation.[9] Most of the approximately $2 trillion in Eurodollar deposits are in fixed-rate bank time deposits with maturities ranging from overnight to six months. Negotiable Eurodollar CDs are actively traded in a secondary market headquartered in London. Arbitrage keeps interest rates closely aligned between Eurodollar deposits and similar deposits at banks located in the United States. For example, the rate on three-month CDs in the United States and the rate on three-month Eurodollar deposits were very close between 1975 and 1990. Some of the fundamental characteristics of the Eurodollar market, also referred to as the offshore market, are: (1) most transactions are among banks, with nonbank participants dealing through a bank; (2) the transactions and the deposits are typically large, generally at least $1 million; (3) the market is largely unregulated, and many countries do not set reserve requirements on Eurodollars; (4) Eurodollar deposits are normally dated for 7 days, 30 days, 60 days, and 90 days, and seldom for longer than 90 days; and (5) the Eurodollar market obtains funds from all over the world and makes loans all over the world.

A number of factors have contributed to the tremendous growth in Eurodollar deposits. One was certainly the Federal Reserve's Regulation Q, which set maximum interest rates that banks in the United States could pay to their depositors. When interest rates increased in the later 1960s and 1970s, many investors put their funds in unregulated Eurodollar banks rather than in domestic banks, Also, many American banks opened up branches in London to sell Eurodollar CDs and then made the funds available to the home office in New York. In addition, most Eurodollar banks do not have to hold non–interest-bearing reserves against their Eurodollar deposits or pay insurance premiums for deposit insurance (required for most banks in the United States), and many countries have low tax rates on the deposits and the interest they generate. The Eurodollar market, or offshore market, is the monetary equivalent of

---

[9]Many workers of these offshore centers actually live and work in New York City, where they maintain the "books" of the financial centers of Nassau and Cayman Islands.

flags of convenience in the shipping business. The relative lack of regulation has enabled the banks to pay higher interest rates on deposits and charge lower rates for loans.[10]

One factor affecting the growth of the Eurodollar market has been the relative riskiness of dollars deposited in U.S. banks versus Eurodollars deposited in banks outside of the United States. Risk comparisons are very complicated, but they include at least the following variables. Although few banks in the world are less risky than large American banks, the citzenship of the depositor has to be considered when evaluating risk. For example, an American might easily conclude that there is less risk of a deposit in a bank located in the United States than in a bank located in a foreign country. A Mexican might also conclude that dollar-denominated deposits in the United States are safer than dollar deposits located in Mexico or Hong Kong. However, an Iranian or Iraqi might decide that a dollar deposit in a Hong Kong bank is far safer than a deposit in a bank located in the United States, where the deposit might be blocked by the U.S. government. Also, deposits in banks located in the United States are insured up to $100,000, whereas most dollar deposits in foreign countries are not insured. Federal Reserve support is available to the banking system in the United States, whereas foreign central banks are much less likely to support dollar-denominated accounts. Further, many banks in foreign countries are affiliated with well-known banks in the United States, but this does not mean that their risks are the same. Foreign governments can pass legislation or regulations affecting foreign affiliates of American banks, which could restrict conversion of principal, interest, or other conditions of the deposit. Also, the legal form of the affiliation might be crucial. A branch office of an American bank in a foreign country is more closely tied to the home office than is a subsidiary. A branch normally cannot fail unless the home bank also fails; however, a subsidiary can fail even though the home bank does not.

Name: Federally Sponsored Credit Agencies' Securities
Alternative names: Federal National Mortgage Association (FNMA), nicknamed Fanny Mae; Federal Home Loan Banks (FHLBs); Federal Home Loan Mortgage Corporation (Freddie Mac); Farm Credit Banks; Student Loan Marketing Association (Sallie Mae)
Agency/Institution: Division of Credit Agencies, Federal Reserve System
Address: Washington, DC 20551

---

[10]In addition to having lower lending rates, the Eurodollar market is not plagued with many of the restrictions American banks have placed on their loans. Consequently, we must be careful in comparing interest rates of the Eurodollar market and American banks. American banks, especially in periods of tight money, require interest-free compensating balances as high as 30 percent as well as promises from the borrowers to conduct future business with the bank.

Telephone number for data and inquiries: Call the Federal Reserve, 202-452-3244, and you will be referred to the currently correct number.
Sources: *Federal Reserve Bulletin* (monthly) and *Annual Statistical Digest* (Federal Reserve System)
Frequency: Data changes almost daily, but the only consistent and complete series is published in the *Federal Reserve Bulletin*.
When available: About a three-month lag in reporting

■ A QUICK LOOK: Federally Sponsored Credit Agencies' Securities

A number of government sponsored agencies occasionally issue short-term securities that are part of the money market. See a description and discussion of these agencies in the "Bond Market" section on page 209. The short-term obligations of the Farm Credit Banks, the Federal National Mortgage Association, and the Federal Home Loan Banks are widely traded in the secondary markets, and the bid and offered spreads are quite narrow. Although securities of the federally sponsored credit agencies are not obligations guaranteed by the U.S. government, they are subject to some of the same regulations as those governing U.S. Treasury securities. Consequently, investors tend to regard them as being as nearly riskless as Treasury securities, and their rates are very close to T-bill rates. The Federal Reserve also buys and sells these securities in open market operations and accepts them as collateral for borrowing at the discount window. Except for the Fannie Mae issues, the securities of federally sponsored agencies are exempt from state and local income taxes.

Name: Money Market Mutual Funds (MMF)
Alternative name: Short-term Investment Pooling Arrangements (STIPs)
Agency/Institution: Federal Reserve, Standard & Poor's, and others
Telephone number for data and inquiries: Call any stockbroker for quotes on specific mutual funds.
Sources: Daily newspapers and financial publications, *Federal Reserve Bulletin* (monthly), *Annual Statistical Digest* (Federal Reserve System), *Lipper Mutual Fund Profiles* (quarterly)

■ A QUICK LOOK: Money Market Mutual Funds

Money market mutual funds began in the early 1970s when Regulation Q still limited the interest rate that banks and depository institutions could pay on deposits. MMFs are simply a pool of funds invested in money market instruments such as those described in this section. MMFs are administered by brokerage houses and banks to attract deposits and brokerage business. They enable small investors to obtain relatively high rates from money market instruments; MMFs are frequently viewed as alternatives to deposits in depository institutions. Since the yields that investors can earn on MMFs have never been regulated, they grew rapidly from their inception during the seventies when interest rates soared but depository rates were regulated. The MMFs easily survived the removal of Regulation Q, and they are now widely used by brokerage firms as the key vehicle in "cash management accounts." Most funds have a checking option that enables members to obtain cash easily and quickly, although there might be some limitations on the number of checks that can be written. MMFs do not have redemption penalties and sales charges because expenses are deducted each day from the gross income. Some MMFs are called "tax-exempts" because they purchase only the securities of state and local governments, which pay interest that is exempt from federal income taxes.

Name: Repurchase Agreements
Alternative name: RPs
Agency/Institution: Federal Reserve System
Address: Washington, DC 20551
Telephone number for data and inquiries: Call the Federal Reserve, 202-452-3244, and you will be referred to the currently correct number.
Sources: *Federal Reserve Bulletin* (monthly) and *Annual Statistical Digest* (Federal Reserve System)
Frequency: Daily
When available: Next day
Revisions: None

■ A QUICK LOOK: Repurchase Agreements

Repurchase agreements have existed for many decades, but they have become significant instruments in the money market only during the past two decades. A **repurchase agreement** is technically an agreement to sell a security—typically a U.S. government security—and to buy it back at some time in the future. It is really a means of providing collateral for loans. The borrower "sells" the securities and obtains the funds from the lender and then "buys" back the securities a day or two later, when the loan is repaid. A corporation with idle funds on Wednesday that will be used to fund a Friday payroll might arrange to purchase a government security from a bank with the agreement that the bank will repurchase the security two days later. Banks, securities dealers, corporations, state and local governments, and the Federal Reserve are major participants in the RP market.

RPs provide perfect collateral and enable the lender to earn interest on excess funds for a few days. Banks, which are not required to hold reserves against their RP borrowings, find them an excellent source of short-term funds. Most RP transactions are in amounts of $1 million or more, and the interest rate on RPs is very close to the federal funds rate, often a bit less because RP transactions are collateralized whereas federal funds are not. Most RPs are overnight transfers or on a special contract that continues until cancelled by either party. The term *reverse RP* (also called *matched-sale-purchase agreement*) is used to change the emphasis from the borrower (seller of RPs) to the lender (buyer of RPs). In a reverse RP transaction, the lender wants to buy a security to hold until maturity or to obtain securities to use in RPs.

Data on RP transactions are included in federal funds data found in the monthly *Federal Reserve Bulletin*. Interest rates on repurchase agreements are not published by the Federal Reserve.

Name: Treasury Bills and the Treasury Bill Rate
Alternative name: T-bills and T-bill Rate
Agency/Institution: Federal Reserve acting as agent for the U.S. Treasury
Telephone number for data and inquiries: Call the Federal Reserve, 202-452-3244, and you will be referred to the currently correct number.
Sources: The *Wall Street Journal* and major daily newspapers, *Federal Reserve Bulletin* (monthly), *Survey of Current Business* (monthly)
Frequency: Daily
Historic data: See below

■ A QUICK LOOK: U.S. Treasury Bills

The following are examples of U.S. Treasury bill rates in the auction (or primary) and the secondary markets:

	1987	1988	1989	1990	Week Ending Nov. 29, 1991
Auction Average					
3-month (91 days)	5.82	6.68	8.12	7.51	4.44
6-month (182 days)	6.05	6.92	8.04	7.47	4.50
1-year (364 days)	6.33	7.17	7.91	7.36	NA
Secondary Market					
3-month	5.78	6.67	8.11	7.50	4.39
6-month	6.03	6.91	8.03	7.46	4.45
1-year	6.33	7.13	7.92	7.35	4.50

Treasury bills: Short-term obligations of the Treasury that are generally sold with maturities of 91 days, 182 days, and 364 days.

Auction market: The primary market in which brand new Treasury bills are auctioned off to investors. The bills go to the investors who bid the highest prices (lowest interest rates) in the weekly auctions held by the Federal Reserve on behalf of the Treasury. The auction averages are the discount rates from 100 percent.

Secondary market: After Treasury bills are purchased in the auction, or primary, market, they may be sold in the secondary market. The rates in the secondary market are the closing bid rates (the rates at which the dealers will buy the bills) obtained from at least five dealers. All rates are discount rates from 100 percent. Many daily newspapers show the bid and asked rates.

■ A CLOSER LOOK: Treasury Bills

Treasury bills, which are short-term obligations of the United States government, are issued for 13 weeks (91 days), 26 weeks (182 days), and 52 weeks (364 days).[11] Treasury bills are issued in bearer form only, which means that the Treasury is not responsible if the bills are lost or stolen. Treasury bills do not pay an explicit interest. Interest is earned as the difference between the price paid for the bill and price received for the bill when sold or redeemed at maturity. Treasury bills are quoted on a discount basis, using a 360-day year and dividing by the par value of the bond. Interest earned on Treasury bills is not subject to state and local income taxes, so Treasury bill rates are always lower than alternative money market rates, which are taxable. For example, if the combined state and local income marginal income tax rate is 20 percent, the investor will be indifferent between a CD paying 8.0 percent and a T-bill paying 6.4 percent [$0.08 \times (1 - .20)$].

Treasury bills are attractive to investors because they are free of default risk; they are readily acceptable as financial assets in many state and federal regulations; they have a high degree of liquidity, which means they can be converted to cash quickly at low transaction costs; and they receive favorable tax treatment in state and local income taxes. The 91-day Treasury bills are the bellwether of short-term interest rates, and many financial institutions tie their own lending rates to it.

The Primary Market

Treasury bills are initially sold in what is known as the primary market. Here the Treasury auctions or sells off its T-bills to the public in minimum denominations of $10,000, with $5000 increments above $10,000. Gener-

---

[11]U.S. Treasury debt instruments with maturities of one to ten years are called *Treasury notes* and long-term Treasury debt instruments with maturities of ten years of greater are called *Treasury bonds*.

ally, the quantity of new three- and six-month Treasury bills that will be auctioned the following week is announced on Tuesday, and the auction is conducted on the following Monday, with delivery and payment on the following Thursday. The maturity dates will also be on a Thursday. Newspapers report the results of the Monday auction on the following Tuesday. One-year bills are auctioned every fourth Wednesday and are issued on the following Tuesday.

Bids can be made on a competitive or noncompetitive basis at the 12 Federal Reserve district banks located around the country. A competitive bid is one that includes the quantity of T-bills desired and the price the investor is willing to pay for each of them. A single investor may enter several bids by listing the various quantities he or she is willing to take at alternative prices. Generally, those making competitive bids are large institutions whose managers are in daily contact with the bills' market. Individual investors generally make noncompetitive bids by indicating the quantity of bills desired but not the price. They will pay the average price of the competitive bids that are submitted. All bids must be made at the Federal Reserve district banks before 1:30 P.M. (Eastern time) on the day of the auction.

The T-bills are first awarded to foreign official institutions, and then an amount necessary to fulfill all noncompetitive bids is set aside. The remainder is then allocated to those competitive bidders submitting the highest bids (lowest interest rates). The Treasury works its way down the price list from highest to lowest bidder until the amount available for competitive bids is awarded. The "stop-out price" is the lowest price, or highest yield, at which the bills are awarded. The average competitive price is then computed for the noncompetitive bids. Generally, about 10 to 25 percent of total sales is awarded to noncompetitive bidders. Information on the results of the primary sales in the weekly and monthly auctions is published in the *Wall Street Journal* and the financial sections of many newspapers. Results are also available in the *Federal Reserve Bulletin*, where the weekly and monthly average auction yields for 13-, 26-, and 52-week bills' averages are reported. The buyer of a T-bill does not receive a certificate; ownership is recorded on the computer at the buyer's bank and, in turn, is recorded on the computers at the Federal Reserve. This book entry system means that bills can trade without shifting pieces of paper. The Fed computer records every sale, and the bank acts as custodian for the owner.

The Secondary Market

Treasury bills cannot be cashed in prior to the maturity date. If the investor wishes to convert his bills to cash, he must sell them in the secondary market. The secondary market in Treasury bills, in which individuals and companies can buy and sell bills to bill dealers, is quite active. The major players in the secondary T-bill market are the Federal Reserve, which buys and sells T-bills in order to make adjustments in the monetary base, and government securities dealers and brokers. There are approximately three dozen dealers, who buy and sell securities for their own account and for trading with other dealers and their customers. Major customers of the dealers are banks, thrift institutions, pension funds, and insurance companies. In addition to T-bills, most dealers deal in other money market instruments and government and private securities.[12]

Dealers do not charge a commission for their services; they make profits by trading on a spread between their buying and selling prices. Spreads are very narrow for T-bills because they are activly traded and involve lower risks of loss than longer term securities. The dealers' buying and selling prices for T-bills are reported on the financial pages of most newspapers. A typical report for the trading day of July 5, 1990, is as follows:

Maturity	Bid	Asked	Bid Chg.	Yld.
May 09 '91	7.49	7.47	−.04	7.96

The maturity date is the date the bill will mature and be redeemed by the Treasury. Since the maturity date is longer than six months from the July 5, 1990, date, you know it was originally issued as a 52-week bill. On Treasury bills, the price is stated as the annualized percentage discount off the face value. The bid price is the price the dealer is willing to pay for the bill; the asked price is the price at which the dealer is willing to sell the security. In order to convert the discount "price" reported in the press into a price per $100 of face value, we have to know the number of days left to maturity. Since this newspaper account was for July 5, 1990, there are 308 days until the maturity date of May 9, 1991. Thus, the bid and asked prices are converted into dollar prices as follows:

$$100 - [\text{discount rate} \times (\text{days to maturity}/360) \times 100] = \text{bid price or ask price}$$

Thus,

$$100 - [0.0749 \times (308/360) \times 100] \qquad = \$93.592 \text{ (bid price)}$$

and

$$100 - [0.0747 \times (308/360) \times 100] \qquad = \$93.609 \text{ (asked price)}$$

---

[12]Some dealers in government securities are large banks that trade in a variety of government securities and money market instruments but are prohibited by the Banking Act of 1933 (Glass Steagall Act) from trading corporate equities and bonds. The Glass Steagall Act separated the activities of commercial banking from investment banking because it was widely believed that the numerous bank failures in the early 1930s were caused by banks speculating in stocks and private bonds.

The dealer is willing to sell a Treasury bill maturing in 308 days for $93.609, and he is willing to buy it for $93.592. The dealer's spread is 1.7 cents per $100 of par value. The bid change is the change in the bid rate from the previous business day. In the quote shown, "Yld." is the yield to maturity, which is 7.96 percent.

Another short-term Treasury security is the tax anticipation bills, generally referred to as TABs, which are designed to attract funds that corporations have set aside for their income tax payments. These bills mature seven days after the corporate quarterly income tax payment dates. Since corporations can turn in these bills at face value when their taxes are paid, they get an extra seven days' interest (a higher effective interest rate). If not used for taxes, they are redeemable at face value on the maturity date.

Since the late 1970s, futures contracts on T-bills have been traded just like futures contracts on wheat, corn, and other agricultural commodities. The value of the trading unit for 90-day T-bills is $1 million and for one-year bills, $250,000. The values of futures contracts closely follow money market interest rates, especially interest rates on T-bills in the secondary markets. Unlike the bills themselves, futures contracts on T-bills are not obligations of the U.S. Treasury.

Historic Data: Annualized Discount Rates on New Issues of 91-Day T-Bills, 1931–1991

1931	1.40%	1947	0.60%	1962	2.78%	1977	5.27%
1932	0.88	1948	1.04	1963	3.16	1978	7.22
1933	0.52	1949	1.10	1964	3.55	1979	10.04
1934	0.26	1950	1.22	1965	3.95	1980	11.61
1935	0.14	1951	1.55	1966	4.88	1981	14.08
1936	0.14	1952	1.77	1967	4.33	1982	10.72
1937	0.45	1953	1.94	1968	5.34	1983	8.62
1938	0.05	1954	0.95	1969	6.69	1984	9.57
1939	0.02	1955	1.75	1970	6.44	1985	7.49
1940	0.01	1956	2.66	1971	4.34	1986	5.97
1941	0.10	1957	3.26	1972	4.07	1987	5.83
1942	0.33	1958	1.84	1973	7.03	1988	6.67
1943	0.37	1959	3.41	1974	7.87	1989	8.12
1944	0.38	1960	2.95	1975	5.82	1990	7.51
1945	0.38	1961	2.38	1976	5.00	1991	5.41
1946	0.38						

CHAPTER 9

FINANCIAL MARKETS AND INSTRUMENTS

I. THE STOCK MARKET

READ ME FIRST

When companies need funds to finance capital expansions, they issue (sell) stocks and bonds, often called *financial securities* or *instruments*. Some economists call the funds procured by the sale of these securities *financial capital*. Although the value of bonds outstanding far exceeds the value of stock, the average person hears more about the stock market than the bond market. Holders of **common stock** own an interest in the company and can vote for the company's directors and on certain other matters. They earn income from dividends and from the appreciation of the market value of their common stock. Holders of **preferred stock** are entitled to receive a fixed dividend each year, which must be paid before any dividends can be paid to common stockholders. Preferred stockholders cannot vote, and they normally cannot share in any profits of the firm which are greater than their fixed dividends. **Convertible preferred stock** enables its owners to exchange preferred stock for common stock within some specified period. **Participating preferred stock** permits the holder to receive preferred dividends plus the right to participate in certain additional earnings.

New issues of stocks or bonds are called *primary issues,* and the process of bringing them to the market generally involves an investment banker. Investment bankers do not make investments or accept deposits or make loans, as normal commercial banks do. The major role of investment bankers is to help corporations bring their bonds and stocks to market, purchase the bonds and stocks from issuing corporations, and then arrange sales to the public.[1] Investment bankers are often called *under-writers* because they guarantee that the issuing company will receive a certain amount for its new securities. Sometimes the investment bankers will not underwrite the issue but will assist in a private placement, which brings buyers together with issuers. For all but the smallest issues of stocks or bonds, investment bankers form groups of underwriters called *syndicates* in order to spread the risks of placing the large issues. Underwriting firms are compensated by the spread between the price they pay for the securities and the price at which they sell the securities to investors.

After the new shares of stock are issued and sold, they can be bought and sold in the secondary market, which comprises the organized exchanges and the over-the-counter markets. The most famous exchange is the New York Stock Exchange, also known as the Big Board, which traces its roots back to 1792, when stockbrokers met under a buttonwood tree just a few blocks from its present location at 11 Wall Street on Manhattan Island. The 1500 common stocks and 750 preferred stocks listed on the exchange represent about 80 percent of the market value of all stocks sold on U.S. exchanges. Other stock exchanges include the American Stock Exchange (Amex), Midwestern Stock Exchange, over-the-counter market, and various small regional exchanges.

About one-half of the total volume of shares traded in the United States are traded in the **over-the-counter (OTC) market**. The term "over the counter" originated in the early part of the century, when securities were sold from dealers' inventories and handed to the buyer over the counter. Now it means a method of trading other than on the organized exchanges. Basically, the OTC market is composed of thousands of brokers (some have memberships on the exchanges) and customers who communicate and trade with each other through computers, telephones, and telegraphs. The OTC is especially important for bond trading. The National Association of Securities Dealers regulates the OTC markets and publishes its Automated Quotations on stock trades, which have become known as the NASDAQ National Markets and the NASDAQ Bid & Asked quotations.

Stocks may be purchased with cash or with credit, but the amount of credit is limited by *margin requirements*, which refers to how much an investor can borrow to buy stocks. Although the Federal Reserve sets

---

[1]The major function of investment banks, such as Solomon Brothers; Goldman, Sachs; Drexel Burnham Lambert; and Morgan Stanley is to sell new issues of securities to the public. They also help arrange mergers and acquisitions. Since the 1930s, the investment and commercial (accepting deposits/making loans) functions of banks have been separated by law, and neither set of institutions is allowed to engage in the activities of the other. Recently, commercial banks have been trying to get congressional approval to engage in various underwriting activities.

minimum margin requirements, brokers are free to adopt higher require-ments.[2] If margin requirements are 60 percent and the investor wants to purchase stock with a market value of $10,000, he must put up 60 per-cent — or $6000 — of his own money. Using the stock as collateral, the buyer can borrow the remaining $4000.

The financial novice gathering data on the stock market is often over-whelmed by the terminology used by more experienced traders. The fol-lowing brief definitions are provided for those who want to understand some of the technical terms used by "Wall Streeters."

Bear/Bull: A "bear" is a trader who expects the market price to fall, whereas a "bull" is one who expects it to increase. Presumably the terms originated during the California gold rush, when the miners would place bets on the outcome of a fight between a bull and a bear that were chained together. The bear's best tactic was to get down as low as possible so that it could grab the bull with its teeth and claws. The bull's best tactic was to raise the bear up so it could pierce it with its sharp horns. When the miners went on to San Francisco and other cities and began hedging and speculating, they remembered the bear's low stance and the bull's high one.

Book value per share of common stock: The total value of assets of a corporation less the total value of its liabilities and less the value of its outstanding preferred stock divided by the number of common shares outstanding.

Calls/puts (see pages 258–262 for a complete discussion of puts and calls):   A *call* is an option to buy a specified number of shares (usually 100) of some stock at a given price within a specified period of time — that is, an option to "call in" shares for purchase. The option seller or writer is the person who receives a price (or premium) for selling an option. An options buyer is the party who pays a price (or premium) to induce the seller to write the option. The purchaser of a call expects the price of that stock to go up and pays for the privilege of getting the option to buy a stock at a specified price. A *put* is an option to sell a certain number of shares at a specified price within a certain time period — that is, an option to "put" shares to someone else. The purchaser of a put expects the price to go down so that he can buy these shares at a low price and sell them at the higher contract price. The exercise price is the predetermined price at which an option may be exercised. If an investor expects XYZ Company's stock to increase from $50 to $80 during the next six months,[3] he might purchase a six-month call of 100 shares for $500. If the price does go to $80 during the six-month period, the investor will make a profit of $2500 [($80 − $50) × (100) − $500)]. If the price does not go up, the investor will simply not exercise the call. The maximum risk to the investor is the $500 paid for the call.

Dividend yield: Dividends paid by the company during the past year divided by the closing price of the stock. Dividend yields are reported daily, monthly, and at year's end. Dividend yields are highest during periods of low stock prices. During

---

[2]Since the margin requirements began in 1934, they have varied from a low of 40 percent to a high of 100 percent. Since 1974, the margin requirement has been 50 percent.

[3]Puts and calls are bought and sold for periods lasting from 30 days to one year.

the years 1969 to 1991, Standard & Poor's 500 companies have had average dividend yields ranging from 2.7 percent (1972) to 5.4 percent (1981).

Earnings per share: The amount obtained by dividing the corporation's total income for some period (quarter, year) by the number of shares outstanding. This, along with the rate of return on common equity, is a good measure of the firm's profitability and an important determinant of the market value of the firm's common stock.

Price-earnings (P/E):   The current price of a share of stock divided by earnings per share for the last 12-month period. A company's stock that is selling for $50 in the stock market and that has a $5 earning per share has a P/E ratio of 10. Generally, P/E ratios range between 10 and 20; the higher the ratio, the lower the yield on the stock. A high P/E ratio generally indicates investor optimism about the future trend of the stock. Standard & Poor's publishes the *S&P's 500 Year End P/E Ratios*. During the 20-year period 1970–1990, it ranged from 8.0 in 1981 to a high of 18.4 in 1972, but it averaged about 12.2.

Rate of return on equity: The income of the corporation available for common stock (after deducting interest on debt and preferred dividends) divided by the book value of common stock.

Short sales: Sales of shares that are not owned by the investor. The stock is borrowed from a broker and then sold, with the hope that the stock can be purchased back at a lower price before the stocks have to be returned to the broker. When the short sales investor borrows stock, he has to pay cash equal to the minimum margin requirement. The short seller is said to be bearish because he expects/hopes the market will decrease. Short sales are risky because there is no limit to the increase in the price of the stock between the time the stock is sold short and the time that it has to be purchased to replenish the broker's portfolio. Assume that XYZ Company's stock is selling at $50 and the investor sells short 100 shares borrowed from the broker. The investor sells short with the expectation that he will purchase the stock at a lower price, say at $40. When the price hits $40 the investor buys the stock and pays back the broker. He has realized a profit of $10 per share, or $1000, less commission and interest. However, if the price rises to $60 instead of falling to $40, the investor loses $1000 plus interest and commission.

Short/long trader: A short trader is one who is in a "stock owing" position and hopes or expects the value of the stock to drop; a long trader is one who is in a "stock owning" position and hopes that the value of the stock will increase. A typical short trader has borrowed stock to sell and has to pay back the stock, whereas a long trader has purchased the stock and is holding it.

Stock right: The privilege granted to a stockholder to buy additional shares in a company. When a company issues new shares, the price of the stock will drop because of the additional supply. Thus, the company often gives current stockholders rights to buy additional stock at a price lower than the current market price. These rights can be sold to other investors as well as exercised.

Stock split: A stock split occurs when the company issues a certain number of shares per share of stock outstanding. A "2-for-1" split is very popular. That is, the holder of 10 shares will receive an additional 10 shares for a total of 20 shares. The primary purpose in issuing a stock split is to reduce the market price so that fewer wealthy investors can buy the stock in blocks of 100s.

Stock warrant: A company's promise to sell common stock at some future date at a stated price. Warrants are sometimes issued to company stockholders for terms from one to five years at prices that might exceed the current value of the stock. Warrants become valuable when the market value of the stock exceeds the stipulated price in the warrant. For example, if the warrant states that the holder may buy a share of XYZ Corporation for $20 and XYZ's stock is currently selling for $15, the warrant has no value. If XYZ's stock should increase to $30, however, the warrant's value increases to approximately $10.

10-K reports: The SEC requires companies that sell stock to file annual reports, which are called 10-K reports (10-Q reports are updated quarterly reports). About 12,000 companies file these reports each year. The 10-K is not a "fill-in-the-blank" form; rather, it is a set of answers to questions posed by the SEC. These 10-K reports are excellent sources of public information about a company. While some of the 10-K information will be in a company's annual report, much of it will not be. The information provided includes income statement, balance sheet, cash flows, description of products, markets, subsidiaries, foreign operations, management's summary of financial conditions, and lists of company directors, officers, major shareholders, insider owners, and so on.

These documents are not easy to obtain. The SEC has public reference rooms in its regional libraries, and many companies mail their 10-K reports to those who request them. Private companies, such as Disclosure, make microfiche, computer tape, CD-ROMs, and paper copies that are available by subscription. Perhaps the best way of gaining access to the 10-K files is to go to a major university library and use the CD-ROM discs to look up any company and print out its entire 10-K.

Name: Dow Jones Industrial Average (DJIA)
Alternative name: The Dow Jones
Telephone number for data: 212-976-4141 for latest recorded update
Sources: *Wall Street Journal* and most newspapers (daily), *Daily Stock Record* and the *Survey of Current Business* (monthly), *The Outlook* (Standard & Poor's; weekly)
Frequency: Every five minutes during market hours for those watching in brokers' offices or financial television channels.
Historic data: See below; for daily Dow Jones high/lows/closings since 1885, see *The Dow Jones Averages, 1885–1980*, edited by Phyllis Pierce (Homewood, IL: Dow Jones-Irwin, 1982)

■ **A QUICK LOOK: The Dow Jones Industrial Average**

The **Dow Jones Industrial Average (DJIA)** is the stock price indicator reported most frequently and the one watched most closely as a general measure of stock market movements. The following is a typical presentation of the DJIA:

Open	High	Low	Close	Chg
2901.49	2906.44	2863.61	2879.21	−32.42

The "Open" reflects the average of the 30 stocks on their opening sale; the highs and lows are averages of the individual highs and lows during the day. This means that the various stocks did not necessarily reach their highs and lows at the same time. In fact, since the "highs" and "lows" are merely the arithmetic sum of the highs and lows of the individual stocks,[4] the "High" and the "Low" reported by Dow Jones may never have happened at all. The "Close" represents the average at the closing time of the exchange and the "Chg." represents the change from the previous day's closing price. On the evening news the television announcer might interpret the above data as: "The Dow Jones was down today. It closed at 2879, off 32 points from yesterday." The common practice is to carry out the "average" to two decimal places, although this gives a spurious accuracy to the series. Some major newspapers and financial publications present the data in graphical form. The top of the solid vertical line represents the high and the bottom point of the line represents the low during the day/week/month/year. The nub, or dash, represents the closing price.

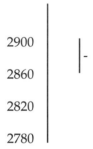

2900

2860

2820

2780

This graph shows the same information as that presented in the DJIA quote. The high was 2906; the low was 2863; and the close was 2879.

■ **A CLOSER LOOK: The Dow Jones Stock Average**

When the stock market was still in its infancy, back in 1884, Charles Henry Dow, first editor of the *Wall Street Journal*, began computing the arithmetic average of the closing prices of 11 stocks that he regarded as representative of the stock market. He published his averages in the "Customer Afternoon Letter" to investors; the letter evolved into the *Wall Street Journal* in 1889. In 1896, Dow published an industrial average consisting of 12 stocks, and he began daily publication of this average. The number of stocks in the index was expanded to 20 in 1916 and to 30 in 1928. That number of stocks, but not the composition, has remained constant

---

[4]The divisor in the Dow Jones average is not the number of stocks. See the "A Closer Look" section that follows.

since then. The 30 stocks (that's right!! only 30!!) that comprise the Dow Jones Industrial Average have changed from time to time, but as of March 1992 they were:

Allied Signal	Dupont	Minn M&M
Alcoa	Eastman Kodak	J.P. Morgan
American Express	Exxon	Philip Morris
AT&T	General Electric	Proctor & Gamble
Bethlehem Steel	General Motors	Sears Roebuck
Boeing	Goodyear	Texaco
Caterpillar	IBM	Union Carbide
Chevron	International Paper	United Technologies
Coca Cola	McDonald's	Westinghouse
Disney	Merck	Woolworth

Not only are there only 30 stocks in the Dow Jones Industrial Average, but many of the 30 firms are not even industrial: McDonald's, American Express, and Woolworth, for example. Furthermore, don't get confused about the name of the famous Dow Jones Index. There are four Dow Jones stock indexes — 30 Industrials, 20 Transportation, 15 Utilities, 65 Composite — and an Equity Market Index.[5] However, *the* Dow Jones Index, even if the TV announcer does not call it by its full title, is the Dow Jones Industrial Average. The others are seldom mentioned on general news broadcasts.

The closing DJIA in our example was 2879.21. Have you ever asked yourself what this figure really means? Surely it is not the average of the 30 stock prices because the average price of the stocks comprising the DJIA would be about $50. If it is not an average, you might think, perhaps it is an index of some sort. Many commentators, in fact, do call it an index. But if it is an index, why haven't we seen the notation of some base year (for example, 1928 = 100). The simple answer is that it is not an index but an average . . . of sorts.[6] The DJIA is a peculiar statistic calculated for the closing prices, as follows:

$$\text{DJIA} = \frac{\text{sum of 30 stocks}}{\text{DJIA divisor}} \quad \frac{\$1609.48}{0.559} = 2879.21$$

Every five minutes the Dow Jones computer sums the prices of the 30 industrial stocks and divides that sum by the DJIA divisor to obtain the

---

[5]The Dow Jones Equity Index is an index of the stock prices of approximately 700 companies that are listed on the NYSE and the American Stock Exchange, and OTC. The index is subdivided into 82 industry groups clustered in the broad sectors of the economy.

[6]Just for kicks, ask your stockbroker, your economics professor, or your friends if they know what that Dow Jones index reported on the news every night really means. If they don't know, buy a copy of this book and give it to them for Christmas.

Dow Jones Industrial Average. Your next question has got to be: How does Dow Jones obtain that divisor? That divisor is simply a way for Dow Jones to maintain compatibility in the series over time. The divisor changes when old firms are dropped and new firms are added and when stock splits or stock dividends are declared by companies in the Index. Suppose there are only three companies (A, B, C) on the DJIA list and their stock prices are, respectively, $20, $30, and $40. The DJIA is:

$$DJIA = \frac{\$90}{3} = \$30$$

This $30 is a simple average, or arithmetic mean, to statisticians. Now assume that company B stock is split 2-for-1. Owners of company B stock have the same wealth but double the number of shares. If the Dow Jones average were a simple average, its value would fall from $30 to $25. A's stock would be selling for $20, C's stock would be selling for $40, but B's split stock would send the price of B's stock to $15. Now $(20 + 15 + 40)/3 = \$25$. If the Dow Jones Company made no adjustment to the divisor, the Dow Jones Index would drop each time there was a stock split even though the investors would certainly be no worse off. Hence, if company B decides to split its stock, the DJ accountants will ask: What divisor will give us the same DJIA the moment after the split as existed the moment before the split? The answer is:

$$\frac{\$75}{2.5} = \$30 \qquad \text{2.5 becomes the new divisor!}$$

A more formal way of determining the new divisor is:

$$\text{New divisor} = \frac{\text{new total of stock prices}}{\text{old total of stock prices}} \times \text{old divisor}$$

In this case,

$$\text{New divisor} = \frac{\$75}{\$90} \times 3 = 2.5$$

Instead of dividing by 3 to get the average, the DJ accountants now divide by 2.5, and will continue to do so until some other change affects the divisor. If one or more of the other companies split their stock, the divisor will fall even further. The divisor is also changed when companies are dropped or added to the list. The significance of these changes can be seen by the extent of the divisor's decline. It has fallen from a value of 30 when the 30-company index was formulated in the 1920s to about one-half of one point (0.559) in 1992. In 1939, it was 15; in 1950, about 9.

The following are major criticisms of the DJIA: It includes very few stocks; it represents only large companies and is not a random sample of all companies; it represents only the companies on the New York Stock

Exchange; it does not adjust for stock dividends of less than 10 percent; it is not composed solely of industrial companies (Disney and McDonald's are included); and it gives more weight to higher priced stocks. Although the criticism that the DJIA consists of only 30 stocks that are not randomly selected is certainly valid, it is not as strong an argument as it might first appear. The reason is that these 30 stocks represent about 25 percent of the total value of all stocks on the New York Stock Exchange, and movements in the DJIA coincide fairly well with broader based measures of the stock market. Perhaps the major advantage of the Dow Jones Industrial Average is its age and continuity. It is the oldest price measure in the United States.[7]

Occasionally, investors compare the stock market, using the Dow Jones Industrial Average, with returns from other investments. This is like comparing apples and oranges since the Dow Jones averages do not include dividend payments. It would be somewhat similar to comparing the return from an apartment house to other returns by considering only the capital appreciation but not the rent.

HISTORIC DATA: Dow Jones Industrial Averages
(Average of monthly high and low closing prices)
1900–1991

1900	61.19	1920	90.10	1940	134.74	1960	618.04	1980	891.4
1901	69.60	1921	73.37	1941	121.82	1961	691.55	1981	932.9
1902	65.14	1922	92.98	1942	107.2	1962	639.76	1982	884.4
1903	55.71	1923	94.57	1943	134.81	1963	714.81	1983	1190.3
1904	54.19	1924	99.82	1944	143.22	1964	834.05	1984	1178.5
1905	79.47	1925	134.21	1945	169.82	1965	910.88	1985	1328.2
1906	93.88	1926	152.92	1946	191.65	1966	873.6	1986	1792.8
1907	76.16	1927	175.56	1947	177.58	1967	879.12	1987	2276.0
1908	74.65	1928	226.45	1948	179.95	1968	906.0	1988	2168.57
1909	92.23	1929	311.24	1949	179.48	1969	876.72	1989	2510.26
1910	84.88	1930	236.34	1950	216.31	1970	753.19	1990	2671.25
1911	82.26	1931	138.58	1951	257.64	1971	884.76	1991	2929.32
1912	88.34	1932	64.57	1952	270.76	1972	950.71		
1913	79.45	1933	83.73	1953	275.97	1973	923.88		
1914	75.00	1934	98.28	1954	333.94	1974	759.37		
1915	74.35	1935	120.0	1955	442.72	1975	802.5		
1916	94.79	1936	162.25	1956	493.01	1976	974.9		
1917	87.72	1937	166.36	1957	475.71	1977	894.6		
1918	81.06	1938	132.44	1958	491.66	1978	817.2		
1919	99.75	1939	142.66	1959	632.12	1979	844.4		

[7]There are price indexes, such as the producer price index, that go back further into history but these indexes were started in the first four decades of the 20th century and were "constructed" for the earlier years.

Name: Mutual Funds
Alternative name: Mutuals
Agency/Institution: Standard & Poor's, Stockbrokers, Federal Reserve
Telephone number for data and inquiries: Call any stockbroker for quotes on specific mutual funds. Some aggregate data are available from the Federal Reserve, 202-452-3244
Sources: Daily newspapers and financial publications, *Federal Reserve Bulletin*, *Lipper Mutual Fund Profiles* (quarterly), *Lipper Mutual Fund Indexes*
Revisions: None
Historic data: *Daily Stock Record*

■ A QUICK LOOK: Mutual Fund Prices

Mutual funds, sometimes called *open investment companies*, are a pool of funds from many investors that are invested in securities. There are approximately 600 stock and bond mutual funds and approximately 300 money market funds. The following are examples of mutual fund prices:

	NAV	Offer Price	NAV Chg
Fidelity Invest:			
HiYld	12.25	NL	. . .
BluCh	13.81	14.09	−.08
Oppenheimer Fd:			
Target	16.78	17.62	−.07
Tax Free	9.20	9.66	+.01

NAV: Net *asset value* per share — the total value of all the securities owned by the fund divided by the number of shares.

Offer price: The price per share with the sales charge added. If the fund is a no-load fund (NL), the price is the NAV.

NAV Chg: The change in the NAV from the previous trading day.

■ A CLOSER LOOK: Mutual Funds

Mutual funds are usually managed by investment firms that receive management fees each year equal to about 1 percent of the market value of the assets. Mutual funds sell their shares to the public and redeem them at the current net asset value (NAV) per share. The NAV per share is computed by dividing the total market value of all the mutual fund's holdings (less any liabilities) by the number of the fund's outstanding shares. Three types of income are generated by mutual funds: (1) interest on bond investments or dividends from common stock; (2) income from change in the fund's total market or net asset value caused by capital gains or losses on the stocks or bonds held by the mutual fund; and (3) capital gains disbursements paid to mutual fund shareholders.

If the funds charge a sales commission, they are called **load funds**. Funds that do not charge a commission are called **no-load funds**. Some funds charge no fees for purchases but charge a fee if investors sell their shares in fewer than five years. **Open-ended mutual funds** continuously issue new shares when investors want to invest in the fund, and it redeems shares when investors want to sell.[8] A **closed-end fund** issues only a fixed number of shares, which usually trade at some discount from the net asset value. Mutual funds specialize in bonds, money markets, income securities, and growth securities. Many companies, such as Fidelity, offer a wide range of mutual funds. Most funds offer reinvestment of income, but the IRS considers reinvested income as taxable income.

Money market mutual funds invest in short-term money market instruments, such as certificates of deposit, Treasury bills, and banker's acceptances with maturities less than 180 days. A number of mutual fund indexes track overall changes in the closing prices of selected mutual funds. See, for example, Lipper Mutual Fund Indexes and Investor's Daily Mutual Fund Index.

Name: New York Stock Exchange Composite Index
Alternative name: NYSE Index
Agency/Institution: New York Stock Exchange
Telephone number for data: 212-976-4141
Sources: *Wall Street Journal* and other newspapers (daily), *Survey of Current Business* (monthly), *Trend Line Daily Action Stock Charts* (weekly)
Frequency: Every 30 minutes
Historic data: See below and *Business Statistics, 1961–1988* (Bureau of Economic Analysis)

■ A QUICK LOOK: NYSE Composite Index

The **New York Stock Exchange Composite Index**, also known as the NYSE Index, includes all 1700 stocks listed on the New York Stock Exchange. Subindexes are provided for industrial, utility, transportation, and financial stocks. The following are sample NYSE indexes:

High	Low		Close	Net Chg	% Chg
201.13	168.88	Composite	176.39	−0.31	−0.18
252.24	210.55	Industrials	221.20	−0.21	−0.09
102.92	80.96	Utilities	82.79	−0.07	−0.08
209.76	134.31	Transportation	140.46	+0.17	+0.12
173.29	119.11	Finance	123.34	−1.10	−0.88

---

[8]For no-load funds, the buying or selling price is pegged at the fund's current net asset value.

This index reflects the total market value of every company listed on the New York Stock Exchange. Thus, like the S&P 500, it avoids the problems of adjusting for stock splits and stock dividends. The NYSE also has separate indexes for industrial, transportation, utility, and financial issues. These series, which were started in 1965, fulfill a particular niche. They are much broader than the 30-stock DJIA and, unlike the S&P 500, they include only stocks listed on the NYSE. The base of these indexes is December 31, 1965 = 50.

HISTORIC DATA
The New York Stock Exchange Composite Index
(Averages of daily closing index levels)
December 31, 1965 = 50

1970	50.23	1985	121.58
1975	47.64	1986	138.58
1980	77.86	1987	138.23
1981	71.11	1988	149.91
1982	81.03	1989	180.02
1983	95.18	1990	183.46
1984	96.38	1991	205.49

Name: Standard & Poor's 500 Composite
Alternative name: S&P 500
Agency/Institution: Standard and Poor's Corporation and others
Other series: Dow Jones Industrial Average; NYSE Composite Index
Telephone number for data: 212-208-8706 for a taped message
Sources: *Wall Street Journal* and most local newspapers (daily), *Survey of Current Business* (monthly)
Frequency: Each trading date
Historic data: See below.

■ **A QUICK LOOK: S&P 500**

The stock index most used by most professionals is *Standard & Poor's 500 Composite Index*. A sample index is given here, with explanations:

	High	Low	Close	Chg
Industrials	423.71	417.85	418.89	−4.82
Transportations	275.37	271.02	271.73	−3.64
Utilities	141.52	138.77	138.92	−2.60
Financials	28.91	28.42	28.51	−0.40
500 Stocks	360.16	354.86	355.68	−4.48

Components: The S&P 500 stocks are composed of the four categories listed in the table. Most newspapers list only the value of the "500" index while a few sources list the component indexes as well.

High/Low: The high and low values report the combined highs and lows of all component stocks during the trading day even though they did not occur at the same time. The S&P stock indexes are based on 1941–43 = 10. Yes, the base number for the index is 10 and not 100 as it is for most indexes.

Close: The index value of the closing values on last trades of all component stocks.

Chg: The change represents the difference between the closing value of the previous business day (Tuesday, July 3) and the closing price of the reporting day (July 5).

■ A CLOSER LOOK: S&P 500

Standard & Poor's published its first index consisting of 233 stocks in 1923. In 1957 the list was expanded to 500 stocks, and, since July 1976, the S&P 500 has been composed of 400 industrial companies, 40 public utilities, 20 transportation companies and 40 financial institutions.[9] Standard & Poor's has kept these numbers constant by replacing dropped stocks with ones from the same grouping. The selected firms may be large or small and many are listed on the American Stock Exchange and the over-the-counter-market as well as on the NYSE. Unlike the Dow Jones Industrial Averages, the S&P 500 is an index and not an average. The index is based on 1941–43 equals 10. Hence, the S&P 500 index in July 1990 was approximately 360, which meant that market value of stocks had increased 36 times (360/10) since 1941–43. The S&P 500 measures changes in the total values of the composite stocks rather than the prices of the stock. The number of shares of each stock is multiplied by the price per share to obtain the market value of each stock. Then the market values of all companies comprising the index are added and indexed to the market value in the base period. (See a discussion of indexes on pages 42–48 of Chapter 3.) By using an index of market values, Standard & Poor's avoids the problems of having to adjust for stock splits and stock dividends. About 80 percent of the total value of the stock listed on the NYSE are represented in the S&P 500 index.

Although the S&P 500 is not as popular among the general public as the Dow Jones Industrial Average, most economists believe it is more representative of the stock market and a much better index to use in following general movements in the stock market. It is the benchmark against which most money managers compare the performance of their portfolios. It is also one of the components of the Department of Commerce's Leading Economic Indicators. In 1983, Standard and Poor's introduced the S&P 100 index (1983 = 100), which is used for trading on the Chicago Board of Exchange's stock index options contract.

---

[9]Standard & Poor's also publishes industrial, financial, utility, and transportation subindexes.

HISTORIC DATA
Index of Common Stock Prices
Standard & Poor's Composite
Monthly Averages of Daily Indexes
1941–43 = 10

1900	6.15	1920	7.98	1940	11.02	1960	55.9	1980	118.8
1901	7.84	1921	6.86	1941	9.82	1961	66.3	1981	128.0
1902	8.42	1922	8.41	1942	8.67	1962	62.4	1982	119.7
1903	7.21	1923	8.57	1943	11.5	1963	69.9	1983	160.4
1904	7.05	1924	9.05	1944	12.47	1964	81.4	1984	160.5
1905	8.99	1925	11.15	1945	15.2	1965	88.2	1985	186.8
1906	9.64	1926	12.95	1946	17.1	1966	85.3	1986	236.3
1907	7.84	1927	15.34	1947	15.2	1967	91.9	1987	286.8
1908	7.78	1928	19.95	1948	15.5	1968	98.7	1988	265.8
1909	9.71	1929	26.02	1949	15.2	1969	97.8	1989	322.8
1910	9.35	1930	21.03	1950	18.4	1970	83.2	1990	334.6
1911	9.24	1931	13.66	1951	22.3	1971	98.3	1991	376.2
1912	9.53	1932	6.93	1952	24.5	1972	109.2		
1913	8.51	1933	8.98	1953	24.7	1973	107.4		
1914	8.08	1934	9.84	1954	29.7	1974	82.8		
1915	8.31	1935	10.6	1955	40.5	1975	85.2		
1916	9.47	1936	15.47	1956	46.6	1976	102.0		
1917	8.5	1937	15.41	1957	44.4	1977	98.2		
1918	7.54	1938	11.49	1958	46.2	1978	96.0		
1919	8.78	1939	12.06	1959	57.4	1979	103.0		

Name: Stock Market Quotes
Sources: *Wall Street Journal* (daily), most daily newspapers, *Standard & Poor's Industry Survey, Moody's, Value Line Investment Survey*, and other financial periodicals
Revisions: The data are not revised except for typographical errors.
Historic data: See below. An excellent source of daily quotes on the major exchanges is the *Daily Stock Price Record*. This three-part reference is published quarterly by Standard and Poor's (25 Broadway, New York 10004) for the New York Stock Exchange, American Stock Exchange, and the over-the-counter market. It lists the volume, high, low, and closing prices of all stocks for all trading days. Monthly averages are also given. It also contains the Dow-Jones averages and the S&P indexes. The *Daily Stock Record* began in 1962. See *Stock Values and Dividends for Tax Purposes* (Commerce Clearing House, Inc., 4025 W. Peterson, Chicago, Illinois) for year-end price and annual dividends.

■ A QUICK LOOK: Stock Market Quotes

The average small investor's acquaintance with the stock market is obtained primarily through the daily quotes of stock prices from the nation's stock exchanges that are given in newspapers and on television. The largest and most famous exchange is the New York Stock Exchange (NYSE); the second largest is the American Stock Exchange (Amex). There are also regional stock exchanges and over-the-counter exchanges. About 80 percent of the stocks listed on the NYSE are also listed on one or more of the other stock exchanges as well. The New York Stock Exchange Composite Transactions, printed in most daily newspapers, includes not only transactions in a stock traded on the NYSE but also those trades of NYSE-listed stocks made on several smaller regional exchanges across the country. (That is why they are called "composite" listings.)[10] The amount of information carried by different newspapers varies, but few publish more information than the following, which is a typical, but hypothetical, newspaper report of a quotation for a stock listed on one of the organized exchanges:

| 52 Weeks | | Stock | Div | Yld | PE Ratio | Sales 100's | High | Low | Close | Chg |
High	Low									
$26\frac{1}{4}$	18	XYZ	.70	3.4	15	1100	$22\frac{1}{8}$	19	$20\frac{3}{4}$	$-\frac{1}{2}$

High: The high price during the past 52 weeks was $26.25 per share.

Low: The low price during the past 52 weeks was $18 per share.

Stock: Name of the stock, sometimes followed by its ticker symbol.

Div: Current dividend for the year.

Yld: Yield, which shows the dividend as percentage of the closing share price — e.g., $0.70/20.75 = 3.4$ percent.

PE: Price-earnings ratio, which is the closing price of the stock divided by its earnings per share for the most recent four quarters.

Sales: Number of shares (in hundreds) traded on this day: 110,000 shares were traded on this day. When a "z" precedes the number, it means this is the actual number of shares traded — e.g., "z30" means 30 shares were traded.

High: The high price for the stock on this trading day was $22.125.

Low: The low price for this trading day was $19 per share.

Close: Price at the close of the trading day was $20.75 per share.

Chg: The change between the closing price on the previous day and the closing price today was $0.50 per share lower.

Symbols following the company's name:

pf: Indicates preferred stock. If "pf" is not shown, the stock is common stock.

wt: Indicates a warrant, which entitles the bearer to buy a share of stock at a specific price.

---

[10]The *Wall Street Journal* includes the word *composite* in its title of the NYSE quotes, whereas many other daily newspapers do not. However, all newspaper reports are reports on the composite transactions.

rt: Indicates a right to buy (generally at less than current market value) new securities in proportion to the number of shares already owned.

un: Indicates a unit share of stock that is sold in combination with another security.

wi: Indicates a conditional transaction in a security authorized for issuance but not actually issued.

The National Association of Securities Dealers (NASDAQ) reports on stocks traded in the over-the-counter (OTC) market, a regulated network of securities dealers linked by telephones and computers. The stocks of larger national companies, known as National Markets issues or Tier 1 OTC stocks, are quoted in basically the same way as the stock traded on the organized exchanges. However, the stocks of companies that are too small or regional to be listed on the National Markets table are shown in a separate section of the newspaper known as "NASDAQ Bid & Asked Quotations." These quotations differ in form from those of the NASDAQ National Markets issues and the stock traded on the exchanges. The following is an example of NASDAQ Bid & Asked Quotations:

Stock	Sales Div	100s	Bid	Asked	Chg
ZXY	.75	32	$12\frac{5}{8}$	$12\frac{3}{4}$	$+\frac{2}{8}$

Stock: Name of the stock.

Div: Annual dividend of 75 cents per share.

Sales: Sales in 100s. There were 3200 shares sold today. When a "z" precedes the number, it means this is the actual number of shares that traded. For example, "z40" means only 40 shares were traded.

Bid: Per-share price of $12.625 at which a dealer was willing to buy 100 shares at closing time.

Asked: Per-share price of $12.75 at which a dealer was willing to sell 100 shares at closing time.

Chg: Net change in bidding price from the previous day. Previous day's bidding price was $12\frac{3}{8}$.

II. THE BOND MARKET

READ ME FIRST

Several data sources referenced in this book show interest rates and financial data pertaining to debt securities. Unless the reader has some fundamental knowledge about bills, notes, bonds, interest rates, yields, discount rates, and other terms, however, the data will be essentially meaningless. The purpose of this section is to provide this fundamental knowledge. Further information is given in the "Closer Look" sections for each financial instrument.

Fixed-income securities such as bonds or bills can pay interest in one of two ways. Most long-term securities, such as bonds, pay interest to the bondholder periodically — for example, annually, semiannually, or quarterly — and are known as interest-bearing securities. Examples of such interest-bearing securities are U.S. Series H savings bonds and most bonds sold by corporations and the U.S. government. Most short-term securities, such as bills, do not pay explicit interest periodically. The holder of a bill (also known as the lender) receives his interest as the difference between what he pays for the bill when he buys it and what he receives when he sells or redeems it. These securities are known as non–interest-bearing securities or discount notes or bills. Examples are Treasury bills, commercial paper, and U.S. Series E savings bonds. The following terms are widely used in the bond and bill markets:

Basis point: A frequently used measure of interest rates on notes and bonds. A single basis point is equal to one-hundredth of one percentage point, so 50 basis points equals 0.005 (0.5 percent) and 100 basis points equals 1 percent. If the interest rate on a bond goes from 7.60 percent to 7.80, it has increased by 20 basis points.

Bill: A short-term obligation can take many forms, such as a Treasury bill, a bank draft, or banker's acceptance. Most bills have no stated interest rates.

Bond: A long-term obligation of a corporation or government that promises to pay a specific amount of interest over a fixed period of time and to repay the principal. Most bonds have stated interest rates called **coupon rates**.

Coupon rate: The annual interest divided by the par value of the bond.

Note: Securities with a medium term of maturity. Treasury notes have maturities of two to ten years.

Par value: The stated, face, or maturity value of the bond, which is generally printed on the face of the bond. The market price of the bond is seldom the actual price for which the bond is sold. Most are sold at a discount or premium.

Yield to maturity (YTM):   The effective or true yield of a security, which should be used for comparisons with the yields on all financial investments. The yield to maturity is that discount rate which makes the future interest payments plus the maturity value equal to the current price of the bond. The YTM will be lower than the current yield when the market price of the bond is above the par value and will be greater than the current yield when the market price of the bond is less than par value.

Assume that the following quote appears in the bond section of the newspaper:

Bonds	Cur Yld	Vol	High	Low	Close	Net Chg
ABC 8½ 95	8.63	55	99	98¾	98½	−1

The name of the company is ABC; 8½ is the coupon rate for the bond, which means that the holder of this $10,000 bond will receive $850 in interest each year. The coupon rate is always the annual interest divided by the par value of the bond. The 95 means the bond will mature in 1995. The current yield is 8.63 percent, the volume sold is 55. The next three figures refer to the price of the bond that day. Bond prices are quoted in percentages of par value or dollars per $100 of par value. The par value is the stated, face, or maturity value of the bond. The par value is not stated here but it most likely is $1000, $10,000, or $100,000. The closing price of the bond on this trading day was 98½, which is the price per $100 of par value. This means that a $1000 bond would sell for $985 and a $10,000 bond would sell for $9850. If the bond price is quoted at 105⅛, it means that a $10,000 bond is selling at $10,512.50. A bond will sell below par value (at a discount) if the market interest rate is above the bond's coupon rate and the bond price will be above its par value (at a premium) if the market interest rate is below the bond's coupon rate. Most bills and almost all tax-exempt bonds are quoted on a yield basis rather than in percentage of par terms. Thus, we might hear about a 90-day Treasury bill selling at 7.3 percent, or a State of Wisconsin bond selling at 6.5 percent. The percentages are annualized discounts from the maturity value which will be explained later.

The **current yield** on a bond is determined by dividing the interest by the current price of the bond — in our example, the current yield of a $10,000 par value bond is: $850/$9850 = 8.63 percent. The current yield is easy to calculate and widely used in the financial world. However, it does not give the true or effective yield, which can be compared with yields on other investments. The effective yield is given by the yield to maturity (YTM), which is found by the following formula:

$$\text{Bond price} = \frac{C}{(1+r)} + \frac{C}{(1+r)^2} + \frac{C}{(1+r)^3} + \frac{C}{(1+r)^n} + \frac{MV}{(1+r)^n}$$

where C is the annual coupon interest, r is the yield to maturity or market interest rate, and MV is the maturity value. If the above quote is for January 10, 1991, and the bond matures on January 10, 1995, the following relationship will hold:

$$\$9850 = \frac{\$850}{(1+0.0896)} + \frac{\$850}{(1+0.0896)^2} + \frac{\$850}{(1+0.0896)^3} + \frac{\$850}{(1+0.0896)^4} + \frac{\$10,000}{(1+0.0896)^4}$$

The yield to maturity is r, or the interest rate of 8.96 percent.[11] The lender will earn the yield to maturity only if he or she immediately reinvests the interest receipts at the YTM and holds the bond to maturity. The easiest way to find the yield to maturity is to look it up in bond yield tables.

---

[11]When the interest is paid semiannually rather than annually, the Wall Street tradition is to cut the discount rate in half and double the time period exponent.

However, if one is not available, try different interest rates in a spreadsheet or calculator until the present value is equal to the market price of the bond.

If we should increase the market interest rate (YTM), from 8.96 percent to 9.5 percent, the market price of the bond will decrease to:

$$\$9680 = \frac{\$850}{(1+0.095)} + \frac{\$850}{(1+0.095)^2} + \frac{\$850}{(1+0.095)^3} + \frac{\$850}{(1+0.095)^4} + \frac{\$10,000}{(1+0.095)^4}$$

If the market interest rate decreases to 8.0 percent, the bond price will increase to:

$$\$10,166 = \frac{\$850}{(1+0.08)} + \frac{\$850}{(1+0.08)^2} + \frac{\$850}{(1+0.08)^3} + \frac{\$850}{(1+0.08)^4} + \frac{\$10,000}{(1+0.08)^4}$$

The change in interest rates, or YTMs, illustrates two very important principles. First, when the market rate is equal to the coupon rate (8.5 percent), the market bond price will be equal to its par or maturity value ($10,000). When the market interest rate is above the coupon rate (8.96 percent > 8.5 percent), the bond price in the market will be less than the par value ($9680 < $10,000). When the market interest rate is lower than the coupon rate (8 percent < 8.5 percent), the market price of the bond will be greater than the par value ($10,166 > $10,000). The second important point is that when market interest rates fall, the price of a security always rises and when market interest rates rise, the price of the security falls.[12] The longer the time to maturity, the greater the change in the price of the security. Compare the market prices, alternative interest rates, and years to maturity of the following:

Par Value	$10,000
Years to Maturity	30
Coupon Rate	8.5%
Market Price at 7.0%	$11,861.36
Market Price at 12.0%	$ 7,180.69

Par Value	$10,000
Years to Maturity	4
Coupon Rate	8.5%
Market Price at 7.0%	$10,508.08
Market Price at 12.0%	$ 8,936.93

When interest rates increase from 7 percent to 12 percent, the price of the 8.5 percent coupon bond with 30 years left to maturity will fall from $11,861 to $7181, a sharp decrease of 39 percent. However, the price of a bond with only four years left to maturity will fall from $10,508 to $8937, a

---

[12]The inverse relationship between security prices and interest rates is also explained in the Read Me First section of Chapter 8, pages 161–163.

decrease of only 15 percent. Thus, if you had purchased the 30-year bond on Monday morning when market interest rates were 7 percent and sold the bond on Tuesday morning when market interest rates were 12 percent, you would have lost $4680 or 39 percent of your investment. Of course, if you held the bond to maturity, you would be able to sell it for $10,000, but you would have foregone the higher interest rates in the meantime. If you had purchased the bond with only four years left to maturity, you would have lost only $1571 or 15 percent of your investment.

IIA. Corporate Bonds

Name: Corporate Bonds—Prices and Yields
Agency/Institution: The National Association of Securities Dealers maintains the National Association of Securities Dealers Automated Quotations (NASDAQ) system. Most bond quotes are taken from this system.
Address: 1735 K Street N.W., Washington, DC 20006
Telephone number for inquiries: 202-728-8000
Sources: *Wall Street Journal* (daily) and most daily newspapers; also see *Survey of Current Business* (monthly), *Moody's Bond Record* (monthly; call 212-943-8200), and *Bond Week* (weekly; call 212-303-3300).
Frequency: Each trading day
When available: Close of business day
Revisions: None, except for clerical errors
Historic data: See below.

■ A QUICK LOOK: Corporate Bonds

The bond prices quoted most often are those existing on the secondary market, where previously issued bonds are bought and sold. A sample of a secondary bond quotation is as follows:

Bonds	Cur Yld	Vol	High	Low	Close	Chg
XYZ 9⅜ 15	13.7	15	68½	68	68¼	+¼

Description of bond: The name of the bond is generally the same abbreviation as in the stock tables. The description that follows the name includes the coupon rate (bond's stated interest rate) and its maturity date (expressed in the last two digits of the year of maturity). The XYZ bond has a coupon rate of 9⅜ percent, which means that a $1000 bond will pay $93.75 in interest each year, normally in two payments of $46.875. The bond will mature in 2015.

Cur Yld: Current yield is the coupon rate divided by the closing price of the bond. (See the discussion of "bond prices" in the following section.) In the case of the XYZ bond, the current yield is $93.75/$682.50 = 13.7 percent.

Vol: Number of bonds traded that day; 15 XYZ bonds were traded.

High/Low: High price for the day was $68.50 per $100 of par value or $685.00 for a $1000 bond. Note that the conventional way of reporting the price is per $100 of bond value, but since bonds are denominated in $1000 increments, the price is often verbally quoted per thousand dollars. A bond with a stated or par value of $10,000 would cost $6850 to purchase. The low price for the day was $68 per $100 of par value, or $680 per $1000.

Close: Price at the close of the trading day was $68.25 (or $682.50 for a $1000 bond).

Chg: The closing price on this trading day was $0.50 (or $5 per $1000 bond) higher than the closing price on the previous trading day.

■ A CLOSER LOOK: Corporate Bonds Prices and Yields

Commercial banks are primary sources of short-term but not long-term funds. Banks are unwilling to make loans for longer than five years because their deposits are primarily short term, and long-term loans would expose them to the risks of changing interest rates. Thus, when corporations want to obtain long-term financing, they issue stock or bonds. Most capital-intensive companies, such as electric utilities, issue bonds almost every year. Bonds are issued for periods longer than 10 years but generally not more than 30 years. The bond issuer promises to make a fixed-interest payment each month, quarter, or year, and to pay back the face or maturity value of the bond. No matter what happens to the price of the bond after it is issued, the interest payments made by the issuer remain fixed. The following are some terms frequently used in the bond market. (Also, see the Read Me First section on pages 183–185.)

Basis point: The interest rates on bonds are often quoted in terms of basis points. A basis point is 1/100 of a percent change in interest rates. A 50 basis point change is equal to a 0.5 percent change and a 100 basis point change is equal to a 1.0 percent change.

Callable bonds: Those that the issuing company can call back before the maturity date. Since bonds are issued for 20 to 30 years, corporations are concerned that interest rates will fall and they will be stuck with bonds paying high-interest rates. Hence, they make the bonds callable, retire early those with high interest rates, and issue new bonds with lower interest rates. Most bonds have call protection, which means that they cannot be redeemed or called for a number of years, usually five to ten years after the issue date.

Closed- and open-end bonds: The safest mortgage bonds are "closed-end" bonds which guarantee that the bondholder will have first claim on the assets even if the corporation sells additional bonds pledging the same security. "Open-end" bonds give all holders the same claim to the common collateral.

Collateral trust bonds: Bonds backed by specific securities held by the corporation.

Convertible bonds: Bonds that can be converted into common shares at the owner's option.

Coupon (or bearer) bonds: Bonds with coupons attached that the bondholder must clip and send to the bank of the issuer. The securities are assumed to be owned by the person who has them in his or her possession.[13]

Coupon rate: The annual interest divided by the par value of the bond.

Current yield: A very rough approximation of the true yield of a bond that is obtained by dividing the coupon rate by the current price of the bond. It is not a good measure of the true or effective rate.

Debentures: Unsecured bonds backed only by the "general assets" and reputation of the corporation. If the corporation should default on its bonds, the holders of debentures would have to wait in line behind the holders of closed-end and collateral bonds. Usually, only financially strong corporations are able to sell debentures, whereas financially weak corporations must resort to pledging specific assets.

Discount: The amount below its par value for which the bond sold. If a $10,000 par value bond is sold for $9000, it is said to have sold "at a discount" or "at a discount of 10 percent."

Equipment trust bonds: A specialized type of bond that is backed by specific types of equipment, such as train cars, trucks, and airplanes. The title to the equipment is held by the bond trustee and is given to the company only after it has paid off the bonds.

Mortgage bonds: Bonds secured by the assets of the corporation which, in the event of default by the corporation, can be sold to satisfy the interest and maturity value of the defaulted bonds. Bonds that pay a stipulated interest each year are generally called coupon bonds even if they are registered bonds.

Par value: The stated, face, or maturity value of the bond, which is generally printed on the face of the bond. The par value is seldom the actual price for which the bond is sold. Most bonds are sold at a discount or premium.

Premium: The amount above its par value for which the bond sold. A $10,000 par value bond that sold for $11,500 is said to have sold "at a premium," or "at a premium of $1500."

Registered bonds: Bonds assigned directly to the bondholders, whose names are listed on the face of the bond and registered on the issuers' books.

Subordinated debenture bonds: Unsecured obligations that are even more risky than general debenture bonds. If the corporation should default on these bonds, the owners of regular debentures would have priority claim on the assets of the corporation and holders of subordinated bonds would have to wait until all debenture bondholders were paid off.

Primary and Secondary Bond Markets

Before bonds can be offered to the public, the company must file documents describing the conditions and affairs of the company and register

---

[13]Bearer bonds are seldom issued anymore because registering bonds is no longer the labor-intensive task it once was. Some are still circulating, however.

the bonds with the Securities and Exchange Commission (SEC). The corporation must also make available to investors a prospectus containing information similar to that sent to the SEC. Private placements of securities (without SEC registration) are possible, but severe restrictions are attached to them and few corporations select private placement.

Corporate bonds and preferred stocks are brought to the market the first time (sold by their issuers) through dealings with underwriting syndicates of investment bankers. These investment bankers may act as a principal or an agent. If they act as a principal, they actually purchase the bonds from the corporation and resell them to the public. Regardless of their subsequent success in selling the bonds to the public, the underwriter must pay the full contractual price to the bond issuer. Generally, only the most reputable and solid corporations are able to have such an arrangement. Less solid corporations, or those unwilling to pay the substantial fees charged for a principal relationship, will have an agency relationship in which the investment banker has no financial responsibility to the issuer but agrees to use its best efforts to sell the bonds. Often a number of investment bankers will form a syndicate to distribute the bonds. The syndicate will "blue-sky" the issue (check out whether the distribution violates any state law), appoint brokers and dealers to act as agents, and stabilize the market.[14] Unlike municipal and state governments, corporations do not have to take competitive bids from investment bankers. Consequently, most corporate bond offerings are negotiated between the corporation and an investment banker or syndicate.

After the bonds are sold by the underwriters to the initial investors, they may be sold again and again through the secondary market. This ability to sell the bonds in the secondary market is what makes them a liquid investment — that is, makes them readily convertible into cash. A substantial number of bonds are listed on the New York Stock Exchange and some trades are executed there, but most corporate bond trading is done in over-the-counter (OTC) trading among dealers and brokers and between these firms and the general public. A *broker* is a firm acting as an agent for its customers, and it buys and sells securities on behalf of the customer for a fixed commission. A *dealer* is a firm acting as a principal that buys and sells for its own account. It makes its profits by selling bonds to customers at a slightly higher price than it purchased them for.

Most firms in the OTC market are both dealers and brokers, and virtually all of them belong to the National Association of Securities Dealers (NASD). Although established by Congress in 1934 and supervised by the Securities and Exchange Commission, the NASD is an independent

---

[14]Manipulating the market prices of securities is illegal except when done by syndicates to facilitate the distribution of new securities. Normally, such manipulation occurs when the syndicate strives to keep the market price from going below the public offering price. Typically, such support lasts for no longer than two weeks.

membership association. NASD administers the National Association of Securities Dealers Automated Quotations (NASDAQ) system, which is an electronic communications network that provides up-to-the-minute quotes on bond prices.

Brokers and dealers buy and sell among themselves for their customers and their own accounts by calling each other and giving and getting bids. If dealer A calls dealer B and asks for a bid price on a certain bond and B replies, "Firm bid is good for an hour, with five," it means that dealer A has one hour to accept the bid price. However, if a third dealer should call B and offer to accept immediately, then B will call A and say that he has only 5 minutes to decide or he will sell to the third dealer. After the deal is struck, the bonds and the money have to be exchanged. There are a number of ways of settling bond market transactions, but the most popular is to pay and deliver within five business days. Since the buyer of a bond receives interest from the corporation for the entire period, even if he bought the bond partway through the period, bond sellers are entitled to receive from the buyer any interest accrued on the bond up to the day before the settlement date.

HISTORIC DATA
Yield on Corporate Bonds
Moody's AAA Rated
1920–1990

		1935	3.6	1955	3.1	1975	8.8
		1936	3.2	1956	3.4	1976	8.4
		1937	3.3	1957	3.9	1977	8.0
		1938	3.2	1958	3.8	1978	8.7
		1939	3.0	1959	4.4	1979	9.6
1920	6.1	1940	2.8	1960	4.4	1980	11.9
1921	6.0	1941	2.8	1961	4.4	1981	14.2
1922	5.1	1942	2.8	1962	4.3	1982	13.8
1923	5.1	1943	2.7	1963	4.3	1983	12.0
1924	5.0	1944	2.7	1964	4.4	1984	12.7
1925	4.9	1945	2.6	1965	4.5	1985	11.4
1926	4.7	1946	2.5	1966	5.1	1986	9.0
1927	4.6	1947	2.6	1967	5.5	1987	9.4
1928	4.6	1948	2.8	1968	6.2	1988	9.7
1929	4.7	1949	2.7	1969	7.0	1989	9.3
1930	4.6	1950	2.6	1970	8.0	1990	9.3
1931	4.6	1951	2.9	1971	7.4	1991	8.8
1932	5.0	1952	3.0	1972	7.2		
1933	4.5	1953	3.2	1973	7.4		
1934	4.0	1954	2.9	1974	8.6		

Source: Moody's Investor's Service.

Name: Corporate Bond Ratings
Agency/Institution: Standard & Poor's and Moody's Investor's Services
Address: Standard & Poor's, 25 Broadway, New York, NY 10004; and Moody's Investor's Service, 99 Church St., New York, NY 10007
Telephone number for data and inquiries: S&P's: 212-208-8000; Moody's: 212-553-0300
Sources: *Standard & Poor's Bond Guide* and *Moody's Bond Record*; also see Standard & Poor's *Debt Rating Criteria*.
Frequency: Periodic

■ A QUICK LOOK: Bond Ratings

Bond prices and their corresponding interest rates are affected by the creditworthiness of the company issuing them. Bond ratings, which are made by Standard & Poor's and Moody's Investor's Services, are ratings of the estimated abilities of the companies to pay the interest and maturity values of their bonds.

Standard & Poor's Corporate Bond Ratings

AAA: Highest grade obligations.

AA: High grade obligations.

A: Upper medium grade, with interest and principal regarded as safe.

BBB: Medium grade bonds, on the borderline between sound obligations and those that have some speculative elements. This group is the lowest that qualifies as investment grade.

BB: Lower medium grade; interest coverages are low.

B: Speculative. Payment of interest cannot be ensured under difficult economic conditions.

CCC: More speculative; interest is paid but questionable in more difficult times.

CC: Outright speculation, with little chance of interest being paid.

DDD–D: All bonds rated with a D are in default; the rating indicates relative salvage value.

Standard & Poor's sometimes uses plus (+) and minus (−) modifiers to show relative standing within a given major rating category.

Moody's Corporate Bond Ratings

Aaa: Best quality bonds.

Aa: High quality by all standards.

A: Possess many favorable investment attributes, but some susceptibility to impairment sometime in the future.

Baa: Bonds are considered medium grade obligations and may lack outstanding investment characteristics; have some speculative characteristics. Lowest investment grade.

Ba: Bonds have speculative elements.

B: Lack characteristics of a desirable investment.

Caa: Poor standing and may be in default.

Ca: Highly speculative and often in default.

C: Lowest rated bonds; very poor prospect of ever attaining investment standing.

Moody's applies the numerical modifiers 1, 2, and 3 to each major rating category from Aa to B to indicate relative ranking within the category. For example, Aa1 indicates that the bond ranks near the top of the category. Bonds falling in the C or D range of Moody's and Standard & Poor's, and even in the lower B rating ranges are called junk bonds. They had a surge of popularity in the mid-1980s, but the subsequent legal troubles of major promoters had a chilling effect on the junk bond market.

■ A CLOSER LOOK: Bond Ratings

Individual and institutional bond buyers do not have the time to follow closely the financial fortunes of all companies that have issued bonds. Most investors depend on the ratings of bonds by Moody's and Standard & Poor's, the two major bond rating agencies. Institutional investors and many individuals will not consider any bond rated less than the minimum investment grade, which is Baa for Moody's and BBB for Standard & Poor's. Only those interested in junk bonds would invest in bonds with lower ratings than a B.

Rating bonds involves examining many variables, but in the last analysis it is a judgment call on the part of those doing the rating. Analysts frequently use and cite in their reports various ratios with which the reader might want to become familiar.

Interest coverage is one of the most important ratios in evaluating bonds but there are various ways of constructing this ratio. Some analysts add preferred dividends to both numerator and denominator and some use pre-tax income while others use after-tax income. Whatever the method of calculation, there is no threshold of "good" and "bad" interest coverages because the quality of the interest coverages depends on the industry and stability of revenues. Here is an example:

$$\text{Interest coverage} = \frac{\text{annual interest charges} + \text{after-tax income}}{\text{annual interest charges}}$$

To illustrate, a firm has $2 million of annual interest expenses and an after-tax profit of $6 million. Thus the interest coverage is:

$$\frac{\$2 + \$6}{\$2} = 4 \text{ times interest coverage}$$

Another ratio used in evaluating bonds is the **capitalization ratio**, which expresses long-term debt as a percentage of total capitalization. Capitalization includes long-term debt and preferred and common stock.

$$\frac{\text{Capitalization}}{\text{ratio}} = \frac{\text{long-term debt}}{\text{total capitalization}}$$

The lower the ratio, the stronger the capital structure and the more able that company is to repay the principal and interest. Again, there is no "correct" capitalization ratio and some industries, such as electric utilities, thrive on capitalization ratios above 60 percent while other industries are considered dangerous if they have 40 percent ratios.

Here is an example: assume that a company has $100 million of debt outstanding, book value of $110 million in common stock, $50 million in common stock, and retained earnings of $200 million. Its capitalization ratio would be:

$$\frac{\$100}{\$100 + \$110 + \$50 + \$200} = 21.7 \text{ percent}$$

The following two ratios are used to gauge the working capital and liquidity position of the company:

$$\text{Current ratio} = \frac{\text{current assets}}{\text{current liabilities}} = \frac{\$10 \text{ million}}{\$5 \text{ million}} = 2.0$$

$$\text{Quick ratio} = \frac{\text{current assets} - \text{inventories}}{\text{current liabilities}} = \frac{\$10 \text{ million} - \$4 \text{ million}}{\$5 \text{ million}} = 1.2$$

Though it is difficult to define acceptable ratios, a widely used standard is 2.0 for the current ratio and 1.0 for the quick ratio.

Name: Dow Jones Bond Averages
Agency/Institution: Dow Jones
Address: 200 Liberty Street, New York, NY 10281
Telephone number for data and inquiries: 212-416-2000
Sources: *Wall Street Journal* and *Barron's*
Frequency: Daily and weekly
When available: 4:30 P.M. (EST) that afternoon

■ A QUICK LOOK: Dow Jones Bond Average

The first Dow Jones Bond Average was published in 1915, and the average is currently composed of 10 utility and 10 industrial bonds. The Dow Jones Bond Average is calculated by taking the simple arithmetic mean of the closing prices of the 20 bonds. The following are examples of bond averages:

	1990				
	High	Low	Close	Chg.	% Yld
20 Bonds	93.04	88.44	90.86	−0.13	9.60
10 Utilities	94.48	89.23	92.85	−0.03	9.49
10 Industrials	91.60	86.43	88.88	−0.23	9.70

The columns above report the high and low bond prices during 1990 and the close and change of the previous day. For example, the 1990 high for 20 bonds was 93.04 per $100 of par value. The closing price was $90.86, a decrease of 13 units. The percent yield (which is a yield to maturity) is also shown.

Name: Moody's Bond Indexes and Yield Rates
Agency/Institution: Moody's Investor's Services
Address: 99 Church Street, New York, NY 10007
Telephone number for inquiries: 212-553-0500
Sources: *Moody's Bond Survey* has the daily bond indexes and averages
Frequency: Weekly
When available: Following day

■ A QUICK LOOK: Moody's Bond Indexes and Yield Rates

Since 1918 Moody's has published a number of bond averages and indexes on a monthly basis. These include Moody's Industrial Bond Averages, Moody's Public Utility Bond Averages, Moody's Railroad Bond Averages, and Moody's Corporate Bond Averages. The best known is Moody's Corporate Bond Averages, which consists of approximately 80 investment grade (Aaa to Baa) corporate bonds. The index is a total-return index, which means that it includes the return or yield on the bond. The index is based on December 31, 1979 = 100.

Name: Standard & Poor's Bond Indexes and Yield Averages
Agency/Institution: Standard & Poor's
Address: P.O. Box 992, New York, NY 10275-0414
Telephone number for inquiries: 1-800-221-5277

Sources: *Current Statistics* (Standard & Poor's Statistical Service; monthly), *Price Index Record* (Standard & Poor's; annually), and many daily newspapers
Frequency: Weekly
When available: Next day

■ A QUICK LOOK: Standard & Poor's Bond Indexes and Yield Averages

Since 1937 Standard & Poor's has published a series of bond yield averages for their investment grade categories of AAA, AA, A, and BBB. The averages are published for S&P Corporate Composite Bond Yield Average and S&P Industrial Bond Yield Average. Standard & Poor's also publishes municipal bond indexes and government bond averages and indexes.

IIB. Government and Municipal Bonds

Name: Government Agency Securities
Alternative name: Federally Sponsored Agency Securities
Sources: *Wall Street Journal* and other daily newspapers, *The Bond Buyer* (daily), and *Bloomberg Financial Markets*
Frequency: Daily
When available: Close of trading day

■ A QUICK LOOK: Government Agency Securities

In addition to Treasury securities traded in the secondary market, a variety of other government-related securities are issued by government agencies and government-sponsored agencies. The prices and interest rates of these securities are listed in the *Wall Street Journal* and in some daily newspapers. Generally they are listed under the heading of "Government Agency Issues," although some of the agency issues, such as Ginnie Mae, might also be summarized under a heading such as "Mortgage-backed Securities." Since many of these agencies have numerous issues, they are identified by their coupon rate and maturity date. The following is a typical quotation:

FNMA Issues

Rate	Mat	Bid	Asked	Yld
10.15	10–90	100–04	100–08	6.63
8.40	8–91	100–11	100–14	7.88
17.00	8–91	108–05	108–09	7.75
7.90	8–96	95–13	95–21	8.86
0.00	10–19	7–03	7–10	9.20

FNMA: These are the initials of the government agency. In this case, it is the Federal National Mortgage Association, also known as Fannie Mae. FNMA is not a federally owned agency; it is an independent agency with some general supervision by Congress. (See the following "A Closer Look" section.)

Rate: Coupon rate on the bonds. The bonds described in the first row have a coupon rate of 10.15 percent. Note that the coupon rate of the bond in the last row is zero. This "zero coupon bond" does not pay annual interest, so the investor obtains a return solely from the difference between the price paid for the bond and the price received when he or she sells or redeems it. An investor could have purchased a $100,000 bond with a maturity date of 2019 in 1990 for only $7312.50. (7–10 means 7 and 10⁄32nds per $100 of face value)

Mat: Maturity date on the bonds. The 10.15 percent bonds will mature in October 1990.

Bid: The bid price of the bond dealer—that is, the price the dealer will pay for bonds bought from investors. As noted earlier, the bid price of 100–04 should be read as 100 4⁄32nds, or $100.125 for each $100 of face value. For example, if the dealer were buying a $100,000 bond he would pay $100,125 for it. The market price can be above par because it is a coupon bond paying a relatively high coupon rate.

Asked: The asked price of the bond dealer—that is, the price the dealer will charge for the bonds that he sells to investors. The asked price of 100–08 should be read as 100 8⁄32nds, or $100.25 per $100 of face value. For example, in selling a $100,000 bond, the dealer would charge $100,250 for it. The 4-point difference represents the spread, which is the dealer's gross profit. In the case of a $100,000 bond, the dealer would have made $125 gross profit.

Yld: The yield to maturity on the bonds given the current asked price of the bond. The YTM is based on the asked price of the bond, its coupon rate, and its time to maturity. The yield to maturity of the 10.15 bond is 6.63 percent.

Note: Security quotes are arranged by maturity date, with the securities closest to their maturity dates listed first. Some of the bonds near their expiration dates might have been issued many years ago. For example, the bond in the first row with a 10.75 percent coupon rate might have been issued in 1980 or 1975, when market interest rates were approximately at this rate. We can be fairly certain that the 17 percent coupon rate bond was issued in 1981, when rates were quite high. Notice that the yields suggest a normal yield curve, with rates getting higher the longer the bond's time to maturity.

■ A CLOSER LOOK: Government Agency Securities

Two types of federal agencies, other than the Treasury, issue securities: (1) federal agencies that are an integral part of the federal government, and (2) federally sponsored agencies with some indirect links to the federal government that are nevertheless owned and governed by private entities. Both types of issues can be purchased and held without limit by national banks and are eligible as collateral for Treasury deposits in commercial banks. Most government agency securities can be used as collateral for loans from the Federal Reserve. Interest rates on these securities closely follow the rates on Treasury securities, except that they are slightly higher. Also, most agency issues are noncallable throughout their entire lifetime, providing protection against redemption should market interest rates decline prior to maturity.

Federal Agencies

The Export-Import Bank (Exim Bank) raises money to provide loans, credit insurance, and various guarantees to facilitate trade between the United States and other countries. It issues short-term discount notes, participation certificates backed by a pool of loans and debentures that have three- to seven-year maturities. Its securities are backed by the full faith and credit of the U.S. government, and all interest and returns are taxable at the federal, state, and local levels.

The Farmers Home Administration, which finances real estate and housing loans to farmers, issues notes and certificates that pay interest annually. The Government National Mortgage Association (GNMA; also known as Ginnie Mae) was established in 1968 and is part of the Department of Housing and Urban Development. GNMA does not originate mortgages or directly issue mortgage-backed securities. Rather, it accomplishes its objective by guaranteeing mortgage-backed securities, thus eliminating the credit risk associated with mortgage investments. The homeowner makes the usual mortgage payments to the savings and loan or bank, which — less a small servicing fee — passes on the payments to GNMA, which, in turn, makes payments to the investors in pass-through certificates. GNMA issues securities against these mortgages, with interest and principal payments made monthly to the investor on a modified pass-through, which means that interest and principal are paid to the investor regardless of whether it has been collected from the mortgagee. The most well known GNMA security is the modified pass-through security, which is based on a pool of FHA- or VA-guaranteed mortgages of the same coupon rate and maturity date and deposited in a custodian bank. Although the original life of these mortgages is 25 to 30 years, the average life is about 12 to 14 years. The minimum purchase requirement is $25,000. The timely payment of principal and interest is guaranteed by GNMA, and the GNMA guarantee is backed by the U.S. government.

The Tennessee Valley Authority (TVA) sells securities to develop its electric power facilities and other programs in the Tennessee Valley. TVA securities are not guaranteed by the U.S. government but TVA does have substantial borrowing power from the Treasury. The TVA issues short-term notes of four-month maturity and long-term bonds.

The Federal Financing Bank (FFB) was created in 1974 to centralize the packaging and selling of securities for federal agencies. The FFB sells its securities and, in turn, provides money to federal agencies that request funds from it. The securities are backed by the U.S. government and are sold in competitive auction similar to the Treasury bills. Government-sponsored agencies are not able to use the FFB.

Federally Sponsored Credit Agencies

Federally sponsored credit agencies are private financial intermediaries established by Congress to supply funds for housing, agriculture, and higher education. Though previously owned by the government, all of these agencies are now privately owned by the institutions and borrowers to which they lend. The securities of these agencies are *not* guaranteed by the federal government.

The 12 Federal Home Loan Banks (FHLBs), created in 1932 and owned by its members make loans to member savings and loan associations and mutual savings banks. These loans, called *advances*, have maturities up to 20 years and are used by the savings and loans to meet liquidity needs and expand portfolios. The FHLBs issue short-term securities with less than 12 months, called *notes*, and securities with greater than 12 months maturity, called *bonds* (note the difference from the U.S. Treasury securities). None are callable prior to par. FHLB securities are not exempt from state and local taxes and are not guaranteed by the U.S. government, but the securities are collateralized by guaranteed mortgages, cash, and government securities.

The **Federal Home Loan Mortgage Corporation** (FHLMC; popularly known as Freddie Mac), provides a secondary market for conventional mortgage loans. It purchases mortgages from loan-originating institutions such as savings and loans, places them in mortgage pools (aggregations of mortgage securities), and issues certificates backed by these loans. It issues mortgage-backed bonds that range in maturity from 12 to 25 years and are not directly guaranteed by the U.S. government but are guaranteed by the Government National Mortgage Association (discussed later), which is backed by the U.S. government. The FHLMC also issues participation certificates backed by pools of conventional mortgages, and the interest and principal payments are passed through to the investor each month.

The **Federal National Mortgage Association** (FNMA; known as Fannie Mae), established in 1938, sells securities in order to finance the purchase of residential conventional mortgages from savings and loan associations, banks, and insurance companies. FNMA securities are not supported by the U.S. government, but FNMA does have close regulatory ties to the Department of Housing and Urban Development and it has the ability to borrow $2.5 billion from the Treasury. Basically, FNMA now buys government-insured or guaranteed mortgages when normal investment funds are relatively scarce and sells them when mortgage funds are more plentiful. FNMA issues discount notes with maturities between 30 and 270 days, debentures (bonds backed by the general credit of the issuer, rather than specified assets), and mortgage-backed bonds, which are secured by mortgages.

Other federally sponsored but not owned agencies include the 12 Federal Land Banks (FLBs), which issue securities to obtain funds to finance loans by the local Federal Land Bank associations to farmers. Their securities are not backed by the U.S. government, but they are backed by the FLBs and the farmers' mortgages. These FLB securities are not recallable and their maturities range from 1 to 15 years. The Student Loan Marketing Association grants loans or advances to financial institutions that make low interest loans to students. The Farm Credit Banks lend to farm-related businesses and to associations and cooperatives that lend to farmers or provide agricultural services.

Name: The *Bond Buyer's* Municipal Bond Index
Alternative name: 40 Bond Index
Agency/Institution: The *Bond Buyer* is a daily newspaper that has covered the municipal bond market since 1891.
Address: One State Plaza, New York, NY 10004
Telephone number for data: 212-943-8543
Telephone number for inquiries: 800-221-7809
Frequency: Daily

■ A QUICK LOOK: The *Bond Buyer's* Municipal Bond Index

The *Bond Buyer's* Municipal Bond Index consists of 40 actively traded, tax-exempt revenue and general obligation municipal bonds. The bond issues included in the index must exceed $50 million, be rated A or higher by Moody's and A- or higher by Standard & Poor's. They must have a maturity of at least 19 years and be callable at par prior to maturity. The index is constructed by contacting five dealers at 3 P.M. each day and asking them the price for each bond. The highest and lowest prices are dropped and the remaining three are averaged. The average is then divided by a conversion factor equal to the price at which each bond would yield 8 percent. The 40 converted prices are then averaged and multiplied by a conversion factor to maintain the continuity of the index when its composition changes. A consistent series is available back to July 1985. The *Bond Buyer* also publishes a weekly 20-bond index that dates back to 1917, an 11-bond index that dates back to 1979, as well as a revenue bond index that dates back to 1979.

Name: Merrill Lynch Bond Indexes
Agency/Institution: Merrill Lynch, Pierce, Fenner & Smith
Address: 250 Vesey St., New York, NY 10281
Telephone number for inquiries: 212-449-0931
Sources: *Wall Street Journal*
Frequency: Every trading day
When available: Next day

■ A QUICK LOOK: Merrill Lynch Bond Indexes

Merrill Lynch publishes information for a variety of bond markets. MLPFS charts the prices of 500 major municipal bond issuers in its tax-exempt security index; the company also maintains indexes of mortgage-backed securities and convertible bonds. The Merrill Lynch 500 Index includes 500 investment grade tax-exempt revenue bonds (25- and 30-year maturities) and general obligation bonds (20 year). One spin-off of the index is the average of bond yields, which is reported separately. The MLPFS bond indexes are based on December 31, 1986 = 100. The following is an example of the Merrill Lynch index of tax-exempt securities:

High	Low (12 mos)		Close	Net Chg	% Chg
123.75	110.82	New 10-yr G.O. (AA)	123.75	+0.02	+0.02
127.70	115.72	New 20-yr G.O. (AA)	127.70	+0.03	+0.02
141.34	126.28	New 30-yr Rev. (A)	141.34	+0.03	+0.02

Name: Merrill Lynch Mortgage-Backed Bond Indexes
Agency/Institution: Merrill Lynch, Pierce, Fenner & Smith
Address: 250 Vesey St., New York, NY 10281
Telephone number for inquiries: 212-449-1000
Sources: *Wall Street Journal* and other financial publications
Frequency: Every trading day
When available: Next day

■ A QUICK LOOK: Merrill Lynch Mortgage-Backed Bond Indexes

Merrill Lynch publishes indexes for a wide variety of bonds, including mortgage-backed securities issued by government agencies. One spin-off of the index is the averages of bond yields, which are reported separately. The MLPFS bond indexes are based on December 31, 1986 = 100. The following are examples of mortgage-backed securities:

141.30	126.23	Ginnie Mae (GNMA)	141.30	+0.31	+0.22
141.64	126.82	Fannie Mae (FNMA)	141.64	+0.30	+0.21
141.20	126.19	Freddie Mac (FHLMC)	141.20	+0.30	+0.21

Name: Municipal Bond Ratings
Agency/Institution: Standard & Poor's and Moody's
Address: Standard & Poor's, P.O. Box 992, New York, NY 10275-0414; telephone
   number for subscriptions: 800-221-5277, for data inquiries: 212-208-1199
   Moody's Investor's Services, 99 Church Street, New York, NY 10007; telephone
   number for subscriptions: 800-342-5647, for data inquiries: 212-553-0500
Sources: *Moody's Bond Record* and S&P's *Municipal Bond Book*
Frequency: Every bond series is reviewed annually; reports are published when
   the bonds are issued.
Revisions: None

■ A QUICK LOOK: Municipal Bond Ratings

Since municipals (securities issued by the state and local governments), unlike governments (federal securities), can be defaulted, investors pay close attention to the ratings of municipal bonds by the two dominant rating companies. Although each rating service appears to emphasize different variables (S&P tends to view the broad taxing powers of a state more favorably), both rating companies tend to look at tax bases, general economic climate, population trends, existing debt burdens, and tax growth and levels.

Standard & Poor's Municipal Bond Ratings

   AAA Prime: Obligations of the highest quality

   AA: High grade—Second highest rating, only slightly marred

   A: Good grade—Principal and interest regarded as safe but some weakness

   BBB: Medium grade—Lowest investment grade; debt service coverage is good, but not exceptional

   BB: Lower medium grade—For the most part, a speculative, non–investment grade obligation

   B: Low grade—Default could be imminent

   D: Defaults—Payment of interest and/or principal is in arrears

   NCR: No contract rating

Moody's Municipal Bond Ratings

Aaa: Best quality bonds

Aa: High quality by all standards

A: Possess many favorable investment attributes but some susceptibility to impairment sometime in the future

Baa: Medium grade obligations that may lack outstanding investment characteristics and have some speculative characteristics; minimum investment grade quality

Ba: Bonds have speculative elements, protection is moderate

B: Lack characteristics of a desirable investment

Caa: Poor standing and may be in default

Ca: Highly speculative and often in default

C: Lowest rated bonds; very poor prospect of ever attaining investment standing

---

Name: Municipal Securities
Alternative name: State and local securities
Agency/Institution: The *Bond Buyer* and Standard & Poor's *Municipal Bond Book*
Address: The *Bond Buyer*, One State Plaza, New York, NY 10004; Standard & Poor's, P.O. Box 992, New York, NY 10275-0414
Telephone numbers for inquiries: The *Bond Buyer* — Municipal bond indexes: 212-943-8543; S&P's: 212-208-1199
Sources: The "bible" of the municipal bond market is the *Bond Buyer*, which is published every weekday. It contains news on municipal bond markets, bond prices, yields, and municipal bond indexes. S&P's *Municipal Bond Book* (bimonthly) is also a good source of municipal bond yields. One source carried in most public libraries is *Moody's Bond Record*, which lists municipals, their bond ratings, and maturity dates, but it does not list their current prices. The *Wall Street Journal* publishes quotes on a few revenue bonds. The *Federal Reserve Bulletin* also reports municipal bond yields.
Historic data: See below.

■ A QUICK LOOK: Municipal Securities

Municipals, also called *tax-exempt securities*, are primarily traded over the counter, and their prices and yields are not widely reported in the daily newspapers. The best source for daily information is a stockbroker. The *Wall Street Journal* lists the prices of a handful of the most actively traded revenue bonds but does not list any general obligation bonds. Unlike Treasury and other government bonds, the general practice is to quote municipal bonds on the basis of yield rather than price. The exceptions are actively traded revenue bonds, which are quoted in percentage-of-par prices.

A typical municipal bond quote looks like the following:

	Coupon	Mat.	Price	Chg.	Bid Yld
Chesapk Bay Br & Tun.	6.375	07-01-22	96⅞	+ ¼	6.61

Chesapk Bay Br & Tun.:   The name or description of the bond.

Coupon: The coupon rate, which tells us that it will pay $6.375 for each $100 of par value.

Mat: Maturity date of the bond, which is July 1, 2022.

Price: This might be stated in bid and asked prices. In this case, the only price listed is the bid price.

Chg: Change (in fractions of a dollar) from the previous trading day.

Bid Yld: The yield to maturity, based on the bid price.

■ A CLOSER LOOK: Municipal Securities

Municipal bonds are those issued by states, counties, cities, villages, school districts, housing authorities, municipal-owned utilities, toll roads, and transit districts. They are generally issued in denominations of $1000 and $5000, and all municipals issued since 1983 must be registered bonds. Most municipal bonds are serial bonds, which means that the maturities of the bonds in a single serial issue will be staggered, with some bonds maturing each year after issue up to 10, 20, or 30 years. There are basically two different types of municipal securities. *General obligations bonds* are secured by the issuer's general taxing abilities; they are said to be "full faith and credit" obligations. The second type of municipal bond is the *revenue bond*, which is secured only by the revenue of the specific project. Special districts, such as airport, highway, transit, or industrial districts issue revenue bonds. Although the supply of revenue bonds has been sharply restricted by the Tax Reform Act of 1986, there has been an increase in municipal securities held by individuals. The main attraction of these bonds — called *munis* or *municipals* — is that they are exempt from federal income tax and, generally, state and municipal income tax if the bondholder lives within the relevant taxing jurisdictions. The following equation can be used to find the taxable equivalent yield of taxable securities:

$$\text{Taxable equivalent yield} = \frac{100 \times \text{yield on muni bond}}{100 - \text{tax-bracket percent}}$$

For example, if an investor were in the 30 percent tax bracket and his tax-exempt muni yielded 8 percent, the above formula would show that the investor would have to earn 11.43 percent on a taxable security to have the same after-tax rate of return:

$$\frac{100 \times 8}{100 - 30} = \frac{800}{70} = 11.43\%$$

Some municipal bonds have zero coupons; these pay all of their interest as the difference between the purchasing and selling (or redemption) price. They are purchased at substantial discounts from par value. The greater the number of years a "municipal zero" has until maturity, the less the investor pays for it. The future value of a zero coupon bond, if held to maturity, is the fixed par value, but its market value will fluctuate between purchase date and maturity date.

Most states and large municipalities issue their bonds publicly through competitive bidding for the underwriting services.[15] A large and active over-the-counter secondary market is centered in New York City, but municipals, especially small issues, are much less liquid than governments.

About a half-dozen insurance companies insure municipal bonds, and more than one-quarter of new municipals are now insured. Municipal bonds can be bought through investment bankers, brokers, and commercial banks. Investors can also buy shares in municipal bond mutual funds, or municipal investment trust (MITs). Municipal bond index futures are also traded.

HISTORIC DATA: Yields on High Grade Municipal Bonds
1920–1991

1920	4.98	1940	2.5	1960	3.73	1980	8.51
1921	5.09	1941	2.1	1961	3.46	1981	11.23
1922	4.23	1942	2.36	1962	3.18	1982	11.57
1923	4.25	1943	2.06	1963	3.23	1983	9.47
1924	4.2	1944	1.86	1964	3.22	1984	10.15
1925	4.09	1945	1.67	1965	3.27	1985	9.18
1926	4.08	1946	1.64	1966	3.82	1986	7.38
1927	3.98	1947	2.01	1967	3.98	1987	7.73
1928	4.05	1948	2.4	1968	4.51	1988	7.68
1929	4.27	1949	2.21	1969	5.81	1989	7.23
1930	4.07	1950	1.98	1970	6.51	1990	7.27
1931	4.01	1951	2	1971	5.7	1991	6.91
1932	4.65	1952	2.19	1972	5.27		
1933	4.71	1953	2.72	1973	5.18		
1934	4.03	1954	2.37	1974	6.09		
1935	3.4	1955	2.53	1975	6.89		
1936	3.07	1956	2.93	1976	6.49		
1937	3.1	1957	3.6	1977	5.56		
1938	2.91	1958	3.56	1978	5.9		
1939	2.76	1959	3.95	1979	6.39		

---

[15]Competitive sales are announced in the *Bond Buyer*.

Name: Shearson Lehman Hutton Treasury Bond Index
Agency/Institution: Shearson Lehman Hutton
Address: American Express Towers, 8th Floor, World Financial Center, New York, NY 10285
Telephone number for data and inquiries: 212-298-2000
Sources: Published daily in the *Wall Street Journal* and some local newspapers and weekly in *Barron's*
Frequency: Daily

■ A QUICK LOOK: Shearson-Lehman Hutton Treasury Bond Index

The Shearson-Lehman Hutton (SLH) Treasury Bond Index is actually a composite index comprising two major subindexes: the Long-Term Treasury Index (the index often reported as the Treasury Long Bond Index), which tracks those issues having maturities from 10 to 30 years, and the Intermediate Treasury Index representing those having maturities longer than 1 year but less than 10 years. The three indexes measure bond price, multiplied by the outstanding amounts of bonds and notes. The composite index uses a base level of December 31, 1980 = 1000. The SLH also produces an index that measures only the price of a long-term bond. The following is an example of SLH Treasury Bond Index rates:

High	Low (12 mos)		Close	Net Chg	% Chg
3082.97	2817.13	Intermediate	3082.97	+ 6.69	+0.22
3630.68	3214.67	Long-term	3630.68	+16.61	+0.46
1378.22	1218.60	Long-term (price)	1316.76	+ 5.71	+0.44
3206.22	2910.48	Composite	3206.22	+ 9.11	+0.28

The two left columns report the index highs and lows for the previous 12 months. The three columns to the right represent the index of closing prices, the net change in the index, and the percentage change from the previous trading date.

Name: Treasury Bond Quotes
Agency/Institution: U.S. Treasury
Address: Bureau of the Public Debt, Washington, DC 20239-0001
Telephone number for data and inquiries: 202-376-4302
Sources: *Wall Street Journal* and most daily newspapers, *Treasury Bulletin* (monthly), *Daily Statement of the United States Treasury* (daily), and most financial publications
Frequency: Daily
When available: Throughout the business day
Revisions: None
Historic data: See below.

■ A QUICK LOOK: Treasury Bonds

The U.S. Treasury issues three types of marketable securities: bonds, notes, and bills. **Treasury bonds** are usually issued in minimum denominations of $1000 and carry a fixed interest rate with interest paid twice a year. They are issued in maturities of 10 to 30 years. **Treasury notes** are issued in maturities ranging from 1 to 10 years and pay a fixed rate of interest payable twice a year. The minimum denomination is $5000 for notes with less than four-year maturities and $1000 for notes with longer maturities. Daily newspapers publish quotes similar to the following:

		Treasury Bonds and Notes			
Rate	Maturity	Bid	Asked	Chg	Yld
8½	Nov91n	100–16	100–18	−1	7.99
14½	Nov91n	106–31	107–03	−1	7.81
6¾	Feb93	96–29	97–05	+2	8.07
10½	Feb95	107–04	107–08	+3	8.50
14	Nov06-11	140–09	140–13	+5	9.16

Rate: This is the coupon rate on the Treasury bond, which was close to the market rate at the time the bond was issued. The coupon rate of the bond in the first line is 8.5 percent and the interest is paid semiannually.

Maturity: The maturity date of the bond. The maturity of the bond in the first row is November 1991, and the "n" denotes that it is a Treasury note. The bond in the fifth line is a callable bond with a maturity date of November 2011, but it is subject to being called by the Treasury any time after November 2006. It was fairly common for 30-year Treasury bonds to be callable after 25 years, but since 1986 the only bonds issued by the Treasury are noncallable 30-year bonds.

Bid: The price that a bond dealer will pay for a bond in terms of dollars per $100 of face value. The number to the right of the dash mark is in 32nds. Thus, the bid price for the 8½ bond is 100 16⁄32nds or $100,500 for a $100,000 bond.

Asked: The price that the bond dealer will charge for a bond sold to investors. The asking price for the 8½ bond is 100 18⁄32nds or $100,562.50. The dealer's spread, or the amount between the bid and asked price, is $62.50. Note that the securities that have coupon rates above the current market rates (the 14 percent bonds) are selling at a premium (above par value) and those with a coupon rate less than the current market rate (the 6¾ bonds) are selling at a discount (less than par value).

Chg: The asked price rose by ⅟32nd since the previous trading date.

Yld: The yield to maturity is based on the asked price, which is the selling price of the dealer, and the price the investor would have to pay. The yield to maturity is the effective rate of interest earned by the bondholder if he or she holds the bond to maturity, the issuer pays all coupons and the principal at maturity, and the investor immediately reinvests the coupon interest receipts at the same rate.

Note that the data suggest a normal yield curve; that is, the yield increases as the time to maturity increases.

■ A CLOSER LOOK: Treasury Securities

There are two categories of Treasury bonds: (1) nonmarketable securities, including the Series E and H savings bonds that many individuals buy at work or their local bank, and (2) marketable securities, which are sold in large amounts and freely traded on the market. Series E bonds, which are issued for five-year periods, provide a fixed yield through a steady increase in the redemption value of the bond. Series E bonds can be turned into cash, but if the investor turns them in before the end of the five-year period, the effective yield will be lower. The interest and thus taxes on the interest of Series E bonds are not payable until the end of the maturity period. Series H bonds have ten-year maturities and pay interest semiannually. If returned prior to maturity, they pay less than their stated rate.

New issues of marketable Treasury bonds are announced about two weeks before their offering date; the formal announcement is made on Wednesday afternoon and subscriptions begin the following Monday. Since 1986 the Treasury has issued only 30-year noncallable bonds; the months of issue are February, May, August, and November. Anyone can submit a competitive or noncompetitive bid with the nearest Federal Reserve bank, and all noncompetitive bidders will pay the weighted average price of the competitive bids. After Treasury bonds are sold in the primary market, they can be bought and sold in the secondary market, where their prices are quoted in terms of percentage of par value but the fraction of a dollar is expressed in terms of 1/32nd of a dollar. Thus, 98-5 means $98.16 per $100 of par value.

All bonds, notes, and bills issued by the U.S. Treasury are fully backed by the U.S. government and are not taxable at the state or local levels. The taxable equivalent yield is the yield that would have to be earned on private bonds in order to yield the same after-tax rate of return as Treasury bonds. If the yield on Treasury bonds is 8 percent and the total state and local marginal tax rate is 20 percent, then

$$\text{Taxable equivalent yield} = \frac{100 \times \text{yield on Treasury bond}}{100 - \text{state and local marginal tax rate}}$$

$$\frac{100 \times 0.08}{100 - 0.20} = \frac{8}{80} = 10 \text{ percent}$$

An 8 percent yield rate on Treasury bonds is equivalent to a 10 percent yield on taxable securities.

HISTORIC DATA: Percent Yields on Long-Term Treasury Bonds
Monthly Averages
1920–1991

1920	5.32	1940	2.26	1960	4.02	1980	10.81
1921	5.09	1941	2.05	1961	3.90	1981	12.87
1922	4.30	1942	2.46	1962	3.95	1982	12.23
1923	4.36	1943	2.47	1963	4.00	1983	10.84
1924	4.06	1944	2.48	1964	4.15	1984	11.99
1925	3.86	1945	2.37	1965	4.21	1985	10.75
1926	3.68	1946	2.19	1966	4.65	1986	8.14
1927	3.34	1947	2.25	1967	4.85	1987	8.63
1928	3.33	1948	2.44	1968	5.26	1988	8.98
1929	3.6	1949	2.55	1969	6.12	1989	8.58
1930	3.29	1950	2.32	1970	6.58	1990	8.74
1931	3.34	1951	2.57	1971	5.74	1991	8.16
1932	3.68	1952	2.68	1972	5.64		
1933	3.31	1953	2.94	1973	6.31		
1934	3.12	1954	2.55	1974	6.98		
1935	2.79	1955	2.85	1975	7.00		
1936	2.69	1956	3.08	1976	6.78		
1937	2.74	1957	3,47	1977	7.06		
1938	2.61	1958	3.43	1978	7.89		
1939	2.41	1959	4.08	1979	8.74		

III FLOW-OF-FUNDS STATEMENT

Name: Flow-of-Funds Statement
Alternative name: Source and Use of Funds
Agency/Institution: Board of Governors of the Federal Reserve
Address: Flow of Funds Section, Division of Research and Statistics, Washington, DC 20551
Telephone number for data and inquiries: 202-862-3780
Sources: The Federal Reserve's statistical releases Z.1, *Flow of Funds Accounts*, and Z.7, *Flow of Funds Summary*
Frequency: Quarterly
When available: Z.1: 23rd of February, May, August, November; Z.7: 15th of February, May, August, November
Revisions: Annually
Historic data: Call 202-862-3780

■ A QUICK LOOK: Flow-of-Funds Statement

The **flow-of-funds statement** released each quarter by the Federal Reserve is the most comprehensive source of information on the credit market. The data, which are extensive, show the sources and uses of funds by sector and market instruments. There are numerous versions of the flow of funds, but the most consistent and easily obtained are those presented in the monthly *Federal Reserve Bulletin*. Individuals desiring more complete data should subscribe to bulletin Z.1, *Flow of Funds Accounts*.

Before discussing the flow-of-funds statements, we need to be aware of two simple but useful rules in financial markets. First, "selling a security" is the same as borrowing funds and "buying a security" is the same as lending. When you go to a bank to borrow funds to finance the purchase of a new car, you are selling your note or security (your signature on the note is your promise to redeem the note in stages or on a single maturity date). The bank that is lending the funds is also buying your security. Thus, when some sector of the economy has increased its holding of securities (for example, bonds, notes, or bills), that sector has also increased its loans to other sectors of the economy.

The second simple useful rule to remember is:

$$\Sigma IOUs = \Sigma UOMes$$

This is read as: "The sum of the 'I Owe You's' must equal the sum of the 'You Owe Me's.'" Someone's financial asset represents someone else's financial liability; total borrowing must equal total lending. When IBM sells a $10 million bond issue, it means that someone must now own an additional $10 million of IBM bonds. The other side of IBM's bond liability is a bondholder's asset of bonds. An analogy that illustrates the significance of the two-sided nature of financial securities is the federal debt, whose significance is often dismissed with the statement that "we owe it to ourselves." If none of the outstanding securities of the U.S. Treasury were held by foreigners, then we would truly owe the national debt to ourselves. As taxpayers, Americans have a collective liability for the outstanding Treasury debt, but as bondholders, Americans also hold the offsetting assets or claims. Since some Treasury securities are held by foreigners, the example is not totally realistic but it does illustrate that we do, in large measure, owe the national debt to ourselves.

Knowing that borrowing is the same as selling a security and that every liability is someone else's asset can be useful in analyzing the nation's finances, but it does not tell us much about the sources of funds or their ultimate destination. For many purposes, we need to know who is providing the funds and who is borrowing the funds. This is the role of a flow-of-funds statement. It shows the sectors of the economy providing the funds (buying the securities) and those borrowing the funds (selling the securities). **Flow of funds** generally refers to the sources and uses of funds during a certain period of time, such as a quarter or a year, but the term is also used for analyses of outstanding debt held by various sectors of the economy.

■ A CLOSER LOOK

Table 9.1 shows the amounts of funds raised, or borrowed, in the U.S. credit market during 1990. Table 9.2 shows the sources of these funds. Together, the two tables show the sources and uses, as well as the flow of funds, in the United States.

There are various types of flow-of-fund analyses, many of them consisting of many pages of complex tables. The following tables are similar to those published in the *Federal Reserve Bulletin*. Some of these terms are to be found in the tables:

Domestic debt: Includes credit market funds borrowed from both domestic and foreign sources. Americans borrowed funds from other Americans and from foreigners.

Foreign debt: Represents amounts borrowed by foreign financial and nonfinancial sectors in U.S. markets. Americans lent money to foreigners, which is "their" debt.

Financial sector: U.S. government–sponsored credit agencies, federally related mortgage pools, and private financial institutions.

Domestic nonfinancial sector: The U.S. Treasury selling securities to finance the national deficit, as well as state and local governments, households, and corporations domiciled in the United States.

Credit market debt: Consists of debt securities, mortgages, bank loans, commercial paper, consumer credit, government loans, and miscellaneous loans.

Financial intermediation: Occurs when individuals or firms place their funds in financial institutions such as banks, savings and loans, credit unions, pensions, and insurance companies, and these funds are then provided to users. The opposite of financial intermediation occurs when individuals buy stocks or bonds directly.

Annual Flow of Funds

The following two tables show the uses and sources of funds during the calendar year 1990. Although it might seem more logical to show the sources of funds in the first table and the borrowings of funds in the second table, we follow the order in which they are listed in the *Federal Reserve Bulletin*. Table 9.1, which shows the amounts raised (borrowed) by all sectors of the American economy, is broken into four major parts. The first section (beginning line 1) lists the amounts borrowed by the nonfinancial sector, primarily households, corporations, and governments.

The second section (beginning line 28) lists the amounts borrowed by the financial sector, principally the credit agencies of the U.S. government, banks, and finance companies. The third section (beginning line 49) lists the different securities through which both the nonfinancial and financial sectors obtained their funds. The fourth and last section (beginning line 62) lists the amounts corporations obtained by issuing preferred and common stock. The individual lines are explained below the table.

TABLE 9.1
Funds Borrowed from the U.S. Credit Market, 1990
(billions of $)

1	Total Net Borrowing by Domestic **Nonfinancial** Sectors	$662.1
2	U.S. Government	272.5
3	Private Domestic Nonfinancial Sectors	389.6
4	Debt Capital Instruments	309.6
5	Tax-exempt obligations	19.4
6	Corporate bonds	61.5
7	Mortgages	228.7
8	Home mortgages	214.4
9	Multifamily residences	(0.7)
10	Commercial	14.8
11	Farm	0.2
12	Other Debt Instruments	80.0
13	Commercial credit	18.4
14	Bank loans, n.e.c.	(3.0)
15	Commercial paper	9.7
16	Other loans	54.9
17	By Borrowing Sector:	389.6
18	State & local governments	14.6
19	Households	260.1
20	Nonfinancial business/firms	114.9
21	Foreign Net Borrowing in the United States	23.3
22	Bonds	21.1
23	Bank Loans, n.e.c.	(2.8)
24	Open-Market Paper	12.3
25	U.S. Govt & other loans	(7.4)
26	Total Domestic plus Foreign Borrowing by Nonfinancial Sectors	685.4
27		
28	Total Net Borrowing by **Financial** Sectors	199.4
29	U.S. Government Related:	170.6
30	Sponsored credit agency securities	22.6
31	Mortgage pool securities	148.0

(continued)

TABLE 9.1 *(continued)*
Funds Borrowed from the U.S. Credit Market, 1990
(billions of $)

32	Private Financial Sectors	$28.8
33	Corporate bonds	44.1
34	Mortgages	0.7
35	Bank loans, n.e.c.	0.7
36	Open-market paper	8.0
37	Fed. Home Loan Bank loans	(24.7)
38	Total by Sector	199.4
39	Sponsored Credit Agencies	22.6
40	Mortgage Pools	148.0
41	Private Financial Sectors	28.8
42	Commercial banks	(1.1)
43	Domestic affiliates	(27.7)
44	Savings and loans	(32.4)
45	Mutual savings banks	(0.1)
46	Finance companies	50.9
47	Real estate investment trusts (REITs)	(0.3)
48	SO issuers	39.5
49	Total Net Borrowing	884.8
50	U.S. Government Securities	443.1
51	Tax-exempt Obligations	19.4
52	Corporate and Foreign Bonds	126.7
53	Mortgages	229.4
54	Consumer Credit	18.4
55	Bank Loans, n.e.c.	(5.1)
56	Open-Market Paper	30.0
57	Other Loans	22.8
58	Memo: U.S. Government, Cash Balance	8.6
59	Totals Net of Change in U.S. Government Cash Balances	
60	Net Borrowing by Domestic Nonfinancial	653.5
61	Net Borrowing by U.S. Government	264.0
62	External Corporate Equity Funds Raised in United States	
63	Total Amount	17.2
64	Mutual Funds	66.9
65	Nonfinancial Corporations	(63.0)
66	Financial Corporations	6.1
67	Foreign Shares Purchased in the United States	7.2

Line 1: Total amounts borrowed by governments, individuals, and nonfinancial firms during the year (line 1 = lines 2 + 3)

Line 2: Total amount borrowed by the Treasury and U.S. govt. agencies.

Line 3: Total amounts borrowed excluding the federal government (line 3 = lines 4 + 12)

Lines 4–16: Amounts borrowed through the following financial instruments, including tax-exempt securities issued by local and state governments. These lines tell us how nonfinancial sectors obtained their funds. Home mortgage loans were the major source of loans in both the nonfinancial and financial sectors. A negative amount, such as the one on line 9, means that there was negative borrowing — that is, more funds were repaid in this category than were borrowed. In line 9, the repayments of mortgages on multifamily residences were greater during the year than the new mortgage loans undertaken by borrowers.

Lines 17–20: Line 17 is the same amount as that shown in line 3, but in these lines the amount borrowed is shown by the classification of the "private" borrower, which includes state and local governments, households, and nonfinancial business firms. Households are major borrowers in the "private" sector, but this sector's $260 billion lags behind the borrowing of $272 billion by the U.S. government (line 2).

Lines 21–25: These lines refer to the funds borrowed by foreigners in U.S. credit markets. Another way of describing this section is to say that these are the values of securities (bonds, notes, paper) sold in the U.S. by foreigners.

Line 26: This shows the total amounts borrowed by foreigners and Americans in the nonfinancial sector (line 26 = lines 1 + 21)

Lines 28–37: Lines 28 through 37 show borrowing in the financial sector by type of financial instrument. The first classification (lines 29 through 31) shows the securities issued by financial agencies, such as Fannie Mae, which are related to the federal government. The second classification (lines 32 through 37) shows the securities issued by the private financial sector.

Lines 38–48: These lines show the funds borrowed by type of financial institution. The institutions shown in lines 39 and 40 are related to the U.S. government. Lines 23–27 of Table 7.2 are a much better source of information on the relative roles of financial institutions in the credit market.

Line 49: This is the total net amount of funds borrowed by the financial and nonfinancial sectors (line 49 = lines 1 + 21 + 28; also line 49 = lines 50 − 57)

Lines 50–57: The following lines show the combined total borrowings by type of securities: Line 50 = lines 2 + 29; line 51 = line 5; line 52 = lines 6 + 22 + 33; line 53 = lines 7 + 34, and so on.

Lines 58–61: This memo is to alert the reader that the cash balances of the U.S. government increased by $8.6 billion during the year. Thus, the net borrowing by domestic nonfinancial sectors was only $653.5 (line 1 – line 58). Federal government net borrowing was only $264.0 (line 2 – line 58).

Lines 62–67: Refers to the funds obtained by corporations through the issue of preferred and common stock. Line 63 = lines 64 + 65 + 66 + 6? Mutual funds issued $66.9 billion of stock, but nonfinancial corporations had a net repurchase or decrease in outstanding stock.

Table 9.1 shows the uses, or the borrowings, of credit market funds. Table 9.2 shows the sources of funds to the credit market that made these borrowings possible. The table shows the sources from many different perspectives, but for most purposes the important part is lines 15 through 49.

TABLE 9.2
Sources of Funds to the Credit Markets,
1990

1	Funds Advanced to Domestic Nonfinancial Sectors	$662.1
2	Total Net Advances by Public Agencies and Foreigners	278.7
3	U.S. government securities	79.9
4	Residential mortgages	179.0
5	FHLB advances to thrifts	−24.7
6	Other loans and securities	44.5
7	Total Advanced by Sector:	
8	U.S. government	34.0
9	Sponsored credit agencies	170.2
10	Monetary authorities	8.1
11	Foreign	66.4
12	Agency and foreign borrowing not in line 1:	
13	Sponsored credit agencies and mortgage pools	170.6
14	Foreign	23.3
15	Total Private Domestic Funds Advanced	577.3
16	U.S. government securities	363.2
17	State and local obligations	19.4
18	Corporate and foreign bonds	67.7
19	Residential mortgages	34.8
20	Other mortgages and loans	67.6
21	Less: Federal Home Loan Bank advances	−24.7

(continued)

TABLE 9.2 *(continued)*
Sources of Funds to the Credit Markets,
1990

22 Private financial intermediation:	
23 Funds Advanced by Private Financial Institutions	$394.1
24 Commercial banking	119.9
25 Savings institutions	−141.0
26 Insurance and pension funds	226.1
27 Other financial institutions	189.1
28 Sources of Funds:	394.1
29 Private domestic deposits	72.8
30 Credit market borrowing	28.8
31 Foreign funds	46.5
32 Treasury balances	5.3
33 Insurance and pension reserves	209.2
34 Other	31.5
35 Private domestic nonfinancial investors:	
36 Direct Lending in Credit Markets	212.0
37 U.S. government securities	198.4
38 State and local obligations	−1.3
39 Corporate and foreign bonds	−26.6
40 Open-market paper	15.9
41 Other	25.6
42 Deposits and currency	100.1
43 Currency	22.6
44 Checkable deposits	−1.0
45 Small time and savings accounts	67.5
46 Money market fund shares	62.4
47 Large time deposits	−45.8
48 Security RPs	−10.5
49 Deposits in foreign countries	4.7
50 Total of Financial Instruments, Deposits, and Currency	312.1
51 Public holdings as percent of total	42.1
52 Private financial intermediation (in percent)	68.3
53 Total foreign funds	112.9
54 Memo: Corporation Equities Not Included Above	
55 Total Net Issues	17.2
56 Mutual fund shares	66.9
57 Other equities	−49.7
58 Acquisitions by Financial Institutions	30.1
59 Other Net Purchases	−12.9

Line 1: Total credit market funds that were made available to nonfinancial sectors. This amount is the same as line 1 in Table 9.1.

Lines 2–11: These lines show the amount of funds provided by public agencies and foreigners. Lines 3 to 6 and lines 8 to 11 both total to $278.7. The most important lines in this section are 8 through 11. Of the total funds made available to domestic nonfinancial entities ($662.1), the U.S. government provided $34 billion directly and $170.1 billion through government-sponsored credit agencies. The monetary authorities (Federal Reserve) provided $8.1 billion and foreigners provided $66.4 billion.

Lines 12–14: These amounts are not included in the funds provided to domestic nonfinancial entities. They are taken from lines 21 and 29 of Table 9.1 and represent funds advanced to the credit market that were not borrowed by domestic entities.

Lines 15–21: These show the funds advanced by private domestic entities. The total of private domestic advances is equal to line 1 less line 2 plus lines 13 and 14:

Line 1 — Funds advanced to domestic nonfinancial sectors	$662.1
Less: Line 2 — Advances from public agencies and foreigners	278.7
Plus: Line 13 — U.S. government-sponsored credit agencies and pools	170.6
Plus: Line 14 — Foreign borrowing in United States	23.3
Equals: Line 15 — Advances from private domestic sources	$577.3

Lines 22–34: Private financial intermediation occurs when individuals or firms place their funds in financial institutions such as banks, S&Ls, pensions, and so on, and these funds are then provided to borrowers. Lines 22–27 show the net funds that flowed through each of the major institutions. Lines 28 through 34 show the sources of funds for the intermediaries. The $72.8 billion provided by deposits is a sharp decrease from previous years.

Lines 35–41: Direct lending is obtained by taking line 15 less line 23 plus line 30. Direct lending funds are those that did not go through intermediaries. The accounts listed in lines 36 through 41 show the securities through which this direct lending took place. That is, they show the securities purchased by domestic, private nonfinancial investors.

Lines 42–49: Show the changes in deposits and currency that occurred during the year.

Line 50: There are two ways of calculating this total that might shed some light on the process involved. One way is to add lines 36 and 42; the other is to add lines 15 + 43 + 49 and to subtract lines 31 through 34.

Line 51: Line 2 divided by line 1. This shows the public and foreign sources of funds as a percent of the total.

Line 52: Line 23 divided by 15. This line shows the significance of financial intermediaries. During 1990 financial intermediaries processed only 68.3 percent of total private domestic funds provided in the private domestic credit market.

Line 53: Lines 11 + 31. This shows the total foreign funds provided to the credit market.

Line 54–59: These lines show the funds provided by the purchase of newly issued corporate equities. These funds are not included in the above data.

CHAPTER 10

OPTIONS AND FUTURES

American financial markets developed organized options and futures markets for commodities such as wheat and corn more than a century ago, but financial option exchanges in the United States are a recent phenomenon. The oldest option exchange, the Chicago Board Options Exchange, began trading financial options in 1973. Other major options exchanges are in Philadelphia, New York, and San Francisco. The largest foreign options exchanges are in London, Amsterdam, and Tokyo. Option contracts are currently available for stocks, bonds, bills, foreign currencies, and even indexes of stocks.

An **option** is simply a legal contract that gives the holder the right to buy or sell a specified amount of something at a fixed price, known as the *exercise* or *strike price*. A **call option** conveys the right to buy something at a fixed price and a **put option** conveys the right to sell something at a fixed price. Options that can be exercised at any time before they expire are called "American-style" options, whereas those that can be exercised only during a specified time period are called "European-style" options. Except for foreign currency options, virtually all options traded on American exchanges are American-style options. Options have standardized features including the size of the contract, the exercise price, and the expiration date. The price at which options are traded is known as the *premium*. Although option markets exist for gold, foreign currencies, Treasury securities (called interest rate options), stocks, indexes, and futures, only the latter three classes of options have much activity.

There are three types of markets for commodities. The first is the **spot**, or **cash**, **market**, where the producer or an intermediary delivers wheat, for example, within a day or two or at some specified time in the future and gets paid in cash or by check. It is a negotiated price influenced by market conditions. When a farmer sells wheat to the local grain elevator for cash or a check, or the elevator sells wheat to a grain mill, the transaction occurs in the spot market. The second market is the **forward market**, in which the buyer promises to pay the seller a fixed price for a specified quantity of some good to be delivered at some date in the future. Like cash contracts, forward contracts are negotiated between a specific buyer and seller, subject to general market conditions. Forward contracts remove some of the risk from both the buyer and the seller, but generally these contracts are not freely traded, and enforcement of the conditions through the courts is costly and time consuming. The third market is the **futures market**, where the price is agreed upon at the time the contract is made but the money and the commodity do not exchange hands until some date into the future. For example, through some exchange, or clearinghouse, Mr. Smith agrees to deliver to Ms. Jones at a warehouse in Chicago 1000 bushels of wheat at $2.10 per bushel in December. Ms. Jones agrees to accept the wheat and to pay that price on delivery. This futures contract might be called a "December contract for Chicago wheat." No money changes hands between the buyer and seller when a trade is made, but both must post collateral ("margin") to demonstrate their good faith that they will fulfill their future obligations. Most margin deposits range between 5 percent and 15 percent of the contract value.

Futures contract markets let businesses shift the risk of losing money to others more willing to bear them. Futures contracts are negotiable financial instruments that can be bought and sold in a secondary market. Most commodity futures in the United States are bought and sold on an organized exchange under terms of a standard contract that sets the grade or quality of the product and the delivery conditions and coordinates all payments. The exchange facilitates trading among buyers and sellers, records the prices, and enforces certain rules to facilitate honest and open trading, but it does not set prices. Members of an exchange gather in a "pit" or "ring" on the exchange floor and make contracts by shouting and using hand signals.

The two largest U.S. futures exchanges are the Chicago Board of Trade and the Chicago Mercantile Exchange. Both have important agricultural and financial futures markets. Other exchanges are located in New York City, Kansas City, London, Tokyo, and Paris. The exchange, or clearinghouse, acts as buyer to every seller and seller to every buyer. For example, if Smith sells a wheat future to Jones, the clearinghouse is really buying from Smith and then selling it to Jones. Smith is obligated to deliver wheat or an offsetting contract to the clearinghouse on delivery day and Jones is obligated to pay the clearinghouse. In most cases, the commodity is not actually delivered; instead the original contract is offset by a reverse contract before delivery time.

Buyers of futures contracts, known as *longs*, hope that prices will rise, whereas sellers of future contracts, known as *shorts*, hope that prices will fall. Futures provide protection against unfavorable price changes through *hedging*, which means taking a position in the futures market opposite from the one taken in the spot or cash market. Futures markets also attract speculators, who hope to make profits by outguessing the market. There are futures markets for a wide variety of commodities, securities, and indexes.

Investors in the stock market who do not have sufficient cash to purchase the stock are required to make a minimum down payment, or margin, on the securities they purchase. Margin also exists in the futures market, but it is much different from margin in the stock market. For example, if Ms. Jones were thinking of buying 10,000 shares of XYZ Corporation for $10 per share, her total investment—ignoring brokerage charges—would be $100,000. Her margin requirement would be 50 percent, which means that she would have to pay $50,000 up front and could borrow the remaining $50,000 at, say, 8 percent interest. If Mr. Smith bought a futures contract on some commodity or financial instrument worth $100,000, he would have a margin requirement of approximately $5000. Since this margin is merely a performance bond, or good faith money, Smith does not have to pay off the rest of the $95,000 at the time of purchasing the futures. In other words, he can buy the futures contract by depositing $5000 of "earnest money" without paying any more than that. Thus, if both investments increase by 15 percent, both investors could earn gross profits of $15,000. However, Ms. Jones would have earned a rate of return on investment (before interest payments) of 30 percent ($15,000/$50,000). Mr. Smith, who put up only $5000, would have a rate of return on investment of 300 percent ($15,000/$5000). This example clearly illustrates the leverage advantage in the futures market. However, leverage works both ways, and Smith could have had a negative 750 percent rate of return if the market turned against him.

Name: Commodity Futures Quotes and Markets
Agency/Institution: Commodity Research Bureau
Address: 75 Wall Street, New York, NY 10005
Telephone number for data and inquiries: 212-504-7754
Sources: *Wall Street Journal*, most daily newspapers, *CRB's Commodity Yearbook* (annual)
Frequency: Every trading day

■ A QUICK LOOK: Commodity Futures

A **futures market** transaction is one in which the price is agreed upon at the time of the contract, but the money and the commodity will not exchange hands until some date into the future. Futures contracts are negotiable financial instruments that can be bought and sold in a secondary market, which is generally a commodities exchange. Most commodity futures in the United States are bought and sold on an organized exchange under terms of a standard contract that sets the grade or quality of the product and the delivery conditions. The following is an example of futures prices for wheat traded on the Chicago Board of Trade in early September:

Wheat (CBT) 5000 bu. is one contract, cents per bu

	Open	High	Low	Settle	Change	LIFETIME High	Low	Open Interest
Sept.	267½	268	264	267¼	−½	377	255¼	1,147
Dec.	284	284¾	280	284	+½	380	272¼	33,000
Mar.	295½	297½	293	296½	+1½	382½	284	14,250
May	301	304	300	303½	+½	373	291	3,953
July	307½	309	306	309	+1	355	298	2,365

Est vol. 10,000; vol. Mon 11,239; open interest 54,810, +361

Commodity: Located immediately above the quotations are the commodity and the exchange on which it is traded, the standardized contract, and the money units in which the quotes are made. In this case, the commodity is wheat, traded on the Chicago Board of Trade (CBT), the standard contract is for 5000 bushels, and prices are quoted in cents per bushel.

Months: Each commodity futures contract has its own standardized delivery months, and the contracts are referred to as September wheat, December wheat, March wheat, and so on.

Open/high/low: The opening, high, and low prices of that trading day in cents per bushel; the opening price for September wheat is $2.675 per bushel.

Settle: The settlement price, which is generally the closing price of that trading day. The settlement price for September wheat was $2.6725 per bushel. It is called a *settlement price* because the margin accounts are adjusted for "marked to market" by this price.

Change: The change in the settlement price from the previous trading day in fractions of one cent.

Lifetime: The highs and lows during the life of that commodity futures being traded on this exchange.

Open interest: The total number of futures contracts of this commodity that have not been offset by opposite transactions or been fulfilled by delivery of the commodity. As the delivery month approaches, traders begin to close out their positions, and the futures price starts moving toward the current spot or cash price. Since this trading day was in early September, most traders had closed out their September contracts so that only 1147 contracts remained opened. However, there were 33,000 open contracts with a March delivery.

Est vol: The number of contracts traded on the trading day and on the previous trading day.

The table showing wheat futures is just one example of quotes on a commodity's future prices. Dozens of commodities are traded on five major commodity futures markets in the United States. The following are some of the major commodity futures and the exchanges on which they are traded:

Corn (CBT)	Oats (CBT)	Soybeans (CBT)
Soybean Meal (CBT)	Soybean Oil (CBT)	Wheat (CBT)
Wheat (KC)	Wheat (MPLS)	Barley (WPG)
Flaxseed (WPG)	Feeder Cattle (CME)	Live Cattle (CME)
Hogs (CME)	Pork Bellies (CME)	Cocoa (CSCE)
Coffee (CSCE)	Sugar (CSCE)	Cotton (CTN)
Orange Juice (CTN)	Copper (CMX)	Gold (CMX)
Platinum (NYM)	Silver (CMX)	Silver (CBT)
Crude Oil (NYM)	Heating Oil (NYM)	Gasoline (NYM)

The exchanges are as follows: CBT: Chicago Board of Trade; CME: Chicago Mercantile Exchange; CMX: Commodity Exchange in New York; CTN: New York Cotton Exchange; CSCE: Coffee, Sugar and Cocoa Exchange in New York; KC: Kansas City Board of Trade; MPLS: Minneapolis Grain Exchange; WPG: Winnipeg Commodity Exchange.

The largest futures exchange is the Chicago Board of Trade, which accounts for more than one-half the total trading in futures; the second largest is the Chicago Mercantile Exchange. A number of commodities, such as wheat, are sold on more than one exchange, and the standards of the contract and prices will vary slightly among the exchanges.

■ A CLOSER LOOK: Commodity Futures

Individuals and firms throughout the country can buy and sell commodity futures through their local brokers. A margin or deposit is required of those who trade in futures, but the margin required in the futures market is different from the margin required in the stock market, where it is the percentage of the total cost of the stock that must be paid in cash. In the commodity futures market, traders generally have to put up 10 percent of the purchase price (margin) of the commodity. Margin deposits in the futures market are not used to buy anything; rather they are "good faith money" to ensure that adequate funds will be on deposit with the broker to cover losses in the advent of an adverse price change. On any day that a net loss is incurred on an investor's futures contract, the margin account is "hit" for the amount of the loss, and additional funds must be promptly deposited to the margin account. Most traders carry excess margin deposits with their broker or make arrangements for instant credit so they don't have to be bothered with frequent margin calls. Interest is earned on this margin, and the margin amount will be returned to investors when their futures contracts are closed out.

Assume that in March a trader "purchases" a futures contract for 5000 bushels of wheat to be delivered in September at $2 per bushel. The original value of the contract is $10,000, but the trader does not actually pay anything now. There is a required margin deposit of $1000, which will be returned to the trader. If the price of wheat falls by $0.20 per bushel, the trader will have to put into the margin account an additional $1000 (5000 bushels × $0.20); if the price should fall by an additional $0.50, he will have to put up another $2500. On the other hand, if the price of wheat increases by $0.20 per bushel, he will have $1000 credited to his margin account; if the price of wheat increases by an additional $0.50 per bushel, he will have an additional $2500 credited to his account. The trader may withdraw these gains at any time and use them to buy a car, a boat, a VCR, or food for the family. However, if the price turns against him in the future, he will have to replenish his account. Note that the contract does not have to be bought, sold, or exchanged in any way for these gains or losses to occur. Each trading day the appropriate adjustments are made to each trader's account. The "street" term for this process is "marking to market." The trader's account is "marked to market" each day, and he will have to come up with the money to cover a fall in futures prices even if he does not sell his contract.

Trading in commodity futures is done by those who are speculating on the future trend of prices or by those who want to protect themselves against the risk of future price changes. *Hedging* is taking a position in the futures market opposite to a position held in the cash market in order to minimize the risk of loss from an adverse price change. The farmer who is about to plant wheat in the spring can protect himself against a price drop by selling a fall wheat contract. If the price of wheat does fall during the summer, the farmer will get less than he anticipated for his wheat when he sells it in the cash market. He will suffer a loss from the fall in wheat prices, but he will have made a profit on his futures contract. An example might help to make this clear.

Assume that it is April and that Mr. Smith, a midwestern farmer, is contemplating whether he will plant and grow 30,000 bushels of corn to be harvested in the fall and sent to market in December. Mr. Smith believes that he can make a satisfactory profit if he is able to sell the wheat at approximately the current price — about $3.05 per bushel — but he is worried that the cash price might fall sharply between now and December. Assume his broker tells him there are futures contracts for delivery of wheat in March, May, July, September, and December. Wheat promised for delivery in each month has its own price, so that the price of September wheat will be different from the price of December wheat. The broker tells Mr. Smith that the price of wheat futures depends on the carrying costs of wheat (storage, insurance, interest), the price of cash wheat, and current and expected supply and demand conditions for wheat. The broker then tells the farmer that the December wheat futures are selling at $3.10 per bushel, and Mr. Smith agress to *sell* six contracts, with each contract involving 5000 bushels. The total value of the contracts is $93,000, so the farmer is asked to deposit $9300 in the margin account he keeps with the broker.

The farmer has obligated himself to sell 30,000 bushels of wheat in December and the buyer of the contract has obligated himself to buy 30,000 bushels of December wheat at $3.10 per bushel. If the price of wheat goes down, the farmer's futures contracts will gain in value and his account will be credited each day. If you are wondering why his futures contract will become more valuable if the price of wheat goes down, the answer is simple. As the price of wheat goes down, Mr. Smith can buy wheat at the low price and deliver it at the agreed futures price of $3.10 on the delivery date. The lower the price he pays for wheat in the market, the greater his profit spread and the more valuable his futures contract to sell wheat at $3.10. Also, a lower cash price of wheat means that the price of futures wheat will be falling as well. Mr. Smith could buy an offsetting contract at a lower price and pocket the difference.

The buyer of a futures contract can sell it at any time prior to the expiration date. Mr. Smith, the seller, cannot get rid of his obligation to deliver wheat by selling his contract, but he can buy an offsetting futures contract to obtain wheat during the same month, and the clearinghouse will cancel his obligation to deliver wheat. If he bought the offsetting contracts at $2.90 per bushel, it would cost Mr. Smith $87,000 ($2.90 × 5000 × 6), and his gross profits would be $6000.

As the delivery date approaches, the futures price approaches the actual cash price, which will be the cash price (assumed to be $2.90) received by Mr. Smith when he sells his wheat in December. Since the cash market price is $2.90 per bushel rather than the $3.10 he expected back in March, Mr. Smith will suffer a "loss" on his cash or spot sales of the wheat he grew and sold in the cash market. He will sell his wheat for 20 cents less per bushel than he expected back in April, which means his revenue in December will be $6000 (− $0.20 × 30,000) less than he expected. However, his gross profits from the futures market ($6000) will offset his losses from the wheat sales ($6000).

A flour mill buyer would hedge on the other side of the market. He would want to protect the mill from a rise in the price of its wheat input. Hence, he will *buy* a futures contract that will increase in value if the price of wheat should increase during the next few months. His gain in the futures market will offset the higher price he will have to pay for wheat inputs.

Name: Futures on Foreign Currencies
Agency/Institution: Foreign Exchange Department and Futures Industry
   Association

Address: Foreign Exchange Dept., Bankers' Trust, 280 Park Avenue, New York, NY 10017; Futures Industry Association, 1825 Eye St., N.W., Suite 1040, Washington, DC 20006

Telephone number for data and inquiries: 212-250-2500 (Foreign Exch. Dept., Banker's Trust)

Sources: *Wall Street Journal* and some daily newspapers in the currency trading section. The Futures Industry Association and Bankers' Trust have explanatory material available.

Frequency: Daily

■ A QUICK LOOK: Foreign Currency Futures

Foreign currency futures are bought and sold on commodities markets, where delivery of the currencies is seldom made. Do not confuse these futures transactions with the forward sales and purchases in the interbank, or foreign exchange, market, where forward deliveries are always made. Although there are differences between the two markets they are, to a large degree, substitutes for each other and their prices generally move in the same direction. Major foreign currencies with active futures markets on the International Monetary Market of the Chicago Mercantile Exchange are: Japanese yen, Canadian dollar, British pound, Swiss franc, Australian dollar, German mark, Mexican peso, Dutch guilder, and the French franc.

Swiss franc (IMM) — 125,000 francs; $ per franc

	Open	High	Low	Settle	Chg	LIFETIME		Open Interest
						High	Low	
Sept.	.7498	.7543	.7493	.7532	−.0063	.7975	.6020	34,334
Dec.	.7487	.7538	.7487	.7527	−.0061	.7965	.6300	15,487
Mr. 91	.7460	.7525	.7460	.7516	−.0059	.7950	.6500	735
June	.7485	.7504	.7485	.7502	−.0058	.7930	.7065	105

Est. vol. 34,785; vol. Mon 36,282; open int. 50,711, +4,436

Description: Swiss franc futures are sold on the International Monetary Market at the Chicago Mercantile Exchange in standardized contracts of 125,000 francs. The prices are quoted in U.S. dollars per franc; for example, the opening September franc is priced at $0.7498.

Months: Most contracts in foreign currency futures are available for delivery in March, June, September, and December. The price on a futures contract is a prediction by the participants of what the exchange rate will be on the delivery day. For example, in the table, September Swiss francs were settled at $0.7532 per franc. The September delivery day is only a few days off, and if the spot market price were not approximately equal to $0.7532, some trader could profit by buying future contract, hold it until delivery day, then buy spot francs and make delivery on the contract. If the spot rate for Swiss francs was higher than the futures rate, he would buy September futures, take delivery of the francs, and then sell them in the spot market. Although this ability to take delivery is not exercised very often, its possibility ties the futures market and the exchange market together.

Open/high/low: The opening, high, and low prices of the futures contracts during the trading day. December francs opened at 74.87 cents per Swiss franc.

Settle: The settlement or closing price for December francs was 75.27 cents per franc.

Chg: The change in the settlement price for December francs from the previous trading day was .61 cent. The settlement price on the previous day was .7588.

Lifetime: Highs and lows for Swiss franc futures since they began trading on the IMM.

Open interest: The total number of contracts that have not yet been liquidated or offset by opposite transactions, or that have not been fulfilled by actual delivery. The open interest contracts include only the number of contracts, not the number of participants.

Est. vol.:   Total volume of contracts sold on the exchange during the trading day.

■ A CLOSER LOOK: Foreign Currency Futures

Futures contracts on foreign exchange can easily get confused with forward contracts on foreign exchange (see "Forward Exchange Markets," pages 422–424.) Foreign currency futures are similar to forward contracts in that both provide for payment and delivery to take place on some date in the future. However, forward contracts virtually always involve the actual delivery of the foreign currency whereas futures contracts do not. A margin or security deposit of about 10 percent must be maintained with the broker on a futures contract. Forward contracts, which have existed for more than 150 years, are usually made through the interbank network of large international money banks; futures contracts, which first appeared in 1972, are made and traded on the floors of the futures exchanges. These futures contracts on foreign currencies can easily be purchased by average individuals through the stock brokerage system. The two markets are somewhat competitive with each other, and a person finding rates and commissions too high in the forward market can use the futures market and vice versa.

Currency futures market contracts are similar to the contracts long used at the commodity exchanges to hedge positions in farm products such as wheat, soybeans, and live cattle. Futures contracts are agreements that are standardized with respect to amount, delivery location, and delivery procedure. The futures currency contract is primarily a means for hedging risk, not for purchasing currencies; thus, futures traders usually (more than 98 percent of the time) settle their accounts by purchasing offsetting contracts before the last scheduled day of trading.

The standard contract amounts are 25,000 British pounds, 100,000 Canadian dollars, 125,000 German marks, 125,000 Dutch guilders, 125,000 Swiss francs, 1 million Mexican pesos, and 12.5 million Japanese yen. The standard delivery dates are the third Wednesday of March, June, September, and December, out as far as 15 months. The standard margin is $10,000 to $20,000. As with most commodities, price movements for the contracts are subject to daily limits. While the futures market has grown considerably during the past few years, it is still attractive to small businesses or investors. Most large multinational companies are hesitant to use it extensively because the large blocks of currency in which they deal will move the rates against them.

Assume that an American importer of BMW cars knows that in six months (June) he will have to pay 10 million German marks (DM) to a German exporter. The importer can choose to hedge in either the forward exchange market or the futures market. He might go to his banker to buy marks six months forward so he will know today what the marks are going to cost him. If the forward rate is, say, $0.60 per mark, he will know today that the dollar cost of his imports will be $6 million. Furthermore, the importer will not have to put anything down. The other option available to the American importer is to hedge on the German mark futures market. Since each futures contract for German marks is 125,000 DM, he will buy 80 contracts for June delivery. If the June DM is trading at .60, he will be contracting to pay $6 million but, of course, he will only deposit about $600,000 as margin. His broker will probably pay some interest on the margin deposit, but this is a deposit requirement in the futures market that the trader does not have in the forward market. If the DM falls in value during the next six months, the importer will suffer a loss on the futures contract, but he will benefit from the more favorable rate of exchange when he buys DMs in the spot market. If the DM rate rises, he will enjoy a profit on his futures contracts and pay a higher price for the spot marks. To summarize:

January: Importer buys 80 contracts of June marks
    @ 125,000 marks per contract. DM = $0.60

                                                $6,000,000

A. Example of DM price increasing:
    June — Importer sells futures contracts

at DM = $0.65	6,500,000
Profit on futures contract	+ 500,000
Importer buys marks on spot market , which now cost 5 cents more per mark	− 500,000

The importer has to pay $500,000 more for the marks on the spot market but he has offsetting profits from hedging in the futures market. Thus, hedging has eliminated the risk of exchange rate fluctuations.

B. Example of DM price decreasing:
June — Importer sells futures contracts

at DM = $0.55	$5,500,000
Loss on futures contract	− 500,000
Importer buys marks on spot market, which now cost 5 cents less per mark	+ 500,000

The importer has lost $500,000 on the futures market but he pays $500,000 less for the German marks. Thus, hedging has eliminated the risk of exchange rate fluctuations.

Name: Futures Options
Agency/Institution: Bankers' Trust and Chicago Board Options Exchange (CBOE)
Address: Bankers' Trust, 280 Park Avenue, New York, NY 10017; Chicago Board Options Exchange, LaSalle at Van Buren, Chicago, IL 60605
Telephone numbers for data and inquiries: 212-250-2500 (Bankers' Trust), 312-786-5600 (CBOE)
Sources: *Wall Street Journal* and some daily newspapers
Frequency: Daily

■ A QUICK LOOK: Futures Options on Commodities, Treasury Bonds, Stock Indexes, Eurodollars, and Foreign Currencies

Trading in options is certainly not new, but trading in options on futures has been taking place only since 1982, when options trading on Treasury bond futures began at the Chicago Board of Trade. Much of the material presented on "Stock Options" (see pages 258–262) are applicable to futures options. As with all options, a call option conveys the right to buy and a put option conveys the right to sell. In this case, the thing being sold is a "Futures Contract" (see pages 234–238 for a discussion of futures) to commodities, bonds, bills, foreign currencies, Eurodollars, or several stock indexes.

The following is an example of commodity futures options rates:

Soybeans (CBT) 5,000 bu.; cents per bu.

Strike Price	CALLS — SETTLE			PUTS — SETTLE		
	Nov-c	Jan-c	Mar-c	Nov-p	Jan-p	Mar-p
600	41¾	57	68½	2⅞	5	6¼
625	23½	38½	50½	9¾	11⅜	12½
650	12¼	25½	36½	23¼	24	22½
675	6¼	17	27	42	40	. . .
. . .	. . .	. . .	. . .	. . .	. . .	. . .

Est. vol. 7,500; Mon vol.: 3,172 calls, 2,021 puts
Open interest Mon: 63,616 calls, 34,045 puts

Description: This table shows the option prices on soybean futures. These options are traded on the Chicago Board of Trade, and the option prices are reported in cents per bushel. A single contract is for 5000 bushels. Delivery months are January, March, May, July, and November, and the option contract expires at least 10 days before the futures contract.

Strike price: This is the price at which the option on the futures is exercised. The strike price in the first line is 600 cents per bushel. If the futures price gets to 600 cents per bushel or higher, then the call option on the futures contract will be exercised. If November soybean futures are selling at 638, or $6.38 per bushel, the call option contracts with strike prices of 600 and 625 are "in the money." This explains why the call options with low strike prices are relatively high priced. If the market price is less than the strike price of the put option contracts, then they will be exercised. With a current market price of 638, the put options with strike prices of 650 and 675 are "in the money" and, thus, they are priced relatively highly.

Months: The expiration months of the put and call options.

Puts/calls settle: The settlement or closing price of the options in terms of cents per bushel. The minimum price change is ⅛, and the value of a single call option contract for November soybeans at a strike price of 625 is $117,500 (23½ × 5000).

The following is an example of Treasury bond futures options rates:

T-Bonds (CBT) $100,000; points and 64ths of 100%

Strike Price	CALLS — LAST			PUTS — LAST		
	Dec-c	Mar-c	June-c	Dec-p	Mar-p	June-p
86	3–48	4–05	. . .	0–49	1–31	. . .
88	2–24	2–55	3–10	1–23	2–11	2–54
90	1–21	1–57	2–15	2–18	3–10	. . .
92	0–42	1–12	1–38	3–38	4–24	. . .
94	0–20	0–46	. . .	5–15	5–56	. . .
96	0–09	0–26	0–46	7–02	7–34	. . .

Est. vol. 47,500; Mon vol.: 26,316 calls, 29,562 puts
Open interest Mon: 321,727 calls, 300,429 puts

Description: This futures option is on Treasury bond futures. Unlike bond and bond futures prices, which are quoted in 32nds of a point, options premiums are quoted in 64ths of a point, with each 64th equal to $15.63. Thus, an option premium of 2–16 would be 2 and ¹⁶⁄₆₄ points, which is $2250 ($100,000 × 0.0225). Delivery months are March, June, September, and December.

Strike price: Price at which the call or put may be exercised by the buyer of the option. This is the price of T-bond futures, which are expressed in percent of par value. For example, the 88 means that a $100,000 bond future is selling for $88,000.

Calls/puts: A call option gives the buyer the right to buy T-bond futures from the writer of the option at a stated price. A put option gives the buyer the right to sell T-bond futures to the writer at a stated price. The word *last* following calls and puts means the price of the last call or put options traded on that day. The option prices are stated in points, or percentages of 100 percent. The call option price, or and selling in the two markets. If the Swiss franc spot rate were less than the futures rate as the delivery day approached, a trader could sell a September franc premium, at a strike price of 86 for expiration in December is 3–48. The "48" means $^{48}\!/_{64}$ths so 3–48 means 3.75 percent, or $3750 ($100,000 × 0.0375) for a standardized contract of $100,000. The put premium for March delivery is 1–31, or $1484.38 for the standardized contract.

Months: Months in the standardized contract when the options expire.

Note: Futures options exist on 10- and 5-year Treasury notes, the Municipal Bond Index, and mortgage-backed securities — all of which are priced and traded essentially the same as futures options on Treasury bonds.

The following is an example of index futures options rates:

S&P Stock Index (CME) $500 times premium

Strike Price	CALLS — SETTLE			PUTS — SETTLE		
	Sept-c	Oct-c	Dec-c	Sept-p	Oct-p	Dec-p
310	13.25	. . .	25.75	1.55	5.35	10.65
315	9.15	. . .	22.30	2.40	6.45	12.10
320	5.60	13.25	19.10	3.85	7.90	13.80
325	2.90	10.10	16.10	6.15	9.70	15.85
. . .	. . .	. . .	. . .	. . .	. . .	. . .

Est. vol. 6,626; Mon vol.: 3,116 calls, 4,000 puts
Open interest Mon: 39,547 calls, 49,917 puts

Description: This table reports the prices for options on the S&P stock index futures. (See pages 256–258 for a discussion of "Stock Index Options" and pages 233–255 for "Stock Index Futures.") These futures options are traded on the Chicago Mercantile Exchange, and the values of the contracts are 500 times premium. For example, a September index at a strike price of 320 had a settlement price of $2800 ($5.60 × 500).

Strike price: The price at which the option is exercised. For example, if the strike price is 315, this is the value of the S&P 500 at which the options may be called or put, at the option of the option holder. If the futures price gets above 315, then the holder of a call option will exercise his option and the writer will have to deliver a standardized futures S&P contract for $157,500 (315 × $500). If the futures price of the S&P 500 index falls below 315, the holder of a put option will exercise his option and the writer will have to buy the futures contract for $157,500.

Calls/puts settle: These are the closing or settlement prices (premiums) for the call and put options. The prices are stated in terms of price per individual index point, but the standard contract is 500 times these prices. If the striking price is "in" or nearly in "the money," the call and put options will increase in price.

The following is an example of Eurodollar futures options rates:

Eurodollar (IMM) $ million; pts of 100%

Strike Price	CALLS — SETTLE			PUTS — SETTLE		
	Sept-c	Dec-c	Mar-c	Sept-p	Dec-p	Mar-p
9150	0.43	0.57	0.60	. . .	0.06	0.14
9175	0.19	0.37	0.43	0.01	0.11	0.20
9200	0.02	0.22	0.29	0.09	0.20	0.30
9225	. . .	0.11	0.18	0.32	0.34	0.43

Est. vol. 18,972; Mon vol.: 17,475 calls, 11,654 puts
Open interest Mon: 244,506 calls, 226,223 puts

Description: This table shows the premiums on Eurodollar futures options. The standard contract is for $1 million of Eurodollar futures. The options are traded at the International Monetary Market (IMM) at the Chicago Mercantile Exchange. Eurodollar options expire at the end of the last day of trading in the underlying Eurodollar futures contract. Delivery months are March, June, September, and December. Option trading terminates at the same date and time as the underlying futures contract (the second business day before the third Wednesday of the contract month).

Strike price: The price at which the option can be exercised. It is stated in dollars per $10,000 deposit, but the more traditional way to read it is in terms of $100 deposit. For example, 9175 is 91.75 per $100 of par value.

Call/put settle: These are the closing or settlement prices for the futures options in terms of percent of value of futures contract. Each point (0.01 percent) equals $25 ($1,000,000 × 0.0001 × 91/365).

Since the Eurodollar futures contract is settled in cash, the final settlement for Eurodollar options follows the cash settlement procedure adopted for Eurodollar futures. To illustrate, suppose the strike price for a Eurodollar futures call option is $91.00 and the final settlement price for Eurodollar futures is $91.50. Exercising the call option at expiration gives the holder the right, in principle, to place $1 million in a three-month Eurodollar deposit paying an interest rate of 9 percent. But since the contract is settled in cash, the holder receives $1250 (50 basis points × $25) in lieu of the right to place the Eurodollar deposit paying 9 percent. Strike price intervals are the same as Treasury bill strike price intervals. The minimum price fluctuation is 1 basis point, and each basis point is worth $25.

The following is an example of futures options rates on foreign currencies:

German marks (IMM) 125,000 marks; cents per mark

Strike Price	CALLS—SETTLE			PUTS—SETTLE		
	Oct-c	Dec-c	Mar-c	Oct-p	Dec-p	Mar-p
6200	1.34	1.93	2.34	0.41	1.00	1.43
6250	1.01	...	...	0.58	1.21	...
6300	0.74	1.38	1.85	0.81	1.45	2.05
6350	0.53	1.16	...	1.11	...	...

Description: This table shows the premiums on German mark futures options. The standard contract is for $125,000 marks. The options are traded at the International Monetary Market at the Chicago Mercantile Exchange. German mark futures options expire on the second Friday before the third Wednesday of the delivery months, which are March, June, September, and December.

Strike price: The price at which the option can be exercised. It is stated in cents per mark. For example, 6250 means that the mark's strike price is $0.625 per German mark, which means that the put or call option can be exercised when the futures price reaches that level.

Call/put settle: These are the closing or settlement prices for the futures options in terms of cents per German mark. For example, the premium for 6200 October is $0.0134 per mark. Since the standard contract is 125,000 marks, the premium per contract is $1675. Each point ($0.0001 per mark) is worth $12.50 per contract.

The primary advantages of futures options over options for actual securities are their ease of trading and the low margin required. As with stock options, the buyer of a put or call need not put down a margin; he or she only has to pay the premium for the option. However, the seller (writer) of a put or call has to post a margin because he or she is committed to deliver the futures contract at the strike price if the buyer exercises the option. The most the option buyer can lose is the price of the option — the premium. The option buyer is never subject to margin calls but option writers are because they will have to sell or buy the futures at the strike price.

Name: Interest Rate Futures (Futures on Treasury Bonds, Treasury Bills, and Eurodollars)
Alternative name: Financial Futures
Agency/Institution: Futures Industry Association (FIA) and Chicago Board of Trade (CBT)
Address: FIA, 1825 Eye St., N.W., Suite 1040, Washington, DC 20006; CBT, La Salle at Jackson, Chicago, IL 60604

Sources: *Wall Street Journal* and many daily newspapers; CBT has various reports on futures trading and it publishes *CBT's Annual Statistical Supplement*, which has futures data; FIA issues monthly reports on futures trading volume
Frequency: Daily
When available: Next day in paper or at 4:30 P.M. EST.

■ A QUICK LOOK: Interest Rate Futures

Financial futures, which were first traded in 1972, are much less well known than commodity futures, but trading activity in them has grown rapidly. The prices of financial futures are reported in many daily newspapers. Following are examples of quotation tables on Treasury bonds, bills, and Eurodollar deposits. A discussion of each instrument is given in the "A Closer Look" section that follows the tables.

Treasury Bonds Futures (CBT) — $100,000; pts 32nds of 100%

	Open	High	Low	Settle	Chg	YIELD		Open Interest
						Settle	Chg	
Sept.	89–08	89–19	89–03	89–15	+3	9.157	−.012	47,618
Dec.	88–28	89–06	88–21	89–01	+3	9.210	−.011	227,298
Mr. 91	88–17	88–26	88–11	88–21	+3	9.255	−.012	14,332
June	88–05	88–14	88–00	88–10	+4	9.297	.016	4,797
Sept	87–26	88–03	87–26	88–00	+5	9.336	.019	2,669
. . .	. . .	. . .	. . .	. . .	. . .	. . .	. . .	. . .

Est. vol. 315,000; vol. Mon 239,316; open int. 297,637, −17,837

Description: Treasury bond futures are traded on the Chicago Board of Trade in standard contracts of $100,000 Treasury bonds, paying a nominal 8 percent, with 20 years to maturity; the numbers to the left of the dash are called **points**; the numbers to the right are called **ticks** and are equal to 32nds of a point (⅟₃₂nd = $31.25 on a $100,000 contract).

Months: The futures contracts are standardized for delivery in the months shown here.

Open/high/low: These are the opening, high, and low prices for the futures contracts. For example, December bond futures opened at 88²⁸⁄₃₂, which is equal to $88,875 for a single contract.

Settle: This is the closing or settlement price at the end of the trading day. For December bonds, it was 89⅟₃₂ or $89,031.25 for a standard contract of $100,000.

Chg: The change in the settlement price from the settlement price of the previous trading day. The change is the number of 32nds. The December bond futures increased in price by ³⁄₃₂, or $93.75 per contract.

Yield: This is the yield of the bond based on the yield of the closing or settle price.

Open interest: The total number of contracts that have not yet been liquidated or offset by opposite futures transactions, or that have not been fulfilled by actual delivery. The open interest contracts are the number of contracts, not the number of participants. Thus, the number of parties involved will be double the open interest listed. Open interest gives some idea of future market activity. The larger the open interest, the greater the activity that will likely occur in the market, especially as the trading date gets close to the delivery date.

Est. vol.:   The estimated volume for this day's trading and the previous day's trading (Mon.) is the number of contracts being traded and not the dollar volume of the contracts traded. The "volume" and "open interest" in the bottom line refer to delivery in all months.

Treasury Bills Futures (IMM) — $1 million; pts of 100%

	Open	High	Low	Settle	Chg	DISCOUNT Settle	Chg	Open Interest
Sept.	92.76	92.76	92.71	92.75	+.04	7.25	−.04	11,263
Dec.	93.06	93.06	92.99	93.03	+.02	6.97	−.02	20,047
Mr. 91	92.99	93.00	92.96	93.00	+.05	7.00	−.05	3,390
June				92.83	−.01	7.17	+.01	254

Est. vol. 5,874; vol. Mon 4,240; open int. 35,015, +785.

Description: The top line describes the futures security. In this case, Treasury bill futures are traded on the International Monetary Market, a division of the Chicago Mercantile Exchange. The contracts are for $1 million, and the prices are quoted in parts of 100 percent. For example, 92.76 means $927,600 for a $1 million contract.

Months: The futures contracts are standardized by month.

Open/high/low: These are the opening, high, and low prices for the trading day. For example, December bills opened at 93.06, or $930,600 for a $100,000 Treasury bill delivered in December.

Settle: The closing or settlement price at the end of the trading day. The settlement price for December bills was $930,300.

Chg: The change in the settlement price from the previous trading day. The settlement price of December bonds on the previous day was 93.01.

Discount: The simple interest rate (discount rate) implied by the day's settlement price. For December bills, it is 6.97 percent, which is obtained by subtracting 93.03 (settle) from 100.

Chg: Reports the change in the discount rate from the previous day.

Open interest: The total number of contracts that have not yet been liquidated or offset by opposite transactions, or that have not been fulfilled by actual delivery. The open interest gives some idea of the market activity. The larger the open interest, the greater the activity that will likely occur in the market, especially as the trading date gets close to the delivery date.

Est. vol.:   The estimated volume for this day's trading and the previous day's trading is the number of contracts being traded and not the dollar volume of the contracts traded. The volume and open interest in the bottom line refer to delivery in all months.

Eurodollar Futures (IMM) — $1 million; pts of 100%

	Open	High	Low	Settle	Chg	DISCOUNT Settle	Chg	Open Interest
Sept.	91.93	91.95	91.90	91.93	−.02	8.07	+.02	145,329
Dec.	92.00	92.02	91.95	92.02	...	7.98	...	235,839
Mr. 91	91.98	92.00	91.92	91.99	...	8.01	...	112,468
June	91.84	91.86	91.79	91.84	−.01	8.16	+.01	65,428
...	...	...	...	...	...	...	...	...

Est. vol. 133,797; vol. Mon. 131,489; open int. 760,168, +2,036

Description: Eurodollar futures are traded on the International Monetary Market at the Chicago Mercantile Exchange. Eurodollar futures are traded in standardized contracts of $1 million and prices are quotes as parts of 100 percent.

Months: The standardized months for delivery of Eurodollars are September, December, March, and June.

Open/high/low: The opening, high, and low prices of the trading day. The prices are stated in percentages. A single contract of $1 million December Eurodollars opened at a price of $920,000.

Settle: The settlement or closing price for December Eurodollars was $920,200.

Chg: The change in the settlement from the previous trading day. The settlement price for December Eurodollars on the previous day was 92.02.

Discount: The interest or discount rate obtained by subtracting the settlement price, 92.02 for December Eurodollars, from 100 to obtain a discount rate of 7.98.

Open interest: The total number of contracts that have not yet been liquidated or offset by opposite transactions, or that have not been fulfilled by actual delivery. The open interest contracts include only the number of contracts, not the number of participants. Thus, the number of parties involved will be double the open interest listed.

Est. vol.:   The total volume and open interest for deliveries in all months are shown at the bottom of the table.

■ A CLOSER LOOK: Interest Rate Futures

Treasury Bond Futures

A **commodity futures contract** is a contract to make or take delivery of a standardized quantity and grade of a commodity during a specific month; a **financial futures contract** is an agreement for the deferred delivery of some standardized financial instrument. Futures contracts are similar to forward contracts in that they both involve deferred delivery. However, there are many differences. Unlike forward contracts, futures contracts are standardized, transferable, and traded on a central market. Also, futures contracts involve margin deposits.

Financial futures includes futures contracts not only for interest rate instruments (which are discussed in this section), but also stock index futures and foreign currencies (which are discussed in the following sections). The term **interest rate futures** refers to contracts on interest-sensitive securities or financial instruments, such as Treasury bonds and bills. Investors can speculate or hedge on future interest rate changes without actually buying and selling bonds.

Assume that Mr. Smith expects interest rates to fall (which means that bond prices will rise) in early December. Mr. Smith could buy "cash bonds" in September, hold them until interest rates fell (bond prices rose) and then sell them for a profit. However, he would have to tie up his capital in the interim. Alternatively, Mr. Smith can buy a futures contract calling for the deferred delivery to him of $100,000 Treasury bonds (a standardized amount) with a coupon rate of 8 percent and 20 years left to maturity.[1] He informs his broker that he wants the bonds to be delivered in December; his broker relays this information to the trading floor of the Chicago Board of Trade, and through a system of shouts and hand and figure language another trader is found who has a customer named Ms. Brown who wants to sell $100,000 of 8 percent Treasury bonds with a 20-year maturity for delivery in December (the standardized months for delivery are March, June, September, and December). The price of the futures contract is stated in percentage of par, with the figures to the right of the decimal point or dash meaning 32nds of a point. For example, if Mr. Smith purchased his bond contract for 65.18, it means that he bought a $100,000 par value bond for $65,562.50. Each full point, or $32/32$ is equal to $1000 and each $1/32$nd (called a **tick**) equals $31.25. Thus, a $100,000 par value bond selling at 65.18 is calculated as:

$$65 \times 1000 = 65,000.00$$
$$18 \times \$31.25 = 562.50$$
$$\text{Sales price} = 65,562.50$$

After the contract is made, Mr. Smith, the buyer of the futures contract, is said to be in a long position and Ms. Brown, the seller, to be in a short position. If the price of Treasury bill futures should drop from 65.18 to 61.18, Mr. Smith, who has promised to pay 65.18, would lose $4000 and Ms. Brown would gain $4000. In fact, Mr. Smith would have to provide an additional $4000 of "margin" to his broker and Ms. Brown would find her account credited with $4000. Crediting the account of the "gainer"

---

[1]Standardized adjustments are made in the price to accommodate different maturities and interest rates.

and debiting the account of the "loser" each trading day is called "marking to market."

Mr. Smith, who has a long position in Treasury futures, has two choices. He can take actual delivery of the Treasury bonds or he can liquidate (cover or offset) his position. If he decides to cover, he would have to sell $100,000 of 8 percent Treasury bonds — the size of a standard contract — for delivery in December. This sale would simply offset his original purchase and he can forget about taking delivery. Mr. Smith has to be sure that he sells the offsetting contract for delivery in December. If he sold the contract for delivery in March, he would still be long in his December contract and short in his March contract. In fact, Mr. Smith would be said to own a "spread" position. If he did nothing to offset these positions, he would have to accept delivery of $100,000 of Treasury bonds in December and he would have to deliver $100,000 of Treasury bonds in March. About 98 percent of all contracts are covered or offset without deliveries being made. Futures markets also exist for 10-, 5-, and 2-year Treasury notes, which are quoted and handled the same way as the 20-year Treasury bonds.

Treasury Bill Futures

Future contracts can also be made for U.S. Treasury bills, which have a standard contract of $1 million and a requirement that bills must have 13 weeks (= 91 days) left to maturity. Delivery months are the same as for Treasury bonds: March, June, September, and December. Price quotations for T-bill futures contracts are based on a formula that involves subtracting the Treasury bill discount yield from 100. For example, if the discount yield on a traded T-bill futures contract is 8.25 percent, then the formula value is $100 - 8.25 = 91.75$ per $100 par. In this case, a $1 million Treasury bill futures contract would be valued at $917,500. These paper prices are predicated on a one-year security, but they are only 91-day securities, so the actual calculations of wins and losses are based on the 91-day maturities. The minimum price fluctuation for these futures contracts is 1 basis point, or $\frac{1}{100}$ of 1 percent, which is $25 on a $1 million contract for a 91-day T-bill ($1 million $\times 0.0001 \times 91/365$).

Assume that in early November Mr. Smith believes that interest rates will fall and that bill prices will increase during the next two or three months. Hence, he buys a March 1991 Treasury bill futures contract at 93.45, which has a nominal value of $934,500. After the transaction is completed, Mr. Smith has an obligation to buy a $1 million (face value) Treasury bill yielding 6.55 percent on a discount basis on the contract delivery date in March. The other party to the transaction — the seller — has agreed to sell a $1 million Treasury bill for $934,500. When Mr. Smith buys the futures contract, he pays nothing but the broker's commission and the margin.

Assume that a few days after purchasing the futures contract, December T-bills drop by 5 basis points so that they are now trading at 93.40. Since each basis point is worth $25, Mr. Smith will have lost $125 if he were to sell the contract today. Even if he continues to hold the futures contract, he will have $125 deducted from his margin account, and the seller will have $125 added to his account. If Mr. Smith's expectations are correct and interest rates fall (price of Treasury bills increases), he will make some gains. If the T-bill price increases to 94.45, Mr. Smith will have gross gains of $2500 ($25 × 100 basis points). This practice of marking futures contracts to market at the end of each trading day means that the trader is forced to realize his loss even though he does not sell the bill. Of course, he doesn't know the final losses (or gains) until the maturity date of the contract because the T-bill price can always change.

Individual investors seldom trade interest rate futures. However, institutions such as banks, pension funds, and investment bankers often use the futures market. For example, if an institution purchases some short-term securities from an issuing corporation with the intent of selling them within a few days, it runs the risk that interest rates could rise and bill prices fall while it is holding these bills. By selling T-bills short on the futures market, however, the firm can hedge against these potential losses. Then, if interest rates do rise and bill prices fall, the firm will take losses on its inventory of bills, but it can also buy back its futures contract at lower bond prices and thus offset those losses.

Eurodollar Futures

A very active market in Eurodollar futures exists on the International Monetary Market in Chicago. The buyer of a Eurodollar futures contract is required to place $1 million in a three-month Eurodollar time deposit, which pays the contracted rate of interest on the contract maturity date. This delivery obligation exists only in principle, however, because the Eurodollar contract is cash settled on the last day of the contract. Eurodollar futures are traded much the same way as Treasury bill futures. Prices are based on the same price index (100 − the discount yield); the same delivery months of March, June, September, and December; and they have the same minimum price fluctuation of 1 basis point equals $25. The final cash settlement is determined by an average of 100 minus the interest rate being paid on Eurodollar deposits on the settlement date. Thus, if the official interest rate on relevant Eurodollar deposits is 8.32 percent, the settlement price on a $1 million Eurodollar deposit would be $916,800.

Name: Spot and Futures Price Indexes
Alternative names: CRB-BLS Spot Price Index and CRB Futures Index
Agency/Institution: Commodity Research Bureau (formerly, together with the Bureau of Labor Statistics) and the Commodity Research Bureau Futures

Address: Commodity Research Bureau, 75 Wall Street, New York, NY 10005
Telephone number for data and inquiries: 212-504-7754
Sources: *Commodity Daily*
Frequency: Daily
When available: Every afternoon at 4:30 P.M. EST.
Historic data: *CRB Commodity Yearbook* (annual)

■ A QUICK LOOK: Spot and Futures Price Indexes

Before 1981, the Bureau of Labor Statistics (BLS) cooperated with the Commodity Research Bureau (CRB) in producing the Spot Price Index for commodities. Although the BLS has not been involved since then, the index, now maintained and published by CRB, is still known as the CRB-BLS Spot Price Index. Based on $100 = 1967$, the index is composed of the spot market prices of 21 commodities, including fibers, metals, livestock, petroleum, and wood.

The CRB Futures Index is a rather peculiar index. Basically, it is intended to track the future prices of commodities. Hence, the future prices of each of 21 commodities (the same ones in the spot price index) are averaged over five months, and then these average prices of the 21 commodities are geometrically averaged. For example, the price of corn is determined by averaging (arithmetic mean) the prices of corn for the following five contract months — that is, the price of corn for delivery in August, the price of corn for delivery in October, the price of corn for delivery in December, and so on. Then these average prices for each commodity are geometrically averaged — that is (corn average × wheat average × cattle average × ⋯)$^{1/21}$. The index is then adjusted for consistency and converted to a number representing changes since the base year of 1967.

Name: S&P 500 Futures Index
Agency/Institution: Standard & Poor's
Address: P.O. Box 992, New York, NY 10275
Telephone number for data: 212-208-1199
Sources: *Wall Street Journal* and many daily newspapers

■ A QUICK LOOK: S&P 500 Futures Index

Although it might be hard for financial novices to believe, an active market exists in futures trading of the S&P 500 Index and several other similar indexes. The following table illustrates typical quotes for one trading day of the S&P 500, which trades on the Chicago Mercantile Exchange. The

New York Stock Exchange Composite Index futures, traded on the New York Futures Exchange (a unit of the New York Stock Exchange) and the Major Market Index futures, traded on the Chicago Board of Trade, are essentially similar to the S&P 500 Index futures.

	Open	High	Low	Settle	Chg	High	Low	Open Interest
Sept.	323.90	325.50	321.40	324.85	+.60	374.90	305.20	114,220
Dec.	327.25	329.25	324.80	328.55	+.60	379.50	308.65	33,253
Mr. 91	330.10	331.80	328.50	331.50	+.35	384.00	312.00	720
June	334.00	336.00	332.60	335.60	+.35	386.00	315.00	19

Est. vol. 53,921; vol. Tues 42,004; open int. 148,212, +336
Index prelim high 324.52; low 320.99; close 324.39, +1.30

Description: The S&P 500 Index futures are traded on the Chicago Mercantile Exchange. The standardized contract is 500 times the index values shown in the table. If someone had purchased a September contract at the opening price, the value would have been $161,950 (332.9 × 500).

Index prelim high/low/close: This information is located on the bottom line of the table, but should be the first line read. It shows the preliminary values for the actual S&P 500 Index on that trading day and the change in the value of the index from the previous trading day. The actual S&P 500 Index closed at 324.39, which was up 1.30 points from the previous day.

Months: The standardized delivery months are March, June, September, and December.

Open/high/low: These are the open, high, and low prices for the index futures for the trading day. The values in the table are the futures values for the S&P 500. The index is based on 1941–43 = 10, but the figures reported in the table, except for the bottom line, are the futures value and not the actual values of the index.

Settle: This is the closing or settlement value for the index futures for this trading day. The standard contract is 500 times the index futures settlement price, so the value for the December index is $164,275.

High/low: These are the highs and lows for the S&P 500 Index futures during the year.

Open interest: Shows the number of contracts that have not been closed out.

■ **A CLOSER LOOK: The S&P 500 Index**

In addition to the futures markets for commodities, Treasury bills and bonds, Eurodollars, and foreign currencies, there has been a futures market in the S&P 500 stock index since 1982. (See Chapter 9, pages 192–194 for a thorough discussion of the S&P 500 Index.) Since that time, the New York Stock Exchange Composite Index futures, traded on the New York Futures Exchange (a unit of the New York Stock Exchange) and Major Market Index futures, traded on the Chicago Board of Trade, have been introduced. They are essentially similar to the S&P 500 Index futures. The futures contract is valued at 500 times the S&P 500 price. If the futures contract is priced at 325, then the contract has a face value of $162,500. Obviously, no actual good or security can be delivered here, so the final settlement is made in cash. Traders can buy and sell index futures as a means of speculating or hedging.

Assume, for example, that Mr. Smith believes the stock market will increase during the next few months. He can buy one S&P 500 futures contract at 325 (worth $162,500) by paying, say, a 10 percent margin of $16,250. If the index goes above 325, then margin payments are made to Mr. Smith by the person who sold the contract. If the index falls below 325, then Mr. Smith has to increase his margin. Just as in all other futures trading, the accounts of each trader are "marked to the market" every trading day. If Mr. Smith sells his contract in December for 340, he will earn $7500; if it drops to 310, Mr. Smith will lose $7500.

S&P 500 futures average on September 5	$ 325
Multiplication factor for one contract	× 500
Value of one futures index contract	$162,500
Margin required and paid (returned)	16,250
If the index futures price rises to 340:	
Mr. Smith sells the contract for	$170,000
Profit from futures trading	7,500
If the Index futures price falls to 310:	
Mr. Smith sells the contract for	$155,000
Loss from futures trading	(7,500)

Mr. Smith could also have used index futures to hedge against changes in the value of a diverse portfolio. Assume Mr. Smith has a diverse portfolio he does not want to sell, but he thinks the general market might move down during the next few months. In order to hedge against this eventuality, he might sell the S&P 500 December, say, for 325. If the index goes down to 310 he will earn $7500, which will offset the loss he would have suffered on the value of his portfolio. Although most individuals would simply keep their portfolio and ride out the market decrease, or sell their stocks at today's higher prices, many institutional investors find this too difficult or expensive to do. Hence, they use the S&P 500 Index futures to hedge against general market declines.

Name: Stock Index Options
Agency/Institution: Chicago Board Options Exchange (CBOE)
Address: La Salle at Van Buren, Chicago, IL 60605
Telephone number for data and inquiries: 312-786-2263
Sources: *Wall Street Journal* and stock ticker tape
Frequency: Every business day
When available: Published in the *Wall Street Journal* the following day

---

■ A QUICK LOOK: Stock Index Options

Since 1983, call and put options on the values of stock indexes have been traded on the exchanges. An investor buys a **stock index call option** with the hope that the underlying stock index (such as the S&P 100) will move higher, and a **stock index put option** with the hope that the relevant index will go down. A number of striking prices are set by the exchange at 5-point intervals, with the contracts set to expire on the third Friday in each of the following three months. Unlike stock commodity options, stock index options are settled in cash and not by the delivery of the stock comprising the index. The following table shows the prices of the puts and calls for the S&P 100, the most popular stock index option, for September 5, 1990, but the other index options work in the same way:

Strike Price	CALLS — LAST			PUTS — LAST		
	Sept.	Oct.	Nov.	Sept.	Oct.	Nov.
285	25$\frac{1}{8}$			1$\frac{1}{16}$	4$\frac{3}{8}$	6$\frac{1}{4}$
290	20$\frac{1}{8}$	24$\frac{3}{8}$		2	5$\frac{1}{4}$	7$\frac{5}{8}$
295	15$\frac{1}{2}$	21		2$\frac{11}{16}$	6$\frac{3}{8}$	9
300	12$\frac{1}{8}$	16$\frac{3}{4}$		3$\frac{5}{8}$	7$\frac{5}{8}$	10
305	8	12	15$\frac{1}{2}$	5	9	11$\frac{1}{2}$
310	4$\frac{7}{8}$	10	12$\frac{3}{4}$	7	11$\frac{1}{2}$	13$\frac{7}{8}$
315	2$\frac{3}{4}$	7$\frac{1}{4}$	10	10	13$\frac{3}{8}$	17$\frac{3}{4}$
320	1$\frac{1}{2}$	5	7	13$\frac{1}{2}$	16$\frac{1}{4}$	18$\frac{1}{2}$

Total call volume: 90,565; Total call open int.: 50,504
Total put volume: 111,358; Total put open int.: 454,811
Total index: high 308.45; low 304.48; close 307.79, +0.68

Description: This stock index option table is for the S&P 100 (quotation symbol-=OEX), which is composed of 100 blue-chip stocks, including AT&T, Eastman Kodac, Exxon, General Electric, and IBM. The S&P 100 Index is computed by multiplying the price of each stock in the index by its number of outstanding shares, and these market values are then summed. The aggregate market value today is divided by the aggregate market value in the base year and multiplied by 100 to obtain the S&P 100 Index, which has a base year of 1976 = 100. In addition to the S&P 100, there are stock options for S&P 500 on the CBOE, the Major Market Index on the American Stock Exchange, the New York Stock Exchange Composite Index, and the Value Line Index on the Philadelphia Exchange.

Strike price: The strike price is the price at which the call or put option can be exercised. The 290 strike price in the second line means that if the holder of this option exercises it on a day when the closing value of the S&P 100 Index is 305, the writer of the option would have to pay the option holder $1500 ($15 per unit × 100 units, which is in the standardized contract). If an investor were holding an option with a strike price of 295 and decided to exercise his option on a day when the index's closing value was 305, he would receive $1000 from the option writer. The exercise prices are set at 5-point intervals to bracket the current value of the index and are quoted as "Sep305" for a September contract with a striking price of 305.

Calls: A call option gives the buyer the right to require the writer of the call to settle in cash an amount equal to the closing price of the index on the exercise day less the strike price. If the closing value of the index is 305 and the strike price is 295, the call option holder would receive $1000 ($10 per unit × 100 units). If the index is valued at 295 or less, the call option holder receives nothing. Index options expire on the third Friday of the month indicated. The price paid for the option is called a *premium*, which is expressed in terms of dollars and fractions of a dollar per single unit of the index, such as the 25⅛, shown at the top of the September call column. Since the standardized contracts are for 100 units, each point really represents $100. Thus, a premium of 25⅛ represents a total payment of $2512.50. Since the S&P 100 Index on this trading date of September 5 is at 307, the value of a 285 October call option, which already permits its owner to receive from the call writer $22 per unit ($307 − $285) and offers good prospects of earning even more as the index increases during the remaining days of the contract. Hence, this particular option is selling at the high premium of 25⅛ because investors are expecting it to increase even further during the few weeks left before expiration of the contract. The higher the striking price, the lower the value of the call options; the farther into the future the expiration date, the higher the value of the call option.

Puts: A put option gives the buyer the right to require the put writer to settle in cash the amount equal to the strike price less the closing index value. Thus, if the strike price is 315 and the closing value is 305, the put option holder will receive $1000 ($315 − $305 × 100). If the index value is 315 or more, the holder of a put option receives nothing. The price of a put option contract at a striking price of 295 in September is $268.75 (2¹⁵⁄₁₆ × $100). Put options increase in value as the striking price increases and also as the expiration date is further away.

Vol: Trading volume for the puts and calls are shown separately. The volume refers to the number of contracts that were traded.

Open int: Open interest is the number of outstanding contracts that have not expired or been liquidated.

Index: The first place to look is at the bottom of the table, where you will find the closing price for the actual S&P 100 Index, which is 307.79. The high for the trading day was 308.45, the low was 304.48, and the closing price of 307.79 was 0.68 higher than the closing price of the previous day.

■ A CLOSER LOOK: Stock Index Options

Stock index options have been traded on the Chicago Board Options Exchange (CBOE) since 1983. They are now also traded on the American Stock Exchange (Amex), the New York Stock Exchange (NYSE), and the Pacific Stock Exchange. While the exchanges use a variety of indexes, the most popular is the S&P 100 Index. Index options are settled by the payment of cash and not by the delivery of the securities that make up the index. When an option holder exercises his option, he receives an amount equal to the difference between the closing dollar value of the index on the exercise date and the aggregate exercise price of the option. In effect, the exercising holder receives the amount by which the option is "in-the-money."

Index options permit investors to take a position on the overall direction of the market. Assume that an investor anticipates that the stock market will increase in value. She could buy a widely diversified mutual fund, but she would tie up her capital and have to pay substantial administrative and brokerage fees. Instead, she can buy a call option on the S&P 100, and if the S&P 100 (OEX) index does increase in value, she can exercise the option and earn a profit. Assume that in September she buys a December 305 OEX call option at a premium of 10, for a total payment of $1000. If the index closes at 327.80 on November 15 and the investor exercises the option, she would have the following profit:

Value of index on November 15: $327.80 \times \$100 =$	$32,780
Less: Exercise price $305 \times \$100 =$	30,500
Gross cash settlement	2,280
Less: Premium paid for the option	1,000
Profits before commissions	1,280

On the other hand, the investor might not have exercised her option and received the settlement in cash, but simply sold the call option on November 15 at, say 22¾, which would equal a gross profit of $2275. The investor's net profit would be $1275 less her broker's commission. Most index option traders would simply sell their option on the CBOE.

Name: Stock Options
Sources: *Wall Street Journal*, many daily newspapers, *Value Line Options* (weekly)
Frequency: Every trading day
When available: Daily
Additional information: Explanatory material on options trading is available from: Chicago Board Options Exchange, La Salle at Van Buren, Chicago, IL 60605

■ A QUICK LOOK: Stock Options

Stock options are widely bought and sold on the commodities exchanges as well as on the traditional stock exchanges. A stock call option gives the buyer the right to buy a certain stock at a stipulated price called the exercise or strike price. The buyer can exercise the option at any time before the expiration date. In exchange for a cash premium (call price), the seller or writer of the call option becomes obligated to sell the securities at the strike price. The buyer of a stock put option has the right to sell a certain stock at the strike or exercise price stipulated by the contract. In exchange for a cash premium (put price), the seller of a put option becomes obligated to buy the security at the strike price at the option of the holder. The following are stock option quotes for September 5.

XYZ Corp. Stock	Strike Price	CALLS — LAST			PUTS — LAST		
		Sept.	Oct.	Nov.	Sept.	Oct.	Nov.
97⅞	85	13	r	r	r	r	r
97⅞	90	7	9⅜		½	1⅝	2¼
97⅞	95	4½	5	7	1⅜	r	3⅞
97⅞	100	1	3	4	r	5¼	r
97⅞	105	r	r	2¼	r	r	r
97⅞	110	r	s	1⅛	r	s	r

Stock: This is the price of the underlying stock at the close of the trading day on the stock exchange. It is shown here solely for information purposes. The closing price of XYZ Company stock on September 4 was 97⅞, which is equal to $97.87.

Strike price: This is the strike or exercise price specified in the option contract at which the buyer can exercise his call or put option. These alternative prices are set by the trading exchange, and the public decides whether they want to buy or sell any options at those strike prices. The first row shows a strike price of $85, which means the holder of a call option can require the writer to sell 100 shares of stock at $85 per share.

Calls: The various prices (premiums) of the call options in dollars and fractions of dollars that were the last transactions on that day. Thus, call options that had a striking price of $95 sold for $4.50, $5.00, and $7.00, depending on whether they expired on the third Friday in September, October, or November. An "r" means that no options were traded for those months at those striking prices. An "s" means that no options were offered for sale — that there simply exist no options with that strike price and expiration date. Note that as the strike price increases from $85 to $90 and on to $110, the prices of call options decrease. This makes economic sense since the right to buy the stock at a lower price is more valuable than the right to buy the stock at a higher price. Wouldn't you be willing to pay more for the right to buy XYZ stock, which is currently selling at 97⅞, at a (strike) price of $85 rather than a (strike) price of $100?

Puts: The various prices (premiums) of the last transactions of put options in dollars and fractions of dollars. Thus, put options with a striking price of $95 sold for $1.375, r, and 3.875 for puts expiring in September, October, and November, respectively. Notice that the price of put options increases as the strike price increases. This, too, is simply common sense. The right to sell stock at higher prices is more valuable than the right to sell stock at lower prices.

■ **A CLOSER LOOK: Stock Options**

Since 1973 a sophisticated stock options market has developed on the Chicago Board Options Exchange (CBOE) and options are now traded on the American Stock Exchange (Amex), New York Stock Exchange

(NYSE), and other exchanges. All exchanges have simplified option contracts with standardized expiration dates, striking prices, and trading blocks. The trading block for most stocks is 100 shares; that is, a single option contract is written to buy or sell 100 shares of the underlying stock at a specific price. The price of the option, often called a *premium*, is determined by competitive auction bidding on the exchange floor, and any option can be sold and resold many times before its expiration date. A **call option** gives the buyer the right to buy the stock at a stipulated price called the **exercise**, or **strike price**, and a **put option** gives the buyer the right to sell (to put) the stock at the strike price. The exchange sets the striking price of an option contract based on recent prices of the stock. Over time, the stock price may change so much that the original striking price becomes irrelevant to current market conditions, and the exchange will create an additional series of options for the same stock but with different striking prices. Thus, for any given stock there will be different contract months, reflecting the various months in which the options expire; in addition, there may be a number of striking price series, reflecting different prices at which the options can be called or put. For example, "XYZ July 45s" means that the option for the stock of the XYZ Company has a maturity in July and a striking price of $45. "XYZ July 50s" states the same information except that the striking price is $50, instead of $45. Options with the same maturity month but with different striking prices are not interchangeable. They are completely separate contracts.

A call option is said to be "in-the-money" when the market price of the stock is above the option's strike price and "out-of-the-money" when the price of the stock is below the strike price. Remember that the holder of an option can exercise the option at *any* time before the expiration date. Hence, if an investor is holding a July call option with a strike price of $45 and the stock is selling at $55 in May, he has to decide whether he should "call" the stock in May for $45 (then sell it for $55) or hold the option, hoping that the price of the stock will increase even more.

The put option is the opposite of a call option. In return for a cash premium (also called a *put price*), the seller of a put option is obligated to buy the underlying stock at the strike price if the buyer requests it. Therefore, the buyer of a put option receives the right to sell the stock at the strike or exercise price stipulated by the contract. A put option is "in-the-money" when the stock's price is below the strike price and "out-of-the-money" when the stock's price is above the strike price. The holder of a put contract wants the price of the underlying stock to decrease so he can buy the stock at a low price and then sell the stock to the option seller, who is obligated to purchase it at the higher strike price.

Buyers of put or call options are not required to deposit funds in a margin account because their risk of loss is limited to the premium paid for the option. Sellers of put and call options are required to maintain margin accounts, however, in order to ensure that they are able to honor their contracts at the strike prices. Most option traders do not expect to actually exercise their options; they will sell their options at an appreciated price if their option is "in-the-money." Are you confused by this babble of new terms and too many words? The following examples should help you understand calls and puts.

Example of a call option:

June 5: Mr. Smith buys 100 shares of XYZ Company stock for 26½ on the New York Stock Exchange.

February 15: Mr. Smith decides to earn some extra income by selling a call option on XYZ. Through his broker, he sells his option on the Chicago Board of Exchange. The option, which is purchased by Ms. Jones for $300, is a three-month call on 100 shares of XYZ, exercisable at 30; that is, the striking price is 30. The premium per share is $3, and Mr. Smith receives $300, less his broker's commission. When Mr. Smith sells the call option, he knows that Ms. Jones might exercise the option at any time before the expiration date and he will have to sell his 100 shares of stock in XYZ for the striking price of $30 per share. Although Mr. Smith sells the option and Ms. Jones buys it, their technical obligations are to the Options Clearing Corporation, which interposes itself between option writer and option buyer. Thus, the clearinghouse is responsible to Ms. Jones for honoring the contract and Mr. Smith is obligated to sell the stock at the striking price to the clearinghouse.

March 15: The price of XYZ stock on the New York Stock Exchange increases to $32 and Ms. Jones sells the call, through the CBOE, to Mr. Charles at a premium of $6, for a total of $600. Ms. Jones has earned a gross profit of $600 − $300 = $300 and is now completely out of this option picture. Mr. Smith is still involved because Mr. Charles might exercise the call. Notice that Mr. Charles was willing to pay an option premium of $6 per share even though the current market price of XYZ stock was only $2 above the strike price. Obviously, Mr. Charles was expecting the market price of XYZ stock to increase even more.

May 17: The stock is now selling for $38 on the NYSE, so Mr. Charles exercises the call (it is above the striking price of $30) through his broker and the CBOE. Mr. Smith now has to sell his XYZ stock to Mr. Charles for $30 per share. If the price of XYZ had been at or below $30 per share until the expiration date, Mr. Charles would not have exercised his call option and it would have simply expired, enabling Mr. Smith to keep his stock. Mr. Charles presumably will sell the 100 shares of XYZ stock for $3800 and will earn a gross profit of $200 ($3800 − $3000 − $600).

Example of a put option:

January 15: Mr. Smith decides to obtain some extra income by writing a put option on 100 shares of QRS stock at a $30 strike price, which will expire on the third Friday in April. Through the CBOE he sells the puts to Ms. Jones at a premium of 3¼, for a total of $325. By writing (selling) this April put option, Mr. Smith has a contractual obligation to buy 100 shares of QRS at $30 per share if the holder of the option exercises the option at any time on or before the expiration date. Because Mr. Smith is a seller of a put option, he has to secure the option by depositing $3000 of Treasury bills with his broker on which he continues to earn interest. Shares of QRS are now selling at 32¼, so he thinks there is a good chance that the price will not fall below $30 and that he will not have to purchase QRS.

February 20: The price of QRS stock has increased to $32 and Ms. Jones, thinking that the price will not fall before the option expiration date, sells the put option to Mr. Charles for 2½, which means that Ms. Jones has suffered a loss of $75, plus commissions. Mr. Smith is smiling more these days.

April 1: Mr. Smith's smile turns to a frown. The price of QRS stock plunges to $22 and Mr. Charles exercises his option to sell 100 shares of QRS to Mr. Smith. Mr. Smith pays $3000 to Mr. Charles and now owns 100 shares of QRS worth $2200. Assuming he sells the stock, he has lost $800 less the $300 premium he received. Mr. Charles has a gross profit of $550 ($3000 − $2200 − $250).

CHAPTER 11

BUSINESS CYCLES AND INDICATORS

Words, as well as sticks and stones, *can* hurt us. One of the most dreaded words in the English language and one that can cause much harm is *depression*. Less dreadful, but still high on a list of "words to avoid" is *recession*. These words, and numerous substitutes, have an interesting history. Prior to the Great Depression of the thirties, "depression" meant only a dip in the ground—it had no connection to the economy. Economic contractions were called "panics" or "crises" because they were generally associated with financial disruptions such as the closures of banks and insurance companies. At the beginning of the economic contraction in 1930, President Herbert Hoover refused to use such harsh terms as *panic* or *crisis* because he didn't want to frighten consumers. He told a nationwide radio audience that the country was only in a "depression." Of course, that word quickly took on a "strongly alarmist" meaning of its own, and the gentler word *recession* became acceptable during the post-World War II period.

President Eisenhower, wishing to avoid the economic and political implications of a "recession," described the contraction of 1958–59 as a "rolling readjustment." The most innovative term ever used to describe an economic contraction was concocted by Alfred Kahn, President Carter's economic adviser. When he mentioned that the economy was going into a slight recession, the president's political advisers strongly chastised him. A repentant Kahn vowed never to use the word again. Snickering audiences soon heard him exuberantly exclaim: "The American economy is heading for a 'banana.'"

Whether we call them panics, crises, depressions, recessions, rolling readjustments, or bananas, we pay much attention to them and we expect our government to avoid them or to shorten their duration. This was not always the case. Prior to the depression of the thirties, most Americans believed that periodic recessions were part of the natural order or were God's plan for imperfect humans and that government action could only make the contractions worse. In fact, most people did not know the current state of the economy because there were few economic data series. There were some rudimentary price indexes, some employment data gathered from the decennial censuses, and fairly good import data, but little else. It might surprise the reader to learn that although we now have annual employment and unemployment series going back to 1870, these were constructed by after-the-fact estimates made after 1930. The systematic collection of current employment and unemployment data did not begin until the late 1930s.

Most of the data series presented in this book are used to analyze the position of the economy in the business cycle as we seek to avoid the depths of the recessions and the peaks of inflation. However, a few data series, also designed to help assess the position of the economy in the business cycle, do not fit logically into other data categories. Hence, they were included in this short chapter.

Economists believe that no economy, socialistic or capitalistic, can completely avoid all recessionary and inflationary pressures. They know that all economies are subject to recurring business cycles in which economic activity expands, contracts, and then expands again. The contraction periods are characterized by increasing unemployment rates for labor and capital and either falling prices or slowly rising prices. Expansionary periods are characterized by falling unemployment rates, higher prices, and temporary shortages of some goods and services.

The first data series, business cycles, explains the meaning and measurement of the business cycle. The second series describes economic indicators, explaining the use of the leading, coincident, and lagging economic indicators, which are used to predict and define the business cycle. The remaining series explain the meaning and use of consumer confidence surveys.

Name: Business Cycles
Alternative names: Economic Cycles (recessions and expansions)
Agency/Institution: National Bureau of Economic Research
Address: 1050 Massachusetts Ave., Cambridge, MA 02138
Telephone number for data and inquiries: 617-868-3900
Sources: *Economic Report of the President* (Council of Economic Advisors), *Handbook of Cyclical Indicators* (Bureau of Economic Analysis), and *Survey of Current Business*
Frequency: Monthly
Historic data: See below.

■ A QUICK LOOK: Business Cycles

The official designator of recessions and expansions is not the Federal Reserve, the Bureau of Economic Analysis, or the Bureau of Labor Statistics. It is the National Bureau of Economic Research, Inc. (NBER), a private, nonprofit economic research organization founded in 1920. The main advantage of having a nongovernmental body designate recessions and expansions is to reduce the possibility that the current administration in Washington will try to define the stages of the business cycle to make the economy and the administration look good and the opposing party look bad. The NBER defines a recession as beginning in the month in which the overall direction of several economic indicators is downward; the beginning of an expansion occurs in the month in which several economic indicators are moving upward. Some of the important indicators are nominal and real gross national product, new capital orders, business sales, industrial production index, unemployment rate, hours worked, and personal income. A recession is often defined as occurring when the quarterly real gross national product declines for two quarters in a row, but this is not a fixed rule and the NBER always looks at other indicators.

The business cycle is divided into four components: (1) a peak, which is also called a *boom*, (2) a contraction or recession, (3) a trough or depression, and (4) an expansion or recovery. The U.S. Department of Commerce uses the NBER system to develop its leading, coincident, and lagging indicators, which are discussed later. **Leading indicators** reach their highs and lows before the cyclical peak and trough. **Coincident indicators** move through the cycle simultaneously with economic activity, and **lagging indicators** reach their highs and lows after the economy has peaked or troughed.

HISTORIC DATA: Business Cycles in the United States

| | | MONTHS OF DURATION | |
| | | --- | --- |
Trough	Peak	Contraction (trough from previous peak)	Expansion (trough to peak)
March 1919	January 1920	7	10
July 1921	May 1923	18	22
July 1924	October 1926	14	27
November 1927	August 1929	13	21
March 1933	May 1937	43	50
June 1938	February 1945	13	80

(continued)

HISTORIC DATA: Business Cycles in the United States *(continued)*

		MONTHS OF DURATION	
Trough	Peak	Contraction (trough from previous peak)	Expansion (trough to peak)
October 1945	November 1948	8	37
October 1948	July 1953	11	45
May 1954	August 1957	10	39
April 1958	April 1960	8	24
February 1961	December 1969	10	106
November 1970	November 1973	11	36
March 1975	January 1980	16	58
July 1980	July 1981	6	12
November 1982	July 1990	16	92

The *trough* is the lower turning point of the business cycle; the *peak* is the upper turning point. This table can be confusing to read and interpret, so let's look at it more closely. In January 1980, the economy reached its peak and fell into a mild recession that lasted until July 1980, when the economy began expanding again. In July 1981, the economy fell off again until November 1982. In November, the economy turned upward and went into its longest peacetime expansion, of 92 months, which ended in July 1990. The longest expansion in the country's history was 106 months during the 1960s, but this expansion was aided by the Vietnam War. The longest single depression occurred during the 1930s, between August 1929 and March 1933.

Note that this table does not indicate the height of the peaks or the depths of the troughs. Although the economy had an expansionary period from March 1933 to May 1937, the economy remained quite depressed during this "expansion." Most economists believe the country did not come out of the depression of the 1930s until 1940.

Name: Index of Leading Economic Indicators, Index of Coincident Indicators, Index of Lagging Indicators
Alternative name: Business Cycle Indicators
Agency: Statistical Indicators Division, Bureau of Economic Analysis, Department of Commerce
Address: Washington, DC 20230
Telephone number for data: 202-898-2450 (3- to 5-minute recorded message available 24 hours and updated weekly, usually on Monday morning.)
Telephone number for inquiries: 202-523-0777

Sources: Used to be published in the *Business Conditions Digest* until that was discontinued. The indicators are now published in the *Survey of Current Business*.

Frequency: Monthly

Available: During the last week of the following month

Revisions: Each month BEA updates the indicators to include the latest available data. These monthly updates revise the indexes of the previous five months. In addition, there are annual updates.

Additional information: See "Business Cycle Indicators: Revised Composite Indexes" in the January 1989 *Survey of Current Business*, pp. 23–28; "Composite Indexes of Leading, Coincident and Lagging Indicators" in the November 1987 *Survey of Current Business*, pp. 24–28; and "A Note on Revisions to the Leading Indicators" in the May 1988 *Survey of Current Business*, p. 21.

Historic data: See below.

■ A QUICK LOOK: Business Cycle Indicators

The recurrent ups and downs in economic activity are called **business cycles**, or **business fluctuations**. Many business and government decisions are based on expectations about where the economy is headed — for example, whether the expansion will continue or whether a recession will dampen economic activity. Economists use a number of data series to predict the direction of the economy. Some use sophisticated econometric models; others simply use their intuition. Most use a combination of sources between these two extremes. One of these sources is the collection of economic indicators widely reported by the media. The origin of leading indicators can be traced back to the work of Arthur F. Burns and Wesley C. Mitchell at the National Bureau of Economic Research, Inc. (NBER), which published its first cyclical indicators in 1938. In 1961, the U.S. Department of Commerce began publishing a monthly report that featured NBER's leading, coincident, and lagging indicators, and the composite indexes of cyclical indicators were first published by the department in 1968.

The BEA uses data from a number of sources to construct three composite indicators: the Index of Leading Indicators, the Index of Coincident Indicators, and the Index of Lagging Indicators. All three indicators are currently based on 1982 = 100, and the BEA reports both the absolute level of the index and the percentage change from the previous month. The components of the leading, coincident, and lagging indicators are changed periodically by the BEA, but an example of the components used are listed in the following table. The BEA has committed itself to improve the leading, coincident, and lagging indicators, so additional changes can be expected during the 1990s.

	Mar.	Apr.	May	June	July
Composite Index of Leading Indicators (1982 = 100)	145.3	145.1r	145.9r	146.1r	146.1p
Percent change over 1-month span	12.3	− 1.6r	6.8r	1.7r	0 p
Percent change over 3-month span	− .5r	5.7r	2.2r	2.8p	. . .
Composite Index of Coincident Indicators (1982 = 100)	134.4	133.9	134.6	134.9	134.6
Percent change over 1-month span	2.7	− 4.4	6.5	2.7	− 2.6
Percent change over 3-month span	3.0	1.5	1.5	2.1	. . .
Composite Index of Coincident Indicators (1982 = 100)	119.2	119.7	119.5	119.0	119.7
Percent change over 1-month span	4.1	5.2	− 2.0	− 4.9	7.3
Percent change over 3-month span	2.0	2.4	− .7	0	. . .

r = revised; p = preliminary

Composite indexes: Each of the composite indexes has many components, which are detailed in the following "A Closer Look" section. The index numbers are based on 1982 = 100.

Percent change over 1-month span: Percentage changes are annualized for one-month and three-month spans. The percentage change immediately below the index number refers to the annualized percentage change from the preceding month. For example, the June leading index increased by 1.7 percent $[(146.1/145.9)^{12} - 1]$ at an annualized rate from May.

Percent change over 3-month span: Contrary to a commonsense assumption, the rate of change over three months is *not* over the three previous months. Rather, it is the rate of change over the previous two months and the following month. For example, the 2.8 percent change under the June leading index refers to the percentage change from April to July $[146.1/145.1)^4 - 1]$. The 2.8 is preliminary because the July index value of 146.1 is preliminary.

■ A CLOSER LOOK: Economic Indicators

The Leading Indicator

The indicator watched most closely by business analysts is the **Index of Leading Indicators**, which signals future changes in the economy. The leading indicator should turn upward a few months before the economy does and downward a few months before the economy starts to dip into a recession. The leading indicator has an average lead of about 9.5 months (with a range of 2 to 20 months) for business cycle peaks, or the beginning of a cycle downturn. One problem with using the leading indicator is deciding how many months the index should move in one direction before concluding that the economy will be heading that way in the coming months. For example, if the Index of Leading Indicators has been climbing for a number of months and then turns down one month, should we conclude that within the next nine months the economy is going to slide off the peak and start heading downward? Most economists, including those at the BEA, say that a one-month drop in the index does not necessarily signal a turning point within the next few months. However, if we wait for the index to fall for 12 successive months, the contraction might already be about finished and the new expansion about to begin.

There is no obvious answer to the number of months one should observe a reversal in the index before reaching a conclusion about the turn in the economy. Many economists use three consecutive monthly increases as an indicator of a forthcoming expansion and three consecutive declines as an indicator of a forthcoming recession. Keep in mind, though, that the leading economic indicator is not perfect and often gives faulty signals. Since 1965 each recession was preceded by a drop in the composite index of leading indicators. The lead time was as much as 15 months and as short as 2 months. The index turned down during each of the nine consecutive months starting in April 1965, but there was no subsequent recession—possibly due to the Vietnam buildup. The index turned down for seven consecutive months during 1984, but again there was no recession; the five-month decline in 1987–88 also did not lead to a recession.

Components of the Leading Indicator

1. Average number of hours worked during week by nonsupervisory workers in manufacturing

2. Average weekly initial claims for state unemployment insurance

3. Manufacturers' new orders for consumer goods and materials in constant 1982 dollars

4. Contracts and orders for plant and equipment in constant 1982 dollars

5. Index of local building permits for new private housing units

6. Vendor performance measured as percentage of companies reporting slower deliveries

7. Changes in manufacturers' unfilled orders for durable goods in constant 1982 dollars

8. Changes in sensitive materials prices

9. Index of S&P 500 common stocks

10. Money supply (M2) in constant 1982 dollars

11. Index of consumer expectations (by University of Michigan's Survey Research Center)

The Coincident Indicator

The **Index of Coincident Indicators** should tell us where the economy is positioned in the business cycle at the present time; that is, it should move with the cycle. If this indicator increases significantly, the economy should be expanding, and if this indicator decreases the economy should be contracting. It is used to confirm or deny the validity of the leading indicator but is not watched nearly as closely as the leading indicator.

Components of the Coincident Indicator

1. Employees in nonagricultural industries
2. Personal income less transfer payments in constant 1982 dollars
3. Index of Industrial Production
4. Manufacturing and trade sales in constant 1982 dollars

The Lagging Indicator

The **Index of Lagging Indicators** is expected to move, after a time lag, in the same direction as the coincident index and thus to confirm the movements in the coincident index and to help define the cycle.

Components of the Lagging Indicator

1. Average duration of unemployment in weeks
2. Ratio of manufacturing and trade inventories to sales in constant 1982 dollars
3. Percentage change in labor cost per unit of output of manufactured goods
4. Average prime rate charged by banks
5. Commercial and industrial loans outstanding in constant 1982 dollars
6. Consumer installment debt as percentage of personal income
7. Change in Consumer Price Index for Services

HISTORIC DATA: Economic Indicators, 1948–1991
(1982 = 100)

	Eleven Leading Indicators	Four Coincident Indicators	Seven Lagging Indicators		Eleven Leading Indicators	Four Coincident Indicators	Seven Lagging Indicators
1948	37.6	38.8	33.4				
1949	36.3	36.2	34.6				
1950	43.3	40.3	35.3				

(continued)

HISTORIC DATA: Economic Indicators, *(continued)*
1948–1991
(1982 = 100)

	Eleven Leading Indicators	Four Coincident Indicators	Seven Lagging Indicators		Eleven Leading Indicators	Four Coincident Indicators	Seven Lagging Indicators
1951	43.2	44.1	41.1	1971	83.3	82.3	87.4
1952	43.0	45.8	44.5	1972	92.3	88.9	86.2
1953	43.3	48.7	48.7	1973	97.2	96.1	92.3
1954	44.0	45.4	47.1	1974	89.0	94.2	100.2
1955	50.3	49.8	47.9	1975	84.5	86.3	93.1
1956	50.5	52.2	55.9	1976	96.2	92.3	87.0
1957	48.6	52.1	59.9	1977	101.0	98.7	89.1
1958	49.3	48.3	56.5	1978	104.6	106.7	94.8
1959	54.8	52.5	59.7	1979	103.6	110.8	102.8
1960	53.8	53.3	64.9	1980	99.2	107.2	105.5
1961	57.2	52.7	62.2	1981	101.2	107.3	102.8
1962	60.2	56.1	63.6	1982	100.0	100.0	100.0
1963	64.2	58.2	66.2	1983	116.2	101.9	91.4
1964	68.7	61.9	69.3	1984	121.7	112.3	100.7
1965	73.0	67.4	73.6	1985	124.0	116.3	107.5
1966	75.0	63.1	79.6	1986	132.4	119.0	111.4
1967	75.1	75.5	82.6	1987	140.1	123.6	110.6
1968	79.8	79.8	84.8	1988	142.4	130.0	114.3
1969	82.0	83.8	90.4	1989	145.0	133.5	119.3
1970	77.2	82.1	92.3	1990	144.0	132.8	119.2
				1991	143.6	126.3	114.5

Name: Consumer Confidence Surveys
Alternative name: Consumer Expectations or Sentiments
Agency: The Conference Board
Address: 845 Third Avenue, New York, NY 10022
Telephone number for data: 202-898-2450
Sources: *Consumer Confidence Survey* (The Conference Board; monthly) and the *Survey of Current Business*
Frequency: Monthly
When available: First week of the following month
Revisions: Each new month there is a preliminary release that is revised the following month.
Historic data: Available from the Conference Board

■ A QUICK LOOK: Consumer Confidence Surveys

The Conference Board publishes *Consumer Confidence Survey*, a monthly report of the results of a survey of 5000 households taken during the first two weeks of every month. The index is based on 1985 = 100 and contains separate indexes for such topics as: expectations of business conditions; employment and income for the next six months; and plans to purchase automobiles, homes, and major appliances during the next six months. The index is available for regions and is broken down by age of household head and household income. Business firms rely heavily on this index when forming their opinions about future consumer spending. The Index of Consumer Expectations (1985 = 100) is included in the *Consumer Confidence Survey*. The following are some index levels:

	1989	1990	1991
Consumer Confidence	116.8	91.5	68.5
Consumer Expectations	104.8	83.7	85.8

Name: Surveys of Consumers
Alternative name: Consumer Expectations and Sentiments
Agency/Institution: University of Michigan Institute of Social Research (ISR)
Address: 426 Thompson, 3254 ISR, University of Michigan, Ann Arbor, Michigan 48106
Telephone number for data and inquiries: 313-764-1817
Sources: *Surveys of Consumers*, (ISR), *Survey of Current Business*
Frequency: Monthly
When available: First week of the following month
Historic data: Available on diskette from ISR, and from *Survey of Current Business*, October 1991

■ A QUICK LOOK: Consumer Expectations and Sentiments

The University of Michigan's Institute for Social Research samples 500 households and reports consumer sentiment in five major categories: current and expected personal finance, current and expected business conditions, and buying conditions. It reports the results in its monthly publication of consumer surveys. The base year is 1966:1 = 100. The following are examples of these index levels:

	1989	1990
Consumer Sentiment	92.8	81.6
Consumer Expectations	85.3	70.2

CHAPTER 12

INDUSTRIAL SECTORS

READ ME FIRST

Most economic data series were started during the decades of the thirties and fifties, when the United States was still the undisputed industrial leader in the world. Thus, it is not surprising that, despite some cutbacks in their number, many more industrial data series are still published than can be included here. Although the United States has lost its preeminent industrial position, it still has manufacturing muscle. About 17 percent of the work force (26 percent in 1970; 40 percent in 1920) and 19 percent of the GDP is produced in the industrial sector. Due to its size alone, the United States is still a major manufacturing nation and is likely to remain one.

In this chapter we present some of the major industrial, manufacturing, construction, and housing data series. Many of the economic censuses, and their related surveys, are described in this chapter, as are productivity and industrial capacity measures. One of the most expensive and useful, but most neglected data series — the input-output tables — are also presented. Before searching through these various series, you might review the section on SIC coding in Chapter 2.

Name: Automobile Production, Sales, and Inventories
Sponsoring Agency/Institution: Federal Reserve Board, Washington, DC 20551; Bureau of Economic Analysis, Department of Commerce, Washington, DC 20230
Telephone: 202-452-3244; 202-523-0819
Sources: Domestic Car Sales, Seasonally Adjusted Annual Rate (Bureau of Economic Analysis, every 10 days), *Wall Street Journal* (monthly), *Ward's Automotive Report* (monthly), and the *Survey of Current Business* (monthly for industrial data and every July for national income and account data)
Frequency: See above.

Revisions: Auto output and sales in the national income and product accounts are revised according to the GDP revisions (see page 122).
Historic data: Available on diskette from the Bureau of Economic Analysis

---

■ **A QUICK LOOK: Automobile Production, Sales, and Inventories**

A wide variety of data are available on auto and truck production, sales, imports, and inventories. Many of these series are watched closely because of the importance of the automobile industry to the national economy. Every month the Federal Reserve's Industrial Production Index includes automotive products and automotive trucks and autos. The current index is based on 1987 = 100, and the figures for 1989 and for August 1990 are:

	1989	1990
Automotive Products	106.9	102.3
Autos and trucks	105.7	97.4
Autos, consumer	101.2	92.2
Trucks, consumer	113.3	106.1
Auto parts	108.7	109.6

"Automotive products" includes the production of tires, brake pads, and repair parts. "Autos and trucks" includes only the production of automobiles and trucks.

The following data are located throughout the blue pages of the *Survey of Current Business*. The wide variety of data on motor vehicles is updated monthly and contains annual data for the two most recent years.

	1989	1990
Manufacturer Shipments:		
Motor vehicles and parts (billions)	$233.0	$226.0
Manufacturer Inventories:		
Motor vehicles and parts (billions)	12.1	13.0
Automotive Products Production Index (1987 = 100)	106.9	102.2
Autos and trucks	105.7	97.2
Consumer Price Indexes (1982–84 = 100)		
New autos	119.2	121.0
Used autos	120.4	117.6
Producer Price Indexes (1982 = 100)		
Motor vehicles and equipment	116.2	118.2
Retail Sales — Automotive Dealers (billions $)	383.6	382.0
Inventories — Automotive Dealers (millions $)	66.4	65.3
Consumer Installment Credit — Automobile (millions $)	290.7	284.8

(continued)

(continued)	1989	1990
Exports—Motor vehicles and parts (mil.$)	23.6	26.7
Imports—Motor vehicles and parts (mil.$)	69.3	69.4
Transportation Equipment:		
Passenger cars		
Retail sales, (millions of units)	9.9	9.5
Domestics (millions of units)	7.1	6.9
Imports (millions of units)	2.8	2.6
Retail inventories (millions of units)	1.7	1.4
Inventory—retail sales ratio	2.8	2.4
Exports (millions of units)	7.7	—
Imports (millions of units)	4.0	3.9
Registrations of new cars (millions of units)	9.9	9.2

The dollar volume of automobile sales is reported as part of the quarterly GDP series as "Automobiles and Parts." (See the GDP series, pages 121–122, for release dates of advance, preliminary, and final estimates.) Auto sales are included in the durable goods section of personal consumption expenditures, which include all new passenger cars purchased during the accounting period, net acquisitions (purchases less trade-ins) of all used cars, and parts and accessories. Imported cars and parts are also included. The data in Table 12.1 are reported with other national income and product account data in the July issue of *Survey of Current Business.* Only the current dollar values are shown here, but the *SCB* also reports constant dollar values for auto output as well as current and constant values for truck output.

TABLE 12.1
Auto Output
NIPA Accounts
(billions of $)

	1990	1991
Auto Output	$130.9	$118.0
Final Sales	135.0	121.0
Personal consumption expenditures	132.4	115.5
New autos	96.6	79.5
Net purchases of used autos	35.8	36.0
Producers' durable equipment	35.5	37.3
New autos	55.0	59.3
Net purchases of used autos	−19.6	−22.0
Net exports	−35.4	−33.7
Exports	10.5	12.4
Imports	45.9	46.1

(continued)

TABLE 12.1 *(continued)*
Auto Output
NIPA Accounts
(billions of $)

	1990	1991
Government purchases of autos	2.5	2.1
Change in Business Inventories	− 4.7	− 3.1
New autos	− 4.2	− 3.8
Used	− 0.6	0.7
Addenda:		
Domestic output of new autos[1]	99.7	94.0
Sales of imported new autos[2]	59.3	54.0

Another automobile sales series, Domestic Car Sales, is compiled by the Bureau of Economic Analysis. The BEA conducts three 10-day samples of unit sales every month: 1–10, 11–20, 21–30. The data include only sales of American-made cars; they are adjusted for seasonal factors and are annualized or converted to annual rates of sale.

Name: Business Inventories
Agency/Institution: Dept. of Business Inventories, Bureau of Economic Analysis
Address: Washington, DC 20230
Telephone number for data and inquiries: 202-523-0784
Sources: *Survey of Current Business*
Frequency: Monthly
When available: Second week of the following month
Revisions: The most recent three months are revised every month; there are also annual revisions
Historic data: Available on diskette from the Bureau of Economic Analysis

---

■ **A QUICK LOOK: Business Inventories**

Inventories are often thought to be both a cause and an indicator of business cycles. High inventory levels are thought to be indications that consumers have decreased consumption and that producers will shortly have to decrease production and employment in order to bring inventories down to acceptable or normal levels. Low inventories are thought to

---

[1]Consists of final sales and change in business inventories of new autos assembled in the United States.

[2]Consists of personal consumption expenditures, producers' durable equipment, and government purchases.

be a sign that consumer demand has picked up and that firms will have to increase production and employment in order to replenish inventories. Research has shown, however, that absolute levels of inventory provide little insight into economic changes since they tend to increase during both the peaks and the troughs. Nevertheless, monthly changes in inventories, although volatile, do tend to fall prior to contractions in the economy. Table 12.2 provides examples of business inventory data.

TABLE 12.2
Business Inventories
(millions of $)

	1989	1990
Manufacturing and Trade Inventories	$810,257	$826,941
Manufacturing, total	383,825	388,811
Durable goods industries	253,261	252,836
Nondurable goods industries	130,564	135,975
Retail Trade, total	238,159	242,563
Durable goods stores	120,663	120,629
Nondurable goods stores	117,496	121,934
Merchant wholesalers, total	188,273	195,567
Durable goods establishments	123,436	128,619
Nondurable goods establishments	64,837	66,948

In addition to monthly and annual inventory data, BEA also provides monthly data on inventory–sales ratios.

Name: Capacity Utilization Rates
Agency/Institution: Federal Reserve Board of Governors of the Federal System
Address: Washington, DC 20551
Telephone number for inquiries and data: Call the Federal Reserve, 202-452-3244, and you will be referred to the currently correct number.
Sources: *Capacity Utilization: Manufacturing and Materials*, G.17, Statistical Release; Federal Reserve and *Federal Reserve Bulletin*; *Handbook of Labor Statistics*; and *Survey of Current Business*
Frequency: Monthly
When available: About 15 days after the end of the month. The June issue of the *Federal Reserve Bulletin* contains the dates for future releases.
Revisions: End of each year; also when industrial production index is revised.
Historic data: Available on diskette from the Bureau of Economic Analysis

---

■ A QUICK LOOK: Capacity Utilization Rates

Capacity utilization rates (CURs) are designed to measure the extent to which firms are producing at their "maximum" output. The capacity utilization rate is the ratio of actual output to potential output. The lower the CUR ratio, the greater the amount of unused capacity. If a factory could produce 1000 pairs of shoes a day, and it is actually producing only 700 pairs, the capacity utilization rate is 70 percent and its unused capacity is 30 percent. If production increases to 800 pairs, the CUR would increase to 80 percent and the unused capacity would decrease to 20 percent. CURs are available for the same industries as the Industrial Production Index: manufacturing, mining, and utilities. Table 12.3 provides examples of CUR data.

TABLE 12.3
Capacity Utilization Rates,
Selected Industries

	PREVIOUS CYCLE		LATEST CYCLE		Oct 1991
	High	Low	High	Low	
Total Industry	89.2	72.6	87.3	71.8	79.6
Manufacturing	88.9	70.8	87.3	70.0	78.6
Durable	88.8	68.5	86.9	65.0	75.9
Lumber	90.1	62.2	87.6	60.9	74.6
Motor vehicles	93.4	51.1	93.0	44.5	74.2
Nondurable	87.9	71.8	87.0	76.9	82.1
Paper products	96.9	69.0	94.2	82.0	87.3
Chemicals	87.9	69.9	85.1	70.1	79.7

Numbers are percents of 100.0 percent of economic capacity.

The current CURs are shown in the far right column. The other four columns show the high and low CURs from the two previous cycles in order to provide relative references for the current CURs.

Interpreting the significance of capacity utilization rates can be difficult, and it is best to consider each industry at a time rather than to generalize from the overall index. Nevertheless, the overall CUR does provide some useful information. Increasing CURs indicate that plants are operating at higher capacity levels, which means that unit costs are decreasing because additional output is being produced without additional plants or equipment. However, increasing production above some level will mean that unit costs will increase because of machinery breakdowns, use of older and less efficient equipment, and the employment of less productive or more costly human and material resources. Thus, until the turnaround point — sometimes called the **flash point** — is reached, additional production will decrease inflationary pressures; above that point, however, additional production will increase inflationary pressures. The exact level at which this turnaround occurs varies by industry and is difficult to identify. A number of economists believe that in many, if not most, industries the turnaround occurs at about 85 percent capacity. They believe that when capacity utilization rates get into the high eighties and low nineties, investment in plants and equipment will increase significantly, whereas capacity utilization in the mid- to low 70s does not generate much new capital construction. Although the series was not intended to be an indicator of economic activity, the CUR often peaks a few months before the economy peaks — but the actual lead time is very unpredictable.

Capacity is an elusive concept to define and even more difficult to measure. One definition states that the capacity of an industry is reached when it is operating 24 hours a day, 7 days a week with a full staff. But this is not possible because periodic maintenance has to be performed on the machinery. If normal maintenance downtime is deducted from theoretical capacity, the result is called **engineering capacity**. This level would be approached only during wartime.[3] The Federal Reserve's capacity utilization ratios measure "practical" or "economic" capacity levels. Except for industries that generally operate continuously, such as utilities and refineries, most industries are assumed to operate 8 hours per day, 5 days per week.

The Census Bureau also publishes annual CURs for manufacturing industries; these CURs are not seasonally adjusted, as are the Federal Reserve's, and are available nine months later.[4] The Census Bureau data are based on establishment surveys and specific definitions of capacity for each industry. The trends of the two indexes are generally the same, but the Census Bureau's CURs are normally about 10 to 15 points below those of the Federal Reserve. The Fed relies on capacity levels obtained from McGraw-Hill, the Census Bureau, and other private and government sources, which it modifies to be consistent with other industry trends.

Name: Construction Data
Agency/Institution: Division of Construction Data, Bureau of the Census
Address: Washington, DC 20233
Telephone number for data and inquiries: 301-763-5435 or 301-763-5717
Sources: Census of Construction, *Construction Review* (monthly), *Value of New Construction Put in Place* (monthly)
Frequency: Every five years in years ending in "2" and "7"
When available: About every two or three years for the Census; about two months for the monthly publications
Historic data: *Construction Statistics 1915–1964* (U.S. Department of Commerce, 1966) and *Value of New Construction Put in Place, 1947–74* (C30-74s)

---

[3]CURs were not available during World War II, but they reached 90–95 percent levels during the Korean War.

[4]The Census Bureau CURs are estimated for the fourth quarter and are not available until the third quarter of the following year.

■ A QUICK LOOK: Construction Data

Data on the construction industry are important to national, state, and local economic analysts, and are reported frequently by the media. The construction industry is composed of firms involved in constructing new homes and other buildings; heavy construction such as highways and waterways; and special trades such as plumbing and electrical work. Many construction data sources, such as the Census of Construction, include subdividers and developers. The three major SIC groups in construction are:

15   Building construction—general contractors and operative builders

16   Heavy construction other than building construction—contractors

17   Special trade contractors

Federal government publications on construction include the following (see "Housing Data," pages 285–288, for data sources of housing starts, completions, sales characteristics, price indexes, authorized):

• *Construction Review:* The most popular and comprehensive monthly source of national, state, and local data on the construction industry apart from the Census of Construction. They include monthly statistics on private new residential and nonresidential buildings authorized for construction, number of buildings, permit valuation, value of construction put in place, permit value data for selected types of buildings for selected SMSA's and construction cost, public contract awards indexes, and contract construction employment. Residential and nonresidential construction activity is shown for the United States, census region, states, and SMSAs.

• *Value of New Construction Put in Place* (series C30): A monthly report on the total value of new private and public construction put in place, including residential and nonresidential buildings, public utilities, nonbuilding construction, and residential additions and alterations. This report is published about two months after the end of the reference month, although press releases are available within four weeks.

This series contains data on the value of private construction by residential, nonresidential, public utilities; value of public construction by residential, nonresidential; highways; military; sewer and water; and conservation for both states and federal governments. Data are reported in current and constant dollars. Construction cost indexes are also included. The following series are available:

Private Construction	Public Construction
Residential	Buildings
New	Housing
Additions	Industrial
Nonresidential	Educational
Industrial	Hospitals
Office	Other
Other commercial	Highways
Religious	Military
Educational	Conservation
Hospitals	Sewer Systems
Farms	Water Supply
Public Utilities	
Telephone	
Gas	
Electric	
Railroads	
Pipelines	
Others	

- *Census of Construction:* The Census Bureau no longer uses receipts as the primary measure of construction activity because advance payments were included in reported receipts even though no work was done during the reporting period. The Bureau now uses "value of construction work done" as the primary measure. The components of the Census of Construction are:

1. Preliminary reports: A preliminary summary report and a report for each 27 four-digit industry in the nation are issued a few months after the end of the census year.

2. Industry series: Each of the 27 industries has its own report, which provides data on the number of construction establishments, value of construction work done, payroll, employment, hours worked, payments to subcontractors, components, supplies and fuels, payments for capital expenditures, and inventories for each state and the nation. A summary report publishes the general data for the nation.

3. Geographic area series: There are nine reports for states grouped by the nine census regions. The data are similar to the industry series, but they are arranged by state instead of by industry. A U.S. summary report presents an overview for the nation.

4. Subject series: Presents number of establishments and total employment for construction establishments, classified by industry and by legal form of organization.

Name: Corporate Income and Financial Data by Industry
Alternative name: Financial Reports by Industry
Agency/Institution: Industry Division of the Census Bureau
Address: Washington, DC 20233
Telephone number for data and inquiries: 301-763-1758
Sources: *Quarterly Financial Report for Manufacturing, Mining, and Trade Corporations*
Frequency: Quarterly
When available: Reports for the first three quarters of each year are released 75
   days after the end of the quarter; the fourth quarter report appears within 95
   days after the end of the quarter.
Revisions: Made in the fourth quarter
Historic data: Available on diskette from the Bureau of the Census

---

■ A QUICK LOOK: Corporate Income and Financial Data by Industry

The *Quarterly Financial Report (QFR)* provides current estimates of income, assets, depreciation, liabilities, number of stockholders, and
equity and financial ratios for corporations classified by industry and asset size. The data are obtained through a national sample of 10,500 firms
in manufacturing, mining, retail, and wholesale companies.

Information is not given in the *QFR* for specific companies, but the
report is a valuable source of industry financial performance by which a
particular company can be evaluated. The Federal Reserve, Department
of Commerce, Department of the Treasury, and the Federal Trade Commission routinely use the *QFR* to evaluate corporate financial structure
and strength. If you are interested in the current income, assets, dividends, and retained earnings of the printing industry, for example, you
can find the data in the *QFR*. Also given are tables showing income-to-
sales ratios of the various industries.

Name: Corporate Profits
Alternative name: Net Profits After Tax
Agency/Institution: Division of Corporate Information, Bureau of Economic
   Analysis
Address: Washington, DC 20230
Telephone number for inquiries: 202-523-0888
Telephone number for data: 202-898-2451 for a 3- to 5-minute tape updating GDP
   data
Sources: *Survey of Current Business* and *Federal Reserve Bulletin*
Frequency: Quarterly
When available: End of the month following the end of the quarter
Revisions: Same as GDP
Periodic revisions: July of following year
Historic data: See GNP/GDP (pages 122 and 149)
Cross-references: Gross National Product (pages 122–158)

■ A QUICK LOOK: Corporate Profits

The *Federal Reserve Bulletin* reports the information in Table 12.4 for the most recent eight quarters and the three previous years.

TABLE 12.4
Corporate Profits
(billions of $)

	1991
Corporate profits with inventory valuation and capital consumption adjustment	$309.8
Profits before tax	312.4
Profits tax liability	124.5
Profits after tax	187.9
Dividends	137.8
Undistributed profits	50.2
Inventory valuation*	3.1
Capital (consumption) adjustment*	−8.7

*See pages 154–158 for a discussion of inventory valuation and capital consumption allowances.

The *Survey of Current Business* reports net profits after taxes for all manufacturing and for major industries. Corporate profit data are available with all complete GDP reports, which are reported quarterly in the *Survey of Current Business*. The data are available on a current-dollar or constant-dollar basis. Corporate profits are a fairly good leading indicator because they have almost always decreased prior to a general decline in economic activity. (See "GDP," pages 154–157.)

Name: Housing Characteristics (other than construction related)
Alternative name: Census of Housing, Current Housing Surveys
Agency/Institution: Division of Housing, Bureau of the Census
Address: Washington, DC 20233
Telephone number for data and inquiries: 301-763-7356
Sources: Decennial Census of Population and Housing, and Current Housing Reports
Frequency: Periodically
When available: Both the census results and the current housing survey results are available about two to three years after the end of the reference year.

■ A QUICK LOOK: Housing Characteristics

The Census Bureau provides nonconstruction data on housing through the decennial census and Current Housing Reports.

The first housing census occurred as part of the 1940 Census of Population and Housing, and each decennial census since then has included a census of housing. The Census of Housing has many reports on housing characteristics, amenities, owners, and so on. Although these were not yet available at the time of publication for the 1990 census, the major reports from that census will become available from 1992 to 1993, and will be similar to the reports from the 1980 census described here.[5]

1. State reports: Reports are issued by states and include statistics for SMSAs, counties, and towns.

   a. General housing characteristics: presents data for the 100 percent items — those data obtained from every respondent. The other questions are answered by random selection of respondents. The 100 percent items in the 1990 census are complete plumbing facilities, number of rooms in unit, owner-occupied or rented, condominium identification, value of home (owner-occupied), rent (renter-occupied), vacancy, for rent, for sale.

   b. Detailed housing characteristics: Provides data for 100 percent and sample housing characteristics.

2. National reports on housing

   a. Subject reports: Provide detailed characteristics on specific subjects such as mobile homes, condominium housing, and households that move continuously.

   b. Components of inventory change: characteristics of changes in housing inventory.

   c. Residential finance: Details on the financing of nonfarm homeowner and rental properties, as well as the characteristics of mortgages, properties, and owners.

Current Housing Reports are periodic reports on housing characteristics, vacancies, and ownership, taken largely from the American Housing Survey, which furnishes statistics comparable to those of the census but with much less geographic detail. You can find whether apartments or homes have telephones, televisions, patios, or recreation rooms, and how long apartments are vacant. Some of the Current Housing Reports cover the United States or major regions while others cover specific metropolitan areas. The American Housing Survey covers MSAs peri-

---

[5]For information on the "Census of Population" see pages 339–344. The Census Bureau has a great deal of data from the Census of Housing on tapes and diskettes. See the *Census Catalog and Guide* for a list.

odically. *Housing Vacancies and Homeownership* (H-111) and *Market Absorption of Apartments* (H-130), which are part of this series, are issued quarterly and annually.

Name: Housing Data
Alternative name: Housing Authorized by Building Permits
Agency/Institution: Bureau of the Census, Department of Commerce
Address: Washington, DC 20233
Telephone number for data and inquiries:
  Building permits: 301-763-7842
  Housing starts: 301-763-5731
  New one-family houses sold and for sale: 301-763-7314
  Prices of new one-family homes sold: 301-763-7842
  Housing completions: 301-763-5731
  New residential construction in selected metropolitan statistical areas: 301-763-7842
Sources: The following are published by the *Bureau of the Census, Department of Commerce*, except as noted:

- Building permits: *Housing Authorized by Building Permits,* series C-40 (monthly); *Construction Review* (monthly); *Economic Indicators* (Council of Economic Advisors; monthly)

- New one-family houses sold and for sale: *New One-Family Houses Sold and for Sale,* series C-25 (monthly); *Characteristics of New Housing* (an annual supplement to series C-25)

- Housing starts: *Housing Starts,* series C-20, (monthly); *Economic Indicators* (Council of Economic Advisors; monthly); *Survey of Current Business* (monthly)

- Prices of new one-family homes sold: *Price Index of New One-Family Homes Sold,* series C-27 (quarterly); quarterly supplements to *New One-Family Homes Sold and for Sale,* series C-25.

- Housing completions: *Housing Completions,* series C-22

- Residential construction in metro areas: *New Residential Construction in Selected Metropolitan Statistical Areas,* series C-21

- Residential upkeep expenditures: *Expenditures for Residential Upkeep and Improvement,* series C-50

Available:

- *Housing Authorized by Building Permits:* Fourth week of following month

- *New One-Family Houses Sold and for Sale:* Press releases appear three weeks after the end of the month; reports are available 3 to 5 weeks later.

- *Housing Starts*: Initial estimates are released in the third week of the following month.

- *Price Index of New One-Family Homes Sold:* Preliminary data appear in a press release 5 weeks after the end of the quarter. Final reports are available 10 to 12 weeks after the end of the quarter.

- *Housing Completions:* Press releases are scheduled to be released 5 weeks after the end of the reference month; reports appear about 9 to 11 weeks after the end of the reference month.

- *Characteristics of New Housing:* Reports are published about six months after the end of the reference year.

- *New Residential Construction in Selected Metropolitan Statistical Areas:* Reports appear about four months after the end of the quarter.

- *Expenditures for Residential Upkeep and Improvement:* Reports appear about six months after the end of the quarter.

Revisions: Most monthly series are revised in the first and third month following month of release and then periodically. Because subsequent revisions can be significant, it is best not to make decisions based on the initial estimates released in the early reports.

Historic data: *Housing Construction Statistics, 1889–1964*

■ A QUICK LOOK: Housing Data

Housing data are found in the following publications:

- *Building Permits* (series C-40): Monthly data include building permits for total private housing units, apartment buildings, one-family units of approximately 3800 localities, and 130 SMSAs. Permit values of homes and contracts awarded for public housing are also presented. Annual data are based on sample surveys of about 16,000 localities; monthly data are reported on about one-half that number. Not all localities require permits for construction, and several months may pass between the permit issuing date and the beginning of construction.

- *Housing Starts* (series C-20): This series represents actual home building activity rather than home building intentions, which are indicated by housing permits. A housing start refers to the breaking of ground and the actual start of construction for a residential structure. The "starts" data include single- and multifamily dwellings, or apartment houses. Each apartment in a multifamily dwelling is considered to be a separate unit. Housing starts are expressed directly in terms of millions of private houses started rather than being based on an index. Monthly housing starts are volatile, and the early estimates are often revised during the following months; these revisions often are significant. Hence, the early estimates should be used with extreme caution, if at all. Monthly data include private and public housing units started and shipments of mobile homes to dealers. Annual data include the characteristics of housing units in new privately owned buildings with five units or more, total time from start of construction to completion, and condominium ownership. Data are available for the United States, census regions, and SMSAs. Data are obtained from a sample survey of 16,000 permit-issuing localities (which account for about 90 percent of residential construction).

- *New One-Family Houses Sold and for Sale* (series C-25): This series is of interest to those interested in the sales of new single-family residences. Data presented include the total number of new one-family houses sold and for sale by region, price categories, stage of completion, median number of months on market, and type of financing.

- *Characteristics of New Housing* (series C-25): An annual supplement to the C-25 series, *New One-Family Houses Sold and for Sale*. This report contains information on selected physical and financial characteristics of new one-family houses completed and sold. Some of the data are square footage, number of bedrooms and bathrooms, type of fuel used, heating systems, price down payment.

- *Price Index of New One-Family Houses Sold* (series C-27): The median and mean prices of homes are available quarterly in the publication *New One-Family Homes Sold and for Sale* (series C-25). The *median price* is the "middle price"; one-half of the homes are more expensive and one-half are less expensive. The *mean price* is obtained by adding up the prices of all homes and dividing by the number of homes sold. The median is a better indicator of the price of a home for an average family; also, its trend over time is more meaningful. The mean price is easily distorted by the sales of a few very expensive homes. The price index, reported in this C-27 series, includes the value of the lot, and is based on holding the following characteristics constant: floor area, number of floors, bathrooms and fireplaces, presence of air conditioning, parking facility, type of foundation, location, and size of lot. Data are available for the country and the four census regions (Northeast, North Central, South, and West.)

- *Housing Completions* (series C-22): A monthly report providing statistics for the United States on new, privately owned housing units completed and under construction, by type of structure. Totals are given for areas inside and outside SMAs. Additional data are provided on a quarterly basis.

- *New Residential Construction in Selected Metropolitan Statistical Areas* (series C-21): A quarterly report containing data for 40 metropolitan areas on new housing units authorized, authorized but not started, started, under construction, and completed.

- *Expenditures for Residential Upkeep and Improvement* (series C-50): Quarterly and annual reports for the United States. The quarterly reports cover expenditures of residential property owners, by number of units on the property. The annual report shows expenditures made by owners of all types of residential property, including owner-occupants of one-housing properties.

Name: Industrial Production Index (IPI)
Sponsoring agency/Institition: Division of Industry, Federal Reserve Board
Address: Washington, DC 20551
Telephone number for data and inquiries: Call the Federal Reserve, 202-452-3244, and you will be referred to the currently correct number.
Sources: *Industrial Production* (Federal Reserve System; G.12.3(414), statistical release); *Federal Reserve Bulletin* (monthly); *Survey of Current Business* (monthly)
Frequency: Monthly
When available: The third week following the end of the month
Revisions: Made during each of the following three months, annually and then every year.
Historic data: *Industrial Production-Year* (Federal Reserve; published periodically)

■ A QUICK LOOK: Industrial Production Index

The Industrial Production Index (IPI) is a monthly indicator of changes in the physical output of manufacturing, mining, and electric and gas utilities. It does not include the construction, transportation, trade, or service industries. The index consists of about 250 different output series constructed from data provided by government agencies, firms, and trade associations. The index has market and industry subgroups, but overall it represents both. This index presents a good overall view of changes in the American industrial sector. A small sample of the data is given in Table 12.5.

TABLE 12.5
Index of Industrial Production,
Selected Products
(1987 = 100)

	1989	1990
Total Index	108.1	109.2
By Market:		
Final products	109.1	110.8
Consumer goods	106.7	107.3
Durables	107.9	106.1
Autos and trucks	105.7	97.2
Nondurables	106.4	107.6
Foods and tobacco	104.2	105.9
Clothing	101.6	95.7

(continued)

TABLE 12.5 *(continued)*
Index of Industrial Production,
Selected Products
(1987 = 100)

	1989	1990
Equipment	112.3	115.5
Business equipment	119.1	123.3
Industrial	113.8	115.2
Office and computing machines	137.2	149.6
Intermediate products	106.8	107.7
Construction supplies	106.1	105.2
Business supplies	107.3	109.4
By Major Industries:		
Mining	100.5	102.5
Metal mining	141.4	153.1
Coal	113.4	113.4
Crude Oil	91.4	87.5
Natural Gas	102.7	104.6
Electric Utilities	108.1	110.8
Manufacturing	108.9	109.9
Nondurables	106.4	107.6
Chemicals and chemical products	108.5	110.1
Rubber and plastic products	108.9	110.2
Leather and products	103.7	99.9
Durables	110.9	111.6
Lumber and wood products	103.1	101.1
Furniture and fixtures	105.3	105.9
Iron and steel	109.3	109.7

To find the annual rate of change based on this index, use the following formula:

$$\text{Annual rate of change} = \frac{\text{Index}_{1990} - \text{Index}_{1989}}{\text{Index}_{1989}}$$

For example, the rate of change for durables production during 1990 was

$$\frac{111.6 - 110.9}{110.9} = 0.6\%$$

(For more on annualizing monthly rates of change, see Chapter 2, pages 18–21.)

■ **A CLOSER LOOK: Industrial Production Index (IPI)**

The Industrial Production Index is widely used to track the business cycle because it is released monthly (the GNP/GDP is released quarterly) and because it measures cyclically sensitive sectors of the economy. The index also enables us to obtain a quick overview of expanding and contracting industries. The crude oil industry, shown in Table 12.5, has obviously contracted since the base year of 1987, while the office and computing machines industry has expanded. The BEA classifies the Industrial Production Index as a coincident indicator, meaning that the peaks and troughs in the series occur at approximately the same time as the economy's peaks and troughs.

The IPI is composed of detailed indexes that are weighted by their relative importance. For example, manufacturing accounts for about 84 percent of the index's major industry weights, mining accounts for 8 percent, and utilities for 8 percent. The weights are determined by the relative values added by each industry in 1987 and are updated, with various lags, every 10 years. When the 1987 census data became available in 1990, the weights, also called proportions, and the index were updated to a 1987 base. One of the problems with the index is that the relative significance of each industry may change considerably before the weights are revised. Thus, the index may not be representative of changes that are occurring in the economy. Until mid-1990, for example, the index was still using the 1977 proportions.

HISTORIC DATA: Index of Industrial Production
(1987 = 100)

1920	8.7	1940	14.4	1960	38.1	1980	84.1
1921	6.9	1941	18.5	1961	38.3	1981	85.7
1922	8.7	1942	21.9	1962	41.5	1982	81.9
1923	10.4	1943	27.1	1963	44.1	1983	84.9
1924	9.8	1944	29.4	1964	47.0	1984	92.8
1925	11.0	1945	24.8	1965	51.7	1985	94.4
1926	11.5	1946	20.2	1966	56.3	1986	95.3
1927	11.5	1947	22.7	1967	57.5	1987	100.0
1928	12.1	1948	23.7	1968	60.7	1988	105.4
1929	13.3	1949	22.3	1969	63.5	1989	108.1
1930	11.0	1950	25.9	1970	61.4	1990	109.2
1931	8.7	1951	28.1	1971	62.2	1991	107.1
1932	6.9	1952	29.1	1972	68.3		
1933	8.1	1953	31.6	1973	73.8		
1934	8.7	1954	29.8	1974	72.7		
1935	10.4	1955	33.6	1975	66.3		
1936	12.7	1956	35.0	1976	72.4		
1937	13.3	1957	35.6	1977	78.2		
1938	10.4	1958	33.2	1978	82.6		
1939	12.7	1959	37.2	1979	85.7		

Name: Input-Output Tables
Agency/Institution: Bureau of Economic Analysis, Department of Commerce
Address: Interindustry Economics Division, BE 51, BEA, U.S. Dept of Commerce, Washington, DC 20230
Telephone number for data and inquiries:
General: 202-523-0792
Benchmark tables: 202-523-0683
Annual tables: 202-523-0867
Methodology: 202-523-0683
Tapes, diskettes, printouts: 202-523-0792
Sources: The most detailed information is available on computer tapes, diskettes, and unpublished printouts from the BEA, but the 85 industry tables are available in the *Survey of Current Business* (generally the April issue).
Frequency: Benchmark tables, based largely on the economic censuses, are prepared every five years; the largest benchmark (1982) was published in 1991. Annual tables are prepared using basically the same procedures as used for the benchmark tables, but with less comprehensive and less reliable source data.
When available: Annual tables have a lag of about four years while the benchmark tables have a lag of eight to nine years.
Revisions: No statistical revisions but, occasionally, BEA issues a definitional revision.
Historic data: Benchmark I-O tables are available from the Bureau of Economic Analysis for 1947, 1958, 1963, 1967, 1972, 1977 and 1982.
Cross-references: See local and state income and employment multipliers, pages 356–362 for information and examples of local and state multipliers based on the national input-output tables.

■ A QUICK LOOK: Input-Output Tables

One of the nation's most extensive and fundamental sources of data is the input-output (I-O) tables, which are generated by complex data gathering and matrix manipulations by the Bureau of Economic Analysis (BEA). Input-output tables are available annually (with a four- to five-year lag) and benchmark tables are published every five years (with a nine-year lag). Tables 12.6–12.8 show a small sample of the data contained in the 1982 benchmark input-output tables of 85 industries published in the July 1991 *Survey of Current Business*. Data for 537 industries are available on tapes and diskettes.

The basic source of all I-O data is the "establishment" — a unit classified as being in a particular industry based on the primary products or services it produces. Many industries produce several products — called secondary products — besides their primary products. Any product can be produced in its primary industry or as a secondary product in any of several other industries. Thus, the paints and allied products industry might produce such secondary products as, for example, farm and garden machinery. Consequently, the I-O tables would include farm and garden machinery in the paints and allied products industry as well as in the machinery industry.

TABLE 12.6
Sample of Commodity-by-Industry Direct Requirements,
Input-Output Table, 1982

	INDUSTRIES				
COMMODITIES	Plastics and Synthetic Products	Drugs, Cleaning, and Toilet Products	Paints and Allied Products	Petroleum Products	Rubber Products
	28	29	30	31	32
28. Plastics and synthetic products	0.02673	0.00287	0.11353	0.00027	0.18727
29. Drugs, cleaning, and toilet preps	0.00608	0.09695	0.00667	0.00170	0.00039
30. Paints and allied products	0.00277	0.00168	0.01037	0.00004	0.00086
31. Petroleum products	0.01455	0.01364	0.01678	0.08465	0.00800
32. Rubber products	0.03343	0.02891	0.00196	0.00152	0.03977
Totals	1.00000	1.00000	1.00000	1.00000	1.00000

Table 12.6, known as a commodity-by-industry table,[6] shows only 5 of the 85 industries published in the *Survey of Current Business* (537 industries are available). The row headings refer to commodities; the column headings refer to industries. The cells contain the input coefficients (also called "direct requirements coefficients," which show the inputs per dollar of output for the industry shown at the top of the columns. If, for example, the plastics and synthetic products industry (col. 28), produces $1 million of output, it will use $26,730 from its own industry (row 28); $6080 of inputs from the drugs, cleaning, and toilet preparations industry (row 29); $2770 from the paint industry; $14,550 from the petroleum industry; and $33,430 from the rubber industry. The column totals always equal 1 because the commodity inputs of all industries are included in the column.

Table 12.6 is called a "direct requirements table" because the coefficients show the inputs that go directly into the industry without including any feedback or indirect effects. *Thus, if we are looking for the composition of inputs in an industry, the place to look is the commodity-by-industry direct requirements table.*

---

[6]The convention employed in I-O accounts is to designate the row first and then the column. Thus, tables in which commodities appear in the rows and industries in the columns are designated "commodity-by-industry" tables. Tables in which industries appear in rows and commodities in the columns are designated "industry-by-commodity" tables.

TABLE 12.7
Sample of Commodity-by-Commodity Total Requirements,
Input-Output Table, 1982

	COMMODITIES				
COMMODITIES	Plastics and Synthetic Products 28	Drugs, Cleaning, and Toilet Products 29	Paints and Allied Products 30	Petroleum Products 31	Rubber Products 32
28. Plastics and synthetic products	1.06069	0.01427	0.12618	0.00228	0.20863
29. Drugs, cleaning, and toilet preps	0.00986	1.10316	0.01074	0.00256	0.00370
30. Paints and allied products	0.00527	0.00311	1.01373	0.00109	0.00293
31. Petroleum products	0.06943	0.03907	0.06299	1.11237	0.04409
32. Rubber products	0.04331	0.03880	0.01607	0.00504	1.05420
Totals	2.65482	2.0556	2.53067	2.39298	2.29425

Table 12.7 is the commodity-by-commodity total requirements table, which shows the production of each commodity required both directly and indirectly to produce the commodities designated at the top of the columns. The cells that represent the same commodity in both the row and a column are called "diagonal cells" and, in this table, are always greater than 1. These entries are greater than 1 because some of the products classified as output from the industry are also inputs to the industry, necessary to produce that output. The production of petroleum products (col. 31) requires $1.11237 of petroleum product inputs, for example, for each $1 of petroleum product output for final customers. That is, an additional $1 of petroleum product input leads to an additional $1 of output from the petroleum industry. In addition, the production process itself, and its secondary effects, use up another $0.11237 of petroleum products to generate that $1 of final petroleum output. Petroleum production requires gasoline and oils to power the pumps and vehicles, for example. This additional outut of petroleum has to be included in the coefficient of petroleum inputs for petroleum products.

This table should be used if you are interested in analyzing the impact of increased production of one product on the various products that constitute its inputs. The way to read this table is to look up the commodity at the head of the column and to read down the column to see the amount of the various commodities necessary as inputs to produce $1 of output of that commodity. For example, if we are interested in the effects of an increase in $1 million of "final demand" (see the *Warning!* below) for petroleum products, we can read down the petroleum products column (31). In order to produce $1 million of petroleum products, $2280 of plastics and synthetic products will be used, $2560 of drugs and cleaners, $1090 of paints, $5040 of rubber products and $1,112,370 of petroleum products. The $1 million of petroleum products will go directly to final demand; the $112,370 of petroleum products will be used to produce these petroleum products.

First Warning! The term *final demand* is used carelessly by the BEA and other users and producers of data series. "Final demand" can mean final demand at the consumer level or final demand at the producer or industry level. The $1 million of "final demand" in I-O tables means the demand in producers' prices at the manufacturing or industry level. It is *not* the final consumer demand in purchasers' prices at the retail or wholesale level. For example, an increase of $2 million in consumer final demand means that prices are expressed at the consumer level and that transportation and trade margins are included. This $2 million increase in "final demand" cannot be applied directly to industries listed in the I-O tables. Transportation costs (including insurance) and trade margins have to be deducted first. If final *consumer* demand for petroleum products increases by $2 million and transportation and trade margins account for $0.8 million, producers' final demand will be $1.2 million, which *can* be applied to the petroleum products column in the table.

Second Warning! Most industries are "driven" by final producer demand or total output, but the trade industry is driven by margins. In order to show the flows among all industries, the trade sector's activity is not measured by its sales but by its margin. Margin is the difference between the purchase cost of an item and the sales price. It consists of the retailer's or wholesaler's operating expenses, profits, sales taxes, excise taxes, and custom duties. The margin associated with a commodity is shown as a separate purchase from the trade sector. If an analyst wants to measure the impact of increased trade activity, he must not enter the value of sales but the amount of the margin associated with the sales.

TABLE 12.8
Sample of Industry-by-Commodity Total Requirements,
Input-Output Table, 1982

	COMMODITIES				
Industries	Plastics and Synthetic Products 28	Drugs, Cleaning, and Toilet Products 29	Paints and Allied Products 30	Petroleum Products 31	Rubber Products 32
28. Plastics and synthetic products	0.87368	0.01710	0.11611	0.00339	0.18352
29. Drugs, cleaning, and toilet preps	0.01891	1.05688	0.01919	0.00349	0.00854
30. Paints and allied products	0.00944	0.00391	0.97862	0.00112	0.00410

(continued)

TABLE 12.8 *(continued)*
Sample of Industry-by-Commodity Total Requirements,
Input-Output Table, 1982

	COMMODITIES				
Industries	Plastics and Synthetic Products 28	Drugs, Cleaning, and Toilet Products 29	Paints and Allied Products 30	Petroleum Products 31	Rubber Products 32
31. Petroleum products	0.15122	0.05207	0.11056	1.07099	0.07023
32. Rubber products	0.04712	0.03753	0.01768	0.00494	0.99924
Totals	2.64367	2.04231	2.51355	2.38616	2.27208

Table 12.8 is the industry-by-commodity *total* requirements table; like the commodity-by-commodity table, it includes both direct and indirect effects. This table shows the production necessary from each of the industries specified in the rows to produce $1 of output of the commodities listed at the head of the columns. *This table is used to assess the impacts on various industries when the output of a commodity is expected to increase.* For example, if demand for paint increases by $1 million, output in the plastics industry (row 28) will increase by $116,110, output in the drugs and cleaning industry will increase by $19,190, output in the paint industry will increase by $978,620, and so on. Unlike the commodity-by-commodity table, the diagonal cells in the industry-by-commodity tables do not have to equal or be greater than 1.

■ **A CLOSER LOOK: Input-Output Tables**

Background

One of the most useful but also the most neglected sources of data provided by the federal government is the input-output tables, which show the inputs each industry receives from each of the other industries and the output each industry provides to all other industries.[7] Essentially, input-output tables portray a from-whom-to-whom breakdown of commodity and service flows, providing much information about each industry's use of materials and the distribution of its products. They show the production of goods and services by each industry, the commodity composition of GDP, and the industry distribution of value added. Values of

[7]Perhaps the reason input-output tables, pioneered by Professor Wassily Leontief of Harvard University, are not widely known is that work began on them during the 1940s and input-output tables became widely available only during the 1960s. Even today, only a few business colleges have courses that delve into the construction and use of I-O tables.

inputs and outputs in I-O tables are based on producer prices, but tables converting producer prices to purchaser prices as used in GDP accounts are also available.[8] The Bureau of Economic Analysis publishes I-O tables every year, but the most reliable and current data are available in benchmark tables that are based on data collected by the economic censuses, which are conducted every five years.

Unfortunately, there is a lag of about four years in the annual input-output tables, and a lag of eight to nine years from the census year until the publication of the benchmark I-O tables. The 1982 benchmark tables, for example, were published in the July 1991 issue of the *Survey of Current Business*.

BEA publishes 85 industry tables at the two-digit SIC level, but 537 industry tables at the six-digit level are available on diskette and tape. The underlying classification of products and firms into industries is based on the SIC classification, but combinations and adjustments are made to fit the 85 industry I-O tables. (See pages 22–23 for a discussion of the SIC codes.) The basic statistical unit, from which the raw data are collected, is the "establishment," which is defined as being located at a single, physical location, and where business is conducted, services are offered, or industrial operations are performed.

After it locates establishments, BEA has to determine the industry in which they should be classified. This classification is based on the primary product or service produced by the establishment. Although there are a number of exceptions, the "primary product" is defined as the one that generates the most gross revenue for the establishment. A farm that receives most of its revenue from raising corn but that also provides horse rides would be assigned to the agriculture industry because its primary product is corn. However, since its secondary product is horse rides, the agriculture industry will now produce a secondary product classified as amusements, which are included in the service industry. If the farmhouse is occasionally used as an inn, the farm establishment would have another secondary product, listed as hotels and lodging, also included in the service industry. If the farm obtained most of its revenue from room rentals, its primary product would be motel services and it would be classified in the service industry. When all establishments have been classified by their primary product, one often finds industries producing secondary products quite unrelated to the primary industry. This mixture of primary and secondary production causes some difficulties in the construction and usefulness of the I-O tables.

---

[8]Producer prices plus transportation, retail and wholesale trade margins, and insurance equal purchaser prices.

The Make Table

I-O tables are not used more frequently because they are very complicated to interpret and understand. The matrix form in which the data are
presented frightens most people and they don't go on. I have attempted
to make the interpretation of I-O tables as simple and brief as possible in
the preceding Quick Look section. However, if you are going to use I-O
tables you will want to read the following material. It is not easy going
and you *will not* understand everything in the first reading. Skim over all
the material, and then come back to this spot and begin again, reading
each sentence very carefully and not going on to the next sentence until
you understand this one. While doing this, constantly refer to the tables
and track down each number and cell as they are mentioned. Taken a step
at a time, this is not difficult material. (Wanna buy a bridge???)

I-O accounts are always presented in matrix form in order to show
relationships among industries, the commodities they produce, and the
inputs they use. The matrices have headings at the top of the columns
and along the left side of the rows. The intersections of the columns and
rows, known as cells, contain the data. Table 12.9, generally the first one
presented in BEA publications, is a hypothetical "Make" table that shows
production of each commodity by each industry. The columns show the
commodities that are produced; the rows show the dollar value of output
of that commodity produced by the industry named at the beginning of
the row. The cells in which the values are denoted by brackets, [ ], are
called diagonal cells. They show the production values of the commodity
for which the industry has been designated the primary producer. The
agriculture industry in Table 12.9, for example, is the primary producer of
agricultural products. The mining industry is the primary producer of
minerals and the construction industry is the primary producer of construction goods. The diagonal cells will have relatively large numbers in
them. As mentioned earlier, several industries produce secondary products, which are products other than their primary products. For example,
in Table 12.9 the agriculture industry produces warehouse services (classified in the transportation industry), which is one of its secondary products; it also produces trade services (for example, retailing of agricultural
products) and services (machinery repair). The row total (at the far right
side of the table) shows the total production of all firms classified in the
agriculture industry. In this hypothetical example, the agriculture industry produces $75 million in its primary industry (the diagonal cell) plus $5
million in transportation, $2 million in trade, and $1 million in services,
for a total output of $83 million. (Please note that all values in this and the
following tables are purely hypothetical and that the I-O tables are much
more detailed than presented here. See the "A Quick Look" section for a
sample of actual data.)

TABLE 12.9
Make of Commodities by Industries,
Hypothetical Values for Any Year
(millions of $ in producers' prices)

| | COMMODITIES | | | | | | | | | |
Industries	Agricultural products	Minerals	Construction	Manufactured products	Transportation	Trade	Finance	Services	Other	Total Industry output
Agriculture	[75]				5	2		1		83
Mining		[57]	2	3						62
Construction		5	[300]	12						317
Manufacturing		1	4	[710]						715
Transportation				1	[120]	3				124
Trade	3			15		[540]				558
Finance							[240]			240
Services					1		3	[610]		614
Other				20	16	7		45	[246]	334
Total Commodity Output	78	63	306	761	142	552	243	656	246	3,047

The entries in the columns represent the value of production by each industry of the commodity named at the head of the column. Agricultural products, for example, were produced by the agriculture industry and by the trade industry. Minerals were produced by the mining, construction, and manufacturing industries. The totals at the bottom of the columns represent the total production of each of the commodities. The $78 million at the bottom of the agricultural column, for example, represents total output of agricultural products.

To summarize, in the make table, the row totals show aggregate production by firms classified in that row's industry; the column totals show the total production of each commodity, regardless of the industry in which it was produced. The sum of the row totals equals the sum of the column totals ($3047). The purpose of the make table is to put the inputs and outputs in matrix form from which subsequent tables can be calculated. The make table is not used as frequently as the coefficient tables that follow, but it is used to estimate the overall size of related markets. For example, a market analyst might be interested in knowing that the total size of the manufactured products market is $761 million and that manufactured products are made in several industries other than manufacturing.

The Use Table

A use table (see Table 12.10) illustrates the mix of commodities consumed by each industry (intermediate users) and by final consumers, and it shows the tie-in between input-output and GDP tables. The industries section shows the value of each commodity input utilized in that industry. For example, the agriculture industry used $5 million of minerals (principally crude oil and gas) in producing agricultural and other products. The mining industry used $2 million of its own mineral production (principally oil and gas to power its pumps, run its shovels and trucks, and so on), and the construction industry used $20 million of minerals. Total minerals used by intermediate industries amount to $69 million, as shown in the column headed "Total Intermediate Use." To the right of the "Total Intermediate Use" column is the GDP section, which shows the value of commodities consumed by end-users in the form of consumption, investment, business inventories, exports, and government. For example, consumers consumed part of the manufactured products industry output when they purchased television sets or watches. Investors consumed part when they purchased computers. The final uses of each of these sectors make up the final GDP component, ($1646) which is shown in the column titled "GDP."

The total value of all commodities available for use in the economy is equal to the total use by industries ("Total Intermediate Use" column)

plus the total use by final users (GDP column). When these two components are summed, the resulting total equals the total produced. Thus,
total commodity output at the far right side of Table 12.10 is the same as
the total of the commodity columns in Table 12.9. Total agricultural output
(a better term would be *total agricultural use*) shown in Table 12.10 is $78
million, which is the same as the total of the agricultural products column
shown in Table 12.9.

National income and product accounts (NIPAs) measure production
in the country, both in terms of final products and in terms of incomes
generated in the production process. The product side includes personal
consumption expenditures, gross private domestic investment (including changes in business inventories), exports, imports, and government
purchases—all of which add up to GDP. The income side includes employee compensation, proprietors' income, rental income, corporate
profits, interest, business transfer payments, indirect business taxes, and
capital consumption allowances. (Only the "compensation of employees" is identified separately in Table 12.10.) (See the GDP discussion
beginning on page 120.) These two sides of the GDP are shown in abbreviated I-O format in Table 12.10. The income side is shown in the bottom
rows under "Value Added," while the product side is shown on the far
right side.

The rows show inputs into the industries identified at the top of the
columns. For example, the agriculture industry (column 1) used $33 mil-
lion of agricultural inputs, $5 million of mineral inputs, $4 million of construction inputs, $15 million of manufactured products, and so on. The
total value of commodity inputs used by the agriculture industry is $76
million.

The value of an industry's output is determined not only by the value
of its commodity inputs but also by the value of all other resources that go
into producing the product. The value of these noncommodity inputs is
determined by their factor payments, which are shown in the bottom
four rows as part of the value-added section. Compensation to employees accounted for $3 million of the value added, indirect business
taxes accounted for $1 million and "Other Value Added," which includes
net interest, depreciation, rentals, corporate profits, and business transfer payments, accounted for $3 million. Total industry output is com-
posed of the value of intermediate inputs ($76 million for agriculture)
plus the total of value added, or income ($7 million for agriculture). These
value-added data are often used as one measure of the income originat-
ing within each of the industries. For example, the total value added (factor incomes) in the agriculture industry totals $7 million, or about one-
half of 1 percent, of the total value added ($1646) in all industries.

The product side of the GDP accounts is shown in the far right columns of Table 12.10. These represent final uses of the products that were
produced in the rows but were not used by the industries. The use by

TABLE 12.10
Use of Commodities by Industries,
Hypothetical Values for Any Year (millions of $ in producers' prices)

Column groups: Industries (Agricultural … Other, Total Intermediate Use); Final Uses (GDP and Its Components): Personal Consumption Expenditures, Gross Private Domestic Investment (Fixed Investment, Business Inventories), Exports, Imports, Government Purchases, GDP, Total Commodity Output.

Commodities	Agricultural	Mining	Construction	Manufacturing	Transportation	Trade	Finance	Service	Other	Total Intermediate Use	Personal Consumption Expenditures	Fixed Investment	Business Inventories	Exports	Imports	Government Purchases	GDP	Total Commodity Output
Agricultural Products	33	2	6	15	1	2	3	1		63	9			5	-2	3	15	78
Minerals	5	2	20	11	13	2	5	9	2	69				1	-8	1	-6	63
Construction	4	5	20	7	4	1	1		4	46		214	-3	1		48	260	306
Manufactured Products	15	11	35	100	7	43	11	35	28	285	321	70	31	9	-6	51	476	761
Transportation	3	3	9	45	17	21	6	21	7	132	4	2	-3	6	-2	3	10	142
Trade	5	2	8	63	2	10	8	11	3	112	425	3		5	-1	8	440	552
Finance	2	1	6	25	1	8	45	21	3	112	116	4		4		7	131	243
Services	5	2	81	50	3	35	39	117	67	399	209	3	2	9	-4	38	257	656
Other	4	2	2	79		9	8	41	38	183	56	2		6	-9	8	63	246
Total Intermed. Value:	76	30	187	395	48	131	126	256	152	1401								
Value Added:																		
Compensation of Employees	3	4	32	210	70	251	95	320	160									
Indirect Business Taxes	1	8	61	12	3	84	10	5	2									
Other Value Added	3	20	37	98	3	92	9	33	20									
Total Value Added	7	32	130	320	76	427	114	358	182	1646							1646	
Total Industry Output	83	62	317	715	124	558	240	614	334	3047								3047

industries is shown in the rows under the "Industries" heading. For example, $33 million of agricultural products were utilized in the agriculture industry (for example, corn to feed pigs), $2 million were used by the mining industry, $6 million by the construction industry, and so on. The total use of agricultural products by all industries is $63 million. We know, however, from the total of column 1 in Table 12.9 that total agricultural output is $78 million. Agricultural output not utilized by industries was sold directly to final users. Consumers directly purchased $9 million, $5 million was sold to foreigners, and government agencies purchased $3 million. Because entries in the industries and final-use portions of the table include imported as well as domestically produced commodities, we deduct imports here in order to obtain commodity output produced in the United States.[9] For that reason, imports are negative items in the "Final Uses" section. The − $2 million in the first row means that $2 million of agricultural products were imported into the country and that total uses of agricultural products totaled $80 million with $78 million being produced in the United States. Deducting the $2 million of imports makes net uses equal to domestic production.

Entries in the industries portion of Table 12.10 do not include capital goods. For example, a newly constructed barn would not be included in agricultural products or in construction. Uses of construction industry products show up as inputs in other industries and products only because "maintenance and repair" construction is included in the construction industry. Thus, the $4 million of construction industry expenditures listed in the agriculture industry cell represent "maintenance and repair" expenditures. "New construction" does not show any uses other than in its own industry; all other construction expenditures are picked up in the investment section. All capital equipment and structures are picked up by entries in gross private fixed investment or government purchases in the "Final Uses" section.

Although I-O tables are based on producers' prices, the "Final Uses" section actually shows the equivalences of purchasers' prices, which are equivalent to the GDP values. All industries, including transportation and trade, are included in the "Final Uses" section so that the total producers' prices and value added will equal the purchasers' prices. Diligent users will want to know that the total of value added equals the sum of the GDP components, shown as $1646 in the lower right-hand side of Table 12.10. This figure, in turn, equals the GDP for that year, which is found in the national income and product accounts.[10]

The entries in the columns of Table 12.10 represent the values of the commodities — raw materials, semifinished products and services — used in the production process by each of the industries identified at the head of the column. Remember that the row total (total commodity output) shows the production of the *commodity*, regardless of which industry actually produced the commodity. The column total (total industry output) shows the production of the industry, regardless of what commodity was produced.

The Commodity-by-Industry Table

Table 12.11 is the commodity-by-industry table[11], which shows products in the row headings on the left-hand side and industries at the head of the columns. It is based on Table 12.10, and, unlike Tables 12.12 and 12.13, it is easy to generate. Each cell in the industries portion of Table 12.10 is divided by the total at the bottom of the columns to obtain the direct requirements coefficients. For example, from Table 12.10 we see that the agriculture industry requires inputs of $15 million of manufactured products. We divide this by the figure for "Total Industry Output" (15/83) to get the direct requirements coefficient (0.181) of manufactured products in the agriculture industry for Table 12.11.

The entries in the cells, called "input coefficient" or "direct requirements coefficients," show the inputs of the products required to produce a dollar of the industry's output. For example, a dollar of output in the agriculture industry requires 39.8 cents of agricultural products, 6 cents of mineral products, 4.8 cents of construction products, 18.1 cents of manufactured products, and so on down the column. To produce a dollar of output of the mining industry, it takes 3.2 cents of agricultural products, 3.2 cents of minerals, 8.1 cents of construction (repair), and so on down the column.

---

[10]This amount is purely hypothetical so it will not equal the GDP of any year. However, the equivalent figure in the BEA's Use Table (row 90; column 99) found in the article "Benchmark Input-Output Accounts for the U.S. Economy, 1982" in *Survey of Current Business*, July 1991, is $3,207,597,000. If you look up the GDP in some other source and find that it is different, do not despair. Remember Chapter 1's discussion about the periodic revisions of data series! Since the 1982 I-O table was not published until July 1991, it was based on the revised GDP for 1982 available in spring 1991.

[11]The convention employed in I-O accounts is to designate the row first and then the column. Thus, tables in which commodities appear in the rows and industries in the column are designated "commodity-by-industry" tables. Tables in which industries appear in rows and commodities in the columns are designated "industry-by-commodity" tables.

TABLE 12.11
Commodity-by-Industry Direct Requirements,
Hypothetical Values for Any Year
(millions of $ in producers' prices)

| | INDUSTRIES | | | | | | | | |
Commodities	Agri-culture	Mining	Construc-tion	Manufac-turing	Transpor-tation	Trade	Finance	Services	Other
Agricultural	0.398	0.032	0.019	0.021	0.008	0.004	0.013	0.002	0.000
Mining	0.060	0.032	0.063	0.015	0.105	0.004	0.021	0.015	0.006
Construction	0.048	0.081	0.063	0.010	0.032	0.002	0.004	0.000	0.012
Manufactured	0.181	0.177	0.110	0.140	0.056	0.077	0.046	0.057	0.084
Transportation	0.036	0.048	0.028	0.063	0.137	0.038	0.025	0.034	0.021
Trade	0.060	0.032	0.025	0.088	0.016	0.018	0.033	0.018	0.009
Finance	0.024	0.016	0.019	0.035	0.008	0.014	0.188	0.034	0.009
Services	0.060	0.065	0.256	0.070	0.024	0.063	0.163	0.191	0.195
Other	0.048	0.000	0.006	0.110	0.000	0.016	0.033	0.067	0.120
Total Intermediate	0.916	0.484	0.590	0.552	0.387	0.235	0.525	0.417	0.455
Value Added:									
Compensation of Employees	0.036	0.065	0.101	0.294	0.565	0.450	0.396	0.521	0.479
Indirect Business Taxes	0.012	0.129	0.192	0.017	0.024	0.151	0.042	0.008	0.006
Other Value Added	0.060	0.323	0.117	0.137	0.024	0.165	0.038	0.054	0.060
Total Value Added	0.084	0.516	0.410	0.448	0.613	0.765	0.475	0.583	0.545
Total Industry	1.000	1.000	1.000	1.000	1.000	1.000	1.000	1.000	1.000

The Industry-by-Commodity Table

We can now begin the tortuous journey of tracing the interconnections among final demand for commodities, production of commodities, and production of the industries producing the commodities. Although the BEA uses more sophisticated techniques, we will use simple arithmetic, which forces us to examine the logic of the underlying process generating the tables. We will assume that consumers increased their demand for agricultural products by $1 million and we will trace through the effects this increase has on the various industries. From Table 12.9, we know that the agriculture industry produced $75 million, or 96.1538 percent, of the $78 million of output of agricultural products. The trade industry produced the remaining $3 million, or 3.8462 percent, of total agricultural products. Based on these proportions, the agriculture industry would provide $961,538 of the $1 million increase in demand and the trade industry would provide the remaining $38,462. Thus, an increase in agricultural demand will initially impact the agriculture and trade industries.

We first trace the effects of this increase in final demand on the agriculture industry. In order to produce this $961,538 increase in agricultural output, the agriculture industry needs to use as input an additional $382,298 ($961,538 × 0.398 from Table 12.11) of agricultural output. Of this additional output, the agricultural industry will produce $367,595 ($382,298 × 0.961538) by itself. Thus, if the demand for agricultural production increased by $1 million, the agriculture industry would have to increase production by $1,329,133 ($961,538 + $367,595). The industry would produce $961,538 of the $1 million demanded by consumers, and, in the process, it would use $367,595 of its own product. For example, if the agricultural product was ham, the agriculture industry would have to produce not only the $961,538 of pigs, but also $367,595 of corn to feed the pigs.

This amount of $1,329,133 is tentatively entered in Table 12.12 as the quantity of output required of the agriculture industry for each dollar of final demand for agricultural products, or 0.1329133.[12] However, we have not yet completed tracing the impact on the agriculture industry because increasing the output of the agriculture industry by $1,329,132 will require an increase in the output of the mining industry of $80,068 ($1,329,133 × 0.060241).[13] This amount, per dollar, is entered in the

---

[12]There will be slight differences in the calculations of the coefficients of Table 12.12 because of rounding.

[13]The number 0.060241 is obtained from Table 12.9, and is also shown (0.060) in Table 12.11. Minerals constitute 5/83 = 0.060241 of each dollar of production in the agriculture industry. Thus, if $1 of final demand for agricultural products is going to require $1.329131 of production in the agriculture industry, the mineral industry will have to produce 0.080068 ($1.329131 × 0.060241).

agricultural cell for the products the mining industry will have to provide if final demand increases by $1.

And we are still not finished with Table 12.12 because we have not accounted for the agricultural products produced by the trade industry. Out of each $1 million of sales of agricultural products, $38,462 will be provided by the trade industry. As we can see from Table 12.10, when its output increases by $38,462, the trade industry itself will require $689 ($38,462 × 0.17921)[14] of additional trade output. It will produce $674 ($689 × .9782608)[15] of this additional output by itself. Thus, if the demand for agricultural products increased by $1 million, the trade industry would have to increase production by $39,316 ($38,462 + $674), or 0.039316. We can now recap the cell entry for the trade industry column:

1. We have shown how each dollar of final demand in the agriculture industry will impact the trade industry. An increase in demand for agricultural products of $1 is going to require an increase of 0.039316 in the trade industry.

2. The trade industry not only produces agricultural products but it also serves as input to the agriculture industry. Tables 12.10 and 12.11 show that the production of $83 million of agricultural products requires $5 million of inputs from the trade industry. Thus, 5/83 = .0602409, which, in Table 12.11, is rounded to 0.060 per dollar of output in the agriculture industry. Thus, each dollar of agriculture industry output requires 0.0602409 of input from the trade commodity. Since each dollar of final demand in the agriculture industry requires the production of 1.3291321 of output in that industry, each dollar of final demand of agricultural products is going to require 0.0800681 (0.0602409 × 1.3291321) of trade production.

Putting these two components together, we see that each dollar of final demand of agricultural products will require 0.1193841 (0.039316 + 0.0800681) of output of trade industry products, which is the direct requirements coefficient for the trade industry in the agricultural products column.

We are still not finished with this table because this recently described increase in trade and agricultural production generates further increases

---

[14]This came from Table 12.10. Look under the column headed Trade and drop down to the row titled Trade. The cell entry is $10, which means that in order to produce a total output of $581 in the trade industry, $10 of inputs from the trade industry itself is required. In other words, 10/558 = 0.0179211 is the percent of the trade industry output that comes from product inputs produced within the trade industry. If trade industry output has to increase $38,462, then an additional $689 of production has to occur in the trade industry.

[15]The trade industry produces $540 of the total output of $552 = 0.9782608.

TABLE 12.12
Industry-by-Commodity Total Requirements,
Hypothetical Values for Any Year
(millions of $ in producers' prices)

| | COMMODITIES | | | | | | | | |
Industry	Agricultural Products	Minerals	Construction	Manufactured Products	Transportation	Trade	Finance	Services	Other
Agriculture	1.3291330	0.0300376	0.0197041	0.0221271	0.0076046	0.0035	0.01463	0.001782	0
Mining	0.0800682	0.9311681	0.0656803	0.0162263	0.0988605	0.0035	0.02438	0.016045	0.0067
Construction	0.0640546	0.0750942	1.040337	0.0103259	0.0304186	0.0017	0.00487	0	0.0134
Manufacturing	0.2402047	0.1652072	0.1149406	1.0547251	0.0532325	0.0767	0.05365	0.062398	0.0938
Transportation	0.0480409	0.0450565	0.0295561	0.0663813	0.9429772	0.0374	0.02926	0.037438	0.0234
Trade	0.1193841	0.0300376	0.0262721	0.0929338	0.0152093	0.9954	0.03901	0.019610	0.0100
Finance	0.0320273	0.0150188	0.0197041	0.0368785	0.0076046	0.0142	1.17055	0.037433	0.0100
Services	0.0800682	0.0600753	0.2660054	0.0737570	0.0228139	0.0624	0.19021	1.394644	0.2179
Other	0.0640546	0	0.0065680	0.1165360	0	0.0160	0.03901	0.073095	1.1197

in the coefficients located in the trade and agriculture industries column as well as in all other industries. The increase in agricultural production in the agriculture industry, among other things, generates increased production in the finance, transportation, and manufacturing industries. Their increased production, in turn, generates further increases in all other industries.

Table 12.12 shows similar calculations for agricultural output, but it does not show the subsequent rounds of feedback effects. These feedback effects are relatively minor — and in the interests of everyone's mental health — we stop our calculations here. The Bureau of Economics Analysis, however, cannot stop calculating at this step. They have to calculate the feedback production in all other industries and the impacts of these on the industries providing the inputs and so on. Fortunately, they have sophisticated procedures using matrix manipulations and powerful computers, which enable them to make these calculations for 85 industries. In fact, Table 12.12 is called the "Industry-by-Commodity *Total* Requirements" table because all direct and indirect effects are supposed to be included.

Proceeding on the assumption that all of these calculations have been made, we can now use the industry-by-commodity table. Assume that we want to know the impact of a $250 million increase in demand for minerals. We go to the minerals column of the industry-by-commodity table and multiply each coefficient by $250,000,000. The resulting increase in sales in each industry will be (in millions):

Agriculture:	$ 7.5
Mining:	232.8
Construction:	18.8
Manufacturing:	41.3
etc.	

The Commodity-by-Commodity Table

There is one more table to construct. Table 12.12 shows the requirements from each industry to service a dollar of demand for each commodity. It answers the question: What is the impact of a $1 million demand for any single commodity on each of the *major industries*? Table 12.13 shows the quantities of each commodity required to produce $1 of final demand for each of the commodities. A typical question it answers is: What is the impact of a $1 million demand for transportation services on each of the *major commodity groupings*? Table 12.13 is constructed by rearranging and recalculating the cell entries into groupings of commodities. The commodity-by-commodity table drops the industry designation and examines only commodity interrelationships. Remembering our example in constructing Table 12.12, in which agricultural products were produced by both the agriculture and trade industries, we can now combine the

TABLE 12.13
Commodity-by-Commodity
Hypothetical Values for Any Year
(millions of $ in producers' prices)

COMMODITIES

Commodities	Agricultural Products	Minerals	Construction	Manufactured Products	Transportation	Trade	Finance	Services	Other
Agricultural	1.2820026	0.0813653	0.0672573	0.2295573	0.0949129	0.1231470	0.0326037	0.0814774	0.0640546
Minerals	0.0300376	0.8512829	0.0915698	0.1597103	0.0395446	0.0297222	0.0155595	0.0559301	0
Construction	0.0199536	0.1435214	1.0228238	0.1248846	0.0282688	0.0260061	0.0226597	0.2478711	0.0065680
Manufactured	0.0248177	0.0323763	0.0241067	0.9892437	0.0705515	0.0928246	0.0373210	0.0765627	0.1165360
Transportation	0.0078936	0.0945258	0.0321828	0.0517953	0.7972416	0.0196200	0.0077871	0.0212321	0
Trade	0.0412577	0.0045970	0.002806	0.0919266	0.0340309	0.9739225	0.0148489	0.0591638	0.0160548
Finance	0.0155585	0.0233134	0.0058917	0.0520553	0.0309805	0.0388720	1.1587892	0.1796208	0.0390183
Services	0.0024602	0.0155193	0.0010839	0.0606119	0.0476205	0.0203240	0.0501254	1.0230667	0.0730951
Other	0.0003821	0.0086290	0.0144756	0.1171577	0.1478876	0.0245101	0.0125513	0.2799157	1.1197604

agricultural production of the two industries. The cell in the first row and the first column reflects the combined agricultural inputs from both the agriculture and trade industries necessary to produce $1 of agricultural products. This table is generated by the same reasoning that was used in constructing Table 12.12, except that the agricultural production characteristics of the primary and secondary industries are now combined with weighted averages.

This table of hypothetical values can be used to determine the inputs required when the demand for any commodity increases. For example, if manufactured goods demand increases by $100 million, the following value of inputs will be required:

Agricultural products	$229,557
Minerals	159,710
Construction	123,885
Manufactured products	989,244
etc.	

Uses and Problems of I-O Tables

The major advantage of I-O tables is that they allow us to measure the direct and indirect repercussions of changes in final demand. The traditional example used to illustrate their benefits is the automobile industry. An increase in automobile demand will lead to an increase in the production of autos, which will lead to more steel production, which, in turn, will require more chemicals, iron ore, limestone, and coal. More fabrics will be required for the upholstery, which will require more synthetic and natural fibers, more sheep and cows for wool and leather seat covers, more corn to feed the livestock, and more electricity and transportation facilities. These are just a few of the repercussions that rumble through the economy when the demand for autos increases. I-O analysis provides individuals with a relatively easy way to trace these effects. Private firms and industry associations use I-O tables to estimate their sales under alternative assumptions about demand for final-use products. One of the most avid users of I-O tables is the federal government, which uses them to estimate the effects of various tax law changes, safety and environmental rules, and shortages in certain raw materials.

Input-output tables are very useful for understanding the flows of commodities among industries and final users, but the data must be used with an understanding of their weaknesses. One weakness — but not the most significant — always cited in the literature is that inputs are proportional to outputs. That is, there are constant returns to scale, so that a 10 percent increase in output requires a 10 percent increase in inputs whether the industry is producing 100 units a year or 100,000 units a year. An *increase* in final demand of $10 million might have a much different impact from the *first* $10 million of production. Because of the proportional relationship, the I-O tables treat the two as being the same. Of more serious concern is the practice of including the inputs of secondary products with the primary industry and vice versa. If an establishment's primary product is manufacturing go-carts, but its secondary product is manufacturing candy, go-cart manufacturing would show sugar as an input and candy would show sheetmetal and rubber tires as inputs. This is a major deficiency in input-output tables that the BEA has lessened somewhat by making the following adjustments (BEA calls them re-definitions) in some industries:

- Construction work performed in any industry is assigned to the construction industry.
- All manufacturing done in the trade and service industries is reassigned to the manufacturing industry.
- Retail trade in service and industries is redefined to the trade industries. Services in the trade industries are redefined to the service industries. Selected services are redefined within the service industry.
- Manufacturers' wholesale sales of purchased goods (resales) are redefined to the wholesale trade industries.
- Rental activities of all industries are redefined to the real estate and rental industries.

When these reassignments are made, the associated inputs are assumed to be those of the primary industry. None of these adjustments, however, would affect the go-cart–candy example, and the I-O tables would continue to reflect these anomalies. Other deficiencies include incomplete and inaccurate data obtained from the establishments.

In addition to the main I-O tables, BEA periodically releases supplementary tables. The *personal consumption expenditures by NIPA category table* expands the personal consumption expenditures (PCE) component on the use table (Table 12.10) to show, in both producers' and purchasers' prices, the detailed PCE categories. This table is essential for those who want to trace changes in the consumption of specific products through the various industries that supply the inputs. The *gross private fixed investment by NIPA category table* expands the gross private fixed investment component to show, in both producers' and purchasers' prices, the detailed categories for structure and producers' durable equipment purchases. This table is essential for those who want to trace changes in investment to industry and commodity output. *The employment and employee compensation table* expands the employee compensation component of the use table to show, by industry, the number of employees, wages, and salaries. This table should be consulted by those who want to relate industry output to employment and to calculate employment multipliers.

The exports and imports by balance of payments category table expands the export and import component of the use table and shows the relationship between the I-O tables and the balance of payments.

Name: Manufacturing Data
Alternative name: Annual Survey of Manufacturers, Census of Manufacturers
Agency/Institution: Bureau of the Census
Address: Chief, Industry Division, Bureau of the Census, Washington, DC 20233
Telephone number for data and inquiries: 301-763-7666
Sources: *Annual Survey of Manufacturers*, Current Industrial Reports, and Census of Manufacturers
Frequency: The *Annual Survey of Manufacturers* is published annually except for years ending in "2" and "7," when the Census of Manufacturers is published; the Current Industrial Reports are published monthly, quarterly, and annually.
When available: The *Annual Survey of Manufacturers* is available about 15 to 18 months after the reference year; the Census is available about two to three years after the end of the census year.
Revisions: Some revisions in the *ASM* are made the following year. Preliminary census material is revised considerably in later publications.
Historic data: Generally, data from earlier censuses are included in the current census. Also available on diskette from the Bureau of the Census.

■ A QUICK LOOK: Manufacturing Data

The Census Bureau publishes numerous reports that contain data on manufacturing industries. The Census Bureau defines *manufacturing* as the mechanical or chemical transformation of materials or substances into new products. Under this definition, some industries are classified as manufacturing that would not be so classified by the average citizen. For example, logging and newspaper, magazine, and book publishing are classified as manufacturing by the Census Bureau. Manufacturing establishments are classified by their principal types of products. There are 20 major SIC groups in manufacturing:

    20 Food and kindred products
    21 Tobacco products
    22 Textile mill products
    23 Apparel and other finished products
    24 Lumber and wood products
    25 Furniture and allied products
    26 Paper and allied products
    27 Printing, publishing, and allied industries
    28 Chemicals and allied industries
    29 Petroleum refining and related industries

30 Rubber and miscellaneous plastics products
31 Leather and leather products
32 Stone, clay, glass, and concrete products
33 Primary metal industries
34 Fabricated metal products, except machinery and transportation
35 Industrial and commercial machinery and computer equipment
36 Electronic and electrical equipment, except computers
37 Transportation equipment
38 Measuring, analyzing, and controlling instruments
39 Miscellaneous manufacturing industries

Some data series distinguish between durable goods manufacturing (SICs 24 and 25 and 32 to 39) and nondurable goods manufacturing (SICs 20 to 23 and 26 to 31). Census Bureau manufacturing data are available from the following reports.

The *Annual Survey of Manufacturers (ASM)* is published in noncensus years because the Census of Manufacturers includes many of the same statistics collected for the *ASM*. The *ASM*'s data are available about 15 to 18 months after the end of the reference year. The *ASM* collects data from a random sample of about 55,000 from the 370,000 plants covered in the census. Although *ASM* reports include many of the same kinds of statistics found in census reports, they do so with much less geographic and product detail.

The *ASM* contains several reports, including the following:

- Statistics for industry groups: Data on employment, hours, payroll, value added, capital expenditures, cost of materials, inventories, and value of shipments. Data are available for the two-, three-, and four-digit levels.

- Value of product shipments: Value of 1500 products shipped, at the five-digit product level, with comparable data for a few previous years.

- Geographic area statistics: SIC three-digit statistics on products and employment for states, SMSAs, large industrial counties, and selected cities.

Current Industrial Reports are nearly 100 monthly, quarterly, and annual reports that contain national and, occasionally, state data on production, shipments, unfilled orders, stocks, inventories, plant capacity, pollution abatement costs, and expenditures.

The reports cover about 5000 products, arranged by SIC codes, representing about 40 percent of U.S. manufacturing. Values and quantities of production, stocks, values of shipments, consumption, receipts, and orders are some of the data reported in the various series.

The Census of Manufacturers (the nation's second oldest census) was first conducted in 1810 and was taken at periodic intervals until 1939. After World War II, this census was conducted in 1947, 1954, 1958, 1963, and 1967, and since 1967, it has been taken every five years for the years ending in 2 and 7. The Census of Manufacturers is easily the most comprehensive industrial census in the world, and it is the first source one should consult for data on manufacturing industries. Unfortunately, because it is conducted only every five years, there is a lag of approximately three years for processing the data. Census data are compiled for all manufacturing establishments with one or more paid employees, and they are published in three final series, by industry, area, and subject. In the 1987 Census of Manufacturers, the Census Bureau obtained mail responses from 220,000 establishments on one of 282 industry-tailored questionnaires. Data for an additional 150,000 small, single-establishment firms were obtained from federal agency records.

The Census of Manufacturers has many component parts and getting through them can be difficult. The following may assist your navigation.

- Preliminary reports: Consist of a summary volume and preliminary industry series. The summary contains statistics for two-, three-, and four-digit manufacturing industries at the national level and for all manufacturing for the 50 states. The Preliminary Industry Series consists of 83 bulletins that present general and historical statistics for three-digit industries on the quantity and value of product shipments and on the quantity and cost of material inputs. You can, for example, discover the number of companies, product shipments, and costs and quantities of the ingredients that went into producing cereal breakfast foods (SIC 2043) in 1982 and 1987.

- Industry series: Consist of nearly 100 separate paper-bound volumes that present data for each of 459 industries on the quantity and value of products shipped and materials consumed; cost of fuels and electric energy; and industry statistics, such as number of establishments, total employment, production workers, hours worked, value added by manufacturing, value of shipments, assets, capital expenditures, rents and labor costs, and cost of purchased services. Also shown are selected operating ratios such as payroll per employee and cost of materials per dollar of shipments. Some data are shown by state and some data from earlier years are made available for comparison purposes. Most data are available on computer tape and diskette.

- Geographic area series: Consist of separate reports for each state. These state reports contain the value of shipments, value added, employment, payrolls, worker hours, capital expenditures, inventories, assets, retirements, depreciations, rents, and number of establishments. Comparable statistics for earlier years are included. Selected statistics are shown for SMSAs, larger counties, and cities, but some statistics, including assets, rents, inventories, and cost of materials, are presented in statewide totals only. All area reports are available on microfiche, and most data are available on computer tape. The location of manufacturing plants by employment-size class for four-digit SIC groups for states, counties, certain geographic areas, and zip codes are available on diskettes and tapes. If you are interested in the value of sausages produced and where they are produced, this is the place to look.

- Subject series: Consist of seven separate, detailed reports with data primarily for the national level. These include corrections and revisions for the geographic area series, textile machinery in place, water use in manufacturing, marketing channels, concentration ratios, and shipments to the federal government.

- Analytical reports: Three analytical reports present information on manufactured exports, related employment, and percent of goods manufactured by specific two-digit industries, but the most important are *Exports from Manufacturing Establishments* and *Selected Characteristics of Manufacturing Establishments That Export*. The third report is the index of production, which measures the change in the physical output of manufacturing and mineral industries between 1982 and 1987.

Name: Mineral Industries Data
Agency/Institution: Department of Commerce, Bureau of the Census
Address: Washington, DC 20233
Telephone number for data and inquiries: 301-763-5938
Sources: Census of Mineral Industries
Frequency: Every five years, for years ending in 2 and 7
When available: About two to three years after the end of the survey year
Historic data: Available in the industry series part of the Census of Minerals Industries

---

■ A QUICK LOOK: Mineral Industries Data

The nation's 31 mineral industries explore, develop, process on site, and extract minerals that occur naturally, whether in solid, liquid, or gaseous form. There are four major groups in the SIC code for mineral industries, and mineral establishments are classified according to the principal mineral they mine or produce:

10 Metal mining
12 Coal mining

13   Oil and gas extraction
14   Mining and quarrying of nonmetallic minerals, except fuels

The Census Bureau has developed a seven-digit classification system that supplements the SIC four-digit codes.

The Annual Survey of Oil and Gas, which was begun in 1973, was discontinued in 1982, and many of the data are now published by the Energy Information Administration. The remaining data in the mineral industries are gathered and published by the Census of Mineral Industries.

The Census of Mineral Industries was first conducted in 1840, and then every ten years through 1940. After World War II, the census was conducted in 1954, 1958, 1963, and 1967. Since 1967, it has been taken every five years in years ending in 2 and 7. Data are compiled for all mining establishments with one or more paid employees. The results of these data-gathering efforts are presented in the following census publications:

- Preliminary reports: There are 13 preliminary reports; one is an overall summary for the nation and the other 12 show preliminary values for quantity and value of shipments by industry.

- Industry series: Twelve reports that contain the following data for 31 four-digit industries: number of establishments, payroll, employment, hours worked, quantity and value of products shipped and supplies used, cost of purchased machinery, capital expenditures, assets, depreciation, amortization, rents, inventories, fuel costs and quantities, and development and exploration costs. Some data are shown by state and offshore area.

- Geographic area series: Nine reports that present state and offshore data on number of establishments, payroll, employment, hours worked, value of shipments, cost of supplies, capital expenditures, assets, inventories, and value added.

- Subject series: This includes a general summary, a report on fuels and electric energy consumed by mineral establishments, and a report on water use in mineral industries.

Name: Productivity Index
Alternative name: Index of Output Per Worker, Multifactor Productivity
Agency/Institution: Department of Production and Technology, Bureau of Labor Statistics
Address: Washington, DC 20212
Telephone number for data and inquiries: 202-523-9294

Sources: *Monthly Labor Review* (Department of Labor), *Employment and Earnings,* and *Survey of Current Business*

Frequency: Quarterly

When available: Nonfarm business and manufacturing become available about one month after the quarter ends; productivity indexes of nonfinancial corporations become available about two months after the end of the quarter

Revisions: No set policy

Historic data: *Productivity Measures for Selected Industries 1954–79,* Bulletin 2093 (Bureau of Labor Statistics, April 1981) and *Handbook of Labor Statistics,* Bulletin 2340 (1989).

Further information: *Productivity Measures for Selected Industries and Government,* Bulletin 2322 (Bureau of Labor Statistics, 1989); and the *BLS Handbook of Methods,* Bulletin 2285.

Cross references: See the "International" section, pages 441–443, for a comparison of productivity rates among countries.

■ A QUICK LOOK: Productivity

The productivity of American businesses and industry is widely discussed but very difficult to measure. The most reliable sources of information on productivity changes are the following indexes. They do not enable us to make absolute comparisons with the productivity measures of other countries, but they do allow us to measure changes in productivity over time and among various industries within the United States.

	Index of Output per Hour of All Persons for 1990 (1982 = 100)
Productivity	
a. Business	111.9
b. Nonfarm business	110.8
c. Nonfinancial business	114.1
d. Manufacturing	136.8

	Index of Multifactor Productivity For 1990
Multifactor Productivity	
a. Private business	111.4
b. Private nonfarm business	110.1
c. Manufacturing	135.1

Industry Productivity
Selected Industries
Index: Output per Hour for
1989
(1982 = 100)

Industry Productivity Series

Iron mining, crude ore	264.4
Footwear	104.4
Motor vehicles and equipment	136.4
Department stores	122.8
Grocery stores	90.6
Hotels, motels	99.1

Productivity: The four categories listed here are measures of productivity for each of the sectors, based on the real output per hour of all employees. Since the measure is by output per hour, it is frequently assumed that the productivity index measures only the productivity of labor. This is not correct—the index was never designed to measure only the production of labor. It is based on dividing total production by the number of labor inputs. An increase in the index could be caused by improved technology, additional investment, more efficient use of resources or management, as well as by the increased efforts of employees.

a. *Business:* The Bureau of Labor Statistics publishes a number of productivity indexes, but the most popular index and the one most frequently quoted by the media is Output per Labor Hour for the business sector, which represents about 80 percent of the GDP. This index measures changes in the real output of the business sector per hour worked. Excluded are the outputs of government, nonprofit organizations, and household workers because their outputs are defined as being equal to their wages and salaries so there can be no change in their productivity. Also excluded are the rental values of owner-occupied buildings. Government enterprises, such as the TVA and the Postal Service, are included in the business sector because their outputs are valued at market prices. Hours of work include the hours of paid employees, self-employed, and unpaid family workers. Vacations, sick leave, and holidays are included in "hours worked."

b. *Nonfarm business:* The output of the nonfarm business sector is equal to the business sector less farming.

c. *Nonfinancial business:* The output of the nonfarm business sector less the output of the financial sector, including banks, savings and loans, credit unions, and insurance companies.

d. *Manufacturing:* The manufacturing sector only. Productivity increases have consistently been highest in this sector.

Multifactor productivity: The Bureau of Labor Statistics recently introduced a new set of productivity indexes called *multifactor productivity indexes*, which attempt to measure output growth that cannot be accounted for by the growth of labor and capital inputs. These multifactor productivity indexes measure non-labor, noncapital productivity increases for private business, private nonfarm, and manufacturing. The indexes are available on an annual basis.

Industry productivity series: Provides information for more than 100 industries at the three- and four-digit levels of the SIC system, of which this is only a small sample. This series differs in methodology and data sources from the other productivity measures because it is developed independently of the national income and product accounts, which are used for the major sector productivity estimates. Generally, productivity indexes refer to the real output per hour of all employees. These data are available on an annual basis.

■ A CLOSER LOOK: Productivity Indexes

Productivity indexes measure changes in the economy's productivity over time and among industries. The major sector productivity indexes are released quarterly, whereas the multifactor and industry productivity indexes are released annually. Productivity generally rises more during economic expansion than during recession because firms tend to keep about the same number of employees during the initial stages of both expansions and recessions. Productivity is volatile and often changes for a particular year without any apparent cause. Although Output per Labor Hour is the most popular productivity index, there is also an index of the Output per Unit of Capital Services. It measures, in constant dollars, the value of goods and services per unit of capital services input.

Measures of labor input are based mainly on the monthly BLS survey of nonagricultural establishments. From it are drawn measures of employment and average weekly hours paid to employees of these establishments. Supplementary information for farm workers, the self-employed, and for unpaid family workers is obtained from the monthly survey of households, the Current Population Survey. These indexes should not be used for comparisons with other countries because productivity indexes can be calculated in many different ways, and such indexes are likely not to be compatible. (See international comparisons of productivity on pages 441–443.)

There are two very important caveats you must keep in mind when using productivity measures. First, productivity indexes do not measure the productivity of labor even if their titles might suggest that they do. For example, the "Productivity Index of Output per Hour, All Persons, Business Sector" might indicate that it is measuring the productivity of workers in the business sector. The index is constructed by dividing total output by the number of persons employed in the business sector. However, an increase in productivity could actually be due to new technology, additional capital, or factors other than labor. That is, changes in productivity might not be caused by the increased efforts of employees.

The second caveat is that all productivity data are based on total production divided by total number of employees; productivity indexes show changes in the average product per employee. They do not reflect marginal changes, which many economists view as being more important. That is, the indexes do not measure changes to productivity when output changes. Average productivity could be decreasing while marginal productivity is increasing.

HISTORIC DATA: Productivity Index of Output Per Hour
All Persons, Business Sector
(1982 = 100)

		1960	65.9	1975	95.6
		1961	68.5	1976	98.3
1947	43.8	1962	71.0	1977	100.2
1948	46.0	1963	73.8	1978	100.7
1949	46.5	1964	77.1	1979	99.5
1950	50.4	1965	79.4	1980	99.2
1951	52.5	1966	81.7	1981	100.7
1952	54.1	1967	84.1	1982	100.0
1953	56.1	1968	86.6	1983	102.3
1954	57.0	1969	86.8	1984	104.9
1955	58.7	1970	87.3	1985	107.1
1956	59.6	1971	90.5	1986	109.5
1957	61.2	1972	93.2	1987	110.7
1958	63.0	1973	95.0	1988	113.2
1959	65.1	1974	93.5	1989	112.6
				1990	111.9
				1991	109.9

Name: Service Industry Data
Alternative name: Census of Service Industries
Agency/Institution: Department of Commerce, Bureau of the Census
Address: Chief, Business Division, Bureau of the Census, Washington, DC 20233
Telephone number for data and inquiries: 301-763-7039
Sources: Census of Service Industries and Annual Reports of Services
Frequency: Every five years, in years ending in 2 and 7
When available: About two to three years after the end of the reference year

---

■ **A QUICK LOOK: Service Industry Data**

Service industries are those engaged in providing services for individuals, business, governments, and other organizations. Examples of service industries are motels, laundries, motion picture theaters, law firms, and repair shops. There are 16 major SIC groupings in the service industry:

70 Hotels, motels, camps, and other lodging places
72 Personal services
73 Business services
75 Automotive repair, services, and garages
76 Miscellaneous repair services
78 Motion pictures
79 Amusement and recreation, except motion pictures
80 Health services
81 Legal services
82 Education services except elementary, secondary, and colleges
83 Social services
84 Museums, art galleries, and botanical and zoological
86 Membership organizations
87 Engineering, accounting, research, management services
88 Private households
89 Other services

The Census of Service Industries does not include most of SICs 82 to 86, 88, and 89. Census data on the service industries are obtained through questionnaires sent to all service industry firms with four or more employees. The data are presented in the following reports:

1. Service annual surveys: Annual reports with estimates of receipts of selected service industries, percentage changes, and employment by kind of business. The report is issued about nine months after the end of the reference year.

2. Census of Service Industries: Conducted every five years in the years ending in 2 and 7.

   a. Geographic area series: Separate reports issued for the United States and each state. Data on receipts, employment, and payroll. Some of the other data contained in these reports are shown here for some major service industries.

      i. Hotels, motels, and other lodging places: Receipts, number of rooms, percentage of occupancy. Data available for United States, states, and selected SMSAs.

      ii. Laundry, cleaning, and garment services: Source of receipts and number and type of machines. Data available for United States, states, and selected SMSAs.

      iii. Motion picture industry: Admissions and capacity, number of screens, receipts, and promotional expenditures of motion picture theatres; receipts, expenses, and film processed for motion picture producers and distributors. Data available for United States, states, and selected SMSAs.

    iv. Legal services: Personnel and payroll by occupation, operating expenses, primary fields of practice, and receipts by class of client. Data available for United States, states, and selected SMSAs.

    v. Engineering, architectural, and surveying services: Number of firms, receipts by source, expenses, personnel by occupation, fees by class of client, type of project, and specialized types of engineering service. Data available for United States and states.

    vi. Arrangement of passenger transportation: Receipts, operating expenses, and size of establishment for travel agencies, tour operators, and other passenger transportation arrangement services. Data available for United States, states, and selected SMSAs.

    vii. Health services: Personnel, payroll by occupation, and other data for offices of health practitioners such as physicians and dentists; nursing and personal care facilities, hospitals; medical and dental laboratories; outpatient care facilities and other health and allied services. Data available for United States and states.

    viii. Tax-exempt service organizations: Number of establishments, expenses, payroll, and employment by kind of business for tax-exempt service establishments. Data available for United States and states.

b. Zip code statistics: Presented only on computer tape and CD-ROMs. These data show the number of establishments in each size class, receipts, payroll, and number of employees by five-digit zip code. The data can be used to develop mailing lists of service industries by zip codes or to evaluate the extent of market coverage by specific services in certain areas.

c. Subject series: These are segmented into four reports:

    i. Establishments and firm size — data for the United States based on size of establishment, size of firm, legal form of organization, receipts, payroll, and employment. This report provides information on concentration in the various service industries. Data available only at the national level.

    ii. Capital expenditures, depreciable assets, and operating expenses — data for the nation on capital expenditures, assets, and selected operating expenses by kind of business.

    iii. Special data on hotels, motels, and other lodging places.

iv. Miscellaneous subjects — check here for data not found elsewhere.

Name: Transportation Data
Agency/Institution: Department of Commerce, Bureau of the Census, Washington, DC 20233
Telephone: 301-763-4364
   Association of American Railroads
   American Railroad Building
   50 F Street NW
   Washington, DC 20001
   202-639-2100

   Federal Railroad Administration
   400 7th Street, NW
   Washington, DC 20590
   202-366-4000

   Interstate Commerce Commission
   12th Street and Constitution Ave. N.W.
   Washington, DC 20423
   202-275-7119

   Federal Aviation Administration
   800 Independence Ave. S.W.
   Washington, DC 20591
   202-267-3484
Sources: *Motor Freight Transportation and Warehousing Survey* (annual) and the Census of Transportation, which is taken every five years, or in years ending in 2 and 7, *Survey of Current Business*
When available: The *Motor Freight Report* is available about 10 to 12 months after the end of the year, and the Census of Transportation is available about two to three years after the end of the reference year.

■ A QUICK LOOK: Transportation Data

The *Survey of Current Business* publishes monthly, quarterly, and annual data (for the previous two years) on passenger-miles, ton-miles, revenues, expenses, and other operating statistics for air carriers, motor carriers, and railroads. It also reports orders, sales, export, import, and registrations for airplanes and motor vehicles. The transportation-related SIC groups are:

   40 Railroad transportation
   41 Local and interurban passenger transportation
   42 Trucking and warehousing

43 U.S. Postal Service
44 Water transportation
45 Air transportation
46 Pipelines, except natural gas
47 Transportation services, including travel agencies, tour operators

Census Bureau surveys cover only SICs 42, 44, 47, which means that data for other transportation sectors have to be obtained from other sources, such as the Interstate Commerce Commission, American Association of Railroads, and Federal Railroad Administration. Census figures for states and metropolitan areas reflect the location of the establishment and not necessarily the location where the trucking or other activities take place.

The two major reports on data collected by the Census Bureau are the annual *Motor Freight Transportation and Warehousing Survey* and the Census of Transportation. Following is a brief description of each:

- *Motor Freight Transportation and Warehousing Survey* is an annual report that provides operating revenues and expenses and inventories of revenue-generating equipment for establishments in SIC 42 for the United States. Comparable statistics are shown for the previous year and year-to-year percentage changes are also shown. Reports are available about one year after the end of the reference year.

- The Census of Transportation, which is the nation's most extensive source of information on transportation and travel, is composed of the following reports:

  1. Geographic area series: This report presents data on number of establishments, revenue, payroll, and employment by varied transportation classifications for the United States, each state, and MSAs.

  2. Subject series: This report presents data showing the size of establishment, size of company, revenue, payroll, employment, and number of establishments operated singly or in multiestablishment companies. These data enable us to see the degree of concentration in the covered transportation sectors.

  3. Truck inventory and use survey: Separate publications for the nation and each state provide data on the number of trucks, their characteristics, and use. Some of the characteristics are annual miles, range of operation, products carried, miles per gallon, truck type, truck fleet size, power steering, air conditioning, and weight. A separate report available only on computer tape shows the details on each individual truck, so numerous cross-tabulations can be built.

CHAPTER 13

ENERGY

Since the Arab oil embargo of the United States in 1973 and the accompanying increase in the prices of crude oil, which were quickly transmitted to other energy sources, economic analysts have been concerned about the production, consumption, and conservation of energy. Energy sources are, at the margin, substitutable for one another, and thus an increase in the price of crude oil quickly produces increases in the prices of other energy sources. The price of crude oil in the United States, in turn, is determined by the price of imported crude oil. As long as the United States imports oil, or exports oil to other countries, U.S. oil prices exclusive of tariffs will be equal to world oil prices.

Individuals using energy data need to know some basic nomenclature, such as *degree days*, and have some basic knowledge of various energy conversion factors. **Degree days** are frequently used measures of average outdoor temperatures over a period of time. They are an important indicator of the demand that will be placed on heating and air conditioning units and of the fuel inputs that will be required. **Cooling degree days** are the number of degrees per day that the daily average temperature is above 65 degrees. The daily average temperature is the mean of the maximum and minimum temperatures for a 24-hour period. Daily deviations from the 65 degrees are summed for some period, usually a month. For example, if the mean temperature is 70 degrees each day for 30 days, there would be 150 cooling degree days [$(70 - 65) \times 30$)] and zero heating days during the month. **Heating degree days** are the number of degrees per day that the daily average temperature is below 65 degrees. If the mean temperature is 50 degrees each day for 30 days, the number of heating degree days during the month is 450 days. Cooling degree days are not subtracted from heating degree days. If the mean temperature is

70 degrees for 15 days and 60 degrees for 15 days, there will be 75 cooling days and 75 heating days during the month. With **population-weighted degree days**, various areas (say a state) are subdivided into smaller sectors with similar climates and assigned weights based on the relative populations they contain. These population-weighted degree days are then summed to obtain state heating and cooling degree days.

Conversion Factors

Energy resources are stated in varying measurement units, including short tons, long tons, barrels, gallons, and BTUs. When comparisons are made among quantities of energy sources, the frequently used common denominator is a British thermal unit (BTU), which measures heat content.

Crude Oil

One U.S. barrel	= 42 U.S. gallons
One short ton	= 6.65 barrels
One metric ton	= 7.33 barrels
Heat content	= 5.8 million BTUs per barrel

Coal

1 short ton	= 2000 pounds
1 long ton	= 2240 pounds
1 metric ton	= 2205 pounds
Heat content	= 21.3 million BTUs per short ton

Electricity

Heat content (steam)	= 10,235 BTUs for steam per kwh

Name: Energy Consumption in the United States
Agency/Institution: Energy Information Administration
Address: 1000 Independence Avenue, S.W., Washington, DC 20585
Telephone number for data and inquiries: 202-586-9160
Sources: *Monthly Energy Review, Minerals Yearbook, Minerals Industry Survey,* and *Quarterly Coal Report* for coal; *Monthly Gas Utility Statistical Report* (American Gas Association), *Petroleum Supply Monthly, Highway Statistics*
Frequency: Monthly
When available: Data are reasonably contemporaneous with the issue date of *Monthly Energy Review (MER)*. However, the actual publication date of the *MER* is about three months after the issue date. For example, the June 1990 issue of *Monthly Energy Review* was sent to the printer on September 26 and was not released until mid-October.
Revisions: Most data are subject to revisions for about one year.
Historic data: See below.

■ A QUICK LOOK: Energy Consumption

The Energy Information Administration provides a wide variety of information on energy consumption by source and by end use. Data are provided on the quantity of energy consumed by residential, commercial, industrial, and transportation sectors; and by electric utilities by major sources such as coal, natural gas, petroleum, hydroelectric power, and electricity. Data include the production, imports, and stock changes for motor gasoline, distillate fuel oil, residual fuel oil, jet fuels, and fuels used by electric utilities. Data on passenger cars include average annual miles traveled, fuel used, and miles per gallon. The following historic data suggest that conservation efforts and the significant increase in energy prices during the 1970s and early 1980s have decreased energy consumption.

HISTORIC DATA: Energy Consumption

	Total Consumption (quadrillion BTUs)	Consumption Per Dollar of GNP (1000 BTU, in 1982 $)	Passenger Cars (miles per gallon)
1973	74.282	27.1	13.3
1974	72.543	26.6	13.42
1975	70.546	26.2	13.52
1976	74.362	26.3	13.53
1977	76.288	25.8	13.8
1978	78.089	25.1	14.04
1979	78.898	24.7	14.41
1980	75.955	23.8	15.46
1981	73.99	22.8	15.94
1982	70.848	22.4	16.65
1983	70.524	21.5	17.14
1984	74.101	21.2	17.83
1985	73.945	20.4	18.2
1986	74.237	20	18.27
1987	76.845	20	19.2
1988	80.202	20	19.87
1989	81.244	19.8	20.31
1990	81.269	19.5	20.92

Name: Energy Imports
Agency/Institition: Energy Information Administration
Address: 1000 Independence Avenue, S.W., Washington, DC 20585
Telephone number for data and inquiries: 202-586-9160
Sources: *Monthly Energy Review, Petroleum Supply Annual, Petroleum Supply Monthly* (all Energy Information Administration publications)

Frequency: Monthly

When available: Data are reasonably contemporaneous with the issue date of *Monthly Energy Review*. However, the actual publication date of the *MER* is about three months after the issue date. For example, the June 1990 issue of *Monthly Energy Review* was sent to the printer on September 26 and was not released until mid-October.

Revisions: Most data are subject to revisions for about one year.

Historic data: See below.

Cross references: Production of Petroleum (pages 333–334), Energy Production in the United States (pages 330–331), and Energy Consumption in the United States (pages 326–327)

■ A QUICK LOOK: Energy Imports

Data on energy imports (and exports) are provided by the Department of Energy and the Bureau of Economic Analysis. Virtually all U.S. energy imports are crude oil and petroleum products, and the only net export is coal. Imports are the receipts of crude oil and petroleum products into the 50 states and the District of Columbia from foreign countries and from Puerto Rico, the Virgin Islands, and other U.S. possessions and territories. It is important to understand that these import data do not measure "dependence" of the United States on imports from OPEC countries because many petroleum products imported from Caribbean and European areas are derived from crude oil imports from OPEC countries. However, the "all countries" data do include refined oil products as well as crude oil.

HISTORIC DATA: Imports of Crude Oil and Petroleum Products
As a Percent of Total Petroleum Products Used

	From Arab OPEC (percent)	From OPEC (percent)	From All Countries (percent)
1973	5.3	17.3	34.8
1974	4.5	19.7	35.4
1975	8.5	22.0	35.8
1976	13.9	29.0	40.6
1977	17.3	33.6	46.5
1978	15.7	30.5	42.5
1979	16.5	30.4	43.1
1980	14.9	25.2	37.3
1981	11.5	20.6	33.6
1982	5.6	14.0	28.1
1983	4.1	12.1	28.3
1984	5.2	13.0	30.0
1985	3.0	11.6	27.3

(continued)

HISTORIC DATA: Imports of Crude Oil and Petroleum Products *(continued)*
As a Percent of Total Petroleum Products Used

	From Arab OPEC (percent)	From OPEC (percent)	From All Countries (percent)
1986	7.1	17.4	33.4
1987	7.6	18.3	35.5
1988	10.6	20.3	38.1
1989	12.3	23.8	41.6
1990	13.2	25.2	42.2

Name: Energy Prices
Agency/Institution: Energy Information Administration
Address: 1000 Independence Avenue, S.W., Washington, DC 20585
Telephone number for data and inquiries: 202-586-1258
Sources: Best central source of energy prices is *Monthly Energy Review*. For more detailed data on prices of retail gasoline, see *Consumer Prices: Energy* (Bureau of Labor Statistics). See the *Lundberg Report* and *Pratt's Oilgram* for detailed data on crude oil prices.
Frequency: Monthly
When available: Data are reasonably contemporaneous with the issue date of *Monthly Energy Review*. However, the actual publication date of the *MER* is about three months after the issue date. For example, the June 1990 issue of *Monthly Energy Review* was sent to the printer on September 26 and was not released until mid-October.
Revisions: Most data are subject to revisions for about one year.
Historic data: See below

■ A QUICK LOOK: Energy Prices

A wide variety of energy prices is reported by a number of sources. The *Monthly Energy Review* is a ready source of general price information, but more detailed and more timely data may be obtained from such publications as the *Lundberg Report* and *Pratt's Oilgram*. These publications include price data on coal, petroleum products, crude oil, natural gas, electricity, kerosene, jet fuel, diesel fuel, and electricity.

One of the most widely quoted energy prices is the price per barrel of oil. Crude oil prices vary, depending on the source and quality of the oil. The so-called wellhead price varies slightly depending on the location of the well and the characteristics of its oil. The official Department of Energy designation for the "wellhead" price is now the *domestic first purchase price*. Those interested in the price of the crude that will have the greatest impact on petroleum product prices should use the *refiner acquisition cost*, which is the weighted price paid by refineries for all crude inputs. Refiner acquisition costs are available for domestic crude, imported crude, and combined weighted-average cost.

The prices of electricity are determined by taking monthly residential revenue and dividing by the sum of monthly residential kilowatt hour sales of 200 utilities randomly selected. Annual data are simply the average of the monthly data.

HISTORIC DATA: Prices of Gasoline, Electricity and Crude Oil

	Leaded Regular Gasoline: 85 Urban Areas (cents/gal including taxes)	Unleaded Regular Gasoline: 85 Urban Areas (cents/gal including taxes)	Retail Prices of Electricity: Residential (cents/kwh)	Crude Oil Price: Refiner Acquisition Cost ($/barrel)
1973	38.8	na	2.54	$4.15
1974	53.2	na	3.1	9.07
1975	56.7	na	3.51	10.38
1976	59.0	61.4	3.73	10.89
1977	62.2	65.6	4.05	11.96
1978	62.6	67.0	4.31	12.46
1979	85.7	90.3	4.64	17.72
1980	119.1	124.5	5.36	28.07
1981	131.1	137.8	6.20	35.24
1982	122.2	129.6	6.86	31.87
1983	115.7	124.1	7.18	28.99
1984	112.9	121.2	7.54	28.63
1985	111.5	120.2	7.79	26.75
1986	85.7	92.7	7.41	14.55
1987	89.7	94.8	7.41	17.90
1988	89.9	94.6	7.49	14.67
1989	99.8	102.1	7.64	17.97
1990	114.9	116.4	7.80	22.23

Name: Energy Production in the United States
Agency/Institution: Energy Information Administration
Address: 1000 Independence Avenue, S.W., Washington, DC 20585
Telephone number for data and inquiries: 202-586-9160
Sources: Best source of general energy production data is *Monthly Energy Review*. More detailed data are to be found in the *Petroleum Supply Monthly* and *Petroleum Supply Annual*.
Frequency: Monthly
When available: Data are reasonably contemporaneous with the issue date of *Monthly Energy Review*. However, the actual publication date of the *MER* is

about three months after the issue date. For example, the June 1990 issue of *Monthly Energy Review* was sent to the printer on September 26 and was not released until mid-October.

Revisions: The latest monthly data are always preliminary, and are usually revised within one to six months.

Historic data: See below.

■ A QUICK LOOK: Energy Production in the United States

Energy production data are important for evaluating the energy "self-sufficiency" of the United States and the relative growth rates of different sources of energy. To make comparisons easy, production data are first converted into quadrillions of BTUs. (See the "Read Me First" section on page 326 for the conversion rates.) Be careful in comparing production and consumption of electricity because both involve considerable losses of energy. For example, about 67 percent of total energy input is lost in converting heat energy into mechanical energy to turn electric generators, and an additional 9 percent is lost in the transmission and distribution process (line losses).

HISTORIC DATA: Production of Energy by Source,
United States
(quadrillion BTUs)

	Coal	Crude Oil	Natural Gas Liquids	Natural Gas Dry	Hydro-electric Power	Nuclear Electric Power	Total
1973	14.0	19.5	2.6	22.2	2.9	0.9	62.0
1974	14.1	18.6	2.5	21.2	3.2	1.3	60.8
1975	15.0	17.7	2.4	19.6	3.2	1.9	59.8
1976	15.7	17.3	2.3	19.5	4.0	2.1	60.8
1977	15.8	17.5	2.3	19.6	2.3	2.7	60.1
1978	14.9	18.4	2.2	19.5	2.9	3.0	61.0
1979	17.5	18.1	2.3	20.1	2.9	2.8	63.7
1980	18.6	18.2	2.3	19.9	2.9	2.7	64.6
1981	18.4	18.1	2.3	19.7	2.8	3.0	64.3
1982	18.6	18.3	2.2	18.3	3.3	3.1	63.8
1983	17.2	18.4	2.2	16.5	3.5	3.2	61.1
1984	19.7	18.8	2.3	17.9	3.3	3.6	65.7
1985	19.3	19.0	2.2	16.9	2.2	4.1	63.9
1986	19.5	18.4	2.1	16.5	3.0	4.2	63.7
1987	20.1	17.7	2.2	17.0	2.6	4.9	64.6
1988	20.7	17.3	2.3	17.5	2.3	5.7	65.8
1989	21.3	16.1	2.2	17.8	2.7	5.7	65.8
1990	22.5	15.6	2.2	18.4	2.9	6.2	67.9

Name: International Energy Production and Consumption
Agency/Institution: Energy Information Administration, Department of Energy
Address: 1000 Independence Avenue, S.W., Washington, DC 20585
Telephone number for data and inquiries: 202-254-5514
Sources: *International Energy Annual*
Frequency: Annually
When available: About ten months after the end of the year
Revisions: None
Historic data: See the *International Energy Annual*.

■ **A QUICK LOOK: International Energy Production and Consumption**

The *International Energy Annual* is an excellent source of data on energy production and consumption by region and country. It shows the production of energy by country and by source — crude oil and natural gas liquids, dry natural gas, coal, hydroelectric, and nuclear. The supply, disposition, reserves, and refining capacity is shown for petroleum and production; trade and reserves are shown for natural gas and coal. Prices are presented for crude oil, premium gasoline, diesel fuel, fuel oil, natural gas, and electricity. Virtually all countries have to pay for their crude oil imports in U.S. dollars. Hence, when the foreign exchange value of the dollar increases, the price of crude imports increases in terms of the country's currency even if the dollar price of oil stays the same. When the foreign exchange value of the dollar increases, as it did in the mid-1980s, major oil importing countries face severe inflationary pressures.

Name: Nuclear Energy
Agency/Institution: Energy Information Administration
Address: 1000 Independence Avenue, S.W., Washington, DC 20585
Telephone number for data and inquiries: 202-254-5514
Sources: *Monthly Energy Review* and various publications of the Nuclear Regulatory Commission
Frequency: Monthly
When available: Data are reasonably contemporaneous with the issue date of *Monthly Energy Review*. However, the actual publication date of the *MER* is about three months after the issue date. For example, the June 1990 issue of *Monthly Energy Review* was sent to the printer on September 26 and was not released until mid-October.
Revisions: Most data are subject to revisions for about one year.
Historic data: See below.

■ A QUICK LOOK: Nuclear Energy

The number of operable nuclear units generating electricity, their capacities, actual generation, number of planned units, and units under construction are available in the *Monthly Energy Review* and various publications from the Nuclear Regulatory Commission.

HISTORIC DATA: Electricity Generated by Nuclear Plants in the United States

	Percentage of Electricity Generated by Nuclear Plants	Operable Nuclear Plants
1973	4.5	39
1974	6.1	48
1975	9.0	54
1976	9.4	61
1977	11.8	65
1978	12.5	70
1979	11.4	68
1980	11.0	70
1981	11.9	74
1982	12.6	77
1983	12.7	80
1984	13.6	86
1985	15.5	95
1986	16.6	100
1987	17.7	107
1988	19.5	108
1989	19.0	110
1990	20.6	111

Name: Production of Petroleum, by Country
Agency/Institution: Energy Information Administration
Address: 1000 Independence Avenue, S.W., Washington, DC 20585
Telephone number for data and inquiries: 202-586-8995
Sources: *Petroleum Intelligence Week, Oil and Gas Journal, Monthly Energy Review,* and *International Energy Annual* (Energy Information Administration)
Frequency: Weekly, monthly, annually
When available: Data are reasonably contemporaneous with the issue date of *Monthly Energy Review (MER)*. However, the actual publication date of *MER* is about three months after the issue date. For example, the June 1990 issue of the *Monthly Energy Review* was sent to the printer on September 26 and was not released until mid-October. The *International Energy Annual* is published about ten months after the end of the year.

Revisions: Most data are subject to revisions for about one year.
Historic date: See below and the *International Energy Annual.*

■ A QUICK LOOK: Production of Petroleum

Oil analysts frequently need to access data on world oil production, relative quantities produced by OPEC countries, or quantities produced by Persian Gulf nations. The most current data on world crude oil production is available in *Petroleum Intelligence Weekly*, but the more widely available *Monthly Energy Review* has monthly and annual data with about a three-month delay. The Soviet Union was the world's largest producer of crude oil between 1974, when it took over the number one spot from the United States, and 1990 when it was dissolved.

HISTORIC DATA
World Crude Oil Production
(thousands of barrels per day)

Year	Total OPEC*	Persian Gulf Nations**	Canada	Mexico	United Kingdom	United States	China	USSR	Other	World Total
1973	30,988	20,668	1,798	465	2	9,208	1,090	8,329	3,804	55,684
1974	30,729	21,282	1,551	571	2	8,774	1,315	8,856	3,862	55,660
1975	27,154	18,934	1,430	705	12	8,375	1,490	9,472	4,139	52,777
1976	30,737	21,514	1,314	831	245	8,132	1,670	9,985	4,355	57,269
1977	31,299	21,725	1,321	981	768	8,245	1,874	10,485	4,616	59,589
1978	29,875	20,606	1,316	1,209	1,082	8,707	2,082	10,950	4,782	60,003
1979	30,998	21,066	1,500	1,461	1,568	8,552	2,122	11,187	5,089	62,477
1980	26,985	17,961	1,435	1,936	1,622	8,597	2,114	11,460	5,204	59,353
1981	22,843	15,245	1,285	2,313	1,811	8,572	2,012	11,552	5,390	55,778
1982	19,145	12,156	1,271	2,748	2,065	8,649	2,045	11,615	5,646	53,184
1983	17,891	11,081	1,356	2,689	2,291	8,688	2,120	11,684	6,248	52,967
1984	17,857	10,784	1,438	2,780	2,480	8,879	2,296	11,576	6,897	54,203
1985	16,634	9,630	1,471	2,745	2,530	8,971	2,505	11,250	7,540	53,646
1986	18,734	11,696	1,474	2,435	2,539	8,680	2,620	11,540	7,850	55,872
1987	18,846	12,103	1,535	2,548	2,406	8,349	2,690	11,690	8,242	56,306
1988	20,899	13,682	1,610	2,512	2,232	8,140	2,728	11,679	8,669	58,507
1989	22,558	14,837	1,560	2,520	1,802	7,613	2,757	11,420	9,338	59,568
1990	23,828	15,295	1,547	2,553	1,813	7,355	2,765	10,715	9,788	60,361

*OPEC countries = Algeria, Ecuador, Gabon, Indonesia, Iran, Iraq, Kuwait, Libya, Nigeria, Qatar, Saudi Arabia, the United Arab Emirates, and Venezuela
**Persian Gulf nations = Bahrain, Iran, Iraq, Kuwait, Qatar, Saudi Arabia, and the United Arab Emirates

CHAPTER 14

COMMERCIAL SECTORS

Data on the retail and wholesale industries are increasingly being disseminated by private companies, such as Donnelley's *Survey of Buying Power.* However, most extensive data are provided by the monthly and annual surveys of the Census Bureau and by the Census of Wholesale and Retail Trade. The Census Bureau has taken a Census of Business for each of the years 1929, 1933, 1935, 1939, 1948, 1954, 1958, and 1963. In 1964, Congress required the Bureau to conduct economic censuses every five years, for years ending in 2 and 7. The title "Census of Business" was discontinued in 1972, when the retail, wholesale, and service industries were separated, and individual censuses were taken for each. However, the collection of business-related censuses is still often called "economic censuses."

Name: Personal Consumption Expenditures
Agency/Institution: Bureau of Economic Analysis, Department of Commerce
Address: Washington, DC 20230
Telephone number for data: 202-898-2452 for monthly and quarterly estimates
Telephone number for data and inquiries: 202-523-0819
Sources: *Survey of Current Business*
Frequency: Monthly
When available: Last week in following month
Revisions: Revised in the following months, each year for three years, and then
    every five years
Historic data: See pages 148–149.

■ A QUICK LOOK: Personal Consumption Expenditures

One of the better indicators of the economy's health is consumer spending, but if you shift through the reams of statistics provided by the federal government, you will not see a "spending" series. However, you will find retail and wholesale trade censuses and surveys, and you will see personal consumption expenditures. **Personal consumption expenditures (PCE)** is part of the national income and product accounts (see pages 131–132), classified as one of the uses of disposable personal income; the other is personal saving. One major advantage of the PCE series is that it is released monthly as part of the personal income series while most of the rest of the GDP data are released quarterly. Personal consumption expenditures are broken down into considerable detail; the major subcategories are given in Table 14.1. Each subcategory is broken down into additional detailed accounts too numerous to include here. See the July issue of the *Survey of Current Business* for a thorough listing:

TABLE 14.1
Personal Consumption Expenditures, 1990
(billions of $)

Personal Consumption Expenditures	$3,657.3
Durable goods	480.3
Motor vehicle parts	213.0
Furniture and household equipment	176.4
Other	90.9
Nondurable goods	1,193.7
Food	624.7
Clothing and shoes	213.2
Gasoline and oil	93.8
Other nondurable goods	261.9
Fuel oil and coal	18.5
Other	243.4
Services	1,983.3
Housing	569.5
Household operation	211.3
Electricity and gas	96.4
Other	115.0
Transportation	136.6
Medical care	483.4
Other	582.5

Name: Consumer Expenditure Survey
Alternative name: Consumer Expenditures

Agency/Institution: Bureau of Labor Statistics
Address: Washington, DC 20212
Telephone number for data and inquiries: 202-272-5060
Sources: *Handbook of Labor Statistics, News, Monthly Labor Review* (all from the Department of Labor)
Frequency: Annually and quarterly
When available: About one year later
Revisions: No established policy

■ A QUICK LOOK: Consumer Expenditure Surveys

The buying habits of American consumers change over time as a result of changes in relative prices, real income, new products, and family size, as well as general tastes and preferences. The Consumer Expenditure Survey is the only national survey that relates family or household expenditures to demographic data.[1]

Until 1980, the Consumer Expenditure Survey had been conducted approximately every 10 years to provide new benchmark data for the Consumer Price Index. Since then, however, the survey has been conducted every year in order to provide a continuous flow of information on the buying habits of American consumers. The survey consists of two components: (1) a diary completed by respondents for two weeks and (2) five interviews of 5000 participants conducted every three months.

Survey participants record expenditures for goods and services purchased during the day; their reported expenditures include all sales and excise taxes for all items purchased. They also include expenditures for gifts and contributions and payments for pensions and personal insurance. Excluded from the survey are all business-related expenditures. The difference between this series and the "Personal Consumption Expenditures" (PCE) series is that this survey shows consumption expenditures and percentage distribution for the average household, whereas PCE shows total expenditures in the country. The survey contains information about households (now called "consumer units"), including number of children, vehicles owned, and income. The average level and percentage distribution of consumer expenditures are presented quarterly and annually. The quarterly data are to be considered preliminary and the sampling errors in quarterly data are much higher than those in annual data.

---

[1]Continuing a valued tradition, the federal government uses many terms interchangeably — which can cause headaches for those who are unaware of the lack of meaningful distinctions among the terms. The words *family, household,* and *consumer unit* mean the same thing.

TABLE 14.2
Data on Consumer Respondents
Percentage Distribution of Total Consumer Expenditures

	1990
Number of consumer units (in thousands)	96,968
Consumer unit characteristics:	
Income before taxes 1/	$31,889
Average number of persons in consumer unit	2.6
Average age of reference person	47.2
Average number of earners	1.4
Average number of vehicles	2.0
Percent homeowner	62
Average annual expenditures	$28,369
Food	15.1%
Food at home	8.8
Cereals and bakery products	1.3
Meats, poultry, fish, and eggs	2.4
Dairy products	1.0
Fruits and vegetables	1.4
Other food at home	2.6
Food away from home	6.4
Alcoholic beverages	1.0
Housing	31.3
Shelter	17.7
Owned dwellings	10.4
Rented dwellings	5.4
Other lodging	1.9
Utilities, fuels, and public services	6.7
Household operations	1.6
Housekeeping supplies	1.4
Household furnishings and equipment	3.9
Apparel and services	5.7
Transportation	18.1
Vehicle purchases (net outlay)	7.5
Gasoline and motor oil	3.7
Other vehicle expenses	5.8
Public transportation	1.1
Health care	5.2
Entertainment	5.0
Personal care products and services	1.3
Reading	0.5
Education	1.4

(continued)

TABLE 14.2 *(continued)*
Data on Consumer Respondents
Percentage Distribution of Total Consumer Expenditures

	1990
Tobacco products and smoking supplies	1.0%
Miscellaneous	2.3
Cash contributions	2.9
Personal insurance and pensions	9.1
Life and other personal insurance	1.2
Pensions and Social Security	7.9

Name: Population and Demographic Data
Alternative name: Census of Population
Agency/Institution: Division of Population, Bureau of the Census
Address: Washington, DC 20233
Telephone number for data and inquiries: 301-763-4251
Sources: Census of Population (Census Bureau), *Sourcebook of Demographics and Buying Power for Every Zip Code in the U.S.A.* by CACI (annual), *Donnelley Demographics* (Donnelley Marketing Information Services)
Frequency: The census is taken every 10 years, but the Bureau of the Census releases annual surveys; the private companies issue quarterly and annually.
When available: Monthly, annually, every 10 years
Revisions: The first census reports to appear after a decennial census are the preliminary reports (issued within six to eight months of Census Day), which are subsequently superseded by the advance reports (released about one year after Census Day), which, in turn, are replaced by the final reports, which are released about two to five years after Census Day). The basic population and housing data go through all three stages, but many reports do not go through the first two stages and appear only as final reports.
Historic data: Some series have historical tables; most do not.
Cross references: The Census of Housing, which is taken at the same time as the Census of Population, is discussed on pages 283–285.

■ A QUICK LOOK: Population and Demographic Data

The word *census* means to count all units. Although about 30 censuses are taken in this country, the most well known one is the Census of Population and Housing, which has been taken every ten years since 1790. The complete results of that first census were published in 56 pages; the 1980 census had about 300,000 pages. The Census of Population is not a single report; it is composed of dozens of individual reports broken down into series. Each census arranges and reports data in its own way and with its own design, but the 1990 Census of Population reports, which will not be available until 1992 to 1995, will be similar to the following. (See "Revisions" in this section for a discussion of preliminary, advance, and final reports. Some of the following reports have these three versions.)

- State reports: Reports issued for each state; they include statistics for SMSAs, counties, cities, and towns within that state.

  1. Number of inhabitants: Includes population counts with historical comparisons.

  2. General population characteristics: Presents data that were obtained from answers to questions asked of all respondents. These are known as complete-count, or 100 percent data, items. The other data items were obtained from questions answered only by those households selected by random sampling. The 100 percent population items are household relationships, sex, race, age, and marital status.

  3. General social and economic characteristics: Presents data on 100 percent items and sample characteristics, including occupation, industry, class of worker.

  4. Congressional districts: Provides selected 100 percent and sample data on the characteristics of persons and housing units by congressional districts.

- Reports issued by SMSA: The focus on small-area statistics.

  1. Block statistics: Presents 100 percent data items by census block

  2. Census tracts: Presents most population and housing data by census tracts

- National reports: Subject reports provide detailed characteristics on such specific subjects as migration, journey to work, earnings, education.

The workers at the Census Bureau do not hibernate between census years. Not only are they processing data for the other nine censuses, but they are busy producing an astonishing amount of data about the people of the United States, which they publish through three separate population series. The first series consists of the many decennial census reports just discussed. The second series is based on the Current Population Survey, which is a continuing survey of the population but with smaller samples or numbers of respondents. The third series is the estimate series, in which estimates are made for various groups of populations.

The Current Population Survey (CPS), which is conducted every month, is the most important source of population statistics between census years. The CPS is primarily directed at obtaining labor market data (see "Labor Market," pages 75–76) for the Bureau of Labor Statistics' employment and earnings data series, but the survey also covers a wide range of population characteristics such as marriage, household composition, migration, work history, and income. The CPS also serves as a vehicle for supplemental studies on subjects other than employment. Every two years the CPS asks respondents whether they registered and voted. The Census Bureau issues three series of publications based on the CPS:[2]

1. Population Characteristics (series P-20): A series of reports covering a broad range of topics. A subscription is possible to the entire series, but individual reports can be purchased separately. The specific reports published will vary from year to year, but they generally cover such topics as geographic residence and mobility, fertility, school enrollment, education, marital status, and other social characteristics. Biennial reports present information on voter registration. P-20 reports are numbered consecutively, with the 400s being the 1990 series. If the report carries the notation "Series (P 20)" on its title page, it is part of this series. One example of the many reports in this series is *Household and Family Characteristics: March 1988* (P-20, No. 437).[3]

2. Special Studies (series P-23): Another report series generated by data obtained through the Current Population Survey. Frankly, it is hard to distinguish between the P-20 and the P-23 series. You are more likely to find reports on methodology and concepts in this series, but it also contains population data — for example, *Population Profile of the United States: 1989* (P-23, No. 159).

3. Household Economic Studies (series P-70): This relatively new series features data on the economic and social characteristics of households. A typical publication in this series is: *Characteristics of Persons Receiving Benefits from Major Assistance Programs* (P-70, No. 14).

The third series of reports put out by the Census Bureau is based not on the Current Population Survey, but on estimates or projections. However, current data obtained from one of the CPS-based publications are

---

[2]In addition to the following P-series publications derived from Current Population Survey data, the Census Bureau sells a number of microdata tapes that have the original answers to the questionnaires, with name and address deleted.

[3]Prior to 1987, a separate series (P-27, Farm Population) published characteristics of the farm population. Since 1987, this series has been integrated into the P-20 series.

often included. Population estimates are made for future years as well as for the years between the census years.

1. Population Estimates and Projections (series P-25): The reports in this series are sometimes called *Current Population Reports*. They are issued periodically and contain estimates of future population trends for varying segments of the population in the United States or the various states. A typical report is *United States Population Estimates, by Age, Sex and Race: 1988 to 2080* (P-25, No. 1018).

2. Local Population Estimates (series P-26): These reports provide population estimates for counties and metropolitan areas. A typical report in this series is *County Population Estimates: July 1, 1987 and 1986* (P-26, No. 87-A).

■ A CLOSER LOOK: Population and Demographic Data

The Census Bureau obtains its basic data in two ways. Most of the data are obtained from questionnaires that are mailed to households, filled out, and returned. About 85 percent of these forms are returned by the deadline. Households that do not return the questionnaire or that do not fill it out completely are visited by an enumerator. Also, some areas are visited directly by enumerators without any questionnaires being mailed. These data are then processed in many ways to eliminate errors made by respondents, enumerators, or typists.

Although the Census Bureau is besieged by thousands of individuals and organizations recommending questions (How often do you bathe? How many pets reside at this residence? What do you eat for breakfast?), the Bureau has an elaborate procedure for sifting through possible questions, and it includes only those that are necessary.

People who have not gathered raw data might not understand the complexities of such items as determining the place of residence. The following discussion merely scratches the surface of the complexity of this single question. Persons are counted at their "usual place of residence," which is where the person sleeps and lives most of the time.[4] Members of the armed forces living on a military installation are counted as residents of the area in which the installation is located; if armed forces members are living off base, they are counted in that locality. Armed forces stationed on patrolling vessels that will be away from port for a considerable period of time and those based overseas are counted in the

---

[4]Economic censuses count people where they work, so discrepancies in population counts often arise among the censuses.

overseas population. College students are counted as residents of the area in which they are living while attending college. Children in boarding school below the college level are counted at their parental home. Inmates of institutions are counted as residents of the locations of the institutions. Persons in hotels and motels on Census Day are assigned to their hometowns. Special enumerations are conducted of missions, homeless shelters, jails, and detention centers, and their inhabitants are counted as members of the area in which the facility is located. Citizens of foreign countries who have resided in the United States for some time are included in the area's population but foreign tourists are not.

The Census Bureau is not able to count everyone who qualifies as a resident. People living on the streets, in dangerous urban housing units, in remote urban areas, or in RVs are obviously difficult to count. The Census Bureau is well aware of these problems, and it has developed a number of programs to minimize its undercount. It is currently estimated that the undercount numbers about 2 percent.

If you are going to dig into the census or survey reports, a knowledge of the following geographical areas will be useful:

Minor civil divisions (MCDs):   Minor subdivisions of counties, such as towns and townships.

Special economic urban areas (SEUAs):   Townships in New Jersey and Pennsylvania and towns in the six New England States with a 1980 population of 10,000 or more.

Incorporated place: A political unit that is legally incorporated as a city, village, or town.

Census designated places (CDPs):   Formerly called unincorporated places, CDPs are closely settled areas of population without legally established limits. They generally have a population of at least 1000 people. There are about 3000 CDPs.

Census tracts: Statistical subdivisions of counties in metropolitan areas that average about 4000 in population. Economic data are widely available for the approximately 45,000 census tracts. A medium-size metropolitan area of around 500,000 population will have about 110 to 125 census tracts. The importance of census tracts, other than the smallness of the area they cover, is that their boundaries basically do not change. When a tract's population increases, the tract is divided into smaller tracts but the boundary of the original tract remains constant. Assume that a certain tract on the fringe of a metropolitan area is numbered census tract 50. As the tract gains population, it could be divided into tracts 50.01, 50.02, and 50.03, with the three tracts comprising the same total area as the original tract 50. Census tract boundaries may cross place and MCD boundaries, but they never cross state or county boundaries. Blocks and block groups do not cross census tract boundaries.

Census blocks: These are the smallest type of census area. They are subdivisions of census tracts that comprise one or a few city blocks that are small rectangular areas bounded by four streets. Blocks generally contain about 70 to 100 people.

They are identified in virtually all urban areas but only in a few rural areas. No sample data are published for blocks, and 100 percent, or complete-count data, are suppressed if they would reveal information about a particular household.

Enumeration districts (EDs): Used where census blocks are not used. Average population in EDs is about 600.

Central business districts (CBDs): Areas of high land value, traffic flow, and concentration of retail businesses, offices, theaters, hotels, and service establishments. They are defined in all SMSA central cities and cities with a population of 50,000 or more that have a sufficient concentration of economic activity.

Major retail centers (MRCs): MRCs are concentrations of retail stores located in SMSAs but outside the CBDs. They must have at least 25 retail establishments and one or more large general merchandise or department stores.

The Census Bureau uses many different terms in its reports to refer to the same thing. For example, the number of households, the number of occupied housing units, and the number of householders will always be the same. Knowing this can save a lot of time and frustration when you can find one term and can't find the others. The number of families and the number of family householders are also the same.

Name: Retail Trade
Alternative names: Market Studies, Buying Patterns
Agency/Institution: Bureau of the Census is the primary source, but private companies sell studies with the same data.
Address: Bureau of the Census, Washington, DC 20233
Telephone number for data and inquiries: 301-763-7038
Sources: From Bureau of the Census: Census of Retail Trade (every 5 years), *Advanced Monthly Retail Sales* (press release), *Monthly Retail Trade*, and *Annual Retail Trade*; from Bureau of Economic Analysis: *Survey of Current Business* (monthly).
When available: The five-year Census of Retail Trade becomes available about two to three years after the end of the target year. The census is taken in every year ending in 2 or 7. The *Advanced Monthly Retail Sales* releases, based on a small sample, are published about 10 days into the following month. *Monthly Retail Trade* contains preliminary data for a month and one-half earlier and revised data for two and one-half months earlier. Advance estimates for the month of September would be released about October 10, preliminary data for October would be reported in the *Monthly Retail Trade* of November and revised data would be in the *Monthly Retail Trade* in December.
Revisions: Revisions are made in the month following original publication and then for the next two months and then in the following year (Revised data for 1991 were released in April 1992).
Historic data: Each April, a ten-year time series is published, with the latest revisions of the previous year. *Revised Monthly Retail Sales and Inventories: January 1980 through December 1989* was published in April 1990.

■ A QUICK LOOK: Retail Trade

About two-thirds of national output is generated initially in the retail sector, so one of the first places to look for data affecting the economy is in that sector. Surveys of retail trade cover establishments engaged in selling merchandise for personal or household consumption in contrast to wholesalers, who sell to other wholesalers or to retailers. If a store sells to both consumers and to wholesalers, it is classified as a retail store if more than one-half of its sales are to the general public.

All government and private retail series report the sales and inventories of all establishments classified as retail establishments in SIC codes 52 through 59.

SIC Code	Retail Sectors
52	Building materials, hardware, garden supply, and mobile home dealers
53	General merchandise stores
54	Food stores
55	Automotive dealers and gasoline service stations
56	Apparel and accessories
57	Furniture, home furniture, and equipment
58	Eating and drinking places
59	Miscellaneous retail trade

The federal government puts out four retail trade publications:

- *Advanced Monthly Retail Sales:* This publication provides rough estimates of the retail sales in the previous month. Based on a small subsample, it is issued only ten days after the end of the month. It contains rough (called "advanced" by the bureaucrats) estimates for the previous month, preliminary estimates for the month before that, and final estimates (they are *not* final) for the month before that. For example, the *Advanced Monthly Retail Sales* report issued on October 10 would contain the advanced estimates for September, preliminary estimates for August, and "final" estimates for July. These estimates are for the kind-of-business groups at the national level only.

- *Monthly Retail Trade: Sales Accounts Receivable, and Inventories:* The monthly report is released about six to seven weeks after the end of the "target" month. The mid-October issue would carry preliminary data for August and "final" estimates for July. Although it is issued a month later than the *Advanced Monthly Retail* report, it has more comprehensive data, including dollar volume and percentage changes summarized by kind-of-business groups for the United States and the 19 most populous states, 15 PMSAs, and four cities. Comparable data are shown for the prior 12 months, along with percentage changes from the previous month and the same month in the previous year. National estimates of end-of-month inventories and inventory-sales ratios are given. A separate report in this series is the annual revised summary (see Historic Data above).

- *Annual Retail Trade:* An annual report of annual sales, year-end inventories, inventory-sales ratios, and accounts receivable balances for the United States. This report becomes available about one year after the reference year.

- The Census of Retail Trade, taken every five years, contains the most comprehensive data on retail trade for the nation, states, counties, MSAs, and many local places. This report becomes available about two to three years after the end of the year. See the following "A Closer Look" section for a more detailed discussion of the census.

During the past two decades a number of private sources of data valuable to the retail industry have emerged. Two of the most significant are:

- *Market Profile Analysis (MPA):* Published annually by Donnelley Marketing Information Services, it contains population, household, income, number of financial institutions, businesses, employees, age, mobility, housing, value of homes, employment by industry, and construction. All of this information is available in federal documents, but this is much handier and more useful. However, your local library is unlikely to have MPAs other than for the local SMSA.

- *Survey of Buying Power:* Published annually by *Sales and Marketing Management Magazine.* It contains 900 pages of maps and figures for states and counties on detailed characteristics of the population, household income, effective buying income, and total retail sales for 12 store groups and 10 merchandise lines. It contains estimates for the current year and data from the previous Census of Retail Trade.

■ A CLOSER LOOK: The Census of Retail Trade

Every five years (covering years ending in 2 and 7), a Census of Retail Trade is taken, but the publications resulting from the census are not released until about three years later. As with all censuses, the Census of Retail Trade is composed of many reports and is difficult to use. This census is composed of four major series:

1. Geographic area series: Composed of separate reports for the United States and each state. This series contains data on the number of establishments (this is "bureaucratese" for stores), employment, payroll,

and sales by the kind of business. The data are provided at the state, county, and SMSA level for cities of more than 2500 population and any other place that has at least 350 retail establishments. The major counties and places are ranked by sales volume within each state. The separate U.S. summary report provides comparative data at the national level, and it ranks the 250 top counties by sales volume. Assume that you are in the hardware business and you are thinking of establishing a new hardware store in Bakersfield, California. One of the first things you would want to know is the number of hardware stores, sales, and per capita hardware sales in Bakersfield. You could turn to the Bakersfield MSA page in the Census of Retail Trade's geographic area series for California and find these data. You might also look at the special report series, described next.

2. Special report series: Profiles selected variables for retail trade for the nation, states, and MSAs, which are not reported elsewhere. Various ratios, rankings, and other comparisons are presented in this series. Comparisons between the last two census years (for example, growth rates between the two most recent censuses) are given only in this series.

3. Zip code statistics series: Includes number of retail establishments by sales, employment, and total kind of store (SIC) for each five-digit zip code. Also, retail sales, payroll, and employees in the retail sector (but not by type of store) is given for each five-digit zip code. These data are available only on CD-ROM and computer tape, but private companies such as Donnelley provide the data in published form. Assume that you are marketing the National Requirer and that you have to develop market areas for your salespeople. By looking at these data, you can determine the number of grocery stores, drug stores, and newsstands in each of the zip code areas.

4. Subject series: There are four reports in this series.

   a. The first report presents data on the number of establishments, sales, payroll, and employment, cross-tabulated by kind of business and size of firm for the United States. This is the place to look if you are interested in the concentration of certain retail markets, such as grocery stores, music stores, and so on.

   b. The second report shows accounting and financial data on the nation's retailers, including sales, purchases, inventories, capital expenditures, depreciable assets, gross margins, value added, operating expenses, and net income. These data are available only at the national level and are based on a separate sample of 20,000 firms. If you are interested in entering a retail business at the national level, you would use this source to give you an idea of the business's assets per dollar of sales, expenses, and net income.

c. The third report reveals what kinds of stores sell which kinds of merchandise and in what quantities. You might think this is obvious. Grocery stores sell groceries and TV stores sell TVs. But the American retail market is not divided into such neat shells. Groceries are sold at grocery stores, drugstores, service stations, bakeries, department stores, vegetable markets, and many more outlets. If you want to learn the amounts and percentages of groceries sold through each of these outlets, check this report. If you are marketing automotive parts, this report might surprise you with data showing that far more automotive repair parts are sold through automotive supply stores and department stores than through new and used car dealers.

d. Miscellaneous: This report changes quite a bit with each census. If you can't find retail data of interest to you in the other reports, check out this report.

Name: Wholesale Trade Reports
Agency/Institution: Bureau of the Census
Address: Chief, Business Division, Bureau of the Census, Washington, DC 20233
Telephone number for data and inquiries: 301-763-7007
Sources: From the Bureau of the Census: *Monthly Wholesale Trade, Annual Trade Survey,* and Census of Wholesale Trade; from the Council of Economic Advisors: *Economic Indicators* (monthly); from the Bureau of Economic Analysis: *Survey of Current Business* (monthly).
Frequency: Monthly, annually, and every five years
When available: The *Monthly Wholesale Report* is available about five to six weeks after the end of the reference month. The *Annual Trade Survey* is available about nine months after the end of the year, and the five-year census report is available about two to three years after the end of the reference year.
Revisions: Revisions are made in the following two months and then in the annual summary contained in the January report.
Historic data: Publications with data for the past 10 to 20 years are released periodically.

■ A QUICK LOOK: Wholesale Trade Reports

Wholesale trade includes establishments or places of business that are primarily engaged in selling merchandise to retailers or to industries, farms, or other wholesalers. Normally a store is classified as wholesale if more than half of its sales are to businesses and institutions. The following SIC codes are included in wholesale trade:

SIC Code	Industry
50	Wholesale trade — durable goods
501	Motor vehicles and automotive parts and supplies
502	Furniture and home furnishings
503	Lumber and other construction materials
504	Sporting, recreational, toys, and hobby goods
505	Metals and minerals
506	Electrical goods
507	Hardware, plumbing, and heating equipment
508	Machinery and equipment
509	Miscellaneous durable goods
51	Wholesale trade — nondurable goods
511	Paper and paper products
512	Drugs, drug proprietaries
513	Apparel, piece goods, and notions
514	Groceries and related products
515	Farm products — raw materials
516	Chemicals and allied products
517	Petroleum and petroleum products
518	Beer, wine, and distilled alcoholic beverages
519	Miscellaneous nondurable goods

The Census Bureau categorizes establishments by type of operation:

Merchant wholesalers who actually take title to the goods they sell. These are wholesalers who are familiar to most people and who account for more than 80 percent of all wholesale establishments.

Sales branches and sales offices maintained by manufacturers to market their products.

Agents or brokers who buy and sell goods for others and receive a commission for the transaction.

The Census Bureau obtains census data on wholesalers from questionnaires mailed to all firms with paid employees. The monthly and annual data are obtained from questionnaires sent to a sample of merchant wholesalers. The Bureau provides the following reports on the wholesale industry:

- *Monthly Wholesale Trade:* This report is issued about five to six weeks after the end of the reference month. It shows sales, inventories, and inventory-sales ratios for merchant wholesalers based on three-digit

SIC classification. The January report shows all final data for the previous year.

- *Annual Wholesale Trade:* This report shows annual sales, year-end inventories, sales-inventory ratios, purchases, and gross margins for selected three-digit SIC industries. Comparable statistics are shown for the previous year, along with year-to-year changes. The report is issued eight to nine months after the end of the year.
- The Census of Wholesale Trade is taken every five years in years ending in 2 and 7.

■ A CLOSER LOOK: Wholesale Trade Reports

Every five years—those ending in 2 and 7—the Census Bureau conducts the economic census, including the Census of Wholesale Trade. The census is composed of many separate reports:

- Geographic area series: Consists of a separate report for each state and for the United States. The state reports contain data for the state and its MSAs, counties, and places with 200 or more wholesale establishments on number of sales, payrolls, and employment by kind of business and type of operation (merchant, agents, brokers). Wholesale data are shown for all incorporated places of more than 2500 population, but these data exclude the kind-of-business detail. If you are interested in the number, sales, and payrolls of furniture wholesalers in Springfield, Missouri, turn to the Springfield MSA in the Missouri geographic area series. The U.S. summary report in this series presents comparable information for the nation and abbreviated comparative data for the states.
- Subject series: There are four reports in the subject series.
  1. The first report presents data on the number of establishments, sales, payroll, and employment, cross-tabulated by kind of business and size of firm for the United States. This is the place to look if you are interested in the concentration of the wholesale industry in certain markets.
  2. The second report shows accounting and financial data of the nation's wholesalers, including sales, purchases, inventories, capital expenditures, depreciable assets, gross margin, value added, operating expenses, and net income. These data are available only at the national level and are based on a separate sample of 5100 firms. If you are interested in entering a wholesale business at the national level, you would use this source to give you some idea of the business's assets per dollar of sales, expenses, and net income.

3. The third report reveals what kinds of wholesale establishments handle which kinds of merchandise and in what quantities. The printed report contains only national data, but the computer tapes and CD-ROMs have data for 15 states and 15 MSAs. If you want to learn the amounts and percentages of lumber products sold through various wholesalers, check this report.

4. Miscellaneous: This report changes quite a bit each census. If you can't find wholesale data of interest to you in the other reports, check out this report.

CHAPTER 15

REGIONAL, STATE, AND LOCAL

READ ME FIRST

During the past two decades regional economic data, which are used by local planners, politicians, media, forecasters, industry analysts, and many others, have grown considerably in quantity, sophistication, and timeliness. One of the most important sources of economic data on the state and county level is the annual *County Business Patterns (CBP)*, published by the Census Bureau. Each state has a separate report, presenting state- and county-level data on number of establishments, employees, payrolls, and the number of establishments by employment-size class. If you want to know the number of establishments, employees, and payroll in your home county or state, *County Business Patterns* is the place to look.

Many state and local data series were presented in other chapters. For example, Chapter 4 contained data series on employment, and unemployment, wages, and hours worked. Production data were presented in Chapter 12, and retail and wholesale data series were shown in Chapter 14. Some significant state and local data series, such as employment and earnings by county, local personal income, gross state product, local shipments to the federal government, and income and output multipliers that were not presented in these other chapters are contained in this chapter.

A valuable topic found in this chapter is an explanation and sample of state and local multipliers. These multipliers show the direct requirement, output, and earnings that will be generated by each $1 increase in final demand. Chambers of Commerce, small businesses, and city development offices do not have to hire economists to do these important studies. Just read the regional multipliers section very carefully and you will have no trouble. Since regional multipliers are based on the national input-output tables, you might want to read "Input-Output Tables" in Chapter 12.

Name: Employment and Earnings by County and State
Agency/Institution: Bureau of the Census, Department of Commerce
Address: Washington, DC 20233
Telephone number for data and inquiries: 301-763-5430
Sources: *County and Business Patterns.* There is a national summary volume and a volume for each state, the District of Columbia, and Puerto Rico.
Frequency: Annually
When available: About two years after the data year
Revisions: None, unless there are serious errors
Historic data: The data series began in 1946 but was revised in 1974, which affected the comparability of the data. The data have been published annually since 1964. Each state volume contains county data on employment and wages by four-digit industries back to 1964 (larger counties back to 1946).

■ **A QUICK LOOK: Employment and Earnings by County and State**

Employment and earnings by county data include employment, payrolls, and number of firms for four-digit SIC groups for states and counties and for two-digit SIC groups for SMSAs. Following is an outline of information provided in *County Business Patterns*:

I. National Publication — Provides data on establishments, employees, and payrolls for the following categories
    A. United States
        1. Major industry groups
        2. Employment size class by industry
        3. Administrative and auxiliary establishments by major industry group
        4. Statewide establishments
            a. Employment size class by major industry groups
            b. Employment size class by state
    B. States
        1. Major industry group
            a. State
            b. Employment size class of 1000 or more by state
            c. Administrative and auxiliary establishments by state
        2. Employment-size class
            a. By counties in each state
            b. By counties having highest employment
    C. Federal Civilian Employment and First Quarter Payroll by State

II. State Publications — A separate report of the *County Business Patterns* is published for each state and the District of Columbia

  A. States

    1. Establishments, employment, and payroll by major industry groups

    2. Employment and payroll by employment-size class

  B. Counties: Establishments, employment, and payroll by industry within each county

The primary source of data are reports filed by firms covered by the Federal Insurance Contributions Act (FICA). Thus, all government employess, self-employed persons, domestic workers, railroad employees, and employees of certain nonprofit organizations are excluded. The reporting unit is an *establishment*, which is a single physical location at which business is conducted or where services of industrial operations are performed. It is not necessarily identical with a company or enterprise, which may consist of one or more establishments. All activities carried on at a location are generally grouped together and classified on the basis of the major reported activity, and all data for the establishment are included in that classification.

Payroll: Total annual payroll includes all forms of compensation, such as salaries, wages, commissions, bonuses, vacation allowances, sick-leave pay, and the value of payments in kind (meals and lodgings) paid during the year. Tips and gratuities received by employees are included. Payroll is reported before deductions for Social Security, income tax, insurance, union dues, and so on.

Employment: Paid employment consists of full- and part-time employees, including salaried officers and executives, if they were on the payroll in the pay period including March 12. Included are employees on paid sick leave, holidays, and vacations.

SIC: The Standard Industrial Classification system for classifying firms into industries. Beginning with the 1988 issue of *County Business Patterns*, the 1987 edition of the SIC manual has been used.

Name: Gross State Product (GSP)
Alternative name: Gross Domestic Product for States
Agency/Institution: Bureau of Economic Analysis, Department of Commerce
Address: Regional Economic Analysis Division, BE-61, Bureau of Economic Analysis, U.S. Department of Commerce, Washington, DC 20230
Telephone number for data and inquiries: 202-523-9180
Sources: Gross state product estimates are available each year in the *Survey of Government Business* and on magnetic tape and personal computer diskettes.

A magnetic tape containing total GSP by two-digit industry in both current and constant (1982) dollars for the United States, BEA regions, and states costs $200. Diskettes cost $20 each and are available by BEA region; a diskette for a region contains estimates for the United States, the BEA region, and each state of the region. (The Southeast region, on two diskettes, costs $40.) Requests should be addressed to: Economic and Statistical Analysis (ESA), BEA (BE-61), U.S. Department of Commerce, 222 Mitchell Street, P.O. Box 100606, Atlanta, GA 30384.

Frequency: Periodically

When available: About two years after the reference year

Revisions: None

Cross references: See the discussion of the gross domestic product on pages 121–149.

Historic data: These estimates were originally published in the May 1988 *Survey of Current Business*, with errata on page 37 of the October 1988 *Survey*. They are available back to 1963 on computer tape.

■ A QUICK LOOK: Gross State Product

Gross state product (GSP) is the gross market value of the goods and services attributable to labor and property located in a state. It is the state counterpart of the nation's gross domestic product (GDP).[1] Gross state product is measured in current dollars as the sum of four components for each of 61 industries: (1) compensation of employees; (2) proprietors' income;[2] (3) indirect business tax and nontax liability (IBT); and (4) other, mainly capital-related, charges ("capital charges"). The estimates, which are given in current and constant dollars, are for all 50 states, nine regions, and the United States.

Name: Regional Multipliers
Alternative name: RIMS II Multipliers
Agency/Institution: Bureau of Economic Analysis, Department of Commerce
Address: Washington, DC 20230
Telephone number for data and inquiries: 202-523-0594

---

[1]Gross domestic product measures the output of goods and services produced by labor and property located in the United States. The income of all productive resources located in the United States — no matter who owns these resources — are included in GDP (see pages 121–149).

[2]Proprietors' income includes inventory valuation adjustment and capital consumption allowances. For an explanation of these terms see chapter 7.

Sources: The actual multipliers are available only on computer printouts and disk-ettes from the BEA's Office of Regional Economics. BEA will produce the print-outs on request for about $1500, but the cost is considerably less if the particular county has been previously processed. Check with your local university's Division of Business Research or check "Sources of Local, State, and Regional Data" in Appendix D.

Frequency: The multipliers are updated annually, but the benchmark revisions, based on the national input-output tables, are updated every five years. However, there is a delay of five to nine years in making those benchmark revisions. The benchmark revisions based on the 1982 census were released in 1991.

Further information: *Regional Multipliers: A User Handbook* and *Regional Input-Output Modeling System (RIMS II)*, both from Department of Commerce

---

■ A QUICK LOOK: Regional Multipliers

Businesses, lobbyists, city planners, and government officials often want to know the impact of a new industry in a local area or in the state. A useful tool for calculating the impact of a new or old industry is the **regional multiplier**. During the mid-1970s, the Bureau of Economic Analysis instituted the Regional Input-Output Modeling System (RIMS), which produced local and state input-output multipliers, by industry, for direct coefficients, output, earnings, and employment. The methodology was improved in the RIMS II model adopted in 1981. These multipliers are probably available in one or more of your state universities or your state data centers (see Appendix D for a list).

There are two sizes of multiplier tables. One table has 39 columns and 39 rows, which means there are 39 industries (columns) that can be subjected to the multipliers and 39 industries (rows) that "feed" the column industries. Another table has 531 columns and 39 rows. This table, which applies to many more industries, and, consequently, has more disaggregated data, enables us to obtain more precise data. The computer printouts provided by BEA contain only the numbers of the industries, so accompanying tables must be used to cross-list the numbers with the names of the actual industries. The RIMS tables are based on the national input-output tables, so anyone interested in better understanding RIMS will want to read the "Input-Output Tables" section in Chapter 12.

These tables are easy to use once you've become acquainted with them. The first step in using the multipliers is to determine the change in final demand in some industry. For each dollar increase in demand in that industry, the multipliers will show the total increase in output, income, and employment in the county, metropolitan area, or state. Let's look at an example.

TABLE 15.1
Hypothetical Output Multipliers

	61.0100	61.0200	61.0300
1	0.0016	0.0012	0.0087
2	0.0008	0.0143	0.0245
3	0.0161	0.1045	0
4	0.0020	0.0043	0
.			
.			
.			
22	1.0984	1.1065	1.0054
.			
.			
.			
39	0.3096	0.5425	0.5172
Total	1.8965	2.0906	1.6941

Table 15.1 is a hypothetical table of output multipliers for the Podunk Metropolitan Statistical Area (MSA). The first thing to do is convert the numbers at the top of the columns and at the left side of the rows into industries. Looking at a table provided by the BEA, we find that 61.0100 is shipbuilding and repairing, 61.0200 is boat building and repairing, and 61.0300 is railroad equipment. The 39 numbers listed along the left-hand side are the industries supplying resources to the industries listed at the top. The data in the cells are the coefficients, or multipliers, which show the increase in output of the row industries when the output of the column industries increases by $1. Thus, if a ship (industry 61.0100) valued at $10 million is constructed in Podunk, the multiplier of 0.0016 means that the shipbuilding industry will require inputs from industry 1 of $16,000; industry 2, of $8000; and so on. Note that industry 22 has a multiplier greater than 1. This is because industry 22 is transportation equipment, which includes the ship, boat, and railroad equipment industries. Thus, an increase in output of $1 in ship construction would result in an increase of at least $1 in the output of transportation equipment plus the value of other resources from transportation that might be used in producing ships. Industry 39 is the household industry, which receives income from the industries numbered 1 through 38. The total does not include income generated in the household sector because the multipliers listed in Table 15.1 in industries 1 through 38 include the income.

■ **A CLOSER LOOK: Regional Multipliers**

Assume that you are an urban planner for the county of Podunk, and the Slippery Chemical Company is going to locate in your community. You would like to determine the economic impact of the new company on other industries in your county and on total income and employment. One option available to you is to conduct very expensive surveys of the inputs used by similar chemical companies, the percentage of such inputs that are available locally, and the wages and salaries in these various industries. However, generally, a more desirable option is to use the RIMS II regional multipliers, which are available for any region of the country composed of one or more counties. There are four tables of different multipliers, depending on the questions you want answered: direct requirements multipliers, total requirements multipliers, earnings multipliers, and employment multipliers.

Direct Requirements Multipliers

The *direct requirements* (or coefficients) multipliers show the inputs of goods and services from the county's industries that will be required to produce a dollar of output in the chemical industry. Table 15.2 illustrates the meaning and significance of these direct requirements.

TABLE 15.2
Direct Requirements (or Coefficients) Multipliers

	PURCHASING INDUSTRY				
	1	2	3	4	Households
1	0.06	0.15	0.07	0.08	0.08
2	.12	.02	.10	.03	.10
3	.08	.08	.09	.02	.12
4	.03	.0	.04	.06	.11
Households	.18	.23	.13	.10	.08
Totals	.47	.48	.43	.29	.49

This table is hypothetical, but the real table would be adopted directly from the national input-output model, which shows the purchasing industries arranged in columns and the supplying industries in rows. Assuming that the chemical industry is industry 3, we look under the column heading of "3" to obtain the direct coefficients for inputs into the chemical industry. For the chemical industry to produce $1 of output, it requires 7 cents worth of input from industry 1 located in Podunk, 10 cents of input from industry 2 located in Podunk, 9 cents from industry 4 located in Podunk, and 13 cents of labor inputs from households located in Podunk. This means that if Slippery Chemical has sales of $10 million, the sales of industry 1 firms in the city will increase by $700,000 and the sales of firms in industry 2 firms will increase by $1 millon. Households will supply labor inputs of $1.3 million. The Totals row shows that chemical firm sales of $10 million will generate a direct increase of $4.3 million in the output of all firms and households in Podunk.

Total Requirements Multipliers

Direct requirements tables provide useful information on the inputs of firms, but they do not show the indirect impact on the local economy. An increase in the output of the chemical firm and in its related direct requirements produce two additional impacts not included in Table 15.2. One is an increase in the production of inputs to those firms that provide the direct requirements (this is called a *secondary impact*) and another is the increase in production of the goods and services demanded by those whose incomes have been increased (called an *induced impact*). In order to "pick up" these secondary and induced impacts, economists have developed *total requirements multipliers*, which include (1) the initial output of the industry in question (the chemical industry), (2) the direct impact produced by firms in the region supplying inputs to the key (chemical) industry and (3) the indirect impact, which includes secondary and induced impacts. See Table 15.3.

TABLE 15.3
Total Requirements or Output Multipliers

	PURCHASING INDUSTRY				
	1	2	3	4	Households
1	1.14	0.22	0.13	0.12	0.15
2	.19	1.10	.16	.07	.16
3	.16	.16	1.16	.06	.19
4	.08	.05	.00	1.09	.15
Households	.29	.34	.23	.17	1.17
Totals	1.57	1.53	1.53	1.34	.65

Table 15.3 is interpreted in the same way as Table 15.2 except that the multipliers now represent indirect as well as direct impacts. Thus, if sales of the chemical industry (industry 3) in Podunk increase by $10 million, total output in industry 1 in Podunk is increased by $1.3 million, the output of industry 2 by $1.6 million, and the output of industry 3 by $11.6 million. Note that an increase of $1 in final demand in the chemical industry will generate a $1.16 increase in total output in the chemical industry. One dollar is the direct increase in output of the chemical industry. The additional 16 cents of output is caused by secondary effects and the fact that chemical products are used in making the $1 of chemical products. The entry in the Households row says that the sum of earnings paid to households in all of the preceding four industries for each $1 increase in output in the chemical industry is 23 cents. Thus, if sales of Slippery Chemical Company increase by $10 million, household income (sales of labor and other resources) will increase by $2.3 million. The total increase in output in Podunk resulting from a $10 million increase in the output of Slippery Chemical Company is $15.3 million.

These output multipliers are contained in every multiplier package provided by the BEA. The output multipliers can provide useful information to regional authorities, but keep in mind that the output values produced by these multipliers are duplicative. Assume that ABC Sand Company supplies $10,000 of sand to Slippery Chemical Company and that a glass company sells Slippery Chemical $5000 of glass. These inputs go into producing chemicals that Slippery sells for $50,000. Thus, the output of the chemical company will be picked up in its industry output (industry 3) in the amount of $50,000, the output of the sand industry will be picked up in another industry (say, industry 1), and the output of the glass industry will be included in yet another industry (say, industry 2). Thus, the reported total output or sales in the community will be $65,000, whereas the final output is actually only the $50,000 of chemicals, which includes the value of the sand and glass that went into its production.

Earnings Multipliers

A third useful multiplier in regional analysis is the *earnings multiplier*, which shows the earnings that arise when the output of a given industry is increased by $1. Look at Table 15.4.

TABLE 15.4
Earnings Multiplier

	1	2	3	4	Households
1	.20	.04	.02	.02	.03
2	.04	.25	.04	.02	.04
3	.02	.02	.15	.01	.02
4	.01	.01	.01	.11	.02
Households	.02	.02	.01	.01	.06
Totals	.29	.34	.23	.17	.17

From Table 15.4 we see that an increase of $1 in chemical sales (industry 3) will generate 2 cents of income in industry 1, 4 cents of income in industry 2, 15 cents of income in the chemical industry, 1 cent of income in industry 4, and 1 cent of income to household employees. When Slippery Chemical Company sales increase by $10 million, total income in Podunk will increase by $2.3 million. Earnings include wages and salaries, proprietors' income, and other labor income; they do not include employer contributions to private pension and welfare funds.

Employment Multipliers

BEA also provides *employment multipliers*, which show the number of jobs (full- or part-time) produced by *$1 million* of output. See Table 15.5.

TABLE 15.5
Employment Multipliers

	1	2	3	4	Households
1	18	4	2	2	3
2	3	18	3	1	3
3	1	1	9	1	1
4	0	0	0	6	1
Households	0	0	0	0	1
Total	22	23	14	10	9

This table shows that for each $1 million of output, the chemical industry (industry 3) requires a total of 14 employees, including 9 in its own industry. In order to use these multipliers, we have to know the change in final demand and the industry in which it occurs. An increase of $10 million of output in the chemical industry (industry 3) will produce an increase of 140 new jobs in Podunk County.

Name: Regional Personal Income
Alternative name: State, County, MSA Personal Income
Agency/Institution: Bureau of Economic Analysis, Department of Commerce
Address: Regional Economics Measurement Division, BE-55, Bureau of Economic Analysis, U.S. Department of Commerce, Washington, DC 20230
Telephone number for data and inquiries:
General: 202-523-0966
State personal income: 202-523-0911
Wage and salary income and employment: 202-523-0945
Proprietors' income and employment: 202-523-0937
Sources: *Survey of Current Business* (quarterly estimates published in the January, April, July, and October issues); an annual publication, *Local Area Personal Income*, presents personal income by major type of payment, earnings by major industry, and total and per capita personal income for states, counties, and metropolitan areas.
Frequency: Quarterly
When available: Month following the end of the quarter; annual data for states are available in the April issue of *Survey of Current Business*
Revisions: Initial revisions of local and state estimates are published in the April issue of *Survey of Current Business*. For the following four years, local and state estimates are routinely revised in the August issue of *Survey of Current Business*. After the fourth year revision, estimates are revised only when benchmark revisions are made to the national income and product accounts, which is every five years.
Historic data: *State Personal Income: 1929–87* — Estimates of annual personal income and disposable personal income, total and per capita, for 1929 to 1987; includes annual personal income by major type of payment and earnings by industry for those years. The estimates are for each state and eight BEA

regions. A comprehensive statement of sources and methods used for estimating state personal income is included.

Cross references: Personal Income and Gross National Product in Chapter 7, beginning on page 121.

■ **A QUICK LOOK: Regional Personal Income**

Personal income is income received by households before the payment of income taxes. It includes income from wages and fringe benefits, profits from self-employment, rent, interest, dividends, Social Security benefits, unemployment insurance, food stamps, and other income maintenance programs. It is one of the best measures of comparative living standards of people living in various regions and states of the country. Personal income is available by region, state, and metropolitan area in the following volumes of *Local Area Personal Income*, published annually by the Bureau of Economic Analysis:

Volume 1. Summary: Regions, States, and Metropolitan Areas

Volume 2: New England, Mideast and Great Lakes Regions (Connecticut, Delaware, District of Columbia, Illinois, Indiana, Maine, Maryland, Massachusetts, Michigan, New Hampshire, New Jersey, New York, Ohio, Pennsylvania, Rhode Island, Vermont, and Wisconsin)

Volume 3: Plains Region (Iowa, Kansas, Minnesota, Missouri, Nebraska, North Dakota, and South Dakota)

Volume 4: Southeast Region (Alabama, Arkansas, Florida, Georgia, Kentucky, Louisiana, Mississippi, North Carolina, South Carolina, Tennessee, Virginia, and West Virginia)

Volume 5: Southwest, Rocky Mountain, and Far West Regions and Alaska and Hawaii. (Alaska, Arizona, California, Colorado, Hawaii, Idaho, Montana, Nevada, New Mexico, Oklahoma, Oregon, Texas, Utah, Washington, and Wyoming).

Each state has personal income data for counties.

Name: Shipments to Federal Government Agencies
Alternative name: Local Purchases Made by Federal Agents
Agency/Institution: Bureau of the Census, Department of Commerce
Address: FOB #4, Room 2232, Washington, DC 20230
Telephone number for data and inquiries: 301-763-2502
Sources: *Shipments to Federal Government Agencies*
Frequency: Annual budget cuts have made this an erratic publication. Year 1992 will be available perhaps in 1993 or 1994.

■ **A QUICK LOOK: Shipments to Federal Government Agencies**

This series has been published since 1963 to measure the impact of federal government spending on geographical areas and to provide data that legislators can use to show their constituents how effective they are in Washington. Data are obtained from a sample of 7000 plants in 92 industries that historically have been major direct suppliers to the federal government. Firms that supply more than $1 million report their shipments to federal agencies. Data are shown by four-digit industry groups and for major states and SMSAs.

CHAPTER 16

GOVERNMENT

Governments are an integral part of the American economy. They tax income and goods; make capital investments in roads, buildings, and education; purchase materials; and employ millions of workers. Some governments, such as the TVA and state liquor stores, even organize and administer business units. The United States is characterized by a large number of independent government units, although that number has decreased significantly since 1942 because of the consolidation movement of the postwar period and the disappearance of some small towns (see Table 16.1).

TABLE 16.1
Number of Government Units in the United States

	1942	1967	1987
Total	155,116	81,299	83,237
States:	48	50	50
Local Governments	155,067	81,248	83,186
County	3,050	3,049	3,042
Municipal	16,220	18,048	19,200
Township and town	18,919	17,105	16,691
School district	108,579	21,782	14,721
Special district	8,299	21,264	29,532

Government budgets receive a great deal of coverage in the media, in corporate and government offices, and in university classrooms, but seldom are we able to find a cogent discussion of the budgetary practices and accounting procedures that underlie the data. Although the accounting profession has rules and guidelines for government accounting, it has not developed suitable guidelines for budgetary procedures. The result is a stream of budgetary changes and much confusion, especially at the federal level, about the meanings, trends, and usefulness of budgetary data.[1] Budgets are detailed documents that present the spending and taxing plans of the administration. They are not the documents that guide and determine the actual spending and taxing of governments; these are determined by bills passed by legislatures. However, generally, most of the detailed data contained in the budget do get legislated because legislatures don't have the time to go over each account. Most budget documents are excellent sources of actual expenditures in prior years.

Name: The Federal Budget
Alternative name: Federal Government Budgets, Expenditures, Receipts, and Deficits.
Agency/Institution: Office of Management and Budget
Address: Old Executive Office Building, Washington, DC 20500
Telephone number for data: 202-395-3080
Sources: *Budget of the United States*
Frequency: Annually
When available: Congress has specified that the budget be available on the first Monday in February.
Revisions: The budget is composed of estimates, but the actual data are given for the current and recent fiscal years. No revisions are published.
Historic data: Historical tables have been available in recent budget documents. See below.

■ A QUICK LOOK: The Federal Budget

The federal budget document contains information on nearly 200,000 federal programs printed on more than 1500 pages crammed with budgetary data, terms, concepts, and program explanations. It contains budget data by program, function, and agency. A cursory reading of the budget document quickly reveals that there are many versions of the budget — and these produce widely different estimates of deficits and surpluses.

---

[1]One of the more comprehensive and readable sources of information on government revenues and expenditures is *Facts and Figures on Government Finance*, published by Tax Foundation, Incorporated (One Thomas Circle, N.W., Washington, DC 20005). The main sources of information on federal revenue and expenditures are the *Budget of the United States*, the *Treasury Bulletin*, the *Annual Report of the Secretary of the Treasury*, and the national income and product accounts. The basic source of data on the operations of state and local governments and all governments combined is the Government Division, Bureau of the Census, Department of Commerce. This division publishes comparable data for local, state, and federal governments. It takes data directly from the various governments and adjusts them to make them comparable.

Even the unified budget, which is the official budget of the United States, can be displayed in many different ways, one of which is shown in Table 16.2. The terms used in this and other variations of the unified budget are also given. For a more thorough understanding of the budget and the budgetary process, read the "Closer Look" section that follows.

TABLE 16.2
The Unified Budget by Fund Groups
(FY 1992)

	1992 Estimates Billions of $
Receipts	
On-Budget:	
Federal funds	712.4
Trust funds	293.4
Interfund transactions	−156.0
Total, on-budget receipts	849.8
Off-Budget:	
Federal funds	
Trust funds	315.3
Total, off-budget receipts	315.3
Total, federal receipts	1,165.0
Outlays	
On-Budget:	
Federal funds	1,119.1
Trust funds	231.1
Interfund transactions	−156.0
Total, on-budget outlays	1,194.2
Off-Budget:	
Federal funds	−1.1
Trust funds	252.8
Total, off-budget outlays	251.7
Total, federal outlays	1,445.9
Surplus or deficit (−)	
On-Budget:	
Federal funds	−406.8
Trust funds	62.4
Total, on-budget deficit	−344.4
Off-Budget:	
Federal funds	1.1
Trust funds	62.4
Total, off-budget surplus	63.6
Total overall federal government deficit	−280.9

Note: Totals may differ slightly because of rounding.

Unified budget: Official budget of the United States since 1969. Generally it shows details for on-budget, off-budget, and total budgets. There are various forms in which the unified budget can be presented — this is only one of them.

Receipts: Collections resulting from the government's exercise of its sovereign power to tax or otherwise compel payment. Receipts include money collected from taxes, duties, and premiums from social insurance programs. Federal government receipts do not include collections from business activities conducted by government. Revenue from business-related activities are deducted from gross outlays rather than included in receipts. For example, the revenue received by the Department of Commerce from its sales of booklets on international trade is treated as a reduction in the net outlays of the Commerce Department instead of an increase in receipts.

Outlays: These measure actual government spending during the fiscal year. Outlays are sometimes equated with cash outlays, but this is not correct. Outlays now include noncash subsidy costs of direct loans and loan guarantees and interest accrued on public debt.

Federal funds: These comprise most expenditures in the budget and include all transactions not classified by law as being in trust funds. The main component of federal funds is general funds, which are those funds used for the general purposes of the government and include all receipts not earmarked by law to finance other funds, including virtually all income taxes, and all outlays financed by these receipts and by general Treasury borrowing.

Trust funds: Funds financed by taxes and other receipts earmarked by law for specific purposes. The major trust funds are Social Security, medicare, unemployment compensation, federal employee retirement, highway construction, and airport and airway development.

On-budget: Programs or agencies that have not been declared by Congress to be off-budget. The net balance of on-budget expenditures and receipts should guide Congress and the administration in determining the nation's fiscal policy. The problem is that many programs or agencies that are not on-budget are very influential in affecting fiscal decisions. Also, there is a "shadow on-budget" list that is not identical with the official on-budget list. (See the further discussion in the "Closer Look" section.)

Off-budget: Programs or agencies that have been excluded from the federal budget by law. Presumably, the receipts and expenditures of these programs do not or should not be included in the formation of fiscal policy. However, many, if not most, of the off-budget deficits/surpluses are actually considered in the "shadow on-budget."

Interfund transactions: The outlays of a fund in one group that are the receipts of a fund in another group, such as the payment of interest on Treasury debt (from a general fund) to the Social Security fund (to a trust fund). Since receipts from interfund transactions are not receipts from the public and outlays are not outlays to the public, these transactions must be netted out so that budget totals for receipts and outlays will include only transactions with the public.

Total budget: Total receipts and expenditures represent all transactions between the federal government and the public.

■ **A CLOSER LOOK: The Federal Budget**

The Budget Document

Warning! Reading and trying to understand the federal budget may be harmful to your mental health. The federal government is so immense and its activities are so numerous and diverse that it is virtually impossible for anyone to obtain complete knowledge of the government budget. The 1992 budget contained 2026 pages, and weighed more than 7 pounds. If you spent only one minute examining each of the 200,000 federal programs, it would take you more than a year and a half, working eight hours a day, five days a week, to go through the accounts — and these are only the summary accounts of other budgetary decisions and allocations. Needless to say, no one has mastered the content of the entire federal budget. And even if you learned its current format, it is as certain as death and taxes that the format will change. In fact, there is a good chance that within the next few years the 25-year-old unified budget (the official budget of the United States) will be replaced by one of several other budget formats currently being discussed. Simply put, there is no such concept as *the* federal budget because there are so many ways of putting a budget together. Thus, we have to be careful in using data on federal revenues, expenditures, and deficits. Every year the budget document reveals some ingenious new ways of putting budgetary data together that provide additional definitions of the deficit. There are baseline budgets, policy budgets, unified budgets, consolidated budgets, national income budgets, funds budgets, and many more. And many of these budgets can be combined with other budgets to produce an almost unlimited number of budget variations.

Generally, every modern federal budget contains the following information:

- Budget message of the president, which is one or two pages of general highlights
- Budget message of the director of the Office of Management and Budget, which is usually an introduction to the budget and the budgetary innovations that are introduced this year
- Explanations of major administrative programs
- Discussions and tables of alternative economic assumptions
- Discussion and tables of alternative budget formats, including receipts, expenditures, deficits, and surpluses
- Budget data arranged by programs, functions, and agencies
- Data on tax expenditures

The most important sections of the federal budget are those showing revenue and expenditure estimates. Based on certain economic assumptions, the revenue section shows estimated budget receipts by major source, such as individual income taxes, corporate income taxes, excise taxes, and custom duties. Most revenue and expenditure tables in the budget give actual revenue and expenditure data for the previous year (a very useful source of reasonably hard data), estimates for the current fiscal year, and estimates for the following two budget years. For example, the FY 1992 budget, sent to Congress by the president in January 1991, showed actual revenues and expenditures for FY 1990, estimates for FY 1991 (which ended on September 30, 1991), estimates for the fiscal year being discussed in this budget (FY 1992), and rough estimates for 1993 and 1994.

Proposed expenditures, also called **outlays**, are displayed in two fundamentally different formats: by function and by agency. For most purposes, the functional presentation of budget spending is the most important because it lists total expenditures for a particular government program regardless of the agencies actually administering the programs. For example, housing, international affairs, health care services, and national defense are listed as separate functions regardless of the agencies providing these services. Expenditures are also shown by agency, such as the Department of Transportation, Department of Defense, and Department of Housing and Urban Development. These agency budgets are most useful for accounting and auditing purposes.

The budget document also contains information and data on tax expenditures. The Congressional Budget Act of 1974 requires that a list of tax expenditures be included in the budget, and it defines tax expenditures as "revenue losses attributable to provisions of the Federal tax laws which allow a special exclusion, exemption, or deduction from gross income, or which provide a special credit, a preferential rate of tax or a deferral of liability." Tax expenditures are one means by which the federal government pursues public policy objectives and are an alternative means of achieving the same objectives pursued by other government policy instruments, such as direct expenditures and regulation. The cost of medical care, for example, is reduced by direct government expenditures for Medicare and Medicaid, and by permitting individuals to exclude from income the medical insurance payments that employers pay for their employees. Government expenditures are made for social welfare purposes, and individuals are allowed to deduct from their taxable income their contributions to social agencies. Tax expenditures include accelerated depletion for oil and gas developments, exclusion of scholarship and fellowship income, exclusion of Social Security benefits, deductibility of medical expenses, and many others. The budget document is an excellent source of information on amounts of recent tax expenditures.

The Budgetary Process

The budgetary process begins deep in the burrows of the federal bureaucracy, with thousands of subagencies assembling data they hope will convince legislators and high-level bureaucrats that their programs should be expanded. The simple process of keeping track of these requests and their relative merits is a complex job. Evaluating these requests is a herculean task. It is difficult to understand today that prior to 1921, federal agencies took their budgetary requests directly to Congress, with virtually no review process by the president or his staff. Today the budget is far too complicated for such a direct approach, so the Office of Management and Budget (OMB) has been assigned the task of evaluating, approving, and modifying the requests of each agency; formulating the budget; and proposing tax changes. It is the OMB's budget that the president submits to Congress every year. After each agency's budget has run the gauntlet of its own department and that of the OMB, it must traverse the mine fields of Congress, which has its own budgetary process independent of the administration. The timing of this combative budgetary process is determined by the fiscal year. Prior to 1977, the federal fiscal year began on July 1 and ended 12 months later on June 30. Beginning in 1977, the federal fiscal year has begun October 1 and has ended September 30; fiscal year 1993 ends on September 30, 1993.[2]

Work on the budget begins about two years before the start of the fiscal year, or about December 1990 for the FY 1993 budget. Around May 1991, OMB discusses the budget with the president and his advisers, the Treasury works up revenue and tax estimates, and OMB begins working more intensively with agencies who have been toiling on their budgets since December. "Revised formal estimates" are resubmitted by the agencies to the OMB during the fall of 1991, when further pruning and refinements are made. The president formally presents the FY 1993 budget to Congress in January 1992. Congress begins preliminary work during the spring of 1992, and the Budget Committee writes up a concurrent resolution establishing temporary expenditure and revenue targets.

The Constitution requires that all appropriations originate in the House, so the House Appropriations Committee and its subcommittees hold hearings in which agency officials and experts are called to testify. The recommendations of each subcommittee are submitted to the Appropriations Committee, which reviews and merges the recommendations before sending the appropriations bill to the House to be voted on. The Congressional Budget Office, which is the congressional counterpart of the OMB, provides budgetary information and analyses to Congress and

---

[2]Most state governments have a fiscal year beginning July 1 and ending June 30, whereas many local governments have a fiscal year ending December 31. Most local government data gathered by the Census Bureau have been adjusted to fiscal years ending June 30.

its numerous committees. After approval by the House, the budget bill is sent to the Senate, where it follows a similar procedure. Differences between the House and the Senate are ironed out in a conference committee. After passage by both houses, the bill is sent to the president, who can sign the bill or veto it but he cannot change or veto individual items. Basically, the president must spend the funds appropriated by Congress. If he does not want to spend all funds approved for a fiscal year or if he wants to delay the spending, he must get the approval of Congress. A *recission* is a presidential proposal not to spend an appropriation and a *deferral* is a presidential proposal to delay spending. Congress must explicitly approve the president's recission within 45 legislative days or the funds must be spent as Congress originally intended. A deferral can take effect unless Congress specifically passes legislation prohibiting it.

Budgetary Concepts

Before discussing the federal budget with your next door neighbor, you must at least know the relevant meanings of *authorization, appropriation, budget authority*, and *budget outlay*. The first step in establishing a new federal program is to have Congress pass an **authorization bill**. This authorization bill does *not* provide the funds for a program or permit a department to make commitments to spend program funds. With an authorization bill, Congress is saying, for example, "We would like to establish the Animal Clean Breath Program, to provide free dental care to dogs." This authorization bill will specify the maximum expenditure, say, $500 million over a period of five years. The authorization bill will also generally place the program in some department, say, in this example, the Department of Health and Human Services (DHHS). If no further legislative action is taken beyond the authorization bill, the Animal Clean Breath program will never exist because there are no funds for staff or expenditures.

Congress must pass another bill, called an **appropriation bill**, to provide funds for the program. The appropriation bill provides **budget authority** (BA) to the relevant agency, which means that the Department of Health and Human Services can now enter into contracts and hire employees for the Clean Breath program. Assume that you dig deep into the budget and find that the Clean Breath program was appropriated $80 million in the FY 1992 budget. Are you to interpret this appropriation to mean that DHHS will actually write checks totalling $80 million during the year? No, the appropriation merely means that DHHS has budget authority to obligate the government to spend this amount. The amount that is actually spent is called **budget outlay** (or expenditures). If Congress appropriates $80 million for FY 1992 but DHHS expects to spend only $60 million, the FY 1992 budget will show:

Budget Authority (appropriations)	$80 million
Budget Outlays	$60 million

Since both budget authority and outlays are found in federal budgetary data, it is essential that the user keep this distinction firmly in mind. Of the two, budget outlays are more important than budget authority because budget outlays are compared with revenues (also called *receipts*) when calculating budget deficits and surpluses.

Another term we frequently find in budget discussions is **obligational authority**, which is the sum of new budget authority obtained from Congress during the one year plus the balance of budget authority from prior years that has not yet been obligated. A related concept is the **obligated balance**, which is the total amount of budget authority obligated for a specific purpose but not yet actually spent or outlayed. Obligational authority and obligated balance are the same if the amount not spent is the same as the amount not obligated. If Congress votes additional budgetary authority of $80 million for the Clean Breath program for FY 1993, DHHS will have an obligated balance of $100 million because it has $20 million of budget authority that it did not spend the previous year. Budget outlays for FY 1993 could be, say, $90 million, which will be $10 million less than obligational authority but $10 million more than the new budget authority.

Figures for both budget authority and outlays are needed because many government activities cannot be completed within a single fiscal year, and it is important to know both the total cost (budget authority) and the amounts actually spent during the fiscal year (outlays). The construction of an aircraft carrier provides a good example of the distinction between budget authority and budget outlay. Budget authority in the first year will be quite large since it will reflect the entire cost of constructing the ship. In the second year there will be no new budget authority because the full cost was provided in the last year's budget. The same will be true for the remaining years of the construction period. Budget outlays will be small in the first year because it takes a long time to start construction. In the following years the outlays will increase even though there will be no new budget authority.

About 30 percent of total budget outlays in most years are the result of budget authority from prior years. Actual data from the FY 1991 budget show that new budget authority recommended for 1991 was $1397 billion, of which $753 billion was to be spent in that fiscal year, with $644 billion to be spent in future years. Total outlays in 1991 were budgeted to be $1233, with $753 coming from new authority in 1991 and $480 from unspent authority from previous years.

A great deal of discussion can be found in the media over "controllable" versus "uncontrollable" federal spending. Actually, all federal spending is controllable in the long run, but parts of the budget appear to be uncontrollable during any single budget year. Most apparently "uncontrollable" spending — about 75 percent of the total budget — results from prior budget authority, entitlements, and budget authority provided through permanent appropriations (for example, interest on the national debt). These expenditures or outlays would exist even if Congress passed no new appropriations during the year. The most frequently mentioned class of "uncontrollable" expenditures are **entitlements**, which are particular types of authorization that require the government to pay benefits to any person meeting the eligibility requirements established by Congress. Although an entitlement requires an appropriation before funds can be spent, it differs from other authorizations because it constitutes a legally binding commitment on the federal government. Examples of entitlement programs are Medicaid, Medicare, Social Security, and veterans' benefits.

Now for the really tough part of understanding federal budget data. The current "official" budget of the federal government, which was adopted in 1969, is called the **unified budget**. It evolved out of the old consolidated cash budget (which included trust funds) and the administrative budget (which excluded trust funds). Although the adoption of the unified budget, which is supposed to include all fiscal transactions of the federal government with the public, was intended to settle the controversy over the budgetary treatment of trust funds, a continuing debate over the content of the budget has grown more vociferous over the years. The ink on the act adopting the unified budget as the "official budget" was not even dry when an exemption was made for the Import-Export Bank, stating that its receipts and expenditures were not to be included in the unified budget. Within a few years, several federal programs and agencies were removed from the budget or created outside of the unified budget. Thus, budgetary accountants, members of Congress, and the media began to increasingly mention "on-budget" and "off-budget" programs. Soon the unified budget itself began incorporating the "on-budget" and "off-budget" distinction.

The "on-budget" versus "off-budget" differentiation often gets confused with other distinctions, such as those between federal funds and trust funds. Federal funds, which comprise most expenditures in the budget, include all transactions not classified by law as being in trust funds. The main component of federal funds is the general fund, which is used for the general purposes of the government and includes all receipts (virtually all income taxes) not earmarked by law to finance other funds. In addition to general funds, federal funds include special funds and revolving funds. **Special funds** are funds financed by revenues earmarked for specific purposes (for example, license fees deposited into the land and water conservation fund); **revolving funds**, such as the Postal Service fund, are funds that use the proceeds from the sale of products or services to finance their own spending. The proceeds of the revolving funds are credited to the fund that makes the expenditure.

Trust funds are financed by taxes and other receipts earmarked by law for specific purposes. The major trust funds are Social Security, Medicare, unemployment compensation, federal employee retirement, highway construction, and airport and airway development. Although these funds are commonly called "trust funds," this term, in relation to government trust funds, has a different meaning from the term "trusts" or "trust funds" as used in the private sector. Unlike the private sector, in which "trusts" mean assets held in a fiduciary capacity for someone else, federal trust funds and their corresponding assets are owned not by the presumed beneficiary but by the federal government, which can change the rules governing receipts and expenditures. Trust funds are really like special funds or revolving funds — they are designated as "trust funds" by Congress more for political than for economic or accounting reasons.

Federal funds programs are often thought to be on-budget, whereas trust fund programs are equated with off-budget. Although many trust funds were off-budget at one time, this simple dichotomy is simply incorrect. Until 1986, Social Security, a trust fund, was included with on-budget items. On-budget receipts and outlays include both federal funds and trust funds, and off-budget accounts consist of both federal funds and trust funds. Social Security, a trust fund, and the Postal Service, a federal fund, have been officially listed as off-budget items since 1986 and 1989, respectively, but this classification can change at any time.

When a budgetary program is off-budget, its receipts, outlays, and surpluses or deficits are supposedly not included in budget receipts and outlays, but this distinction often becomes blurred if not meaningless. On-budget and off-budget totals may even be added together to arrive at total receipts, outlays, and surplus or deficit of the federal government. This is done in most presentations of the unified budget. Off-budget does not mean "not reported" or "not viewed" or "not considered" because off-budget items are included in the unified budget. In fact, despite the number of debates and laws related to placing programs on-budget or off-budget, it is difficult to explain the ramifications and distinctions of on-budget versus off-budget. Among the most important of recent laws pertaining to the budgetary classification of Social Security and other programs have been the Gramm-Rudman-Hollings Act, the Omnibus Act of 1989, and the Omnibus Act of 1990. The Balanced Budget and Emergency Deficit Control Act of 1985 (the Gramm-Rudman-Hollings Act, or G-R-H) placed on-budget all programs that were then off-budget. However, it moved Social Security from on-budget to off-budget.[3]

After the passage of G-R-H, it seemed reasonable to expect that when Congress was contemplating and attempting to "balance" the budget, it would be concerned only with on-budget items, which now excluded

---

[3]Social Security, which had been on-budget since the origin of the unified budget in 1969, had been scheduled by a 1983 law to go off-budget in 1993, but G-R-H accelerated the movement to get it off-budget in 1986. Social Security consists of Old Age and Survivors' Insurance (OASI), disability insurance (DI), and hospital insurance (HI). The 1983 law required that all three be put off-budget by 1993, but the G-R-H law allowed only HI to stay on-budget until 1993 while requiring that OASI and DI be taken off-budget in 1986.

Social Security. However, this was not the case. The G-R-H Act moved Social Security off-budget, but it retained the program in a "shadow budget" for purposes of calculating G-R-H deficit targets. Hence, the largest off-budget program was still, in effect, an integral part of budget deliberations and calculations. Budgetary confusion had increased by a couple of notches. The G-R-H Act, which required the federal government to move toward a balanced budget by 1994, was dealing not just with the on-budget items but rather with all on-budget programs plus Social Security. Budgetary chaos was increased another notch when the Omnibus Budget Reconciliation Act of 1989 moved the Postal Service from on-budget to off-budget. Nearly 30 percent of the federal government's total revenue and 20 percent of its outlays were now off-budget.

Before discussing two bills passed in 1990 that might help alleviate this budgetary confusion, we need to identify other sources of budgetary confusion. In addition to the clutter and bewilderment arising from the distinction (or lack of it) between on-budget and off-budget items and between the items that are (or should be) included in the deficit targets, there are off-off-budget outlays that do not get picked up even in the off-budget category. Many of these programs are related to the credit activities of government-sponsored enterprises that are financial intermediaries and totally excluded from the budget on the grounds that they are private. Loan guarantees generally do not result in budget outlays except in the case of default; and insurance, whether credit related or not, does not result in budget outlays unless the insured event actually occurs.

The major source of budgetary chaos, however, is politics and the lack of time-honored professional standards of how new government activities should be treated on the accounts' ledger sheets. One indication of the political implications of budget composition is given by the FY 1991 budget. Off-budget items (primarily Social Security) for FY 1991 had an estimated surplus of $78.6 billion, but on-budget items had an estimated deficit of $141.7 billion. If the on-budget and off-budget accounts were consolidated, the federal deficit would be "reduced" to only $63.1 billion. The Republicans, representing the administration, would then claim that the budget deficit was $63.1 billion. The Democrats, however, would reject such a consolidation and would claim that the deficit was $141.7 billion. And those who lobby for larger government expenditures would claim the size of the deficit to be only $63.1 billion, and would claim that now the country could afford to increase government expenditures.

The lack of agreement on the content of the federal budget has not only produced confusion among those who have to make budgetary decisions but it has made life difficult for researchers who analyze trends in budgetary receipts, outlays, and deficits and surpluses. Our discussion should have made it clear that we cannot compare deficits and surpluses over time unless the budgetary methodology is consistent over the years.

The composition of various accounts in the official budget is reasonably clear if we dig through the 2000 pages of the budget itself, but secondary data are often foggy because they seldom mention whether Social Security, credit subsidies, and other off-budget items are included in the net budgetary data. Even after carefully examining the descriptions and definitions accompanying the data, it is often difficult to determine what is included in the budget's totals, deficits, or surpluses.

Two bills passed by Congress in 1990, which are to take effect between FY 1992 and FY 1995, will, hopefully, streamline the budgetary process, lessen the confusion in the data series, and make budget comparisons more meaningful. The Omnibus Budget Reconciliation Act of 1990 (OBRA) and the Budget Enforcement Act of that same year substantially modify the Gramm-Rudman-Hollings (G-R-H Act) deficit reduction targets and make some major changes in budgetary compositions.

First, OBRA not only keeps Social Security off-budget but removes it from future deficit targets and sequestration; that is, it "really" takes Social Security off-budget by excluding it from inclusion in any targets for deficit reductions. In addition, the act includes so-called "fire wall" provisions intended to make it slightly more difficult for Congress to spend the projected buildup of Social Security reserves on higher benefits or lower Social Security taxes. The purpose of the "fire wall" is to protect the surplus of the Social Security trust fund and, hopefully, to encourage saving.

Perhaps a few sentences explaining the importance of Social Security in the budgetary process will clear away any confusion. If Social Security revenues and expenditures are included in the calculation of the budget deficit, the deficit will be reduced because significant surpluses in Social Security are now accumulating to help pay for the retirement of the baby boomers. However, these "lowered" deficits, it is feared, will simply encourage Congress and the administration to spend more or to reduce Social Security taxes. If Social Security is truly placed off-budget — not included anywhere in the budget — the government's deficit cannot be reduced by the surplus in the Social Security account. It is always tempting for current politicians to reduce the deficit by including Social Security in the budget or to gain political favor by voting to reduce Social Security tax rates. The "fire wall" guarding the isolation of Social Security is necessary to avoid congressional tampering with the budgetary treatment of Social Security or with Social Security rates. Hopefully, the larger deficits that result from actually placing Social Security off-budget will encourage Congress to reduce the deficit. If the federal budget is gradually brought into balance, the surpluses will be used to reduce publicly held federal debt, add to private capital formation, and increase real GNP.

The Budget Enforcement Act (BEA) does much more than take Social Security out of the budget and remove it from deficit reduction targets. It extends and substantially revises the budget targets and sequestration process that were part of the G-R-H Act. The BEA divides the budget into two mutually exclusive categories: discretionary programs and direct spending and receipts. **Discretionary programs** are those whose program levels are established annually through the normal congressional appropriations process. The BEA limits budget authority and outlays available for discretionary programs each year through 1995. Appropriations that exceed the BEA limits will trigger a **sequester**,[4] and budgetary authority and outlays in that category will be reduced. Limits are specified for three categories of discretionary programs: defense, international, and domestic. The limits (also called *caps*) on each of these three categories are enforced independently. Savings in defense, for example, cannot be used to increase spending in domestic programs. These separate categories for discretionary programs disappear after 1995, when there will be an overall cap for total discretionary budget authority and outlays. These limits are adjusted for inflation and changes in budgetary accounting.

The nondiscretionary part of the budget is direct spending and receipts; these are subject to a pay-as-you-go requirement, which means that direct spending and receipts must either be deficit neutral or must reduce the budget. The BEA defines direct spending as all budget authority other than normal annual appropriations acts, entitlement authority, and the food stamp program. Deficit neutrality of direct spending programs is also enforced through sequesters. As legislation of direct spending and receipts is passed during the year, a sequester "scorecard" is kept, and at the end of the legislative year the scorecard reports the estimated cumulative net impact on the deficit of those actions for both the fiscal year that just ended and the fiscal year just beginning. If the estimated deficit exceeds the maximum deficit amounts by more than the allowed margin there will be an enforced sequester of authority and expenditure in that budget year. Social Security, Postal Service, certain low-income programs, retirement programs, veterans' benefits, and the FDIC are exempt from sequester. Other programs, such as Medicare, are not exempt, but a sequester reduction is limited to 4 percent annually.

Credit Reforms in the Budget

The federal government is the largest source of credit and the largest underwriter of risk in the country. At the end of 1990 the amount of outstanding federal and federally assisted credit and insurance was $6.2 trillion (113 percent of GDP). About one-half of all nonfederal borrowing is

---

[4]A sequester is an automatic decrease in government expenditures.

related to federal credit programs, government-sponsored enterprises (GSEs), or federal deposit insurance. Federal insurance programs include deposit insurance, pension guarantees, flood insurance, federal crop insurance, aviation war risk insurance, veterans' life insurance, and maritime risk insurance. Federal credit and GSEs extend direct or indirect credit for housing, education, and agriculture.

Previously, federal credit activities were excluded from the budget (both on-budget and off-budget) at the time the loans were made or guaranteed. Thus, loans and loan guarantees were made without any budgetary evaluation of likely defaults. Appropriation bills were passed to pay for defaults only after such defaults had actually occurred, and Congress could do little else but legislate the funds. The Federal Credit Reform Act of 1990, part of OBRA, made ground-breaking changes in the budgetary treatment of these credit activities.

Let's look at some background information on federal loans and guarantees. Unlike private loans, federal direct loans and loan guarantees are not made on the premise that the present value of repayments, interest, and fees will be at least as large as the amount of the loans made. Rather, federal credit programs exist to provide benefits to certain classes of borrowers or to channel resources to certain political or economic sectors and, in most cases, they are expected to produce losses to the government. Consequently, a subsidy and a loan or guarantee are combined in a single transaction. As mentioned earlier, federal budgeting and accounting until now failed to recognize this dual nature of credit programs, but the Federal Credit Reform Act of 1990 requires that all future losses (subsidies) be officially recognized at the time the loans or guarantees are made. The expected costs resulting from loan defaults — a measure of the credit subsidy — will now be included in the outlays of the programs and the agencies that conduct the credit program.

The new law requires that federal agencies include in their requested budget authority an amount to cover the estimated subsidy costs of all federal direct loans and all guarantees when they are made. The subsidy costs are calculated as the difference between the present value of the expected cash outflows from the government and the present value of the expected cash inflows, each discounted by the interest rate on marketable Treasury securities of like maturity at the time of loan disbursement.

The credit reform provisions of OBRA will be effective for direct loan obligations and loan guarantee commitments made in 1992 and beyond. Unfortunately, historic data cannot be converted to this new measurement basis. Thus, data prior to 1992 are based on a cash flow or pre–credit reform basis. Data for 1992 and beyond will reflect the subsidy cost of post–credit reform concepts for the 40 or so budget programs providing direct loans or loan guarantees.

Government-sponsored enterprises (GSEs), which are privately owned entities originally established and chartered by the federal government to provide certain loans and loan guarantees, are not covered by the credit reform laws. Their loans and loan guarantees are still not picked up in the federal budget. Most GSEs borrow in the securities market and lend their borrowed funds for specifically authorized purposes either directly or by purchasing loans originated by private lenders. Government sponsorship gives GSEs various benefits. Their securities can collateralize Treasury deposits, and they can be held in unlimited amounts by banks and thrifts. GSEs are exempt from SEC registration, and their corporate earnings are exempt from state and local income taxation. At the discretion of the Treasury, they may borrow up to $4 billion, and because of their special treatment GSEs can borrow at lower interest rates in the bond market.

GSEs include, among others, Federal Home Loan Banks, the Federal National Mortgage Association (Fannie Mae), the Federal Home Loan Mortgage Corporation (Freddie Mac), the Student Loan Marketing Association, and the Farm Credit System. The Federal Credit Reform Act has not required any significant changes in accounting for GSE loans, but it has required an analysis of the financial exposure they pose to government, and the OMB and Congress are now considering whether to extend recent credit reforms to GSEs.

HISTORIC DATA: Summary of Federal Receipts, Outlays, and Surpluses or Deficits (millions of $)

	TOTAL BUDGET				TOTAL BUDGET		
	Receipts	Outlays	Surplus Deficits ()		Receipts	Outlays	Surplus Deficits ()
1901	$ 588	$ 525	$63	1919	$5,130	$18,493	$(13,363)
1902	562	485	77	1920	6,649	6,358	291
1903	562	517	45	1921	5,571	5,062	509
1904	541	584	(43)	1922	4,026	3,289	737
1905	544	567	(23)	1923	3,853	3,140	713
1906	595	570	25	1924	3,871	2,908	963
1907	666	579	87	1925	3,641	2,924	717
1908	602	659	(57)	1926	3,795	2,930	865
1909	604	694	(90)	1927	4,013	2,857	1,156
1910	676	694	(18)	1928	3,900	2,961	939
1911	702	691	11	1929	3,862	3,127	735
1912	693	690	3	1930	4,058	3,320	738
1913	714	715	(1)	1931	3,116	3,577	(461)
1914	725	726	(1)	1932	1,924	4,659	(2,735)
1915	683	746	(63)	1933	1,997	4,598	(2,601)
1916	761	713	48	1934	2,955	6,541	(3,586)
1917	1,101	1,954	(853)	1935	3,609	6,412	(2,803)
1918	3,645	12,677	(9,032)	1936	3,923	8,228	(4,305)

(continued)

HISTORIC DATA: Summary of Federal Receipts, Outlays, and Surpluses or Deficits *(continued)*
(millions of $)

	TOTAL BUDGET			ON-BUDGET			OFF-BUDGET		
	Receipts	Outlays	Surplus Deficits ()	Receipts	Outlays	Surplus Deficit ()	Receipts	Outlays	Surplus Deficit ()
1937	$5,387	$7,580	$(2,193)	$5,122	$7,582	$(2,460)	$265	$(2)	$267
1938	6,751	6,840	(89)	6,364	6,850	(486)	387	(10)	397
1939	6,295	9,141	(2,846)	5,792	9,154	(3,362)	503	(13)	516
1940	6,548	9,468	(2,920)	5,998	9,482	(3,484)	550	(14)	564
1941	8,712	13,653	(4,941)	8,024	13,618	(5,594)	688	35	653
1942	14,634	35,137	(20,503)	13,738	35,071	(21,333)	896	66	830
1943	24,001	78,555	(54,554)	22,871	78,466	(55,595)	1,130	89	1,041
1944	43,747	91,304	(47,557)	42,455	91,190	(48,735)	1,292	114	1,178
1945	45,159	92,712	(47,553)	43,849	92,569	(48,720)	1,310	143	1,167
1946	39,296	55,232	(15,936)	38,058	55,022	(16,964)	1,238	210	1,028
1947	38,514	34,496	4,018	37,055	34,193	2,862	1,459	303	1,156
1948	41,560	29,764	11,796	39,944	29,396	10,548	1,616	368	1,248
1949	39,415	38,835	580	37,725	38,408	(683)	1,690	427	1,263
1950	39,443	42,562	(3,119)	37,337	42,038	(4,701)	2,106	524	1,582
1951	51,616	45,514	6,102	48,496	44,237	4,259	3,120	1,277	1,843
1952	66,167	67,686	(1,519)	62,573	65,956	(3,383)	3,594	1,730	1,864
1953	69,608	76,101	(6,493)	65,511	73,771	(8,260)	4,097	2,330	1,767
1954	69,701	70,855	(1,154)	65,112	67,943	(2,831)	4,589	2,912	1,677
1955	65,451	68,444	(2,993)	60,370	64,461	(4,091)	5,081	3,983	1,098

(continued)

HISTORIC DATA: Summary of Federal Receipts, Outlays, and Surpluses or Deficits (continued)
(millions of $)

	TOTAL BUDGET			ON-BUDGET			OFF-BUDGET		
	Receipts	Outlays	Surplus Deficit ()	Receipts	Outlays	Surplus Deficit ()	Receipts	Outlays	Surplus Deficit ()
1956	$74,587	$70,640	$3,947	$68,162	$65,668	$2,494	$6,425	$4,972	$1,453
1957	79,990	76,578	3,412	73,201	70,562	2,639	6,789	6,016	773
1958	79,636	82,405	(2,769)	71,587	74,902	(3,315)	8,049	7,503	546
1959	79,249	92,098	(12,849)	70,953	83,102	(12,149)	3,296	8,996	(700)
1960	92,492	92,191	301	81,851	81,341	510	10,641	10,850	(209)
1961	94,388	97,723	(3,335)	82,279	86,046	(3,767)	12,109	11,677	432
1962	99,676	106,821	(7,145)	87,405	93,286	(5,881)	12,271	13,535	(1,264)
1963	106,560	111,316	(4,756)	92,335	95,352	(3,967)	14,175	14,964	(789)
1964	112,613	118,528	(5,915)	96,247	102,794	(6,547)	16,366	15,734	632
1965	116,817	118,228	(1,411)	100,094	101,699	(1,605)	16,723	16,529	194
1966	130,835	134,532	(3,697)	111,750	114,817	(3,067)	19,085	19,715	(630)
1967	148,822	157,464	(8,642)	124,421	137,040	(12,619)	24,401	20,424	3,977
1968	152,973	178,134	(25,161)	128,056	155,798	(27,742)	24,917	22,336	2,581
1969	186,882	183,640	3,242	157,929	158,436	(507)	28,953	25,204	3,749
1970	192,807	195,649	(2,842)	159,348	168,042	(8,694)	33,459	27,607	5,852
1971	187,139	210,172	(23,033)	151,294	177,346	(26,052)	35,845	32,826	3,019
1972	207,309	230,681	(23,372)	167,402	193,824	(26,422)	39,907	36,857	3,050
1973	230,799	245,707	(14,908)	184,715	200,118	(15,403)	46,084	45,589	495
1974	263,224	269,359	(6,135)	209,299	217,270	(7,971)	53,925	52,089	1,836

(continued)

HISTORIC DATA: Summary of Federal Receipts, Outlays, and Surpluses or Deficits (continued)
(millions of $)

	TOTAL BUDGET			ON-BUDGET			OFF-BUDGET		
	Receipts	Outlays	Surplus Deficits ()	Receipts	Outlays	Surplus Deficit ()	Receipts	Outlays	Surplus Deficit ()
1975	$279,090	$332,332	$(53,242)	$216,632	$271,892	$(55,260)	$62,458	$60,440	$2,018
1976	298,060	371,779	(73,719)	231,671	302,170	(70,499)	66,389	69,609	(3,220)
1977	355,559	409,203	(53,644)	278,742	389,782	(111,040)	76,817	19,421	57,396
1978	399,561	458,729	(59,168)	314,170	378,013	(63,843)	85,391	80,716	4,675
1979	463,302	503,464	(40,162)	365,308	413,807	(48,499)	97,994	89,657	8,337
1980	517,112	590,920	(73,808)	403,903	490,942	(87,039)	113,209	99,978	13,231
1981	599,272	678,209	78,937	469,096	563,880	(94,784)	130,176	114,329	15,847
1982	617,766	745,706	(127,940)	474,299	610,510	(136,211)	143,467	135,196	8,271
1983	600,562	808,327	(207,765)	453,242	656,923	(203,681)	147,320	151,404	(4,084)
1984	666,457	851,781	(185,324)	500,382	704,673	(204,291)	166,075	147,108	18,967
1985	734,057	946,316	(212,259)	547,886	780,503	(232,617)	186,171	165,813	20,358
1986	769,091	990,258	(221,167)	568,863	813,451	(244,588)	200,228	176,807	23,421
1987	854,143	1,003,830	(149,687)	640,741	820,332	(179,591)	213,402	183,498	29,904
1988	908,954	1,064,051	(155,097)	667,463	870,219	(202,756)	241,491	193,832	47,659
1989	990,691	1,144,069	(153,378)	727,025	941,378	(214,353)	263,666	202,691	60,975
1990	1,031,308	1,251,703	(220,395)	749,652	1,026,711	(277,059)	281,656	225,065	56,590
1991	1,054,260	1,323,750	(269,492)	760,377	1,082,067	(321,690)	293,883	241,685	52,198

On- and off-budget data are available only from 1937.

Name: Federal Debt
Alternative name: National debt; Government Debt
Agency/Institution: U.S. Treasury
Address: 1500 Pennsylvania Ave., N.W., Washington, DC 20220
Telephone number for data and inquiries: 202-395-3000
Sources: Federal budget (annual), *President's Economic Report* (annual), *Treasury Bulletin* (monthly), and *Monthly Statement of the Public Debt of the United States*
Frequency: Monthly
When available: Two weeks after target month
Revisions: No policy
Historic data: See below.

■ **A QUICK LOOK: The Federal Debt**

There are many definitions of the federal debt and even more ways of showing its trend over time. Table 16.3 shows some of these definitions and presentations.

TABLE 16.3
Public Debt at End of Fiscal Year

	BILLIONS OF DOLLARS						PERCENTAGE OF GDP	
	Gross Public Debt	Less: Amount Held by Federal Government Accounts	Equals: Amount Held by Public	Less: Amount Held by Federal Reserve	Equals: Amount Held by Other Public	Foreign Held Debt As % of Net Other Public	Gross Federal Debt	Net Other Public
1990	3,365	828	2,539	260	2,277	18.5%	61.0%	41.3%
1991	3,802	969	2,833	288	2,545	18.0%	67.0%	44.9%

Public debt: Government debt can be issued by the Treasury or by government agencies. *Federal debt* is the total of the two, but *public debt* is only the debt that is issued by the Treasury. Securities issued by government agencies are called *agency debt*. None of the debt data reported in this table contain agency debt, which is only about 1.5 percent of total government debt. Generally, when the media refer to the debt of the federal government they mean the public debt.

Gross public debt: All Treasury debt, including securities held by government agencies, the public, the Federal Reserve Bank, and foreign residents and institutions.

Debt held by government accounts: Treasury debt held by government agencies, usually trust funds such as Social Security.

Debt held by the public: Treasury debt held by the public, including the Federal Reserve Bank.

Size of federal debt: There are many ways of reporting the size of the federal debt. First you have to decide what debt you want reported (total government, gross federal, net publicly held debt, or whatever) and then how you want to measure it. One meaningful measure is net publicly held debt as a percent of GDP (in Table 16.3, 41.3 percent), but there are many others.

■ A CLOSER LOOK: The Federal Debt

If you have read other sections of this chapter, you should be ready for the warning that the amount of the federal debt is not a simple, readily determinable number. The national debt varies significantly, depending on the source of the debt, the holder of the debt, and way in which the debt is measured.

The primary source of federal government debt is government budget deficits, which occur when government expenditures or outlays are greater than government receipts during one or more years. While a deficit can be financed by several other means, such as a decrease in the Treasury cash holdings, seignorage[5] on coins, and changes in checks outstanding, these are relatively insignificant. The primary means of financing a deficit is for the Treasury to sell bills, notes, and bonds.[6] These Treasury securities, which constitute most of the national debt, are known as the *public debt*. Another kind of federal debt, known as *agency debt*, results from certain government agencies issuing securities to finance their own activities. Agency debt outstanding in 1991 was less than 2 percent of total federal debt. The term *agency debt* has a different meaning for budgetary purposes than the broader *agency debt* used in the securities market. Financial analysts and brokers often use the term *agency debt* to include the securities not only of government agencies but also of government-sponsored enterprises. Statistics on the "federal debt" almost always exclude the debt of all government-sponsored enterprises, which is not included in agency debt.

Federal debt can be differentiated according to the "holders" of public debt. The most popular distinction is between debt held by the public and the debt held by federal government agencies. Many government agencies, such as Social Security and employee retirement trust funds, invest their surplus funds in Treasury securities. In fact, they are required to do so by law. However, the largest part of the debt is the debt held by the

---

[5]Seignorage is the profit on producing coins that is earned by the Treasury. It is the difference between the monetary value of the coins and the costs of producing them.

[6]The total deficit of the federal government includes not only the budget deficit but also the surplus or deficit of off-budget federal entities, which have been excluded from the budget by law. Under present law, off-budget federal entities are the old-age and survivors' insurance trust fund, the disability insurance trust fund, and the Postal Service fund. Since these funds had a large combined surplus during the past few years, they have reduced the requirement for the Treasury to borrow from the public.

public, which, for some reason, is defined to include the debt held by the Federal Reserve. Gross federal debt consists of both the debt held by the public (borrowed from the public) and the debt held by government accounts. Borrowing from the public, whether by the Treasury or some other federal agency, has a significant impact on the economy. It is a rough approximation to federal dissaving, which has to be financed by the saving of households and businesses, the state and local sector, or the rest of the world.[7] Treasury borrowing from the public also affects interest rates, crowding out of private investment, the size and composition of assets held by the private sector, and the perceived wealth of the public. It affects the amount of taxes required to pay interest outlays to the public. Borrowing from the public is therefore an important concern of federal fiscal policy. Debt sold to government agencies does not have any of the economic effects of borrowing from the public. It is an internal transaction between two accounts, both within the government. It does not represent either current transactions of the government with the public or an estimated amount of future transaction with the public.

During most of American history, the federal debt was held almost entirely by individuals and institutions residing within the United States. Foreign holdings of government debt began to increase in 1970, and by the end of 1991, foreign holdings of Treasury debt were $418 billion or 18 percent of the total debt held by the public. Foreign holdings of U.S. securities are now about one-fifth of the foreign-owned assets in the United States; and about 65 percent of the foreign-held debt is held by foreign central banks and other foreign institutions.

Debt held by the public was formerly measured as the par (face) value of the security, which is the principal amount due at maturity. This method of valuing outstanding federal securities overstated the amount of the national debt because the Treasury actually borrowed much less. If Treasury sells a bill with a $10,000 par value at a price of $9300, it raises $9300 in cash and finances $9300 of the deficit. For both budgetary and economic analysis, it is more meaningful to say that the government has borrowed $9300 than to say that it has borrowed $10,000. However, until 1990 the federal government reported the entire face value of $10,000 as the amount of the national debt. In 1990, the OMB corrected its procedures by adopting the accrual method of measuring all Treasury debt.[8] At the time of sale, the accrual value equals the sales price of the security.

---

[7]Actually the federal sector for the national income and product accounts (chapter 7) provides a better measure of the deficit for analyzing federal dissaving than does the budget deficit or federal borrowing from the public.

[8]The new accrual method applies only to Treasury bills and to zero-coupon bonds. Coupon bonds, which can sell at a premium or a discount, are recorded only at par value. Agency debt continues to be recorded at par.

Subsequently, the accrual value equals the sales price plus the amount of the discount that has been amortized up to that time. In equivalent terms, the accrual value equals the par value less the unamortized discount. Data series on national debt were revised back to 1956.

Debt Limits

Legislated limitations on the outstanding debt of the federal government have been in existence since 1917. The amount of debt subject to limit was formerly the par value of the securities, but since 1990 Treasury bills and zero-coupon bonds have been measured on an accrual basis. During the 1960s, Congress changed the statutory debt limit 13 times; during the 1970s, it changed the debt ceiling 18 times; and during the 1980s, it changed the ceiling 24 times. The current debt ceiling is $4145, which should be sufficient until 1993.

HISTORIC DATA: Federal Debt At End of Fiscal Year

	Gross Federal Debt	Less: Amount Held by Federal Government Accounts	Equals: Amount Held by Public	Less: Amount Held by Federal Reserve	Equals: Amount Held by Other Public	Foreign Held Debt As % of Net Other Public	Gross Federal Debt	Net Other Public
			BILLIONS OF DOLLARS				PERCENTAGE OF GNP	
1940	$51	$8	$43	$2	$41		52.9%	42.1%
1941	58	9	49	2	47		50.9	40.7
1942	79	11	68	3	65		55.7	45.8
1943	143	15	128	7	121		81.1	68.6
1944	204	19	185	15	170		101.0	84.1
1945	260	25	235	22	213		122.5	100.5
1946	271	29	242	24	218		127.3	102.4
1947	257	33	224	22	202		115.0	90.5
1948	252	36	216	21	195		101.7	78.7
1949	253	38	215	19	196		95.7	73.9
1950	257	38	219	18	201		96.3	75.2
1951	255	41	214	23	191		81.0	60.7
1952	259	44	215	23	192		75.7	56.0
1953	266	48	218	25	193		72.7	53.0
1954	271	46	225	25	200		73.3	54.0
1955	274	48	226	24	202		71.0	52.5
1956	273	51	222	24	198		65.2	47.5
1957	272	53	219	23	196		61.8	44.6

(continued)

HISTORIC DATA: Federal Debt At End of Fiscal Year *(continued)*

		BILLIONS OF DOLLARS					PERCENTAGE OF GNP	
	Gross Federal Debt	Less: Amount Held by Federal Government Accounts	Equals: Amount Held by Public	Less: Amount Held by Federal Reserve	Equals: Amount Held by Other Public	Foreign Held Debt As % of Net Other Public	Gross Federal Debt	Net Other Public
1958	$ 280	$53	$ 227	$25	$ 202		62.1%	44.6%
1959	287	53	234	26	208		59.7	43.3
1960	291	54	237	27	210		57.3	41.5
1961	293	54	239	27	212		56.5	40.7
1962	303	55	248	30	218		54.3	39.2
1963	310	56	254	32	222		52.8	37.8
1964	316	59	257	35	222		50.2	35.3
1965	322	62	260	39	221	5.6%	47.9	33.0
1966	328	65	263	42	221	5.2	44.5	30.0
1967	340	74	266	47	219	5.2	42.8	27.7
1968	369	79	290	52	238	4.5	43.4	27.9
1969	366	88	278	54	224	4.6	39.4	24.1
1970	381	98	283	58	225	6.2	38.5	22.8
1971	408	105	303	66	237	13.4	38.7	22.5
1972	436	114	322	71	251	19.6	37.8	21.8
1973	466	125	341	75	266	22.3	36.4	20.7
1974	484	140	344	81	263	21.6	34.2	18.6
1975	542	147	395	85	310	21.3	35.6	20.3
1976	629	152	477	95	382	18.3	37.0	22.5
1977	706	157	549	105	444	21.5	36.5	23.0
1978	777	169	608	115	493	24.5	35.8	22.6
1979	829	189	640	116	524	23.0	33.9	21.4
1980	909	199	710	121	589	20.7	34.0	22.0
1981	994	210	784	124	660	19.8	33.3	22.1
1982	1,137	218	919	134	785	17.9	36.2	25.0
1983	1,371	240	1,131	156	975	16.4	41.3	29.4
1984	1,564	264	1,300	155	1,145	15.3	42.4	31.0
1985	1,817	318	1,499	170	1,329	16.8	46.0	33.6
1986	2,120	384	1,736	191	1,545	17.2	50.7	37.0
1987	2,346	457	1,889	212	1,677	16.7	53.0	37.9
1988	2,601	551	2,050	229	1,821	19.0	54.4	38.1
1989	2,868	677	2,191	220	1,971	20.0	55.9	38.4
1990	3,365	828	2,537	260	2,277	18.5	61.0	41.3
1991	3,802	969	2,833	288	2,545	18.0	69.0	44.9

Name: Government Data
Agency: Bureau of the Census, Department of Commerce
Address: Washington, DC 20233
Telephone number for data and inquiries: 301-763-7789
Sources: Census of governments and annual and quarterly reports listed below.
Frequency: Every five years, in years ending in 2 and 7
When available: The census reports are available about three years after the end
   of the census year, while annual reports are available about five or six months
   after the end of the year.

■ A QUICK LOOK: Government Data

The federal government provides some very basic information on the
nation's government sector through the following publications:

* United States Dicennial Census
  The census of governments' coverage is broader than the coverage of
  the SIC category for public administration (major groups 91 through
  97); census coverage includes many activities in the service sector such
  as education and health care. Census data are published in the
  following:

  a. *Government Organization:* This is the first publication you should
     browse through if you are unfamiliar with governments and gov-
     ernment data. It presents detailed data on government units and
     public school systems for the United States, states, and counties;
     county, municipal, and township governments by type and popula-
     tion size; school systems by enrollment, area served, grades pro-
     vided, and number of schools operated. The names and addresses
     of all 83,000 local governments are provided on tape.

  b. *Popularly elected officials:* No other country in the world elects as
     many officials, or as often, as the United States. From dogcatcher to
     sheriff to mayor to president, this report shows the officials elected
     to office by type of office and by type of government, by county and
     state.

  c. *Taxable Property Values:* This report covers the aggregate gross and
     net assessed valuations for all taxable real and personal property in
     the United States.

  d. Government employment: Four census reports cover government
     employment. *Employment in Major Local Governments* provides em-
     ployment, payroll, and average earnings as of October 1987 for
     county governments, municipal governments having 10,000 or
     more population, school systems with 5000 or more students, and
     special districts with 100 or more employees. You go to this report to

compare size of governments, payrolls, and earnings. You can, for example, determine the number of full-time employees in your state's higher education (or other function) per 10,000 population. *Compendium of Public Employment* contains national and state data on federal, state, and local government employment and payroll by function and type of government. You look here to see how many government employees reside in your state and what kind of jobs they have. The other two employment reports in the census series have self-explanatory titles: *Labor-Management Relations in State and Local Governments* and *Government Costs for Employee Benefits*.

e. Government finances: This series of reports presents detailed financial and expenditure data for fiscal year 1986 87, including revenue by source, expenditure by function and object, indebtedness and debt transactions, and cash and security holdings. There are six separate reports, with national, state, and local data:

1. *Finances of Public School Systems*

2. *Finances of Special Districts*

3. *Finances of County Governments*

4. *Finances of Municipal and Township Governments*

5. *Compendium of Government Finances* (includes basic statistics and a summary of local governments in each county)

6. *Employee Retirement Systems of State and Local Governments*

f. Topical studies has four publications: (1) *Historical Statistics on Government Finances and Employment*, (2) *State Payments to Local Governments*, (3) *Government Statistics for Puerto Rico*, and (4) *Graphic Summary*.

• Annual census publications on government employment and finances

a. Government Employment (GE) Series

1. *City Employment*

2. *Public Employment*

3. *County Government Employment*

4. *Local Government Employment in Local County Areas*

b. Government Finances (GF) Series

1. *Chartbook on Governmental Finances and Employment*

2. *City Government Finances*

3. *Compendium of State Government Finances*

4. *Finances of Employee Retirement Systems of State and Local Governments*

5. *Government Finances*

6. *Local Government Finances in Selected Metropolitan Areas*

7. *State Tax Collections*

8. *Summary of Governmental Finances*

9. *Summary of State Government Finances*

- *Federal Expenditures by State for Fiscal Year:* This is an annual report covering grants to state and local governments, salaries and wages, procurement, direct payments for individuals, and per capita and percentage distributions of expenditures by state. These data, which are collected from all federal departments, tell you your state's share in the federal largesse.

- Private sources of government data

  1. *Facts and Figures on Government Finance* (Tax Foundation, Washington, DC; annual)

  2. *Fiscal Survey of the States* (National Association of State Budget Officers, Washington, DC; semiannual)

  3. *State Expenditure Report* (National Association of State Budget Officers, Washington, DC)

  4. *Statistical Yearbook of Municipal Finances by Public Securities Association, New York*

Name: Government Receipts and Expenditures in the National Income and Product Accounts

Agency/Institution: Bureau of Economic Analysis, Department of Commerce

Address: Government Division, BE-57, BEA, Washington, DC 20230

Telephone number for data and inquiries:

General government: 202-523-0715

Federal: 202-523-0744

State and local: 202-523-0725

National defense: 202-523-5017

Sources: Quarterly estimates appear in the *Survey of Current Business* in the month following the end of the quarter. The detailed accounts and first annual revision are available in the July issue of *Survey of Current Business*. The February issue of *SCB* usually contains an article on the federal, state, and local fiscal programs for the next fiscal year. NIPA budgetary information is also available in the federal budget of the United States.

Revisions: The first advanced release is made in the month following the end of the quarter. A revision of the first release (called the *preliminary estimate*) is published in the following or second month; this is revised again the following month with the final estimate. No further revisions are made until the annual revisions, which are published in July. Annual revisions are made for the next two years, and then no further revisions are made until the comprehensive revisions, which are usually made every five years. For example, the advance estimate for the first quarter data of 1992 (1992:I) will be released in April 1992.

The 1992:I data will be revised in May 1992 (preliminary estimate) and June 1992 (final estimate). No further revisions of 1992:I will be made until July 1993, when the annual estimates are revised. The 1992 annual estimates will be revised in the July issues of *SCB* for the next two years and then will not change until the five-year benchmark revisions are made.

Frequency: Quarterly

When available: Month following the end of the quarter

Historic data: See below.

Cross references: Federal Government Budget; National Income and Product Accounting

---

■ A QUICK LOOK: Government Receipts and Expenditures in NIPAs

The national income and product accounts (NIPAs) measure the nation's total current production of goods and services, known as gross domestic product (GDP) and the income generated in its production. GDP is the sum of the net products of the household, business, government, and foreign sectors. Federal, state, and local transactions are included in NIPAs as part of the government sector. The NIPA federal sector is not itself a budget or a financial plan for proposing, determining, or controlling the fiscal activities of the government. It is supposed to measure the impact of government receipts, outlays, and deficits on the national economy. Government purchases of goods and services are included in GNP as part of final output, together with personal consumption expenditures, gross private domestic investment, and net exports. Government expenditures in the form of transfer payments, grants to state and local governments, subsidies, and net interest payments are not part of final output, so they are not included. Rather, they are transfers of income to others, whose consumption and investment are part of final output. See Table 16.4 for an example of this data series.

TABLE 16.4
Government Receipts and Expenditures in the National Income and Product Accounts,
1991
(billions of $)

	Total Govts	Federal	State & Local
Receipts	$1,739.0	$1,120.1	$771.7
Personal tax and nontax receipts	616.1	470.4	145.7
Income taxes	569.2	458.4	110.8
Estate and gift taxes	11.0	11.0	—
Nontaxes	17.7	1.0	16.7
Other	18.2	—	18.2
Corporate profits tax accruals	124.5	102.9	21.6

(continued)

TABLE 16.4 *(continued)*
**Government Receipts and Expenditures in the National Income and
Product Accounts,**
1991
(billions of $)

	Total Govts	Federal	State & Local
Indirect business tax and nontax revenue	471.0	78.8	392.2
Sales taxes	188.8	—	188.8
Excise taxes	46.3	46.3	—
Property taxes	162.1	—	162.1
Other	41.2	—	41.2
Custom duties	17.2	17.2	—
Nontaxes	15.3	15.3	—
Contributions for social insurance	527.4	468.0	59.4
Federal grants in aid	—	—	152.8
Expenditures	**$1,910.6**	**$1,321.7**	**$741.7**
Purchases of goods and services	1,087.5	445.1	642.4
Compensation of employees	434.1	—	434.1
Other	208.2	—	208.2
Transfer payments	700.0	513.5	186.5
To persons	—	546.6	—
To foreigners	—	−33.1	—
Grants in aid to state and local govts	—	152.8	—
Net interest paid	131.6	188.7	−57.1
Interest paid	284.6	220.1	64.5
To persons and business	—	181.1	—
To foreigners	—	39.0	—
Less: Interest received by govts	153.1	31.5	121.6
Less: Dividends received by govts	9.2	—	9.2
Subsidies less current surplus of govt	0.6	21.5	−20.9
Subsidies	27.4	27.8	0.4
Less: Surplus of govt. enterprises	27.6	6.3	21.3
Surplus or deficit, NIPA	−171.6	−201.6	30.3
Social insurance funds	108.7	43.4	65.3
Other	−280.3	−245.0	−35.3

Note: The total of federal, state, and local government receipts and expenditures are greater than the amounts reported in the total government column because $152.8 billion of federal grants-in-aid are included in state and local receipts and expenditures. Federal grants to state and local governments are expenditures of the federal government and revenue receipts for state and local governments. When the receipts and expenditures of all governments are aggregated, the $152.8 billion gets cancelled out on both the expenditure and receipts side.

Personal taxes and nontaxes: Taxes include taxes on income, including realized net capital gains, taxes on transfers of estates and gifts, and taxes on personal property. Nontaxes include tuitions and fees paid to government schools and hospitals, and fees, fines, and donations paid to governments.

Corporate profits tax accruals: Federal, state, and local income taxes on all corporate earnings, including realized capital gains.

Indirect business tax and nontax accruals: Excise taxes on sales, property, and production. Excise taxes at the federal level include taxes on alcohol, tobacco, and gasoline. Corporate income taxes and social insurance contributions are not included. Nontaxes include regulatory and inspection fees, fines, rents, and royalties.

Contributions for social insurance: Employer and personal contributions for social insurance to Social Security, unemployment insurance, and railroad retirement.

Purchases of goods and services: Purchases from business, compensation of government employees, and purchases from foreigners. Does not include transfer payments, interest paid, subsidies, or transactions in financial assets and lands.

Transfer payments: Income payments to persons for which they do not render current services. These include Social Security benefit payments, Medicaid, unemployment insurance, military and federal workers' retirement, veterans' benefits, food stamps, and disability.

Net interest paid: Interest paid to persons, business, and foreigners less the interest received from them.

Dividends received: Dividends received by state and local governments, primarily by their social insurance funds.

Subsidies less current surpluses: Monetary grants paid by governments to business. Subsidies include those paid to agriculture, housing, maritime industry, Amtrak, and mass transit in cities. The current surplus of government enterprises is their operating revenue and subsidies received from other levels of government less their current expenses. Subsidies and current surplus are shown as a combined entry because deficits incurred by government enterprises may result from selling goods to business at below-market prices in lieu of giving them subsidies.

Surplus or deficit: The sum of government receipts less the sum of government expenditures. A surplus is designated by the absence of a sign; a deficit is designated by a minus sign. The surplus or deficit of social insurance funds is shown separately. If there had not been a large surplus ($109 billion) in social insurance funds, the 1991 deficit would have been $280 billion.

Detailed data are available on tax revenues, social insurance contributions, and state and federal government expenditures by type and function.

■ A CLOSER LOOK: Government Receipts and Expenditures in NIPAs

The national income and product accounts (NIPAs) include the government sector as part of their measurement of the nation's gross national product. Recall that data reported in NIPAs are adjusted to reflect the reporting goals and nature of NIPA, and, thus, these government sector data will differ considerably from data in the federal and state budgets. Some of the differences between the federal budget and the NIPA reporting of federal receipts and expenditures are:[9]

1. NIPA accounts are based on calendar quarters, whereas the federal budget is based on a fiscal year extending from October 1 to September 30.

2. The budget includes receipts and expenditures from U.S. territories and Puerto Rico, whereas NIPA considers the territories to be outside the United States.

3. The budget does not include certain government entities, such as the Postal Service and TVA, that are included in the NIPA accounts. Basically, NIPA includes both on-budget and off-budget items. NIPA excludes all financial transactions such as loans, loan repayments, and loan guarantees on the grounds that such transactions involve an exchange of assets with no production involved. Beginning in 1992, the budget has included an estimate of the subsidies involved in loan guarantees. Also, insurance outlays for "resolving" failed banks and thrift institutions are excluded from NIPA on the grounds that there are no offsetting current income flows.

4. Generally, budget outlays are based on a cash basis, whereas most NIPA accounts are recorded on an imputed and accrual basis. National defense expenditures, for example, are recorded by the budget when they are made, whereas they are recorded in the NIPAs when the goods are delivered.

5. The budget includes net lending and sale of land, whereas the NIPA accounts do not include them because they are considered to be an exchange of existing assets rather than the creation of new ones.

6. The budget records certain transactions as offsets to outlays, whereas they are recorded as receipts in the NIPAs. Government contributions for employee retirement is one example. The budget offsets these payments against outlays while the NIPAs treat the federal government as any other employer and show contributions for employee social insurance as expenditures by the employing agencies; they receipt the appropriate social insurance funds.

It is difficult to state when one should use the NIPA government data or the federal/state budgetary data. The fundamental rule is to use NIPA

---

[9]Similar adjustments are made for state and local budgetary data. For example, state and local expenditures or revenue associated with financial transactions and sale of land are excluded from NIPA.

data when assessing the impact of government receipts and expenditures on the national economy. However, when analyzing the impact on financial markets or examining the detailed expenditures of certain agencies or programs or evaluating the control over resources, the budgetary data should be used.

HISTORIC DATA: Government Receipts and Expenditures:
National Income and Product Accounts*
(billions of $)

	Total Govt. Expend.	Total Govt. Receipts	Total Govt. Surplus Deficit	Federal Govt. Expend.	Federal Govt. Receipts	Federal Govt. Surplus Deficit (−)	State & Local Govt. Expend.	State & Local Govt. Receipts	Local Govt. Surplus Deficits (−)
1929	10.3	11.3	1.0	2.7	3.8	1.1	7.8	7.6	− 0.2
1933	10.7	9.4	− 1.3	4.0	2.7	− 1.3	7.2	7.2	0.0
1939	17.6	15.4	− 2.2	9.0	6.8	− 2.2	9.6	9.6	0.0
1940	18.5	17.8	− 0.7	10.0	8.7	− 1.3	9.3	10.0	0.7
1941	28.8	25.0	− 3.8	20.5	15.5	− 5.0	9.1	10.4	1.3
1942	64.1	32.7	− 31.4	56.1	23.0	− 33.1	8.8	10.6	1.8
1943	93.4	49.2	− 44.2	85.9	39.3	− 46.6	8.4	10.9	2.5
1944	103.1	51.2	− 51.9	95.6	41.1	− 54.5	8.5	11.1	2.6
1945	92.9	53.4	− 39.5	84.7	42.7	− 42.0	9.0	11.6	2.6
1946	47.2	52.6	5.4	37.2	40.7	3.5	11.1	13.0	1.9
1947	43.4	57.8	14.4	30.8	44.1	13.3	14.4	15.4	1.0
1948	51.1	59.6	8.5	35.5	43.9	8.4	17.6	17.7	0.1
1949	60.0	56.6	− 3.4	42.0	39.4	− 2.6	20.2	19.5	− 0.7
1950	61.4	69.4	8.0	41.2	50.4	9.2	22.5	21.3	− 1.2
1951	79.5	85.6	6.1	58.1	64.6	6.5	23.9	23.4	− 0.5
1952	94.3	90.5	− 3.8	71.4	67.7	− 3.7	25.5	25.4	− 0.1
1953	102.0	95.0	− 7.0	77.6	70.4	− 7.2	27.3	27.4	0.1
1954	97.5	90.4	− 7.1	70.3	64.2	− 6.1	30.2	29.0	− 1.2
1955	98.5	101.6	3.1	68.6	73.1	4.5	32.9	31.7	− 1.2
1956	105.0	110.2	5.2	72.5	78.5	6.0	35.9	35.0	− 0.9
1957	115.8	116.7	0.9	80.2	82.5	2.3	39.8	38.5	− 1.3
1958	128.3	115.7	− 12.6	89.6	79.3	− 10.3	44.4	42.0	− 2.4
1959	131.9	130.3	− 1.6	91.7	90.6	− 1.1	47.0	46.6	− 0.4
1960	137.3	140.4	3.1	93.9	96.9	3.0	49.9	50.0	0.1
1961	150.1	145.9	− 4.2	102.9	99.0	− 3.9	54.5	54.1	− 0.4
1962	161.6	157.9	− 3.7	111.4	107.2	− 4.2	58.2	58.6	0.4
1963	169.1	169.8	0.7	115.3	115.6	0.3	62.9	63.4	0.5
1964	177.8	175.6	− 2.2	119.5	116.2	− 3.3	68.8	69.8	1.0
1965	189.6	190.2	0.6	125.3	125.8	0.5	75.5	75.5	0.0
1966	215.6	214.4	− 1.2	145.3	143.5	− 1.8	84.7	85.2	0.5
1967	245.0	230.8	− 14.2	165.8	152.6	− 13.2	95.2	94.1	− 1.1
1968	272.2	266.2	− 6.0	182.9	176.9	− 6.0	107.8	107.9	0.1
1969	290.2	300.1	9.9	191.3	199.7	8.4	119.3	120.8	1.5
1970	317.4	306.8	− 10.6	207.8	195.4	− 12.4	134.0	135.8	1.8
1971	346.8	327.3	− 19.5	224.8	202.7	− 22.1	151.0	153.6	2.6
1972	377.3	374.0	− 3.3	249.0	232.2	− 16.8	165.8	179.3	13.5

(continued)

HISTORIC DATA: Government Receipts and Expenditures: *(continued)*
National Income and Product Accounts*
(billions of $)

	Total Govt. Expend.	Total Govt. Receipts	Total Govt. Surplus Deficit	Federal Govt. Expend.	Federal Govt. Receipts	Federal Govt. Surplus Deficit (−)	State & Local Govt. Expend.	State & Local Govt. Receipts	Local Govt. Surplus Deficits (−)
1973	411.7	419.6	7.9	269.3	263.7	− 5.6	182.9	196.4	13.5
1974	467.4	463.1	− 4.3	305.5	293.9	− 11.6	205.9	213.1	7.2
1975	544.9	480.0	− 64.9	364.2	294.9	− 69.3	235.2	239.6	4.4
1976	587.5	549.1	− 38.4	393.7	340.1	− 53.6	254.9	270.1	15.2
1977	635.7	616.6	− 19.1	430.1	384.1	− 46.0	273.2	300.1	26.9
1978	694.8	694.4	− 0.4	470.7	441.4	− 29.3	301.3	330.3	29.0
1979	768.3	779.8	11.5	521.1	505.0	− 16.1	327.7	355.3	27.6
1980	889.6	855.1	− 34.5	615.1	553.8	− 61.3	363.2	390.0	26.8
1981	1,006.9	977.2	− 29.7	703.3	639.5	− 63.8	391.4	425.6	34.2
1982	1,111.6	1,000.8	− 110.8	781.2	635.3	− 145.9	414.3	449.4	35.1
1983	1,189.9	1,061.3	− 128.6	835.9	659.9	− 176.0	440.2	487.7	47.5
1984	1,277.9	1,172.9	− 105.0	895.6	726.0	− 169.6	475.9	540.5	64.6
1985	1,402.6	1,270.8	− 131.8	985.6	788.7	− 196.9	516.7	581.8	65.1
1986	1,491.5	1,347.4	− 144.1	1,034.8	827.9	− 206.9	563.5	626.3	62.8
1987	1,575.0	1,464.9	− 110.1	1,072.8	911.4	− 161.4	604.8	656.1	51.3
1988	1,658.8	1,562.7	− 96.1	1,118.3	972.4	− 145.9	651.9	701.6	49.7
1989	1,778.7	1,673.8	− 104.9	1,196.7	1,046.8	− 149.9	701.6	746.6	41.1
1990	1,836.7	1,697.1	− 139.6	1,270.1	1,104.8	− 165.3	698.8	724.5	25.7
1991	1,910.6	1,739.0	− 171.6	1,320.4	1,119.9	− 200.5	741.9	771.5	29.6

*Annual values are averages of the quarterly values; total government receipts and expenditures are reduced by the grants-in-aid.

CHAPTER 17

INTERNATIONAL TRADE AND FINANCE

Most countries keep track of the transactions of their residents with the residents of other countries, and the United States is no exception. The United States maintains a sophisticated data collection system that includes the balance of payments, international capital flows, international investment position, indexes of import and export prices, changes in foreign exchange rates, and many other data series related to foreign trade and investment. The international trade database is growing as the importance of international trade grows. In 1960, imports were only 4.5 percent of the nation's gross domestic product; today they are about 13 percent.

One of the most closely watched international data series is the balance of payments. When the United States and other western countries went on a flexible exchange rate system in 1973, it was thought that economists, the media, and even average citizens would lose interest in the balance of payments and shift their attention to the levels of exchange rates. This view has proven to be incorrect. There has been less interest in certain versions of the balance of payments, but the merchandise trade balance and the current balance are at least as closely watched as they ever were.

A widely reported number in the financial media is the international value of the dollar, which changes continuously as it is bought and sold on exchange markets throughout the world. Since 1973, when the world officially abandoned fixed exchange rates, the dollar has fluctuated in value. Now, supply and demand forces in the market, as well as the continual intervention in the exchange market by central banks, determine its value. Since 1973, the dollar has appreciated sharply against currencies such as the British pound and the Italian lira and depreciated rather sharply against other currencies such as the German mark and the Japanese yen. Movements in the exchange value of the dollar have important consequences for all Americans. When the U.S. dollar increases in value (appreciates), foreign goods and services become less expensive to American importers and to Americans traveling in foreign countries. Don't cheer too loudly, though, when you learn the dollar has appreciated — a lengthy period of appreciation just might eliminate your job. When the dollar appreciates, American-made goods cost more in foreign currencies and U.S. exports drop. When the dollar depreciates, U.S. goods and services become less expensive in foreign countries, thus increasing exports. But all those electronic products, clothes, and automobiles we buy from other countries become more expensive, and we have to pay more for them in our stores. All of this, and much more, will be explained in the foreign exchange section later in the chapter.

Warning! Don't Miss This!! As the "world continues to shrink" and we massage our shekels with our bahts, ringgits, wons, takas, and escudos,[1] we are increasingly confronted with comparisons of prices, incomes, gross domestic products, savings, and investments among countries. "The average Japanese earns only $6 per hour while the average American earns $12 per hour" is a typical example. Sometimes, such comparisons have merit; most of the time, however, they are as real — and almost as humorous — as Bugs Bunny. Although the better studies attempt to ensure that similar concepts of "earnings" are used, perfect compatibility has not been achieved in any study or data series seen by this author. Fringe benefits such as pensions, vacation, health, and retirement plans are generally included in the better studies, but unusual benefits such as "free parking" (a Japanese worker would part with many yen for free parking) at work, subsidized lunches, travel, and expense accounts are generally ignored. The important point to all this, however, is that the writers (reporters) and readers of these studies fail to realize the simple fact that Japanese workers work for yen and not for dollars. That is, someone somewhere is using some kind of figures to convert those yen to dollars and the figures that are used will significantly affect (distort??) the final results. If the average[2] Japanese worker earns 1,300,000 yen per year, what is the equivalent amount in dollars? If the author of the study uses the hypothetical end-of-year exchange rate of 130 yen per dollar, then the average Japanese worker will "earn" $10,000. If he uses the midyear exchange rate of 115 yen per dollar, the average Japanese worker will "earn" $11,304; if the daily closing average of 105 yen per dollar is used, the Japanese worker will "earn" $12,380. Exchange rates fluctuate during the year and over the years. At times, speculative rumors will drive them unusu-

---

[1] I know you're curious. Shekel is the currency of Israel, bahts are from Thailand, ringgits from Malaysia, wons from South Korea, takas from Bangladesh, and escudos from Portugal.

[2] Reread the meanings of averages on pages 9–12.

ally high or low. Exchange rate conversions are seldom reliable for comparisons of many data series among countries.

Because exchange rates fluctuate widely for many reasons other than the relative growth rates in domestic prices, many economists prefer to use the comparative purchasing power parity (PPP) of each country's currency as a means of converting foreign currency values to dollars. PPPs show how many units of a currency are needed in one country to buy the same amount of goods and services that one unit of currency will buy in the other country. For some countries, conversion by the exchange rate and by the PPP produce about the same results. The 1989 per capita income (PCI) of the United Kingdom, for example, was $14,345 when converted by current exchange rates and $14,005 when using PPP. However, the Japanese per capita income was much different when the yen income was converted to dollars by the exchange rate and by PPP. If you wanted to "prove" that Japan had a higher PCI than the United States, you would use current exchange rates to make the yen-to-dollar conversion. This would have yielded a PCI of $22,896. If you wanted to "prove" that income in the United States was higher, you would use the PPP conversion, which produces a Japanese PCI of $15,501. Although, for most purposes and for most data series, the PPP conversion method is more scientifically correct than the exchange rate method, the overwhelming majority of comparative international data series continue to use exchange rates.

Name: Balance of Payments
Alternative name: International Transactions; Balance of Payments, BPA version
Agency/Institution: Bureau of Economic Analysis
Address: Balance of Payments Division, BE-58, Bureau of Economic Analysis, U.S. Department of Commerce, Washington, DC 20230
Telephone number for data: The most recent balance of payments and merchandise trade are updated by a 3- to 5-minute telephone tape at 202-898-2453.
Telephone number for inquiries:

Current-account analysis	202-523-0621
Current-account estimates	-0625
Merchandise trade	-0668
Capital-account transactions	-0603
Government transactions	-0615

Sources: *Survey of Current Business, Federal Reserve Bulletin, Wall Street Journal*
Frequency: Quarterly
When available: Current estimates, including estimates of merchandise trade on a balance of payments basis, are reported in the March, June, September, and December issues of the *Survey of Current Business*. Thus, for example, first quarter data are reported in June, second quarter data are reported in September. Estimates include details of the current and capital accounts, classified by type of transaction and by country of trade.
Revisions: Each June the balance of payments estimates are revised back at least four years, and improvements are made in the collection and presentation of data, sometimes for the entire historical series.

Historic summary: June issues of the *Survey of Current Business* currently present adjusted and revised data back to 1960.

Cross references: Balance of Payments, NIPA version (page 413)

■ A QUICK LOOK: The Balance of Payments

The **balance of payments (BOP)** is a record of the transactions between the residents of one country and residents of the rest of the world during some period of time. Every international transaction causes an increase in credits (+) and an increase in debits (−). A **credit transaction** is one that generates an increase in the demand for dollars and an increase in the supply of foreign currencies. For example, an increase in U.S. exports (a credit) to Germany would generate an increase in demand for dollars to pay for the exports and an increased supply of German marks. A **debit** transaction is one that generates an increased demand for foreign currencies and an increased supply of dollars. An increase in imports from Britain will generate an increased demand for British pounds and an increased supply of dollars.

The inevitable result of this double-entry bookkeeping is that the total of debits equals the total of credits. Hence, the balance of payments always balances and any apparent "imbalance" has been generated by looking only at certain accounts.

Thus, there are different balances (one is the **merchandise trade balance**) depending on the accounts that are totaled. If you look at 1991 BOP data during some future year (say 1995) and the numbers you have for 1991 don't agree with the numbers in Table 17.1, don't worry—it is perfectly normal. As with many other data series, the 1991 BOP data will be adjusted for many years into the future. (See the Revision section.)

TABLE 17.1
Balance of Payments, 1991
(millions of $)

	Credits +	Debits −
A. Merchandise trade		
Exports	$416,517	
Imports		− $490,103
Merchandise Trade Balance		− 73,586
B. Services:	144,675	− 108,796
Military sales/gifts	10,429	− 15,709
Travel	45,551	− 39,418
Passenger fares	13,836	− 9,289
Other transportation	23,114	− 23,467
Royalties and license fees	16,330	− 3,409
Other	35,415	17,504

(continued)

TABLE 17.1 *(continued)*
Balance of Payments, 1991
(millions of $)

	Credits +	Debits −
C. Income earned/paid on assets	115,306	− 105,943
Direct investment (+ = U.S. earnings)	51,754	− 361
Other private receipts/payments	56,011	− 66,743
Receipts (+)/payments (−) by governments	7,541	− 38,839
Balance on Goods, Services and Income		− 28,344
D. Unilateral transfers, net	19,728	
Government	21,924	
Private		− 2,196
Current Account Balance		− 8,616
E. U.S. assets abroad (increase = capital outflow = " − ")		− 67,747
U.S. official reserve assets	5,763	
Gold	No change	
Special drawing rights		− 177
Reserve position in IMF		− 367
Foreign currencies	6,307	
U.S. government assets, other than official reserves	3,572	
U.S. credits and other long-term assets		− 11,916
Repayments on U.S. credits and other long-term assets	16,466	
U.S. foreign currencies and short-term assets		− 979
U.S. private assets (increase = " − ")		− 77,082
Direct investments		− 29,497
Foreign securities		− 46,215
Nonbank claims on foreigners		− 4,798
Claims on foreigners by U.S. banks	3,428	
F. Foreign assets in the U.S. (increase = capital inflow = " + ")	79,503	
Foreign official assets in the U.S.	20,585	
U.S. government securities	19,549	
Other U.S. government liabilities	1,603	
Liabilities of the U.S. banks		− 1,856
Other foreign official assets	1,289	
Other foreign assets in the U.S.	58,918	
Direct investment	22,197	
U.S. Treasury securities	16,861	
Other U.S. securities	35,417	
U.S. nonbank liabilities to foreigners	—	
U.S. banks liabilities to foreigners		− 15,046
G. Allocation of special drawing rights		511
H. Statistical discrepancy		− 3,139

A. Merchandise Trade: This account includes only merchandise trade between residents of the United States and residents of other countries. Wheat, lumber, cars, stereos, and computers are included in this category. Merchandise exports are credits (+) because they stimulate a demand for dollars and a supply of foreign currency. Merchandise imports are debits (−) because they stimulate a supply of dollars and a demand for foreign exchange. The merchandise trade balance is one of the most widely reported balances in the balance of payments.

B. Services: Services include a variety of accounts, including travel, tourism, transportation, business, and consulting activities as well as royalties and income from copyrights, patents, and licenses. When an American travels in a foreign country, the amounts paid for hotels, food, and entertainment are debited to the travel account. Expenditures by a foreigner traveling in the United States are credited to the travel account. When a foreigner travels on an American airplane or ship between countries, the ticket prices are credited to passenger fares. When an American exporter ships goods on a Norwegian ship, there is a debit to "other transportation."

C. Income Earned/Paid on Assets[3]:   When individuals invest in foreign countries, they receive income from these assets. For example, an American may own stock in a British company from which he receives dividend income. When the American buys British stock, the transaction is *not* reported in this account (it is reported as a direct investment under Private Assets). However, when the American receives dividends, rents, or distribution of profits from these foreign direct investments, the amounts are credited to Investment Income-Direct Investment. When foreigners receive income on their investments in the United States, the amounts are debited to Investment Income-Direct Investment. This account does not include earned profits that are reinvested in the same or another country. The United States has consistently run a surplus (+'s > −'s) in income from direct investment but the surplus is diminishing, and within a few years the United States will have a deficit in this account as it already does on the Other Private Income Flows. The large deficit (−'s > +'s) in the government income payments represents interest payments on the large quantity of U.S. government securities held by foreigners.

D. Unilateral Transfers: These are transactions in which there is no "quid" for the "quo." One party has given another party something of value but does not expect anything in return. Unilateral transfers, in effect, are gifts. For example, if the United States ships wheat to India under a foreign aid program, Merchandise Exports will be credited (wheat is exported to a foreign country) and Unilateral Transfers will be debited (nothing was received or expected in return for the wheat).

E. U.S. Assets Held Abroad: The debits and credits to these accounts represent *changes* in the assets and not the total value of the assets. Thus, a debit to one of these accounts occurs when there is an increase in the value of foreign assets held by Americans and a credit occurs when there is an increase in the value of foreign-

---

[3]Prior to spring 1990, the income earned on investments in foreign countries was included as part of services. Since then, however, such income has been segmented into its own area, where it properly belongs.

owned assets in the United States. An outflow of capital from the United States that is invested in another country is a debit or a "minus" transaction. The fact that a capital outflow is a debit is generally confusing to students because imports of goods and services are also debits. When an American invests funds in a foreign country (say, an American purchases a business firm), he is demanding foreign exchange and supplying dollars just as if he were purchasing goods from a foreigner. In effect, he is importing a security or ownership interest.

U.S. Official Reserve Assets: These are assets held by the Treasury and the Federal Reserve. They consist primarily of gold and foreign currencies. The gold is left over from the post–World War II era (up to 1971), when the United States redeemed foreign official holdings of dollars with gold. Thus, the central bank of France, say, could turn in its dollar holdings for gold. However, the United States no longer redeems its dollars in gold, and the amount of gold in the official reserves has remained fairly constant since 1971. The gold is valued at $42.22 per ounce. It is still included in official reserves because the Federal Reserve or the Treasury could sell the gold and purchase foreign currencies or other assets. Foreign currencies are obtained when the Federal Reserve supports the international value of the dollar by buying foreign currencies. Remember that a debit $(-)$ is an increase in the official reserves and a credit $(+)$ is a decrease.

Special drawing rights are one component of U.S. Official Reserve assets that merit a more lengthy discussion. Special drawing rights (SDRs) are an international reserve asset that was introduced in 1970 as a substitute for gold; they are often called "paper gold." Unlike gold, which had to be mined, panned, or dredged, and then transported and stored, the International Monetary Fund can create SDRs out of thin air—that is, by crediting and debiting the appropriate accounts. Actually, the delegates at the numerous conferences establishing the SDRs could not agree whether to call these ledger sheet entries "money," "credit," or "assets." Using ever-popular clichés, they decided to call them "special drawing rights" and then defined the newly created "rights" as "reserve assets."

SDRs are nothing more than entries on the books of the IMF and central banks throughout the world. The amount allocated to each central bank is based on its country's proportional contribution to the IMF. These accounting entries can be used to obtain hard currencies and to settle imbalances in the trade accounts. SDRs were originally valued in terms of gold, but since 1974 they have been valued in terms of the weighted average of the value of five major currencies. Even some commercial contracts are now valued in terms of equivalent values of SDRs. For example, an American firm selling computers to a German customer might require that payment be made in 60 days in dollar equivalents of SDRs. If the dollar were to depreciate during the 60 days, it would take more dollars to equal one SDR and the American firm would get more dollars for its computers.

The major purpose of SDRs is to help countries with balance of payments or exchange rate difficulties by giving them an asset that can be converted into strong currencies. If, for example, Mexico is importing far more goods than it is exporting, its currency will depreciate. Mexico can then "sell" some of its SDRs to Japan for yen and then use the yen to buy Mexican pesos, thus driving up the international value of the Mexican peso. Countries such as Japan have to accept SDRs up to a certain maximum level. The −$177 million in SDRs shown in the 1991 balance of payments were probably "sold" to the Fed in exchange for dollars; they represent an increase in the Fed's official reserve assets.

The reserve position in the IMF is a legally defined proportion of the U.S. quota to finance the IMF. The United States can draw (borrow) on this position virtually without any restrictions. During 1991, the United States added (paid back) to its reserve position at the IMF by $367 million.

U.S. Government Assets Other than Official Reserves: These are assets that various government agencies buy in the normal conduct of their business.

U.S. Private Assets: These are assets in foreign countries owned by private American citizens and corporations. An increase in these assets is generated by American exports of goods and services, and they generally show an increase (−) each year. Direct investments are investments in real estate, companies, and subsidiaries. When Americans purchase foreign bonds or securities, the Foreign Securities account is debited. The largest increase in foreign assets owned by Americans was caused by the large increase in foreign deposits owned by American banks. The best way to conceptualize these transactions is through an example. Assume that an American exporter sells a computer to a British firm. The British firm sends a check drawn on its London bank to the American exporter. The American firm sends the check to its local bank, which, in turn, credits (increases) the export firm's account and debits (increases) deposits in the London bank, and then sends the check back to the London bank.[4] An American bank now owns a deposit in a foreign bank. The balance of payments entries for this transaction would be: credit (+) to merchandise exports for the export of the computer and a debit (−) to claims on foreigners by American banks. Most of these debit claims are American-owned deposits in foreign countries or loans made by American banks to foreign banks, which generate an asset (Loans Receivable) for the American banks. They are assets to American banks but liabilities of foreign banks.

F. Foreign Assets in the United States: These are assets held by foreigners representing obligations of Americans. When Americans import goods they pay for these goods by increasing their obligations, or IOUs, to foreigners. Such an increase in foreign-owned assets in the United States is represented by a credit (+). Thus, we can say that an increase in these accounts represents the financing of America's current-account deficit or that it represents an inflow of foreign capital. Foreign-owned assets are divided into official reserves and others. The largest increase in capital inflows was in the form of foreigners increasing their holdings of U.S. private securities ($35 billion). American bank liabilities to foreigners actually decreased by $15 billion.

G. Allocation of Special Drawing Rights   The IMF periodically allocates SDRs to its member countries or makes adjustments. A small adjustment was made in 1991.

H. Statistical Discrepancy (The Fudge Factor)   The BOP is based on the *concept* of double-entry bookkeeping, but, unlike firm accounting, it is not possible to record the debits and the credits at the same time. The BOP is actually constructed from a wide variety of data collected from around the world, some of which are based on best "guess-ti-mates." Export data, for example, are collected from cus-

---

[4]The London Bank would debit (reduce) the account of the importer and credit (increase) its deposit liabilities to American banks.

toms records (plus allowances for smuggling and undocumented exports), whereas the offsetting payments are picked up from surveys of bank deposits and other financial information. The debits and credits are not recorded at the same time, and no particular debit can be traced to any particular credit. In fact, it's a marvel that the BOP can be constructed at all. Many slippages, omissions, errors, and unobtainable data are involved in BOP construction. The statistical discrepancy entry is the explicit recognition of such "inaccuracies" — but it does not distract from the concept that debits equal credits. The statistical discrepancy is simply the number that will make total debits equal total credits. In this case, we know that before the statistical discrepancy amount was entered into the BOP, credits exceeded debits by $3.1 billion.

■ A CLOSER LOOK: Balance of Payments

The **balance of payments (BOP)** is a record of the transactions between the residents of one country and the residents of the rest of the world during some period of time. Despite its name, it has virtually no similarity to a private firm's balance sheet because the BOP does not summarize total assets and liabilities as does a balance sheet. The BOP has more in common with the income statement of a private firm because it shows transactions over a period of time, but the BOP does not show profits or losses.

Two widely held myths about the balance of payments need to be dispelled quickly and firmly. The first is that the balance of payments can have a net overall deficit or surplus. Rather, like any accounting ledger sheet, the sum of the debits in the balance of payments will always equal the sum of the credits. A deficit or a surplus can be derived only by isolating certain accounts in the balance of payments and adding up their debits and credits. The second myth is that the balance of payments shows the international assets and liabilities of the United States in the same way a corporation's balance sheet shows the equality of assets and liabilities plus net worth. The balance of payments is *not* an international balance sheet. It is also *not* a statement of international indebtedness, showing the amounts Americans owe to foreign residents and the amount they owe to us. The balance of payments records only the transactions between Americans and foreign residents for a particular period of time, usually a quarter of a year.

The balance of payments is based on double-entry bookkeeping, as used in accounting. And every student learns, in principles of accounting, that: Every debit must have an equal and corresponding credit. Unlike accounting, however, a credit in balance of payments accounting is a plus (+) and is placed on the left-hand side of the ledger sheet, and a debit is a minus (−) and is placed on the right-hand side. It is especially important to remember the plus (credit) and minus (debit) signs because they are widely used in BOP statements. A credit (+) is recorded for a transaction that increases the demand for dollars and increases the supply of foreign currency. A debit (−) is recorded for a transaction that increases the demand for foreign currency and increases the supply of dollars. This accounting convention is somewhat similar to that used by private firms, which record a sale as a credit. Exports, similar to sales, are recorded as a credit. Imports, similar to goods placed into inventory, are recorded as debits. The balance of payments is often segmented into current-account transactions, capital transactions, and reserve transactions. Current accounts record trade in goods, services, investment income, and exchange of gifts. Capital accounts record changes in the level of capital and financial assets; reserve accounts record changes in the level of international reserves held by the Federal Reserve. The following hypothetical transactions will show the fundamental double-entry bookkeeping nature of the balance of payments.

Current-Account Transactions

(1) Assume that an American imports a case of Scotch from Britain for $5000, which he pays by a check written on his bank. The Scotch is a merchandise import so the account appropriately named Merchandise Imports is debited (increased). The British clear the check by sending it to their bank in the United States, so an American bank now has an increase in its liabilities to foreigners.[5] In effect, Americans are exporting demand deposits to foreigners. This increase in the liabilities of American banks to foreigners is a credit (+) in the balance of payments. If someone invested in your firm, you would credit Accounts Payable to reflect that you now have a liability to the investor. When a foreign resident "invests" in the United States by depositing funds in an American bank, the transaction is recorded as an Increase in Short-term Liabilities to Foreigners. We can show this entry as:

	Credit (+)	Debit (−)
(1) Increase in short-term liabilities to foreigners (American bank's liability to a foreign bank)	$5,000	
Merchandise imports		$5,000

(2) If Americans export $4000 of wheat to Britain, there is a credit to Merchandise Exports and a debit to Short-term Capital assets. Now Americans are investing in foreign banks, so Americans have increased their short-term claims (Accounts Receivable) on foreigners.

---

[5]When the American bank receives the check from the British bank, it will debit (decrease) the deposits of the American importer and credit (increase) the deposits of the British bank. Foreign investment in the United States has now increased, and this will be recorded in the BOP as a credit to Short-term Liabilities to Foreigners. In the terminology employed by BOP accountants and shown in Table 17.1, U.S. banks' liabilities to foreigners increased.

	Credit (+)	Debit (−)
Merchandise exports	$4,000	
Increase in short-term claims on foreigners		$4,000

If we consider only these two transactions, we have the following balance of payments:[6]

Balance of Payments

Credits (+)		Debits (−)	
Merchandise Exports	$4,000	Merchandise Imports	$5,000
Increase in American banks liabilities to foreigners	$5,000	Increase in for. banks liability to Americans	$4,000
Totals	$9,000		$9,000

Notice that there is no overall balance of payments deficit or surplus; the credits equal the debits. The only way to get a deficit or surplus is to draw a line under Merchandise Imports and Merchandise Exports, and then say we have a merchandise trade deficit because imports (debits) are greater than exports (credits). That's right! We get a deficit or surplus by singling out some accounts and then calculating the net balance of those accounts. However, before we can describe the process of singling out these accounts, we will discuss a few other transactions in the balance of payments.

(3) A Japanese tourist flies to Las Vegas on an American airline (fare: $1000) and spends $4000 on hotels, food, camera film, and the blackjack table. He converts his yen into dollars at an American bank. Americans are exporting transportation and travel services to a foreigner, which are credits in the BOP. The American bank is now holding Japanese currency (or a yen deposit at a Japanese bank), so Americans have increased their claims on foreigners (on the Japanese central bank if currency; on a Japanese commercial bank if it is holding a deposit).

	Credit (+)	Debit (−)
Transportation	$1,000	
Travel	4,000	
Increase in short-term claims on foreigners (yen holdings)		$5,000

If the Japanese tourist had been holding dollars and he used these to pay for his trip, there would have been a decrease in Foreigners' Short-term Claims on Americans, as well as a debit to Short-term Capital.

(4) IBM pays $300 in dividends on stock held by a French resident. The payment of investment income to a foreign resident is a debit to Investment Income. The Frenchman deposited his check for $300 in an American bank, which meant there was an increase in American liabilities to foreigners.

	Credit (+)	Debit (−)
Increase in U.S. bank's liabilities to foreigners	$300	
Investment income earned by foreigners		$300

(5) An Italian-American sends a pizza dough machine, with a market value of $400, to her uncle in Naples as a birthday gift.

	Credit (+)	Debit (−)
Merchandise exports	$400	
Unilateral transfers — Private		$400

Unilateral transfers are "quids without quos." They are gifts made by the residents of one country to the residents of another country without expecting anything in return. Gifts made by American residents to foreign residents are recorded as debits (−). Since the Italian-American's gift is a commodity, the credit is to exports. If she had sent a $400 check instead and her uncle had deposited the check in the local bank, the bank would have sent the check to its American correspondent bank, and an Italian bank would have had a claim on an American bank. The BOP credit would have been to (increase) Foreigners' Short-term Claims on the United States.

Capital-Account Transactions

Capital-account transactions record *changes* in the value of international assets owned by Americans and the value of American-based assets owned by foreigners. The Capital account is further divided into the subaccounts of Direct Investment, Portfolio Investment, and Private Short-term Investment.[7] An example of a direct investment (debit) would be for an American to purchase a foreign company and take on management responsibilities for that company; portfolio investment involves the purchase of securities such as stocks or bonds, with little or no management responsibilities. Short-term capital flows involve investments in money

---

[7]Balance of payment data can be presented in many ways; in Table 17.1, the capital accounts are shown in sections E and F.

market instruments, bank deposits, and currency and other securities that have a maturity of less than one year.

(6) Assume that an American buys a $10,000 bond issued by a German company with a check that the German company deposits in an American bank.

	Credit (+)	Debit (−)
Increase in U.S. bank liabilities to foreigners (the check)	$10,000	
Increase in direct investment in foreign country (the bond)		$10,000

The purchase of the German bond, which involves an increase in the demand for deutsche marks, is a debit. The offsetting credit is an increase to Short-term Liabilities of U.S. banks because the German firm deposited the check in a German bank, which now has a claim on an American bank.

(7) A British bank buys a $2000, three-month Treasury bill by writing a check on its account at the Chase Manhattan bank.

	Credit (+)	Debit (−)
Increase in short-term liabilities to foreigners (Treasury bill)	$2,000	
Decrease in short-term liabilities to foreigners (decrease in bank account)		$2,000

Official Reserves Transactions

Official Reserve accounts measure changes in international reserves owned by the country's central bank. The major reserves are gold and foreign currencies that are convertible and readily marketable in the foreign exchange market.

(8) Assume that the U.S. Federal Reserve bank sells Japanese yen to a British foreign exchange dealer and gets $1500 of dollar balances in return. The decrease in the Federal Reserve's holdings of yen is a decrease in Official Reserves, or a credit.[8] Since the British foreign exchange dealer is decreasing its holdings of dollars, there is a decrease in American liabilities to foreigners, or a debit.

	Credit (+)	Debit (−)
Decrease in official reserves (yen)	$1,500	
Decrease in short-term liabilities to foreigners (dollars)		$1,500

---

[8] Official reserve transactions will test your mental concentration. An increase in the official reserve position of the United States is recorded as a debit, which is a minus (−). A decrease in official reserves is recorded as a credit, which is a (+).

The balance of payments statement in Table 17.2 is derived from the eight hypothetical transactions just listed. Note that the account descriptions are slightly different from those used before but the concepts are identical. The precise wording and format of balance of payments presentations differ over time and among publications. The memo at the bottom of the table shows four alternative measurements of the balance of payments based on these transactions.

TABLE 17.2
Hypothetical
Balance of Payments

	Credits +	Debits −
A. Merchandise Trade		
Exports	$4,000(2)	
	400(5)	
Imports		−$5,000(1)
B. Services:		
Travel	4,000(3)	
Passenger fares	1,000(3)	
C. Income earned(+)/paid on assets(−)		− 300(4)
D. Unilateral transfers, net		− 400(5)
E. U.S. assets held abroad (increase = " − ")		
U.S. official reserve assets		
Foreign currencies	1,500(8)	
U.S. private assets (increase = " − ")		
Direct investments		
Foreign securities		− 10,000(6)
Claims on foreigners by U.S. banks		− 4,000(2)
F. Foreign-owned assets in the U.S. (increase = " + ")		
Direct investment		
U.S. Treasury securities	2,000(7)	
U.S. banks' liabilities to foreigners	5,000(1)	
	300(4)	− 1,500(8)
	10,000(6)	− 2,000(7)
		− 5,000(3)
	$28,200	$ − 28,200
	Credits +	Debits −
Memo:		
Merchandise Trade Balance (A)		− $600
Balance on Services (B)	5,000	
Balance on Goods, Services, and Income (A + B + C)	4,100	
Current Account Balance (A + B + C + D)	3,700	

The total of the balance of payments debits equals the total of the credits. There can be no imbalance in the overall balance of payments. There can be a deficit or surplus only if some accounts are singled out and their debits and credits are added and compared independently of the other accounts. In the merchandise trade balance, we draw a line below merchandise exports and imports and add up the amounts in the accounts above the line. If the credits, or plus items, above that line are greater than the debits, or minus items, above the line, there is a surplus; if the debits above the line are greater than the credits above the line, we have a deficit. Thus, we can make the balance of payments surplus or deficit whatever we want merely by drawing the line in the appropriate place. In fact, at one time or another, the lines have been drawn in almost every conceivable place. There are still a large number of alternative places to draw that line, but in the remainder of this section, we discuss the most popular ones and the names of the balances that are associated with them.

The line for the **merchandise trade balance** is simply drawn under merchandise exports and imports. If the credits or pluses above the line are greater than the debits or minuses above the line, there is a merchandise trade surplus. If the debits above the line are greater than the credits above the line, there is a merchandise trade deficit. Since there is only one account on each side of the ledger sheet, we can more simply say that if merchandise exports exceed merchandise imports there is a surplus.

Another BOP balance is the **balance on goods and services**, which adds transactions in services to the merchandise trade balance. Until 1990, the service sector included investment income, but investment income has now been separated out and accorded a position of equal importance with the service sector. Thus, there are now balances on goods and services and balances on goods, services, and investment income. One significance of this latter balance is that it represents the values used in computing a nation's GDP. The net export statistic in the GDP will be close to the balance on goods, services, and investment income.

Next to the merchandise trade balance, the balance that is reported most frequently by the media is the **current-account balance**, which is the balance on goods, services, and investment plus private and government transfer payments. **Transfer payments** are gifts and aid sent from one country to another. When a government or private agency sends food to Africa, the accounting transactions are: debit (−) to Unilateral Transfers and credit (+) to Merchandise Exports. Thus, a net debit (−) balance in transfer payments means that Americans have transferred more or given more aid to foreigners than foreigners have transferred to us. The current-account balance probably gives the clearest interpretation of a change in the nation's international position by showing the net non-financial flow of resources in international trade. If the current account has a net debit balance (−), it means that the United States is importing or consuming more than it is exporting or giving up to the rest of the world. Thus, the United States has increased its net international debt as shown in the International Investment section (see pages 428–434).

HISTORIC DATA: Alternative Balances in the Balance of Payments,
Selected Years, 1960–1991
(billions of $)*

	Balance on Merchandise Trade	Balance on Services	Balance on Goods, Services, and Income	Balance on Current Account
1960	$4,892	($1,385)	$6,886	$2,824
1961	5,571	(1,376)	7,949	3,822
1962	4,521	(1,151)	7,664	3,387
1963	5,224	(1,014)	8,806	4,414
1964	6,801	(779)	11,063	6,823
1965	4,951	(287)	10,014	5,431
1966	3,817	(877)	7,987	3,031
1967	3,800	(1,196)	7,878	2,583
1968	635	(385)	6,240	611
1969	607	(516)	6,135	399
1970	2,603	(349)	8,486	2,331
1971	(2,260)	(957)	5,969	(1,433)
1972	(6,416)	973	2,749	(5,795)
1973	911	989	14,053	7,140
1974	(5,505)	1,213	11,210	1,962
1975	8,903	3,501	25,191	18,116
1976	(9,483)	3,401	9,894	4,207
1977	(31,091)	3,845	(9,285)	(14,511)
1978	(33,947)	4,164	(9,639)	(15,427)
1979	(27,536)	3,003	5,603	(991)
1980	(25,481)	3,093	9,467	1,119
1981	(27,978)	11,852	15,223	6,892
1982	(36,444)	12,101	3,907	(5,868)
1983	(67,080)	9,469	(30,188)	(40,143)
1984	(112,522)	2,744	(86,385)	(99,006)
1985	(122,148)	(877)	(106,859)	(122,332)
1986	(145,058)	4,706	(129,384)	(145,393)
1987	(159,500)	6,434	(147,739)	(162,314)
1988	(126,986)	11,519	(113,857)	(128,862)
1989	(114,864)	2,463	(95,314)	(110,034)
1990	(108,115)	26,376	69,794	(92,123)
1991	(73,586)	35,879	(28,344)	(8,616)

* + = surplus; (−) = deficit.

The data in the Historic Data table clearly show that the United States ran fairly consistent surpluses in merchandise trade and current-account balances until the 1980s, when they quickly deteriorated into deficits. One major cause of the deficits was the significant increase in the international value of the dollar during the early to mid-eighties. This lowered the dollar price of imports, which encouraged imports, and increased the foreign currency price of U.S. exports, which discouraged exports. The table also shows that although the alternative balances do differ, they tend to move in the same direction.

Name: Balance of Payments, NIPA version
Agency/Institution: Bureau of Economic Analysis, U.S. Department of Commerce
Address: Balance of Payments Division, BE-58, Bureau of Economic Analysis, Washington, DC 20230
Telephone number for data: 202-898-2453
Telephone number for inquiries: 202-523-0620
Sources: January, April, July, October issues of the *Survey of Current Business*. The most complete information is published in the July issue.
Frequency: Quarterly
When available: The month following the end of the quarter
Revisions: Same as the GDP, page 122.
Cross references: Balance of payments

■ A QUICK LOOK: Balance of Payments, NIPA Version

The balance of payments version reported in the previous section, the BPA version (pages 399–413), is the one most commonly used. However, an alternative source of information about the balance of payments is the BEA's national income and product accounts, which also record the GDP. The data are available by quarters and are published in the *Survey of Current Business*. The most complete data are available in the *SCB*'s annual NIPA issue in July. Although both versions use the same fundamental methodology, the NIPA balance of payments estimates differ from the BPA balance of payments data because of the different treatment of some transactions, timing differences, and varying schedules for data revisions. Thus, the data in Table 17.3, from the NIPAs, will vary from those given in the BOP accounts. Most of the time, the BOP data are the most appropriate data to use. However, if comparisons are being made to other accounts in NIPA, such as gross national product or personal income, it is better to use the NIPA balance of payments data. In addition to the data in the table, the NIPA accounts provide much detailed data on commodity exports and imports.

TABLE 17.3
Foreign Transactions in the National Income and Product Accounts,
1990, 1991

	1990	1991
Receipts from Foreigners (+)	698.2	726.3
Exports of goods and services	550.4	591.3
Merchandise	398.2	427.2
Durables	262.6	283.8
Nondurables	135.6	143.4
Services	152.2	164.1
Receipts of Factor income	147.8	135.0
Payments to Foreigners (−)	698.2	726.3
Imports of goods and services	624.8	622.0
Merchandise	507.4	500.5
Durable goods	314.3	316.0
Nondurable goods	193.1	184.5
Services	117.4	121.5
Payments of Factor income	137.0	121.8
Transfer payments (net)	20.0	− 25.1
From persons (net)	2.9	3.2
From governments (net)	12.6	− 33.1
From business	4.5	4.9
Net foreign investment	− 83.6	7.6

Note: The plus and minus signs shown after "Receipts from Foreigners" and "Payments to Foreigners" were added by the author to show correctly the relationship of the NIPAs to the BOP accounts described in the previous section and to avoid confusion, which can result from the misuse of these signs. The NIPAs normally do not carry plus or minus signs, as do the BOP accounts. This can confuse readers who are dealing with both sets of data and the BEA should reconsider its practice of not using them. For example, in the March 1992 issue of the *Survey of Current Business*, there were no minus signs on any of the categories except for net foreign investment in 1990. The BEA meant this minus to be interpreted as a deduction from the payments to foreigners category ($624.8 + $137.0 + $20 − $83.6 = $698.2). However, in normal balance of payments accounting, a minus net foreign investment of $83.6 billion means that Americans have invested in foreign countries $83.6 billion more than foreigners have invested in the United States. This is exactly the opposite of what actually occurred.

Factor income: Income for services rendered by American residents to foreigners, including income on investments in foreign countries or income paid to foreign residents for services provided to Americans, including payments made to foreigners on their investments in the United States.

Transfer payments (net):   Transfer payments made to foreigners minus transfer payments that foreigners made to Americans. The net transfer is the excess of the transfer payments made to foreigners.

Net foreign investment: The investment Americans made in foreign countries less the amount foreigners invested in this country.

Name: Detailed Data on U.S. Export and Import Merchandise
Alternative name: Merchandise Trade Flows
Agency/Institution: Bureau of the Census
Address: Washington, DC 20212
Telephone number for data and inquiries: 301-763-5140
Sources: *Summary of U.S. Export and Import Merchandise Trade* (FT-900) and the FT-900 supplement, *U.S. Merchandise Trade: Exports, General Imports, and Imports for Consumption; SITC Commodity by Country* (FT-925)
Frequency: Monthly
When available: About 6 to 8 weeks after the end of reference month
Revisions: Every month
Historic summary: Available on disks

These three monthly publications provide a great deal of detail about the value of exports and imports and trade balance by SITC (Standard International Trade Classification, SIC-based). For example, if you want to know the imports, exports, and trade balance for August in forestry product (yes, we have a deficit in forestry products!), look in FT-900, *Summary of U.S. Export and Import Merchandise Trade*. If you want to see which countries sent us forestry products and which countries received our forestry products, check out FT-925. Probably the most useful publication in this series is the FT-900 supplement, which shows the international trade flows by state. If you want to know if your state exported forestry products, or any other good, look in this supplement, which is a separate monthly report from FT-900 and is issued about two weeks later.

Name: Indexes of U.S. Import and Export Prices
Alternative name: International Price Indexes
Agency/Institution: Department of International Affairs, Bureau of Labor Statistics
Address: Washington, DC 20212
Telephone number for data inquiries: 202-272-5038
Sources: Most complete listing is in *U.S. Import and Export Price Indexes* and the *Monthly Labor Review*
Frequency: Quarterly
When available: About 2–3 weeks after the reference quarter
Revisions: When benchmark weights are changed; about every 5 years
Historic summary: *Handbook of Labor Statistics* and diskettes

---

■ A QUICK LOOK: Import and Export Price Indexes

These quarterly indexes (1985 = 100) measure trends of import and export prices for nonmilitary goods traded between the United States and other countries. They are used to determine the relative competitiveness of American products in international trade, to check on trends in import prices for specific goods, and to determine trends in terms of trade. The terms of trade basically tell us how many units of some commodity American residents will have to export in order to get one unit of a certain import. How many bushels of wheat do we have to export in order to be able to import one 20-inch Sony TV? If the import price index is increasing faster than the export price index, the terms of trade are said to be moving against the United States.

Table 17.4 shows a small sample of the price indexes available.

TABLE 17.4
Import and Export Price Indexes
(1990:II)

1. U.S. Export Price Indexes by Standard International Trade Classification

	SITC	Index
All commodities		113.3
Food	0	108.8
Grains and grain preparations	04	101.8
Vegetables and fruit	05	115.6

2. U.S. Import Price Indexes by Standard International Trade Classification

	SITC	Index
All commodities		119.0
Food	0	111.7
Grains and grain preparations	04	147.4
Vegetables and fruit	05	126.2

3. U.S. Export Indexes by End-Use Category

Foods, feeds, and beverages	108.8
Industrial supplies and materials	118.2
Capital goods	110.5
Automotive	111.6
Consumer goods	

4. U.S. Import Indexes by End-Use Category

Foods, feeds, and beverages	112.6
Industrial supplies and materials	97.6
Capital goods	65.4
Automotive	128.1
Consumer goods	133.1

Standard International Trade Classification (SITC): This is an international system for classifying industries that is similar to the standard industrial classification used in the United States. Classification of products by SITC facilitates the comparison of U.S. price and production trends with similar data from foreign countries. Price indexes are available for the four- and five-digit level of detail.

End-use Categories: Imports and exports are grouped by end-use detail to enable readers to observe trends in broad categories.

Only a small sample of the detail for SITC and end-use categories are given in Table 17.4. These indexes are calculated on the dollar prices of imports and exports, but the BLS also publishes indexes on the foreign currency prices of imports and exports. In addition, a complete index series is published showing the product classification of the Standard Industrial Classification.

■ **A CLOSER LOOK: Import and Export Price Indexes**

The **export price index** measures price changes for all products sold by U.S. residents to foreign buyers; the **import price index** measures price changes for all goods purchased from other countries by U.S. residents. Goods whose prices are measured by the indexes are raw materials, agricultural products, and semifinished and finished manufactured goods, including both consumer and capital goods. The data are collected by mail each quarter directly from importers and exporters. Survey respondents are requested to list all discounts, allowances, and rebates so that the prices used in the index are the actual prices for which the goods were bought and sold.

Export prices are based on f.a.s. (free alongside ship), which means that the prices include transportation from point of origin to the port or airport. Import prices are based either on the f.a.s. price at the foreign point of exportation or the c.i.f. (cost, insurance, and freight) price, which means that the price includes the costs of getting the product to the U.S. port. Import duties are never included. The f.a.s. basis is used for some imports while the c.i.f. basis is used for other imports. For any given imported product, however, only one basis is used.

Name: Foreign Exchange Rates, Prices of Foreign Currencies
Alternative name: Foreign Currencies, Spot Rates, Forward Rates
Agency/Institution: Federal Reserve System, International Monetary Fund
Address: Federal Reserve System, Washington, DC 20551
Telephone number for data and inquiries: 202-452-3244
Sources: *Wall Street Journal* and most daily newspapers, Federal Reserve Statistical releases (H.10, weekly; G.5, monthly), and the *Federal Reserve Bulletin* (monthly). The most complete listing of exchange rates of most of the world's currencies is contained in *International Financial Statistics* (monthly) published by the International Monetary Fund.

Frequency: Daily; the Fed's H.10 statistical release is made available each Monday.
When available: Next day in newspapers
Cross references: Foreign Currency Futures (page 246), Index of the Value of the Trade-Weighted Dollar (pages 426–427)
Historic summary: See below.

■ A QUICK LOOK: The Foreign Exchange Market

The countries of the world use different currencies. The British sell fish 'n chips for pounds, the French sell wine for francs, the Germans sell bratwurst for deutsche marks, the Norwegians sell sardines for krone, and the Thai sell rice for baht. Although much of the world's trade is initially conducted in American dollars, most international traders eventually have to exchange their dollars for local currencies. Furthermore, final consumers almost always must pay for internationally traded goods in local currency. Anyone who engages in international trade must eventually get involved in trading foreign currencies — also called *foreign exchange* — and watching changes in foreign exchange rates. A **foreign exchange rate** is the rate at which one country's currency exchanges for another. For example, the exchange rate of the dollar can be expressed in terms of the number of units of foreign currency that can be purchased with one U.S. dollar. If one dollar will purchase 235.25 Japanese yen, the exchange rate is $1:Y235.25. If $1 will purchase 1.7342 German marks, the exchange rate is $1:DM1.7342. The exchange rate can also be expressed in terms of the dollar value of a single foreign currency unit. For example, the value of one Japanese yen would be $0.00425 (1/235.25) and the value of a German mark is $0.57663 (1/1.7342). Thus, the value of a dollar in terms of German marks is the reciprocal of the value of the German mark in terms of dollars. Foreign exchange rates are reported in daily newspapers in both forms:

Exchange Rates

	U.S. $ EQUIVALENT		CURRENCY PER U.S. $	
	Tues.	Mon.	Tues.	Mon.
Argentina (austral)	.0001940	.0001946	5154.80	5140.00
Australia (dollar)	.7780	.7795	1.2853	1.2829
. . .				
Britain (pound)	1.9280	1.9155	.5187	.5221
30-day Forward	1.9188	1.9063	.5212	.5246
90-day Forward	1.9037	1.8917	.5253	.5286
180-day Forward	1.8842	1.8273	.5307	.5341

These exchange rates are the closing prices of actual trades amounting to more than $1 million among the major foreign exchange banks in New York. These rates are lower than the retail prices charged to corporations and correspondent banks for foreign currency. The closing prices of the past two trading days are generally shown for comparison. The two columns under "U.S. $ Equivalent" are the dollar prices per unit of a foreign currency. For example, a single Australian dollar costs about 78 cents in American dollars and the British pound traded at $1.93 per pound. The two columns on the right show the value of a dollar in terms of units of foreign currency. It would have taken 5154.8 Argentina australs to buy one American dollar. The quotes for Britain also show the forward rates, which are the rates for currency delivery at that designated number of days in the future.

■ A CLOSER LOOK: Foreign Exchange Markets

Since 1973, many industrialized countries have allowed their currencies to fluctuate in response to general supply and demand forces in the international exchange market. Such "free-floating" rates are a radical departure from earlier practices. Under the classic gold standard, which Congress officially adopted in 1879 and abandoned in 1933, nations defined their currencies in terms of gold and allowed their currency to be freely exchanged for gold. Thus, as long as the countries maintained a fixed price of gold for their currencies, the exchange rates among the countries were fixed. For example, if the British government declared one ounce of gold to be worth 5 British pounds, the German government said one ounce of gold was worth 120 deutsche marks and the American government said one ounce of gold was worth $20, then $1 = DM6; $4 = £1; and £1 = DM24. Though fluctuations of about 2 percent were possible around these "mint par" ratios, the exchange rates among countries were fairly well fixed by the gold standard. This international gold standard persisted until the depression years of the 1930s, when it was abandoned as countries tried to depreciate the international value of their currencies in order to stimulate exports and discourage imports. The result of this competitive depreciation was a sharp drop in the quantity of trade among countries.

Most countries credited the expansion of trade during the first decades of the 20th century to the fixed rates of the gold standard, and the decline of trade during the 1930s to flexible rates. However, it was soon obvious that the world's supply of gold was insufficient to support the expected growth in international trade after World War II. Furthermore, returning to the classic gold standard would have created many other problems, which are beyond the scope of this book. Thus, the major Western countries, meeting at Bretton Woods, New Hampshire, in 1944, decided to adopt fixed rates—but without the slavish dedication to the gold standard.

The famous Bretton Woods agreement established the International Monetary Fund and a new international exchange standard. Between 1944 and 1973, most industrialized countries maintained fixed exchange rates in what was known as the **adjustable peg system**. Western governments thought they could avoid the 1930s' problems of fluctuating exchange rates by establishing pegged values for the world's currencies based on the U.S. dollar. The dollar, in turn, was pegged to gold at $35 per ounce. By pegging the values of their currencies to the dollar, the countries also pegged their currencies to each other. For example, if British pounds were pegged at £1 = $4 and French francs were pegged at FF8 = $1, then £1 = FF32. The central banks were pledged to maintain these pegged values within plus or minus 1 percent by buying and selling their own currencies and the currencies of other countries.[9] If the price of a country's currency reached the upper limit of the band, the country was supposed to sell its currency in the foreign exchange market, and if it reached the lower limit of the band, it was supposed to buy its currency. If a country's currency was under persistent downward pressure in the foreign exchange market, it would have to use other countries' currencies to buy back its own currency and thus maintain its price. Since it was recognized that countries whose currency was under downward pressure would quickly run out of foreign exchange, elaborate arrangements were made to provide loans to weak currency countries through the International Monetary Fund. If the downward pressures persisted, the country would devalue its currency — that is, officially declare that its par value relative to the dollar would now be decreased.

For various reasons, the adjustable peg system of the International Monetary System was abandoned in 1971 and the world officially went on a **flexible rate system** in 1973. The world's major currencies are now said to be flexible or floating against most other currencies. This means that they are not controlled through administrative edicts of the individual governments or determined by international treaties, conventions, or by some fixed relationship to metals such as gold or silver. Theoretically, the international values of these currencies, like the price of potatoes and shirts, are determined by fluctuations in supply and demand.[10]

Foreign exchange — the currencies of the various countries — are now bought and sold on the foreign exchange market. This "market" does not have one single or even a few physical locations, as do the various stock exchanges around the world. The foreign exchange market is a worldwide market of foreign exchange dealers — generally large money center banks — connected by telephone and telex. In the United States, about a dozen banks in New York and another dozen spread around the country

---

[9]Between 1971 and 1973, the support band was plus or minus 2.25 percent of par.

[10]The world's currencies are not fluctuating as much as indicated by this brief overview. At the beginning of 1991, about 26 currencies were freely floating; 23 had a managed float; 3 were adjusted to a set of indicators; 9 currencies were subject to the cooperative arrangements of the European Monetary System; and 25 currencies were linked to the U.S. dollar, 14 to the French franc, 7 to the SDR (special drawing rights), and 37 to a composite of other currencies. Most major Western currencies are either part of a cooperative arrangement that limits flexibility against certain currencies (the European Community) or are fairly flexible.

have foreign exchange traders. These banks deal in about 15 major currencies that are reasonably convertible. Most currencies are not freely convertible, which means they are not exchangeable for other currencies without some restrictions. These nonconvertible currencies play a negligible role in the foreign exchange market. Banks dealing in foreign exchange buy and sell major currencies (usually in blocs of $1 million and more) for their own account and for the accounts of their customers, such as other banks or corporations.The foreign exchange banks in the United States tend to deal with each other through the intermediation of about six brokers; this arrangement preserves the anonymity of both seller and buyer until the deal is concluded. However, American banks deal directly with banks in other countries, without intermediation by brokers.

Although most Western central banks do not fix the prices of their currencies in the foreign exchange market, they all intervene in the market to maintain short-run price stability and they occasionally "nudge" their currencies upward or downward, for extended periods of time. Central banks buy and sell their own currencies, as well as the currencies of other countries, in order to influence the exchange rate value of their currency. When central banks engage in extensive intervention for more than a few days, the currency in question is said to be in a **dirty float**. If the central banks do not try to influence the exchange value of their currency over the long run, the currency is said to be in a **clean float**.

The foreign exchange market is active, complicated, and quite stressful to those who participate in it. More than 100 banks and dealers trade more than 200 currencies, although most active trading occurs in about a dozen currencies. Traders have to keep the various rates and cross rates straight and be ready to buy or sell when they get just slightly out of alignment. **Cross rates** are indirect rates of exchange between two currencies, given in terms of a third currency. To illustrate this concept, assume that $1 = .6144 pound and that one deutsche mark will purchase .3248 pound (DM1 = £.3248). Thus, the dollar-deutsche mark cross rate is $1 = DM1.8916 (1/0.3248 × 0.6144).

Transactions in foreign currencies are motivated by the demands of trade and by speculation. Foreign exchange speculators, like speculators in the stock or commodities markets, hope to buy at a low price and sell at a high price. Because speculators tend to buy when net demand and prices are low and to sell when net demand and prices are high, their transactions tend to stabilize the market. Transactions arising from the needs of trade are caused by the simple fact that countries use different currencies, so international trade eventually involves exchanging the currency of the importer for the currency of the exporter. If an American firm is going to import Scotch whiskey and the firm's contract with the Scotch exporter requires that the importer pay in British pounds, the importer has to take the initiative and sell dollars for pounds. If the contract specifies payment in dollars, the exporter will receive dollars and will have to take the initiative to exchange dollars for pounds. If the American importer has to pay in pounds, the firm begins the process of converting dollars to pounds by going to its local bank. If the bank is not a major player in the exchange market, it will contact its correspondent bank in New York. The importer tells the bank that it wants to obtain 100,000 British pounds by March 15, and the bank forwards the order to the New York foreign exchange dealer/bank. On March 13, the dealer/bank probably sells the pounds to the importer out of its own inventory, charging the current dollar price of pounds plus a fee or commission. If this New York bank doesn't have enough pounds in inventory, it calls another major bank or broker and asks, "How do you make pounds?" The answer might be: 1.6120; 1.6150. The first, or lower, quotation is the price at which the responding bank will buy pounds, and the second, or higher, quotation is the price at which it will sell pounds. The dealer/bank might call around to other banks around New York or even in other countries to get the most favorable rate. The local bank charges the importer its cost, plus a fee (say $1600) for its own services. The bank tells the dealer/bank where to wire the pound balances. In this case, we can assume that the pounds will be wired to a British branch of the New York bank. The importer then tells the New York bank to transfer the funds to the bank of the Scotch exporter. Although there will be several intermediary accounting entries, we know that the British exporter will have its pound account credited by £100,000 and the importer will have its bank account decreased by $163,100 (100,000 × 1.6150 + $1600).

Sometimes foreign exchange dealers and their customers, usually banks, agree to exchange a set amount of two currencies on one date and then to complete an opposite transaction at a later date. These are known as **foreign exchange swaps**. Their purpose is to give each party the use of the currency for a few days. The swap is widely used by central banks to obtain the currencies they need to shore up their own currencies in the market. For example, the Central Bank of Japan and the Federal Reserve might arrange a swap of 200 million yen for $1 million to occur on March 10 and to be reversed on March 20. On March 10, the Federal Reserve would credit the Bank of Japan with $1 million and the Bank of Japan would credit the Federal Reserve with 200 million yen. On March 20th, the entries would be reversed, but in the meantime the banks would have been able to use these deposits to buy foreign currencies.

The Forward Market

When foreign currencies are bought and sold for delivery within two days of the contract, the transaction is said to be a **spot market transaction**; when the delivery is a number of days in the future, the transaction is said to be in the **forward market**. In the forward market, parties agree today on the quantities and the prices of the foreign exchange they will be trading some date in the future. They also agree on the date that the currencies will be exchanged. For example, the American importer could have purchased its £100,000 in the forward market by agreeing on the price today (say, $1.5152 per pound), but postponing delivery of the dollars and receipt of the pounds until some time in the future. Delivery can be made a standardized number of days in the future — 30, 60, 90, or 180 days — although customized delivery days, say 42 days, can be arranged for major currencies. Assuming that the American importer doesn't have to pay the Scotch exporter for 90 days, the firm could buy pounds 90 days forward. That is, the firm would enter into a contract today agreeing to deliver $151,520 in 90 days, and it would get £100,000 in return. No money or foreign exchange changes hands today, only a verbal promise, possibly followed by a written confirmation. However, the importer has protected itself against exchange rate risk. Even if the spot price of British pounds should increase during the interim period, the importer's price remains the same because of the forward contract. The American firm knows that in 90 days it will get £100,000 by paying $151,520. Similarly, its foreign exchange trading partner, who is selling pounds (buying $) forward, knows that in 90 days it will get $151,520 by paying £100,000. Both parties have reduced their exchange risk by trading in the forward exchange market. When participants protect themselves against exchange losses that could result from normal trading activities, they are said to be **covering, or hedging**.[11]

The forward rate can be used as an indicator or estimate of what foreign exchange dealers think the exchange rate for two currencies will be in the future. If the price of the British pound is lower for the 30-day forward contract than it is for a spot sale; and if the 60-day forward pound is even lower than the 30-day forward, this is a good indication that the international financial community is expecting the pound to depreciate over the next few weeks.[12] For example, consider the following illustration:

	Foreign Currency in $	Dollar in Foreign Currency
Britain (spot)	1.9162	.5219
30-day Forward	1.9068	.5244
60-day Forward	1.8991	.5266
90-day Forward	1.8920	.5214
Germany (spot)	0.6611	1.5126
30-day Forward	.6616	1.5114
60-day Forward	.6624	1.5096
90-day Forward	.6629	1.5086

[11]Traders can also hedge by trading foreign currency options and futures. See pages 238–241 in the Options and Futures chapter.

[12]Estimates of future exchange rates can also be obtained from the prices of futures contracts, which are traded on the floors of commodity exchanges. Like forward contracts they involve future delivery but, unlike forward contracts, they rarely result in actual delivery.

The British pound is selling at a lower price in the forward market than it is selling in the spot market; that is, the pound is selling at a forward discount. Obviously, the international financial community, based on current information, expects the British spot price to fall (the $ to rise) over the next few weeks. On the other hand, the deutsche mark is selling at a forward premium, which means that the financial community is expecting the DM to appreciate in value (the $ to depreciate) over the next few weeks. Sometimes forward rates are quoted on the basis of a discount or premium. The formula for deriving the forward premium (discount) is:

$$\text{Forward premium} = \frac{\text{forward rate} - \text{spot rate}}{\text{spot rate}} \times \frac{12}{\text{number of months forward}}$$

$$= \frac{0.6629 - 0.6611}{0.6616} \times \frac{12}{3} = 1.09\% \text{ premium}$$

Exchange Rates and International Trade

Although most consumers do not follow closely the movements of foreign exchange rates, they are affected by them in their daily lives. When the value of the dollar appreciates in the foreign exchange market, the dollar prices of goods imported into the United States tend to fall and the foreign currency price of American exports tends to increase. For example, assume that the United States exports computers to Germany, priced at $2000, and imports German wine, priced at DM600. If the exchange rate between the dollar and the deutsche mark is DM4 = $1, American computers will be priced in Germany at DM8000 and German wine will be priced in the United States at $150. Now assume that the dollar appreciates (the DM depreciates) to DM6 = $1. Prices of American computers in Germany would increase from DM8000 to DM12,000. This higher DM price of computers would decrease American exports because German consumers would buy fewer American computers at these higher prices. The domestic price of German wine would fall from $150 to $100 and the quantity of imports into the United States would increase. Thus, an appreciation of the dollar and a depreciation of the deutsche mark would reduce American exports to Germany and increase imports from Germany. A depreciation of the dollar (appreciation of the deutsche mark) would have the opposite effect. In this way, the average consumer and worker are affected by movements in the exchange value of the dollar.

The dollar's value is not simply determined by fluctuations in supply and demand. Central banks enter the foreign exchange market continuously to stabilize short-run fluctuations in the international value of their currencies. Many central banks, including the Federal Reserve, also intervene to affect long-term exchange rates. American importers and exporters are usually aware of the Federal Reserve policies on exchange rates, but most Americans are not because international trade does not affect them as much as the citizens of many foreign countries. In countries such as Great Britain, where significant percentages of food are imported, and a large proportion of their GDP is exported, the foreign exchange policy of the central bank is a well publicized—and much politicized—issue. If any central bank buys large quantities of its own currency in the foreign exchange market, the exchange value of the currency will appreciate and imports will be relatively cheap while exports will be relatively expensive. Importers will cheer as consumers buy more; exporters will moan as their sales fall. If the central bank sells the country's currency, its exchange value will depreciate and imports will be relatively expensive and exports relatively cheap. Exporters will thrive on the increased sales while importers will do without.

Exchange rates are important for a number of reasons other than imports and exports of goods and services. They are used to value foreign assets on corporate and banking balance sheets, and they are used in a wide variety of international wealth, income, and capital comparisons. The particular exchange rates used in making such calculations or comparisons are often vitally important to a firm's bottom line. Because of central bank policies and many other variables, the exchange rate may not reflect the comparative purchasing power of the respective currencies. Thus, a number of "rules of thumb" are used to make purchasing power comparisons or to indicate whether a particular currency is over- or under-valued.

Big Mac Index of International Prices

McDonald's Big Mac® hamburger—"Two all-beef patties, special sauce, lettuce, cheese, pickles, onions, on a sesame seed bun"— has been used as a somewhat humorous but also serious indicator of over- and undervalued currencies. The index converts the local currency prices into dollar prices, using the current exchange rates and then compares the converted dollar prices of Big Macs with the prices of Big Macs in New York. For example, if the Big Mac's price in Japan is 450 yen and the exchange rate is 150 yen to the dollar, the dollar price of a Tokyo Big Mac is $3. But if the New York price of a Big Mac is only $2, then the Japanese yen is overvalued by 50 percent. The *Wall Street Journal* found that most Western European currencies were overvalued. However, these kinds of comparisons are highly sensitive to the type of product selected. If sake, instead of Big Macs, was used, the conclusions would probably be much different. See the "Read Me First" section at the beginning of this chapter for an explanation and application of the purchasing-power-parity theory.

HISTORIC DATA: Selected Exchange Rates,
1971–1990

Year	UK Exchange Rate Per US $	West Germany Exchange Rate Per US $	Italy Exchange Rate Per US $	Japan Exchange Rate Per US $
1971	0.4092	3.4673	616	347
1972	0.4005	3.1889	584	303
1973	0.4084	2.6719	582	271
1974	0.4277	2.5873	651	292
1975	0.4521	2.4614	653	297
1976	0.5567	2.5184	833	296
1977	0.5733	2.3225	882	268
1978	0.5214	2.0089	849	210
1979	0.4720	1.8331	831	219
1980	0.4304	1.8183	857	227
1981	0.4978	2.2606	1,137	220
1982	0.5727	2.4281	1,353	249
1983	0.6601	2.5545	1,520	237
1984	0.7521	2.8483	1,758	238
1985	0.7792	2.9443	1,909	238
1986	0.6821	2.1711	1,491	168
1987	0.6117	1.7976	1,297	145
1988	0.5621	1.7561	1,302	128
1989	0.6111	1.8792	1,371	138
1990	0.5630	1.6159	1,198	145
1991	0.5658	1.6610	1,241	135

Note: To find the number of dollars per unit of foreign currency, simply take the reciprocal of the rates — for example, U.S. $ value of the British pound in 1989 was $1/0.6111 = \$1.64$.

Name: Trade-Weighted Dollar
Alternative name: Federal Reserve Trade-Weighted Dollar, International Value of the Dollar
Agency/Institution: Division of International Monetary Affairs, Federal Reserve
Address: Washington, DC 20551
Telephone number for data: 202-452-3244
Sources: *Federal Reserve Bulletin, Wall Street Journal*
Frequency: Daily in newspapers; monthly in the *Federal Reserve Bulletin*
When available: Next day
Revisions: None
Historic summary: See below.
Cross references: Foreign Exchange Rates

■ A QUICK LOOK: Trade-Weighted Value of the Dollar

On any given day, the U.S. dollar might rise or fall by differing percentages against the world's various currencies. When reporting the net change in the value of the dollar, it is too clumsy and time-consuming to report its value relative to all major currencies. Therefore, in order to assess the change in the value of the dollar relative to an average of the most important of these currencies, the Federal Reserve releases an index on the weighted-average exchange value of the dollar. The index takes into account the currencies of 10 major industrialized countries with extensive trade relations with the United States.[13] The importance, or weight, of each country's currency is based on the relative amount of trade each country had with the United States in the early 1970s. The base of the index is March 1973 = 100. When the index goes up, the dollar is getting stronger relative to the average of the other currencies; when it goes down, the dollar is getting weaker. The index fluctuates constantly as currencies are traded around the world, and it can make significant movements over a few years. The lowest monthly index value of the dollar was 82.12 in February 1991 and the highest was 158.430 in February 1985.

HISTORIC DATA: Trade-Weighted Value
The U.S. Dollar, 1967–1991
(1973 = 100)

1967	120.0	1981	103.3
1968	122.1	1982	116.5
1969	122.4	1983	125.3
1970	121.1	1984	138.3
1971	117.8	1985	143.2
1972	109.1	1986	112.3
1973	99.1	1987	96.9
1974	101.4	1988	92.8
1975	98.5	1989	98.5
1976	105.6	1990	89.09
1977	103.3	1991	89.84
1978	92.4		
1979	88.1		
1980	87.4		

Name: International Investment Position of the United States
Alternative name: Statement of International Indebtedness, United States Assets Abroad, and Foreign Assets in the United States

---

[13]The countries are Belgium, Canada, Germany, Japan, France, United Kingdom, Italy, Netherlands, Sweden, and Switzerland.

Agency/Institution: International Investment Division, Bureau of Economic Analysis
Address: Washington, DC 20230
Telephone number for data and inquiries: 202-523-0966
Sources: The June issue of the *Survey of Current Business*
Frequency: Annually
When available: June of every year
Revisions: Year following publication and then periodically as revisions are made in the series
Historic summary: Annual data from 1975 are available in the June issue of the *Survey of Current Business.*

■ A QUICK LOOK: U.S. International Investment Position

The net international investment position of the United States has recently undergone some radical changes. The previous method of placing values on American-owned assets in other countries and foreign-owned assets in the United States was the historical cost method. Such assets as buildings, equipment, gold, and inventories were valued at their historical costs, which reflected the value of the assets at the time they were acquired. In order to correct the resulting undervaluation, the Bureau of Economic Analysis now issues two series on the international investment position of the United States: one based on current replacement costs of assets and the other based on market value of the equity interest. Table 17.5 shows the United States' international investment position valued only at current cost.

When reviewing the international indebtedness position of the United States, always remember that the values of the various assets and liabilities depend on the exchange rates used in converting the foreign currency value of the assets to United States dollars. When the value of the yen, say, decreases relative to the dollar, the dollar value of U.S.-owned assets denominated in yen will be lower. When the value of the yen appreciates (dollar depreciates), the value of U.S.-owned assets denominated in yen will increase. Thus, the net indebtedness position of the United States, depends, in part, on the international value of the dollar.

TABLE 17.5
United States International Investment Position
Valued at Current Cost
(millions of $)

	1980	1990
Net International Investment Position	$379,623	$ (412,163)*
U.S. assets abroad (at current cost):	921,527	1,764,055
U.S. official reserves assets	171,412	174,664
Gold	155,816	102,406
Special drawing rights	2,610	10,989

(continued)

TABLE 17.5 (continued)
United States International Investment Position
Valued at Current Cost
(millions of $)

	1980	1990
Reserve position in IMF	2,852	9,076
Foreign currency	10,134	52,193
U.S. government assets, other than official reserves	63,865	81,209
U.S. credits and other long-term assets	62,023	80,661
U.S. foreign currency holdings; short-term assets	1,842	548
U.S. private assets	686,250	1,508,182
Direct investment abroad	385,059	589,062
Foreign securities	62,653	222,317
Bonds	43,487	129,062
Corporate stock	19,166	93,255
U.S. claims on unaffiliated foreigners reported by U.S. nonbanking concerns	34,672	33,518
U.S. claims reported by U.S. banks not included elsewhere	203,866	654,285
Foreign Assets in U.S (at current cost)	541,904	2,176,218
Foreign official assets in U.S.	176,062	369,607
U.S. government securities	118,189	296,036
U.S. Treasury securities	111,336	285,767
Other	6,853	10,269
Other U.S. government liabilities	13,367	17,052
U.S. liabilities reported by U.S. banks not included elsewhere	30,381	39,494
Other foreign official assets	14,125	17,025
Other foreign assets in U.S.	365,842	1,806,611
Direct investment in U.S.	124,120	465,916
U.S. Treasury securities	16,113	134,391
U.S. securities other than Treasury securities	74,114	475,120
Corporate and other bonds	9,545	343,964
Corporate stock	64,569	231,156
U.S. liabilities to unaffiliated foreigners reported by U.S. nonbanking concerns	30,426	44,143
U.S. liabilities reported by U.S. banks not included elsewhere	121,069	687,041

*( ) indicates net liabilities of U.S. residents to foreigners

Net international investment position: This is the net international indebtedness of the United States. It reflects total value of U.S. assets in foreign countries less the total value of foreign assets in the United States. In 1980, the U.S. owned $380 billion more claims on foreigners, than the value of claims on the U.S. owned by foreigners. By 1990, foreigners held $412 billion more claims on the United States than claims on foreigners held by U.S. residents.

U.S. official reserve assets: Changes in SDRs, reserve position, and foreign currencies are often due to changes in the exchange rates at which they are converted to dollar values.

Gold: The gold stock, which was valued at $42.22 per ounce, is now valued at market prices for purposes of calculating international debt. Thus, while the quantity of the gold stock remains stable, its value now fluctuates. Its current cost value in 1990 was $102 billion, but its 1990 historical cost value was about $11 billion.

Special drawing rights: Paper credits, also known as "paper gold," created by the International Monetary Fund to alleviate shortages of foreign exchange. They are distributed to central banks in proportion to their IMF quota. Their values are based on the weighted average of the currencies of the five largest exporting countries. Central banks may use these SDRs to purchase foreign exchange, subject to a set of complicated rules. (See page 403, for a more thorough discussion of SDRs.)

Reserve position in the IMF: The United States has automatic borrowing rights on these funds, which represent part of the U.S. contribution to the International Monetary Fund.

Foreign currency: The primary source of foreign currencies is the Federal Reserve's intervention in the foreign exchange market. When the Fed is trying to depreciate the international value of the dollar, it sells dollars and buys foreign currencies such as Japanese yen and German marks. (See Foreign Exchange Rates, pages 417–426.)

U.S. government assets: Certain tangible assets located in foreign countries, including military and other loans made by the U.S. government to foreign countries. They do not include official reserves, which are detailed above.

U.S. private assets: Claims on foreigners held by private firms, institutions, and individuals.

Direct investment abroad: Direct investment includes most investments other than securities, most unaffiliated stocks, and loans and bank deposits. They include ownership of foreign land, firms, and affiliates. An affiliate is a foreign business enterprise in which an American investor owns at least 10 percent. This is one of the accounts that is now valued at replacement or current cost and at the net market value of the firm or asset.

Foreign securities: General stocks and bonds of foreign private entities and foreign governments that are held by American institutions and individuals.

U.S. claims on foreigners: Claims held by nonbanks and banks that are primarily loans to foreign countries and firms and deposits in foreign banks.

Foreign assets in U.S.:   These represent claims on U.S. residents or governments held by foreigners. Foreign official assets include Treasury securities, as well as bank deposits held by foreign *governments* or *central banks*. Claims on the U.S. government, U.S. banks, companies, or individuals held by *private* individuals or institutions residing in foreign countries is shown in "Other foreign assets in U.S."

In 1980, the United States was a net creditor (+) by the net amount of $380 billion, but, by 1990, it had become a net debtor (−) of $412 billion. The 400 percent increase in American-based assets held by foreigners (these are IOUs of Americans) during the 1980s was caused by large deficits in the United States' current-account balance. As long as there is a net deficit in the current account, the debtor position of the United States will continue to grow. This international indebtedness position has increased from a positive 14 percent (net creditor) of GDP in 1980 to a negative 7.5 percent of GDP (net debtor) in 1990.

■ A CLOSER LOOK: International Investment Position of the U.S.

Since the United States became a net international debtor in 1984 and the world's largest debtor in 1987, there has been considerable interest in this series. The methodologies and presentations of the net international investment position of the United States recently underwent major revisions.[14] Economists at the Bureau of Economic Analysis had become quite concerned about the quality of international investment data — so concerned, in fact, that they did not release the 1989 figures. The media responded by accusing the administration of covering up bad news.

The problem addressed by the BEA was a real one, but it was not a new one. In fact, it was one that had divided economists and accountants for generations. About one-half of the components of international investment assets (such as portfolio investments and reserve assets) was valued at current period prices, a pricing method universally supported by economists. The other half of the international assets (such as direct investment and gold reserves) was valued at historical costs, a pricing method generally supported by accountants. The problem with historical cost is that it reflects only the value of the asset at the time it was acquired and not its current replacement cost or market value. This problem was exacerbated in the 1980s by the effects historical cost pricing had on the value of U.S. assets abroad versus the effects it had on the value of foreign investments in the United States. Because a larger percentage of American-owned assets in foreign countries had been purchased many years ago, American-owned assets tended to be relatively more undervalued than foreign-owned assets in the United States.

In 1991, the Bureau of Economic Analysis announced that it had developed two new concepts to measure the value of U.S. direct investment abroad (USDIA) and foreign direct investment in the United States (FDIUS). The **current value method** uses various techniques to estimate

---

[14]If you have unanswered questions after reading this section, you might want to look at "Valuation of the Net International Investment Position" by J. Steven Landefeld and Ann M. Lawson, *Survey of Current Business* (May 1991).

direct investment at current replacement costs. It focuses on estimating the asset value of the balance sheet. The **market value method** uses various indexes of stock market prices to estimate the equity side of the balance sheet. The following example shows the major differences between the methods.

Table 17.6 shows the balance sheet of a hypothetical wholly owned subsidiary of an American company operating abroad, with its assets and liabilities valued at the historical costs the BEA had been using for many years. Historical cost pricing does not produce any problems for cash, accounts receivable, and deposits because these "historical" costs were recorded very recently, and cash-denominated assets always have the same value, whenever recorded. However, historical valuation can produce severe distortions in the valuations of inventories, and especially property, plant, and equipment (tangible assets), which were purchased many years ago. A high percentage of the assets of this American-owned firm is tangible assets, which means that a historical cost valuation of the assets will seriously underestimate the real value of this American investment in a foreign country.

TABLE 17.6
Balance Sheet at Historical Cost

Current Assets:		Liabilities:	
Cash, deposits, notes rec.	$200,000	Current liabilities and long-term debt	$500,000
Inventories	100,000		
		Other liabilities	110,000
Total	300,000	Total	610,000
Noncurrent Assets:			
Property, plant and equipment (PP&E)	650,000	Owners' equity	390,000
Less: Accumulated depreciation	(200,000)		
Net PP&E	450,000		
Other	250,000		
Total	700,000		
Total Assets	$1,000,000	Total Liabilities and Equity	$1,000,000

Let's first correct for the undervaluation inherent in the historical cost method (Table 17.6) during periods of inflation by using the current value method of estimating replacement costs for tangible assets. This current cost method is shown in Table 17.7, where the value of inventories has been adjusted upward to $120,000 and the net value of property, plant, and equipment (net PP&E) has been revalued to $570,000. Financial assets (cash, deposits, accounts receivable) do not have to be revalued because their historical value will equal or approximate their current period values. Since these adjustments increased total assets to $1,140,000, owners' equity had to be increased to $530,000, which is the net value of the firm's investments abroad using the current value method.

TABLE 17.7
Balance Sheet Using Current Cost Method

Current Assets:		Liabilities:	
Cash, deposits, notes rec.	$200,000	Current liabilities	$500,000
Inventories	120,000	and long-term debt	
		Other liabilities	110,000
Total	320,000	Total	610,000
Noncurrent Assets:			
Property, plant and equipment (PP&E)	800,000	Owners' equity	530,000
Less: Accumulated depreciation	(230,000)		
Net PP&E	570,000		
Other	250,000		
Total	820,000		
Total Assets	$1,140,000	Total Liabilities and Equity	$1,140,000

The second method of adjusting for the distortions produced by the historical cost method is to estimate the market value of the equity account by revaluing it to reflect year-end stock market prices. In Table 17.8, the equity account has been revalued from $390,000 in Table 17.6 to $600,000. The offsetting account on the asset side is Goodwill, which, generally, is the balancing item used to reflect differences between the acquisition price of a firm and the net value of the firm's assets minus its liabilities. If the market value method is used, then, the BEA will estimate the American firm's investment in a foreign country as $600,000.

TABLE 17.8
Balance Sheet Using Market Value Method

Current Assets:		Liabilities:	
Cash, deposits, notes rec.	$200,000	Current liabilities	$500,000
Inventories	100,000	and long-term debt	
		Other liabilities	110,000
Total	300,000	Total	610,000
Noncurrent Assets:			
Property, plant and equipment (PP&E)	650,000	Owners' equity	600,000
Less: Accumulated depreciation	(200,000)		
Net PP&E	450,000		
Other	250,000		
Goodwill	210,000		
Total	860,000		
Total Assets	$1,210,000	Total Liabilities and Equity	$1,210,000

The BEA now reports the net international investment position of the United States with direct investment positions at current cost ($-$ $412,163 in 1990) and with direct investment positions at market value (−$360,598). It has revised its historical data back to 1982 for market value–based positions and back to 1976 for current cost–based positions.

BEA publishes separate tables in this data series that show direct investments by country. Canada and the United Kingdom are the recipients of the largest amounts of U.S. direct investment. The United Kingdom is the owner of the greatest amount of direct investment in the United States — about twice as much as Japan. The runners-up are Japan and the Netherlands.

HISTORICAL DATA: The International Investment Position of the United States
Historical Costs Method: 1869–1975
Current Costs Method: 1976–1991
(billions of $)

	U.S. Investment Abroad	Foreign Investment In U.S.	Net International Investment Position of U.S.		U.S. Investment Abroad	Foreign Investment In U.S.	Net International Investment Position of U.S.
1869	$0.1	$1.5	$ − 1.4	1965	$120.4	$58.8	$61.6
1897	0.7	3.4	− 2.7	1966	125.2	60.4	64.8
1908	2.5	6.4	− 3.9	1967	134.7	69.7	65.0
1914	5.0	7.2	− 2.2	1968	146.8	81.2	65.6
1919	9.7	3.3	6.4	1969	158.1	90.8	67.3
1924	15.1	3.9	11.2	1970	165.4	106.9	58.5
1927	17.9	6.6	11.3	1971			0.0
1930	21.5	8.4	13.1	1972			0.0
1935	23.6	6.4	17.2	1973			0.0
1940	34.3	13.5	20.8	1974	255.7	197.0	58.7
1945	36.9	17.0	19.9	1975	295.1	220.9	74.2
1946	39.4	15.2	24.2	1976	457.6	281.7	175.9
1947	48.3	13.8	34.5	1977	519.0	328.5	190.5
1948	52.5	14.4	38.1	1978	627.3	398.8	228.4
1949	53.9	14.8	39.1	1979	792.9	450.0	342.9
1950	54.4	17.6	36.8	1980	936.3	453.7	392.5
1951	56.4	18.7	37.7	1981	1,004.2	629.9	374.3
1952	59.1	20.8	38.3	1982	1,119.2	740.2	378.9
1953	60.2	21.9	38.3	1983	1,169.2	831.8	337.4
1954	62.4	25.0	37.4	1984	1,177.5	944.7	232.9
1955	65.1	27.8	37.3	1985	1,252.5	1,113.6	138.9
1956	70.8	30.5	40.3	1986	1,410.1	1,391.5	18.7
1957	76.4	30.7	45.7	1987	1,564.7	1,591.4	− 26.6
1958	79.2	34.4	44.8	1988	1,654.6	1,838.3	− 183.7
1959	82.2	39.1	43.1	1989	1,794.7	2,107.0	− 132.3
1960	85.6	40.9	44.7	1990	1,884.2	2,179.0	− 294.8
1961	92.0	46.0	46.0	1991	1,960.3	2,321.8	− 361.5
1962	96.5	46.3	50.2				
1963	103.9	51.5	52.4				
1964	114.7	56.9	57.8				

Name: Labor Market Comparisons Among Countries
Alternative name: International Comparisons of Unemployment Rates

Agency/Institution:
Division of International Labor
Bureau of Labor Statistics
Washington, DC 20212
Telephone: 202-523-9294

International Labour Organization (ILO)
(based in Geneva)
U.S. branch office:
1828 L Street
Washington, DC 20036
Telephone: 202-653-7652

Organization for Economic Cooperation and Development (OECD)
Suite 700
2001 L Street NW
Washington, DC 20036
Telephone: 202-785-6323

Sources: *International Comparisons of Unemployment, Bulletin 1979* (annual) and periodic issues of the *Monthly Labor Review* (both from the BLS); *Yearbook of Labor Statistics* (annual) and *Bulletin of Labor Statistics* (quarterly) (both from the ILO); and *Employment Outlook* (annual), *OECD Observer* (every two months), and *Main Economic Indicators* (monthly) (all from the OECD).

Historic summary: *Handbook of Labor Statistics*

Cross references: Employment, Unemployment, Unemployment Rates

---

■ A QUICK LOOK: International Labor Markets

The U.S. Bureau of Labor Statistics currently reports comparable data on domestic labor markets for 10 countries: United States, Canada, Australia, Japan, France, Germany, Italy, the Netherlands, Sweden, and the United Kingdom. The data reported on each country include the following:[15] labor force, employment–population ratio, participation rate, employment, unemployment, and unemployment rate.

Each country maintains its own labor market database, so the definitions and methodologies of each country differ considerably from the others and from the United States. The purpose of this BLS series is to make these data reasonably comparable to U.S. definitions. Some major areas where the data remain incomparable are the following:

1. The youngest labor market age is defined in each country as the age at which compulsory schooling ends. This is 16 years in the United States, France, Sweden, and, since 1973, in the United Kingdom; 15 and over in Canada, Australia, Japan, Germany, and the Netherlands; and 14 and over in Italy.

---

[15]The reader is advised to obtain the definitions of these terms from pages 71–72.

2. The institutionalized population is included in the labor force in Japan and Germany but excluded in other countries.

3. Persons on layoff who are awaiting recall to their jobs are classified as unemployed in the United States but not in other countries.

Another important source of data, analyses, and policies on labor issues is the International Labour Organization (ILO), which was formed by the Treaty of Versailles in 1919 and became affiliated with the United Nations in 1946. It provides assistance in social policy and administration and in manpower training and utilization and fosters cooperative organizations and rural industries. It conducts much research and data gathering on labor and employment issues. Generally pro-labor, it has emphasized protection of international migrants, safeguarding of trade union rights, and an increased labor influence in national and international decisions. It has a large research staff and runs a Center for Technical and Vocational Training in Turin, Italy. It issues papers and books at irregular intervals as well as its *Yearbook of Labor Statistics* and its quarterly *Bulletin of Labor Statistics*.

The *Yearbook of Labor Statistics* and the *Bulletin of Labor Statistics* contain a wide variety of labor market information. They include data on labor force, employment, unemployment, union memberships, wages, fringe benefits, unemployment benefits, occupational accidents, sicknesses, education levels, migration, participation ratios, layoffs, and part-time employment. These two publications are the ones to use when you need labor market information on countries not covered by the U.S. Bureau of Labor Statistics publications or the OECD's *Employment Outlook.*

The *Employment Outlook*, an annual publication of the OECD, provides a wide variety of labor market data for the 24 member countries of this Paris-based organization. Often data and analyses are presented for other countries as well. Recently, the *Employment Outlook* has begun reporting labor market data for the Pacific-rim Asian countries. The major advantage of using *Employment Outlook* as a source of international labor market information is that the publishers make a concerted effort to make the data comparable. When they are unable to do so, they clearly caution the reader about the incompatibilities.

Data series include labor force, employment, unemployment, union memberships, wages, fringe benefits, unemployment benefits, occupational accidents, education levels, migration, participation ratios, layoffs, flexitime, average weekly hours worked, part-time employment, and nonstandard employment. Some of these data series are also available in two other valuable OECD publications: the *OECD Observer* (bimonthly) and *Main Economic Indicators* (monthly).

See Chapter 4 for a discussion of concepts, terminology, and problems in labor market data.

RECENT HISTORIC DATA: Comparable Unemployment Rates Among 10 Countries

	1980	1985	1986	1987	1988	1989	1990
U.S.	7.1	7.2	7.0	6.2	5.5	5.3	5.5
Canada	7.5	10.5	9.5	8.8	7.8	7.5	8.1
Australia	6.1	8.3	8.1	8.1	7.2	6.2	6.9
Japan	2.0	2.6	2.8	2.9	2.5	2.3	2.1
France	6.4	10.4	10.6	10.7	10.2	9.7	9.2
Germany	2.8	7.2	6.6	6.3	6.3	5.7	5.2
Italy	4.4	6.0	7.5	7.9	7.9	7.8	7.0
Netherlands	6.0	10.2	10.0	9.9	9.5	9.0	8.0
Sweden	2.0	2.8	2.6	1.9	1.6	1.3	1.5
U.K.	7.0	11.2	11.2	10.3	8.6	7.0	6.9

Name: GDP Comparisons Among Countries
Agencies/Institutions:
International Monetary Fund
700 19th Street N.W.
Washington, DC 20431
Telephone: 202-623-7000

Organization for Economic Cooperation and Development (OECD)
Suite 700
2001 L Street N.W.
Washington, DC 20036
Telephone: 202-785-6323

United Nations
1st Avenue and 46th Street
New York, NY 10017
Telephone: 212-963-1234

Sources: *International Financial Statistics* (*IFS*; monthly with an annual supplement, from the IMF); *Quarterly National Accounts, OECD Observer* (bimonthly with an annual supplement), and *Main Economic Indicators* (monthly) (all from the OECD); and *United Nations, National Accounts Statistics* (annual)

Historic summary: Some historical data are provided in the source publications. The OECD produces a historical data series (Main Economic Indicators — Historical Statistics) every five years. The most recent one is for 1969–1988.

Cross references: Gross Domestic Product, Chapter 7.

■ A QUICK LOOK: Gross Domestic Product

International Financial Statistics, a monthly publication of the International Monetary Fund, is divided into two sections: (1) a 70-page section containing data on industrial and developing countries arranged by continent, and (2) a country section that lists in alphabetical order a wide range of data for about 145 countries. The world tables do not contain

GNP data but the country section compares gross domestic products and gross national products.

The best source of national income accounting data for the 24 members of the OECD[16] is the *Quarterly National Accounts*, although the monthly *Main Economic Indicators* also contains some national income data such as gross and domestic products by major economic sectors and implicit price indexes. There is a delay of about 1.5 years before reliable data are available.

The United Nations has established a "System of National Accounts" (SNA), which is supposed to be followed by all countries reporting their data to the U.N. The quality of the data has improved in recent years, but, for certain countries, the data are still quite unreliable.

See Chapter 7 for a discussion of some of the concepts, terminology, and problems in national income accounting.

HISTORIC DATA: Gross Domestic Product at Market Prices
per Capita Gross Domestic Product
at Current Dollar Prices Using PPPs

	1970	1975	1980	1985	1989
Australia	$3,474	$5,477	$ 8,514	$11,738	$14,304
Austria	2,722	4,563	7,825	10,745	13,407
Belgium	3,003	4,920	8,174	10,680	13,587
Canada	3,976	6,750	11,153	15,464	19,305
Denmark	3,545	5,344	8,613	12,369	14,594
Finland	2,907	4,873	8,105	11,509	15,030
France	3,204	5,275	8,735	11,707	14,565
Germany	3,430	5,231	8,948	12,105	14,985
Greece	1,564	2,730	4,567	6,009	7,253
Iceland	2,938	5,247	9,911	13,161	15,867
Ireland	1,818	3,010	5,069	6,883	8,984
Italy	3,046	4,666	7,983	10,966	13,902
Japan	2,812	4,533	7,958	11,805	15,501
Luxembourg	3,780	5,889	9,444	13,143	17,192
Netherlands	3,543	5,554	8,798	11,339	13,709
New Zealand	3,283	5,155	7,176	10,106	11,446
Norway	3,127	5,331	9,553	13,963	16,663
Portugal	1,462	2,326	4,308	5,516	7,360
Spain	2,178	3,821	5,775	7,597	10,263
Sweden	3,848	6,024	9,156	12,655	15,533
Switzerland	4,770	6,829	10,775	14,436	17,695
Turkey	890	1,619	2,481	3,606	4,484
United Kingdom	3,265	5,051	7,881	10,971	14,345
United States	4,922	7,334	11,804	16,581	20,629

---

[16]See OECD in the Glossary for a list of members.

Name: Price Change Comparisons Among Countries
Agencies/Institutions:
International Monetary Fund
700 19th Street N.W.
Washington, DC 20431
Telephone: 202-623-7000

Organization for Economic Cooperation and Development (OECD)
Suite 700
2001 L Street N.W.
Washington, DC 20036
Telephone: 202-785-6323

Statistical Office
United Nations
1st Avenue and 46th Street
New York, NY 10017
Telephone: 212-963-1234

Division of International Labor
Bureau of Labor Statistics
Washington, DC 20212
Telephone: 202-523-9294

Sources: *International Financial Statistics* (IFS; monthly with an annual supplement, from the IMF); *Quarterly National Accounts, OECD Observer* (bimonthly with an annual supplement), and *Main Economic Indicators* (monthly) (all from the OECD); *Monthly Bulletin of Statistics* and *Statistical Yearbook* (both from the UN); and *Monthly Labor Review* and *Handbook of Labor Statistics* (periodic) (both from the BLS)

Historic summary: Some historical data are provided in the source publications. The OECD produces a historical data series (Main Economic Indicators — Historical Statistics) every five years. The most recent one is for 1969–1988.

Cross references: Consumer Price Index

■ A QUICK LOOK: Price Changes

International Financial Statistics, a monthly publication of the International Monetary Fund, is divided into two sections: (1) a 70-page section containing data on industrial and developing countries arranged by continent, and (2) a country section that lists in alphabetical order a wide range of data for about 145 countries. The world tables contain comparisons of percentage changes in consumer prices: on a monthly basis for the current year, quarterly for the previous year, and annually for the previous four years. The country tables contain monthly consumer and producer (or wholesale) indexes for the current and past years — quarterly for the past three years and annually for the most recent seven years. Both the Consumer and Producer Price Indexes have a base year of $1985 = 100$.

The *Main Economic Indicators*, published by OECD, reports on producer prices for a number of producers and consumer prices. Price indexes are available by month, quarter, and year.

HISTORIC DATA: Consumer Prices:
Average Annual Rates of Change for
Selected Countries

	1970–75	1980	1985	1989	1990
Argentina	72.50%	100.80%	672.10%	3,079.80%	2,314.0%
Australia	10.30	10.10	6.70	7.60	7.3
France	8.90	13.40	5.80	3.50	3.4
Germany	6.10	6.30	2.20	2.80	2.7
Japan	11.70	8.00	2.00	2.30	3.1
Mexico	12.30	26.40	57.70	20.00	26.7
Norway	8.40	10.80	5.70	4.60	4.1
Switzerland	7.70	4.00	3.40	3.20	5.4
United Kingdom	13.20	18.00	6.10	7.80	9.5
United States	6.80	10.40	3.60	4.80	5.4

Name: Wage Rate Comparisons Among Countries
Alternative name: Hourly Compensation
Agencies/Institutions:
  Division of International Labor
  Bureau of Labor Statistics
  Washington, DC 20212
  Telephone: 202-523-9294

  Organization for Economic Cooperation and Development (OECD)
  Suite 700
  2001 L Street N.W.
  Washington, DC 20036
  Telephone: 202-785-6323

  International Labour Organization
  (based in Geneva)
  U.S. branch office:
  1828 L Street
  Washington, DC 20036
  Telephone: 202-653-7652
Sources: *Report 771*, August 1991 (annual) and *Monthly Labor Review* (both from the BLS); *Main Economic Indicators* (from the OECD); and *Yearbook of Labor Statistics* (from the ILO)
Historic summary: OECD's *Main Economic Indicators* — Historical Statistics data series

■ **A QUICK LOOK: Wage Rate Comparisons Among Countries**

Perhaps the best source of data on wage comparisons in manufacturing is the Bureau of Labor Statistics, since it makes reasonable attempts to make the data comparable and it reports on many countries. The OECD is also a good source for indexes of manufacturing for its 24 member countries. Be careful about the comparability of compensation, however, because many variables may be included in the compensation data of some countries or industries but left out in others. In the BLS data, compensation includes direct pay, employer expenditures for legally required insurance programs and contractual and private benefit (such as pension) plans, and certain labor taxes. The BLS uses an index that compares foreign compensation rates with those of the United States. The OECD uses indexes (1980 = 100) so that comparisons of growth rates in compensation can be made among countries but comparisons of absolute levels cannot be made.

**HISTORIC DATA: BLS Indexes of Hourly
Compensation Rates for Production Workers
in Manufacturing**
Compared with U.S. Compensation

	1975	1980	1985	1990
United States	100	100	100	100
Brazil	14	14	9	18
France	71	91	58	103
Greece	27	38	20	46
Hong Kong	12	15	14	22
Japan	48	57	50	86
Mexico	31	30	16	12
Taiwan	6	10	11	27
United Kingdom	52	76	48	84
West Germany	100	125	74	146

Name: International Comparisons of Manufacturing Productivity
Agency/Institution: Bureau of Labor Statistics
Address: Washington, DC 20212
Telephone number for data and inquiries: 202-523-9301
Sources: *Monthly Labor Review, Economic Report of the President*
Frequency: Only annual data are shown.
When available: About three to six months after the end of the year
Revisions: Frequently
Historic summary: Available on diskettes from the Bureau of Labor

■ A QUICK LOOK: Productivity

Absolute productivity measurements cannot be directly compared among countries, but the BLS has developed indexes of productivity for manufacturing output per hour for 12 countries. Consequently, at least the trends in productivity among countries can be compared. "Hours worked" refers to all employed persons including the self-employed in the United States and Canada; in all other countries, this refers solely to hours worked by wage and salary employees. The United States measures hours paid, whereas other countries count the hours worked.

Productivity data are available for the following countries: United States, Canada, Japan, Belgium, Denmark, France, Germany, Italy, the Netherlands, Norway, Sweden, and the United Kingdom.

The specific data presented are: output per hour, output, total hours, compensation per hour, unit labor costs (national currency basis), and unit labor costs (U.S. dollar basis).

Compensation includes all payments in cash plus legally required insurance payments and taxes. For most countries, the data refer solely to the manufacturing sector, but, in France, Italy, and the United Kingdom, they refer to manufacturing and mining, less energy-related products.

HISTORIC DATA: Index of Output per Hour
Among Countries
(1982 = 100)

	1960	1970	1980	1985	1990
United States	58.4	77.2	96.6	114.8	136.6
Canada	51.6	76.9	99.9	119.8	121.2
Japan	18.6	52.0	92.1	112.0	138.1
Belgium	24.2	44.3	87.5	116.4	—
Denmark	32.4	57.2	98.0	105.0	105.1
France	30.7	58.5	90.6	108.8	127.7
Germany	38.5	67.0	98.4	112.9	124.8
Italy	29.1	54.6	95.5	122.3	138.8
Netherlands	26.9	53.5	95.1	121.1	133.3
Norway	47.8	74.5	96.3	116.0	127.1
Sweden	36.2	69.1	96.4	112.6	118.2
United Kingdom	49.4	70.8	89.9	117.8	145.1

Name: Interest Rates in Various Countries
Agencies/Institutions:
International Monetary Fund
700 19th Street N.W.
Washington, DC 20431
Telephone: 202-623-7000

Organization for Economic Cooperation and Development (OECD)
Suite 700
2001 L Street N.W.
Washington, DC 20036
Telephone: 202-785-6323

Federal Reserve System
Washington, DC 20551
Telephone number: 202-452-3017

Statistical Office
United Nations
1st Avenue and 46th Street
New York, NY 10017
Telephone: 212-963-1234
Sources: *International Financial Statistics* (*IFS*; monthly with an annual supplement, from the IMF); *OECD Observer* (bimonthly with an annual supplement) and *Main Economic Indicators* (monthly and annual supplement) (both from the OECD); *Federal Reserve Bulletin*; and *Monthly Bulletin of Statistics* and *Statistical Yearbook* (both from the UN)
Other sources: *Wall Street Journal* and many private investor services
When available: Monthly publications have a two-month lag
Historical data: Every five years the OECD releases its *Main Economic Indicators —
Historical Statistics* data series, which contains 20 years of data.

■ A QUICK LOOK: Interest Rates in Various Countries

Although there is a lag of two to five months, the most complete source of international interest rate information is *International Financial Statistics*, published monthly by the International Monetary Fund. *International Financial Statistics* is divided into two sections: (1) a 70 page section of data from industrial and developing countries arranged by continent; and (2) a country section that lists in alphabetical order a wide range of data for about 145 countries. The world table on international interest rates reports London interbank offer rates on deposits denominated in SDRs, U.S. dollars, French francs, German marks, Japanese yen, and Swiss francs. These rates are simple, unweighted averages of quotations by major international banks. There are also comparisons of various interest rates (central bank discount rates, money market rates, bank lending and deposit rates, Treasury bill rates, and government bond rates) for about 30 countries.

Many of the country tables for the 144 countries have data for the central bank's lending rate (discount rate), money market rate, interbank deposit rate, Treasury bill rate, bank deposit and lending rates, government bond rate, and mortgage yield rate. These rates are available monthly for the most recent year, quarterly for up to four years, and annually for seven years.

The *Main Economic Indicators*, published by OECD, reports monthly, quarterly, and annual data for money call rates, Treasury bill rates, commercial paper rates, prime rates, and long-term government rates for the OECD countries.

The *Federal Reserve Bulletin* (monthly) reports the discount rates of foreign central banks and the short-term interest rates of the United Kingdom, Canada, Germany, Switzerland, the Netherlands, France, Italy, Belgium, and Japan.

HISTORIC DATA: Government Bond Yields
Selected Countries

	1960	1970	1975	1980	1985	1990
United States	4.2%	6.9%	8.2%	11.5%	10.6%	8.6%
Canada	5.3	7.9	9.0	12.5	11.0	10.9
Japan	—	7.2	9.2	9.2	6.3	7.4
France	5.2	8.1	9.5	13.0	10.9	10.0
Italy	5.2	9.0	11.5	16.1	13.0	11.5
Sweden	4.6	7.4	8.8	11.7	13.1	13.1
Switzerland	3.1	5.8	6.4	4.8	4.8	6.7
United Kingdom	5.4	9.2	14.4	13.8	10.6	11.1
West Germany	6.4	8.3	8.5	8.5	6.9	8.9

Name: Money Supply and Banking Deposits
Agencies/Institutions:
  Division of Monetary Affairs
  International Monetary Fund
  700 19th Street N.W.
  Washington, DC 20431
  Telephone: 202-623-7000

  Organization for Economic Cooperation and Development (OECD)
  Suite 700
  2001 L Street N.W.
  Washington, DC 20036
  Telephone: 202-785-6323
Sources: *International Financial Statistics* (*IFS*; monthly with an annual supplement, from the IMF) and *Main Economic Indicators* (monthly, from the OECD)
Frequency: Monthly
When available: Lag of two to five months after the reported period
Historic summary: Every five years the OECD releases its *Main Economic Indicators — Historical Statistics* data series, which contains 20 years of data.

■ A QUICK LOOK: Money Supply and Bank Deposits

The *International Financial Statistics* is the best source for international information on money supply and banking deposits. The *IFS* is divided into two sections: (1) a 70-page section containing data from industrial and developing countries arranged by continent, and (2) a country section that lists in alphabetical order a wide range of data for about 145 countries. The world tables contain direct comparisons of M1 money stock for most countries of the world, and the individual country sections provide data for M1 and M2 as well as for domestic credit. Foreign assets and liabilities of domestic deposit money banks (these banks are similar to the commercial banks in the United States) are reported in the world section in billions of U.S. dollars and in the country section in domestic currency (country tables). Seasonally adjusted and nonadjusted monetary data are reported for most industrial countries.

The country section contains data on the assets and liabilities of the central banks and central governments and on the assets and liabilities of deposit money banks. The listed liabilities of the banks include demand deposits, time deposits, foreign liabilities, bonds, and so on. Assets listed include reserves and claims on central governments, foreigners, and private entities. Some countries list additional data, such as on life insurance and pension funds.

OECD's *Main Economic Indicators* (monthly with an annual supplement) is a good source of data on M1, M2, credit, and savings deposits for the organization's 24 member countries.

Name: Foreign Trade Statistics
Alternative name: Imports, Exports, Balance of Payments
Agencies/Institutions:
  International Monetary Fund
  700 19th Street N.W.
  Washington, DC 20431
  Telephone: 202 623-7000

  Organization for Economic Cooperation and Development (OECD)
  Suite 700
  2001 L Street N.W.
  Washington, DC 20036
  Telephone: 202-785-6323

  Department of International Economic and Social Affairs
  United Nations
  New York, NY 10017
  Telephone: 212-963-1234
Sources: *International Financial Statistics* (*IFS*; monthly with an annual supplement, from the IMF); *Main Economic Indicators* (monthly) and *Monthly Statistics of Foreign Trade* (both from the OECD); and *Commodity Trade Statistics* (annual, from the U.N.)
When available: A lag of two to five months after the reported period for the monthly publications
Historic summary: Every five years the OECD releases *Main Economic Indicators —Historical Statistics* data series, which contains 20 years of data.

■ A QUICK LOOK: Foreign Trade Data

International Financial Statistics, a monthly publication of the International Monetary Fund, is one of the best, most easily available sources of international trade data. The *IFS* is divided into two sections: (1) a 70-page section of data from various industrial and developing countries arranged by continent, and (2) a country section that lists in alphabetical order a wide range of data for about 145 countries. The world section contains comparative data on exports, imports, export price indexes and import price indexes. The country data contain not only export and import data but also detailed data on the components of the balance of payments, such as merchandise trade, direct investment, portfolio investment, and services.

OECD's monthly, *Main Economic Indicators*, together with its annual supplement and its five-year *Historical Statistics* issue, reports imports and exports for OECD countries as well as data on merchandise trade and current and capital balances. A more complete listing of the origin and destination of trade statistics is contained in OECD's *Monthly Statistics of Foreign Trade*.

A massive amount of trade flow data is contained in the U.N.'s *Commodity Trade Statistics* for each of about 50 countries, which details values and quantities of commodities (classified according to the Standard International Trade Classification). For example, in the 415-page 1990 Italy edition of *Commodity Trade Statistics*, we can find that Italy exported 3241 tons of unpickled frozen vegetables worth $2.8 million to the United Kingdom.

HISTORIC DATA: Current Account Balances,
Selected Countries
(millions of $)

	1970	1975	1980	1985	1990
United States	$ 2,320	$ 18,130	$ 1,860	($122,250)	($92,160)
Canada	1,078	(4,696)	(953)	(1,470)	(13,647)
Japan	2,000	(690)	20,800	49,170	35,870
France	55	—*	(4,208)	(35)	(9,875)
Italy	902	(580)	(9,801)	(3,540)	(10,808)
Mexico	(1,068)	(4,042)	(8,162)	1,130	(5,251)
Sweden	(265)	(342)	(4,404)	(1,608)	(5,833)
Switzerland	72	2,288	(1,555)	6,040	8,500
United Kingdom	1,975	(3,476)	8,690	3,972	(23,538)
West Germany	852	4,093	(16,000)	17,052	43,986

"—" indicates a deficit.

Name: External Debt of Developing Countries
Agency/Institution: International Finance Division, International Economics Department, World Bank
[also known as the International Bank for Reconstruction and Development]
1818 H Street, N.W., Washington, DC 20433
Sources: *World Debt Tables*
Frequency: Annually

When available: About 2½ years after end of reference year
Historic summary: Each issue has data for the previous eight years and then back to ten and twenty years earlier.

■ A QUICK LOOK: External Debt

The most consistent and comparable set of data on external debt is contained in the three volumes of *World Debt Tables*. About 110 countries file reports with the World Bank's Reporting System, which form the bases of the data. All debt figures are converted to U.S. dollars based on market exchange rates. The following are terms frequently used in the *World Debt Tables* and other sources quoting these tables.

Debt service: Annual interest payments and the amortization (payments on principle) of the outstanding debt.

Debt service to exports ratio: A widely used measure of the debt-paying ability of a country.

Long-term external debt: Debt that has an original maturity of more than one year, that is owed to nonresidents, and that is repayable in foreign currency, goods, or services.

Public debt: External obligation of a public debtor, including the national government, a political subdivision, and autonomous public bodies.

Publicly guaranteed debt: External obligation of a private debtor that is guaranteed by a public entity.

Private nonguaranteed external debt: External obligation of a private debtor that is not guaranteed by a public entity.

Short-term external debt: Debt that has an original maturity of one year or less. Available data permit no distinction between public and private nonguaranteed short-term debt.

The following are some of the data reported for each country: total debt stocks (outstanding debt), debt flows (including repayments), interest payments on long-term and short-term debt, amounts owed to various creditors, GNP, exports, imports, international reserves, and current account balances. Data on short-term debts are particularly weak.

Other criteria used to evaluate debt-paying ability are external debt to GDP, interest payments to exports, and debt–equity ratio.

Name: Comparisons of Government Finances
Agencies/Institutions:
  International Monetary Fund
  700 19th Street N.W.
  Washington, DC 20431
  Telephone: 202-623-7000

Organization for Economic Cooperation and Development (OECD)
Suite 700
2001 L Street N.W.
Washington, DC 20036
Telephone: 202-785-6323

Sources: *International Financial Statistics* (*IFS*; monthly with an annual supplement) and *Government Finance Statistics Yearbook* (both from the IMF); and *National Accounts* and *OECD Observer* and its annual supplement (all from the OECD)

Historic summary: See current and past issues of *Government Finance Statistics Yearbook*

■ A QUICK LOOK: Government Finances

International Financial Statistics, a monthly publication of the International Monetary Fund, is divided into two sections: (1) a 70-page section containing data from industrial and developing countries, and (2) a country section that lists in alphabetical order a wide range of data for about 145 countries. There are no government finance statistics in the world tables, but the country tables show, for most countries, national government deficits or surpluses, revenue, expenditures, net borrowings, and outstanding debt of central governments.

The most extensive source of information on government finances is the *Government Finance Statistics Yearbook* (*GFSY*), published by the International Monetary Fund. If one is interested in reasonably comparable data on government expenditures for virtually all countries in the world, this is the place to look. As with the IMF's *International Financial Statistics*, the *GFSY* is split into two parts. The first approximately 120 pages comprises the world section, which presents data on revenue, expenditures, grants, specific expenditures by function in absolute values and by percentages, domestic financing of government deficits, and deficits (surpluses) as a percentage of GNP. Considerably more detailed information is provided in the individual country section, including data on financing deficits by short-term securities, long-term securities, changes in cash and deposits, and foreign versus domestic debt. Ten years of comparative data are provided in both sections.

The OECD publications, including the annual supplement to the *OECD Observer*, provide information on government expenditures and revenue as a percent of gross domestic product, distribution of expenditures by sector (defense, public safety, health, and so on), government employment as a percent of total employment, percent of taxes by source (personal income, corporate income, sales, and so on), lowest and highest rate of taxation, and disposable income of the average production worker as a percent of gross pay.

HISTORIC DATA: Central Government Deficits and Surpluses as Percentages of Gross Domestic Product

	1975	1980	1985	1988
United States	−3.58	−2.91	−5.43	−3.27
Canada	−3.20	−3.34	−5.90	−2.84
Australia	−3.83	−1.64	−3.13	0.49
France	−2.58	−0.07	−2.72	−2.23
Italy	−15.50	−10.70	−13.35	−10.56
Mexico	−4.91	−3.13	−8.73	−10.19
Sweden	−2.71	−8.83	−5.58	2.95
Switzerland	−0.46	−0.20	—	—
United Kingdom	−7.31	−4.63	−2.88	1.35
West Germany	−3.61	−1.81	−1.08	−1.76

APPENDIX A

Terms Often Found in Economic and Financial Research

GLOSSARY

Accrual basis: a method of keeping the books in accounting. Revenues are recorded for the period in which goods are sold or services performed, and expenses are recorded for the period when costs are incurred or obligated. A different way of keeping records is known as the *cash basis*.

Accrued interest: interest accumulated on a bond or note since the last interest payment.

Accumulated depreciation: the depreciation expense charged off each year that is accumulated and reported as an offset (deduction) to the property or equipment account to which it pertains.

Adjustable rate mortgages (ARMs):   mortgage instruments that permit the lender to vary the interest rate during the period of the loan.

American-style options: stock options that can be exercised at any time before they expire; those that can be exercised only during a specified time period are called "European-style" options.

Amortize: to systematically pay off the principal and interest of a debt during the life of the note or loan.

Annualization: converting daily, weekly, monthly, or quarterly data to an annual basis. If two million cars are sold in one quarter, the annual rate of sales will be eight million. With annualized data, it is easier to compare monthly, quarterly, and annual data.

Annuity: a series of equal money payments made at equal intervals during a designated period of time.

Appreciation of the dollar: a term generally meaning that it takes more foreign currency to purchase a dollar in the international exchange market (for example, it takes fewer dollars to buy, say, 5000 yen than it did previously); often incorrectly used to indicate that the dollar has gained domestic purchasing power because of domestic deflation.

Area wage surveys: average straight-time earnings reports for standard workweeks by sex and by occupation within various industries for about 90 metropolitan areas as well as major geographic regions (Northeast, South, Midwest, and West). Thirty-two of the largest Standard Metropolitan Statistical Areas (SMSAs), are surveyed annually; the remaining 58 are surveyed every two years.

Arithmetic mean: the most popular meaning of "average"; the sum of all the numbers in a set divided by the total number of elements in the set. In the set of 1, 2, 2, 4, 6, the arithmetic mean is 3.

450

Asked price: price at which a dealer is willing to sell a security; that is, the price at which you will buy the security.

Balance on goods, services, and investment: one of the "balances" in the balance of payments. This balance includes merchandise trade plus services plus investment income; it represents the values used in computing a nation's GNP. The net export statistic in the GDP will be very close to the balance on goods, services, and investment.

Balance of payments: a record of the transactions between the residents of one country and the residents of the rest of the world during some period of time. Every international transaction causes an increase in credits (+) and an increase in debits (−). The inevitable result of this double-entry book-keeping is that the total of debits equals the total of credits. Hence, the balance of payments always balances; an "imbalance" can be measured only by looking at certain accounts. Thus, there are different balances (one being the merchandise trade balance) in the balance of payments, depending on the accounts totaled.

Balance sheet: the basic financial statement that discloses the assets, liabilities, and equities of an entity at a specified date (for example, December 31, 1992) using GAAP (generally accepted accounting principles).

Basis point: a frequently used measure of interest rate changes on bonds and notes. A single basis point is equal to one-hundredth of 1 percent, so 50 basis points equals 0.005 (0.5%) and 100 basis points equals 1 percent. If the interest rate on a bond goes from 7.60 percent to 7.80 percent, it has increased by 20 basis points.

Bear: one of those creatures who believes that prices are going to fall.

Benchmark revision: that which is completed by a government data agency after all data for a major economic research study have been set in type. Just kidding!!! A benchmark revision is a major revision in a data series based on new source data that are available only at infrequent intervals (such as the decennial census), changes in methodology, and/or new base periods for indexes. Generally, the entire historical series is revised when benchmark revisions are made.

Bid price: price at which a dealer is willing to buy a security; that is, the price at which you can sell a security to the dealer.

Big board: a nickname for the New York Stock Exchange, which traces its roots to 1792, when a few brokers met under a buttonwood tree just a few blocks from the exchange's present location at 11 Wall Street on Manhattan Island. The 1500 common stocks and 750 preferred stocks listed on the exchange represent about 80 percent of the market value of all stocks sold on U.S. exchanges.

Bills of exchange: orders to pay a specified amount at a specified time; these are generally drawn on well-known financial institutions.

Bond: a written promise to pay a specified sum of money (the face value or principal amount) at a specified date (the maturity date), together with periodic interest at a specified rate (the coupon rate). The difference between a note and a bond is that a bond runs for a longer period of time and requires greater legal formality.

Bond discount: the amount by which the face value of a bond exceeds the actual price for which it is bought or sold; occurs when the market interest rate is above the bond's coupon rate.

Bond premium: the amount by which a bond's sales price is above its par (face) value; results when market interest rates are below the bond's coupon rate.

Bond ratings: ratings of the estimated abilities of companies and governments to pay the interest and maturity values of their bonds.

Book value per share of common stock: total value of assets of a corporation less the total value of its liabilities and the book value of its outstanding preferred stock, divided by the number of common shares outstanding. Book value is almost never equal to a firm's market value.

Bretton Woods: small town in New Hampshire where the International Monetary Fund, the World Bank, and the fixed exchange rate system were established in 1944.

Broker: firm acting as an agent for its customers; it buys and sells securities on behalf of its customers for a fixed commission.

Bull: one of those creatures who believes that prices are going to increase.

Business cycle: a recurrent cycle of economic activity divided into four components: (1) a peak, also called a boom, (2) a contraction or recession, (3) a trough or depression, and (4) an expansion or recovery.

Business transfer payments: payments made by businesses to persons who did not perform any current services. Examples are liability payments for personal injuries, corporate contributions to nonprofit institutions, and defaults by consumers on their debts to businesses.

Call option: an option that conveys the right to buy a specified quantity of a stock at a particular price. For example, an option to buy 100 shares of ABC Corporation at a particular price is a call option.

Callable bonds: bonds that the issuer can redeem prior to maturity. When interest rates drop, the issuer can redeem the older, high-interest bonds and issue new bonds at lower rates.

Capacity utilization rate (CUR):   measures the extent to which firms are producing at their maximum output; the ratio of actual output to potential output. The lower the CUR ratio, the greater the amount of unused capacity.

Capital: the amount invested in a company by its owners; can also mean the amount of money needed by a company to finance a particular project. In economics, *capital* is the stock of real goods, such as buildings, plants, computers, and vehicles that produces other goods and services.

Capital consumption adjustments (CCAdj):   adjustments that convert depreciation charges to a consistent accounting basis of straight-line depreciation, uniform service lives, and current replacement costs. When corporations depreciate their capital assets, they charge off part of their capital costs in the current reporting period. Many assumptions have to be made in determining the depreciation rate, and different corporations make different assumptions, so reported data are not uniform or correct for national accounting purposes. Generally, firms use the fastest possible depreciation rates to lower their corporate income taxes.

Capital consumption allowances: fancy term for *depreciation* used by the Bureau of Economic Analysis.

Cash basis: a method of keeping the books in accounting. Revenues are not recorded until cash has been received, and expenses are not recorded until payment has been made. Many small firms and virtually all governmental units maintain their records on a cash basis rather than an accrual basis.

Cash flow: the increase or decrease in a company's cash during a period of time. A cash flow statement shows the sources and uses of cash.

Cendata: the Census Bureau's database, which is accessible only through Dialog and Compuserve, on-line computer service companies.

Census blocks: the smallest type of census areas. They are subdivisions of census tracts that comprise one or a few city blocks; small rectangular areas bounded by four streets. Census blocks include about 70 people.

Census tracts: statistical subdivisions of counties in metropolitan areas and large counties that average about 4000 in population. Economic data are widely available for the approximately 45,000 census tracts in the United States. A medium-sized metropolitan area of around 500,000 will have about 100 to 150 census tracts.

c.i.f.:   literally means "cost, insurance, and freight." If a good is sold "c.i.f.-City X," it means the shipper or seller is paying the costs of getting the good to that city. When c.i.f. is used without any qualifiers, it usually means that the seller will pay the costs of insurance and freight to the buyer's dock.

Civilian labor force: comprises all noninstitutionalized persons 16 years of age or over who are either employed or who meet the conditions for unemployment. Students in school, housewives, retirees, those unable to work because of health problems, and those discouraged from seeking employment are excluded, as are members of the armed forces. Those persons who keep house, or are voluntarily idle, unable to work, or seasonal workers in the "off" season are also not included.

Civilian noninstitutional population: includes all residents of the United States who are 16 years of age and over and who are not inmates of hospitals, homes for the aged, or prisons, or members of the armed forces.

"A Closer Look":   a segment of each data series in this book, which provides a relatively thorough explanation and background on the data series. The "A Closer Look" segments are minicourses on the data series.

Coefficient of variation (CV):   a measure of relative variation, which is calculated by dividing the standard error by the mean.

Commercial paper: short-term unsecured promissory notes sold on a discount basis to institutional investors and corporations. Commercial paper is unsecured, which means that it has no collateral and is backed only by the reputation of the issuer; thus, it is generally sold by large corporations with high credit ratings. It is sold by corporations and finance companies to raise large sums of money quickly and for short periods of time.

Consumer credit: the credit extended for the purchase of goods by consumers; includes all credit card and consumer charge accounts, as well as consumer loans from automotive finance subsidiaries, general finance companies, banks, savings and loans, and credit unions.

Consumer price index: a measure of the average change in prices paid by urban consumers for a fixed market basket of goods and services. There are two monthly CPIs: one for a group consisting only of urban households employed as wage earners and clerical workers (CPI:W) and the other for all urban households (CPI:U).

Convertible currencies: about 15 major currencies in the world that have few restrictions on being bought and sold.

Convertible preferred: preferred stock that enables its owners to exchange preferred stock for common stock within some specified period.

Cooling degree days: the number of degrees per day that the daily average temperature is above 65 degrees. The daily average temperature is the mean of the maximum and minimum temperatures for a 24-hour period. For example, if the mean temperature is 70 degrees each day for 30 days, there would be 150 cooling degree days ($70 - 65 \times 30$) and zero heating days during the month.

Correspondent bank: a bank that has a business relationship with another bank or depository institution. Funds are generally kept in a correspondent bank to facilitate check clearing and fund transfers.

Coupon equivalent yield: the difference between the face value and the purchase price of a Treasury bill, divided by the purchase price, and annualized using 365 (days of the year).

Coupon rate: the interest rate specified on coupons attached to a bond; equal to the annual coupon payment divided by the face value of the bond.

Credit: an accounting entry that goes on the right-hand side of a ledger sheet; used to report an increase in liabilities (amounts owed to creditors) and increases in capital or ownership interest.

Currency in circulation: Federal Reserve notes and coins (together called *currency*) that must be outside of depository institutions, the Treasury, and the Federal Reserve to be considered in circulation and part of the money supply. Currency consists of coins issued by the Treasury (pennies, nickels, dimes, and quarters) and Federal Reserve notes (paper notes) that are issued by the 12 district banks of the Federal Reserve System. Currency constitutes only about 29 percent of the M1 money supply and a much lower percentage of the other money definitions.

Current assets: those assets that can be made readily available to finance current operations or to pay current liabilities; also, those assets that will be used up or converted into cash within one year. Some examples are cash, temporary investments, and notes receivable that will be collected within one year.

Current liabilities: liabilities that will have to be paid during the operating cycle, including accounts payable, short-term loans payable, taxes payable, and accrued wages and salaries. Current assets are often compared with current liabilities to determine the short-run financial position of the company.

Current Population Survey: a monthly survey of about 60,000 households, randomly selected to represent the U.S. population 16 years of age and older. Each month, one-fourth of the households in the sample are changed so that no single family is interviewed more than four consecutive months. A group of 1500 Census Bureau workers interview the sample families on their labor force employment and activities for the week that includes the twelfth day of the month.

Current yield: annual interest (as determined by the coupon rate) divided by the current market price of a bond.

Dealer: firm acting as a principal, buying and selling for its own account.

Debentures: unsecured bonds backed only by the general assets and reputation of a corporation. If the corporation should default on its bonds, the holders of debentures would have to wait in line behind the holders of closed-end and collateral bonds. Usually, only financially strong corporations are able to sell debentures, whereas financially weak corporations must resort to pledging specific assets.

Debit: an accounting entry made on the left-hand side of a ledger sheet, or a minus entry on the right-hand side. Debits are used to record an increase in assets (resources owned by the business) or a decrease in liabilities (amounts owed to creditors) or capital.

Debt monetization: occurs when the central bank (Federal Reserve in the United States) "monetizes" government debt by increasing the money supply when the government is selling bonds. In the United States this occurs when the Fed buys bonds in the secondary market (thus increasing bank reserves) while the Treasury is selling bonds in the primary market. Interest rates are — temporarily at least — kept lower by this monetization of the debt.

Debt service: annual interest payments and the amortization (payments on principal) of the outstanding debt of a company or a country. One very widely used measure of the debt-paying ability of a country is the debt service to exports ratio.

Deficit: Expenses or costs in excess of revenue being received over a measured period of time.

Demand deposits: deposits at a bank that can be converted into currency on demand without prior notice. A major component of the money supply.

Depository institutions: financial institutions, such as banks, savings and loans, and credit unions, that accept deposits and lend out funds.

Depreciation: (1) the cost of property and equipment that occurs during each accounting period; (2) the expensing of an asset over its estimated useful life on a systematic basis. Depreciation results from physical wear and tear and technical obsolescence, but actual depreciation charges generally are not related to the actual wear and tear.

Depreciation of the dollar: a term generally meaning that it takes less foreign currency to purchase a dollar in the foreign exchange market (for example, it takes more dollars to buy, say, 5000 yen than it did previously); sometimes incorrectly used to indicate that the dollar has lost domestic purchasing power because of domestic inflation.

Diffusion index: one measurement of the dispersion of some data. The diffusion index for employment data represents the percent of industries in which employment is rising, plus one-half of the industries with unchanged employment. Thus, a diffusion index of 50 percent indicates an equal balance between industries with increasing and decreasing employment.

Dirty float: a term referring to the practice of central banks buying and selling their currencies in the foreign exchange market in order to influence the long-term trend of the exchange rate.

Discount rate: (1) the interest rate the Federal Reserve charges for its loans to banks and depository institutions; (2) the interest rate charged when discounting the price of securities when there is no coupon rate.

Discounting: a method of charging interest in which the borrower receives less than the principal amount of a loan or note; interest equals the difference between the amount borrowed and the amount received.

Disintermediation: removal of funds from depository institutions and their placement in primary securities such as notes, bonds, and stocks.

Disposable personal income: personal income less income and estate and gift taxes. It represents the actual purchasing power available to consumers from current income.

Dividend yield: current annual stock dividend divided by the current price of the stock.

Dow Jones Industrial Average: popular indicator of changes in stock prices. It is composed of 30 stocks, many of which are not industrial.

Durable goods: goods that are expected to last at least one year, including furniture, cars, and televisions; nondurables are food, clothing, and other goods expected to be totally consumed within one year.

ECU (European currency unit):   monetary unit of the Common Market countries introduced in 1978 and already widely used as a unit of account and store of value among banks and firms. It is expected to reduce the role of the dollar in international trade and to be an actual circulating medium of exchange by the late 1990s.

Edge Act corporation: an international banking subsidiary of a U.S. bank; located in the United States and exempt from prohibitions against interstate banking. These subsidiaries facilitate financing of international investment and trade.

EEC (European Economic Community): also known as the Common Market; founded in 1958 to integrate the economies of Western Europe. Since then it has made uneven progress toward reducing tariffs, increasing mobility of labor and capital, and integrating European monetary systems. The EEC established the European Monetary System (EMS) in 1978 and the European currency unit (ECU) in 1978. All trade barriers are supposed to be eliminated by 1993.

Employed persons: those (1) who worked at least 1 hour for pay or profit during the survey week as paid employees or in their own business, profession, or farm; or (2) who worked at least 15 hours as unpaid workers in a family-owned enterprise; or (3) who were temporarily absent from their jobs due to illness, strikes, bad weather, vacation, or personal reasons. A person working at more than one job is counted only in the job in which he or she worked the greatest number of hours. Persons who work 35 hours or more are classified as full-time; those who work 1 to 34 hours are classified as part-time workers.

Employment Cost Index: measures quarterly changes in wages, salaries, and benefits in the private nonfarm economy, while holding fixed the industrial, occupational, and geographical mix of workers.

Employment–population ratio: number of employed persons divided by the civilian noninstitutional population. Provides about the same information as the labor participation ratio, which is much more popular.

Establishment: an economic unit, generally at one physical location, where business is conducted, services performed, or goods manufactured. Examples of establishments are a factory, a mine, a store, a motel, a warehouse, and an office.

Eurodollar deposits: dollar deposits in banks located outside the United States; for example, a dollar deposit in a London bank.

Face value: stated, par, or maturity value of a bond that must be paid on the maturity date.

Fannie Mae: a nickname for the Federal National Mortgage Association, a private corporation with loose ties to the federal government that buys mortgages from thrift institutions and then sells its own bonds to finance these mortgage purchases. The bonds sold by Fannie Mae are secured by its mortgage holdings.

f.a.s.: literally means "free alongside ship." If a good is sold f.a.s., it means the seller (exporter) pays the costs of getting the goods to the port. The buyer pays the cost of getting the goods loaded onto the ship and transported to the importer's location.

Federal (U.S. government) debt: There are many ways of defining the debt of the federal government, including the following:
- Public Debt: government debt issued by the Treasury or by other government agencies. "Federal debt" is the total of the two, but "public debt" is only the debt issued by the Treasury. Securities issued by government agencies other than the Treasury are called "agency debt." A more accurate name for public

debt is "gross public debt," which includes all Treasury debt — securities *held* by government agencies, the public, the Federal Reserve Bank, and foreign residents and institutions.

- Debt held by government accounts: Treasury debt held by government agencies, usually trust funds such as Social Security.
- Debt held by the public: Treasury debt held by the public, including the Federal Reserve Bank.
- Net public debt: sometimes the same as "debt held by the public," but usually Treasury-issued debt held by the public, excluding the Federal Reserve. Also called "net other public" debt.

Federal funds: reserve deposits, usually held at the Federal Reserve, that one depositary institution (bank, savings and loan, and so on) lends to another, generally overnight. The annualized rate charged on these loans of federal funds is the federal funds rate.

Federal Information Processing Standards: *See* FIPS.

Federal Reserve: the central "bank" of the United States, which consists of 12 district banks plus the Board of Governors in Washington, D.C. It conducts monetary policy, regulates banks, lends funds to depository institutions, and buys and sells dollars and foreign exchange.

Fiat money: money not backed by any commodity such as gold or silver. Most money in the world today is fiat money backed only by the faith in its general acceptance and not by any commodity.

FIFO (First In, First Out):   a method of inventory valuation that assumes the units that were purchased first are sold first; thus, the units remaining in inventory at the end of the accounting period are those purchased more recently. Whenever prices are rising in the economy, the use of the FIFO method tends to understate the cost of goods sold and to overstate operating income and income taxes.

Final sales GNP (GDP):   GNP (GDP) less the change in business inventories. This alternative way of calculating the GNP, or GDP, focuses on the demand in the marketplace as evidenced by sales. For example, if sales levels fall and firms increase their inventories, the regular GNP would show a growing economy. In final sales GNP, an increase in business inventories does not show up, so it tends to show changes in the underlying aggregate demand.

Financial Accounting Standards Board (FASB):   independent, private (nongovernmental) authority for establishment of accounting principles in the United States; funded by the Financial Accounting Foundation (FAF), which derives its support from CPA firms, industry, commerce, and other private sources.

FIPS: the *federal information processing standards* code, a widely used numeric coding structure for presenting state and local data. For example, two digits are used for states; Alabama is 02.

Fiscal year: a period of any 12 consecutive months used as an accounting period. Prior to 1977, the federal fiscal year started on July 1 and ended 12 months later, on June 30. Beginning in 1977, the federal fiscal year has begun October 1 and ended September 30. Most state governments have a fiscal year beginning July 1 and ending June 30, whereas many local governments have a fiscal year ending December 31.

Fixed assets: assets of a long-term character that are intended to continue to be held or used, such as land, buildings, machinery, and equipment.

Fixed-weight price index: obtained from the NIPA accounts. It measures changes in the prices of a fixed market basket over the years; similar to the Consumer Price Index, in that it uses fixed-period weights or a market basket from some base period.

f.o.b.:   literally means "free on board." If a good is sold f.o.b., it means that the buyer pays the freight insurance of getting the products from the seller's dock.

Foreign exchange market: the international market in which foreign exchange — currencies of the various countries — is bought and sold. This "market" does not have a physical location as do the various stock exchanges around the world. The foreign exchange market is a worldwide market of foreign exchange dealers; generally, large money center banks connected by telephone and telex. In the United States, about a dozen banks in New York and another dozen spread around the country are foreign exchange traders.

Forward market transaction: transaction in which foreign currencies are bought and sold for delivery at some time in the future. The essence of the forward market is that the parties agree today on the quantities and the prices of the foreign exchange they will be trading at some date in the future. They also agree on the date that the currencies will be exchanged.

Freddie Mac: a nickname for the Federal Home Loan Mortgage Corporation, a subsidiary of the Federal Home Loan Bank, which sells debt instruments backed by pools of conventional mortgages. Freddie Mac bundles together a group of conventional mortgages and then sells them like conventional bonds

Full faith and credit: a pledge of the general taxing power to pay municipal debt obligations. Bonds carrying such pledges are referred to as general obligation bonds or full faith and credit bonds.

Futures market: a market in which people agree to exchange a specific commodity for a specified price on some specific future date.

General fund: a government's fund used to account for all financial resources except those required to be accounted for in specific funds.

General obligation bonds: municipal bonds secured by the taxing power of the issuing municipality. *See also* Full faith and credit.

Generally accepted accounting principles (GAAP):   uniform minimum standards of and guidelines to financial accounting and reporting. GAAP govern the form and content of the basic financial statements of an entity and encompass the conventions, rules, and procedures necessary to define accepted accounting practice. They include not only broad guidelines of general application, but also detailed practices and procedures.

Geometric mean: number determined by taking the nth root of the produce of N elements (for example, price $1 \times$ price $2 \times$ price $3 \times \cdots \times$ price $N)^{1/n}$). The geometric mean is used when there is a large spread between the lowest and highest values of a set.

Ginnie Mae: a nickname for the Government National Mortgage Association, a part of the Department of Housing and Urban Development. Pools of FHA- and VA-insured mortgages are put together by thrift institutions or mortgage bankers; Ginnie Mae guarantees these pools, which are known as "pass-through securities" and which look very much like bonds and are sold to investors. Ginnie Mae securities have become very popular because of their government guarantees and liquidity.

GNP vs. GDP: In late 1991, the Bureau of Economic Analysis changed the emphasis of its national income accounting reports from gross national product (GNP) to gross domestic product. GNP, and other "national" measures (such as net national product) relate to production by labor and other factors *supplied* by residents of the United States. Thus, the income earned by U.S. residents on their investments in other countries is included in the gross national product. Gross domestic product (GDP) and other "domestic" measures relate to production by factors physically *located* in the United States no matter who owns them. The relationship between GNP and GDP is as follows:

> Gross national product
> Less: Factor income received from nonresidents
> Plus: Factor income paid to nonresidents
> Equals: Gross domestic product

Gross domestic product (GDP):   the market value of the goods and services produced by resources located in the United States. GDP can be measured from the input (income) side and the output (product) side because the GDP, or NIPA, accounting system is designed to replicate double-entry bookkeeping. This means that the total income generated in the economy equals the total output produced. At the end of 1991, the Bureau of Economic Analysis began emphasizing GDP, rather than GNP. *See* GNP vs. GDP for an analysis of the differences between GNP and GDP.

Gross national product (GNP):   the market value of the final goods and services produced by resources supplied by residents of the United States. GNP can be measured from the input (income) side and the output (product) side because the GNP, or NIPA, accounting system is designed to replicate double-entry bookkeeping. This means that the total income generated in the economy equals the total output produced. In the latter part of 1991, the Bureau of Economic Analysis began emphasizing gross domestic product (GDP) rather than GNP. *See* GNP vs. GDP, for an analysis of the differences between GNP and GDP.

Gross state product (GSP):   the gross market value of the goods and services attributable to labor and property located in a state; the state counterpart of the nation's gross domestic product (GDP).

Harmonic mean: number obtained by taking the reciprocal of the arithmetic means of the reciprocals of the individual elements $\{(N/[(1/\text{price } 1) + (1/\text{price } 2) + (1/\text{price } N)])\}$. The harmonic mean is always less than the geometric mean.

Heating degree days: the number of degrees per day that the daily average temperature is below 65 degrees. The daily average temperature is the mean of the maximum and minimum temperatures during a 24-hour period. If the mean temperature is 50 degrees each day for 30 days, the number of heating degree days during the month is 450 days ($65 - 50 \times 30$).

Historical costs: also known as assigned cost because the cost carried "on the books" is the cost recorded when an asset was purchased. This is the opposite of replacement or current cost.

IBRD: International Bank for Reconstruction and Development. *See* World Bank.

IEA: *See* International Energy Agency.

IMF: *See* International Monetary Fund.

Implicit price deflator: a price index that results from dividing nominal GNP by total real GNP; also known as the GNP (GDP) deflator because it is obtained as a by-product from constructing constant-dollar GNP (GDP). The value of GNP (GDP) before correction for price changes is called current-dollar GNP (GDP), or nominal GNP (GDP). The GNP (GDP) adjusted to eliminate price changes is called real GNP, or constant-dollar GNP (GDP). Real GNP (GDP) is obtained by deflating the various component commodities and services in GNP (GDP) with individual price indexes. These deflated components are added to obtain real GNP.

Income statement: also called the profit and loss statement, or operating statement, it reports the revenue, expenses, and profits of the firm during some specific period of time, such as a month, quarter, or year.

Index: converts some raw number into a base number so that future changes in the raw numbers can be reflected as changes relative to that base value. Index numbers are based on some period equalling a number that is usually but not always 100. If the base period is 1980 ($1980 = 100$), for example, and the index value for the current month is 165, we immediately know there has been a 65 percent increase in the underlying data between 1980 and the current month.

Index of Leading Indicators: an index composed of 11 data series that signals future fluctuations in the economy. The leading indicator should turn upward a few months before the economy does and downward a few months before the economy starts to dip into a recession. The leading indicator has an average lead of about 9.5 months (with a range of 2 to 20 months) for business cycle peaks, or the beginning of a cycle downturn.

Indirect business taxes: taxes paid by businesses, such as sales, excise, and property taxes. Corporate income taxes are not included. Property taxes paid by homeowners are included here because their homes are treated as businesses.

Industrial Production Index (IPI):   a monthly indicator of changes in the physical output of manufacturing, mining, and electric and gas utilities.

Industrial revenue bonds: bonds issued by governments, the proceeds of which are used to construct facilities for a private business enterprise. Such bonds may be in the form of general obligation bonds, combination bonds, or revenue bonds.

Inflation: a sustained rise in the weighted average of prices over time.

Input-output tables: tables that show how industries interact with each other by displaying the inputs industries received from other industries and the output provided to all other industries. Essentially, I-O tables portray a from-whom-to-whom breakdown of all commodity and service flows.

Intangible asset: an asset having no physical existence but having value because of the rights conferred as a result of its ownership and possession, such as trademarks, patents, and so on.

Interest rate futures: futures contracts on interest-sensitive securities or financial instruments such as Treasury bonds and bills.

Interfund transactions: the outlays of a fund in one group that are the receipts of a fund in another group, such as the payment of interest on Treasury debt (from a general fund) to the Social Security fund (a trust fund). Since receipts from interfund transactions are not receipts from the public and outlays are not outlays to the public, these transactions are netted out so that budget totals for receipts and outlays include only transactions with the public.

Intergovernmental revenues: revenues from other governments in the form of grants, entitlements, shared revenues, or payments in lieu of taxes.

International Bank for Reconstruction and Development (IBRD): *See* World Bank.

International Energy Agency (IEA): organization dedicated to coordinating energy policies and developments and to operating an energy information system; founded in 1974 after the first "world oil shock." Members: Australia, Austria, Belgium, Canada, Denmark, Germany, Greece, Iceland, Ireland, Italy, Japan, Luxembourg, the Netherlands, New Zealand, Norway, Portugal, Spain, Sweden, Switzerland, Turkey, United Kingdom, United States.

International Monetary Fund (IMF): organization created by the Bretton Woods (New Hampshire) Conference in 1944 to promote international monetary cooperation and exchange rate stability. The major purpose of the "old" IMF was to limit exchange rate fluctuations and to lend funds to member countries to enable them to support these exchange rates. When the IMF's system of fixed exchange rates gave way to floating rates in the early 1970s, the IMF adopted new policies designed to help it control floating rates by exercising "firm surveillance" over exchange rates, whatever that might mean. In reality, the IMF turned its attention to promoting economic development, growth, and price stability in developing countries, which meant it was invading the territory of the World Bank. During the late 1960s, the IMF established currency reserve units called *special drawing rights* (SDRs), also known as "paper gold." Members are allocated SDRs in proportion to their contributions to the Fund. From 1974 to 1980, the value of SDRs was based on a weighted average of the values of the currencies of the 16 leading trading nations. Since 1981, the SDR has been based on the currencies of the five largest exporting nations: Germany, France, Japan, U.K., U.S.

International reserve assets: certain assets owned by the Federal Reserve that can be used to settle international imbalances. They include gold, special drawing rights, and foreign exchange.

Inventory valuation adjustment (IVA):   system for converting the value of inventory withdrawals from the total of historical and current replacement costs to the more analytically correct system of current replacement costs. When goods are sold by corporations, they have to charge off the cost of the goods sold, that is, the cost of goods withdrawn from inventory. Some corporations use the most recent prices (LIFO or replacement costs) in valuing these withdrawals whereas others use earlier (FIFO or historical) prices. IVA is used to reconcile these.

Investment: a term whose meaning varies depending on who is using it and the context in which it is being used. When stockbrokers, accountants, and Wall Street types are using the term, they most probably mean expenditures by individuals or firms to acquire some old or new property or a security that will yield some income, interest, or profits. When economists, government accountants, and news releases mention investment, they most probably are referring to expenditures for new plants, buildings, equipment, and inventories. Economists do not consider the purchase of financial securities or the purchase of previously constructed capital equipment to be economic investment. When reference is made to "investment in the United States economy," the meaning is economic and not financial investment.

Investment bank: a financial institution specializing in designing and marketing new issues of stocks and bonds. Due to federal law, an investment bank cannot also be a commercial bank, although numerous bills have been introduced in recent sessions of Congress to change this law.

Keogh Plan: a pension plan for self-employed individuals that receives special tax treatment.

Labor force participation ratio: the ratio of the civilian labor force to the civilian noninstitutional population.

LIBOR (London interbank rate):   the Eurodollar rate most frequently quoted in Europe and in news reports throughout the world. It is the arithmetic average of the offer rates quoted by six major banks in the London wholesale market; that is, it is the rate at which these banks lend to each other at a certain time in the morning. The LIBOR plus a small fee is the lending rate to borrowers of Eurodollars.

LIFO (Last In, First Out):   a method of inventory valuation that assumes the units taken out of inventory during the period were the last units purchased; hence, most of the units remaining in inventory must be the units purchased at the earlier price. Whenever prices are rising, the use of the LIFO method tends to overstate the cost of goods sold and to understate operating income and income taxes.

Liquidity: ability to convert an asset into cash without much risk of a substantial loss.

Long-term debt: debt with a maturity of more than one year after the date of issuance.

Long-term liabilities: normally, liabilities that are paid off over a period of many years. Long-term bonds and mortgages are examples of long-term liabilities.

Margin: the percentage of the purchase price of a stock or bond that a customer must pay when funds are borrowed to finance the purchase. If an investor buying $100,000 of securities is required to put down $60,000, the margin is 60 percent.

Market risk: the risk of price fluctuations for a security. The market risk for a bill, note, or bond is associated with changes in the interest rate. When interest rates increase, the market prices of debt securities always go down. The longer the security's term to maturity, the greater the market risk.

Marketable securities: the balance sheet title for negotiable stocks, bonds, and Treasury securities carried as an asset by a company.

Mean: *See* Arithmetic mean, Geometric mean, Harmonic mean.

Median: the number that divides a set of numbers so that half of the elements of the set are larger and half are smaller. In the set of 1, 2, 2, 4, 6, the median is 2.

Merchandise trade balance: the net balance of merchandise trade between residents of the United States and residents of other countries. Wheat, lumber, cars, stereos, and computers are included in this category. When merchandise trade exports exceed merchandise trade imports, there is a merchandise trade surplus in the balance of payments. When merchandise trade imports exceed merchandise trade exports, there is a deficit. The merchandise trade balance is one of the most widely reported balances in the balance of payments.

Metropolitan statistical area (MSA):   a city with 50,000 or more inhabitants, or an urbanized area with 50,000 population plus a total MSA area population of at least 100,000.

Mode: the number in a set of numbers that occurs most frequently. In the set of 1, 2, 2, 4, 6, the mode is 2.

Monetary base: total bank reserves plus currency in circulation; also called (incorrectly) the reserve base and high-powered money.

Money: anything that is commonly accepted as money. In the United States there are three widely used definitions of money: (1) M1: checkable deposits plus currency in circulation, (2) M2: M1 plus savings and small denomination time deposits, and (3) M3: M2 plus large denomination time deposits.

Money market: the market in which short-term securities (maturity of less than one year) are bought and sold.

Money market deposit accounts (MMDAs):   deposits at commercial banks and thrift institutions that often earn higher interest rates than other deposit accounts. They were introduced in 1982 to compete with money market mutual funds offered by brokerage firms. The accounts are insured up to $100,000, but usually only a limited number of checks may be written against these accounts.

Money market mutual funds (MMMFs):   mutual funds that invest in short-term government and corporate bonds. Started in 1974, these funds compound interest daily and they have no redemption penalty. Checks may be written against these accounts, but some restrictions might apply.

Money multiplier: the number by which a change in reserves is multiplied in order to calculate the maximum potential change in deposits. The simple money multiplier is the reciprocal of the required reserve ratio.

National Association of Securities Dealers (NASD) Market: often referred to as the "over-the-counter-market," or the NASDAQ market. NASDAQ stands for the National Association of Securities Dealers Automated Quotation System, which is a computerized system for displaying bid and asked prices. The National Association of Securities Dealers is a regulated network of securities dealers linked by telephones and computers. NASDAQ National Market Issues, listed in most newspapers, are daily stock tables. NASDAQ Bids & Asked Quotations is the name of a table for small over-the-counter stock.

National income: income that originates in the production of goods and services attributable to labor and other factors supplied by residents of the United States.

National income and product accounts (NIPAs):   a broad system of accounts that generates data on the gross national product, gross domestic product, national income, investment, savings, and a wide variety of other national economic issues.

Negotiable order of withdrawal (NOW) accounts: interest-bearing savings accounts on which checks can be written.

Obsolescence: the decrease in the value of fixed assets resulting from economic, social, technological, or legal changes.

OECD: *See* Organization for Economic Cooperation and Development.

Off-budget: programs or agencies that have been excluded by law from the federal budget. Presumably, the receipts and expenditures of these programs do not or should not be included in the formation of fiscal policy. However, many, if not most, of the off-budget deficits/surpluses are considered in budget deliberations. The most notable off-budget account is Social Security.

Official settlements balance: the sum of the current account balance and the capital account balance plus errors and omissions.

On-budget: programs or agencies that have not been declared by Congress to be off-budget. Presumably, the net balance of on-budget expenditures and receipts should guide Congress and the Administration in determining the nation's fiscal policy. The problem is that many programs or agencies that are not on-budget are very influential in affecting fiscal decisions.

OPEC: *See* Organization of Petroleum Exporting Countries.

Open market operations: the buying and selling of government securities by the Federal Reserve. This is a method of influencing interest rates, the monetary base, bank reserves, and the money supply.

Organization for Economic Cooperation and Development (OECD):   organization composed of industrialized, market economy countries to promote economic and social welfare of member countries. OECD publishes many factual and analytical periodicals and books relating to the economies of its member countries. Members: Australia, Austria, Belgium, Canada, Denmark, Finland, France, Germany, Greece, Iceland, Ireland, Italy, Japan, Luxembourg, the Netherlands, New Zealand, Norway, Portugal, Spain, Sweden, Switzerland, Turkey, United Kingdom, United States.

Organization of Petroleum Exporting Countries (OPEC):   created by Iran, Iraq, Kuwait, Saudi Arabia, and Venezuela in Baghdad on Sept. 14, 1960, to counter falling market prices for oil. By 1970, it had begun to act like a typical cartel by withholding production in order to force up prices. During 1973–74, OPEC prices quadrupled. Prices stabilized between 1974 and 1978 but doubled in 1979. Demand slackened at the higher prices, and non-OPEC producers increased production. OPEC production quotas broke down during the 1980s as members increased production to sustain earnings in the face of dropping prices. One indication of the lessening power of OPEC is its declining share of world production. OPEC countries produced 66 percent of world petroleum in 1979, but they produced only 33 percent of world output in 1990. Member countries are Algeria, Ecuador, Gabon, Indonesia, Iran, Iraq, Kuwait, Libya, Nigeria, Qatar, Saudi Arabia, the United Arab Emirates, and Venezuela.

Par value: an arbitrary value placed on a share of stock at the time the corporation seeks authorization of the stock; also, another term to describe the face value of a bond.

Participating preferred: preferred stock that permits the holder to receive preferred dividends plus the right to participate in certain additional earnings.

Penny Benny: a nickname for the Pension Benefit Guaranty Corporation, which is to pension funds what the FDIC is to bank deposits. It guarantees some pension benefits in case the company is unable to make the payments.

Persian Gulf nations: Bahrain, Iran, Iraq, Kuwait, Qatar, Saudi Arabia, and the United Arab Emirates.

Personal consumption expenditures: goods and services purchased by individuals; operating expenses of nonprofit institutions; and the value of food, fuel, clothing, housing, and financial services received in kind by individuals. Net purchases of used goods are also included.

Personal income: income received by households before the payment of income and estate taxes. It is obtained from wages and fringe benefits, profits from self-employment, rent, interest, dividends, Social Security benefits, unemployment insurance, food stamps, and other income maintenance programs. It is the most accurate measure of income flows to individuals even though it does not include capital gains or losses, which occur in financial markets. Personal income less income, estate, and gift taxes equals disposable personal income.

Personal saving: the savings of all households, including financial savings (except capital gains), increase in the cash value of insurance and pension reserves, and personal equity ownerships in land and physical resources. It is calculated by subtracting one large number (personal consumption expenditures) from another large number (disposable personal income). Relatively small errors in either of the two large numbers have a disproportionately large impact on the accuracy of personal saving.

Petrodollars: dollar revenues or deposits obtained by oil-exporting countries from the sale of oil.

Present value: the value today of future payments made either in a lump sum or in a series. The present value of these future payments is almost always less than the actual cash outlay because money has a time value.

Price–earnings ratio (PE):   one important evaluation of the attractiveness of a stock. It is computed by dividing the stock's price by the earnings per share of common stock during the past four quarters.

Primary market: the first market in which a stock or security is sold by the original issuer; generally, this market is an auction (governments) market or one dominated by investment bankers. Subsequent purchases and sales are made in the secondary market.

Prime rate: interest rate charged by banks on short-term loans to their most creditworthy customers. Each bank sets its own prime rate.

Pro forma: a favorite term of accountants, it refers to an "as if" financial statement—that is, a financial statement modified to show the effects of some proposed transaction or reshuffling of the accounts. A pro forma reflects how these statements might look.

Producer durables: machinery and equipment—computers, table saws, bulldozers, and the like—that have useful lives longer than one year and are depreciated by companies.

Productivity: a term that has many meanings but, generally, it refers to labor productivity, which is the value of goods and services in constant prices produced per hour of labor input.

Put option: an option that conveys the right to sell a specified quantity of a stock at a particular price. An option to sell 100 shares of ABC Corporation at a particular price is a put option.

"A Quick Look":   a segment of each data series in this book, which provides a relatively short explanation of the data series and how to read it.

Real interest rate: the interest rate in terms of purchasing power over real goods and services. It is approximated by subtracting the rate of inflation from the market interest rate.

Recession: a decrease, or very slow growth, in economic activity. Also, a condition of the economy when *you* are unemployed; if your neighbor is unemployed, it is a "normal cyclical adjustment in the economy." The National Bureau of Economic Research (NBER) defines a recession as beginning in the month in which the overall direction of several economic indicators is downward. Some of the important indicators are nominal and real gross national product, new capital orders, business sales, Industrial Production Index, unemployment rate, hours worked, and personal income. A recession is often defined as occurring when the quarterly real gross national product declines for two quarters in a row, but this is not a fixed rule and the NBER always looks at other indicators.

Replacement cost: the cost at current prices in a particular market area of replacing an item of property or a group of assets. This is the opposite of historical cost, which is the cost of an asset when it was purchased.

Repurchase agreement (repo or RP):   an agreement to sell government securities coupled with an agreement to repurchase them at a price that includes accumulated interest. Most RPs have durations of 1 to 10 days. Repos are often associated with open market operations by the Federal Reserve.

Required reserves: a percentage of deposits that a depository institution is required to hold in vault cash or at the Federal Reserve.

Revenue bonds: bonds (municipals) issued by states or local government agencies that are secured by revenues from the project being financed.

S&P (Standard & Poor's) 500:   an index of stock prices, first published in 1923 with 233 stocks. In 1957, the list was expanded to 500 stocks representing 400 industrial companies, 40 public utilities, 20 transportation companies, and 40 financial institutions. Unlike the Dow Jones Industrial Averages, the S&P 500 is an index and not an average. The S&P 500 is based on 1941–43 equalling 10.

Sampling error: the error arising from the use of a sample rather than a census (a complete enumeration) to estimate data. An estimate of the sampling error, also called the standard error, gives us the odds that the sample value is correct.

Seasonal adjustments: statistical adjustments that attempt to remove the effects of seasonal variation in a data series. For example, retail sales normally increase in December, and home sales are seasonally high in June. Seasonalization removes the effects of these seasonal impacts. If the series is seasonally adjusted, then any week, month, or quarter can be compared with any other week, month, or quarter, or with annual data. If the series is not seasonally adjusted, then comparisons can be made only with the same week, month, or quarter of another year.

Secondary market: the market in which previously issued securities are bought and sold. The New York Stock Exchange, for example, is part of the secondary market for stocks.

Securities and Exchange Commission (SEC):   an agency of the federal government that regulates the public trading of securities; sets broad accounting standards and reporting requirements for all corporations whose stocks and bonds are publicly traded. Also regulates (to some extent) the CPA firms that serve these corporations.

Serial maturity: scheduled retirement of a portion of a bond issue each year until the entire issue is eventually retired. Municipal governments usually issue bonds with serial maturities rather than bonds with a single maturity date, which is what corporations and the Treasury do. Each portion of a bond issue with a serial maturity carries its own interest rate and is almost totally separate from the other portions of the issue. When a municipal or state government issues a ten-year serial bond, it is really selling a series of bonds with different maturities: one-year maturities, two-year maturities, three-year maturities, and so on.

Series E bonds: nonmarketable Treasury bonds issued for five years, which provide a fixed yield through a steady increase in the redemption value of the bond. Series E bonds are not marketable (they cannot be sold); they can be turned into cash before the maturity date, but the effective yield will be lower. The interest and thus taxes on the interest of Series E bonds are not payable until the end of the maturity period.

Short position: an outstanding obligation to buy back a security, option, or future.

Short sales: sales of shares not owned by the investor. Stock is borrowed from a broker and then sold with the hope that it can be purchased at a lower price before it has to be returned to the broker.

Special drawing rights (SDRs):   paper credits, also known as "paper gold," created by the International Monetary Fund to alleviate shortages of foreign exchange. They are distributed to central banks in proportion to their subscription or quotas. SDR values are based on the weighted average of the values of the currencies of the five largest exporting countries (Germany, France, Japan, U.K., U.S.). Central banks may use these SDRs to purchase foreign exchange, subject to a set of complicated rules.

Spot market transaction (foreign exchange market):   a transaction in which foreign currencies are bought and sold for delivery within two days.

Spot price: the price at which something can be purchased for immediate delivery, or delivery within a day or two.

Standard industrial classification (SIC):   a system of classifying firms into industry groupings based on the primary activity of that firm or establishment. A single company might consist of several establishments. The broadest level of industrial classification is among 11 divisions denoted A through K. These divisions are further segmented into major groups that have 2-digit SIC codes, then into industry groups that have 3-digit codes, and finally into industries with 4-digit codes.

Standard international trade classification (SITC):   an international system for classifying firms and industries that is similar to the standard industrial classification used in the United States.

Standard & Poor's 500:   *See* S&P 500.

State data centers: centers cooperating with federal agencies. They receive data from the federal government and make them available to the residents of the states.

Stock split: occurs when the company issues a certain number of shares per share of stock outstanding. A "2-for-1" split is very popular. The holder of 10 shares receives an additional 10 shares for a total of 20 shares. The primary purpose in issuing a stock split is to reduce the market price so that less wealthy investors can buy the stock in blocks of 100.

Strike price: the strike or exercise price specified in an option contract at which the buyer can exercise a call or put option. These alternative prices are set by the trading exchange, and the public decides whether it wants to buy or sell any options at those strike prices.

Stripping: a term whose meaning on Wall Street, as opposed to rumored definitions in Times Square, is the removing of the interest coupons from bonds and reselling them as separate zero-coupon bonds. A newly issued 20-year Treasury bond can be stripped into 41 separate zero-coupon securities, including two coupon payment dates each year (40 separate maturity dates) plus the final maturity date for the body of the bond.

Tax anticipation notes (TANS):   short-term municipal securities issued to raise temporary funds that will be paid off from forthcoming tax receipts.

Tax credit: a direct reduction in the amount of tax liabilities.

Tax and loan accounts: U.S. Treasury accounts at depository institutions throughout the country into which the Treasury deposits the revenue it obtains from taxes and loans. The Treasury transfers funds from these accounts to its account at the Federal Reserve when it has to pay bills by writing checks on the Fed.

10-K reports: annual reports that are required to be submitted to the Securities and Exchange Commission (SEC). About 12,000 companies file these reports each year. The 10-K is not a "fill-in-the-blank" form; rather, it is a set of answers to questions posed by the SEC. The information provided in 10-K reports includes income statements; balance sheets; cash flows; descriptions of products, markets, and subsidiaries; foreign operations; management's summary of financial conditions; and lists of company directors, officers, major shareholders, and insider owners.

Thrift institutions: mutual savings banks, savings and loan associations, and credit unions.

TIGRS: Treasury investment growth receipts, which are zero-coupon securities created by stripping Treasury bonds.

Time deposits: interest-bearing bank deposits, by law requiring 14 days notice prior to withdrawal.

Trade-weighted value of the dollar: the value of the dollar relative to the weighted average of the values of the ten most important currencies in the world. The weight of each country's currency is based on the relative amount of trade each country had with the United States in 1973 (March 1973 = 100). When the index goes up, the dollar is getting stronger relative to the average of the other currencies; when it goes down, the dollar is getting weaker.

Treasury bills: an IOU of the Treasury that matures in one year or less and is sold on a discount basis; that is, the bill is sold at less than its par value calculated on the basis of a 360-day discount rate.

Treasury bond: an IOU of the Treasury that matures in more than ten years. It normally pays interest twice each year and carries a coupon rate of interest.

Treasury Investment Growth Receipts: *See* TIGRS.

Treasury note: an IOU of the Treasury that matures in one to ten years, normally pays interest twice each year, and carries a coupon rate of interest.

Trust funds: funds financed by taxes and other receipts earmarked by law for specific purposes. The major trust funds are Social Security, Medicare, unemployment compensation, federal employee retirement, highway construction, and airport and airway development.

Underground economy: billions of dollars in unreported income that results from cash payments for products and services, barter exchanges of one good or service for another, or services rendered by business firms and independent contractors that are not recorded in the firms' accounting statements. The underground economy also includes income from illegal activities such as drugs, prostitution, stealing, and gambling.

Underwriting: services provided by an investment banker or other agent to bring a newly issued security to market.

Unemployed persons: those who (1) actively looked for work during the past four weeks, (2) are currently available for work, and (3) do not have a job.

Unemployment rate: number of unemployed persons divided by the civilian labor force.

Unified budget: official budget of the United States since 1969. Generally, it shows details for on-budgets, off-budgets, and total budgets.

Unilateral transfers: international transactions in which there is no "quid" for the "quo." One country (or resident in that country) has given another country (or resident) something of value but does not expect anything in return.

Working capital: capital in current use in the operations of a business. The excess of its current assets over its current liabilities is generally referred to as a company's working capital. The amount of working capital has long served as a credit test and often as a measure of the debt-paying ability of a company.

World Bank: although its official name is the International Bank for Reconstruction and Development (IBRD), it is better known as the World Bank. It was established along with the International Monetary Fund (IMF), by the Bretton Woods Agreement (1944). The World Bank, which has 150 members, and its close affiliates — the International Finance Corporation and the International Development — makes loans and provides other assistance to developing countries. Loans are made directly to member governments or to private companies if the government guarantees the loan. Decisions on loans are made by the board of directors, where most votes are weighted by the members' capital contributions—this means that the World Bank is controlled by the wealthier nations.

Yankee CD: a dollar-denominated certificate of deposit that is issued by a branch of a foreign bank located in the United States.

Yield: the effective interest rate or rate of return on a given investment.

Yield curve: the relationship that exists at a specific time between nominal interest rates earned by securities with similar risks but different maturities.

Yield to maturity (YTM):   the effective or true yield of a security, which should be used for comparisons with the yields on all financial investments. The yield to maturity is that discount rate that makes the future interest payments plus the maturity value equal to the current price of the bond. The YTM will be lower than the current yield whenever the current price of a bond is less than the par value and greater than the current yield whenever the current price of the bond is above par.

Zero-base budgeting: a budgeting approach under which each expense starts at zero for each planning period. Each dollar in a zero-base budget must be justified on its own.

Zero-coupon bond: a bond that does not carry a coupon interest rate, which means it does not make periodic interest payments. Interest is earned through appreciation in the market price of the bond.

APPENDIX B

RELEASE DATES OF SOME IMPORTANT DATA SERIES

The following schedules show the regular release dates of some important economic data series. Release dates are the dates when new data are released to the public and to other government agencies, generally in the form of a press release. If one is going to rely on traditional published sources, such as the *Federal Reserve Bulletin*, the *Survey of Current Business*, or the *Monthly Labor Review*, to obtain the data, there will be a further lag of at least one to six weeks. Newspapers and financial programs on television normally report some data releases but only in very short summaries. Most agencies will send you detailed data releases, but the subscriptions are quite expensive. One quick and relatively inexpensive way of obtaining most new data releases is to subscribe to the Department of Commerce's "Electronic Bulletin Board" (see page 496). Most releases are posted to the EBB the same day.

The following release dates are approximate because they often vary by one to four days. The reference period, denoted in brackets, "[ ]," is the period covered by the newly released data. Most, but not all, releases also include data for some earlier periods as well. The department releasing the data is shown in braces "{ }."

Abbreviations:
BEA — U.S. Department of Commerce, Bureau of Economic Analysis
BLS — U.S. Department of Labor, Bureau of Labor Statistics
Census — U.S. Department of Commerce, Bureau of the Census
CEA — U.S. Council of Economic Advisors
DOE — U.S. Department of Energy
FRB — Federal Reserve Board
HUD — U.S. Department of Housing and Urban Development
ILO — International Labor Office
IMF — International Monetary Fund
OMB — U.S. Office of Management and Budget

Daily Data Releases

Time	Description	Source
9am	Treasury rate quotations	{FRB-NY}
	Contains yesterday's prices and yields on *all* U.S. securities as well as Federal funds rates, CD rates, and yields on commercial paper.	
9am	State and local government bond rate	{Treasury}
1pm	Trade opportunities	{Commerce}
	Trade contacts and opportunities listed by country.	

4pm	Yield curve points	{Treasury}
4pm	Daily Treasury statement	{Treasury}

      Shows deposits and withdrawals to the Treasury account at the Federal Reserve and its tax and loan accounts. Also shows public debt transactions.

Weekly Data Releases

Monday

    Assets and Liabilities of Banks (H.8) [period ending three weeks previous] {FRB}

    Foreign Exchange Rates (H.10) [week ending the previous Friday] {FRB}

    Selected U.S. interest rates (H.15) [week ending previous Saturday] {FRB}

Wednesday

    Selected Borrowings of Large Commercial Banks (H.5) [week ending previous Thursday] {FRB}

Thursday

    Aggregate Reserves and the Monetary Base (H.3) [period ending eight days earlier — Wednesday] {FRB}

    Factors Affecting Reserves (H.4.1) [week ending yesterday — Wednesday] {FRB}

    Money stock, liquid assets, debt measures (H.6) [period ending ten days earlier — Monday] {FRB}

Friday

    Actions of the Board: Applications and Reports Received (H.2) [previous week] {FRB}

    Condition Report of Large Commercial Banks (H4.2) [week ending previous Wednesday] {FRB}

Monthly Data Releases

Date   Name of Data Release

1 — Value of New Construction Put in Place-C30 [two months previous] {Census}

1 — Foreign Exchange Rates (G.5) [previous month] {FRB}

1 — International Finance Statistics [three months previous] {IMF}

3 — Manufacturers' Shipments, Inventories, and Orders [previous month] {Census}

4 — Selected Interest Rates (G.13) [previous month] {FRB}

5 — Labor Market and Employment Data [previous month] {BLS}

6—Monthly Wholesale Trade: Inventories and Sales [previous month] {Census}

7—Consumer Installment Credit [two months previous] {FRB}

10—Producer Price Index [previous month] {BLS}

12—Debits and Deposit Turnover at Commercial Banks (G.6) [previous month] {FRB}

12—Housing Completions (C22) [two months previous] {Census}

12—IMF Survey (bimonthly) [recent information] {IMF}

13—Consumer Price Index [previous month] {BLS}

14—Manufacturing and Trade: Inventories and Sales [two months previous] {Census}

14—Advance Monthly Retail Sales [previous month] {Census}

15—Industrial Production and Capacity Utilization [previous month] {FRB}

16—Local Area Employment and Unemployment [two months previous] {BLS}

18—Advance Report of U.S. Merchandise Trade (FT 900) [two months previous] {Census}

19—Housing Starts and Building Permits (C20) [previous month] {Census}

22—Loans and Securities at Commercial Banks (G.7) [previous month] {FRB}

22—Major Nondeposit Funds of Commercial Banks (G.10) [previous month] {FRB}

23—Monthly Treasury Statement [previous month]

24—Yield on FHA-Insured New Home Mortgages [previous month] {HUD}

25—Advanced Reports on Durable Goods [previous month] {Census}

26—Advance Report on Durable Goods, Manufacturers' Shipments and Orders [previous month] {Census}

27—U.S. Import and Export Indexes [previous month] {BLS}

27—IMF Survey (bimonthly) [recent information] {IMF}

28—Employment Cost Index [previous month] {BLS}

28—Monthly Energy Review {DOE}

30—Indexes of Leading, Lagging, and Coincident Indicator [previous month] {BEA}

30—Personal Income and Outlays [previous month] {BEA}

30 — New One-Family Houses Sold and for Sale [previous month] {Census}

Quarterly and Annual Release Dates

January

9 — Quarterly Financial Report for Retail Firms [3rd quarter of previous year] {Census}

10 — Annual Energy Outlook, Long Term Projections [future years beginning in this year] {DOE}

23 — State Personal Income [3rd quarter of previous year] {BEA}

24 — Housing Vacancies [4th quarter of previous year] {Census}

28 — Major Collective Bargaining Settlements [4th quarter of previous year] {BLS}

28 — Employment Cost Index [4th quarter of previous year] {BLS}

28 — Gross Domestic Product — Advance (GNP) [4th quarter of previous year] {BEA}

29 — Import and Export Indexes [4th quarter of previous year] {BLS}

February

1 — Budget of the United States (annual) [next fiscal year] {OMB}

1 — Government (International) Finance Statistics (annual) [previous year] {IMF}

2 — Balance of Payments Statistics (annual) [previous year] {IMF}

6 — Productivity and Costs [4th quarter of previous year] {BLS}

10 — Economic Report of the President (annual) [previous year and historical data] {CEA}

15 — Flow-of-Funds Summary (Z.7) [4th quarter of previous year] {FRB}

23 — Flow-of-Funds Accounts (Z.1) [4th quarter of previous year] {FRB}

28 — Gross Domestic Product — Preliminary [4th quarter of previous year] {BEA}

March

1 — Merchandise Trade (BOP basis) [4th quarter of previous year] {BEA}

2 — Direction of Trade Statistics [4th quarter of previous year] {IMF}

6 — Productivity and Costs, Revised [4th quarter of previous year] {BLS}

6 — Plant and Equipment Expenditures [4th quarter of previous year] {Census}

15 — Assets and Liabilities of Major Foreign Branches of U.S. Banks (E.11) [4th quarter of previous year] {FRB}

15 — Quarterly Financial Report for Manufacturing, Mining, and Whole-saling [4th quarter of previous year] {Census}

15 — Summary of International Transactions [4th quarter of previous year] {BEA}

16 — Bulletin of Labor Statistics [previous quarter] {ILO}

16 — Terms of Bank Lending to Business (E.2) [quarter ending in February] {FRB}

28 — Corporate Profits — Preliminary [4th quarter of previous year] {BEA}

28 — Gross Domestic Product — Final (GNP) [4th quarter of previous year] {BEA}

29 — Agricultural Finance Databook [quarter ending in January] {FRB}

April

9 — Quarterly Financial Report for Retail Firms [4th quarter of previous year] {Census}

9 — Plant and Equipment Expenditures [4th quarter of previous year] {Census}

14 — International Energy Outlook (annual) [projections beginning with this year] {DOE}

15 — Balance Sheet for the U.S. Economy (semiannual) [previous year] {FRB}

23 — State Personal Income [4th quarter of previous year] and Preliminary Per Capita PI [previous year] {BEA}

24 — Housing Vacancies [1st quarter of this year] {Census}

28 — Corporate Profits, Revised [4th quarter of previous year] {BEA}

28 — Major Collective Bargaining Settlements [1st quarter of this year] {BLS}

28 — Employment Cost Index [1st quarter of this year] {BLS}

28 — Gross Domestic Product — Advance (GNP) [1st quarter of this year] {BEA}

May

5 — Metropolitan Area Personal Income [two years previous] {BEA}

6 — Productivity and Costs [1st quarter of this year] {BLS}

15 — Flow-of-Funds Summary (Z.7) [1st quarter of this year] {FRB}

23 — Flow-of-Funds Accounts (Z.1) [1st quarter of this year] {FRB}

28 — Corporate Profits — Preliminary [1st quarter of this year] {BEA}

29 — Gross Domestic Product — Preliminary [1st quarter of this year] {BEA}

June

1 — Merchandise Trade (BOP basis) [1st quarter of this year] {BEA}

2 — Direction of Trade Statistics (quarterly) [1st quarter of this year] {IMF}

6 — Plant and Equipment Expenditures [1st quarter of this year] {Census}

6 — Productivity and Costs, Revised [1st quarter of this year] {BLS}

15 — Assets and Liabilities of Major Foreign Branches of U.S. Banks (E.11) [1st quarter of this year] {FRB}

15 — Quarterly Financial Report for Manufacturing, Mining, and Wholesaling [1st quarter of this year] {Census}

15 — Summary of International Transactions [1st quarter of this year] {BEA}

16 — Terms of Bank Lending to Business (E.2) [quarter ending in May] {FRB}

16 — Bulletin of Labor Statistics [previous quarter] {ILO}

28 — Gross Domestic Product (GNP) — Final estimates [1st quarter of this year] {BEA}

28 — Corporate Profits, Revised [1st quarter of this year] {BEA}

29 — Agricultural Finance Databook [quarter ending in April] {FRB}

July

9 — Quarterly Financial Report of Retail Firms [1st quarter of this year] {Census}

15 — Direction of Trade Statistics Yearbook [previous year] {IMF}

23 — State Personal Income [1st quarter of this year] {BEA}

24 — Housing Vacancies [2nd quarter of this year] {Census}

28 — Major Collective Bargaining Settlements [2nd quarter of this year] {BLS}

28 — Employment Cost Index [2nd quarter of this year] {BLS}

28 — Gross Domestic Product (GNP) — Advance estimates [2nd quarter of this year] {BEA}

August

6 — Productivity and Costs [2nd quarter of this year] {BLS}

15 — Flow-of-Funds Summary (Z.7) [2nd quarter of this year] {FRB}

20 — State Per Capita Personal Income, Revised (annual) [previous year] {BEA}

23 — Flow-of-Funds Accounts (Z.1) [2nd quarter of this year] {FRB}

28 — Gross Domestic Product (GNP) — Preliminary [2nd quarter of this year] {BEA}

28 — Corporate Profits — Preliminary [2nd quarter of this year] {BEA}

September

1 — Merchandise Trade (BOP basis) [2nd quarter of this year] {BEA}

2 — Direction of Trade Statistics (quarterly) [2nd quarter of this year] {IMF}

6 — Productivity and Costs, Revised [2nd quarter of this year] {BLS}

6 — Plant and Equipment Expenditures [2nd quarter of this year] {Census}

15 — Assets and Liabilities of Major Foreign Branches of U.S. Banks (E.11) [2nd quarter of this year] {FRB}

15 — Quarterly Financial Report for Manufacturing, Mining, and Wholesaling [2nd quarter of this year] {Census}

15 — Summary of International Transactions [2nd quarter of this year] {BEA}

16 — Terms of Bank Lending to Business (E.2) [quarter ending in August {FRB}

16 — Bulletin of Labor Statistics [previous quarter] {ILO}

20 — International Finance Statistics, Yearbook Issue [previous year] {IMF}

28 — Gross Domestic Product (GNP) — Final [2nd quarter of this year] {BEA}

28 — Corporate Profits, Revised [2nd quarter of this year] {BEA}

29 — Agricultural Financial Databook [quarter ending in July] {FRB}

October

9 — Quarterly Financial Report for Retail Firms [2nd quarter of this year] {Census}

15 — Balance Sheet for the U.S. Economy (semiannual) [previous year] {FRB}

23 — State Personal Income [2nd quarter of this year] {BEA}

24 — Housing Vacancies [3rd quarter of this year] {Census}

28 — Gross Domestic Product — Advance estimates [3rd quarter of this year] {BEA}

28 — Major Collective Bargaining Settlements [3rd quarter of this year] {BLS}

28 — Employment Cost Index [3rd quarter of this year] {BLS}

November

6 — Productivity and Costs [3rd quarter of this year] {BLS}

15 — Flow-of-Funds Summary (Z.7) [3rd quarter of this year] {FRB}

23 — Flow-of-Funds Accounts (Z.1) [3rd quarter of this year] {FRB}

28 — Gross Domestic Product — Preliminary [3rd quarter of this year] {BEA}

28 — Corporate Profits — Preliminary [3rd quarter of this year] {BEA}

December

1 — Merchandise Trade (BOP basis) [3rd quarter of this year] {BEA}

2 — Direction of Trade Statistics (quarterly) [3rd quarter of this year] {IMF}

6 — Productivity and Costs, Revised [3rd quarter of this year] {BLS}

6 — Plant and Equipment Expenditures [3rd quarter of this year] {Census}

15 — Assets and Liabilities of Major Foreign Branches of U.S. Banks (E.11) [3rd quarter of this year] {FRB}

15 — Quarterly Financial Report for Manufacturing, Mining, and Wholesaling [3rd quarter of this year] {Census}

15 — Summary of International Transactions [3rd quarter of this year] {BEA}

16 — Bulletin of Labor Statistics [previous quarter] {ILO}

16 — Government Finance Statistics Yearbook [previous year] {IMF}

16 — Terms of Bank Lending to Business (E.2) [quarter ending in November] {FRB}

22 — Gross Domestic Product (GNP) — Final [3rd quarter of this year] {BEA}

22 — Corporate Profits, Revised [3rd quarter of this year] {BEA}

28 — Balance of Payments Statistics Yearbook [previous year] {IMF}

29 — Agricultural Finance Databook [quarter ending in October] {FRB}

APPENDIX C

SOURCES OF DATA SOURCES

The following publications provide comprehensive lists and descriptions of economic and financial sources of data.

American Statistics Index (ASI). *A Comprehensive Guide and Index to the Statistical Publications of the United States Government.* Bethesda, MD: Congressional Information Service. Annual with monthly supplements. The *ASI* publication has two segments providing useful information on statistics published by the federal government: (1) an index by subject, name, category, city, nation, state, and report number; (2) a section with multiparagraph abstracts of federal publications. This is the master source of all statistical publications of the U.S. government and is a better source than the monthly catalog of the Government Printing Office. It is a useful publication and should be the first place one goes to look up government sources of statistics. *ASI* does not cover highly technical and scientific data that would be of interest only to specialists in those areas.

Board of Governors of the Federal Reserve System. The Fed has available nearly 200 publications which are listed in the *Federal Reserve Bulletin* (see below), about four pages in from the back cover. A list may also be obtained by writing to the Board of Governors at the address listed at the bottom of page 482. Some of these publications are released from the Washington office, but many are released by Federal Reserve district banks. Each district bank releases its own monthly, bimonthly, or quarterly review, and many banks publish other series and reports.

Publications Services, MS138
Board of Governors
Federal Reserve System
Washington, DC 20551
202-452-3244

Each Federal Reserve district bank also issues its own publications. Unfortunately, the only way to obtain a complete list of these publications is to write to the public information office of each bank:

Federal Reserve Bank of Boston
Boston, MA 02106
617-973-3459

Federal Reserve Bank of New York
33 Liberty Street
New York, NY 10045
212-791-6314

Federal Reserve Bank of Philadelphia
P.O. Box 66
Philadelphia, PA 19105
215-574-6115

Federal Reserve Bank of Cleveland
P.O. Box 6387
Cleveland, OH 44101
216-241-2000

Federal Reserve Bank of Richmond
P.O. Box 27622
Richmond, VA 23261
804-643-1250

Federal Reserve Bank of Atlanta
P.O. Box 1731
Atlanta, GA 30301
404-586-8788

Federal Reserve Bank of Chicago
230 South LaSalle Street
Chicago, IL 60690
312-322-5112

Federal Reserve Bank of St. Louis
P.O. Box 442
St. Louis, MO 63166
314-444-8321

Federal Reserve Bank of Minneapolis
250 Marquette Avenue
Minneapolis, MN 55480
612-340-2446

Federal Reserve Bank of Kansas City
925 Grand Avenue
Kansas City, MO 64198

Federal Reserve Bank of Dallas
400 South Akard Street
Dallas, TX 75222

Federal Reserve Bank of San Francisco
P.O. Box 7702
San Francisco, CA 94120
415-544-2184

Census Bureau Guides to Statistics.   The Census Bureau publishes a number of guides to its publications. These guides contain descriptions of the census programs in each area and information on how to find relevant data in each sector. These guides can be a useful starting place for those who are not familiar with census data publications and statistics, and they will probably be updated for each new census.

Customer Services
Data Users Service Division
Bureau of the Census
Washington, DC 20233
301-763-4100

Census Catalog and Guide.   Annual. This catalog and guide provides information on publications that provide current census statistics. Most entries contain a brief abstract of the census publication or computer tape. The catalog also lists the federal depositories and state data centers that make census and other government publications available to citizens. Available for a $19 subscription from GPO. This is updated by the *Monthly Product Announcement*, which is free.

CIS Index.   Bethesda, MD: Congressional Information Service. Monthly and annual. The major work of Congress is done in the hearing rooms and offices of the nearly 300 congressional committees. These committees turn out a massive number of reports, hearings, and documents — more than 800,000 pages each year. CIS indexes and abstracts these congressional publications, including the publications of the Congressional Budget Office and the Office of Technology but excluding the *Congressional Record*. Abstracts of witness testimony are provided, along with the name and credentials of the witness. Every month CIS publishes the *CIS Index*, which catalogs, abstracts, and indexes publications issued by Congress during the previous month. Each *CIS Index* is in two sections. The Abstracts section contains abstracts of the month's publications. The Index section contains subject, title, bill number, report number, document number, hearing number, and print number indexes. The annual *CIS Index* cumulates and publishes 10,000 abstracts and more than 100,000 index references. The annual also includes legislative history citations for all public laws enacted during the year. The *CIS Index* is on Dialog's database and CD-ROM.

Directory of Federal Statistics for Local Areas: A Guide to Sources.   Washington, DC: U.S. Bureau of the Census, 1978. Guide to information on local areas published in U.S. government publications.

Encyclopedia of Associations.   3 vols. Gale Research. Annual. Volume 1 contains details on more than 22,000 national and international nonprofit trade and professional associations; social welfare and public affairs organizations; religious, sports, and hobby groups; and other types of organizations that consist of voluntary members and are headquartered in the United States. Entries are arranged by subject, and there is a name and key word index. The description includes name of the organization, address, telephone number, publications, members, budgets, dues, conventions, meetings, purpose, and executive director. Volume 2 lists by state and city all the associations in Volume 1. Volume 3 is a supplement to Volume 1, containing newly formed associations not yet listed in Volume 1.

Encyclopedia of Associations, International Organizations.   Gale Research. Annual. This work provides contact information and descriptions for multinational organizations and national groups based outside the United States. It has detailed descriptions of more than 9700 international nonprofit organizations. The description includes name of organization, conventions, meeting address, telephone number, publications, members, budgets, dues, purpose, and executive director.

Encyclopedia of Associations, Regional, State, and Local Organizations.   Gale Research. Annual. This five-volume guide to nearly 48,000 regional, state, and local nonprofit membership organizations in the 50 states and the District of

Columbia provides an alphabetical listing by state and city. The descriptions are similar to those provided in the international *Encyclopedia of Associations* listed above but is briefer.

Encyclopedia of Business Information Sources.   6th ed. Edited by James Woy. Detroit, MI: Gale Research, 1986. Contains bibliographies, directories, online databases, periodicals, newsletters, research centers, statistics sources, trade associations for most industries, and certain subjects. Good source for industry research.

Federal Statistical Directory: The Guide to Personnel and Data Sources.   Irregular publication. Lists by subject and by organizational unit within each agency, the names, office addresses, and telephone numbers of key personnel engaged in statistical programs of the federal government. Available for $32.50 from Oryx Press, 2214 N. Central, Phoenix, AZ 85012 (1-800-457-ORYX).

A Guide to Statistical Sources in Money, Banking and Finance.   Edited by M. Balachandran. Phoenix, AZ (85012): Oryx Press, 1988. This is a guide to detailed monetary data, banking statistics, consumer finance, bank deposits, assets, liabilities, and so on for nations, states, and localities.

A Guide to Trade and Securities Statistics.   Edited by M. Balachandran. Ann Arbor, MI: Pierian Press.

Guide to U.S. Government Statistics.   By John L. Androit. McLean, VA (22101): Documents Index, Inc. Annual. All publications containing statistical data are fully listed under department and issuing bureau, with a description of the publication, type of statistics, and frequency of publication. An annotated guide to 14,500 U.S. government statistical publications. An effectively organized and logically arranged presentation of data available from the federal government. Data are arranged by department/bureau with an extensive index.

National Trade & Professional Associations of the U.S.   Columbia Books. Annual. Lists more than 6000 trade and professional organizations, including trade unions. Contains address, telephone numbers, budget data, and officers of the organizations.

Predicasts Forecasts.   Reports on publications that forecast future economic activity. It also summarizes the information presented in the publication. Most of the publications are technical or trade journals. Available from Publ. Predicasts, 11001 Cedar Avenue, Cleveland, Ohio 44106 (1-800-321-6388).

Regional Statistics: A Guide to Information Sources.   Edited by M. Balanchandran. Detroit, MI: Gale Research, 1980. Lists regional, state, and local data sources that are primarily nongovernment sources.

Sources of Statistics.   2d ed. rev. By Joan M. Harvey. Hamden, CT: Shoe String Press, 1971.

Sources of World Financial and Banking Information.   Edited by G.R. Dicks. Westport, CT: Greenwood Press, 1981.

Standard & Poor's Register of Corporations, Executives and Industries.   Annual. One of the oldest and best-known directories of corporations. It lists about

50,000 companies by the names, addresses, directors, offices, products produced, and relevant SIC codes are provided for about 50,000 companies.

Statistical Reference Index.   Bethesda, MD: Congressional Information Service, 1980–. This is a guide to certain statistical sources other than the U.S. government. It is indexed by subject, name, and category and published in monthly index and abstract issues with an annual cumulation. It includes statistics on business, economics, finance, social conditions, governments, politics, and populations.

Statistics Sources.   *A Subject Guide to Data on Industrial, Business, Social, Educational, Financial and Other Topics for the United States and Internationally.* 13th edition (1990). 2 vols. Edited by Jacqueline Wasserman O'Brien and Steven R. Wasserman. Detroit, MI: Gale Research. Annual. The 13th edition has more than 3700 pages with more than 10,000 subjects. It indexes many topics, including economic and financial data. It does not explain the meaning or use of the data, but it can be a first place to search for data not listed in this book or in other sources listed here. A typical entry is:

Income—Disposable Income per capita—U.S. Department of Commerce, Bureau of Economic Analysis, Washington, DC 20230, "The National Income and Product Accounts of the United States, 1929–1982. *Survey of Current Business,* April and July issues.

Available from Gale Research, Book Tower, Detroit, MI 48226.

Where to Find Business Information.   2d ed. By David M. Brownstone and Gorton Carruth. New York: Wiley, 1982.

APPENDIX D

GOLDEN NUGGETS OF ECONOMIC AND FINANCIAL DATA

Basic Economic Statistics. By M. Balachandran. Monticello, IL. Council of Planning Librarians, 1976.

Budget of the United States of America. Annual. Generally available in February from the Government Printing Office.

Major publications of the Bureau of Economic Analysis (Department of Commerce):

1. *Survey of Current Business* (SCB). If you can afford to subscribe to only one economic data source, this monthly should be the one. The *Survey of Current Business* contains articles on the national and international economy and is the primary publication for national income and product accounts (GNP data), which are contained in every issue, with revised annual data published in the July issue. Its current business statistics, otherwise known as the "blue sheets" or the "S-pages," are located in the back half of the publication. The blue sheets contain information (mostly monthly series) on nearly 1900 major economic series, including personal income, industrial production, business sales, manufacturer's shipments, orders and inventories, business incorporations and failures, consumer and producer price indexes, construction, housing starts and permits, mortgages, retail trade data, labor employment and earnings, banking, finance and monetary data, government budgetary data, transportation data, foreign trade data, and information for a number of specific industries. A section (yellow pages) on business cycle indicators, which was previously published in the *Business Conditions Digest* (no longer published), is now given in the *Survey of Current Business*. Currently, the subscription price is $29 per year second class and $52 first class.

2. BEA reports can be obtained at a combined subscription rate of $110, or individually at $24/year except for the regional report, which is $12. Many of the data contained in these reports are published in the SCB, but the advantage of BEA reports is that they are mailed the day after the estimates are made. Data in the SCB are 30 to 60 days late.

   a. *Gross national product.* Monthly reports with summary national income and product account estimates, including corporate profits. (BEA-15-S)

   b. *Personal income and outlays.* Monthly reports of personal income and outlays. (BEA-14-S)

c. *Regional papers* are issued six times a year and present estimates of state personal income (quarterly and annually) and of county and metropolitan area personal income. (BEA 17-S)

d. *International reports* are issued 13 times a year and present estimates of merchandise trade, international transactions, investment, and related topics. (BEA-18-S)

e. *Composite indexes of leading, coincident and lagging indicators.* Monthly reports with summary estimates of the composite indexes. (BEA-16-S)

3. *Business Statistics, 1961–88.* Contains annual data for all the series that appear in the S-pages, or blue pages, of the *Survey of Current Business.* These series include business sales, inventories, prices, employment, construction, banking, finance, transportation, and many other industries and commodities. An appendix provides data for major national income and product accounts and U.S. international transactions. It also contains definitions of terms, sources of data, and methods of compilation.

Major publications of the Bureau of Labor Statistics (Department of Labor):

1. *Employment and Earnings.* This is the most valuable publication of BLS. It contains data on employment, hours, and earnings for the United States, states, and more than 200 local areas. It has an annual supplement that contains revised data for recent years. $25. (GPO 729-004-00000-6)

2. *Monthly Labor Review.* Contains articles on the labor force, wages, prices, and so on, but its real value is the current labor statistics in the back section. $20. (GPO 729-002-00000-3)

3. *Handbook of Labor Statistics.* An excellent annual source of data on the labor market, prices, and foreign labor statistics. $29. (GPO 029-001-03009-6)

Major publications of the Census Bureau. Census publications of the Census Bureau are too extensive for an individual to purchase or even to list here. However, there are two worthwhile monthly census publications many people might want to subscribe to. I have found the following address a better source for procuring census publications than the Government Printing Office:
Customer Services
Bureau of the Census
Washington, DC 20233
301-763-4100

1. *County Business Patterns.* A series of 53 reports covering the United States, each state, the District of Columbia, and Puerto Rico that con-

tain detailed employment, payroll, and establishment data by county and states. Prices vary by state.

2. *Census and You.* Previously a rather dry and boring publication called *Data User News*, this work has had a title and content change and is now an interesting and informative monthly. It contains some key economic indicators (for example, housing starts, retail sales, CPI) and keeps readers informed of Census Bureau developments and publications. If you are interested in local or national data, you should subscribe to this monthly publication, which costs $18/yr. (GPO No. C3.238)

Dictionary of Economic and Statistical Terms.   U.S. Social and Economic Statistics Administrations, 1972.

The Dow Jones Averages 1885–1980.   Edited by Phyllis Pierce. Homewood, IL: Dow Jones-Irwin, 1982. Presents 95 years of the monthly averages for industrials, transportation, and utilities.

The Dow Jones-Irwin Business and Investment Almanac.   Edited by Sumner K. Levine. Homewood, IL. Annual since 1977. This covers such topics as largest corporations, stock and commodities markets, price data, population, and GNP by country. Contains a day-to-day accounting of the business year in review.

Economic Indicators.   President's Council of Economic Advisors, 1948–. Monthly. Presents basic statistical series produced by federal agencies on total output, prices, employment, wages, production, credit, money, and federal finance. Also contains some recent historical data. Write to: Superintendent of Documents, Washington, DC 20402.

Economic Report of the President.   An annual published in February since 1945. It contains the annual economic report of the president and his Council of Economic Advisors. (Pr41.9)

Major publications of the Energy Information Agency (Department of Energy):

1. *Annual Energy Review.* If your data needs are in energy, this is a "must." It provides data on energy supply, production, disposition, and consumption in total and by specific sources and uses. It presents energy indicators and has data on exploration, development, reserves, natural gas, coal, oil, wood, nuclear, waste, solar, and geothermal. It also has some comparative data on international energy production and uses. $18. (GPO 061-003-00615-9)

2. *International Energy Annual.* Similar to the *Annual Energy Review*, except that it provides data for the world and individual countries. $18. (GPO 061-003-00642-6)

Federal Reserve Bulletin. Published monthly by the Board of Governors of the Federal Reserve System. The *Bulletin* contains articles on the domestic and international economy, monetary and financial statistical series, and extensive data series on prices, money, banking, production, interest rates, federal budgets, securities, credit, gross national product, balance of payments, foreign exchange rates, housing, and construction. Write to:

Publications Services, Mail Stop 138
Board of Governors of the Federal Reserve System
Washington, DC 20551
Call: 202-452-3244
Cost: $25 per year (in 1990)

A Guide to Consumer Markets. By Helen Axel. New York, The Conference Board, 1970–. Annual. Statistics on consumers and the consumer market are organized into six broad categories: population, employment, income, expenditures, production, distribution, and prices.

Handbook of United States Economic and Financial Indicators. Edited by Frederick M. O'Hara, Jr. and Robert Sieignano. Westport, CT: Greenwood Press, 1985. An alphabetical index of key economic indicators containing information on the indicator, derivation, source, frequency, and contact.

Historical Statistics of the United States, Colonial Times to 1970. There is no better single source of historical data of the United States between 1610 and 1970. However, many of the series have been revised since the book was published so those in the book may not be strictly compatible with more recent data. Nevertheless, *Historical Statistics* is a valuable source of historical data that, unfortunately, has not been updated. Order No. 003-024-00 120-9, $56 for 2 vols. Order from Supt. of Documents.

Statistical Abstract of the United States. Published annually by the U.S. Department of Commerce. This work has nearly 1000 pages of information on population; vital statistics; health; education; law enforcement; elections; federal, state, and local governments; employment; social insurance; income; prices; banking and finance; business; transportation; agriculture; construction; manufacturing; and international trade and finance. It presents national, state, and local data for many series. Published since 1878, it is one of the oldest and best sources of general statistical data.

Statistical Yearbook of the United States. Department of Housing and Urban Development. Washington, D.C., 1969–. Annual. Available from the Government Printing Office.

Survey of Buying Power.   New York: Bill Communications, 1918–. Annual. Published each year in the July and October issues of *Sales and Marketing Management*.

Trade and Securities: Statistics.   New York: Standard and Poor's Corporation. More data on the stock market than you could ever use. It is published in two parts: the annual *Basic Statistics* and the monthly update called *Current Statistics*.

Major publications of the U.S. Department of Treasury:

1. *Statistics of Income.* Internal Revenue Service, 1916–present. Annual. Presents summary financial information taken from tax returns of individuals and corporations.
2. *Treasury Bulletin.* 1939–. Monthly. This major publication of the Treasury Department contains information on federal fiscal operations, federal debt, ownership of federal securities, average yields and prices of Treasury securities, and international financial statistics.

U.S. Industrial Outlook.   Department of Commerce, Washington, DC 1965–. Published each January or early February for that year. It contains projections for a number of industries in the United States. The "Outlook" also contains a summary forecast of the national and international economies for the following year. Much historical industrial data are contained for 350 industries it covers. Write to: Superintendent of Documents, Washington, DC 20202-9325. $28. 202-377-4356. (SN 003-009-00586-8)

SOURCES OF LOCAL, STATE, AND REGIONAL DATA

Almanac of the 50 States.   *Basic Data Profiles with Comparative Tables.* Edited by Alfred N. Garwood. Palo Alto, CA: Information Publications, 1985.
   Annual City Data: A Catalog of Data Sources for Small Cities. By Stephen J. Carroll et al. Santa Monica, CA: Rand Corporation, 1980. Data sources are arranged into categories ranging from population and economy to recreational services.

Book of the States.   Council of State Governments, 1935–. Biennial. Lexington, Kentucky. Statistics of legislative actions, finances, services, expenditures, and so on.

BEA reports: regional reports.   Good general sources of state and local data that contain summary estimates of state personal income (quarterly and annual) and county and metropolitan area personal income (annual). The reports are available on the BEA's Electronic Bulletin Board and in printed reports for $12 per year. (BEA-17-S)

Public Information Office BE-53
Bureau of Economic Analysis
U.S. Department of Commerce
Washington, DC 20230
202-523-0777

County Business Patterns   (See Census Bureau publications.)

County and City Data Book, 1988.   Bureau of the Census. Washington, DC This handy book is published about every five years. It presents more than 200 bits of information for each city having 25,000 or more population and 15 data items for places of 2500 or more inhabitants. Retail trade, finance, population, personal income, federal funds and grants, local government finances and employment, vital statistics, housing, crime, and education. It is also available on diskette. Write to:

Customer Services
Bureau of the Census
Washington, DC 20233
301-763-4100

County Year Book.   Washington, DC National Association of Counties and the International City Management Association. 1975–. Annual. Contains comprehensive information on county governments.

Editor and Publisher Market Guide.   New York: Editor and Publisher Company, 1901–. Annual. Each city entry includes such data as population, market area, transportation, housing, banks, auto registration, numbers of electric and gas meters and telephones, employees, average weekly pay, colleges and universities, climate, retailing, and so on.

Facts and Figures on Government Finance.   New York: Tax Foundation, 1974–. Biennial. Data on revenues and expenditures of local, state, and federal governments.

Local Area Personal Income.   Bureau of Economic Analysis. Washington, DC Personal income by type, major industries, population, and per capita income by states, counties, BEA areas, and SMSAs.

Market Profile Analysis.   Published by Donnelley Marketing Information Services. There are several private publishers of regional data, but Donnelley is one of the major companies. The reports contain figures on population, household, income, number of financial institutions, businesses, employees, age, mobility, housing, value of homes, employment by industry, and construction. All of this information is available in federal documents, but this is handier and much more useful. Your local library, however, is unlikely to have MPAs for any other than your local SMSA.

State and Metropolitan Area Data Book, 1986. A wide variety of statistical information for states, regions, and metropolitan statistical areas. Write to:

Customer Services
Bureau of the Census
Washington, DC 20233
301-763-4100

State Personal Income: 1929–87. The best source of historic information on total and per capita personal income and earnings by industry for each state. It is available in most university libraries and from the Government Printing Office for $16. The stock number is 003-010-00197. The BEA periodically updates the series. Call to see if they have added recent years: 202-523-0966.

INTERNATIONAL STATISTICS

Annual Report of the Bank for International Settlements. Provides much data on economic developments, money, credit, capital market conditions, Eurocurrency, and balances of trade and payments for major countries. Write to:

Bank for International Settlements
P.O. Box 262
4001 Basel, Switzerland

The following are important publications of the International Monetary Fund; they can be obtained by writing or calling:

Publication Services
International Monetary Fund
Washington, DC 20431
202-623-7430

1. *International Financial Statistics* is the standard source of data on international and domestic finance. It includes data on exchange rates, international liquidity, prices, production, government budgets, interest rates, bank deposits, and exports and imports for most of the 144 countries. Subscription prices are $188 ($94 to faculty and students). Data are also available on magnetic tape.

2. *Balance of Payments Statistics.* 1949–. Annual. Extensive data on the balance of payments for over 110 countries. Write to:

Publication Services
International Monetary Fund
Washington, DC 20431
202-623-7430

3. *Direction of Trade Statistics*. Monthly and annual.

The following are important publications of the United Nations. (United Nations data publications have had a poor reputation but they have improved quite a bit during the past two decades.) Write to:

Publishing Division
United Nations
New York, N.Y. 10017

1. *United Nations Statistical Yearbook*. 1949–. Annual. International coverage of population, employment, production, mining, construction, energy, trade flows, communications, GNP, health, education.

2. *Handbook of International Trade and Development Statistics*. Annual. Data on trade flows, balance of payments, debt, population, growth rates, industrial production, and employment.

3. *World Economic Survey*. 1948–. Annual. Comprehensive annual review and analysis of world economic conditions and trends. Most of the publication is composed of written analyses of trends in international trade, oil, finance output, social conditions, and special issues, but there are many tables that summarize world economic data of the past year.

4. *Demographic Yearbook*. 1948–. Annual. Population, birth and death rates, population densities, life expectations, infant mortality, and social and economic characteristics of the population of the world and most of the world's countries.

The following are important publications of the World Bank; these can be obtained by writing or calling:

World Bank
Publishers Department
1818 H Street, N.W.
Washington, DC 20433
202-473-7561

1. *World Bank Atlas*. 1966–. Provides estimates of population, GNP, and average annual growth rates for 184 countries.

2. *World Debt Tables: External Debt of Developing Countries*. 1973–. Annual.

APPENDIX E

GETTING YOUR HANDS ON THE DATA

1. Libraries. A large urban library should have many of the sources listed in Appendixes C and D. University libraries and many of the 1400 government depositories located throughout the United States will have most of the data sources. If you want only a couple of numbers, you can call most local libraries for the information since most have a research or reference desk.

2. State data centers and business/industry data centers. These centers are located in every state. They receive data from the federal government and share it with the residents of the states. A number of affiliated centers throughout the state may be more capable of providing assistance than the main center, or lead agency. The ability and willingness of these centers to help data users vary widely, but they can be a valuable resource. Following is a list of lead agencies and their telephone numbers, which you can call to get the list of affiliated centers in your state:

State	Lead Agency	Telephone
Alabama	University of Alabama	205-348-6191
Alaska	Department of Labor	907-465-4500
Arizona	Department of Economic Security	602-542-5984
Arkansas	University of Arkansas-LR	501-569-8530
California	State Census Data Center	916-322-4651
Colorado	Division of Local Government	303-866-2156
Connecticut	Office of Policy and Management	203-566-8285
Delaware	Development Office	302-736-4271
D.C.	Office of Planning	202-727-6533
Florida	State Data Center	904-487-2814
Georgia	Office of Planning and Budget	404-656-0911
Hawaii	Department of Economic Development	808-548-3067
Idaho	Department of Commerce	208-334-2470
Illinois	Bureau of the Budget	217-782-1381
Indiana	State Data Center	317-232-3733
Iowa	State Library	515-281-4105
Kansas	State Library	913-432-3919
Kentucky	University of Louisville	502-588-7990
Louisiana	Office of Planning	504-342-7410
Maine	Department of Labor	207-289-2271
Maryland	Department of State Planning	301-225-4450
Massachusetts	Institute for Economic Research	413-545-3460
Michigan	Information Center	517-373-7910

Minnesota	State Planning Agency	612-297-2360
Mississippi	University of Mississippi	601-232-7288
Missouri	State Library	314-751-3615
Montana	Department of Commerce	406-444-2896
Nebraska	University of Nebraska–Omaha	402-595-2311
Nevada	State Library	702-885-5160
New Hampshire	Office of State Planning	603-271-2155
New Jersey	Department of Labor	609-984-2593
New Mexico	Economic Development and Tourism	505-827-0276
New York	Division of Policy and Research	518-474-6005
North Carolina	State Data Center	919-733-7061
North Dakota	North Dakota State University	701-237-8621
Ohio	Data Users Center	614-466-2115
Oklahoma	State Data Center	405-841-5184
Oregon	Portland State University	503-725-3922
Pennsylvania	State Data Center	717-948-6336
Rhode Island	Office of Municipal Affairs	401-277-2886
South Carolina	Division of Research and Statistics	803-734-3780
South Dakota	University of South Dakota	605-677-5287
Tennessee	State Planning Office	615-741-1676
Texas	Department of Commerce	512-472-5059
Utah	Office of Planning	801-538-1036
Vermont	Office of Policy Research	802 828-3326
Virginia	Employment Commission	804-786-8624
Washington	Office of Financial Management	206-586-2504
West Virginia	Office of Community Development	304-348-4010
Wisconsin	Demographic Service Center	608-266-1926
Wyoming	Department of Administration	307-777-7505

3. Government Printing Office. If you use data regularly, you eventually will have to order some publications from the Government Printing Office. You can order by mail, phone, or fax, and charge the orders to your VISA or MasterCard, or you can set up a deposit account at the GPO. There are 24 GPO bookstores, all in large cities. The Government Printing Office has most current federal government publications, but it often does not sell older publications. If you cannot order something from the GPO, call the government agency that issued the publication, or write:

Superintendent of Documents
Government Printing Office
Washington, DC 20402
(202-783-3238)

4. Bureau of Economic Analysis. The Bureau has recorded telephone messages lasting 3–5 minutes that summarize key estimates for the following:

| Leading indicators | 202-898-2450 |
| Gross national product | 202-898-2451 |

Personal income and outlays   202-898-2452
International trade transactions 202-898-2453

For other information on data series, subscriptions, and so on, call or write (also see information below on the BEA Economic Bulletin Board):

Public Information Office, BE-53
Bureau of Economic Analysis
U.S. Department of Commerce
Washington, DC 20230
202-523-0777

5. *Online Databases.* Online databases are modern electronic libraries that are accessed by computers equipped with modems, which enable the computers to communicate with virtually every type of computer anywhere in the world. Modems are available for every type of computer, and 2400-baud modems (don't buy a modem with a lower baud, that is, a slower transfer speed) are sold for a street price of less than $100. You will need a simple communications program to enable you to communicate with the other computers, but they, too, are inexpensive and are included in some modem packages. Once you are connected to the host computer (a simple task), you can read the data and text while online, or you can download huge files and look at them later. You can even load them into your spreadsheets or word processors. Many of the following will enable you to hook up for a few minutes of free time:

   a. *The Bureau of Economic Analysis (BEA) Economic Bulletin Board.* One of the best and certainly most reasonable online sources of general economic information. An annual $25 fee covers two hours of connect time on the system; additional time is charged by the minute, which is 10 cents per minute after 6 P.M. BEA is placing an increasing amount of its own data, as well as data from other federal agencies, on the board. News releases are available on the Bulletin Board shortly after their release to the media. Selected estimates and articles from the *Survey of Current Business* are also available. For further information, contact (instant hookup is available):

   Bureau of Economic Analysis
   202-377-1986

   b. *Cendata. (Census Data).* Instead of developing its own electronic bulletin board as BEA did, the Census Bureau opted to put its immense database of construction, housing, business, and population data on Cendata, which is available *only* through Dialog and Compuserve, two expensive online service companies. Thus, to access Cendata, you have to belong to one of these services. You can obtain information on Cendata by calling the Census office at 301-763-2074.

   c. *State electronic bulletin boards.* Many states have electronic bulletin boards and at least some of these are toll free. Check with the office of economic development or the state data center in your state to see if there is an electronic bulletin operating in your state.

d. *National electronic bulletin boards:*

BRS Information Technologies
1200 Rte. 7
Latham, NY 12110
1-800-833-4707

DIALOG Information Services
3460 Hillview Avenue
Palo Alto, CA 94304
1-800-227-1927

SDC Information Services
2500 Colorado Avenue
Santa Monica, CA 90406
1-800-421-7229

Compuserve Business Information Service
5000 Arlington Centre Blvd.
Columbus, OH 43220
1-800-848-8990

Data Resources, Inc. (DRI)
1750 K Street N.W.
Washington, DC 20006
202-633-7720

Dow Jones News/Retrieval
P.O. Box 300
Princeton, NJ 08540
1-800-257-5114

Census Microcomputer Information Center
Bureau of Census
Washington, DC 20233
301-763-4100

Citicorp Database Services
P.O. Box 966
Wall Street Station
New York, NY 10268
212-968-6912

Control Data Corporation
Business Information Services
500 W. Putnam Avenue
Greenwich, CT 06836
203-632-2000

General Electric Information Services (GEISCO)
401 N. Washington Street
Rockville, MD 20850
301-294-5405

Index

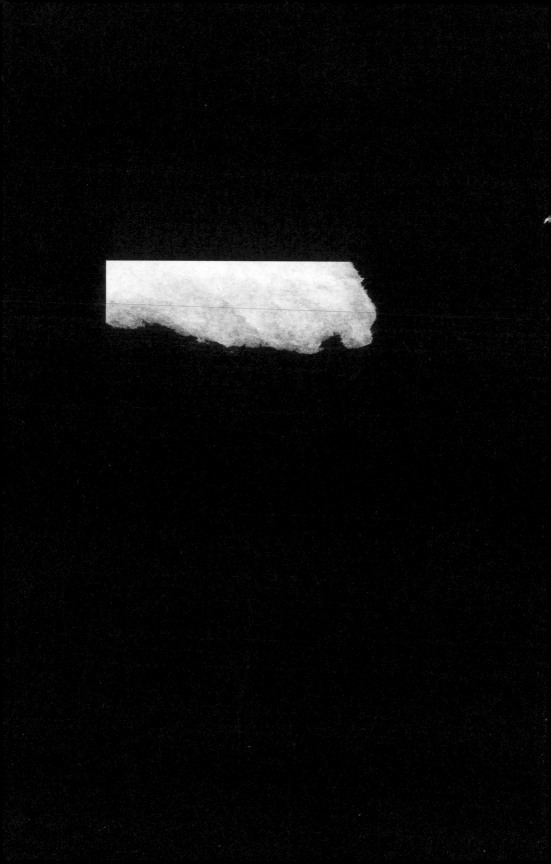